"This is the single finest description of the Vietnam War at the grunt level. Overwhelming in its detail, *Hill 119* brings the reader into battle, day after day, month after month. The readers leave exhausted, wondering how anyone survived and how and why grunts on both sides—Marines versus Viet Cong guerrillas and North Vietnamese soldiers—had the grit and resolve to hammer away at each other day and night, neither side relenting or backing down. It's all here—the smothering heat, the AK rounds zipping past, the peaches in the C-rations, the mistakes, the small triumphs, the dead-body stink, the blessed artillery blasting the bush in front of you, the rear echelon disconnects, the carefully planned inserts ending in hasty extracts. Everything you wanted to know about that jungle war is here in one book that grabs you and doesn't let you go. Colonel Mike Fallon guides the reader through the land of warriors."

—Francis J. "Bing" West Jr. is an American author, Marine combat veteran and former Assistant Secretary of Defense for International Security Affairs during the Reagan Administration

"Mike Fallon, one-time patrol leader, platoon commander, outpost commander, and company commander in 1st Reconnaissance Battalion in Vietnam, has written an amazing story of combat, up close and personal. In writing this book, Mike has two purposes. First, he wanted to share the lessons we learned, often at a high price in blood, body parts, and even our lives, in hopes of passing those lessons on to current day warriors who now serve as the defenders of America. Mike tells us how in 1st Recon, we did the business of patrolling right: patrol orders, inspections, immediate action drills, rehearsals, and test fires. The result was that in face-to-face gunfight, we outshot the enemy by perhaps 20 to 1. Technology may have in some ways changed the way we fight, but some things remain unchanged. The sinking feeling when a booby trap (now an IED) goes off in the distance, and you know that some of your Marines have likely been killed or injured. Or the jolt of fear that shoots through your heart when you make point-to-point contact on a jungle trail with an enemy mere yards away. On a jungle trail, the point of an enemy fire team looks just like the point of an enemy platoon, and you have no idea which it is until the gunfire has already started. Mike tells us what that was like. Second, Mike wanted to tell the story of and honor those young Americans who fought in Vietnam. In the time that Mike writes of, there was not much support for the war nor for those of us who had been sent to fight. I was never spat upon, but it happened to others. In spite of the fact that much of America didn't seem to care, Mike and his Marines kept going back out on patrol day after day, night after night, at risk of life and limb. Even if America didn't seem to care, those Marines will always be my heroes. And Mike Fallon has told us their story."

—Robert Fawcett, Colonel, U.S. Marine Corps (Ret). A thirty-year Marine infantry officer. He served as the Commanding Officer of The Basic School. After retirement he became the Chief Academic Officer at Expeditionary Warfare School. In Vietnam he served as a platoon commander in 2nd Battalion, 1st Marines, and as a patrol leader and platoon commander in 1st Recon Battalion, 1970–71

"If ever a book was written about the tactical importance of a single terrain feature in the Vietnam War, it is *Hill 119*. Further, it is a tribute to the courageous Reconnaissance Marines and the vital importance of their intelligence gathering, interdiction, and observation missions at the grunt level. The author's years of fastidious research, including the hundreds of interviews of the Marines who manned the OP on Hill 119 is staggering in its detail. This is a book for warfighters. It reminds us of the 'indispensable' role of tactical reconnaissance in ground combat. You don't win battles without it!"

—William M. Matz, Major General, U.S. Army (Ret.)

HILL 119

HILL 119

Defending a Reconnaissance Marines' OP, Vietnam, 1969–70

COLONEL MICHAEL O. FALLON, U.S. MARINE CORPS (RET.)

CASEMATE
Pennsylvania & Yorkshire

Published in the United States of America and Great Britain in 2025 by
CASEMATE PUBLISHERS
1950 Lawrence Road, Havertown, PA 19083, USA
and
47 Church Street, Barnsley, S70 2AS, UK

Hardback Edition: ISBN 978-1-63624-592-8
Digital Edition: ISBN 978-1-63624-593-5

A CIP record for this book is available from the British Library

Printed and bound in the United Kingdom by CPI Group (UK) Ltd, Croydon, CR0 4YY

Typeset in India by Lapiz Digital Services, Chennai.

For a complete list of Casemate titles, please contact:

CASEMATE PUBLISHERS (US)
Telephone (610) 853-9131
Fax (610) 853-9146
Email: casemate@casematepublishers.com
www.casematepublishers.com

CASEMATE PUBLISHERS (UK)
Telephone (0)1226 734350
Email: casemate@casemateuk.com
www.casemateuk.com

Cover images: (Front) American flag over Hill 119, CH-53 delivering a Water Buffalo, fall 1969. (DoD public domain, Corporal W. P. Berger); (back) The American flag flies over Hill 119, looking southwest with Que Son Mountains looming in background, fall 1969. (J. Hackett); (back flap) Author at Mess Night with Marines, 2024. (M. Fallon)

The Publisher's authorised representative in the EU for product safety is Authorised Rep Compliance Ltd.,
Ground Floor, 71 Lower Baggot Street, Dublin D02 P593, Ireland.
http://www.arccompliance.com

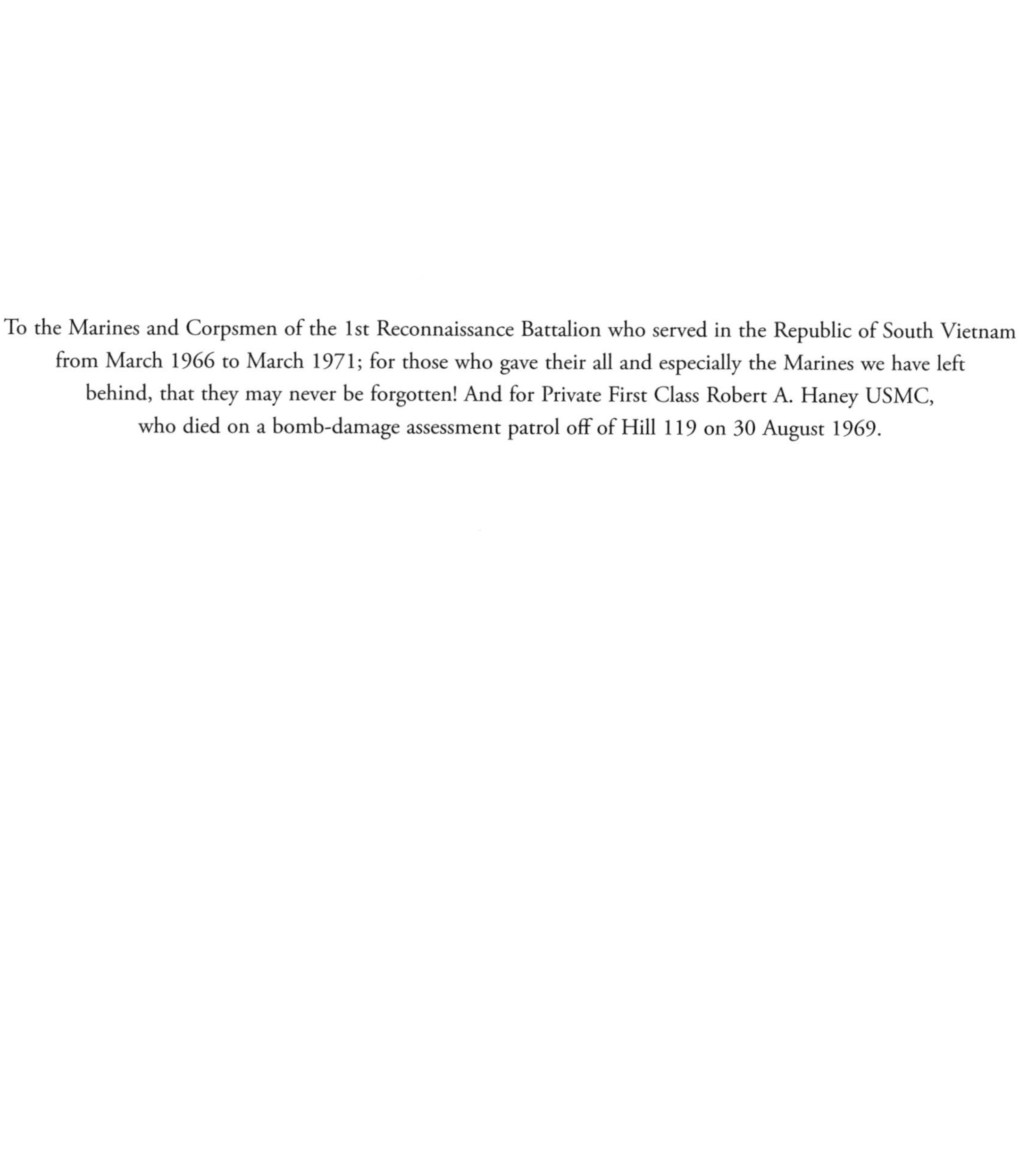

To the Marines and Corpsmen of the 1st Reconnaissance Battalion who served in the Republic of South Vietnam from March 1966 to March 1971; for those who gave their all and especially the Marines we have left behind, that they may never be forgotten! And for Private First Class Robert A. Haney USMC, who died on a bomb-damage assessment patrol off of Hill 119 on 30 August 1969.

Contents

List of Maps

Orientation Maps

Tactical Maps

Maps not reproduced to scale.

List of Sketches

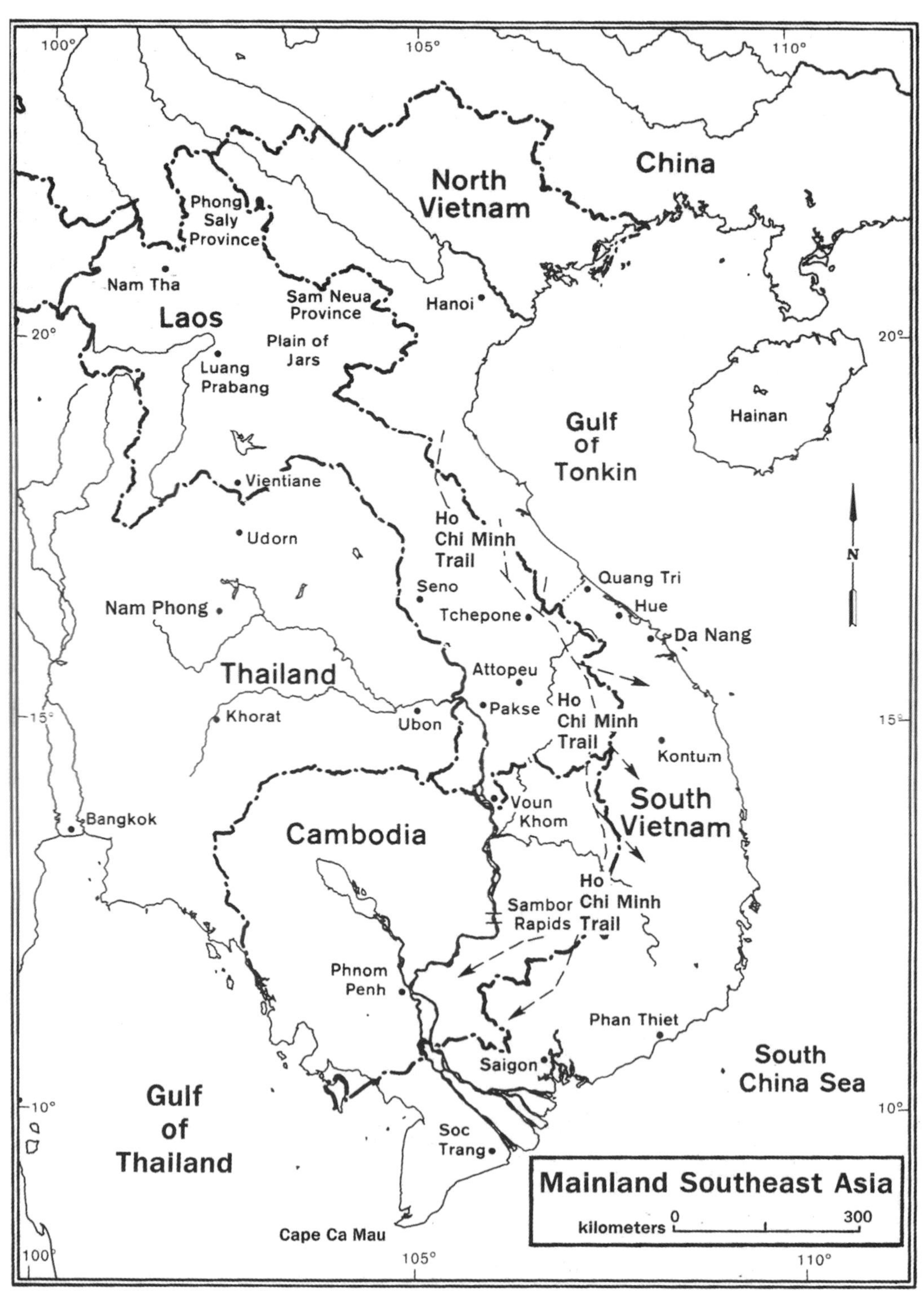

Mainland Southeast Asia. (History & Museums Division, HQMC Naval Historical Center)

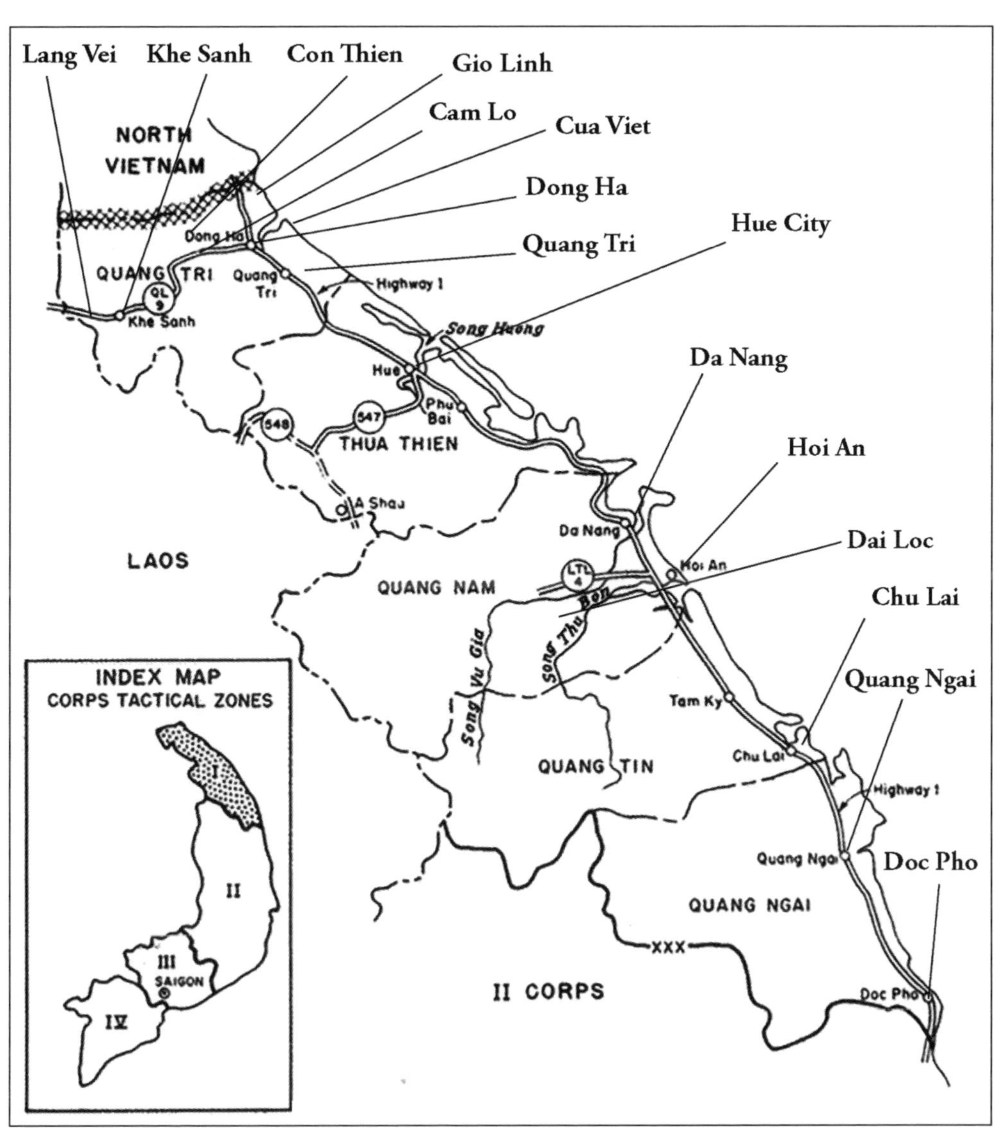

Locations around I Corps. (Courtesy of Vietnam Battlefield Tours)

Foreword

This is the single finest description of the Vietnam War at the grunt level. Overwhelming in its detail, Hill 119 brings the reader into battle, day after day, month after month. The reader leaves exhausted, wondering how anyone survived and how and why grunts on both sides—Marines versus Viet Cong guerrillas and North Vietnamese soldiers—had the grit and resolve to hammer away at each other day and night, neither side relenting or backing down. It's all here—the smothering heat, the AK rounds zipping past, the peaches in the C-rations, the mistakes, the small triumphs, the dead-body stink, the blessed artillery blasting the bush in front of you, the rear-echelon disconnections, the carefully planned inserts ending in hasty extracts. Everything you wanted to know about that jungle war is here in one book that grabs you and doesn't let go.

Colonel Mike Fallon guides the reader through the land of warriors. By diligence and at the sacrifice of his own time, he tracked down and interviewed more than a hundred grunts who served with him on Hill 119. With a shrewd eye and eye-popping candor, he relates fight after fight, pointing out who performed admirably and who made mistakes, some inadvertent and some culpable. Always, his focus is upon both the peril and verve—there's no other word for it—of recon in the bush and observation from Hill 119, seeking to kill the tough North Vietnamese jungle fighters hiding in their natural lair.

There are no intellectual theories or airy strategic thoughts in this gritty book. There are few Marines and, wherever they fight, they are outnumbered, so they need to hone an attitude that prizes innovation and flexibility on the battlefield. Throughout Mike's career, he passed on to others the idea of relating all tasks to improving the lethality of the individual grunts of the front lines. Those he led and counseled benefited from his perspective.

And due to his prodigious effort extending over a decade, we as readers can all admire and benefit from understanding how Marine Recon adapted step by step and became so feared by our enemies. It's execution—the plodding tasks of a thousand small details—that turns an idea into successful practice in battle. This book isn't just about the history of one unit; it is a description of how to adapt and triumph in the most unforgiving business on earth: attacking a much-larger enemy on his home ground. As we confront an aggressive China, this book has relevance for the future as well as standing as the classic history of Recon's achievements and sacrifices in war.

It is regrettable to write this, but the United States chose to lose in Vietnam. Soldiers and Marines in the conventional units, and in Recon, had shattered the guerrilla movement called the Viet Cong and had driven the hundred thousand North Vietnamese back far into the jungles and into Laos. President Nixon promised that as the troops withdrew, the U.S. would provide military aid and bomb the enemy should they attack. When Nixon resigned, Congress reneged on both promises, slashing aid, and ordering American pilots never again to bomb the enemy. South Vietnam fell. Units like Recon on Hill 119 won the battles; the politicians chose to lose the war.

Our beloved nation will be challenged. We will again be called out to fight. Lethality must remain the bellwether of our military forces. Mike Fallon shows what that means in real terms. Let me pose the question every reader should ask as he or she turns the pages, and is drawn into patrol after patrol and clash after clash: Does our culture have that same warrior spirit today?

Francis J. "Bing" West Jr.
Author, Marine combat veteran, and former Assistant Secretary of Defense
for International Security Affairs in the Reagan Administration

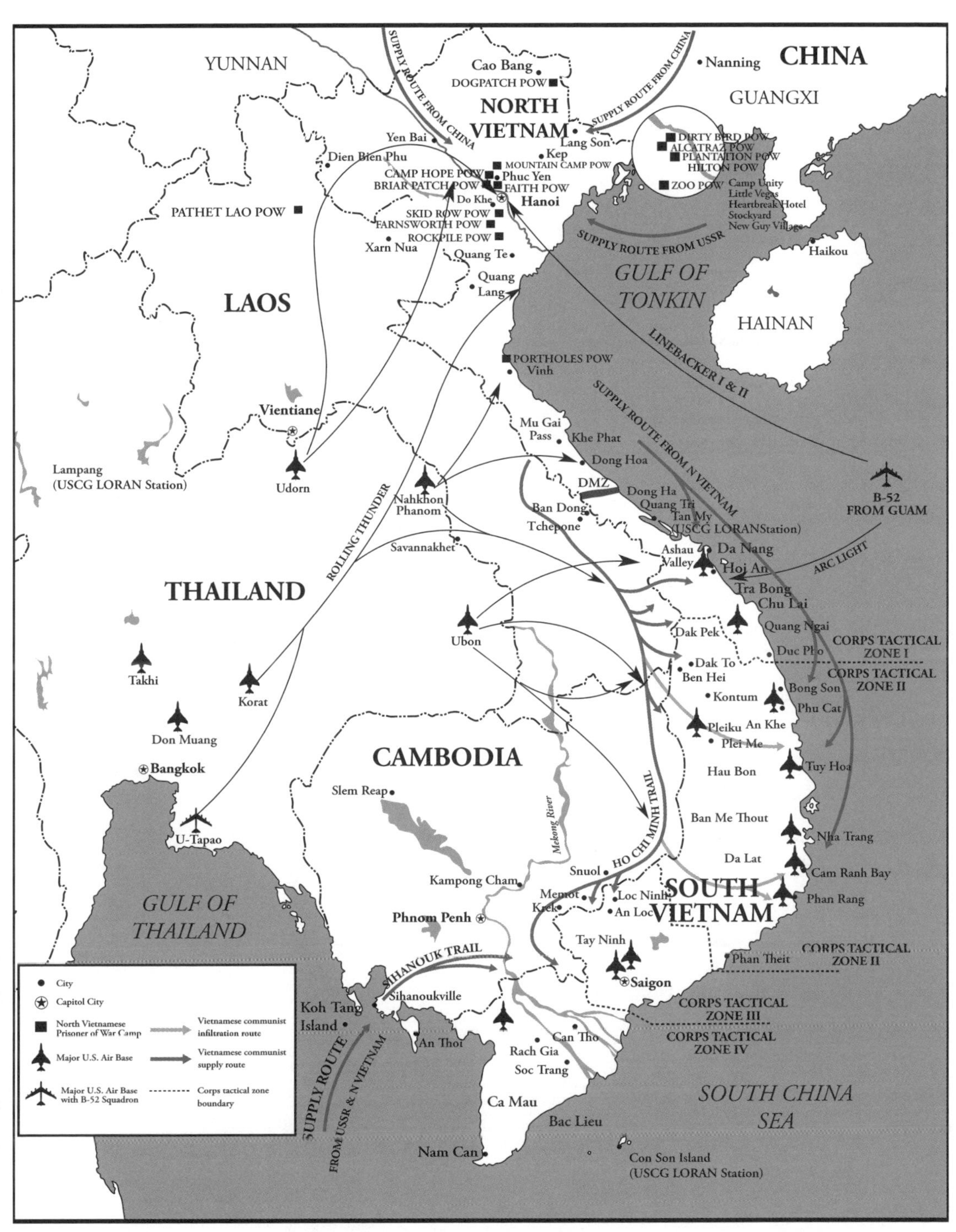

Overview of Vietnam War. (50th Anniversary of Vietnam War Commemorative Commission)

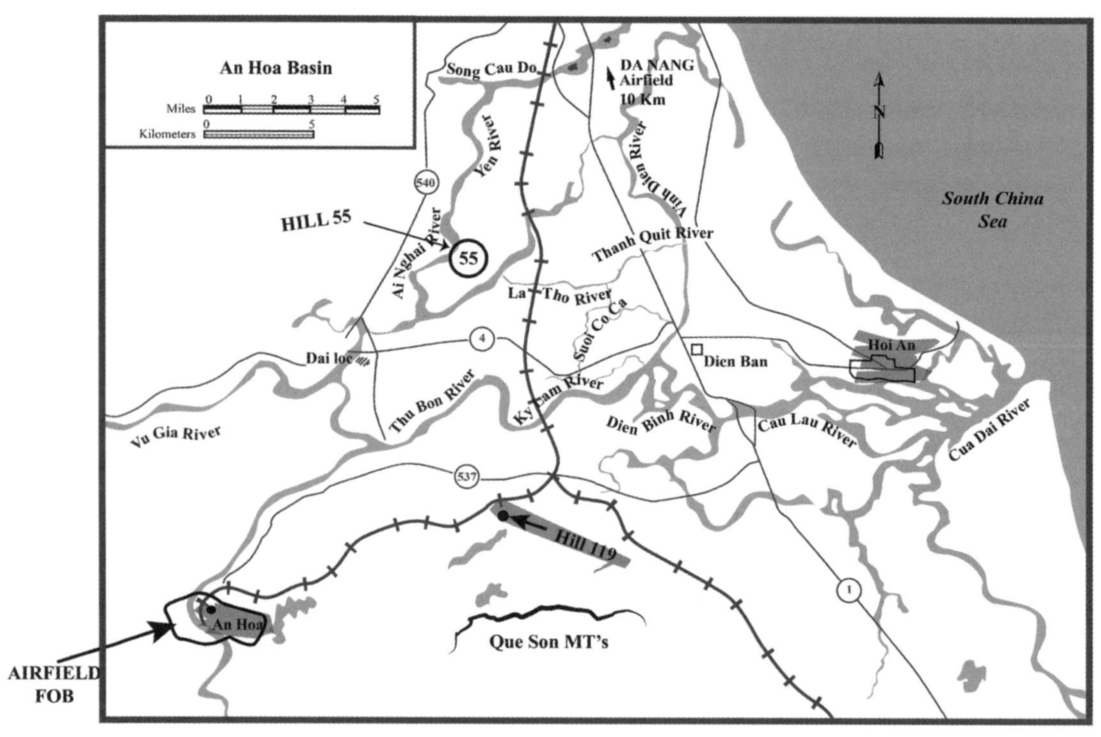

An Hoa Basin. (History & Museums Division, HQMC Naval Historical Center)

Preface

This book has been written to remember the sacrifices Marines and Corpsmen made for each other during the Vietnam War and to shed light on a small community of Reconnaissance Marines, who, by any measure, fought far above their weight. The primary objectives of this book are: that today's Marines may learn from the hard-earned lessons of those who went before; that this story will serve as a reminder to future leaders not to cut the human reconnaissance element from the Marine Corps structure; and to close the circle and honor veterans who served in Vietnam by sharing their stories of service.

This effort started ten years ago as research into Delta Company, 1st Reconnaissance Battalion's contribution to the Vietnam War, or the "American War" as the Vietnamese call it. As discussions with Delta Company Marines and Corpsmen continued, there came the realization that, in the Recon genre, there had not been a thorough and statistical look at the role of the observation post (OP). Delta Company's OP was Hill 119 and, as you will see, it and the men who served on it had stories and statistics to share. Besides interviewing every person from the Recon and Artillery communities that I could find who had served on Hill 119, one-hundred-plus and counting, I analyzed each platoon's tour of duty on the hill as it was written up in debriefing reports. Beginning at Camp Reasoner, the home of 1st Recon Battalion, we follow these Marines on long-range patrols, and then up to the OP on Hill 119. This is their story.

Their patrol reports served as reliable fact checks to the beer-and-bar stories that merged and have grown in drama over the past 50 years. Remember, veterans telling war stories always tell them from their perspective and there is always the inclination to spin the story toward the point the teller is making. Memory morphs over time and, even with good intentions, events or incidents often turn into merged stories. For this book, I have cross-walked every story with a patrol report, a debriefing document, a command chronology, and/or those events recorded in the Marine Corps History and Museums Division series, *U.S. Marines in Vietnam*. The events happened, the dates are accurate, Marines placed there are factual. I have done my best to reconstruct the dialog around some of the happenings. A few of the individuals' names have been changed to protect them or their family from undue ugly memories. I believe I have told it "like it is," as we used to say in Vietnam. All mistakes or differences of opinion are solely mine. My hope is you will enjoy the read and that future young Marines and Corpsmen learn a little that may allow them to sidestep a booby trap, self-firing device, improvised explosive device, or the next name change for increasingly popular remote unmanned ambushes.

Semper Fidelis
Mike "Deli" Fallon, Colonel of Marines (Ret.)
Paradise Valley, Arizona; Buena Vista, Colorado 2025

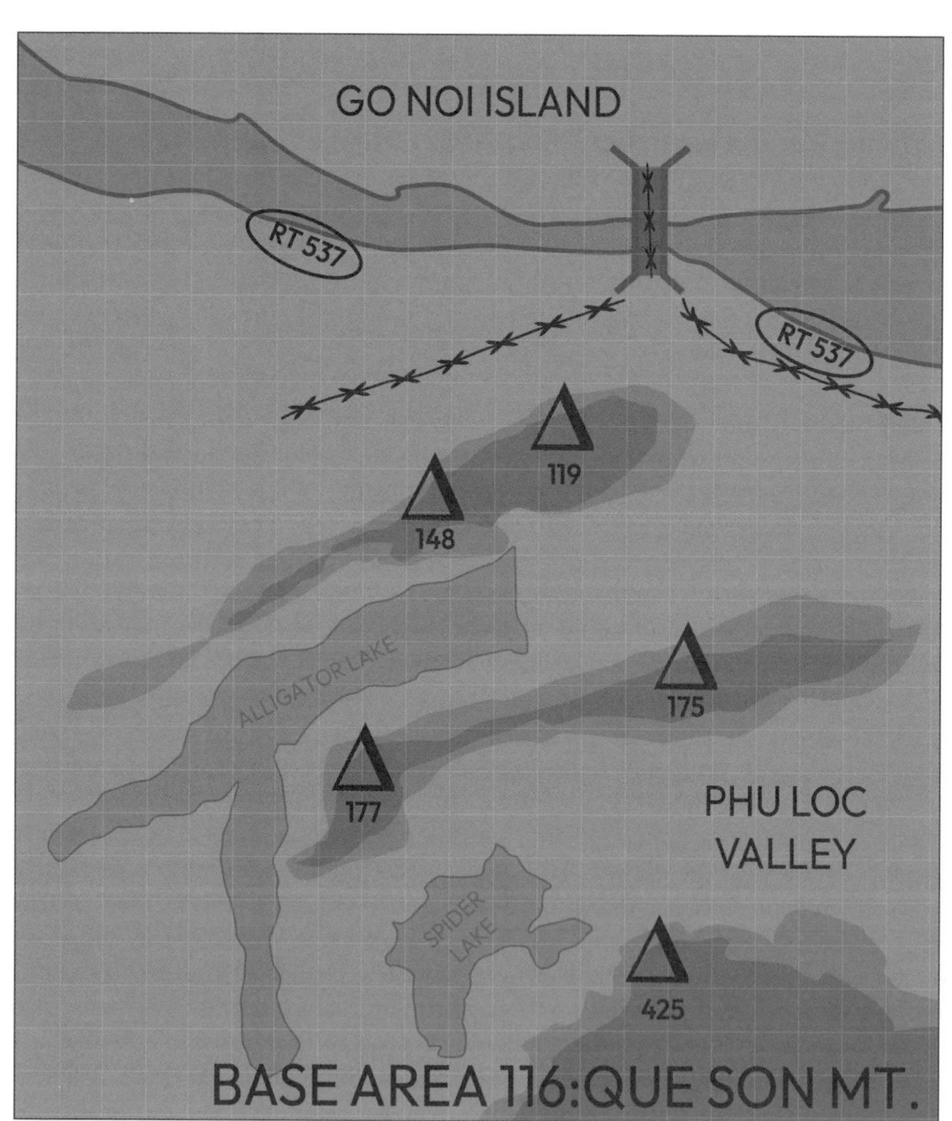

Hill 119 area. (W. Denham)

Introduction

A platoon of Reconnaissance Marines manned an observation post (OP) surrounded by the North Vietnamese Army (NVA) and Viet Cong (VC). Their lifeline was the Marine helicopters that flew out every other week bringing water, ammunition, food, and their replacement platoon. Delta Company, 1st Reconnaissance Battalion, 1st Marine Division, manned the OP for 600 continuous days in 1969 and 1970.

Hill 119, "Doi Chiem Son" in Vietnamese, is a barren slight rise on a finger of terrain. Located 25 kilometers south of Da Nang, it overlooks the Thu Bon River Basin and Go Noi Island. The ancient port town of Hoi An lies to its east on the East Sea (Bien Dong), part of the South China Sea. The hill provided the Marines with an excellent 360-degree view of the region, known as "Indian Country," surrounded by their lethal adversary. Da Nang was a strategic deep-water port and a major airfield; the epicenter of logistics for the five northern provinces of South Vietnam. Located one night's march south of Da Nang was Go Noi Island. The island was a stronghold for the VC and NVA, as it had been for the Viet Minh in the previous French Indochina War. Hill 119, the Reconnaissance OP, was located just 1,200 meters south of Go Noi Island. The OP's original mission was to support Operation *Taylor Common*, which was Task Force *Yankee*'s push west into General Binh's Base Area 112. The OP produced immediate results with supporting arms inflicting casualties on the NVA. Based on its immediate and enduring success as a tactical obstacle for the NVA, the OP became a key piece in the defense of the Da Nang Vital Area.

Patrolling deep in the jungle on hard-dirt trails, or living in wet, sand-bagged bunkers, the Marines and Corpsmen operated in three environments:

"The Rear" was Camp Reasoner, named for Medal of Honor recipient, 1st Lieutenant Frank Reasoner, who died on patrol saving the lives of his Recon Marines 15 kilometers south of the battalion's base camp.

"The Bush" was adrenaline-filled long-range patrols where a six-man team went behind enemy lines into their base areas seeking information, capturing prisoners of war (POW), or creating havoc with supporting arms.

"The Hill" was where, for two weeks every other month, one of four Delta Company platoons would man the OP.

A Recon Marine would run multiple 4–7-day patrols deep into enemy territory in small teams for six weeks and then serve for two weeks on the OP. They defended the OP by calling air strikes and artillery on their enemy, patrolling at night, and setting deadly ambushes. From a Marine's perspective The Rear was chickenshit, spit and polish, with incidents like Lance Corporal Paul Freeman's non-judicial punishment for visiting the infamous "Dog Patch." The Bush was adrenaline-filled sleepless days, always being outnumbered on the enemy's home turf, like Team

Pal Joey's conduct of a POW snatch. The Hill was a relaxing break. Like Lance Corporal "Big I" Iantonio's missed triple-gainer dive attempt into Alligator Lake which resulted in a broken knee cap, it was often extremely dangerous, lulling one into being lazy and paying the price by hitting a booby trap or getting overrun by the bad guys. The enemy was the 2nd North Vietnamese Army Division's T89 Sapper Battalion, who General Binh tasked with neutralizing the Marine OP.

Late in 1969, the Marines deployed to the hill the new, classified secret, technology of the laser range finder. The Office of Naval Research integrated it into observation equipment called the Integrated Observation Device (IOD). Together, these devices dramatically increased the accuracy of an artillery call for fire. One of the first IODs was placed on Hill 119. Even looking through the "Big Eyes" of the IOD, the most difficult challenge for the Marines was distinguishing civilian farmers from military soldiers. Many times, the same person wore different clothes and uniforms at different times, day, and night. This led to serious incidents on Hill 119 like the Lieutenant Lee Article 32 Investigation and general court-martial for the manslaughter of a Vietnamese woman. We will follow the events for over five months resulting from the lieutenant's sniper shot from the hill, killing the young woman, through the Naval Investigative Service's detailed investigation to the Article 32 hearing, and his general court-martial.

From a leadership perspective, six battalion commanders are covered in the book: Lieutenant Colonels Sharon, Mickelson, Grace, Drumright, Regan, and Leftwich. Each impacted the battalion with their personalities as well as their planning and execution of multiple missions with the always-changing enemy situation, from classic *Keyhole*, snoop-and-poop patrols, to aggressive *Sting Ray* patrols designed to inflict casualties.

The common thread for the Recon Marines and Corpsmen was a trip to Hill 119 once every two months. During the 600 days the Marines occupied the OP, they called supporting arms every day and every night. They rained fire down on the NVA. They killed 1,089 of General Binh's soldiers, both North Vietnamese regulars as well as motivated Viet Cong. Hill 119 is the history of Delta Company's Marines, Corpsmen, officers, and staff non-commissioned officers from the ground level during the life of the OP.

Tactical Maps

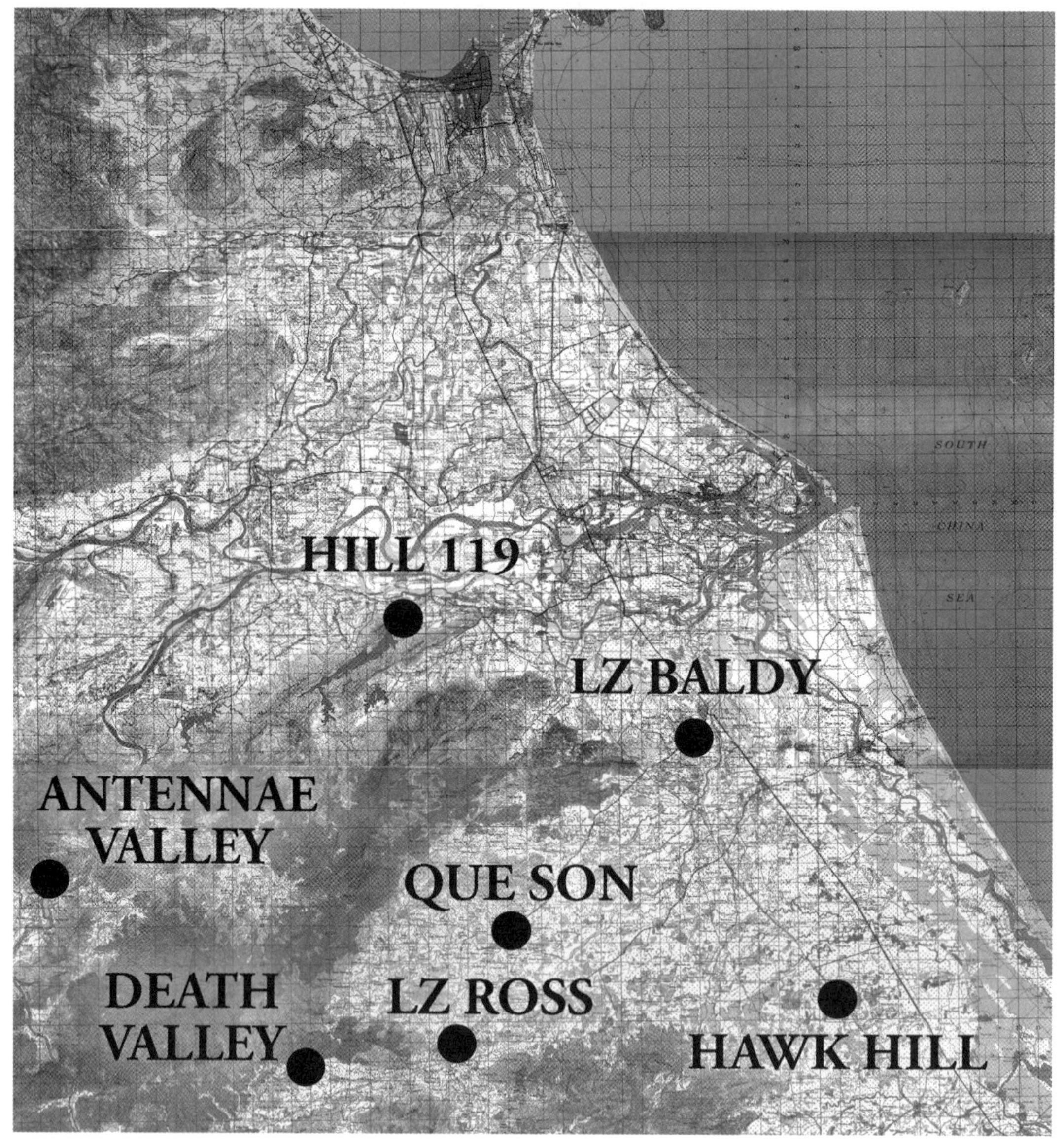

Da Nang and Que Son Mountains, 1:250,000 aviation map. (Vietnam Battlefield Tours)

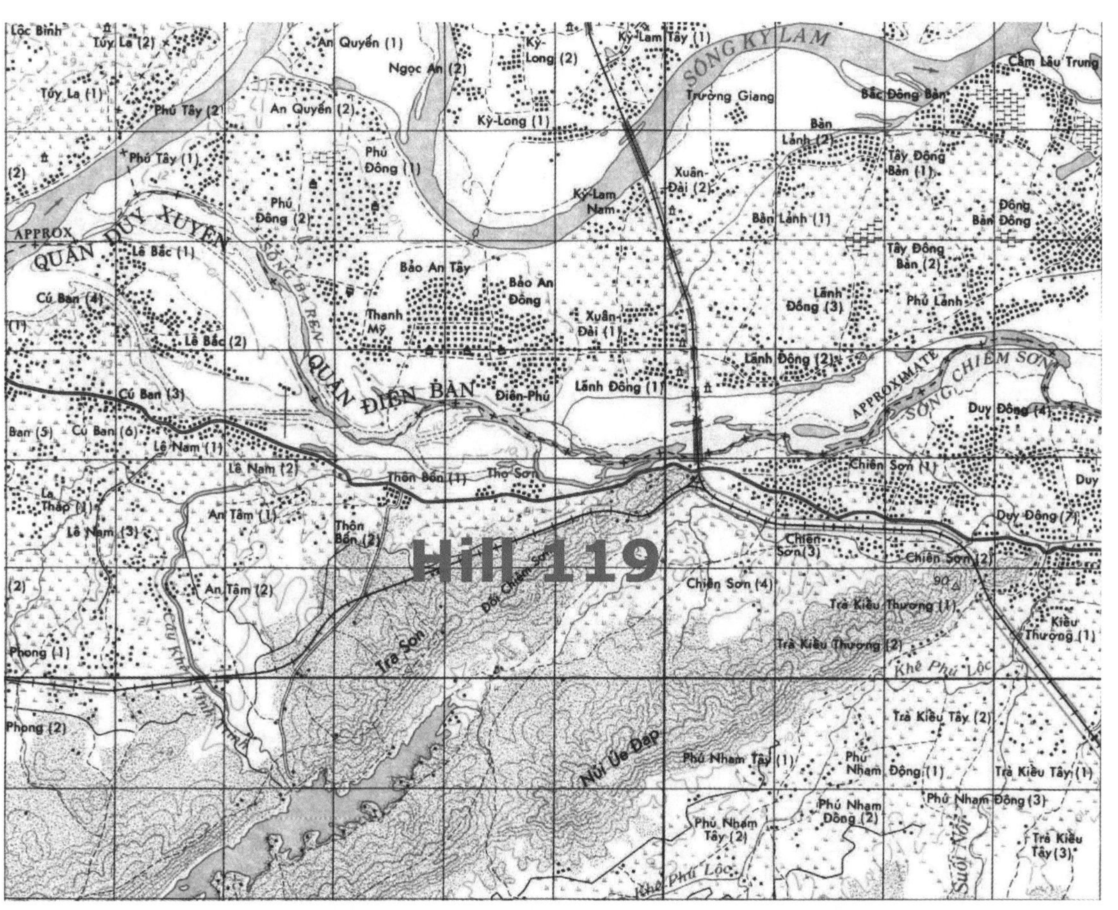

Go Noi Island and Hill 119, 1:50,000. (Vietnam Battlefield Tours)

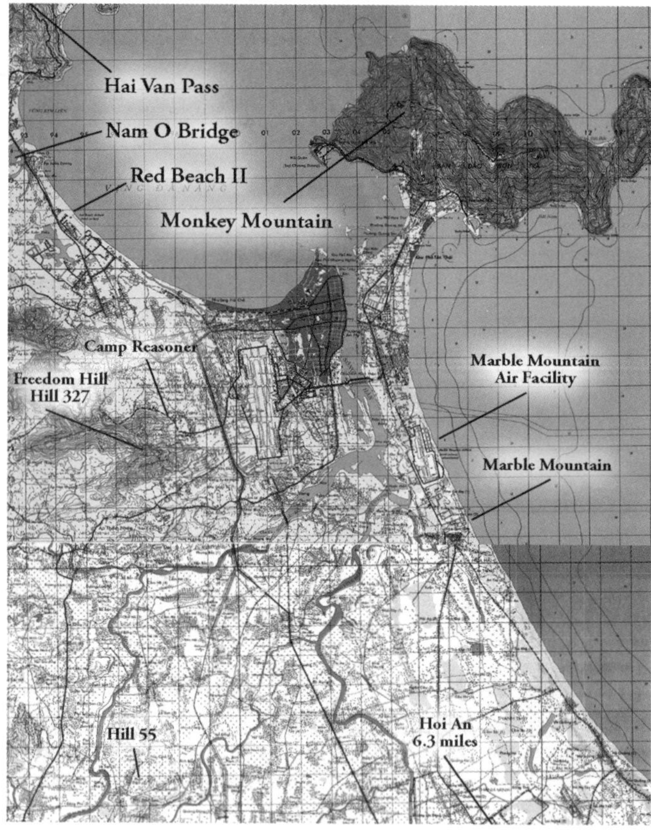

Da Nang, Camp Reasoner, 1:50,000. (Vietnam Battlefield Tours)

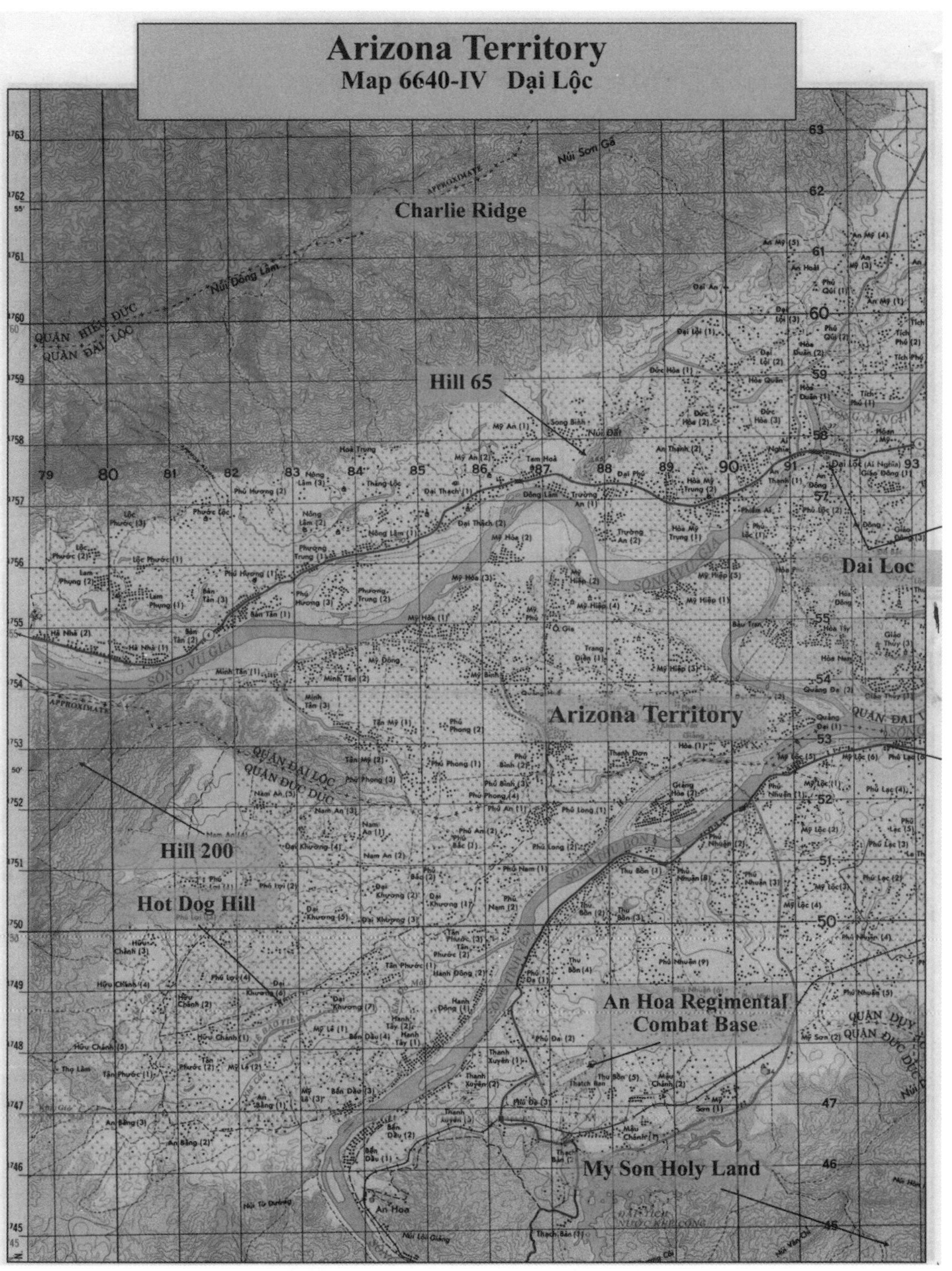

Arizona Territory, 1:50:000. (Vietnam Battlefield Tours)

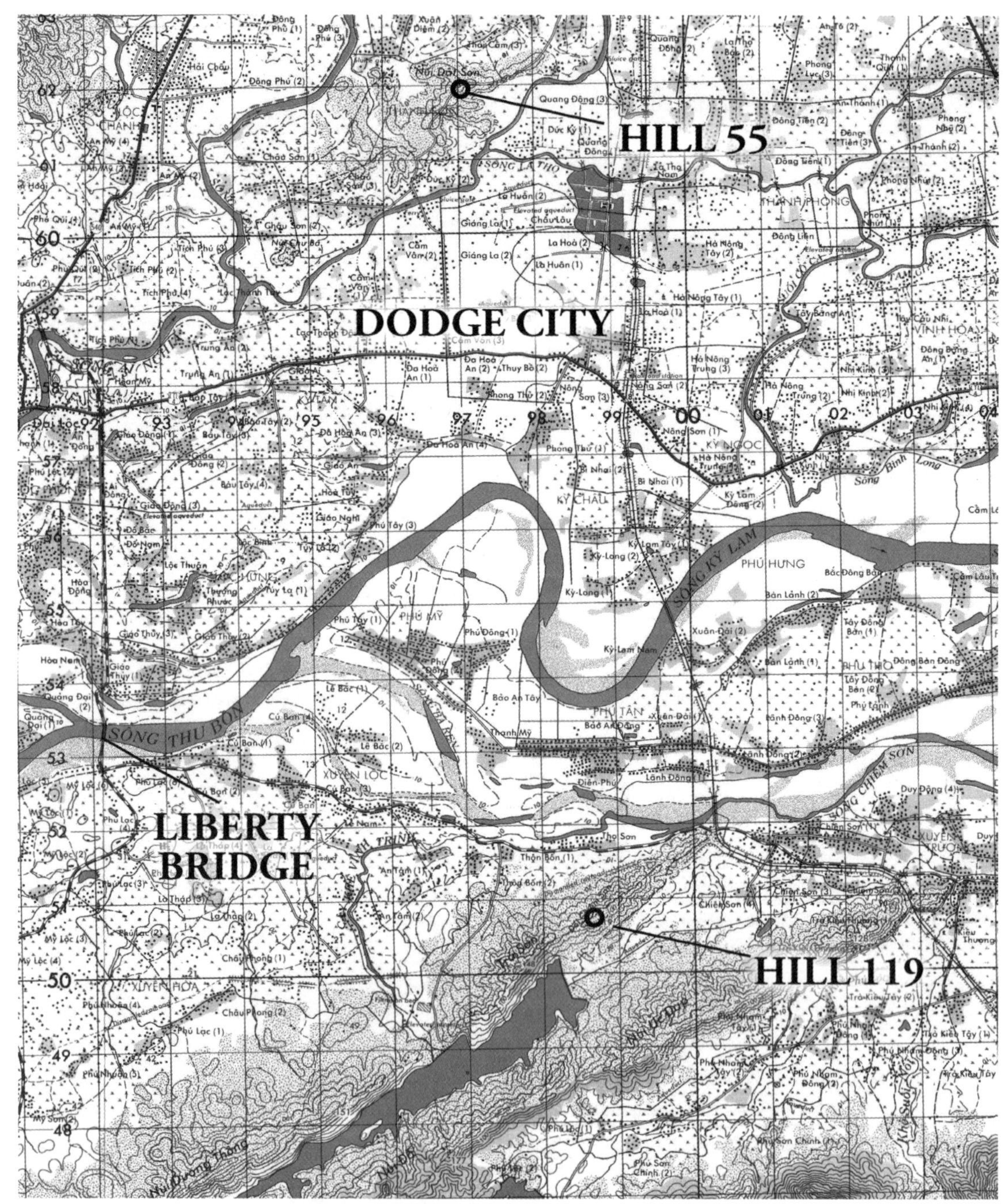

Dodge City, 1:50,000. (Vietnam Battlefield Tours)

CHAPTER I

Year of Decision—1969

The American citizenry had decided in the presidential election of 1968, with Richard M. Nixon winning in November. Nixon had promised an end to the Vietnam War achieving "Peace and Prosperity." On 20 January 1969, he was inaugurated as President of the United States, declaring in his inaugural address: "The greatest honor that history can bestow is the title of peacemaker."

The question for him and his administration was how to honorably end the Vietnam War, to make peace and support our ally, the South Vietnamese Government, and its people. Shortly after the election, President-elect Nixon ordered a review of the Vietnam War. The newly appointed Commandant of the Marine Corps, General Leonard F. Chapman Jr., reported on the situation in Vietnam, as he found it during the inspection visit, at the 15 January 1969 meeting of the Joint Chiefs of Staff. He likened the situation to a pioneer who settles in the wilderness and begins the arduous task of cultivating a crop. In the fall, after being ravaged by Indian raids, weather, and vermin, the crop was ready for harvest. Like the pioneer, who had to decide whether to remain or move on, the time had come for America to decide. He concluded 1969 "would be the year of decision."[1] What General Chapman and the Joint Chiefs of Staff failed to realize was that Nixon and Henry Kissinger, Nixon's national security advisor, had already decided not to remain; they were moving on. After a publicly stated thorough review, President Nixon adopted a policy of seeking to end United States military involvement in Vietnam either through negotiations or by turning the combat role over to the South Vietnamese. It was this decision that began the administration's plan to increase both the number and training of South Vietnamese forces and to turn over fighting of the war and areas of responsibility to them. This approach was called "Vietnamization."

Under pressure from Nixon's new ambassador, Henry Cabot Lodge, the South Vietnamese President, Nguyen Van Thieu, suggested the Army of the Republic of Vietnam was ready to replace part of the allied forces in 1969. Vietnamization was step one. Step two was to interdict the North Vietnamese supplies lines; President Nixon ordered secret B-52 bombing raids in Laos of base camps and the Ho Chin Minh Trail which became known as *Menu* bombings. The third piece of the strategy was the peace talks in Paris. Kissinger thought the public peace talks in Paris were being used as propaganda theater and that progress could only be made in private discussions, which he initiated with his counterpart. The Paris Peace Talks, as they became known, had begun under President Johnson in May 1968. They would continue until the Paris Peace Accords were signed in 1973. The year 1969 marked a major change and watershed in United States policy for the Vietnam War.

After four years at Fleet Marine Force, Pacific, Lieutenant General Victor H. "Brute" Krulak, who had influenced much of the Vietnam policy for the previous six years, was forced to retire after not being selected for commandant. He was replaced by Lieutenant General Henry Buse, a trusted General Chapman ally. The Marines of III Marine Amphibious Force (III MAF), the largest combat command in Marine Corps history, continued to be commanded by Lieutenant General Robert E. Cushman.[2] III MAF continued the full range of military and pacification activities within I Corps' tactical zone during what would start a period of transition for the Marines. In Quang Nam Province, the 1st Marine Division, under Major General Ormond R. Simpson, continued both mobile offensive and pacification operations to protect population centers. The division was tied to the defense of the Da Nang Vital Area first before mounting other operations. The Marines faced General Binh and Front 4's estimated force of 24 enemy infantry and support battalions.[3] The enemy adhered to a defensive pattern established during late Summer 1968, a posture of refusal to engage friendly forces in a large-scale confrontation. The enemy, after heavy losses during the 1968 Tet Offensive, was rebuilding and conserving his troops by remaining in his base areas south and west of the Da Nang Vital Area. At Hill 327, below the division command post and across the road at Camp Reasoner, Lieutenant Colonel P. L. Sharon, the Korean War veteran, had General Simpson's full faith as he and his Marines conducted *Keyhole* patrols, named for spying through a keyhole to gain information. These patrols, working clandestinely and designed to report locations of base camps and enemy movements on the major avenues of approach to Da Nang, represented the division's early warning system.

CHAPTER 2

Genesis of Hill 119, "Doi Chiem Son"

Go Noi Island was the geographic, agricultural, and operational genesis for putting an observation post (OP) on Hill 119, "Doi Chiem Son." The island is 15 miles due south of Da Nang International Airport. It was the traditional staging area for the Viet Cong (VC) and People's Army of North Vietnam (PAVN), better known as the North Vietnamese Army or NVA, when preparing to attack Da Nang, just as it had been for the Viet Minh who used the fertile delta island as their staging area against the French during the Indochina or French War in Vietnam. As with the real-estate saying "Location, location, location," Go Noi Island had it in spades. Just west of the small Hoi An port and five miles east of An Hoa combat base, the island was at the center of the An Hoa drainage basin. Its 7,144 acres of rice paddies and hedgerows consisting of enclosed vegetable gardens in the numerous small villages was not only a bread basket, it was also one night's march from the Da Nang vital complex of airfields and port in what is the third largest city of Vietnam.

Since the time of the Viet Minh, the villagers had built family shelters with three-foot-thick earthen roofs. These underground bunkers were basic living areas that provided safety for every family. Whether a thatched hooch on the western side of the island or red-brick house on the eastern side, every home had a family shelter below ground. These provided safety from all sides for the 27,000 farmers of the island.[1] Early in 1966, the Government of Vietnam (GVN) moved the population off the island and located them east along Route 1 in secure hamlets. Over the years, the departed shelters had been connected and utilized by the VC and NVA, protecting them from supporting-arms fires in every instance except a direct hit. Coupled with the numerous hedgerows, and manmade irrigation systems of dikes, channels, narrow canals, and creeks, these obstacles to movement meant the island was easy to defend with small arms. The hidden trenches, hedgerows, and bamboo thickets favored the defender.

Go Noi Island was the principal staging area for the VC and NVA preparing for any assault on Da Nang. Geographically, the island is bounded on the northwest by the Song Thu Bon, on the north by the Song Ky Lam, on the south by the Song Chiem Son, and on the east by the elevated national highway Route 1 running north and south. The island was split in half by the six railroad bridges connected by above-ground causeway berms running north to south. The western half was diked irrigated rice paddies while the eastern half had sand dunes, bamboo, and hedgerows dividing family vegetable gardens as well as groomed rice paddies. The fertile delta, with its annual flooding, supported two full growing seasons a year which produced an excess of rice and vegetables along with some sugar cane. It alone could feed Da Nang's population or an NVA division. The island's agricultural production was more than enough to support both sides of the war.

Just as the Viet Minh, the VC, and now the NVA, knew of Go Noi Island's advantages, as did the local GVN. Moving the entire population off the island allowed the area to become a free-fire zone (FFZ). FFZs were areas with no friendly population; anyone discovered inside an FFZ was considered the enemy because they were not supposed to be there and were therefore legitimate targets. In late April 1968, the G-2 (intelligence) section of the 1st Marine Division identified and placed three VC battalions (R-20, V-25, and T3 Sappers) and the 36th Regiment of the 308th NVA Division on the island.[2] Prisoners of war and "Chieu Hoi" (VC or NVA who were repatriated and joined the Allied side) had reported a large hospital and extensive training complex on the island, as well as a number of food-production organizations. Overall NVA command and control of Go Noi fell under the Quang Da Zone Headquarters known as Group 4, or Front 4.[3] The Quang Da–Da Nang Special Zone was established in November/December 1967 to take charge of all military/political activities within the zone at the request of the Central Vietnam Staff which was the organization that ranked over the PAVN/VC Military Region V. Its creation was in response to the large GVN and Allied presence in the area, including the large logistics installations in the Da Nang municipality.

The enemy's Special Zone was comprised of 11 districts and ran from Hue in the north to Tam Key in south-central Vietnam. Within the zone, District 2 Da Nang was considered the most critical and was composed of VC cadre of the Da Nang Administrative Committee who were designated to run Da Nang after a successful offensive. The Special Zone had both a headquarters base-camp staff and a mobile staff. The mobile staff was composed of 20 officers who had one 15-watt radio and operated in the Duy Xuyen, Dai Loc, and Go Noi areas. The command-level HQ base camp was in the Que Son Mountains. A field-grade political officer led it, Ho Phuoc, who was also a committee member of Military Region V. The military commander was Colonel Vo Thu, also known as NGOC, Military Chief of Special Zone. He had the following units available at his disposal for the conduct of operations: the T87 Sapper Battalion, located north of Da Nang in Hai Van/Nam O area, and the T89 Sapper Battalion located south of the city in Hao Tho and Hoa Thai villages, each had 350 trained sappers; two rocket regiments, the 575th and the 577th, located west of the city in Charlie Ridge, west Happy Valley areas, had 2,400 soldiers; Mobile Battalion R20, composed of approximately 500 people, operated in Go Noi and Duy Xuyen along with NVA Regiment 31 which had infiltrated from North Vietnam via the Ho Chi Minh Trail branch through Base Area 112, arriving January 1968 to An Hoa village/Arizona Territory and spreading out east into Duy Xuyen District and western Go Noi; and one Special Mobile Company operated inside Da Nang's limits. Company Commander Hien and Assistant Commander Thanh led it. Thanh was also a Da Nang City Security Committee member. This latter company had 40 men aged 16 and 17. Their mission was to sabotage gas stations and power stations. Additionally, they targeted and discovered enemy intelligence personnel and assisted in kidnapping or assassinating them. Finally, the Special Zone had a Combined Operational Section charged with the mission of proselyting both GVN military and all classes of civilian personnel within the zone.[4]

With corroborated intelligence of an enemy build up and the increased U.S. troop strength provided by President Johnson's 1968 buildup, the 1st Marine Division had received a fourth infantry regiment, the 27th Marines, fresh from forming in Camp Pendleton. This meant the division had sufficient forces to move beyond the defensive perimeter encircling Da Nang, the Da Nang rocket belt. Its purpose was to cordon the vital complex at a distance further than the range of a 122-mm rocket, thereby employing distance alone to protect the airport runways and harbor. On 4 May 1968, Operation *Allen Brook* commenced, under the command of the 7th Marine Regiment, 2nd Battalion, 7th Marines (2/7), pushing out east from Liberty Bridge and starting a multi-battalion sweep of the western end of Go Noi Island.[5] Except for Reconnaissance Marines, no Marines had been on the western side of the island in over a year. By 9 May, 2/7 was approaching the north–south railroad embanked bridges cutting the island. The fight stalled out with 2/7 killing over 80 NVA as they approached the six bridges.[6] At this time, based on new intelligence, III MAF (Marine Amphibious Force), the division's higher headquarters, ordered the 1st Division to send a large force west into Quang Tin Province. This operation was to kick off near Thuong Duc and push both east and west. This operation became known as *Mameluke Thrust* and caused the 7th Marines to pull 2/7 out of Go Noi in order to participate.[7] They would be replaced by the recently arrived 3rd Battalion, 27th Marines (3/27), who would be given the western half of the island while an ARVN (Army of the Republic of Vietnam) multi-battalion force would take the eastern half with the boundary between the two forces being the north–south railroad cutting through the island.[8]

On 13 May 1968, I Company of 3/27 was helo-lifted onto a small landing zone (LZ) on top of Hill 148 on the closest finger overlooking Go Noi Island.[9] It was obvious that grunts[10] had used the hill previously, as there were old, partially filled-in, fighting holes, and, where the hard rock existed, old split, or sliced, sandbags used for fighting positions. While going to retrieve old sandbags to improve his machine-gun position, Lance Corporal Tim Davis tripped a booby-trapped land mine and immediately lost a leg, the other just hanging on. India Company called its first medevac of the operation from its insertion LZ on top of Hill 148.[11] Operation *Allen Brook*, a multi-battalion operational sweep of Go Noi Island would also include, and feature, engineers clearing the land with large bulldozers nicknamed "Roman Plows." Additionally, the supporting operation, *Trail Dust*, included an airborne herbicide-spraying using Agent Orange to kill the foliage. *Allen Brook* ended in August 1968, recording 917 NVA/VC killed and claiming that Go Noi was now void of the enemy and the NVA/VC infrastructure and food supply had been severely disrupted.[12] The Marines then withdrew from the FFZ and went onto other operations and duties.

Colonel Adolph Dolph Schwenk (later a lieutenant general), who had been the commanding officer of the 27th Marines on *Allen Brook*, found himself in November 1968 as the G-3 (Operations) officer for the 1st Marine Division. Six months later, the intelligence community once again reported Go Noi Island was infested with the enemy harvesting rice, training, and staging for an upcoming attack on the Da Nang complex during Tet '69; this despite the earlier successful operations. Schwenk now became the architect for a new operation in the Go Noi area. Operation *Meade River*, another multi-battalion operation (seven infantry battalions) would encircle Dodge City/Go Noi Island and conduct sweeps through the area from 20 November to 9 December 1968. *Meade River* resulted in 1,023 enemy killed in action and 123 captured.[13]

On 20 December, as 1968 closed out, the Marine Corps' normal rotation process assigned Major General Ormond R. Simpson to command of the 1st Marine Division, relieving Major

General Carl Youngdale. Simpson was a Texan who entered the Marine Corps in 1936 and had served during World War II in the Pacific. He was familiar with Southeast Asia, having commanded the 3rd Marine Expeditionary Brigade during the 1962 Laotian Crisis. Simpson and his staff faced a new situation going into 1969. With the administration's announced drawdown, and new Vietnamization Program, his smaller division (the division had already lost the 27th Marine Regiment that had returned to Camp Pendleton) had four infantry regiments for the upcoming year's campaign, but the same missions. The 1st Division's primary mission was the protection and security of the Da Nang Vital Area and its over one million Vietnamese residents in and around the city. Without Da Nang's logistical infrastructure, airfields, and port, the entire U.S. and Allied effort simply could not have operated in the I Corps' tactical zone. Centered on Da Nang, the division employed its four infantry regiments—1st, 5th, 7th, and 26th—in a series of concentric belts around the vital area. In the north, the 26th Marines were anchored on Hai Van pass providing security for National Route 1, the Esso plant, Nam O Bridge, and Hill 190, which overlooked the eastern mouth of Elephant Valley.[14] The 7th Marines patrolled the rocket belt, rice paddies, foothills, and jungles due west of Da Nang into Sherwood Forest, Happy Valley, and Charlie Ridge. The 5th Marines were headquartered at An Hoa Combat Base and patrolled the southwest including the Arizona Territory and the Song Thu Bon drainage basin. Due south of Da Nang, and north of the South Korean (RoK) Marines anchored in the small port of Hoi An, were the 1st Marines who secured Route 1 south of the city and the rice-paddy area known as Dodge City out to the East China Sea and the coastal lowlands. The division was tied into a defensive posture guarding Da Nang and National Route 1, south to north throughout its tactical area of responsibility (TAOR), which protected the southern half of MACV's (Military Assistance Command, Vietnam) I Corps territory.

In early December, intelligence had placed the 2nd NVA Division and its higher HQ, Front 4, in Base Area 112, which was west of An Hoa, and organized around Thuong Duc stretching west up the valley to Laos and the Ho Chi Minh Trail. Military Assistance Command, Vietnam suggested, and III MAF ordered, that the 1st Marine Division prepare a plan to go on the offensive to neutralize Base Area 112's infrastructure and disrupt the enemy's supplies lines into Da Nang and Tam Kay prior to the expected 1969 Tet offensive. This operation would be executed by Task Force (TF) *Yankee*, commanded by Brigadier General Dwyer, one of the two assistant division commanders. The task force would consist of the 5th Marines and its three battalions plus Battalion Landing Team 2/7, a small field-artillery group, and 1st Force Recon Company. Operating in coordination with TF *Yankee* for the new Operation *Taylor Common* would be three ARVN Ranger Battalions and one U.S. Army brigade of the Americal Division.[15]

Pulling a regiment composed of four maneuver battalions out of the concentric belt defense of the vital area left Go Noi Island as a gap in the outer belt between An Hoa/Arizona Territory (to be included in Phase 1 of *Taylor Common*) and the RoK Marines in the east next to the South China Sea. To cover this gap, an economy-of-force concept was needed. The division staff recalled that, in June 1968, a Reconnaissance team, callsign *Parallel Bars*, had major success by using Hill 425, located six kilometers south of Go Noi Island, as an OP. In the clear weather on the evening of 25/26 June, Team *Parallel Bars* had observed four separate groups (100, 80, 16, and 27 men strong) of NVA moving off Go Noi Island and had successfully engaged them with both air strikes and artillery.[16]

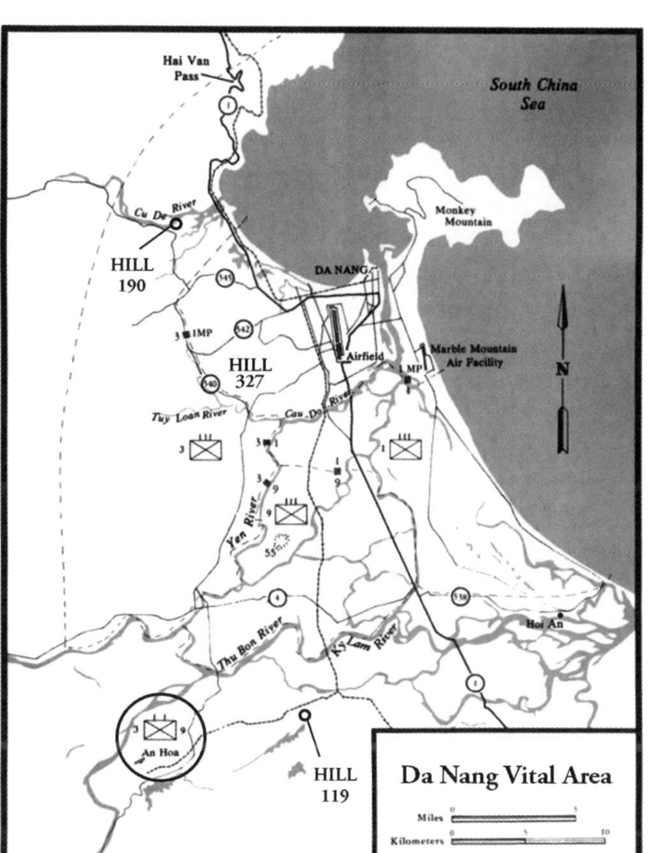

Da Nang Vital Area. (History & Museums Division, HQMC Naval Historical Center)

While Recon Battalion still maintained the OP on Hill 425, it was unrealistic to believe they could monitor Go Noi Island from a distance of 6 (southern river) to 11 kilometers (northern river) in the monsoon season, not to mention night observation at that distance. However, during both Operation *Allen Brook* and *Meade River*, the infantry had routinely used Hill 148, two kilometers due south of the island, as an insertion LZ and battalion jumping-off point for moving onto Go Noi. As an economy-of-force measure to observe and control by fire the western half of the Go Noi gap in the outer belt, the 1st Reconnaissance Battalion was tasked in January 1969 to determine if an OP could be established on Hill 148.[17] For the eastern half of the railroad-divided island, General Simpson decided it should be permanently occupied and provide a barrier to National Route 1. He coordinated with the Allies to build and man two firebases, one to be manned by the ARVN's 3rd Battalion, 51st Regiment, and the southern one to be the new home of the 1st Battalion of the RoK Marine Brigade.[18] The closest prominent terrain feature with enough elevation to observe Go Noi Island was a narrow finger two kilometers south of the Song Chiem Son, the southern boundary of the FFZ. This northernmost finger of the Que Son Mountains featured two small humps as it ran east northeast from Alligator Lake like a dagger pointed directly toward the railroad bridges across the island. These humps were Hills 148 and 119.

At 1st Reconnaissance Battalion, Captain G. R. Willson would get the mission. A Naval Academy graduate, Class of 1964, from South Dakota, he was on his second tour in Vietnam and would later retire as a lieutenant colonel. In 1966, he had been a platoon commander in Bravo Company, 3rd Recon, where, for actions on 15 March, he received the Silver Star for his tactical competence and savvy tactics in extracting his platoon from a point-on-point contact along a river trail near the village of Duc Bo.[19] The Delta Company commander, on 8 January 1969, received Operations Order #24-69 from the S-3A (assistant operations officer), 1st Lieutenant Art Weber. Earlier, Willson had been given a heads up by the battalion commander, Lieutenant Colonel P. L. Sharon, with the suggestion he personally lead the patrol to Hill 148. The mission was the regular mission: "conduct reconnaissance and surveillance operations within your assigned haven." However, it added a task: "to check the possibility for an Observation Post on either Hill 148 or Hill 119. Be prepared to call and adjust Arty/air on targets of opportunity in support of Operation Taylor Common."[20]

The execution paragraph stated they would be inserted in two days on the morning of 10 January and be extracted the same day; additional instructions would be verbal. Returning to the company area, Willson called Staff Sergeant Jones in and told him to pull together a larger team for the one-day site-survey mission. He would take nine Marines and a corpsman. He told Jones he wanted an M60 machine gun on the patrol.[21] Willson went to the S-2 (intelligence) shop for maps but also got a camera to take photos of the approaches and views from both hills. He would give Jones and the entire team a complete patrol order that afternoon and have rifle inspection and immediate-action drills on the following morning of 9 January. On 10 January, Captain Willson had Team *Empire State-A* on the battalion LZ after breakfast, waiting for their turn to be inserted.

It was a short 20-minute flight due south and Willson watched as they flew over Division Ridge (Hill 327), south over Dodge City, and then directly over Go Noi Island. The pilot had landed on Hill 148 during Operation *Allen Brook*, so he took it in a fast, low, straight approach to the top of 148 and set the CH-46 down on the crown at 1051[22] (military time, a 24-hour system where time is represented by a unique four-digit number. The first two digits represent the hour, and the second two digits represent the minutes). The team came off forming a 180-degree defense facing north, laying down as the bird departed. There was absolutely no cover. The crest was an old infantry position. Willson immediately did not like it. After the bird departed, he called the team close and told them the position was booby-trapped so they were going to move off the crest and head east off-trail. He pointed for Corporal Hicks, the point man, to depart.

They moved 200 meters into grass and scrub brush 2–3-feet high and stopped to form a 360 defense. Willson then took a series of pictures from 148's northeast military crest. It was a good OP position that could observe most of Go Noi Island, but the team could not see the dual-railroad inverted "Y" entrance to the first southern bridge going to the island. Willson called over Hicks, who was walking point, and explained they would cross over the finger to the south side and drop below the ridgeline so as to not be silhouetted and observed from the northern Go Noi side. He was to move extra slowly, off-trail, looking for booby traps. Willson showed him the saddle and then Hill 119, 800 meters to their east-northeast. They moved out slowly and uneventfully over to Hill 119.

Arriving on 119, the team moved from the southside of the finger to the north side and down to the military crest. Willson left two members on the crest of the finger facing outward to provide security on the game trail that ran along the spine of the finger. He told Staff Sergeant Jones to set security, split the team 50/50, taking meal/water breaks, while he moved around and took photos of each avenue of approach and the view in all directions. The team was only one-kilometer due south of Go Noi Island. To the north, Willson could see both sides of the island, east and west, and the distinctive six railroad bridge spans and elevated berms that spilt it in half. He could easily see all three rivers forming the island in the west, north, and south. He also could detect vehicle movement with his 7 × 50s on Route 1 to the east-northeast. Directly below and northeast, the finger's terrain shape caused a blind spot on the approach to the southern bridge for approximately 500 meters, but he could see both going into and coming out of the blind spot before the first bridge. Due north of the hill, running east to west, was old French Route 537 which had become a two-wheel dirt track. Just below the hill were the leveled ruins of two hamlets: Tho Son and Thon Bon (1). Looking northwest, he could follow the path of Route 537 west to where it met the Liberty Bridge Road. He could easily see Liberty Bridge itself as well as the compound on the north side of the river. Willson finished taking photos on the north side and moved up and over the crest of the finger, sitting next to Corporal Hicks, who pointed out Hill 425, Hon Coo Mountain. The permanent Recon OP on the northern side of the Que Sons had been established on 8 December 1967 and served as both an OP and radio relay and was just four kilometers from them across the Phu Loc Valley. From a security perspective, 425 would be able to watch 119's south side. Also in view was Spider Lake, just below and to the west of Hill 425, and directly below them and to the southwest was the Alligator Lake dam and lake. The lake was only about 500 meters down a draw.

Hill 119 was three kilometers due west of the heavily populated Chien Sons (1, 2, 3, and 4) that were positioned on both sides of the east-running rail line next to Route 537 and running out to Route 1. This hill was a great OP, but what about the defensive on the bald finger? Hicks pointed out three hills to the south, southwest, and west of Hill 119. All were higher and within small arms and 60-mm mortar range. Hill 148 was less than 800 meters away on the same finger and across one small saddle. Hill 177 was on the south side of Alligator Lake to the southwest. Willson thought the hills would not be an issue. However, almost due south at just under two kilometers, was Hill 175. It was another bald finger that both 119 and Hill 425 could easily observe the crest of. The north side had a large boulder field down to the valley floor which was blind to 425. This boulder field would later prove to be a thorn in the backside of Hill 119.

Willson sketched the Hill 119 finger, noting it had six obvious avenues of approach, and the three hills that overlooked it would have to be defended. These included two draws on the north side, the southwest crest trail across the saddle, the northeast crest trail, and two draws on the south side, especially the one southwest to Alligator Lake that Hicks now pointed out had a trail coming up to it and over the saddle, running down the northside toward the two destroyed hamlets. The other notable terrain features north and below the hill 500 meters away was the abandoned railroad berm that ran from An Hoa, in the west, northeast all the way across the entire front of Hill 119, and directly below to the railroad-bridge intersection just south of Go Noi Island. Two hard-packed trails could easily be seen from the hill, paralleling each side of the elevated railroad berm. This obviously was an east–west axis for the NVA/VC and the trails that, six months earlier, Team *Parallel Bars* had had success calling supporting arms on from Hill 425. Willson finished his sketch, called over the radio operator, and told him to call *Benchmark Zulu*, their radio relay to arrange for their extract helicopter.

An hour later, their bird was inbound. Willson had moved the team back to the crest of 119 for the extract. At approximately 1600, they boarded and were back at LZ Finch, the battalion LZ, below Hill 327, by 1630, 5½ hours after they had departed. Willson kept Jones and Hicks with him for the debrief at the S-2 hooch. In the debrief, his recommendation was unequivocal: "Recommend Hill 119 as a permanent OP."[23]

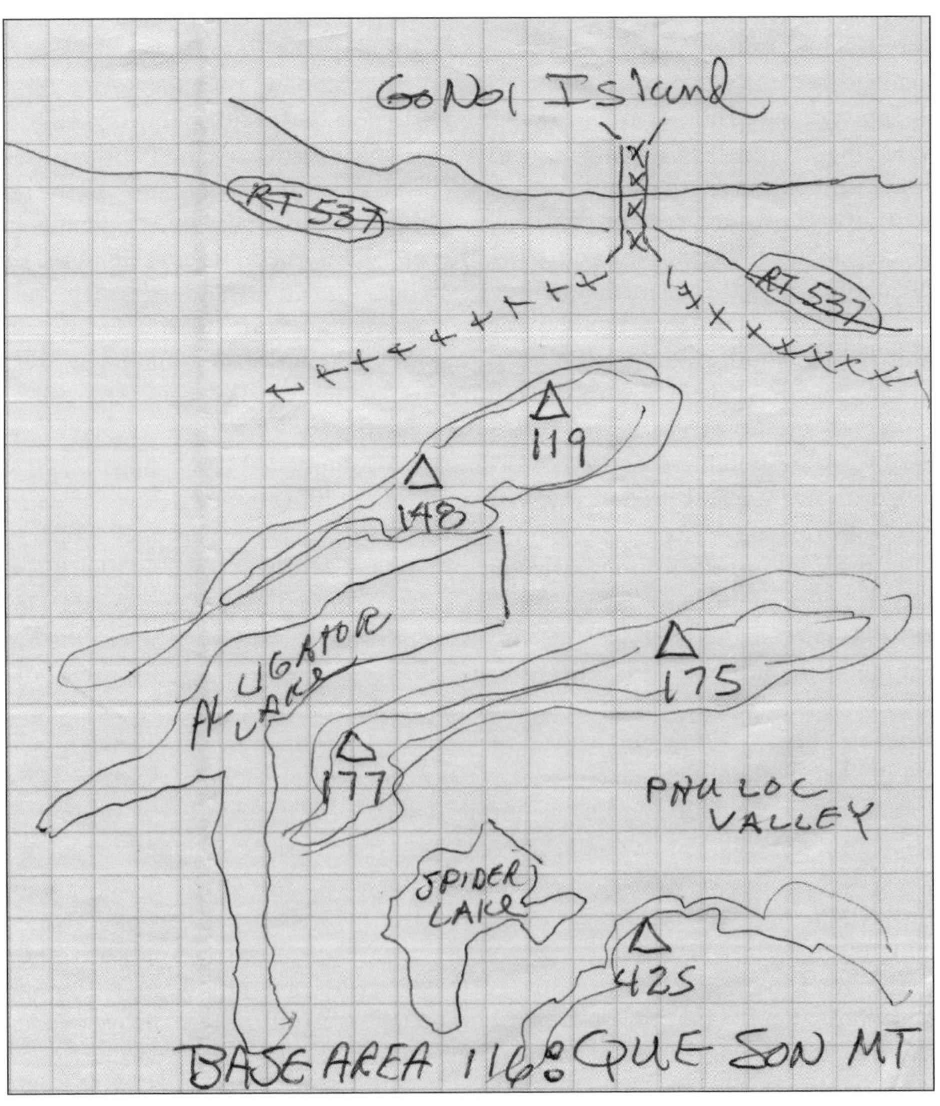

Willson's debrief sketch. (M. Fallon)

He turned in the camera and the sketches. Then he walked back down the hill to the S-3 bunker to find Major D. White and give him a verbal debrief. The 1st Marine Division's nightly situation report to III MAF for 10 January 1969 reported that Team *Empire State-A* had been inserted in the vicinity of grid AT9750 (Hill 148's grid square) at 101031H (the first two numbers represent the date; while the last four represent the time, and the letter the time zone) and extracted at 101620H from the vicinity of grid square AT9850 (military map coordinates) for Hill 119 in support of Operation *Taylor Common*.[24] It was now Phase 3 of *Taylor Common*, which would target Go Noi Island once again with another infantry sweep. The battalion, in consultation with the division staff, concurred with Captain Willson's recommendation. As an economy-of-force measure to observe and control the western half of the Go Noi gap in the outer defensive belt, the 1st Reconnaissance Battalion was tasked to cover the gap with observation and fires from Hill 119. The battalion would build and man its permanent OP.

The next week would be busy for Delta Company as they had not previously had an OP responsibility and were now assigned to construct and man one. Captain Willson set up a planning table on the porch of the Delta Company office. It was his place to sit, plan, and enjoy a Coke from his vintage red, top-opening, Coke machine.[25] It had rails holding glass-bottled Cokes in a tub of ice. One had to slide the Coke bottle along the rail to one end to fish it out and open with the opener on the side of the chest. Willson paid a Vietnamese mama-san to keep the cooler full

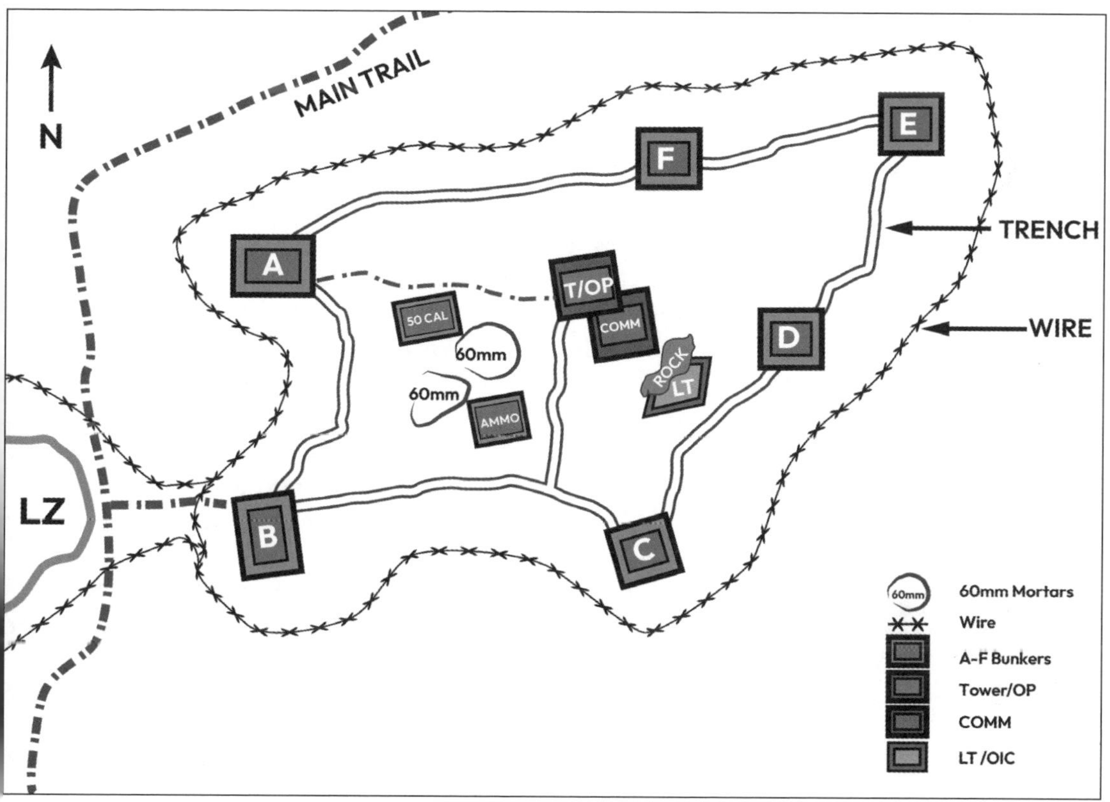

Overhead sketch of Hill 119 bunkers. (W. Denham)

and iced. Known for his tactical competence, Willson was a detailed planner. He sketched out the hill's defenses, built around a communications bunker and mortar pit, with six bunkers around the perimeter, which he labeled A through F, to cover each of the six avenues of approach to the hill. The hill's defensive scheme was planned for one Reconnaissance platoon of three six-man teams, plus a headquarters element, to man the hill.

The need for the OP was reinforced in early January when Team *Fig Newton* of Echo Company, operating in southern Dodge City, identified an NVA antiaircraft (AA) position on the Go Noi Island railroad berm firing at helicopters as they were flying over the island.[26] This happened while Willson was running the OP survey and planning to build the OP. The battalion was covering the Go Noi gap with patrols. One of his Delta Company lieutenants, 1st Lieutenant John Mann from Washington, D.C., who had matriculated through the enlisted commissioning program (ECP), Officer Candidate School (OCS) and graduated from The Basic School (TBS) Class 8-68. Mann was leading Team *Vesper Bells* who had walked in from a truck insert off Route 4 into the Dodge City area just north of Go Noi. On 11 January, they made contact three times with NVA wearing new uniforms and new rain gear. The team suffered four minor wounded-in-actions (WIA) from shrapnel which his tall, lanky, corpsman Dave Snider took care of while the team backed away and broke contact.

They reported a major bunker complex in grid square AT9955 and the AA position dug into the side of the berm at the northern bridge to Go Noi.[27] This site fired at 90 percent of aircraft flying overhead. The team was emergency extracted under fire from small arms and AA fire. At the same time, Team *Paddy Shell*'s patrol leader, Corporal Brunner, reported, upon his extract 500 meters northwest of the northern Go Noi bridge, that they took .30-caliber machine-gun fire from the bridge.[28]

On 15 January, Charlie Company's Lieutenant Carpenter, leading Team *War Cloud*, supporting 1st Marines, walked in off Route 4 into Dodge City across the open rice paddies during the hours of darkness, heading south while patrolling for three hours toward Go Noi parallel and east of the railroad. They moved to the river, Song Ky Lam, arriving about 2300. Following the river west, they moved 300 meters east of the railroad bridge. At 0100, they discovered a hole covered by a poncho and their Scout Dog Prince alerted them. An NVA popped up from the hole, opening fire with an AK-47, killing the dog and dog handler, Armstrong. Following that exchange of fire, the rest of the tree line opened up. The NVA threw a frag grenade, killing another Marine and wounding another. With two dead Marines and two wounded, Lieutenant Carpenter regrouped the team next to the river for cover. He had brought an M60 machine gun for this patrol. As the enemy got on-line and tried to push them into the river, the M60 opened fire along with the team throwing M26 grenades. Eight NVA were killed directly in front of the team. The exchange was over. Carpenter moved the team back east from where they came along the bank. He called for an immediate emergency extract and requested air support. He got a *Spooky* (AC-47 fire-support aircraft) overhead to work over the area prior to his extraction. The team was recovered from the riverbank at 0420 with the extract bird taking heavy AA fire, believed to be a .50-caliber from across the river to the south on Go

"Doc" Dave Snider in the bush. (D. Snider)

Noi Island's north side. Team *War Cloud* suffered two Marines killed and two WIA.[29] Between 9–16 January, Recon Battalion had four teams shot out of their insertion LZs, never getting on patrol near the northern railroad bridge complex of Go Noi.

The need for a full-time OP that could direct supporting arms was now even more urgent. With the death of two of his Marines, Lieutenant Colonel Sharon pushed Captain Willson for a plan and schedule to man the OP overlooking Go Noi Island. Willson, who had already submitted two requisitions to the battalion S-4 (logistics), 1st Lieutenant R. L. Wiggins, wanted to get all the pioneer gear, explosives, sandbags, and lumber for construction pre-staged to take up to the hill when they occupied it. That did not happen. On the morning of 16 January, after Team *War Cloud*'s emergency extract early that morning, Willson was given a verbal warning order to expedite the OP occupation. Two days later, on 18 January, Willson got the written Operations Order from 1st Lieutenant Art Weber, the S-3A.[30] Weber, who enlisted in the Marine Corps in January 1967, graduated from Parris Island and, scoring high on the ASVAB Test (Armed Services Vocational Aptitude Battery Test), became an ECP, and was sent on OCS and TBS. Arriving in Vietnam, he had been assigned to B Company, 1st Recon and spent five months patrolling, accumulating 18 patrols before being reassigned as the assistant operations officer. The battalion had a policy of keeping a recent and experienced patrol leader in the S-3 role in order to not only talk to teams on the radio but to advise Command on their utilization. Art's initiative, that every patrol leader appreciated, was his establishment of an insert/extract officer from S-3 to ride with the heliborne packages on inserts for teams to ensure they were being put in the correct LZs. This double check of the pilot's map reading got patrols started where they thought they were being inserted. Later in his tour, Weber would command Alpha Company. Art remained in the Marine Corps for a career, later commanding the 9th Marine Corps District as a colonel. He would retire from the Staff of the Naval War College in Newport, Rhode Island, and now resides in Middletown.

Captain Willson's team callsign going up to Hill 119 was *Empire State*. The operation order read:

> Mission: Conduct reconnaissance and surveillance operations within your assigned haven to detect possible VC/NVA troop movement or arms infiltration from **Hill 119. Build defensive positions to fortify the hill** [author's emphasis]. Be prepared to call and adjust Arty/air on targets of opportunity in support of Operation Taylor Common. See references (a), (c), and (d).
>
> Execution: Depart LZ 401 on 19 Jan.; insert Haven (UL AT 9852; LR BT0050). Extract when Hill is properly fortified within same Haven. Coordinating Instructions are contained in reference (b) and (e).[31]

A Reconnaissance "Haven" is a fire support coordination measure and deconfliction tool using map coordinates to create areas between friendly units. It was a grid-coordinated box indicated by "UL" (upper left corner) and "LR" (lower right) of the box on the map. Inside this haven or TAOR (tactical area of responsibility), no friendly units could enter or fire inside without specific permission from the unit that owned the area; no one could fire direct or indirect weapons into the haven without first coordinating with the owner. It was a protection zone from friendly fire around the hill. In this case, Willson was provided with a four-grid-square box encompassing Hill 119. It included the abandoned railroad-berm crossing, the hill's north slope, the unoccupied Tho Son hamlet, and ended at the river dividing it from Go Noi. He had recommended a nine-grid-square box, that would have included the four he received plus adding squares to the west (Hill 148) and south (Alligator Lake dam), so he would control all the avenues of approach to the hill with an adequate buffer. Havens were also fire-support coordination boundaries that represented who owned the coordination responsibility and with whom to coordinate. The 5th Marines owned west of Hill 119, the RoK Marines owned east of the hill, and the 11th Marines coordinated fires into the FFZ (Go Noi Island). The small size of Hill 119's haven would continue to plague Hill Commanders and have operational impacts.

Captain Willson had decided he would lead the fortification efforts since he had made the defensive plan. He would take 2nd Lieutenant Lawrence's platoon along with an engineering detachment and a dog team to the hill. Departing at 0900 and flying up from LZ 401 in two CH-46s and a CH-53 would be two officers, 40 Marines, a corpsman, and the Scout Dog Coco. Besides each Marine's M16 rifle, the Recon Marines took three M79s (40-mm grenade launcher), an M14 rifle, one M40 (Remington 700 bolt-action sniper rifle), one M12 (Winchester model 1912 pump shotgun), and three M60 machine guns. For communications, they loaded three PRC-25s and two 292 antennas. To facilitate observation, they brought three 7 × 50 binoculars, one M49 scope, and two nighttime starlight scopes.[32] The CH-53, with the engineer detachment, carried spools of barbed wire, metal engineer stakes, demolitions, and crates of Claymore mines. Prior to departing that morning, Captain Willson had personally briefed the entire group to expect the area to be booby-trapped since the VC had a pattern of booby-trapping former infantry positions as they knew the infantry always returned to hills they had used, and the Americans favored the high ground for their defensive positions.

Upon landing on the hill's crest and unloading, Willson had Lieutenant Lawrence push out two-man security positions east and west and established a two-man OP, while everyone else dug fighting holes around the perimeter in an elongated oval at the military crest on the finger. They soon found, after less than a foot of digging, they hit the solid rock of the finger.[33] They would need more sandbags. By 1445 that afternoon, the Marines had found five booby-trap M26 grenades off the east end of the finger and just off the game trail. They blew each in place. The first day was about getting the defensive fighting holes dug and setting a defense before the sun set. Surely the VC had seen the helicopters arrive and now knew they were on Hill 119. What the NVA/VC did not know was that the Recon Marines had come to stay.

The evening was quiet. The next morning, Captain Willson called the Marines together and explained they were building their own defense. The engineering detachment would start constructing a triple-apron fence around the perimeter which meant the Marines needed to clear all the brush away because the wire fence needed to be on cleared ground so they could see their fields of fire. He closed with, "Always be wary of booby traps!" Further out, Lawrence would have security on all sides of the hill. While they were doing that, he had the communications Marines putting up the 292 antennas and beginning to dig out a comms bunker. Willson walked around with a pole and started outlining the bunker and trench plan for the hill on the ground. This would be a work in progress for some time. Hospital Corpsman Second Class Dagley recommended getting some leather gloves for the Recon Marines like the engineers had as most were developing blisters after only one day of digging. After spending a day on the hill, Captain Willson asked to speak to the S-4, who would have to be summoned to the S-3 bunker to talk on the radio. He wanted to send a message directly to the S-4 about a list of construction items they needed immediately, including the gloves. About forty-five minutes later, he got a return call from the battalion's supply officer, 2nd Lieutenant R. L. Weigand, which was just as well as he would be putting in the requisitions. Willson used all the authority he could muster over the radio to explain the urgency around why they needed not only the gloves, but additional Claymores, and more M60 machine-gun ammunition, and all the items from the construction list not yet filled. He stressed the need for additional sandbags and at least twenty more 5-gallon cans of water. The radio call for resupply completed, Willson went back to digging. He had started a bunker just below the communications-bunker site and was digging out a place to sleep.

The hill fell into a daily routine of security out, brush burn-and-chop detail, and wire detail. The priority was to get the defensive-wire layer out in daylight and let the Marines improve their fighting holes, in which they were living, during the late afternoon/evening. By now, all the holes had a poncho structure overhead and at least two rows of sandbags but were not deep enough to provide real protection. At 1845 hours on 20 January, they got their first sighting—due north about thirteen hundred meters out—on the island's south bank where they sighted twenty or more VC in black "PJs" moving south to southeast towards Tho Son hamlet. They had packs, mortar rounds, and a mortar tube. A fire mission could not be called due to friendly forces operating in the area. Captain Willson made a note that the OP needed to know who was operating in their vicinity, along with their radio frequencies. On the 21st, they continued working defenses and had four separate sightings, totaling 15 NVA/VC with weapons, but again could not call fire missions due to friendlies working the area. They called in the coordinates for the S-3 shop to pass along. On their fourth day, at 1245, they sighted 11 NVA just across the Song Chiem Son, approximately seventeen hundred meters northeast of the hill. They were moving from the north towards them, carrying packs and rifles, in khaki uniforms. The team sniper with the M40 Remington 700 bolt-action sniper rifle took a shot and got a confirmed kill which stopped the column's movement as they went to ground. Lieutenant Lawrence had a fire mission on the way and got good coverage of the static NVA. The spotters saw six bodies on the ground.[34] Hill 119's first enemy kill was with the Remington 700 sniper rifle fired into the Go Noi Island FFZ, followed by an artillery fire mission.

The remaining enemy moved into the tree line and bunkers therein. Close to the sun going down, the Marines spotted six NVA in khaki uniforms with packs and rifles, 12 kilometers north of them in Dodge City on the north side of Route 4. Had Captain Willson not looked through the M49 spotting scope himself he would not have believed what he was seeing. The day was clear, and they had the sun on their western shoulder providing good light. They called a fire mission but were denied clearance due to infantry operating off Hill 55 in the local area.[35] That one sighting confirmed to Willson Hill 119 was going to be a good OP. It was time to add more observers and rotate them every hour, giving all the Marines an opportunity to observe with fresh eyeballs. Going forward, they would have four observers, three with 7 × 50s and one with an M49. He assigned sectors and challenged the Marines to find the targets. Not ten minutes later, Lance Corporal Franklin was calling for everyone to look to the northwest two kilometers out, just off Route 537 near the Song Ba Ren river branch. He had a larger group of NVA moving, northwest to southeast, toward them. The four observers counted 54 NVA wearing packs and rifles. Lawrence, on the radio calling the fire mission, was again denied clearance.[36] It seemed to Captain Willson that the fire-support coordination system had not realized the new OP existed. He would talk with the commanding officer and the S-3 to see if they could talk with the 11th Marines, the artillery regiment. For now, he told his observers to stay vigilant; their day would come.

The next morning, 23 January, at about 0945, after security was out and all the working parties were deployed stringing perimeter wire, the OP team spotted six NVA wearing khaki uniforms with packs and rifles moving east to west on Go Noi Island just across the river from them and about two kilometers due north. The enemy moved into tall grass and out of sight before a fire mission could be called. At 1245, they spotted six more NVA moving next to a thatched hooch in the middle section of the island. The enemy then changed from khaki uniforms into black PJs, which was routine before they moved into rice paddies to work the fields as farmers. They placed their rifles and packs in the hooch. *Empire State* called a fire mission with good coverage of the hooch resulting in two confirmed kills and two probables. Later, at 1615, the hill observed eight NVA dressed in khaki with rifles, and what appeared to be two heavy automatic weapons, disappear into the ground on Go Noi just north of the hamlet Thon Bon (1). They could not call a fire mission on the underground bunker complex due to a 1st Battalion, 5th Marines, platoon patrol base operating in the area.[37] As the sun was setting, they observed, due north just across the river, ten NVA working around a hooch, wearing khaki uniforms, and carrying rifles. They called a fire mission with good target coverage but could not observe results due to darkness.

On the 24th, the engineer detachment continued the wire detail, stringing the three-tier apron fence while the hill Marines provided security and filled sandbags for the machine-gun bunkers. At 1645, on the railroad berm between Bridge 1 and 2 on the island, they observed seven NVA in khaki uniforms with three rifles and seven packs. They called a fire mission with outstanding coverage, resulting in four confirmed kills and three probables. At 1705, they observed one NVA, in green utilities east of the first railroad bridge, wading in the river; he moved into the foliage before they could call for artillery. Forty minutes later, the OP team spotted 11 NVA in khakis and camouflaged with bushes moving to the west on the island's center section along an old east–west dirt track. They called a fire mission but were put into check fire before rounds were fired; the NVA moved out of sight.[38] The next morning at 0905, in an area on the western part of the island the Marines had started calling "the camel's hump" for the way the river bend was shaped, they spotted five NVA in new khaki uniforms and three civilians moving west towards the Song Thu Bong. They had packs, rifles, and four mortar tubes. The hill called a fire mission but were put into check fire; the enemy moved out of visual observation before the check fire was lifted. At 1715, due north of the hill 2,100 meters and just across the southern Song Chiem Son, the team observed, in the same bunker complex, three NVA in green utilities, and five in black PJs with rifles, working around the hooch. With the impact of the first artillery rounds, the enemy moved underground into bunkers. Just as darkness was falling, the Marines observed two NVA in khakis with packs and rifles moving west on the old road on Go Noi. The team was unable to observe further due to darkness.[39]

January 26 would be a resupply day and partial change out of personnel on the hill. Captain Willson would depart with the engineering detachment. During the first eight days on the hill, the Marines and their engineers had completed clearing an LZ on the saddle between Hills 148 and 119. The primary wire was erected and staked out with Claymores in the lower crawl areas. Three bunkers were dug and built out with wood but not sandbagged, and Bunkers 4 and

5 had been started. No trench line existed yet but fighting holes ringed the hill. Trip flares had been strung.[40] An open two-hole shitter, with diesel fuel for burning, had been built with plywood, and furnished with two 55-gallon drums cut in half. A trash pit had been established outside the wire in the deep draw to the northwest. Staff Sergeant Jones would bring an additional corpsman and three new Recon Marines for Lieutenant Lawrence's platoon. Lawrence was now the hill commander with his platoon of 25 Marines and two corpsmen as the callsign changed to *Vesper Bells*.[41] During the first eight days for the OP, *Empire State* had 20 sightings of 133 NVA, 33 VC, and three civilians with NVA escorts. The hill had been partially fortified. The OP had called artillery fire missions, resulting in six confirmed kills and 11 probables; the sniper rifle had claimed two confirmed kills.[42]

Team *Vesper Bells* would have the same haven and same mission with special emphasis in their mission statement to "continue building fortifications on the Hill and to call and adjust Arty/air in support of Operation *Taylor Common*."[43] Jones, the former embassy security guard, had remained in the rear for the first week, at Captain Willson's behest, to scrounge construction items but most importantly to trade for a .50-caliber machine gun.[44] He arrived on 26 January with an old, but functioning, .50-cal he had gotten from the Seabees (Naval Construction Battalion) in exchange for two AK-47s. He also brought up a fourth M60 machine gun. On the second packed CH-46 was a load of construction materials and a pallet of unfilled sandbags. That night, the Marines observed six lights moving to their south on the finger of Hill 175, two kilometers away. They called a fire mission, and the lights went out. Their sister OP to the south on Hill 425 confirmed but saw nothing further that evening.

During a wire check the next morning the team found three booby-trapped grenades on the front northeast slope 100 meters outside the wire in the draw.[45] The Marines stated the draw had been clear two days prior. The patrol also found an old LAAW (Light Anti-Armor Weapon), that appeared to be booby-trapped, just off the game trail to Hill 148. It was blown in place. Lieutenant Lawrence did not like being penned into the OP by booby traps. He would recommend the hill be turned into a platoon patrol base with a larger haven and the authority to patrol off the hill. This would be the first of numerous recommendations by hill commanders to expand their haven in order to improve their own security. The haven would remain the same size for the first eight months and, when the change came, it would get smaller. The issue was deconfliction with the infantry units operating in the area to the west and the RoK Marines operating to the east. They owned their TAORs and would not give up the territory. This meant every patrol from the hill going outside the haven needed to be cleared by higher headquarters in advance, for specific times and locations, to prevent a friendly-on-friendly firefight.

The routine of construction was ongoing and a sighting or two continued daily. On 29 January, the hill had a front-row seat while observing the 1st Battalion, 7th Marines debark trucks and move across the Song Ky Lam onto Go Noi Island. They had observed an NVA force of 300-plus on the island and directed an artillery barrage against them as they were pushing them west.[46] The NVA moved west but were boxed in by D Company, 1st Battalion, 5th Marines, who had moved east from Liberty Bridge in a coordinated trap, as part of Phase III of *Taylor Common*.[47] Hill 119 could watch the fighting continue all night with the NVA shooting green tracers and attempting to break contact, and Marines shooting red tracers. One could watch the flow of the battle. After midnight, the enemy split into small groups to exfiltrate south to avoid the Marines' pincer movement. That morning, the grunts found 72 NVA bodies with numerous additional blood trails.[48]

The next day, 30 January, at 1215, the OP picked up eight VCs dressed in dark clothing carrying packs and rifles. One had a cartridge belt. They were on Go Noi Island, 2,000 meters due north of the hill and were moving southeast towards the river. A fire mission could not be cleared by the FDC (Fire Direction Center) at An Hoa due to friendlies being reported in the area. At 1400, watching the same eight VC, *Vesper Bells* called a new fire mission and was granted clearance to adjust fire. Instead, they fired a battery-two (six guns firing twice) immediately fire-for-effect, resulting in one confirmed kill and four probables. The VC went to the ground. At 1705, the Marines observed seven NVA wearing green utilities carrying packs and rifles on Go Noi, 3,200 meters northwest near the Song Ky Lam. At 1745, the observer team picked up three NVA, wearing dark utilities and carrying packs and rifles, at grid coordinates AT987526 just outside the Dien Phu hamlet, 1,900 meters due north just across the river. Lieutenant Lawrence decided to engage with the team's sniper. Several shots were fired with the M40 Remington 700 and observed with the spotting scope, reporting one NVA hit and down as the other two went behind a dike.[49]

Twenty-five minutes later, seven Vietnamese civilians departed the hamlet of Tho Son below the hill and on the main trail, in the open, walking slowly up the hill. They were carrying a body. They stopped about 300 meters from the wire on the trail and just stood there. After ten minutes, they turned around and returned to the hamlet and were out of sight due to darkness. This was the first incident of villagers coming toward the hill.[50] Villagers approaching the hill on the main trail leading to the saddle that went over to Alligator Lake would become a recurring issue with which hill commanders would have to deal.

On 31 January, the sun rose early and bright in a clear sky. The aviators would call it good flying weather. At 0845, the OP spotted a large group of VC moving around the center bridge/railroad tracks halfway across the island, heading north. Staff Sergeant Jones started counting and stopped at 44. This target was large enough. Lieutenant Lawrence sent a request for air up the chain while he worked up a fire mission. The VC were wearing mixed PJs and all carried rifles. They were getting into an ambush position on the third bridge. Twelve minutes later, Lawrence got a call from an aerial observer (AO) who said he had heard they had a good target. The lieutenant passed him a nine-line close-air-support brief he had written up and talked the aircraft on to Bridge 3 on Go Noi Island. He put the artillery on hold as the hill got to observe its first fixed-wing airstrike by a pair of Marine A-4s with multiple bomb runs on the VC.[51] After the aircraft pulled off and departed, the AO fired an artillery fire mission. *Vesper Bells* had not called the supporting arms, nor did they hear the results on the radio. It was a good show to watch with morning coffee and warm sunshine.

At 1100, the OP picked up multiple targets. With an OV-10 aircraft in the area, Lawrence dialed up the back-seat AO *Cowpoke* on the net and talked him on to three NVA on the north side of the island, running south. They were wearing dark uniforms and carrying very heavy packs with camouflage bushes on top. They looked like three bushes moving down the trail. The OV-10 rolled in hot, using its guns, and scored a direct hit; the three bushes stopped, dead on the trail. While he had the aircraft, Lawrence talked the AO onto a second target of six NVA who had been observing the AO's previous run with binoculars. These enemy soldiers were wearing green utilities and carrying rifles. The *Hostage* OV-10 worked them over with its rockets, scoring hits, and claiming three confirmed kills. About 1400, back between Bridges 3 and 4 on the island, the OP picked up five NVA moving west away from the railroad. All five had rifles and each was carrying a body.[52] They were departing from the area of the early-morning fight with the RoK Marines on the eastern portion of the island. The NVA always removed their dead and wounded from the battlefield to deny their enemy any thought of victory or gain any intelligence from the bodies. Once removed from the battlefield, it was their practice to strip the bodies and bury them in shallow unmarked graves to let nature consume the bodies in secret. Later in the afternoon, at about 1700, the OP observers spotted one NVA in cammies observing the hill from old Route 537 northeast of the hill. They engaged with the sniper rifle, but the soldier was savvy and faded back below the elevated dirt track out of sight.

At about 1715, the Marines picked up 17 NVA moving along the railroad berm halfway across the island in the vicinity of the morning air strike. They were all camouflaged with fresh-cut bushes and carrying packs and rifles. The hill worked up and called a fire mission but could not see results. Later, with sunlight gone at 1845, they picked up eight VC in three boats moving east on the Song Chiem Son, headed toward the RoK sector.[53] The boats were full, and rifles could be seen. They called in a spot report as the boats faded downstream. Lawrence made a note to tell all the observers at the evening coordination meeting to start watching for boat traffic. That night he put out three 2-man listening posts east, west, and southwest down the Alligator Lake trail. On Hill 119, the first sighting of the day was just south of the first railroad bridge on the Song Chiem Son, where 11 small boats were sighted shuttling soldiers, two per boat, across the river. The NVA were wearing dark-green utilities and carrying heavy packs and rifles. The hill requested air and got an AO flying south from Marble Mountain Air Facility to check out the target. There were at least 15 NVA visible in boats and on both shores. This unit had not finished its nighttime crossing and was caught in the morning daylight. The AO got a flight of two F-4s and worked over the ferry crossing site and both banks. The OP overheard the report by the AO to the jets of five probable kills.

For the remainer of the day, the OP had five more sightings totaling 32 NVA with weapons. They had difficulty getting fire-support clearances due to Operation *Taylor Common* owning Go Noi Island with both the 2nd Battalion, 7th Marines and the 1st RoK Marine Battalion working west and east of the rail line, respectively. For the entire week, the OP had a total of 187 sightings of NVA/VC. That afternoon, the platoon cleaned up the hill and packed up their gear. Tomorrow would be their flip day when they returned to Camp Reasoner to be replaced by another Delta Company platoon. These platoon flips would take place every two weeks between the four platoons of Delta Company for the next two years (*see* Appendix 2 for Hill Commanders and Platoon flip dates) Lieutenant Lawrence worked on his notes for the debrief. He would recommend a larger haven and pitch the concept that the hill platoon should run a platoon patrol base and actively patrol in all directions coming off the hill. *Vesper Bells* had found three booby traps on wire checks and one booby-trapped LAAW missile. The VC were booby-trapping the Marines on avenues of patrol coming out of the wire. Actively patrolling off the hill was a standard security measure that needed to be implemented as a counter to the enemy moving freely close to the OP.

CHAPTER 3

New Month, New Leadership at Recon, February 1969

Two songs dominated the charts in the U.S. in February 1969—"Crimson and Clover" by Tommy James & the Shondells and "Everyday People" by Sly Stone of Sly and the Family Stone. Across the Pacific Ocean in Da Nang, South Vietnam, Lieutenant General R. E. Cushman continued to command III Marine Amphibious Force (III MAF). He had four infantry maneuver divisions to orchestrate. In northern I Corps' tactical zone, the 3rd Marine Division and 101st Airborne Division countered the 1969 Tet offensive, while in southern I Corps, the 1st Marine Division and the Americal Division were both on the offensive. III MAF personnel strength was 139,600.[1]

At the 1st Marine Division, Major General O. R. Simpson was moving Operation *Taylor Common* to Phase III. Task Force *Yankee* and the 5th Marines, under Brigadier General R. T. Dwyer had gone west of the combat base at An Hoa into the enemy's Base Area 112. Now, in Phase III, they were cleaning up the Arizona Territory and Go Noi Island, once again, with a multi-battalion sweep. At Camp Reasoner on 8 February, the battalion had a change of command. Lieutenant Colonel P. L. Sharon was relieved for cause by the commanding general and replaced with Lieutenant Colonel R. D. Mickelson.[2]

This early turnover was precipitated by an incident on battalion Landing Zone (LZ) 401 in preparation for a nighttime emergency extraction of Team *War Cloud*, at 0300 on 16 January.[3] As the S-3 (operations) shop was organizing the emergency extract and briefing the pilots on LZ 401, Sharon came down the trail to the LZ from his hooch, dressed in just flip-flops and his boxer-short skivvies, yelling: "What the fuck is going on?" and "Who the fuck authorized the extraction?" He was obviously very drunk and had to be escorted back to his hooch while the assistant operations officer (S-3A), 1st Lieutenant Art Weber, completed the extract brief for the pilots, along with the warning they should expect a hot LZ.[4] Weber would ride the birds as the battalion's emergency extract officer for *War Cloud*, who had four Marines down, two of whom succumbed before the birds arrived.[5] Because it was a night extract, both the lead CH-46 and the lead gunship were piloted by their respective squadron commanders, lieutenant colonels, as they had the experience flying this dangerous mission and had self-assigned themselves.

After the successful extract and drop off of wounded and two dead Marines at the 1st Medical Battalion's LZ, the squadron commanders returned to Marble Mountain Air Facility and went directly to breakfast with their group commander. They reported the actions of Sharon earlier that night. The air group commanding officer took it to his boss, the wing's commanding general, Major General C. J. "Chick" Quilter, who spoke with his peer, Division Commander Major

General O. R. Simpson.[6] Sharon was a direct report, meaning he worked directly for Simpson. After confirming the behavior, and Sharon's pattern of heavy drinking, Simpson relieved him.[7]

Lieutenant Colonel Mickelson was a seasoned combat veteran with clandestine experience with the CIA. He was pulled from his staff job and flown into Da Nang as soon as his replacement could be found, approved, and moved to Saigon. Mickelson arrived on 8 February and was briefed by the commanding general of 1st Marine Division and the division's chief of staff. He immediately proceeded down Division Hill across the road and through the gate at Camp Reasoner to take command.

After the battalion changed leadership, "Mick" Mickelson refocused the battalion. In the field, they would conduct classic *Keyhole* patrols in direct support of infantry operations. In the rear, he put a new emphasis on training. He added experienced Recon Marines as instructors in the S-3 Training Section, which was responsible for the Recon Indoctrination Course (RIC), and extended the course to a full two weeks. Every new enlisted Marine and Corpsman would now go through the course, with no exceptions. RIC 1-69 for 36 newly joined battalion members, which had started on 4 February, was extended until 16 February.[8] RIC 2-69 started 18 February with 31 new members and graduated after a patrol on Monkey Mountain. The Pre-SCUBA Course also started on 16 February for a period of one week.[9] This course, conducted both in the classroom and in the water, was screening and prep to ensure all battalion Marines/Corpsmen/officers headed to the Navy's dive school in Subic Bay, passed the course. SCUBA School seats were cherished and used by the battalion as incentives, normally for a person to extend his tour for six months. During February, operationally, the battalion continued direct support to Operation *Taylor Common* with teams on patrol, and now the observation post (OP) on Hill 119, watching the infantry's back when they swept Go Noi Island. The 1st Force Recon Company had been chopped (operationally assigned) to Task Force *Yankee*, the higher headquarters responsible for the operation.[10] It was to patrol deep to the west of Operation *Taylor Common*'s tactical area of responsibility. Simultaneously, the battalion provided teams for the newly kicked off Operation *Linn River*.

Supporting *Taylor Common* on Hill 119 from 2 February would be 2nd Lieutenant Ed Wietecha and his 2nd Platoon, callsign *Rudder*.[11] They were the second platoon to man the OP and the first to be probed by the enemy. Their flight of two CH-46s landed at 0900; Lieutenant Lawrence and his platoon would depart at 1000 hours. Meanwhile, the two helos departed Hill 119's new LZ and had gone over to An Hoa to refuel. It would be a short turnover. Lawrence had guides assigned and he and Wietecha split up his platoon on the LZ for a guide to each bunker. At the bunkers were C-ration carton sketches and notes including final protective fires. Wietecha had brought 22 Marines and a corpsman along with a dog handler and his dog. He also had two more M60 machine guns that brought the total on the hill to six M60s and one 50-cal.[12] To aid in observation of the enemy forces, his Marines had scrounged two M49 tripod-mounted spotting scopes and a third starlight scope for night observation. He also brought an additional PRC-25 radio, making it four radios on the hill.[13] This was needed to monitor four separate networks, simultaneously, which enabled the OP to act both as an artillery forward observer and aircraft adjuster while maintaining a radio-relay station between Battalion and the Recon teams patrolling in the Que Son Mountains. This trend of bringing additional firepower, observation improvements, and radio capabilities would continue as every platoon wanted to increase its operational capabilities. Weapons and equipment migrated to the hill, not off the hill.

The increased firepower and radio coordination improved the defensive and offensive capability of the hill. On the early evening of 4 February, at approximately 2045, the scout dog alerted on the northeast draw. Movement could be heard in the draw just below the wire. Lieutenant Wietecha called for artillery illumination, which proved ineffective. This was an active probe of the wire.[14] So as not to give away the machine-gun positions, the Recon Marines used gas and frag grenades thrown down the draw. This caused a lot of scrambling movement sounds away from the hill, with the sound of rocks falling in the draw. The OP had received its first enemy probe and learned it needed its own organic illumination capabilities on the hill.

Captain Willson had talked about a mortar.[15] (Mortars are organic equipment for infantry units but were not on the Table of Equipment for a reconnaissance battalion). Wietecha knew they needed to trade for a mortar so they could put up their own illumination rounds and not have to wait and adjust artillery illumination. He would also order illumination rounds for the M79s. On 6 February, the hill was probed again at 2100 in the same northeast draw.[16] One enemy could be seen in the starlight scope. The Marines fired M79 rounds into the draw and heard movement away from the hill.

On the morning of 7 February, nine Vietnamese civilians approached the hill on the main north access trail from the Tho Son hamlet on Route 537 at the base of the hill.[17] Wietecha sent Sergeant Loper and a security team out with a radio. They met the villagers at the abandoned railroad berm partway up the hill. He radioed they wanted medical assistance. As a result, Corporal Stout took the corpsmen down; they treated minor infections and told the villagers to return to their hamlet. During the course of Wietecha's nine-day flip on the hill, the platoon had 32 spot reports with 29 sightings of 139 North Vietnamese Army/Viet Cong, calling 20 artillery fire missions that resulted in two confirmed kills and seven probables. They had two probes of their wire.

The hill had its second visit of civilians from Tho Son, where the grunts had reported to them a discovery of 55 tons of stored rice.[18] In his patrol report, Wietecha noted the grunts appreciated the coordination and the OP watching their backs during the sweep of western Go Noi Island, which was a part of Operation *Taylor Common*.[19] Wietecha made note that the hill needed more wire and recommended a second apron strand outside the first with special emphasis on the northeast draw. He went into detail and stated a determination should be made on the status of Tho Son as both he and the grunt lieutenant he spoke with were under the assumption it was not supposed to be occupied.[20] It had been leveled during Operation *Mead River* but now villagers from Chien Son were rebuilding thatched structures while the OP continued to observe VC (Viet Cong) and NVA (North Vietnamese Army) in the hamlet. Wietecha's report also stated the hill needed an interpreter and that it should be considered for a full-scale MedCAP event. A Medical Civic Action Program is a pre-planned and advertised event for the local population to come to a secure location to receive ad-hoc medical treatment.

Recently assigned Lieutenant Phil Downey had been told by Captain Willson, the Delta Company commander, that his 3rd Platoon would be next to the OP. He needed to start preparing his Marines to go up the hill. What the captain formerly meant was to get his requisition for construction materials into the system as that took time. What he implied was they should also use the Marine Corps' tradition of scrounging items the supply system could not produce. Willson was teaching his young lieutenants the process and art of supporting their Marines. Downey got his Operation Order #110-69 from 1st Lieutenant Art Weber in the S-3 shop at 0930 on 9 February.[21] The order number indicated this would be the 110th patrol run by the battalion since 1 January; their callsign would be *Mad Hatter.*

Downey called his platoon together that afternoon after chow and gave them his patrol order and wish list of materials. They would be going up the hill in two days. They had the same mission, supporting *Taylor Common*, and would continue to fortify the OP. He was a little under strength. He would be taking 20 Marines, two corpsmen and a dog.[22] With six bunkers to man, he assigned each of his six-man teams two bunkers each and kept his platoon sergeant, corpsmen, and dog handler with him. Later, when he got on the hill and realized the amount of radio work needed, he put the dog and handler in the northeast bunker and assigned the corpsmen to help out all night bunker watches. This enabled him to bring four radio operators back to man the small communications/command bunker. It put three men in each bunker and four radio operators in the command bunker.

The platoon had its first sighting during the noon meal on 11 February when they spotted 13 VC in "PJs" and khakis with packs moving out on the eastern half of Go Noi Island.[23] They started the process of calling a fire mission but, with the clearance going slowly through the South Korean (RoK) Marine Brigade HQ and then down to 1st RoK Battalion, it took time and the VC had moved out of the area before clearance was granted. Language was not the issue slowing the process as the RoK had Marines assigned from ANGLICO (Air Naval Gunfire Liaison Company) to coordinate their fires and call fires for them outside the brigade's organic fires. The issue was the layered process of multiple commands being involved in the clearances. The next afternoon, they got an aerial observer (AO), *Mayfly Seven-Fifteen*, who ran a flight of fixed-wing on nine Viet Cong in the center of Go Noi. It was an excellent airshow to watch just 2,100 meters to the north. The AO gave the BDA (bomb-damage assessment) back to the aircraft as two confirmed kills, one probable, and a destroyed bunker.[24] Lieutenant Downey brought his three team leaders and platoon sergeant up to watch and learn as the fixed-wing aircraft made their runs across the front of the hill. He called them "The 4 Corporals": May, Boyle, McQuade, and Castellano. They conducted one additional fire mission before sundown.

The next day, the morning was slow and overcast so Downey had the Marines run a wire check and continue construction of the bunkers; filling sandbags was a never-ending task. The OP now had six fighting bunkers with one layer of sandbags on the roof. Each fighting bunker was also the Marines' home for two weeks. Therefore, internal digging and shaping of the inside continued for safety and comfort. It was also important to design a drainage system for one's bunker, to ensure that, during heavy rains, it did not become a swimming pool and then mud swamp. The lieutenant also worked at his bunker and a separate radio/command one. The actual OP watch was on the roof of a bunker on the hill's crest in the center of the oblong oval defense. A tower was built above this bunker but not until October.

Radios were remoted from the OP to the communications bunker. When a sighting was made, one could immediately get on the radio at the OP and request supporting arms. That afternoon of 13 February, they had three sightings; the first two they used artillery and, on the third, they got *Deerlodge Six-Zero* flying overhead in an O-1 Bird Dog aircraft to run a fixed-wing mission on four VC and a bunker. They could not observe the results on the VC, but confirmed the bunker was destroyed. The next day, they observed four VC south of the hill but could not get clearance to fire artillery. Later that afternoon, with clear skies, they got *Lopez One-Seven*, an AO on station orbiting over the free-fire zone of Go Noi Island, for over an hour searching for a target. Finally, at 1630, the hill picked up 23 NVA in the far northeast corner of the island with heavy packs, cartridge belts, and rifles. *Lopez One-Seven* ran fixed-wing and provided a BDA of six probable kills with two bunkers destroyed.[25]

February 15 was a clear day. Downey had told the morning wire-check patrol to drop off the finger in the southeast and check out the area below them because it was a visual blind spot. There the patrol found recently used three thatched hooches with fighting holes and bunkers underneath two of them. They found a well-hidden 7' × 4' metal storage bin that held approximately fifty pounds of rice. They also found six empty 81-mm mortar boxes. The patrol destroyed all and caved in the bunkers.[26] Back up on 119, late that morning, the OP watch observed movement and VC on Go Noi Island but could not get clearance to engage. By mid-afternoon, AO *Headcold Six-Four* checked in with the hill. The hill had a bunker midisland that the AO's aircraft made a rocket run on and destroyed. That flushed three VC, which the *Headcold* bird engaged, resulting in three probable kills. At 1520, the Marines observed nine NVA on western Go Noi, but all the firing batteries were in check fire and the enemy moved out of sight.

At 1630, an OV-10, *Cowpoke Six-Zero*, checked into the hill and reported 13 NVA/VC on the eastern portion of the island; however, before they could get the bird oriented it had to depart low on fuel. The crew said they would be back. After refueling and dinner at Marble Mountain Air Facility, *Cowpoke* was back. The hill had spotted 82 NVA/VC and teed them up for the AO. They were just northeast of the southern railroad bridge and were moving into a hedgerow, hiding from the aircraft. The hill talked the bird onto the target. The artillery was still in check fire, so *Cowpoke Six-Zero* got a flight of fixed-wing. It was dark when the fourth and final run of two aircraft headed east, therefore no results were observed. For the day, the hill had seven sightings with some significant numbers.[27] The sweeps by the grunts and RoK Marines were pushing the NVA/VC south and off the island. With daytime movement, they were observable to the OP and became targets. Everyone knew the NVA continued to move all night.

That next morning, 16 February, the hill picked up two VC scouting the OP from the northeast. Thirty minutes later, they picked up 12 VC moving in column south of the first railroad bridge. They could not get clearance to engage. Clearly Operation *Taylor Common* was pushing the enemy south towards the OP with the enemy moving from the island back to the Que Son Mountains and their underground or cave base camps there. Just after lunch, the OP picked up nine VC moving and called AO *Headcold Seven-Four* overhead to engage. *Headcold* got a flight of Navy birds to run on the target. He called it one confirmed kill, four probables, and four who escaped into a tree line.[28] Lieutenant Downey thought the AO was being generous to the Navy but, hey, that's how AOs got aircraft willing to come back to them. Between 1700 and 1915, Team *Mad Hatter* counted 168 NVA/VC in mixed uniforms carrying heavy packs and rifles moving off the island.[29] They could not get clearance to fire. They got *Headcold Six-Three* on station, but he also could not get artillery clearance or a flight of birds to service the target because all the allocated aircraft had flown their sorties for the day. *Headcold* gave the OP a detailed description of the trail network on both sides of the first railroad bridge as they were beaten down and heavily used at nighttime when they could not be observed. As he departed, *Headcold* reported a boat coming out of the brush near the bridge on the Song Chiem Son.[30]

The morning of the 17th broke bright and sunny; with the morning light, the OP picked up approximately 150 VC in small groups of 10–15 moving south on the island.[31] They could not get a fire mission due to a local political Tet ceasefire in the area. *Headcold Six-Three* was back overhead supporting the observations. Later in the afternoon, with the ceasefire lifted, the Marines called four fire missions, the last one at 1830, on 20 VC but could not observe results in the dark.[32] Clearly, the VC were moving. Lieutenant Downey knew more would move past him that night heading back to the Que Sons. The next day was overcast with poor visibility. Downey pushed out a wire patrol and a second security patrol south of the hill. He could not get clearance to push a patrol north of the hill due to the ongoing Operation *Taylor Common,* now in Phase III, working Go Noi Island.

The only sighting of the day came at 1810 and was northeast of the OP near the first railroad bridge. There were 11 VC in black PJs, with packs and rifles, moving southeast. The OP called a fire mission and got good coverage of the target area but by the time firing ceased it was dark so impacts on the ground could not be observed, although flashes in the darkness as each round impacted could be seen. Downey called for a ceasefire.[33] That night, 19 February, at 0430, Scout Dog Alos alerted on the northeast steep draw below Echo Bunker.[34] The bunker could not determine the number of enemy that were probing, but at least two were seen. The Marines threw M26 grenades and fired M79 40-mm high-explosive rounds. After a wind-direction check, Echo Bunker fired 40-mm CS gas (tear gas) down the draw. Meanwhile, Downey had called for artillery illumination. However, the probe was over by the time the illumination lit up the night with parachute flares over Hill 119. The Vietnamese villagers would get new silk from the parachutes the illumination rounds used. That day, the Marines had two sightings near the bridge of seven and 20 VC, respectively.

The next day, 20 February, they had only one sighting of two VC out on the island. The large enemy movements had ceased, at least during daylight hours. On the 21st, the Marines picked up 29 NVA/VC moving on a trail on the southeast part of the island toward the RoK positions.[35] They called in a spot report to 1st Recon Battalion and then changed radio frequencies to call directly to the two ANGLICO Marines supporting the 1st RoK Battalion and gave them a heads-up and grid location of the enemy moving towards them. The next afternoon, they sighted nine VC on the northeast side of the island moving into a bunker. They got *Cowpoke One-Five* overhead to check it out, with negative results. The activities of the enemy slowed down with the hill having no observations on the 23rd and only one sighting each day on the 24th and 25th.[36] Lieutenant Ed Wietecha and 2nd Platoon of Delta Company were due to return on the 24th. They arrived at 1300.[37] Captain Willson had arranged for a one-day turnover so that evening there would be two platoons on the hill with Downey's departing on the 25th. The Marines liked the overnight turnover as the two platoons got to spend time together and the evening watches were only an hour long. This was Wietecha's second trip up the hill, so he knew what to expect. He and Downey reviewed the latter's spot reports over a warm C-ration dinner.

CHAPTER 4

NVA Flags, March 1969

As February 1969 was ending at Camp Reasoner, 2nd Lieutenant Ed Wietecha had received his Operation Order #148-69 from 1st Lieutenant Art Weber (S-3A), three days before heading to the hill; except for the dates, it read the same as his last patrol to Hill 119.[1] The platoon would continue observing and call supporting arms in support of Operation *Taylor Common.* Wietecha's callsign for this flip would be *Aunt Mable.* He would not have chosen it, but the troops did not seem to mind. They arrived at 1300 hours in two CH-46 helos flown by the *Purple Fox* Squadron. On the tail of each CH-46 was a white-painted oval with a large head of a fox painted bright purple. In black letters around the bottom of the oval was the squadron motto, "Give A Shit." Recon Battalion had an enduring admiration for the squadron that got them out of the shit!

Lieutenant Downey had guides for the arriving platoon as the Marines spilt up and went to their assigned bunkers. Wietecha followed Downey over to the hill commander's bunker. It had two cots inside and a front porch, with a trench looking south and an outside cooking station. He settled in. Downey wanted to talk so Wietecha listened. Downey also wanted to know what was going on in the rear.

The two lieutenants talked most of the night, as did the Marines in each bunker. Downey and his platoon departed the next day. Wietecha had prebriefed his platoon sergeant, Sergeant Smith and three corporal team leaders (Boyde, Stout, and Mortimer) on what he expected. They would all

Purple Fox Squadron. HMM 364's courtesy calling card, 1970. (M. Fallon)

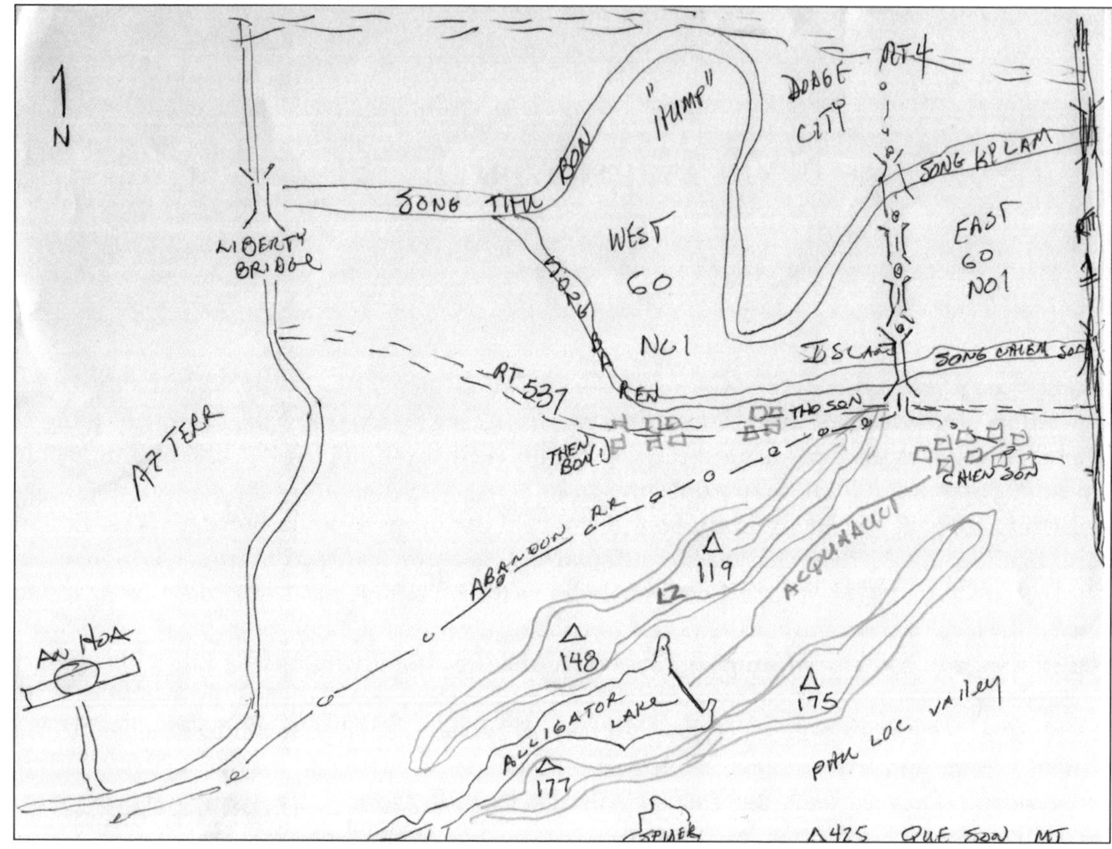

Go Noi Island railroad bridge and berm. (M. Fallon)

continue to improve the defenses. He would run two listening posts each evening and a daily wire patrol each morning. He challenged his leaders to observe life around the hill and try to identify patterns of life below the hill and on Go Noi Island. He wanted to be notified immediately if anyone observed friendly units as he still did not trust the friendly deconfliction processes with the new observation post (OP) and the infantry/Allied units operating in the area. Team *Aunt Mable* fell into a daily routine. There were 68 daylight sightings during their two-week flip, resulting in 425 North Vietnamese Army/Viet Cong (NVA/VC) being observed. *Aunt Mable* called in 46 artillery fire missions and four fixed-wing aircraft missions, accounting for 11 confirmed kills and 79 probables.[2] Wietecha worked up his notes for the S-2 (intelligence) debrief as he wanted to stress the increase in the number of small boats and sampans they had observed that were not fishing but transporting NVA/VC and villagers. It was evident a water-transport system existed on and off the island as well as in some canals on the island. Eight of the boat sightings were at sundown with one group numbering 25 VC and, another evening, 30-plus NVA in uniforms and carrying rifles. There were also two additional sightings at sunrise.[3] It was obvious the enemy was using the rivers, creeks, and canal system during the hours of darkness to move their forces and supplies on, off, and around Go Noi Island. Wietecha's highlight for the upcoming debrief

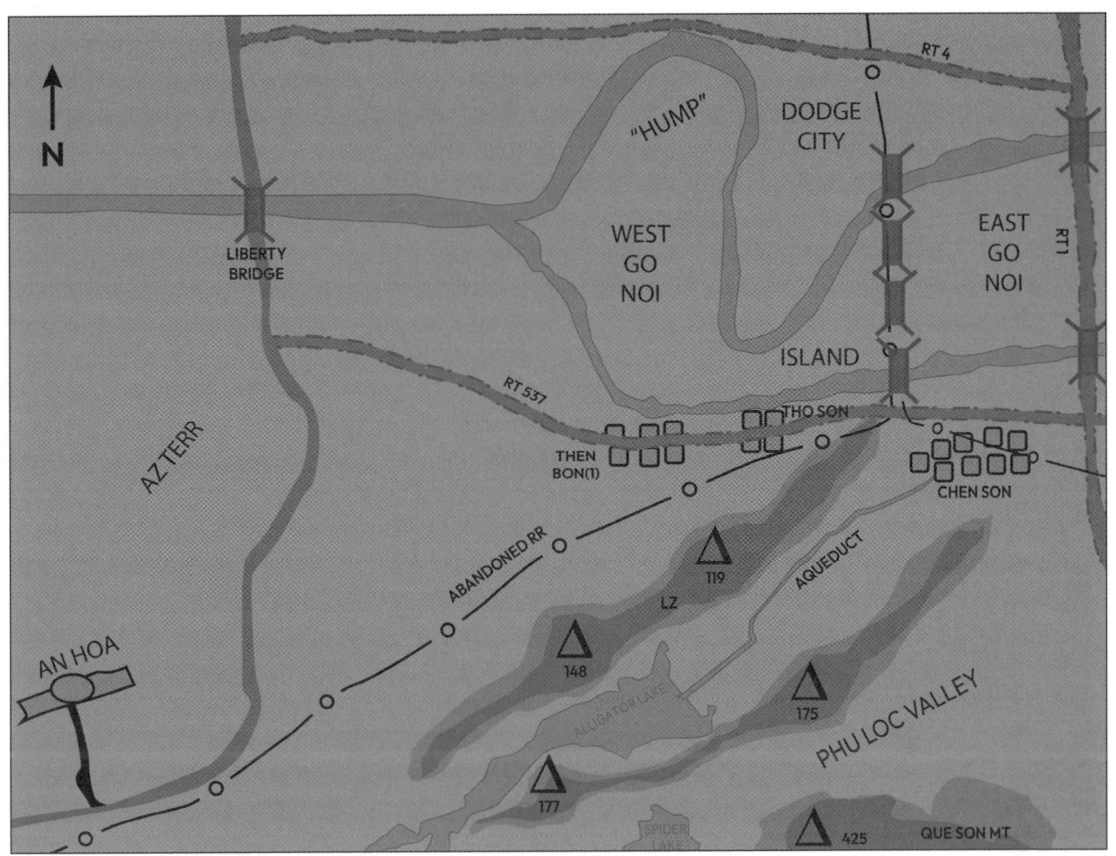

An Hoa, Go Noi Island, railroad bridges, 1970. (M. Fallon and W. Denham)

was the OP's observation of seven NVA flags flown during a Tet celebration near the northern railroad bridge leading off the island.[4]

He had called an aerial observer (AO) who ran an air strike but, due to darkness, neither the OP nor the AO could confirm anything except that the flags disappeared as soon as the air strike began. The planes took green tracer fire with each pass.[5] Because military flags represent a military unit, the S-3 (operations) shop had many questions on the flags, none of which could be answered. From ancient warfare through the American Civil War, flags were used by the leadership of infantry units for movement or to guide their assaults. Capturing an enemy's flag was always an objective and a great morale boost. Sitting on Hill 119, the Marines could only wish they could engage. Wietecha would never know what happened to those NVA "Tet holiday flags." It was a clear statement that, for that moment, the NVA controlled Go Noi Island. Tomorrow, 9 March, was their flip day. Coming up would be 3rd Platoon led by 2nd Lieutenant Jim Unsworth.[6]

CHAPTER 5

Grim Reaper, *Pennywise*, and *Spooky*, March–April 1969

The number of Americans killed in action in the Vietnam War by the end of March 1969 was 33,994, which surpassed the 33,629 killed during the Korean War.[1] President Nixon, frustrated by trying to end the war, authorized bombings in Cambodia to try to cut North Vietnam's supply lines and base camps on and around the Ho Chi Minh Trail. He kept this decision and the subsequent bombing operations classified secret from both Congress and the American people.[2] In Da Nang, Republic of South Vietnam, on 26 March 1969, the III Marine Amphibious Force (III MAF) would change command. A future Commandant of the Marine Corps, Lieutenant General R. E. Cushman Jr. relinquished command to Lieutenant General Herman Nickerson Jr.[3] And, on 30 March, the III MAF engineers completed construction of Liberty Bridge over the Song Thu Bon, opening the road to An Hoa Combat Base.[4]

During March, the 1st Reconnaissance Battalion continued providing teams in direct support of Operation *Taylor Common*, including the three teams assigned as a platoon to Hill 119. Lieutenant Colonel "Mick" Mickelson continued to stress training at the battalion and company level for both newly assigned Marines and for those between patrols. He spoke to the Recon Indoctrination Course 3-69 on their first day, 2 March.[5] Midmonth, on the 14th, the 1st Marine Division Commander, Major General Simpson, spent a half day with the battalion getting both operational and training briefs. He finished with an award ceremony on the battalion street.[6]

In Delta Company, Captain Willson briefed 2nd Lieutenant Jim Unsworth, two days prior to the flip, at his Coke-machine planning table on the side porch of the company office. Fifty-five years later, Jim could not recall the specifics but could recall he was impressed with the detail, thoroughness, and professionalism of the brief and how good the cold bottled Coke tasted.[7] Jim was a stud, collegiate wrestler, and a physical-fitness nut. He fit the mold and was assigned directly to Recon in February 1969 after graduation from The Basic School Class 2-69. This would be Jim's first trip to Hill 119. Water was an issue on the hill. Each Marine would take a metal 5-gallon water can plus his own canteen, his water for two weeks. No showers, just drinking and cooking water.

Arriving 9 March, Jim's 1st Platoon had 24 Marines and two corpsmen, with a dog and dog handler attached.[8] Additionally, he would have two forward observers (FO) from the 11th Marines to assist on the observation post (OP) calling fire missions. Their platoon's callsign was *Night Scholar*.[9] Immediately after landing on the hill, during turnover, the FOs spotted over fifty North Vietnamese Army/Viet Cong (NVA/VC), on the far side of Go Noi Island, walking a trail next to the Song Ky Lam headed towards the railroad.[10] Unsworth confirmed with Wietecha, who was staying behind one night without his platoon to help Unsworth's turnover.[11]

As Wietecha's platoon headed to the LZ (landing zone) to depart, the lieutenants both thought the large enemy group deserved an air strike. Unsworth got on the battalion radio with the air-liaison officer in the S-3 (operations) shop and told him what he had. He was told to wait out. At 1530, an aerial observer (AO) showed up and called *Night Scholar*, asking for the target and the brief. After briefing the AO, Jim and 1st Platoon got to watch, between 1545 and 1800, five pairs of aircraft running strikes on the northern river and northernmost railroad bridge of Go Noi. It was close to sunset when the AO's aircraft departed for Marble Mountain Air Facility and dinner. The AO called the BDA (bomb-damage assessment) as five probable enemy kills.[12]

On 10 March, the hill had five sightings, calling three fire missions, and utilizing one AO. For the day, they had seen 32 NVA/VC, resulting in six confirmed kills, two canoes destroyed, and one secondary explosion observed.[13] Jim walked the lines to all the bunkers, each of which had one layer of sandbags on the roof. He was a new guy or FNG (Fucking New Guy). His only real comparison was An Hoa Combat Base, home of the 5th Marine Regiment. After arriving in-country, Jim hitchhiked a helo ride to An Hoa to visit his brother Andy who was a private first class in the 3rd Battalion, 5th Marines at the large combat base and refueling strip. That afternoon and evening, he got caught up with his brother and filed the paperwork to get Andy transferred to Okinawa.[14] The Marine Corps had a policy that only one family member should be in the war zone at a time without a waiver. Now that Jim was in-country, Andy could be transferred out.

During that trip, Jim noted how thick the bunkers in An Hoa were sandbagged. Three layers were the norm on the outer line of defense and many bunkers in the interior next to the SEA (Southeast Asia) Huts had six layers of sandbags. Using An Hoa as a standard, he pushed his platoon on Hill 119 to add a layer to their individual bunkers.[15] Jim started filling bags for his bunker. The hill's crest was hard and rocky. Dirt had to be imported from below the military crest which meant filling and then moving bags back to your bunker. The weather closed in around the hill in fog and rain. Three days of rain proved none of the bunkers were watertight, and all needed better drainage. The platoon dug drainage ditches out of every bunker towards the side of the hill. The hill was wet and muddy, as was every member of the platoon. Unsworth had his corpsmen running feet checks every afternoon to check for trench foot.

The sun broke out on the fourth day, 14 March. With clear weather they could see the island and they had two sightings that day of six and eight enemy.[16] The first group were moving while carrying packs and rifles, and the second group was busy digging a bunker. The FOs called two fire missions and claimed three confirmed kills and 11 probables. The next day, the FOs, in the early afternoon, spotted ten VC in four sampans on the Song Chiem Son east of the railroad bridge, moving upstream toward the bridge. They called a fire mission and could clearly see four destroyed sampans and claimed ten probable kills.[17] Sergeant Peai, the big Samoan platoon sergeant, was up early on the 16th and had the wire detail out at sunrise.[18] The hill had two sightings that day, for eight total VC.

On St. Patrick's Day, the hill was wet and cold. The Marines had nothing to celebrate with the Irish. They did have four sightings totaling 23 NVA/VC, firing two fire missions with no clear observation. March 18, traffic on Go Noi picked up, with three sightings and a tally of 40 NVA/

VC. They managed to get one fire mission cleared, which resulted in 17 probable kills and a destroyed bunker.[19] The next morning, looking south, they picked up a lot of movement directly below the OP on Hill 425. They radioed 425, who could not observe below them due to the angle of the sheer cliff. The NVA were wearing khakis and carrying rifles. They were approximately 500 feet directly below and at the north face of the hill. Hill 119 called a coordinated fire mission with Hill 425 but, because of the terrain, could not observe the results.

At 1330, three kilometers due west of Hill 119, observers picked up 50-plus VC running southeast away from a grunt sweep. They called the 5th Marines' Combat Operations Center (COC) in An Hoa and reported grid AT955514, requesting the unit's callsign and frequency.[20] At 1715, they picked up 13 NVA in khakis with rifles on Go Noi. The FOs called an artillery mission and reported eight probable kills.[21] Somehow, the Arty observers always saw more kills than the Recon observers. The measure of effectiveness (MoE) in Vietnam for the Americans was body count. The MoE was driven from the top, by Secretary of Defense Robert S. McNamara. Artillery FOs got credit and rewards for more kills. In Recon, they tended to respect a Marine with a higher number of patrols in the bush. There would always be a difference on Hill 119 between Recons responsible for security and Artillery Marines calling fire missions. At this point in the war, Hill 119 only had Arty observers about one flip every other month. Those flips tended to have more kills reported than during a pure Recon flip.

At last light, looking south, at 1918, they were observing below Hill 425. Hill 119 picked up NVA moving and reported the observation to their fellow Recon Marines on that OP. At 2300, just outside the north wire of 119, they picked up a light. Firing M79s from two bunkers, the light went out.[22] The wire checks the next morning found nothing. The next afternoon, they picked up VC in black "PJs" and armed with rifles in a trench and bunker just below the north face of Hill 425. The FOs called a fire mission but could not walk it in due to the angle of the gun target line of the firing battery and the face of the hill. An AO was in the area, so they handed it off to him, who ran an air strike and destroyed the bunker and trench on the valley floor. At 1630, Lieutenant Jim Unsworth was summoned to the observation deck and watched below their hill a column of VC wearing straw coolie hats and black PJs.

The VC were carrying chow baskets, returning from the fields, and heading into the hamlet of Tho Son on Route 537 directly below the OP. The tell on these farm workers was they were also carrying rifles they had taken to the fields.[23] The OP tried but could not get clearance to fire. At 1900, they picked up 13 VC with rifles coming out of the village on the dirt road, turning south on the main trail and coming up the hill towards the OP. Unsworth himself got on the radio to the Fire Direction Center at An Hoa and got the fire mission cleared. They had a preregistered target with the battery where the trail crossed over the abandoned railroad. He timed it well and had good coverage with a battery-one (six guns, one round each) fire-for-effect. When the dust cleared, they could see no VC, who were both hit by the Arty and jumped into the holes dug along the railroad berm.

On the 21st and 22nd, the Marines on the hill had seven sightings, totaling 36 NVA/VC moving around, out on Go Noi Island. They called four fire missions and one air strike but, due to vegetation, could not see the results.[24] The night of the 22nd, at 2300, the team picked up two flashlights moving across the trail on their LZ. They opened fire with M16s as the lights went out as the enemy ran down the trail towards Alligator Lake.

Second Lieutenant Jim Unsworth on the tower with Lance Corporal Service plotting targets. (J. Unsworth)

On 23 March, as a weather front was moving in from the sea, they picked up four NVA wearing camouflage utilities, with packs and rifles, moving east on a Go Noi trail towards the South Korean (RoK) positions, which were further east. They executed a fire mission with four probable kills.[25] That evening, there was zero/zero visibility and rain. It rained all night, and the Marines began to worry they would not have flying weather for their scheduled flip out the next day. It was overcast on 24 March but not enough to prevent flying. They got a radio call just prior to noon from LZ 401 that the flip was on. It would be a hot flip, and they were to be prepared to mark with smoke the placement location of the water buffalo (water tank on a trailer). Fifteen minutes later, a CH-53, with the trailer slung under it, could be seen coming toward the hill.

Lieutenant Unsworth picked a small, level spot above the trash pit on the forward north slope for the buffalo. The Marines watched it come in. Something was not right. Finally, when the giant CH-53 was hovering to put it down, Unsworth realized it was blue, or blueish green. Back at Camp Reasoner early that morning, well before sunlight, Corporal McQuade had been busy with the ¾-ton personnel carrier from the Recon motor pool. He had made the midnight requisition of an Air-Force-blue water buffalo from Da Nang airfield. Then he and "Doggie" McBride painted it green before taking it to LZ 401 to be flown out to the hill where no air force would ever see it. The paint had not dried and, as the helicopter flew south, the green buffalo was turning blue with every mile as the paint peeled off. Now that Hill 119 had a water buffalo, it would be traded out once a month for a full one in the routine shuffle that replaced empty buffalos for full at every fire-support base around Da Nang. From a quality-of-life point of view for the hill's Marines, the McQuade/McBride midnight requisition was the most significant upgrade to occur.

The upcoming platoon with water buffalo arrived at noon; Unsworth and his Marines were off the hill before 1230, headed for Camp Reasoner, hot chow, and cold showers. Coming up to the OP was 3rd Platoon and 1st Lieutenant John Mann. His mission, of observing and interdicting the NVA/VC movements with supporting arms, would continue.[26] With Operation *Taylor Common* moving off Go Noi Island, the direct-support mission was dropped. There would be no grunts sweeping the island, which once again became a free-fire zone. The platoon liked their callsign: *Grim Reaper*. Mann would have 21 Marines, a dog, and dog handler.[27] The FOs went back to the 11th Marines, so he and Staff Sergeant Jones would be calling the Arty and air. Jones had been up with the captain at the start, so he knew the hill and had the Marines organized for their arrival by Bunkers A through E. Shortly after they were settled in, they observed a large group of civilians depart the village and move up the main trail toward the hill. The group remained at the railroad berm, except for six Vietnamese who continued to come up the trail. They were wearing the standard farmers' clothes of black PJs, and a couple had white tops and coolie hats.[28] Mann did not like the tactical situation that was developing. He did not know their intent, especially the larger group below which they really could not observe well behind the railroad berm. It was 1620. Mann called Jones and Sergeant Castellano for a conference. All three agreed the civilians should not be allowed close to the hill. Jones suggested warning shots to push them away or at least see how they would respond. Jones went to A Bunker and Castellano went to Echo; on Mann's signal, both bunkers opened fire in the dirt just outside the wire. It sounded like a mini FPF (final protective fire), and Mann thought they over did it. That said, the civilian group of six turned around and the entire group returned to Tho Son hamlet. Mann would write up a spot report in order to report the incident to Battalion.[29]

Over the first four days, the OP observed only light movement on the island. On 27 March, things picked up and, as the sun was setting, they observed 41 NVA/VC near the southern bridge to the island, along with a sampan moving out into the river. Mann thought they were NVA as they were wearing green utilities, carrying packs and rifles, and wore helmets. It was dark by the time they got clearance and executed the fire mission.[30] Mann shot it into the dark out of frustration. Afterward, he called Battalion and asked that they have the assistant operations officer (S-3A), 1st Lieutenant Art Weber, come to the radio. Mann was concerned with night movement in his blind spot below the east end of the finger between the bridge and the village of Chien Son. When Weber called him an hour later, he proposed a walk-off patrol into grid squares AT9951 and BT0051. Weber said he would work on the proposal, and all the clearances with the grunts and the RoKs. Mann could plan the patrol but had to wait for the order and the grid clearances prior to stepping out to the east.

On the evening of 3 April, Mann set out a night ambush led by Corporal Wayne and five other Marines. They were inside his haven on the northwest side of the trail next to the abandoned railroad tracks. At 0330, three VC moving along the trail walked into the ambush site. The team engaged with small arms. After waiting ten minutes, they moved over to the kill zone below them, finding only blood trails and discarded towels. They moved back up the hill and awaited the morning light. Returning to the ambush area for a daylight search, they followed blood trails and found a dead woman, wearing black PJs, with a small pack. The pack contained personal gear and a small shovel.[31] They left the body and returned to the OP.

On 4 April, nine days after Mann's request to patrol to the east, and a 121 NVA/VC sighting later, Weber radioed with a clearance for a walk-off and a frag order. He gave him the frag order and patrol haven east for two kilometers. He added guidance that Mann could not lead the patrol; as hill commander, he must remain at the OP. He should pick his best patrol leader and let him run the patrol. The walk-off patrol would be called *Pennywise*,[32] was led by Sergeant Castellano, and included six other Marines. The patrol exited the west gate of Hill 119 after dark on the evening of 5 April by walking across the LZ and dropping down the trail to the south towards the lake. Once off the skyline, they got off-trail to avoid booby traps and cut back east on the sidehill just below the OP. *Pennywise* had prebriefed this route to Mann to ensure the hill would not misidentify them as they walked just outside the wire before dropping into the valley. They moved into the valley for two hours and found a game trail heading east. They could see the lights of the well-populated Chien Son village on the valley floor below. They set in above a north–south, hard-packed, high-speed trail that led straight to the railroad bridge 800 meters to their north. At 2215, they first heard the enemy. *Pennywise* started counting NVA, who were moving slowly, just walking, talking, and smoking cigarettes. They were in groups of 10–12, well-spaced on the same trail, moving south and a little west back towards the Phu Loc Valley. *Pennywise* called *Grim Reaper* twice with no response. Then they got a radio call from *Coffee Time*. They recognized Mann's voice on the radio. They had not been briefed about the callsign change.[33] Whispering over the radio, they informed the lieutenant they had multiple groups of NVA moving west. The count was now over 200 and they were still on the move,[34] too many for the team to engage. The team was told to move away, back up the finger, and get down. The hill would take control and engage the large target. Mann called the battalion COC and requested an air strike while simultaneously working up a fire mission. They fired the artillery for 20 minutes until *Spooky* arrived.[35] *Spooky* was the callsign for the AC-47 aircraft with three Gatling guns firing out one side. Flying an orbit so the guns pointed at the ground, it could put down 1,000 rounds a minute, with every fifth round being a red tracer. At night, it looked and sounded incredibly scary—a red line, or three red lines from the sky with all three guns going. The sight earned *Spooky* the nickname "Puff, the Magic Dragon." Before *Spooky* started, *Pennywise* was sitting on top of the finger ready to watch. *Pennywise* called *Coffee Time* and reported *Spooky* was taking groundfire. The next morning, they went back down to the high-speed trail and found blood trails leading away towards the large boulder field on the north slope of Hill 175. It was out of their haven, so they returned to the hill.[36] The platoon was due to come off the hill on 8 April. For *Grim Reaper/Coffee Time*, during the two weeks they occupied the OP, they observed 164 NVA/VC, called 16 fire missions and four air strikes, accounting for six confirmed kills and 17 probables.[37] The two walk-off patrols had resulted in one confirmed kill and over 200 NVA engaged by *Spooky*. Clearly the enemy knew the hill was manned and was, therefore, moving around it at night to avoid being seen.

Upon returning to Camp Reasoner, Lieutenant Mann felt like crap and looked worse with a yellowish skin color. After the patrol debrief, he went to the battalion aid station and was diagnosed with malaria and a lymph-node infection. He would end up spending the next month in a 1st Medical Battalion ward for malaria, recovering and trying to regain his weight. Returning from the hospital with 23 patrols under his belt, he was transferred to become the battalion's S-2 (intelligence).[38] In July, with the departure of Art Weber, who had become Alpha Company's commander, Mann became his replacement, or *Alpha-Six,* until his 10 September 1969 rotation to Camp Lejeune, North Carolina.[39] He served there for another year until his discharge. Getting out, he used the GI Bill and earned a degree in forestry engineering from the University of West Virginia. Moving to the Pacific Northwest, he spent the next 25 years in the forest and logging business with a 17-year run on Vancouver Island in its large virgin forest, harvesting lumber. Today, he lives in Bend, Oregon.[40]

CHAPTER 6

Booby-trapped Bodies and Civilian Medevacs, April 1969

Playing in movie theaters and drive-ins across the United States in April was *Midnight Cowboy*. On 3 April, Secretary of Defense Melvin Laird formally announced the United States would reduce its involvement in the war. The new policy of "Vietnamization," a word made up by the Pentagon, was intended to reduce American involvement and turn the war over to the South Vietnamese Government and its military forces.[1] The announcement was not sufficient enough for the antiwar movement which was already coordinating a massive demonstration in major cities on 5 April.[2] The country was quickly becoming divided over the Vietnam War.

On 17 April, III Marine Amphibious Force (III MAF) received its first 175-mm guns.[3] The increased range over the 155-mm guns would be a direct help supporting reconnaissance teams employed on the Laos border. On 27 April, a controlled grass fire got out of control at the Navy/Marine Ammunition Supply Point #1 in Da Nang, resulting in its complete destruction.[4] A huge fire with exploding ammunition, it burned for three days. Anyone who saw it on the first day would never forget the inferno.

At Camp Reasoner, training continued to be emphasized. Recon Indoctrination Class 5-69 commenced, as did Pre-SCUBA 4-69.[5] Lieutenant Colonel Mickelson took one Recon team up to Division Hill on 9 April to serve as a static display for Senator John Tower of Texas.[6] Major D. White, who was the S-3, had also been the previous battalion commander's drinking buddy. While he attended the MACV (Military Assistance Command, Vietnam) Recondo Conference in Nha Trang in early April, he was subsequently transferred.[7] Major P. J. Cole, personally selected by Mickelson, became the new S-3 Operations Officer for the battalion.[8] Next at bat for Hill 119 would be 2nd Platoon Delta Company led by Staff Sergeant Hall as the company was short of officers. He would bring 21 Marines, two corpsmen, a dog, and dog handler to the hill for their two-week watch.[9]

The flip had only taken 30 minutes, with 2nd Platoon arriving at 1130 and 3rd Platoon departing on two CH-46s at 1200, but it had been long enough for 3rd Platoon to brag on the successes they had had with walk-off patrols. They had sighted over 200 NVA (North Vietnamese Army) in the south valley and had *Spooky* work out a great sound and light show.[10] They had bragged about bagging a VC (Viet Cong), whose body was just off the northwest trail by the railroad berm. It was ripe and still there to smell and see![11] Not long after they had settled into their bunkers, a group of Marines approached Hall and wanted to go check out the body and take photos. Hall was an excellent Recon Marine on his second tour in Recon. He was not infantry or observation-post (OP) savvy. He said fine. So, a group of ten Marines, not really an organized patrol, dressed in shorts and shirts, with cameras and bandoleers of ammunition across their chests, walked across the LZ (landing zone) and down the northwest trail. At 1410, the hill heard a large explosion.[12] Looking across the LZ and down the trail, they saw the gray smoke of the explosion drifting away; Marines were down. Sergeant Gawlaki yelled for "Doc" Dana, and they ran across the LZ and down the trail. Immediately, they saw three men down hard. Doc jumped on the worst-looking body and cleared his airway as the Marine went into shock. Gawlaki sent Private First Class Urnes back up to tell Hall to call for a medevac. Gawlaki organized the Marines to carry the three wounded back to the LZ. Doc worked to stabilize all three on the LZ. By 1435, the one emergency and two routine medevacs were complete.[13] By 1600, Captain Willson was on a bird to Hill 119. He arrived to confront Hall. The company commander had cooled off by the time he arrived. Had Hall been in the grunts on his first tour, he would know what all grunts knew: all bodies, friendly and enemy, found on, or left on, the battlefield was going to be booby-trapped. Willson spoke softly in the commander's bunker for the 30 minutes he was on the hill. He had no officers available for command of the hill. He knew Hall was a solid staff non-commissioned officer who had made a mistake. It had cost them three Marines.[14] Willson explained to Hall what he expected for the next two weeks and was extremely specific about no walk-off patrols. The platoon was now down three men and had to maintain security of the hill. It was not the best solution, but it was today's solution. Captain Willson departed on the CH-46. He would have dinner with Lieutenant Colonel Mickelson and Major Cole, explain what happened, and the plan going forward.

That night, at sundown, the OP spotted 15 NVA/VC moving on the island. They called their artillery FDC (Fire-Direction Center) to fire into the free-fire zone. *Ladyman*, the battery, fired two battery-twos, or twenty-four 105-mm rounds, with favorable effect. The OP saw three enemy moving away. Twelve were on the ground dying. They gave *Ladyman* 12 probable kills as darkness fell.[15] The morning of 9 April, they had multiple observations on the southeast side of the island near the river. They also saw five boats. The boats always got the chain of command excited and, soon after, the Direct Air Support Center, co-located with the 1st Marine Division's Fire Support Coordination Center, radioed out to see if the boats were still on the river. When they got an affirmative answer, they said an aerial observer (AO) would be out shortly. That day, the Marines had a series of three spotter aircraft overhead. Each would work multiple air strikes and fire missions on the eastern free-fire zone.[16] On the 10th and 11th, there was boat traffic on the northern river of the island, the Song Ky Lam. Boat traffic and VC were sighted on both banks. The OP got an AO up both days to work the northern river as they focused their own observations south.

At 1000 on 11 April, seven women brought five children up the main trail and stopped just past the railroad berm. Hall sent a security detail down. They wanted medical care. The corpsman, Doc Dana, said three of the Vietnamese needed to go to the hospital. The OP contacted battalion, and the air officer arranged for a medevac. Three wounded casualties were subsequently evacuated at 1121.[17] A precedent had been set; the villagers of Tho Son hamlet would use the hill for medevacs for the next two years.

At approximately 1500, *Black Ace One-One*, an Army O-1 Bird Dog with an AO, came on station, calling the hill for targets. The hill talked him over to some bunkers midisland. Within fifteen minutes, *Black Ace* had fixed-wing aircraft running passes and dropping bombs on the bunkers. The air strikes stirred the nest, and the OP was soon counting NVA moving south at high speed. They radioed *Black Ace* with a count of over 200 NVA. That got more air on station. A Marine OV-10 with an AO, *Cowpoke Three*, came on station to relieve *Black Ace*. *Cowpoke* ran air and got secondary explosions which *Hanover Sue*, the OP's new callsign, could see from Hill 119.[18] When the air departed, *Cowpoke* called two fire missions and then departed due to darkness. There had been an aircraft over the island from 1500 to sundown.

One-armed woman and two village boys, December 1969. (T. Mullins)

On 12 April, the village women were back, led by an elderly one-armed woman.

It was the same seven women, this time with two children. The security team and corpsmen met them 300 meters outside the wire. Three needed medevacs, which were completed before noon.[19] Later that night, at 0435 on the 13th, Alpha Bunker could hear voices coming from the abandoned railroad bed below the hill. The OP called a fire mission, and the voices ceased. On the morning of the 15th, the village women were back. This time, five were wearing traditional black bottoms and white tops. They had four children. Two of the children were extremely sick, with a high fever, and were malnourished. The OP radioed for a medevac. Two women and two sick children remained sitting all day on the north slope off the LZ, waiting for their lift to the hospital. The others returned to Tho Son 800 meters below the Marines' position. The medevac bird came in late afternoon and flew the two children and two women out.[20] The OP had nine sightings between the 15th and 17th, each receiving a fire mission or attempted fire mission. A typical day on the OP was five hours of boredom, or filling sandbags, broken by an occasional sighting and an attempt to get a fire mission cleared. It was easy to fall into a lazy routine.

On the evening of the 17th, at sundown, the OP observed 13 NVA/VC, wearing black PJs and carrying heavy packs, moving into the east side of Thon Bon (1) hamlet northwest of Hill 119. No civilians lived in the empty hamlet. The Marines called a fire mission but, due to darkness, could not observe the results.[21]

On the 18th, at 1530, eleven Vietnamese civilians approached the hill. Seven were woman and four were military age men. They all wore the mixed PJs of farm workers, and coolie hats. They stated they were sick and hungry. None had South Vietnamese ID cards. All were detained. At 1615, they were flown to LZ 20 and escorted to the III MAF prisoner compound for questioning.[22] At 1900, two Army gunships, *CP Six-Eight* and *CP Six-Nine*, checked in with the hill looking for targets. The hill had spotted a cooking fire on Go Noi Island. They vectored the birds over to check it out. They took small-arms green tracer fire, so they worked over the area, reporting they had expended all their ordnance, and departed. At the end of the day on the 20th, one woman and two children walked up the north main trail to the outside meeting point. They asked for medical treatment. After Doc Dana confirmed they were sick, they were medevac'd at last light by a bird coming out of An Hoa and headed for Marble Mountain Air Facility (MMAF).[23]

At 1915, the OP picked up 23 NVA/VC moving on the trail next to river on the island side. A fire mission was attempted but, prior to clearance, the enemy went into the hedgerow and out of observation. With the fire mission cancelled, the spot report was radioed into Battalion.[24] On the morning of 21 April, three female and one male Vietnamese moved up the trail. The security team went out and checked for ID cards. They had none. All four were evacuated later that day as suspected and hungry VC.

On the 22nd, the day broke with bright sunlight and the OP immediately picked up multiple parties moving on Go Noi Island. At 0745, they counted 75 NVA/VC in PJs carrying packs and rifles and moving into bunkers, in a complex in the center of the island. *Hostage Dog*, an OV-10 Bronco, was up and started working the area with its own ordnance until they got a flight of F-4s on station. The fixed-wing fighters made multiple runs with 500-pound bombs. They worked over the target area, destroying the bunkers. Not being able to see any enemy, they presumed to have killed most inside the bunkers. At 1635, the OP picked up 13 NVA moving with rifles on the island and got *Cowpoke Six-Nine*, an AO overhead, to run two flights of fixed-wing aircraft followed by two fire missions. The enemy dispersed into the thicket in four directions. The next two days were slow with only four sightings. On the evening of 24 April, at 2100, the OP observed heavy machine-gun fire aimed at every aircraft flying north over the railroad berm on Go Noi. *Spooky One-One* came down from MMAF and started working the berm from north to south. It took heavy machine-gun fire from close to the southern bridge over to the island before departing the area having expended all its ammunition.[25] For their two weeks on the hill, 2nd Platoon had 382 NVA/VC sightings. More significant was the multiple visits from the women of Tho Son and Chien Son, totaling 26 women and 11 children.[26] The OP had become a de facto medical-evacuation site.

After completing his flip out at noon on 25 April and finishing his S-2 (intelligence) debrief, Staff Sergeant Hall got the Delta Company jeep and, along with Sergeant Gawlaki and Doc Dana, drove down to 1st Med Battalion to visit their wounded Marines. The Marine who was the subject of the emergency medevac had lived but was already in the naval hospital on Guam. They found their other two Marines in a convalescent ward.

Flipping up to Hill 119 that day was 2nd Lieutenant Jim Unsworth for his second trip. He would have the callsign *Bag Shaw* this time around.[27] Delta Company's 1st Platoon had 18 Marines and two corpsmen. Sergeant Peai remained Unsworth's platoon sergeant, but he was pleased to also have Sergeant Mendez along for this trip. Jansen and Kenner, both hospital corpsmen third-class, were strong and experienced corpsmen.[28] Corporal Cantrell had graduated from the 1st Marine Division Sniper School and had his own assigned rifle, an M40 equipped with a scope. It was a Marine Corps purpose-built bolt-action sniper rifle based on the Remington 700. He had zeroed the rifle specifically for him at the school. Unsworth told Cantrell, if they had the opportunity, he would use the sniper.[29] The first opportunity came four days into the flip, at 1500. While experiencing good sunlight, the OP spotted seven Vietnamese, wearing black-and-white PJs, digging a pit on the side of a trail next to the aqueduct that ran towards the village of Chien Son (4) east of the hill. It was a 1,600-meter shot. Cantrell put several shots towards the diggers. When they heard the shots, the Vietnamese scattered east back towards Chien Son (4). There were no hits or any casualties.[30] His next opportunity came the next day, 30 April. The OP spotted two NVA/VC with rifles walking west on the aqueduct trail due south of the hill approximately 700 meters out. Cantrell laid on top of Bravo Bunker and zeroed in. He fired two rounds and got one confirmed kill which he logged into his sniper logbook.[31] The second man hid behind the aqueduct. The same day, ten Vietnamese villagers came up the north trail and waited at the abandoned railroad berm. The security team and corpsmen went out to meet them. None had ID cards, but most had infected shrapnel wounds. All were heli-lifted out to LZ 20 and escorted to the III MAF compound for treatment and questioning.[32] During their 19 days on the hill, *Bag Shaw* had 72 separate sightings consisting of 527 NVA/VC. They fired 51 fire missions and called 11 air strikes.[33]

On 5 May, during the morning wire check at 0715, the team found a freshly planted M26 grenade with pin pulled and a rock holding the spoon in place.[34] It was 75 meters west of the LZ on the side of the trail leading up to Hill 148. It had clearly been put there the prior evening. The team tipped it over and the grenade rolled down the draw, exploding with no casualties. They had been extremely lucky it rolled away downhill. During his S-2 debriefing with Corporal Sizemore, Unsworth stressed the point that the hard-packed trail south and below the OP, between the hill and the aqueduct, was being used nightly by the NVA moving in and out of the Que Son Mountains. To make his point, he asked Sizemore to highlight his spot report of 1 May on his debriefing report. The report occurred at 2230 where the OP's southern listening post had counted over one hundred NVA moving east carrying packs and rifles.[35]

CHAPTER 7

Team *Barkeep* and Night Fighting, May–June 1969

In the United States, the top rock music hit for May was "Get Back" by The Beatles. It became a most-requested song on the Armed Forces Vietnam Network (AFVN). On 6 May, Marine Lieutenant General R. E. Cushman, just back from commanding III Marine Amphibious Force (III MAF), was reassigned and became Deputy Director of the Central Intelligence Agency.[1] At III MAF on the same day, the command began its fifth year in Vietnam.[2] And in the northern A Shau valley, the 101st Airborne Division captured Hill 937, or "Hamburger Hill," as the troops called it, on 20 May.[3]

In the 1st Marine Division, the G-2 (intelligence) reported that Front 4 had moved significant elements of the 2nd North Vietnamese Army (NVA) Division forward. The 36th NVA Regiment—comprising the R-20, V-25, T3 Sapper, and T89 Sapper Battalions, as well as what remained of the 38th NVA Regiment—was back on Go Noi Island.[4] Colonel James Ord, the former commander of 5th Marines, was now the division's operations officer.[5] Knowing the island well, he had a personal hand in developing the scheme of maneuver and operations plan for the upcoming Operation *Pipestone Canyon* that, once again, had the objective of clearing the enemy from Go Noi. This operation would be a large one involving a combined infantry force of ten maneuver battalions from the U.S. Marines, Army of the Republic of Vietnam, and South Korean Marines. In mid-May 1969, 1st Division briefed the 1st Marine Regiment that its mission would be to completely clear and neutralize Go Noi Island, and Dodge City just north of the island, and reopen Route 4 from the coast highway to Dai Loc village and Hill 65. *Pipestone Canyon* would run from 26 May to 7 November.[6]

At 1st Recon, the month found both organizational change and personnel change at Camp Reasoner. 1st Force Recon Company, under Major Simmons, had been assigned to Task Force *Yankee* and the 5th Marines. Living and working out of An Hoa Combat Base, they were released from being attached to *Yankee*. They now came under the operational control of 1st Reconnaissance Battalion. Force Recon also moved the company from An Hoa back to Hill 34, commencing a rehabilitation and training period.[7] At Camp Reasoner, Lieutenant Colonel Mickelson rewarded the diligent, sleep deprived, assistant operations officer (S-3A), 1st Lieutenant Art Weber, by assigning him as the company commander of Alpha Company.[8] First Lieutenant Porpotage came out of the bush as an experienced patrol leader and became S-3A. In Delta Company, Captain G. R. Willson was headed to 1st Force Recon Company to become their S-3. He was replaced by another experienced patrol leader, 1st Lieutenant A. T. Bouts.[9] In an example of Major General Simpson's trust in Mickelson, he had the battalion host Secretary of the Navy John Chaffee for briefings and a static display of Recon Marines with war paint on and carrying patrolling weapons and equipment.[10]

The teams on Hill 119 were tasked to support Operation *Pipestone Canyon* on Go Noi Island and Dodge City. Second Lieutenant Jim Unsworth flipped back from Hill 119 to Camp Reasoner with his platoon on 13 May.[11] He was replaced by 3rd Platoon, Delta Company, now led by 2nd Lieutenant Schanck, who assumed command of the hill at 1200 upon Unsworth's departure. Schanck would have with him the experienced Staff Sergeant Jones, making his third trip to the observation post (OP). He had 21 of his Marines with him, plus two corpsmen and two attached engineers.[12] The engineers were delivering razor wire and explosives. Their goal was to get another string of wire entirely around the hill in this two-week period and to blow some rock, forming what would become a mortar pit. Captain Willson had scrounged a 60-mm mortar for the hill before his departure.[13] The platoon also carried a PRC-47 radio, a high-frequency radio for long-haul communications.[14] On a clear night, using a sky wave bounce, the PRC-47 could talk with Camp Pendleton in California. Although the hill was not supposed to just pass gossip, it was called a comm check and represented training to the lieutenant. Schanck's Operations Order was #401-69, identifying this was the 401st patrol of the year for 1st Recon Battalion.[15] His callsign was *Segment* for this two-week flip to Hill 119.

Life on the hill settled into a routine. The following morning, after wire check, the engineers, with assigned working party and security detail, moved out and started clearing brush and stringing wire. The OP watch manned the spotting scopes and 7 × 50s and were getting sightings of small numbers of enemy. On 20 May, the OP watch picked up three NVA in khakis with rifles stowed at stack arms (arranged in a pyramid, standing on their butts). They were working the center trestle of the railroad bridge mid-island, digging a shaft into the berm with pioneer gear, picks and shovels, and a wheelbarrow. Team *Segment* worked up a fire mission. With the first adjustment round, the NVA went down the shaft or tunnel. *Segment* requested an end of mission and waited. An aerial observer (AO) came on station and asked for targets; *Segment* handed off the tunnel.[16] The AO had the heavy cruiser USS Newport News (CA-148), and its 8" guns dialed up to provide naval gun fire (NGF). The 8" rounds came in sounding like a freight train, firing from out of sight in the East China Sea. Shooting NGF was more art than science. A naval gun is a large rifle that shoots projectiles in a direct-fire mode. Shooting at the side of an object, like another ship or a mountain, where there was a vertical surface to impact, was what it was designed to do. Shooting at a flat island, where short and long rounds could be as much as five kilometers off, took skill and/or luck. The only vertical face on the flat Go Noi Island was the railroad berm sticking 20 feet above the water level. One NVA was standing in the tunnel entrance on the west side of the berm when the third round scored a direct hit on the east side of the trestle/berm. The NVA disappeared in a cloud of dust. Whether luck or skill, the AO took credit and gave the ship one confirmed NVA killed along with a destroyed tunnel and bunkers.[17] That battle-damage assessment would be the topic of discussion in the ship's wardroom and the chief's mess. After sundown on 22 May, about 2130, the watch, Lance Corporal LaRue in Alpha Bunker, overlooking the main trail to northwest of the LZ (landing zone), picked up noise and then heard movement. He soon observed six enemy walking in a low, slow crouch. LaRue was using the starlight scope which magnified ambient light from the moon or stars. The bunker waited until they were one hundred feet from the wire and then fired M16s at the group and yelled for illumination rounds from the 60-mm mortar.[18] It took some time to get the illumination fired; when it went up, there was no enemy to be observed. They had run back down behind the old railroad berm and were gone. Schanck and Jones needed to assign and train a mortar team. They needed to have illumination rounds broken out and ready to drop. Discussing the incident with Jones, and Sergeants Castellano and Gwinn, they felt this was more a probe, the enemy checking the wire, or a sapper trying to set a booby trap in the new-wire construction field.

On the early evening of 25 May, at approximately 1915, Bravo Bunker saw movement across the saddle in the draw outside the northwest side of Alpha Bunker. They counted nine people in black "PJs" in the long draw carrying gear and bales of unfilled sandbags back down the draw. The OP watch was notified and called for artillery illumination. In the morning, the construction materials, which had been stored outside the wire on the north side of the landing zone, had been raided or stolen by the villagers or Viet Cong (VC) to be used on their own projects.[19] On the evening of 26 May, Schanck worked up his statistics for the S-2 debrief in the morning. For *Segment*'s 14-day stay on Hill 119, there were 44 separate sightings of 285 NVA/VC; the Marines called 32 fire missions and one air strike.[20] They were scheduled to flip the next morning with 2nd Platoon, callsign *Barkeep*, led by 2nd Lieutenant Ron Pfeiffer.[21] Pfeiffer was a woodsman from Maine. He had already acquitted himself well on patrol and was respected for his bush savvy by his Marines. While this would be Pfeiffer's first trip to the hill, the platoon had some hill veterans in Sergeants Gawlaki, Gwinn, and "Doc" Dana. Gunnery Sergeant Hall was the new platoon sergeant and a career infantry leader. Pfeiffer had already told the "gunny" he was to hold mortar classes with live-fire training and to pick two mortar men for the hill's 60-mm mortar. *Barkeep* took over the hill at noon on 27 May.[22] The engineers departed. They had finished placing the second strand of wire completely around the hill. They also left thousands of sandbags to be filled. For night surveillance, the Marines had three starlight scopes farmed out to the corner bunkers. The starlight scope, or AN/PVS-2 Night Vision Sight, had been designed as a rifle night scope with four-times power. It was heavy and bulky when mounted on a rifle so, in the bunkers, they were used as a standalone on the bunker parapet. Battery operated, they were passive sights that used the ambient light of the moon or stars, which meant on clear, bright, nights you could see out to 400 meters; objects or people appeared as a green–black profile picture in the scope. On cloudy nights, a range of 200 meters would be good but, if it was raining the sights were not as good as the "Mark 1 eyeball" of a human observer. *Barkeep* also brought a Night-Observation Device (NOD) on a standing tripod.[23] This big brother of the starlight scope was heavy, at 50-plus pounds, and bulky. The seven-power battery operated scope could reach out 1,800 meters on a clear moon-filled night. It was a major upgrade to help the defense of the hill and its offensive nighttime-spotting capability. The NOD was placed on a tripod at standing height on the roof of the observation bunker. It was kept under a tarp during the daytime to hide its existence from the enemy. The NOD's range on a clear night meant the OP could watch the abandoned railroad berm or see Route 537. It could also see the finger and hills south and observe as far as the Alligator Lake dam.

On their first full day, 28 May, Alpha Bunker sent a runner over to the command bunker and asked for the leadership to come over to see the exceptionally large group of Vietnamese moving up from Tho Son hamlet. As they started out of the hamlet, they appeared to be women and children wearing traditional field workers' black PJs, with white tops for the women. The kids were in shorts, t-shirts, and flip-flops.[24] Pfeiffer was perplexed and asked for opinions. Sergeant Gawlaki said small groups had previously come to the hill for medical care; he had never seen such a large group. He suggested they stop the group on the flat space just south of the railroad berm on the north side of the hill. The lieutenant told Gunnery Sergeant Hall to organize a detail and to take Gawlaki and Doc Dana down to stop the group. Pfeiffer went to the radio to discuss with the battalion S-3 shop, which told him to sort by age and sex and determine whether or not they had ID cards. Those who needed aid, or were without ID, would be evacuated to Da Nang for processing at LZ 20. Hall had taken a radio. After posting security, they got a head count of 34 women, two old men, and 57 children, all with no ID cards. They were asking to go to Da Nang to get away from the VC. Pfeiffer called the information back to Battalion. It took all morning but, by 1320, two CH-53s came out from Marble Mountain Air Facility (MMAF) and, with two separate landings on the 119 LZ, took the 93 Vietnamese to LZ 20 at the southern end of MMAF for processing.[25] The next day, continuing their primary mission, the Marines got an OV-10 *Hostage*[26] aircraft with *Cowpoke Three-Zero*, the AO, in the back seat. It was flying over Go Noi Island and worked over some bunkers the OP had pointed out.

On the night of 3 June, the weather was clear, and the stars were out. At 2015, through the NOD, they observed five NVA/VC moving on Route 537 some twelve hundred meters below the hill. It was their first NOD sighting at distance.[27] They radioed their direct-support artillery battery (Echo Battery) at An Hoa and got a fire mission with good coverage of Route 537. They then learned that, when an Arty round impacts the ground, the observer gets a bloom of light inside the NOD scope, and it blacks out. So, they could not immediately see what happened to the enemy. The next night, the NOD team spotted another six NVA/VC on the south side of the hill just below Alligator Lake dam. They were moving along the aqueduct trail to the east. *Barkeep* called a fire mission and waited to watch the enemy move a kilometer down the trail while the clearances were being worked through. When the clearances came, the enemy soldiers were out of sight around the bend in the finger that was a blind spot to the OP. They needed on-call preregistered targets on known enemy routes. At 0500, that morning, the NOD observers picked up 12 NVA/VC with packs moving on the dirt track that was Route 537 on the north side of the hill.[28] They worked up a fire mission but, due to a slow clearance or a slow battery response, the enemy was soon out of sight. The NOD clearly confirmed what they knew. The enemy was moving at night around the hill between Go Noi Island and the Que Son Mountains.

On the morning of 5 June, the hill observed four VC walking into Tho Son with rifles. They were wearing blue and black PJs. At one hooch, they stacked arms. One of them remained with the weapons and the other three got sickles out and headed to the fields behind the village near the river to harvest. With the success of the NOD sighting, Pfeiffer, after dialog with his leaders, decided to switch the main effort to nighttime operations and periods of observation. They would keep a minimum-security watch, and one daytime observer awake, while the remainder slept in the bunkers. The lieutenant would maximize the nighttime observation with the NOD, three starlight scopes, and 7 × 50s, using four to six observers, each with a one-hour watch. The next three nights they saw groups of NVA/VC from two to 32 moving in all directions around the hill!

The enemy knew the hill was an OP and avoided all daytime movement within sight of it. Their tactic for the hill was to avoid being seen, and have the VC, or VC sympathizers, in Tho Son village watch and observe the Marines. Additionally, they would booby trap trails close to the OP's exits, penning in the Marines. At night, the enemy thought they could not be seen outside the wire without illumination overhead. Now, with the NOD, they could be seen below the hill and further than they realized. All the trails at the base of the hill, on both sides, were well worn and had the appearance of being used nightly. Each of these could be observed with the NOD.

On the evening of 9 June, traffic picked up south of the OP where the east aqueduct trail met the cross-valley trail at the base of the dam. Alligator Lake was 700 meters below the hill and the NOD could see the intersection. Pfeiffer had his Marines take turns counting the number of NVA moving through the intersection at 0100. By 0145, they had counted over 100. The lieutenant worked up a fire mission and also radioed battalion requesting they use the land line to the Direct Air Support Center to request air support. By 0200, the enemy was moving in both directions at the intersection, shuttling loads. The count was 300 when Pfeiffer called for an artillery time on target at the intersection. They got excellent coverage but could see no results from the bloom effect inside the NOD that was caused by the Arty air burst.[29] When the aircraft arrived about 30 minutes later, Pfeiffer ran them anyway because they had flown out but had no real observations. At 0440, the NOD picked up a group of 30 NVA/VC at the south intersection. They were carrying bodies west. Pfeiffer called the Arty on-call intersection target and within two minutes got good coverage while the enemy was still on the trail at the base of the dam.[30] That morning, Pfeiffer and Hall talked about going down to the intersection. Hall was against the idea, but Pfeiffer was gung-ho. He talked himself into the need for a battle-damage assessment (BDA) patrol.[31] He said Hall could remain on the hill and he would lead the patrol. He told Sergeant Gawlaki to pick a team and that they would go down and check out the intersection. Gawlaki was worried about booby traps, so Pfeiffer agreed they would move Recon style, off-trail, and not grunt style down the trail, either going down or heading back to the OP. It took them two hours to move southeast, sidehill down the hill to the valley floor where they picked up the aqueduct and came back west towards the dam. They were 300 meters east of the dam when they heard Vietnamese talking. They were on the north high side of the trail and Pfeiffer signaled his point to move higher and stop. They stopped on-line and watched nine NVA below them in shorts, khaki shirts, and sandals. They were well armed with AK-47s, SKSs, and at least one B40 rocket launcher. The team had them in a downhill kill zone 20 feet below them. Pfeiffer called out to the enemy to "Chieu Hoi," meaning to give up. That action gave away their position and the enemy initiated firing uphill and over the team. The Recon Marines responded immediately with the first sound of fire, sweeping the kill zone. Eight enemy lay dead. The team captured the ninth as a prisoner.[32] Setting security in both directions on the trail, Pfeiffer had Gawlaki search the bodies while he tied up the prisoner. He had a decision to make, return to the OP with what they had or continue down the trail to the intersection at the dam base to conduct the BDA. Worried this enemy group might be a rear-security element of the NVA clean-up detail from the previous night's larger unit, Pfeiffer decided to get the rifles and equipment and move back up the hill to the OP. He would have Hall call the on-call intersection target as soon as he had moved out of the area and got some elevation away from the intersection. The patrol back up the hill took time as they now had the prisoner, and six AK-47s, three SKS semi-automatic rifles, a B40 with sight, one #15 shape charge, 11 Chi-com grenades, two mines, bayonets, and the enemy packs with personnel letters. They also recovered some documents and two diaries.[33]

When they got back, three hours later, the battalion in the rear wanted to talk to Pfeiffer. There would be a bird out to pick up the prisoner and all the gear. Pfeiffer acknowledged on the radio. He called Gawlaki over and told him to stage the prisoner, the nine enemy packs, documents in the packs, and one AK-47 and one SKS, along with the B40, for what the rear called the exploitation team, which would also interview them. He told Gawlaki to distribute the rifles and bayonets to every patrol member and that he wanted the B40 rocket sight. He did not know why he wanted the sight. He wanted a souvenir, but he also wanted to look the exploitation interviewers, or REMFs (rear-echelon motherfuckers) in the eye and tell them he had not taken any weapons. During the hill interviews, the exploitation team wanted to know why there were not nine weapons as reported. Pfeiffer said he did not know what might have happened to the weapons during the confusion of the ambush but that he had no enemy weapons. The REMF team could not push it as the sun was going down and their helo was returning to take them back to a hot shower and dinner. Every field Marine knew that if you gave up a captured weapon to the intel or exploitation teams, regardless of the cardboard tags of ownership put on each, the Marine who captured it would never see the weapon again! Pfeiffer had taken care of his Marines.[34]

On 10 June, they observed an infantry unit supported by tanks pushing east from Liberty Bridge and down Route 537 toward Go Noi Island. Unbeknown to Hill 119, Operation *Pipestone Canyon* had begun. All morning, the OP had picked up enemy moving and running east back towards Thon Bon (1) hamlet where they disappeared into thatched huts and bunkers. Hill 119 could not get clearance for fire missions due to the infantry sweep now in progress. They called the spot reports, with specific grids and movement, into both Recon Battalion and the 5th Marines Combat Operations Center at An Hoa. On their last night on the hill, at 2345, they observed lights east of their position on the crest of their own finger some three hundred meters outside their wire. Echo Bunker responded with M79 high-explosive rounds followed by M79 illumination rounds.[35] The lights went out and the movement ceased. Since this was on the finger crest proper with no bush cover in the open, the OP Marines did not believe this was a probe, rather an enemy who took the wrong trail. The hill was in a festive mood, and AFVN transistor radios were blaring rock and roll in all the bunkers. The Marines would be flipping out in the morning of 12 June. For their two weeks on the OP, *Barkeep* had 13 sightings of 475 NVA/VC. They had called seven fire missions and one air strike. *Barkeep-A*'s walk-off patrol had netted eight confirmed NVA killed and one prisoner of war.[36] The patrol members were returning to Camp Reasoner with five AK-47s, two SKSs, and nine bayonets as personal souvenirs. Pfeiffer had his B40 sight.[37] He did not know what to do with it but, for now, he would put it on his ammo box bookshelf next to his cot.

CHAPTER 8

Operation *Pipestone Canyon* and Team *Grade Level*, June 1969

On 8 June 1969, President Nixon flew to Midway Island, in the middle of the Pacific Ocean, for secret talks with the President of South Vietnam, Nguyen Van Thieu. Following the meeting, Nixon announced that 25,000 troops would be out of Vietnam by the end of August.[1] Defense Secretary Laird announced on 13 June that the 9th Marines would be out of country by July.[2]

III Marine Amphibious Force (III MAF) now had to manage the withdrawal of forces coupled with the shift north of U.S. Army and Army of the Republic of Vietnam (ARVN) units to cover positions formerly occupied by the Marines. In-place hand offs of fire bases and base camps had to be scheduled and coordinated prior to moving troops to the staging areas near the airfield in Da Nang and their heavy equipment to the port of Da Nang. The 1st Marine Division continued Operation *Pipestone Canyon* as it moved from Phase II to Phase III on 10 June.[3]

At 1st Reconnaissance Battalion, Lieutenant Colonel Mickelson continued his training emphasis, with pre-SCUBA 6-69 starting 1 June and Recon Indoctrination Course 7-69 beginning on 17 June. The III MAF commander visited the morning of 8 June for briefings and a static display of one team and their equipment. Captain G. R. Willson, formerly of Delta Company, had moved over to 1st Force where he became the S-3 (operations) for Major Simmons. As a result, 1st Lieutenant A. T. Bouts became the new commanding officer at Delta Company.[4] The company's observation post (OP) on Hill 119 had now been operational for five months. It had thousands of enemy sightings and hundreds of kills, but it had not prevented the North Vietnamese Army (NVA) from returning to Go Noi Island after the infantry departed. By the end of May, Allied intelligence organizations placed 8–10 enemy battalions operating back in the Go Noi area. Most were there for what the NVA called the "production campaign," which meant putting every soldier in the rice paddies harvesting rice. The estimate was 2,500 NVA from the 2nd Division, supported by 300 to 500 local-force Viet Cong (VC), were working the rice harvest.[5] The idea, or tactical concept, that Hill 119 could cover-by-fire the gap in the Da Nang Rocket Belt was exposed and had not held up. The cork in the bottle did not work, and the railroad bridges across Go Noi Island had continued to be used as an elevated highway at night. The OP was more like a plastic fishing bobber that bobbed when the fish swam by and around. It reported large numbers of NVA moving out of the Que Son Mountains, along with the OP at Hill 425, but it did not prevent the enemy from reoccupying the fertile river delta.

Major General O. R. Simpson, the 1st Marine Division commander, decided the enemy presence was a threat and required a major operation to address; thus, Phase III of *Pipestone Canyon*. This time, he would commit the maneuver battalions but, following their sweep, he Operation added three engineering battalions to level the island. The operation would run until 7 November 1969. It was clear the grunts had hit the hornets' nest with a large stick. On the evening of 9 June, at 0021, the OP on Hill 425, with 1st Lieutenant Gary Allord aboard, had picked up over five hundred NVA moving between Hill 119 and themselves. The NVA, in double column, were moving southeast over Hill 175. Allord had coordinated a time-on-target (ToT) with seven artillery battalions to fire on this moving target.[6] Neither OP could observe the results due to low cloud cover and darkness. When the Arty ToT was over, *Cowpoke One-Nine* came on station and worked over Hill 175 with naval gunfire (NGF), shooting up the long access of the Phu Loc Valley toward Spider Lake.[7] At 0718, the morning sunlight allowed the OP on Hill 425 to pick up another formation of 200 NVA in the valley making a high-speed march for the Que Sons where the steep rock draws and caves would provide cover from the Allies' supporting-arms fire. They were wearing green utilities and carrying packs and rifles. They were caught in open rice paddies. Allord got a *Cowpoke* aerial observer (AO) overhead. *Cowpoke* reported one group was carrying at least 100 bodies, presumed from the strike earlier that evening.[8] The NVA moved into an OP blind spot, as a second AO, *Cowpoke Six-Nine*, came on station and started working Arty and NGF up the draws of the Que Sons as the enemy ran for the caves in the mountains. On 10 June, at 0627, Lieutenant Pfeiffer got called to the radio.[9] He recalled the time, having walked the lines just prior to sunrise and laying back down in his cot. As the runner came over, lifting the blackout-flap front door to his bunker and calling him, he had checked his watch. Walking in shower shoes and shorts to the communication bunker, he took the radio to get a heads up that the "Heavies" (Marine term for senior officers) were coming to the hill that day and to hold police call (a thorough clean-up of the area). Leaving the bunker, he called for Gunnery Sergeant Hall. This is what "gunnies" did. He told Hall about the heads up of the VIP visit. They needed the hill policed. Pfeiffer added they should burn the shitters and get extra rolls of shit paper in the ammunition box next to the open-air two-hole toilet. It was located on the hill just above the trash pit on the northwest side of the hill, where everyone could watch you do your business. He wondered who was coming but decided he needed coffee, and a sugar boost, so he returned to his bunker. Pulling out a metal canteen cup, he put four packs of instant C-ration coffee granules in the bottom, poured in water, and set it on his heat-tab stove. When the water was boiling, he poured in one large cocoa package, six sugars, and stirred. Burning his mouth with the first sip, he saw Hall had everyone up and moving. Pfeiffer knew he needed to shave so he heated more water as he got into a dirty set of utilities.

At 0915, he could see four Huey helicopters flying in formation, first circling Liberty Bridge, then over a column of tanks on Route 537 between the bridge and the hill. Then *Scarface One-Three* called the hill and asked for a zone brief. Sergeant Gwinn ran their little landing zone (LZ). He gave the inbound birds the short LZ brief as he walked to the center of the zone. He had a backpacked PRC-25 radio, goggles, and popped green smoke as the first bird headed in for a landing.

The four Hueys landed, and the file of Heavies stretched from the LZ to the flat observation platform. Pfeiffer saluted as the group was led by a two-star general. The general waved off the salute, walking to the top of bunker and shook his hand, introducing himself as O. R. Simpson. Pfeiffer recognized the name as being the commanding general of the division. He had never seen nor met the man. In fact, this was the first general he had met in country. The tactical, or

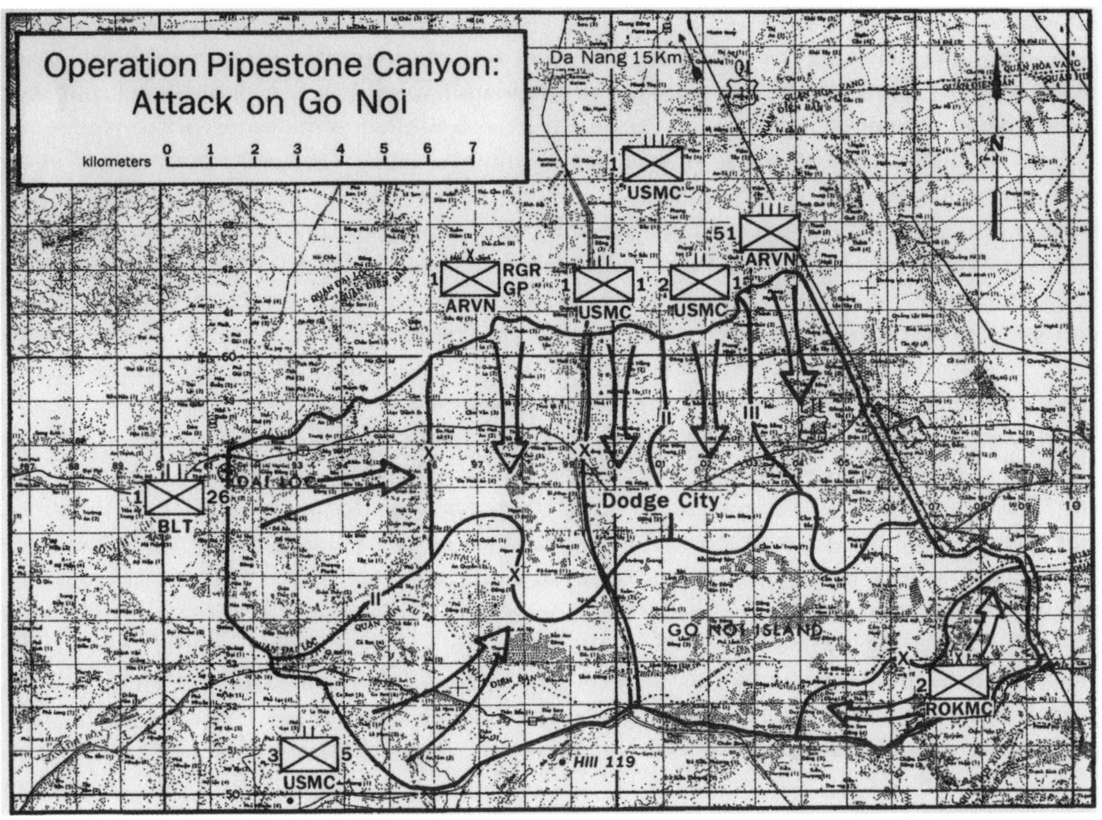

Operation *Pipestone Canyon*: Attack on Go Noi. (DoD public domain; History Division HQMC)

jump, command-post staff of both the division and the regiment were now on the hill, at least fifteen officers and senior enlisted plus a fire team of security with shotguns. Pfeiffer wondered what hot dog had gotten the shotguns and allowed it. They were military police (MP). Pfeiffer, an infantry officer, had been assigned to the 3rd MP Battalion before he escaped the rear and joined 1st Recon. The day was bright and hot. The general followed with a colonel in tow who was the commanding officer of the 1st Marines, Colonel C. E. Walker. He was pointing out units on the battlefield in front of them and narrating what could be seen from the hill by unit and its leader's name for the general.

To the northwest towards Liberty Bridge, Marines were on-line on both sides of the tanks coming down Route 537. This was 1st Battalion, 1st Marines, led by Lieutenant Colonel W. P. Morgenthaler. Across and north of the Song Thu Bong, with 7 × 50 binos, they could see Marines jumping off trucks and sweeping from west to east of Thunder Road into Dodge City. This would be 2nd Battalion, 1st Marines, commanded by Lieutenant Colonel Harold Glasgow. Along the railroad berm in eastern Dodge City, 3rd Battalion, 5th Marines, was occupying blocking positions.[10] The staff could also see the Korean Marines east and south of Go Noi Island. North on Route 1, the staff knew the ARVN (Army of the Republic of Vietnam) were dug in. While the command group watched from Hill 119, fixed-wing aircraft followed by helo gunships prepped two large LZs. Following the end of air prep were two attack aircraft, flying at 200 feet, laying down a smoke screen on the southern side of the island. This allowed 22 CH-46 helicopters to fly in behind the smoke to land, with the enemy's vision limited to the center of Go Noi, where the operational forces were trying to encircle and trap the enemy. The helicopters landed in the two LZs on the bank of the southern river.[11] After the landing, the units began to tighten the cordon around the entire island. The VIP delegation departed. The first two Hueys took the commanding general's party off the hill. Ten minutes later, a CH-46 came in and picked up the commanding officer of the 1st Marines and his jump staff, to return them to their forward command post for the operation. On Hill 119, it was time to watch the grunts do their thing. Two days later, it was time to flip platoons on the OP. On 12 June, at 1030, Pfeiffer's platoon boarded their two CH-46s to head back to Camp Reasoner.[12]

Arriving an hour earlier at 119 was 2nd Lieutenant Jim Unsworth on his third trip with 1st Platoon, callsign *Defend*.[13] Unsworth had talked with 1st Lieutenant Gary Allord of Echo Company who was headed to their OP on Hill 425, on the north shoulder of the Que Son Mountains. They agreed they would observe each other's hill and its surrounding base.[14] Both had blind sections below them that could be seen by the other OP. They set up a direct radio-coordination frequency between the two hills. On Hill 119, it was clear to Unsworth that the NVA had gone to ground due to the large infantry operation. All the hill's sightings were one VC, or two NVA, moving quickly in all directions. They were mostly messengers, which was the NVA/VC's primary means of communications at the tactical level. However, over on Hill 425, on 12 June, Allord had two sightings of 200 and 180 NVA respectively moving into the mountains.[15] On the night of 15 June, both OPs picked up many NVA skylined on the crest of Hill 175.[16] At 2145, enemy wearing packs and carrying rifles could be seen by both OPs. They were moving southeast on the high-speed trail. Neither OP could get supporting-arms clearances as there was a Korean Marine unit to the east. The Koreans fired 81-mm mortars that caused the column to disperse in four directions.

At 0930 on 18 June, Unsworth, while watching the northwest with 7 × 50 binos and laying in the prone position on top of the observation bunker, picked up two NVA/VC moving into Thon Bon (1) hamlet. They were carrying packs and rifles and wearing "PJs." Unsworth got *Cowpoke One-Zero*, who was flying overhead, on the radio. *Cowpoke* could not flush out the two enemy. However, Unsworth changed radio frequencies to an infantry unit, *Gunsmoke Two-Bravo*, who were patrolling down Route 537 toward Thon Bon (1). He was able to vector the grunts into the thatched hooch where the two had been seen. The infantry captured the two hiding in the bunker below the hooch.[17]

On 20 June, at 1712, the OP watch picked up 37 NVA moving into Tho Son hamlet just below the hill to the north side. These were clearly NVA as they were wearing new green utilities and carrying packs and rifles. Unsworth got *Cowpoke Six-Eight* to start working over the village with his on-board ordnance. The NVA had gone to ground in the bunkers. Shortly after *Cowpoke Six-Eight* had expended all ordnance, he handed off to *Cowpoke One-One* who relieved him on station and got fixed-wing aircraft on station to make some runs on the village using 500-pound bombs with good coverage. With the air off station, he called artillery and fired a battery-two (six guns, two rounds each) into the village. Neither the AO nor the OP could report results due to the heavy smoke and fires burning in the village as the sun set.[18]

One of the duties on the OP was to serve as a radio relay. As such, the hill monitored Recon frequencies to send messages between teams on patrol and the battalion command center in the underground bunker just above LZ 401 at Camp Reasoner. On 21 June, Hill 119's radio relay, callsign *Defend*, was busy as two other Delta Company teams were being inserted. They were relaying for Teams *Mayfly* and *Grade Level*. Lieutenant W. Garry Schanck was taking two of his platoon's teams into the jungle of the Que Son Mountains. Schanck had grown bored with college and dropped out of the University of Rhode Island after three semesters to enlist in the Marine Corps. Completing boot camp at Parris Island, he was selected for Officer's Candidate School. A fitness enthusiast, upon graduation from The Basic School in Quantico, Schanck joined Delta Company, 1st Recon, in late December 1968.[19] He had run five patrols and done one Hill 119 flip. Two teams were being inserted, based on intelligence, they believed they needed 14 Marines in the patrol haven. Corporal Evans, leading *Mayfly*, was experienced and had been into the Que Sons on prior patrols. He was on the lead bird going into a one-bird LZ, which was an alternate zone. The primary, a two-bird LZ, had been in the clouds, so they were going down low into a stream bed, only half an LZ. It would be a ramp jump from the bird to the ground.

The LZ turned hot. They were taking fire from the hillside on the other side of a streambed. The bird hovered at 10 feet as the team jumped into the LZ. The bird took small-arms hits going into and coming out of the LZ. The team moved off the LZ, and into the canopy where it began suppressive fire across the streambed. The second CH-46 approached the same LZ from below and down the draw. It was coming up fast and low. The bird started its hover, lowering itself into the zone, the tail ramp coming down, with high canopy on all sides. The CH-46 was now taking heavy small arms from the ridgeline south and above it while both of its .50-caliber machine gunners raked the sides of the draw. Aborting the insert, the pilot started to pull out when the bird was hit with some heavy caliber ordnance in both engines. The bird started down and crashed east of the LZ into the canopy, 125 meters away, and burst into flames. Fifteen minutes after the crash, Team *Mayfly*'s eight Marines, led by Corporal Evans, reached the downed aircraft to look for survivors.[20] The wreckage was still burning and extremely hot. The team could not get close to the wreckage due to the fire and heat. Evans stayed on the radio, coordinating the two gunships making gun runs on the opposite ridgeline. When they pulled off, an AO had arrived and was overhead. The AO took over, keeping the enemy at bay and off of *Mayfly*. He had fixed-wing aircraft cover the ridgeline with snake and nape[21] (standard load out for aircraft: two "Snake Eye" bombs, and two napalm canisters). They had taken the heavy fire from that ridgeline.

Mayfly moved to the high ground above the burning crash site where the team found five wounded Marines. They had been thrown off the bird as it went down and were in bad shape. Two Recon Marines and three Marine aircrew needed immediate first aid. *Mayfly* moved them back to the LZ and called for an emergency medevac. They got the five evacuated and returned to the crash site. The enemy fire had stopped due to the close air support. The enemy was now some distance away on the ridgeline south of the team, but Evans knew it was only a matter of time before they closed again.

Back at the crash site, he set up security on the avenues into the site and put out Claymore mines. At 1230, after a tense wait, a reaction force from Recon Battalion arrived at the original primary LZ higher up the ridgeline as the morning fog had burned off. Two CH-46s brought 32 Marines. It took the reaction force 30 minutes to come down the hill. They took over security from *Mayfly*. On Hill 119, in the communications bunker, the operators could only relay the messages and pray for their brothers in the Que Sons. The reaction force now set a perimeter and started enlarging the lower LZ. It was eerily quiet. The air power had pushed away the NVA, at least for now. At 1245, another helo arrived with a Graves Registration team and body bags.

The fire was out on the crashed bird. The graves team recovered eight bodies, six Recon Marines and two pilots. The reaction force gathered the charred machine guns and radios from the burned-out CH-46, including the bodies, and moved to the original LZ as night approached; everyone was extracted on four CH-46s at 1800. The second insert bird had been carrying Team *Grade Level,* led by 2nd Lieutenant Schanck. He, Lance Corporals Bosco and Well, and Privates First Class Hall, Council, and Crites were all killed in action (KIA). Hospital Corpsman Third Class Rucker and Private First Class Harlicka were seriously wounded along with the three surviving crew members of the crashed CH-46. The two pilots were KIA at the crash site.[22] On Hill 119, the communication bunker had put *Mayfly*'s primary radio frequency on the squawk-box speaker as members of Delta Company listened to their brothers from 3rd Platoon in trouble in the mountains for six hours. It was a quiet mood on the hill that evening. The next evening, 22 June at 2045, the hill picked up 17 NVA/VC wearing black PJs and moving around Tho Son just below them.[23] They had packs and rifles. Lieutenant Unsworth now had the hamlet as a preregistered fire mission with Echo Battery, a 105-mm howitzer battery due west in An Hoa. He fired a battery-two without any adjustment rounds to try to catch the enemy outside their bunkers. The twelve 105 rounds impacted on target inside the village, but he could not see due to dust blown up by the barrage. They were due off the hill on 24 June. Unsworth had earned a trip to Embarkation School. He would spend July in school at Camp Hanson, Okinawa.

Replacing them was 2nd Platoon and Lieutenant Pfeiffer, who was now a hill veteran. He had the same mission and haven with the added task to coordinate with, and support, the infantry in Operation *Pipestone Canyon*, still operating on Go Noi Island.[24] The *Pipestone Canyon* operations were in the engineering plowing-and-clearing phase where bulldozers were leveling the land, caving in bunkers and trench lines.[25] The OP was to watch the 30 bulldozers' backs for VC snipers and their fronts for VC planting landmines. Although Pfeiffer knew the mines would be placed at night, his Marines made a maximum effort to watch out for the engineers.

The platoon arrived at 0900 on the 24th in two CH-46s for their two-hour turnover.[26] Due to the effectiveness of the night-observation device (NOD), they got three sightings that evening. All three were to the north of the OP, with the last sighting at 2115. They picked up 11 enemy moving west on Route 537 below them. They tried their own 60-mm mortar, since the sighting was inside their haven.[27] The Marines enjoyed firing the mortar as it was not normally in Recon's weapons inventory. Pfeiffer noted they clearly needed training on fire direction and practice on how to employ and adjust fire. They had time on the OP for both. On 25 June, Pfeiffer observed five Vietnamese, wearing black PJs and carrying sickles, moving from the fields as the sun was coming down over Tho Son hamlet. Twenty minutes later, he saw five VC moving out of the hamlet, carrying rifles and headed east on Route 537.[28] The next night, Pfeiffer sent Corporal Evans and Team *Mayfly* out for a night ambush/prisoner snatch inside their haven. Evans had volunteered, as he did not want to sit on the OP and think about *Grade Level.* Team *Mayfly* was out to get some! The team moved out of the east gate after sundown and dropped off-trail over the north face of the finger, moving until they intersected the main trail up to their hill. They were planning to go to the abandoned railroad-berm trail but heard noise as they came to the dangerous open area of the main trail up to the OP. Evans got the team into a hasty on-line ambush. As two VC moved up the trail, Evans and Lance Corporal Dowers tried to move forward with the intention of executing a prisoner snatch by tackling the two VC while being covered by the rest of team. The VC saw them and opened fire. In 15 seconds of two-way fire, one was killed, and the other was seen running back to Tho Son. Disappointed with no prisoners, Evans gathered a dropped enemy pack, and the team moved back up the hill to the OP.[29] Inside the communication bunker, they searched the pack and found numerous documents, a cartridge belt with a 9-mm pistol, first-aid pack, and civilian clothing. The pack had belonged to an officer. They called in the spot report of one KIA with documents.[30] Evans kept the pistol; it was a prized souvenir great for trading and easy to get permission to bring back to the States at the end of his tour. At 2345, while Evans was in the communication bunker with the lieutenant looking at the documents, Sergeant Cronk on the NOD spotted a large group of NVA moving west on the south aqueduct trail. He called an artillery mission but could not observe due to the trail hitting a blind spot in front of the Alligator Lake dam where the enemy would turn due south. Cronk radioed over to Hill 425 and gave them a heads up on the large group of NVA headed in their direction and back toward their base camps in the Que Sons. The next morning, Pfeiffer had the morning wire check drop down the north main trail to the previous night's hasty ambush site. The body was gone, recovered sometime during the night. Pfeiffer thought next time he would set an ambush for a VC body recovery.

The next night, 27 June, the NOD watch at 2300 picked up 31 NVA/VC moving into Tho Son hamlet. They were moving through without stopping. The OP called an on-call fire mission for the hamlet. After the mission, through the NOD, they could clearly see two bodies lying on the trail.[31] The OP had no sightings on the 28th. On 29 June, at 0900, through the BC-Scope (ballistic coefficient scope), they observed, two kilometers east, seven NVA/VC sitting on rocks near the village of Chein Son (4). They were wearing black PJs. The OP called a fire mission and got excellent coverage. The enemy scattered and went to ground. One body remained visible, slumped over the rock on which he had been sitting. Close to sundown, they picked up seven NVA/VC moving, with three rifles and one pack, back into Tho Son. They lost the enemy in the grass between the hamlet and the river. At 2115, the NOD watch picked up 24 moving west out of Tho Son. The hill fired their own 60-mm mortar, and the enemy disappeared into the high grass next to the river. At 2205, the NOD picked up another 51 NVA/VC moving on the north–south trail below the Alligator Lake dam. They were all carrying packs and rifles.[32] The OP requested an on-call target for the trail but the enemy, hearing the incoming, sprinted west out of the concentration and into the dark of night towards Hill 425. Hill 119 called the OP on Hill 425 and gave them a heads up. On 30 June, at 1100, three Vietnamese men in civilian clothing walked up the main north trail to the hill. The OP almost opened up on them but noted they were waving leaflets while their weapons were across their backs. A security team went out and met them. They were "Chieu Hois" giving up and changing sides. The security team recovered one M1 rifle, an M14 rifle, and seven grenades (four of which were Chi-com and three were M26s).[33] The men were told to sit, then given water and watched as the hill called for a helo to evacuate them to the III MAF prisoner compound for their processing as Chieu Hois. The bird returning from a resupply run to An Hoa that afternoon picked them up for the short flight to LZ 20 at the compound.

On 1 July, the watch picked up 12 NVA/VC moving west out of Thon Bon (1) on Route 537. They were walking directly toward an infantry unit moving east. The hill notified the infantry, who set an ambush. Over the next three days, the hill had five sightings totaling 38 enemy. All were inside their haven, so they engaged each with the 60-mm mortar followed by M60 machine-gun fire. Each time the first mortar round hit, the enemy went to ground and crawled into thick brush or underground pre-dug bunkers, escaping along each trail.[34] The platoon flipped at 1430 on 4 July. During his debriefing with Corporal Page, the S-2 (intelligence) debriefer, Pfeiffer explained he wanted his recommendation in writing to emphasize that the OP be allowed to patrol off the hill in all directions. He was sure nighttime patrolling would reap solid results; the location was perfect for the conduct of a prisoner snatch since they had the friendly LZ uphill from any potential snatch extract.[35]

CHAPTER 9

"We've Landed on the Moon!" July 1969

The first U.S. troop withdrawals of the war began on 8 July 1969. On 20 July, American citizens, along with an estimated 650 million people worldwide, watched live television of the *Apollo 11* astronauts plant the American flag on the surface of the moon.[1] On 25 July, President Nixon declared the "Nixon Doctrine" which began "Vietnamization" of the war.[2] Nixon, in a surprise visit on 30 July to South Vietnam, held a meeting with President Nguyen Van Thieu to cover his new doctrine and inform Thieu that the fight would be shifted to him, the South Vietnamese Government and Army.[3] The day prior, on 29 July, there were race riots at Marine Corps Base Camp Lejeune, North Carolina. One person was killed during the riots.[4]

III Marine Amphibious Force's contribution to the July troop withdrawal was the departure of Battalion Landing Team 1/9, by ship, for Okinawa on 14 July. These were the first Marines to execute Nixon's withdrawal plan.[5] The 1st Marine Division continued Operation *Pipestone Canyon*.[6] Based on new intelligence, on the morning of 15 July, Lieutenant Colonel H. Glasgow's 1st Battalion, 1st Marines (1/1), conducted a four-rifle-company helo assault into four separate landing zones (LZ) in order to cordon off Tay Bang An village in the eastern Dodge City area. All four zones were hot and taking fire as the helicopters came in to land. Two zones were shifted to alternates. The cordon was closed in two hours. After sweeping the villages and surrounding fields, 1/1 was lifted out on the morning of 17 July. The cordon had killed 20 North Vietnamese Army (NVA) personnel and captured 14 prisoners.[7]

In Lieutenant Colonel Mickelson's Recon Battalion, training continued to be the watchword. Pre-SCUBA Class 7-69 commenced as the precursor for Marines and Corpsmen headed off to SCUBA school in the Philippines. Reconnaissance Indoctrination Course 9-69 commenced to train newly joined Marines and Corpsmen in patrolling techniques as well as insert/extract methods.[8] The summer personnel-turnover season was in full swing. First Lieutenant R. E. Miller assumed command of Charlie Company, Captain D. C. MacCaskill took over Echo Company, and 1st Lieutenant J. W. Mann from S-2 (intelligence) assumed command of Alpha Company from 1st Lieutenant Art Weber,[9] who then rotated back to Quantico to be assigned to Schools Demonstration Troop. This was the unit that provided the aggressors, or enemy, for newly commissioned lieutenants at The Basic School. Reflecting on the split atmosphere of the United States, Weber also got involved with additional duties as part of a riot-control unit in the nation's capital. This included deployments to the basement of the Capitol building during riots in Washington, D.C.[10] Meanwhile in Delta Company, 1st Lieutenant A. T. Bouts remained in command, sending platoons to the observation post (OP) on Hill 119 while providing patrols in support of 1st Marine Division operations.

On 17 July, Mr. Geran, a Special Representative from the Department of Defense, spent a day at 1st Recon trying to understand the challenges with communications in deep jungle or, rather, the lack of communications through triple-canopy forest.[11] On 1 July 1969, Sergeant James Hackett and four of his Marines from the 11th Marine Regiment G-2 Section landed on Hill 119[12] and were immediately struck by the stark reality of the OP. It had no vegetation, no shade, and was a rocky spine with a few boulders. It was hot, with heat rising from the ground. It was like a moonscape to the new Marines.

The CH-46 landed in the saddle between Hills 148 and 119. Sergeant Hackett, or "Hack" as his Marines called him, helped his men unload their packs, rifles, support equipment, and the Korean-era AN/PPS-6. This Army hand-me-down radar, known as the "People Sniffer," was the reason Hack and his Marines had been sent to Hill 119.[13] The 1st Marine Division's intelligence shop thought the hill was going to be hit or attacked and this radar would provide early warning. The dome on a tripod was supposed to detect movement 300 feet away. After the helo departed and the dust settled, Hackett walked through the wire and up onto the hill. There he met Lieutenant Pfeiffer, the hill commander, who had been expecting him. The lieutenant said he could set up wherever he wanted but recommended he check out the observation platform first. He said they could use the bunker below the platform to carve out their living space. The platform was a plywood stage on top of a bunker in the center of the hill. It had a tripod with the night-observation device (NOD) sitting on its roof. After looking the area over, Hack selected a ground position due to down-look angle. The AN/PPS-6 and its tripod was positioned on the ground next to the observation platform.

There was an issue with the angle facing downhill that needed to be worked out.[14] Hackett and his Marines fell into a routine for their watch on the People Sniffer. They all knew it did not work.[15] Every morning, Recon would go outside the wire with a small patrol and circle the OP, checking the wire for signs of the enemy trying to cut through defenses or turning the claymore mines back toward the hill. On these patrols, the AN/PPS-6 only picked up the Marines if they stood right in front of it and did jumping jacks. The box powered on, but the 11th Marines did not have the parts, nor were the Marines sufficiently trained, to keep it calibrated. The Marines who manned the radar thought OP duty was okay, as it was not the rear with inspections, and the Recon guys left them alone. If they wanted to join in what they called a daytime stroll, they could join a walk-off patrol with Recon.

On 4 July, 2nd Lieutenant Klein and 2nd Platoon Delta flipped to Hill 119, arriving at 1400 for the fast turnover.[16] It was Klein's first trip to the hill. He would bring along 21 Marines led by the experienced Sergeant Gwinn, now a hill veteran. "Doc" Dana was also aboard and breaking in a new corpsman, Hospital Corpsman Third Class Daugherty. In addition to observation, fire missions, and radio relay, the platoon would remain in direct support of the grunts and engineering units on Operation *Pipestone Canyon*. Daily, they could see the dust trails being raised by the "roman plows" flattening the hedgerows and bunkers on Go Noi Island. Klein's welcome to the hill would be one "Chieu Hoi." He had walked up the trail from Alligator Lake with his hand over his head holding a leaflet ("Chieu Hoi," "give up"). He was wearing dirty, tattered, dark "PJs" and had a basket, with a pouch full of his personal effects.[17] Gwinn explained to the lieutenant that Chieu Hois and villagers coming to the hill was a constant issue that needed to be addressed. The OP, now callsign *Beech Nut*, radioed the Battalion Combat Operations Center (COC) and got word to put the Chieu Hoi on the next bird to LZ 401. On the Fourth of July, entertainment and fireworks were provided by the NVA in the boulder field on the northern slope of Hill 175 to their south. The NOD watch picked up 35 moving west across the hill towards the Que Son Mountains. The OP got *Spooky One-One*, with its red tracer rounds from three Gatling guns, trade fire as the enemy shot green tracers back at the aircraft.[18] It was not only a remarkable visual sight at night, but the OP could easily hear the pepper-grinding sound of the Gatling guns. The AC-47 flying at 3,000 feet was above the effective range of small arms and only had to worry if they got tracers from a heavy machine gun coming in their direction. After their first sighting, the OP could not observe anyone on Hill 175. It was a nice airshow for the Fourth of July as every Marine thought of their own hometown fireworks celebration. On the morning of 5 July, the hill watched in frustration as a CH-53 departing An Hoa airfield took ground fire and multiple rocket-propelled grenade hits as it was lifting off. The bird was on fire and crashed hard into grid square AT9652 northwest of Thon Bon (1) hamlet just off Route 537.[19] There were grunts in the area that quickly moved to the burning wreckage. The hill did not know the fate of the passengers and crew. The charred wreckage became a navigation landmark just off Route 537 as it was never removed.

On 6 July, Gwinn led an eight Marine walk-off patrol down to the Alligator Lake dam intersection and then followed the aqueduct trail back east; 500 meters east of the dam, they picked up blood trails leading to a draw. Upon checking out the draw, they found a small rest station. There was a decaying body in a partially destroyed bunker. The body wore green utilities and had an NVA belt buckle which Gwinn gave to Doc Dana. The Marines always took care of their corpsmen; this prized souvenir was an example of taking care of the men who took care of the Marines. There were two small, shallow wells and a cooking fireplace with pots, pans, and eating utensils for four. The patrol destroyed the wells and collapsed the bunker. Lance Corporal LaRue picked up an old AK-47 magazine.[20] It would make for good trading materials in "Dog Patch," the Vietnamese village just outside the west gate at Da Nang International Airport. It had numerous stalls and thatched shacks along the road where Marines and airmen could buy or trade for just about anything. The Air Force guys would always pay higher prices for a souvenir from the field, such as an AK-47 banana magazine.

Back at 119, the hill fell into a daily routine. The morning had a fire team wire check circle the hill while an eight-man walk-off patrol headed in a different direction each day within the haven. Lieutenant Klein, advised by Sergeant Gwinn, had pushed security out away from the hill. This was done by patrolling off-hill, limited by the size of the haven. On 10 July, the walk-off patrol was *Beech Nut-Charlie*, meaning it was Charlie Bunker's turn for a walk-off patrol. They departed on the north side, led by Corporal Griffin. They had planned to check out the Tho Son hamlet below the hill. None of the Charlie Bunker team had been there before. They went off-trail to avoid booby traps and took an hour-and-a-half to get there after departing the east gate. They entered the hamlet from the east and heard pans banging.[21] It was the hamlet's signal that Marines had entered the enclave of thatched huts. They found no villagers present, so Griffin started searching the individual huts. They found one on the riverside of the hamlet with a bunker and a trench that led to a bunker complex between the hamlet and the river. They subsequently discovered 16 bunkers. The first five along the trench line had earthen roofs and were easily collapsed. The primary trench led to a second trench that, in turn, led to 11 bunkers that paralleled the river. They all had steel-reinforced roofs covered with earth. All were empty. In the largest one, Griffin found a message in Vietnamese dated 10 July.[22] They had started the patrol at 0530; it was now 1420, so Griffin had the team saddle up and head back up the hill. The Vietnamese knew they were there, so the patrol moved out of the hamlet and proceeded straight up the hill off-trail and decided to head to the LZ to return since the villagers knew that was an entrance. It was after 1600 when they were through the wire and Griffin showed the Vietnamese message to the lieutenant, telling him and Gwinn about the steel-reinforced bunkers.

That night Typhoon *Tess* came ashore from the East China Sea. The commanding officer of the 1st Marines had pulled all units off the below-sea-level Go Noi Island, including the heavy bulldozers.[23] It rained hard for the next 36 hours. Every bunker had standing water on its dirt floor. At sundown on 11 July, in the rain, the OP picked up two Viet Cong (VC) scrounging around an old infantry position in the center of Go Noi Island. They were searching each fighting hole. *Beech Nut* got *Hostage Delta,* an OV-10, on the radio; it came over and worked the area over with its rockets. He then handed off to *Hostage Zulu,* who was headed back to Marble Mountain Air Facility and had rockets to expend. When *Zulu* was rounds complete, he handed off to an aerial observer, *Cowpoke Six-Nine,* in the back of a new OV-10 coming out for the evening. They also expended their rockets on the old infantry position.[24] The Marines on the hill had their own private airshow during its rainy dinner hour while sitting on top of their bunkers in ponchos. Many of them took the opportunity in the warm rain to strip down and take a rain shower.

Klein and Gwinn spent the next day discussing the Tho Son hamlet, believing they did not have the full picture of what was going on there. They decided to send another walk-off patrol on the morning of 12 July. Gwinn would lead and take two full teams with him; one would be used for security and the other would be used for searching. He would take Griffin's team, which had been down and found the bunkers, and Corporal McCommon's team. They departed at 0430, got off the hill okay, and were entering Tho Son by 0600. They must have surprised the villagers as there was no banging of pans. The team rounded up one old man, six women, and eight children in the center square of the hamlet along Route 537.[25] The elderly woman with one arm seemed to be speaking to the villagers and she would be the one to talk to the Marines via a young girl who could speak a few words of English. The adults all had ID cards and said they were from Chien Son three kilometers to the east. The patrol team told them they should not be in Tho Son. The security team put them in one hut with two Marines to watch and posted two Marines east and west on Route 537 for security. Griffin took Gwinn to the back side of the hamlet facing the Song Chiem Son. There they started the slow search process. Slow not because the bunkers were hard to find, but because they had to check for booby traps. They hoped that, since they surprised the villagers, no booby traps were set in the hamlet. They searched for seven hours, finding a bunker complex starting under the hamlet and running to the river.

There was a 4-foot-deep × 4-foot-wide open trench, essentially a hard-packed walled high-speed trail running from the hamlet to the river. With bunkers on both sides, the trench had a T junction

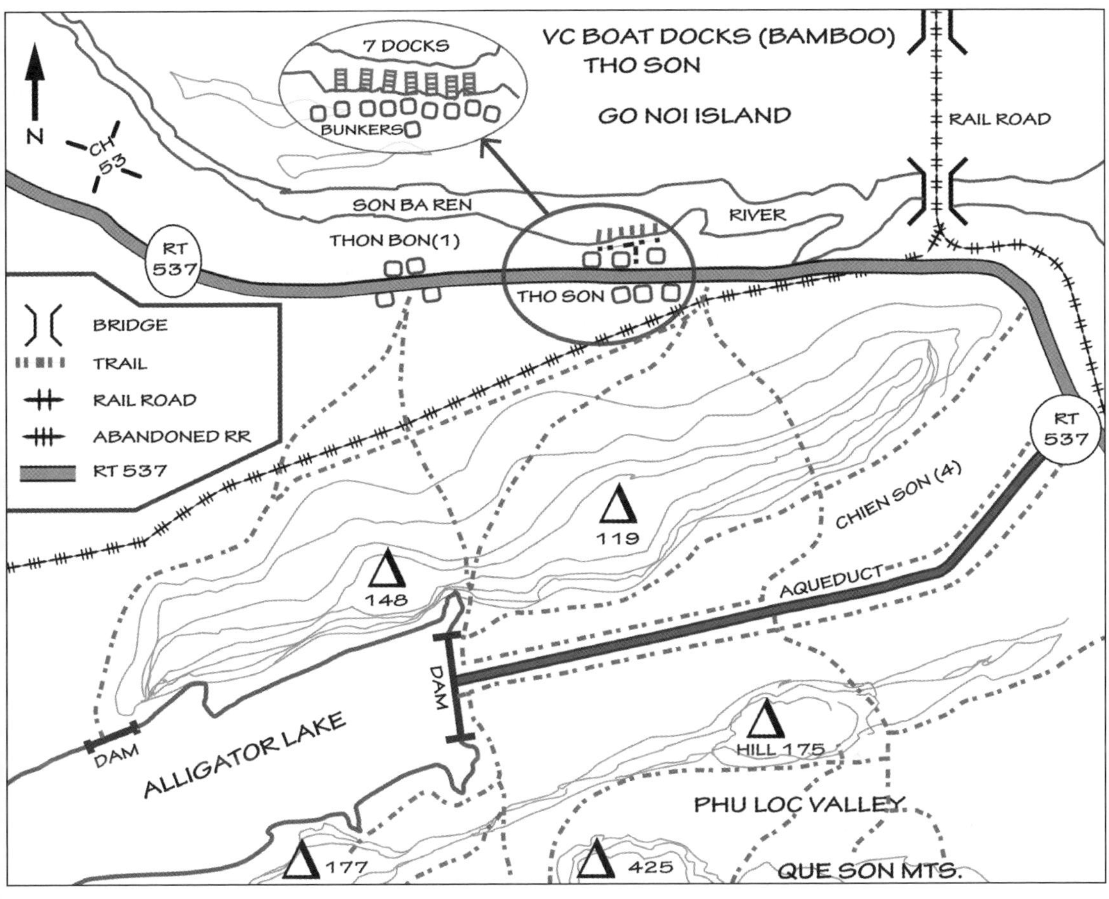

Boat terminal, docks, and bunker complex, Tho Son hamlet, 1970. (M. Fallon and W. Denham)

at the river and went east–west along the southern bank of the Song Chiem Son. They found seven boat landings that led directly into reinforced bunkers on the riverside and out to the trench line on the hamlet side. In total, there were 50 bunkers with the largest riverside ones capable of holding ten Vietnamese-size people. These bunkers were constructed with reinforced-steel beams, timbers, and sheet-metal roofs covered with three feet of earth.[26] Mostly empty, it was clear this was a major transportation hub between the southern bank and Go Noi Island. The search found one decaying body in civilian clothes in a bunker at the western end. They also found documents, and official papers with stamps, in the center bunker.[27] *Beech Nut-Charlie* had called the hill earlier and asked the lieutenant what to do with the villagers. Klein was not sure, so he radioed the battalion and asked for guidance. After some time, Battalion radioed back and said, since they had ID cards, to warn them not to come to this restricted area and send them back east down the Route 537 dirt track to Chien Son (1).[28] This was another recorded encounter with the one-armed woman who had a total black/red betle-nut set of teeth which she proudly displayed with smiles. There were many rumors and stories in the Delta Company club, the "Stagger Back

Inn," about the one-armed woman, particularly that she had lost her lower left arm during the French War fighting for the Viet Minh. This was just one of many encounters with her and the children of Tho Son. The patrol returned to the hill late that afternoon. Klein spent the next day, 13 July, calling for artillery fire missions from *Pony Boy* in An Hoa. He targeted between the hamlet and the river, trying to destroy the bunkers. At the end of the day, he estimated eight of 50 bunkers had been destroyed. He also observed one large secondary explosion.[29]

Delta Company's 2nd Platoon would depart at 1130 on 14 July. They were replaced by 4th Platoon for the next two weeks.[30] On 15 July, Reconnaissance Indoctrination Course (RIC) 8-69 commenced at Camp Reasoner. Delta Company had nine new Marines attending: Lance Corporal T. Williams, and eight Privates First Class: R. L. "Bob" Grossman, Randy Lowery, M. E. Huber, J. E. Diaz, D. R. Euclide, W. C. Berry, L. R. Calvert, and J. M. McCarrell. All would become stalwarts in Delta Company over the next year.[31] RIC was designed to familiarize newly joined personnel with the principles, techniques, and tactics of ground-reconnaissance patrolling in the Republic of Vietnam. The course included immediate-action drills for small patrols, live firing their own M16 rifle after zeroing the weapon and rappelling off the battalion water tank. The students were also taken to the 11th Marines' artillery cantonment down Division Road to observe a fire mission on the gun line. This was followed by a class on how to call fire missions. Radio procedures were also covered. The class finished with a three-day patrol, led by the instructor cadre, on the Monkey Mountain jungle peninsula east of Da Nang harbor. More monkeys than people were encountered on the outer peninsula of Da Nang Bay. It was a controlled location to break in new Recon personnel on how to live and sleep without talking, smoking, or cooking in the field. The class graduated on 24 July with 30-plus new Marines and Corpsmen returning to their parent companies.[32]

Back on Hill 119 on 20 July, as Sergeant Hackett recalled, one of his Marines was on the platform monitoring the People Sniffer and listening to AFVN (Armed Forces Vietnam Network) Radio, when they had breaking news announcing, "Man had landed and walked on the moon." Excited, the Marine yelled the news from the centrally located platform to the rest of hill. "Marines, attention," he yelled, "We've just landed on the Moon!" A Marine sunbathing on top of Charlie Bunker on the south side of the hill yelled back, "Hey, asshole, you're already on the moon!"[33] Marines did not give each other much slack, especially if they were just hanging out on a hot rock in Vietnam.

On 26 July at 0600, Lieutenant Pfeiffer and 3rd Platoon were sitting on LZ 401 waiting for their helo lift. They were returning to Hill 119. Pfeiffer was bringing 25 Marines, a corpsman, and Scout Dog Harvey Baby.[34] He was also bringing a new NOD. The previous one had gotten soaked in the rains of Typhoon *Tess* and was inoperable. The OP's mission and haven size remained the same, even though Pfeiffer had lobbied the S-3 (operations) shop for an enlarged haven and additional patrols. They would remain in direct support of the grunts in Operation *Pipestone Canyon.* On their first night with the new NOD, they picked up two NVA/VC with packs on the trail just south of the Alligator Lake dam. Rather than wait for artillery clearance, Pfeiffer engaged them with the hill's 60-mm mortar and .50-caliber machine gun. The gun clearly hit and wounded one of the enemy as they disappeared off the trail.[35] The next afternoon, two civilian villagers approached the hill. One male and one female, they asked permission to search for and remove construction material from the bombed-out hamlet below the hill. Permission was not granted. However, Pfeiffer did tell them he would find construction material for them to be delivered to their village, Chien Son (4).

On 28 July after dark, at about 2215, the NOD watch picked up 12 NVA/VC moving east to west on the aqueduct trail southeast of the hill, 400 meters away. The Marines put up 60-mm mortar illumination and engaged with the .50-caliber machine gun.[36] They shot up the trail, but the enemy, as soon as the first rounds impacted, went to the opposite (south) side of the cement aqueduct for protection. The aqueduct was a USAID project to irrigate the rice paddies east of the Alligator Lake dam. It served the entire village of Chien Son and ran for over 4,000 meters. Because of enemy inactivity, and the priority of artillery fires being allocated to the infantry in Operation *Pipestone Canyon*, Pfeiffer did not call any fire missions during his platoon's two-week flip. Instead, he relied on the hill's organic weapons, which he and the Marines enjoyed firing. On the morning of 29 July, five female villagers led by the one-armed woman approached the hill on the main north trail. They were carrying a Vietnamese in a stretcher made of parachute silk. The injury was shrapnel in the knee and the wound was infected. Through a young boy, acting as interpreter, they requested a medevac and treatment. Hospital Corpsman Third Class Sanders cleaned out the wound. Pfeiffer explained they were not supposed to be there, rather they should go out to Route 1 for road medevacs. The villagers said the Koreans on Route 1 always shot at them and turned them away, so they came to "The Good Hill." They got the medevac.[37]

Pfeiffer pushed out an ambush, for the south side of the hill, on the night of 30 July. While nobody came through the ambush site, the team could confirm movement to the east in the blind spot caused by the terrain. On 31 July, the five villagers, led by the one-armed woman and a boy, approached the hill with two parachute stretchers. A six-man security detail with "Doc" Sanders was sent down the trail to meet and access the wounded. The two men on the stretchers needed to be medevac'd. The team reported they were young men without ID cards. Pfeiffer called the medevac and told Sergeant Keen to inform the crew chief of the evac bird their passengers were VC. He also called in a spot report.[38] Later that day, the medevac bird came. The one-armed women headed back to Tho Son, with the other Vietnamese, as soon as the hill agreed to take the men.

On the evening of 2 August, Pfeiffer was awoken by the sound of incoming mortar rounds. Jumping up and out of his bunker, he saw the rounds impacting 50 feet down the slope inside the first-string wire. The rounds were coming from the northeast and sounded like 81-mm mortars. Sprinting to the communications bunker, he called An Hoa COC and called for a check-fire of all mortar fire missions. The firing stopped. Afterwards, the Marines said it had been between 18 and 20 rounds of friendly fire. Pfeiffer radioed both 5th Marines and Recon Battalion to complain.[39] He then did a complete walk around the hill, as everyone was wide awake, telling every Marine it was friendly fire. He never got an explanation. He was up, and wide awake, so he took a turn at the NOD.

Shortly after midnight, he saw movement on the trail just east of Tho Son hamlet and started counting. At five enemy, he had Sergeant Keen get the mortar and .50-caliber ready. At 17, he called for fire. As sound of the 60-mm mortar dropped, and the sound could be heard in the quiet night, the .50-cal fired and the enemy went to ground in the bunker complex located within Tho Son hamlet.[40] On the evening of 3 August, the hill sent an ambush team down to Route 537 to set in between Thon Bon (1) and Tho Son. They were well inside the hill's designated haven. At approximately 2315, the team spotted four NVA/VC coming along the wide dirt road. Before they entered the kill zone, the team heard the thump of mortar rounds being dropped. So did the enemy who immediately ran right through the ambush, while the Recon team went to ground as the 81-mm mortars impacted 25 meters west of them. The VC were wearing black shorts and black t-shirts, carrying full packs, with rifles at sling arms. The team called the hill, and Pfeiffer told them to come back in. He got on the radio again to 5th Marines and to Recon Battalion to file the second friendly fire incident into the haven.[41] Pfeiffer knew the grunts knew he was on the hill, but he did not believe they had his haven plotted in their battalion's Fire Direction Center. His Marines had been at grid coordinates AT987518, which was 700 meters inside the western boundary line between them and the grunts.

That night, Pfeiffer wrote up his notes for the S-2 debrief on 5 August. He would speak plainly. The artillery unit at An Hoa, callsign *Pony Boy,* had been non-responsive, not on the net, and did not respond to even a routine request to register on-call fires. He knew they were busy; however, they should have been able to find time to register on-call fires for the defense of the hill. Additionally, he wanted to make it clear there was a disconnect in the coordination-control figures and zones between Recon Battalion and the 5th Marines' COC.[42] The good news was that he had no injuries from the two 81-mm mortar incidents, but that was random luck. Pfeiffer was a detailed professional. He had sought out Recon as he could control his own territory (haven) and control his own risk in relationship to the enemy. He was frustrated with friendly violations of his area as it could lead to friendly casualties.

CHAPTER 10

Phu Loc Airshow, August 1969

In the United States, the number one movie in August 1969 was *Butch Cassidy and the Sundance Kid*; the Woodstock Music Festival took place from 15–18 August.[1] The Marines would hear about both events on the Armed Forces Vietnam Network but would not be able to comprehend the effect of either event on American pop culture.

In Vietnam, at III Marine Amphibious Force (III MAF), on 14 August, the 9th Marines' Regimental Landing Team completed its redeployment departure.[2] At the 1st Marine Division, the regiments were busy. First Marines continued with Operation *Pipestone Canyon* in Dodge City and Go Noi Island. Fifth Marines, out of An Hoa, launched into Operation *Durham Peak*.[3] And, the 7th Marine Regiment redeployed south to the Que Son district of Quang Tin Province.[4] At 1st Recon, Camp Reasoner was a crowded place and new hooches were being built by the Seabees. This also meant the Marines from each company were trading or providing the Seabees with war souvenirs they would never have access to—such as bayonets, magazines, enemy rifles, and pistols—in exchange for additional construction in their respective company areas. Delta Company had a nice club, the "Stagger Back Inn," with bar tables and a sound system, in a Southeast Asia Hut.

Charlie Company had an above-ground swimming pool built out of an old water bladder. Officially, they said it was to check out SCUBA gear. It had a sundeck and was a popular place, in the summer, to drink beer. The Battalion Sergeant Major had a handball court built. As a result, Camp Reasoner founded by 3rd Recon Battalion had been built up over time and was a comfortable place. Nonetheless, it was now crowded as the battalion had a fifth patrolling company—Echo Company—and 1st Force Recon Company, with its six platoons, had moved back in as well as two platoons from Alpha Company, 5th Recon. On 1 August, Major General Thrash, the commanding general of the 1st Marine Aircraft Wing, attended the morning briefing provided to the pilots of the insert/extract helo package that had flown over to LZ 401 and shut down.[5] He had come over in his Huey and shut down on the LZ (landing zone). He stood in the back and listened as 1st Lieutenant Porpotage, the assistant operations officer (S-3A), briefed which teams were to be inserted where and who was scheduled for extraction that day. Porpotage also recommended a sequence and route based on experience. The pilots had the final say but they normally went with the battalion's recommendations. The daily insert/extract package was two CH-46s and two gunships. After the eight pilots had finished and departed, General Thrash took a quick walk through the S-3 bunker before returning to his bird and departing. Recon relied on the helos to get them into their patrol areas, known as havens, but, more importantly, to get them out! The pilots and their crews took pride in getting Recon out of bad situations. Many Recon Marines owed their lives to the brave pilots and crews that willingly flew directly into enemy fire to get them out of dangerous situations, putting the aircraft at risk of being shot down.

Later, on the same morning, Lieutenant Colonel Mickelson played host to two newly arrived Colonels, N. L. Beck, and H. L. Wilkerson, who had joined the division staff. They received a brief from Mickelson on how reconnaissance operations were conducted and a current ops brief from the S-3, Major Cole, on what was happening that week. Towards the end of the month, on 20 August, the battalion rolled out its best static display of Recon Marines in cammie-painted faces and full loads of equipment for The Honorable John W. Warner, Under Secretary of the Navy, who also took an operational brief.[6]

Headed to Hill 119, was 2nd Platoon, callsign *Spillway*, under 2nd Lieutenant Klein, for his second flip to the observation post (OP). He took 23 enlisted Marines along with Hospital Corpsman Third Class Semararo. He was pleased to have a dog handler and dog with him for this trip.[7] The mission had not changed and would continue to support Operation *Pipestone Canyon*.

After being the first lift of the day out of LZ 401, they arrived for their one-hour turnover at 0800 on 5 August. Klein did not know why but they were only scheduled for nine days. The lack of artillery support continued. As a result, he did not call for, or execute, any fire missions. The only real activity was multiple visits to the hill by the local Vietnamese. Midmorning on 8 August, two Vietnamese males came up to the wire from the east trail.[8] They were wearing white "PJs," both top and bottom. They had bundles of personal items but no IDs, military gear, or weapons. They were of military age and very hungry. They "Chieu Hoi'd" to get fed. Later, at 1345, another male came up the same east trail to the wire to turn himself in. He was wearing a white shirt and green shorts. He turned in two Chi-com grenades and an M26, one U.S. cartridge belt, one rain suit, rifle cleaning gear, a wallet, and an extra set of clothes. He said he had come during the night from Go Noi Island and waited for daylight to come forward.[9] All three Chieu Hois were evacuated to LZ 20 and the Interrogator Translator Team co-located with the III MAF prisoner compound. On 11 August, in the early afternoon, three males, one female, and an infant baby came up the north trail. Klein sent a security team, including the dog and "Doc," down to investigate. They had a bamboo-pole parachute stretcher for the woman and baby. Both required medevacs. Klein arranged them and also sent the three fighting-age males to the rear as possible NVA or VC.[10] Once again, at 0700 on the 14th, which was the platoon's scheduled flip day, two males came up the north hill wearing black trousers and white tops, hands held high. Their ID cards were dated January 1963. They had Chieu Hoi'd. Klein cuffed the pair, surrounded them with security, and took them out on the scheduled flip.[11]

Next up on the schedule was Delta-1. The Marines of 1st Platoon were now led by Staff Sergeant Ommondson.[12] The third-tour Recon Marine was salty, a term that could be a compliment or derogatory depending on context. The troops loved him. He wore a knit cap on patrol and carried a Thompson submachine gun. Some of the junior officers thought he was cocky but, in truth, they were afraid of him.[13] With the loss of Team *Grade Level*, Delta Company needed an experience leader for 1st Platoon. The Recon-savvy Ommondson had been 2nd Lieutenant John "Jack" Holly's platoon sergeant in Charlie Company on his previous tour.[14] He had taught Jack some of the finer points of patrolling. The staff sergeant would take 25 Marines, Hospital

Corpsman Third Class Vineyard, dog handler Sergeant Segundo and his dog, Baron (Marine dog 943X), to the OP.[15] The hill's callsign would be *Spillway*. Their Arty support would come from *Page Avenue*. During their 11-day stay, the OP had only eight sightings of 51 NVA/VC total.[16] Fire missions remained difficult to obtain as the artillery priority-of-fire remained with Operation *Pipestone Canyon*. The hill continued the use of its own 60-mm mortar and .50-caliber machine gun as they had done on 19 August when they observed 30 NVA/VC carrying packs and rifles moving east to west on the aqueduct trail to their south.[17] Ommondson was happy to be the radio relay for Team *Road Test* operating in the Que Son Mountains. He immediately recognized the voice of Lieutenant Holly whispering "Alpha Sierra" for "all secure" in the late-night hours.[18] His flip day arrived on 23 August with 3rd Platoon arriving at 0800.[19]

Ommondson had prepared a written turnover document for Lieutenant Pfeiffer. He emphasized the lack of artillery support. He wished the lieutenant luck and moved down to the saddle LZ between Hills 119 and 148 to await his ride to the rear. Third Platoon sergeant was Herman Diaz, a second-Vietnam-tour career Marine. He was a hardworking, no-nonsense noncommissioned officer that the gung-ho Bob Pfeiffer really appreciated. He would let Diaz run the platoon, and he would focus on off-hill coordination which, in his view, needed improvement. By being a perfectionist pest on the radio, he could ensure better fire-support coordination. The hill would keep the callsign *Spillway*. In some sense, this helped as the friendly artillery units could associate the callsign with the OP. His primary artillery support remained the 105-mm batteries out of An Hoa Combat Base 12 kilometers to his west-southwest; their callsign remained *Page Avenue*. At the same time, 1st Recon Battalion callsign had changed over to *Summer Breeze*. Before coming up to the hill, Pfeiffer had gone down to the S-3 bunker and walked the S-3A, 1st Lieutenant Porpotage, through the fire-support issues with Hill 119's haven and the artillery. Porpotage said he would speak to the battalion's artillery liaison officer from the 11th Marines. Pfeiffer's 3rd Platoon would have 20 Marines and two corpsmen, Hospital Corpsman Second Class Lee and Hospital Corpsman Third Class Sanders.[20] No dog this trip meant he did not have to worry about water for the dog in the summer heat. Water on the OP was rationed as it all came in by air.

Pfeiffer was physically fit even by Marine Corps standards. He was aggressive by nature. He would actively patrol from the hill inside his haven as he thought that was the best security for the OP. After arriving, Pfeiffer spent the entire day on the radio with *Page Avenue* updating their list of pre-registered targets. He had requested to shoot one round at each of them but had been denied. At 2025, the night-observation device (NOD) watch picked up six NVA/VC carrying packs on the aqueduct trail south of the hill. Pfeiffer tried calling a pre-registered fire mission but could not get quick clearance.[21] He engaged the enemy with the .50-caliber machine gun. In response, the enemy jumped over the cement aqueduct and was gone. The 24th was a quiet day. That evening, just after sunset, at 2012, the NOD watch was focused on the Alligator Lake dam and picked up four NVA/VC moving about on the trail heading east. The hill immediately engaged with 60-mm high-explosive (HE) rounds and the machine gun. They covered the trail but could not observe results.[22] The enemy had been on that trail two nights in a row. Pfeiffer discussed it with Sergeant Diaz. They agreed it would be a good location for an ambush. Pfeiffer did not ask; he said he would take out the first team with Corporal Cob. As the sun was setting on the 25th, they pushed out the east gate and dropped into the southern valley, patrolling off-trail. They took their time, worked across the aqueduct, and moved uphill to the high side of the aqueduct trail, which was on the south side of the structure. There was a trail on each side, so one had to pick. They set in 500 meters east of the dam, about fifteen feet above the trail in a group of scattered boulders.

This was a small six-man team, and it would be a straight ambush. Pfeiffer had discussed a prisoner snatch with Diaz who pointed out they had not rehearsed it, and it would take a bigger team to pull off, thus leaving the hill shorthanded. Straight ambush it was. They set in on-line, Pfeiffer was in the center a little forward. He could see both ways on the trail. They were in position at 2000. At 2037, they heard noise coming down the trail from the dam. There was VC in a tight column. Pfeiffer had two Claymore mines set for the kill zone. When the VC were in the kill zone, Pfeiffer closed each hellbox, one in each hand. The backblast put up a lot of dust. When it settled, he put out security in each direction and he and Cob went to the zone and searched the six dead bodies. They had been wearing shorts, sandals, PJ tops, and helmets. Were they NVA? The team collected the gear quickly and put it in a couple of packs they took off the bodies. Cob told the lieutenant he had seen one enemy soldier who was not in the kill zone run back towards the dam.[23] Pfeiffer knew from his own observations that large units used this trail. It was time to collect the gear and head back up the hill to the OP. They were gone from the ambush site in under five minutes, breaking brush moving toward the OP. They called *Spillway* and told them it had been their ambush they heard, and they would be coming in fast and loud. *Spillway* should fire the Arty target on the trail behind them, to cover their withdrawal. They would use the LZ as it could be accessed off the trail, thereby avoiding any potential booby traps. That evening in the communications bunker, Cob's team, with Pfeiffer and Diaz, went through the captured gear. They had to determine what to report and what the team got to keep. They had captured one radio that clearly would be turned in. The haul also included a .45-caliber pistol and a Russian 9-mm pistol. The lieutenant said the .45 would be turned in as intel would be able to trace where it had been lost, stolen, or captured, and investigate a lead. Cob could keep the 9-mm which would not be reported. The three diaries, 200 sheets of writing paper, one Chi-com grenade, a mine, and extra clothing would be turned in. Diaz and Pfeiffer were surprised they got no rifles. This was clearly a communications team; security teams would have been on the trail before and after them. It had been a successful ambush. They also kept the 25 pounds of tea for the hill. Pfeiffer told Cob to write up the spot report and for Diaz to check it.[24] He was bone tired and departed for his bunker.

The next evening, they decided to put out an ambush on the north side. Diaz said he would go but he wanted to birddog and let Corporal Horton lead the team. They formed up in the mortar pit for a sound inspection. Horton had everyone jump up and down; nobody rattled. Diaz told him to wait until the sun was over the crest of Hill 148. They would go out west across the LZ and pick up the trail that went over the saddle. They had just cleared the LZ when they heard movement coming up the Alligator Lake trail towards the saddle. They moved off-trail on the west side of Hill 148 with a plan to set up a hasty ambush; they were too late. The VC spotted the team just setting into the site and fired first up the steep draw with all the fire going high. The team returned fire down the draw as the VC column withdrew down the draw towards the lake. One VC lay dead. They had seen five VC in black PJs and coolie hats. They recovered a rifle, and a pack filled with rice.[25] Diaz told Horton to bring the team back across the LZ and into the OP. Later that evening, at 2240, the NOD watch picked up six NVA/VC, approximately thirteen hundred meters east, carrying two satchels.[26] The hill fired 60-mm mortar HE rounds and the .50-cal machine gun. The enemy had disappeared. On the night of the 27th, they again picked up groups moving north to south coming off the trestles of the southern bridge to Go Noi Island. They engaged with the machine gun, at a distance of over two kilometers, with no effect. The following evening, 28 August, at 2115, the OP watch, using the NOD, picked up five NVA sitting on the east side of the military crest of Hill 148. They wore utility uniforms and were carrying rifles and demolition gear. They were setting booby traps. The hill had a night ambush out on the saddle trail 200 meters away, between Hill 119 and Hill 148. Pfeiffer radioed the ambush telling them to get down and wait in the ambush. The hill was going to engage over the top of them. Diaz went down and supervised the 60-mm mortar mission to ensure they would fire on the far west side and top of Hill 148, which was past the NVA but allowed for a safe distance from his friendly ambush site. He expected the NVA to move when mortared; the question would be in which direction. With the bloop of the mortar being fired, the enemy group split and moved out. Four NVA ran into the ambush kill zone. The ambush was initiated by one Claymore set five feet from the kill zone. However, it was defective. The blasting cap blew, and a lot of dust went up as three of the NVA fled. One lay dead, killed by rifle fire. The team searched the body, recovered two AK-47s from the site, one M26 grenade, and a box with three blasting caps.[27] Pfeiffer had the ambush team return to the OP. Clearly, the enemy had been elite sappers.

***

Meanwhile, the in-ground sensor strings planted in the Phu Loc Valley and monitored on Hill 425's OP were getting nightly activities. Military Assistance Command, Vietnam (MACV) was a major proponent of sensors. This was because the Department of Defense was a proponent and funded the sensors. Secretary of Defense McNamara, coming from a background of industry, was a big advocate of data and technology. He was a believer in using sensors to detect the enemy's movement. The Department of Defense had a large sensor budget for Vietnam. Sensors were an integral part of creating barriers to infiltration. The Marines, at the behest of MACV, had built a barrier south of the demilitarized zone, which was a wide bulldozed strip of land. It was seeded with sensors to detect enemy movement. Similarly, they had created a bulldozed strip of land around Da Nang, called the Da Nang Defensive Belt or Da Nang Trace. It was also seeded with sensors. The ground sensors were seismic, audio, and metallic, and were meant to detect enemy crossings over the cleared piece of land. Marines patrolled the near sides and shot artillery at sensor read outs in both belts with marginal results when compared to the number of rounds expended. More effective were hand-placed sensors along trails and avenues of approach. The SCAMP (Sensor Control and Management Platoon) Platoon, which was part of the 1st Marine Division's G-2 (intelligence) Section, had placed battery operated seismic sensors on trails in the Phu Loc Valley leading into the Que Son Mountains and Base Area 116. There was also a string of sensors along the finger of Hill 175. These sensor strings needed to be monitored with radio readouts that were line-of-sight radio feeds from the sensor strings. Hill 425 was the sensor-readout position for the Phu Loc Valley set of strings.[28] The readouts were monitored by Marines from the SCAMP Platoon stationed with collection equipment at the Recon OP. When a detection occurred, two events happened. Immediately, the OP was notified as to the location and preregistered artillery fire was shot at these original moving-target indicators. Secondly, the times, locations, and durations of the sensor activation were recorded and sent to the SCAMP Platoon's analytical section on Hill 327. They analyzed the data and presented trend analysis on enemy movements, directions, and flows to the G-2 Section for inclusion in the weekly intelligence summaries. The Phu Loc sensor strings were continually active and calibrated as being accurate with visual sighting from both OPs on Hill 425 and Hill 119 overlooking the valley. Artillery ambushes based on sensor readings became a regular occurrence. The enemy movement during June and July became quite heavy with the SCAMP analysis indicating large units moving into and out of the Phu Loc Valley. The G-2 analysis interpreted these activities as the effects of Operation *Pipestone Canyon* having pushed the NVA off Go Noi Island and back into the Que Sons' Base Area 116, and to the enemy's need to harvest and store the rice crop from the Phu Loc Valley rice paddies. By day, the NVA lived in caves and tunnel complexes within the mountains. At night, they moved in large columns down one of six draws out of the mountains and into the valley to work the fields harvesting rice.

The NVA ran their "production operation" for the harvest as a military operation. With enemy counts in the hundreds every night, the intelligence section suggested it could be a lucrative aviation target. Further, if they could run air strikes in marginal and nighttime weather, which the NVA always used to their advantage for nighttime harvesting, they could catch them in the open. The Marines had developed an all-weather bombing system, the TPQ-10. ASRT (Air Support Radar Team) were the personnel that ran the TPQ-10. This radar, like an air-control radar, produced a directed beam or vector with a 30-mile distance from the radar. An aircraft with the correct electronics package could lock onto the beam and do precision bombing at predetermined grid locations highlighted by the vector of the radar or offset from it. The ASRT team could get Marine and Navy A-6 aircraft, each with a capacity for thirty-two 500-pound bombs, to a location in bad weather, at night, or both. The SCAMP sensor fields were preregistered as known locations for the ASRT team. Then the Marine pilots could drop bombs on those fields or in a predetermined targeted box or rectangle at a given time. With aircraft in the air or on strip alert at Da Nang, and a sensor-field activation being read out on the OP at Hill 425, the Recon Marines could radio the Direct Air Support Center (DASC) for the bombing package and give them the selected rectangle box and time on target based on the enemy's rate of march or direct observation from the OP. This was a high-tech ambush which could use both artillery and air. It required coordination between all the participating units. The coordinator was 1st Lieutenant Sharman leading the Recon team on Hill 425.[29] Because of the amount of assets being utilized in this high-tech fire support ambush, a bomb-damage assessment (BDA) was always planned. BDAs took three forms: visual observation from the OP, observation from an aircraft, or, preferred by the analyst, boots on the ground with a patrol to the targeted area to count the bodies they expected to find after a successful strike.

On the night of 28 August, while Team *Spillway* was dealing with NVA sappers mining nearby Hill 148[30] and Lieutenant Pfeiffer was getting his night-activities team and its partially blown ambush back to his OP, they were watching with interest to their south over the Phu Loc Valley, seeing and hearing an OV-10 and then another aircraft, callsign *Basketball Seven-Six-Two*, light up the entire valley with flares. On Hill 425 was Echo Company's Team *Turf Club*. Sharman and Sergeant Brown were coordinating a high-tech ambush over the valley.[31] They were monitoring a sensor string that triggered a prescripted fire-support ambush of the nightly visitors to the valley from Base Area 116. Just after sundown, the SCAMP Marines on the OP picked up heavy movement on four of the six sensor strings leading out of the Que Sons. *Turf Club* called the DASC, requesting that night's package of eight A-6 aircraft loaded wing to wing with thirty-two 500-pound bombs, each to be allocated for TPQ-10 strikes. An OV-10 *Hostage* aircraft with a *Cowpoke* aerial observer (AO) had been dedicated to help with this coordinated strike.

An OV-10 came out first with a *Basketball* aircraft and contacted *Turf Club* who were already firing preplanned artillery in front of a group of 100 NVA moving on to Hill 175 by firing forward of the enemy columns moving into the rice fields to slow them down. With the arrival of the *Cowpoke* AO, *Turf Club* turned the artillery off. The air strike was handed off to the Marines of MASS-2 (Marine Air Support Squadron-2) who manned the TPQ-10 radar and radios on Hill 10 south of Da Nang. This ASRT team had the radar dialed in for a direct line-of-sight shot to the Phu Loc Valley and the predetermined bombing boxes. The OV-10 set up its observation orbit west over Alligator and Spider Lakes at 3,000 feet, to be out of the way but still observing the valley. They were flying just west of the Phu Loc Valley. The A-6s were receiving direction-to-target from the ASRT by radio and the radar's vector. The MASS-2 Marines, callsign *Devastate Charlie* (Charlie was a shorthand reference meaning "Victor Charlie" or VC), were directing the aircraft to fly north to south at 10,000 feet, turning east and exiting over the South China Sea. Each pair of A-6s would take two passes at their designated targets boxes. The four TPQ-10 runs that night were made at 1945, 2325, 0020, and 0100 on reported SCAMP sensor counts of 100, 60, 8, and 25 enemy in their respective target boxes. The aircraft would service four target boxes, each being guided to its release point by the vector provided by the TPQ-10. The valley was lit up with the ordnance being dropped, followed by *Basketball*'s flares to support observation on the ground. The "Phu Loc Airshow" was on. Visible to Marines on both OPs, they could clearly see and hear the 500-pound bombs exploding and the smoke rising. After the last bird departed, the OV-10 made a few passes identifying bodies on the trails before departing low on fuel. Hill 425 then called preregistered artillery targets into all six draws leading back into the Que Sons. After an initial battery-two (six guns, two rounds each) in each draw, they called a ceasefire. Through the NOD, they observed NVA gathering wounded and dead and moving them into the draws and back into the Que Sons for the remainder of the night.[32] This was reported to Recon Battalion by the OP and to the DASC by the OV-10. The air wing called the division at some point during the night and requested a ground BDA of the four target-box fields. The division agreed. Later that evening, an order was passed from 1st Division to 1st Recon to conduct a BDA at first light. Normally, Recon Battalion's procedure for a BDA was to fly out a team or two by helo and insert directly on the target area. This was not going to happen, perhaps because no teams were available.

At approximately 0200, *Summer Breeze* (Recon Battalion's callsign) called *Spillway* on Hill 119, the S-3A, Porpotage, radioing out to talk to Pfeiffer. The radio watch went and roused the lieutenant. Battalion Command had a lot of confidence in Pfeiffer as a proven patrol leader. Although Hill 119 was further from the air strike, it would get the BDA mission. The target boxes were a three-kilometer, direct-south trek from Hill 119. Hill 425 was straight down and straight up but pulling a BDA team from them would leave them vulnerable to an attack from the NVA in the Que Sons above them, close, and in large numbers. Porpotage asked Pfeiffer if they had watched the Phu Loc Airshow? Pfeiffer acknowledged it was a good show. "Great," said the S-3A and gave him the order to conduct the BDA of the four target boxes on the ground and to get there as soon as possible. Acknowledging the mission, Pfeiffer called Sergeant Diaz and his three team leaders in for a quick review of the mission. A plan had formulated in the bush-savvy lieutenant's mind. The rear had wanted him to push out immediately as it was three to four kilometers to each of the four bombed-out areas. Pfeiffer had waffled his response and said he would push when ready and let the rear know prior to his departure. He also wanted a precleared haven of the BDA area where he controlled all fires. He also wanted direct coordination with *Turf Club* on Hill 425. Almost immediately, he got a three-by-three-grid-square box for his haven, Upper Left AT9850 and Lower Right BT0147. He called *Turf Club* and said he would let them know when he pushed off Hill 119 and told them to watch his back as he planned to run a straight-up infantry patrol. Meeting with his team leaders, he said he was leading a BDA patrol.

This would be no snoop-and-poop Recon patrol. They would go out heavy, wearing flak jackets and helmets. Along with two radios, Pfeiffer wanted guns and ammunition to include an M60 and water for the one-day BDA mission. Diaz would stay on the hill and cover them with the 60-mm mortar and the .50-caliber machine gun between them and the Hill 175 crest. From there, Hill 425 could easily see them and each of the four target boxes they would cover looking for bodies. The planning group broke up at 0300. He told the team leaders to let him know who had volunteered shortly and that they would assemble at 0545 and push after first light. Pfeiffer did not want to trip booby traps exiting the OP in the dark. The entire platoon volunteered, so he and Diaz conferred on what the best split would be for the patrol and the hill defense. He ended up taking six Marines and a corpsman, "Doc" Sanders, with him.[33] Eight going out would leave Diaz with 14 to guard the hill. Pfeiffer was glad to see Privates First Class Swick and Lowery volunteer. They were both good fieldcraft Marines. Private First Class Haney, a new man to the platoon, along with Privates First Class Grossman and Christian, and Lance Corporal Bowers, plus one other Marine, would round out the patrol. Pfeiffer met the Marines in the mortar pit at 0545. It was still dark, so he told them they would wait. He also told them to hydrate as it would be a hot day. He went back to the communications bunker and had *Spillway* do to a comm check on both radios with *Spillway-A.* He then had *Spillway-A* do a communication check with *Turf Club*. Pfeiffer called the battalion's Combat Operations Center and *Turf Club* on the battalion network to tell them he was pushing out.

It was 0608 when the patrol departed Bravo Bunker and headed out the gate to the LZ.[34] They went off the south side of the LZ, off-trail, breaking brush for 400 meters straight downhill. They were walking slowly in a single column. Pfeiffer stopped them as they had gotten bunched up going downhill. He gave them the "spread out" hand and arm signal with both arms. They were at Alligator Lake dam within 45 minutes. Pfeiffer figured they could walk the trail here, as the NVA did it every night, with less fear of a booby trap. They headed straight across the first valley toward the Hill 175 finger on a hard-packed two-foot-wide trail. After the valley floor,

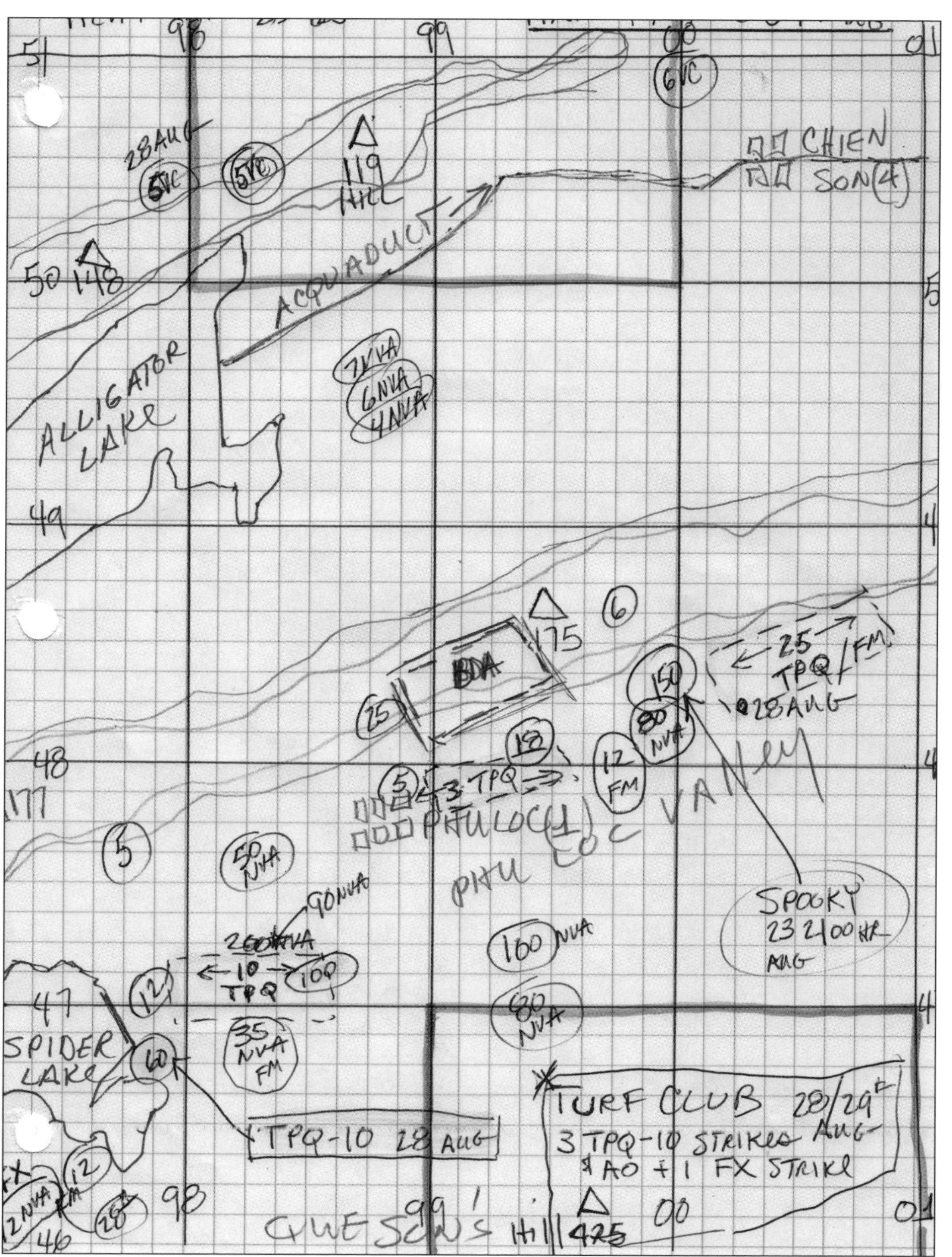

Original sketch of the TPQ-10 bombing boxes as used for the BDA patrol. (M. Fallon)

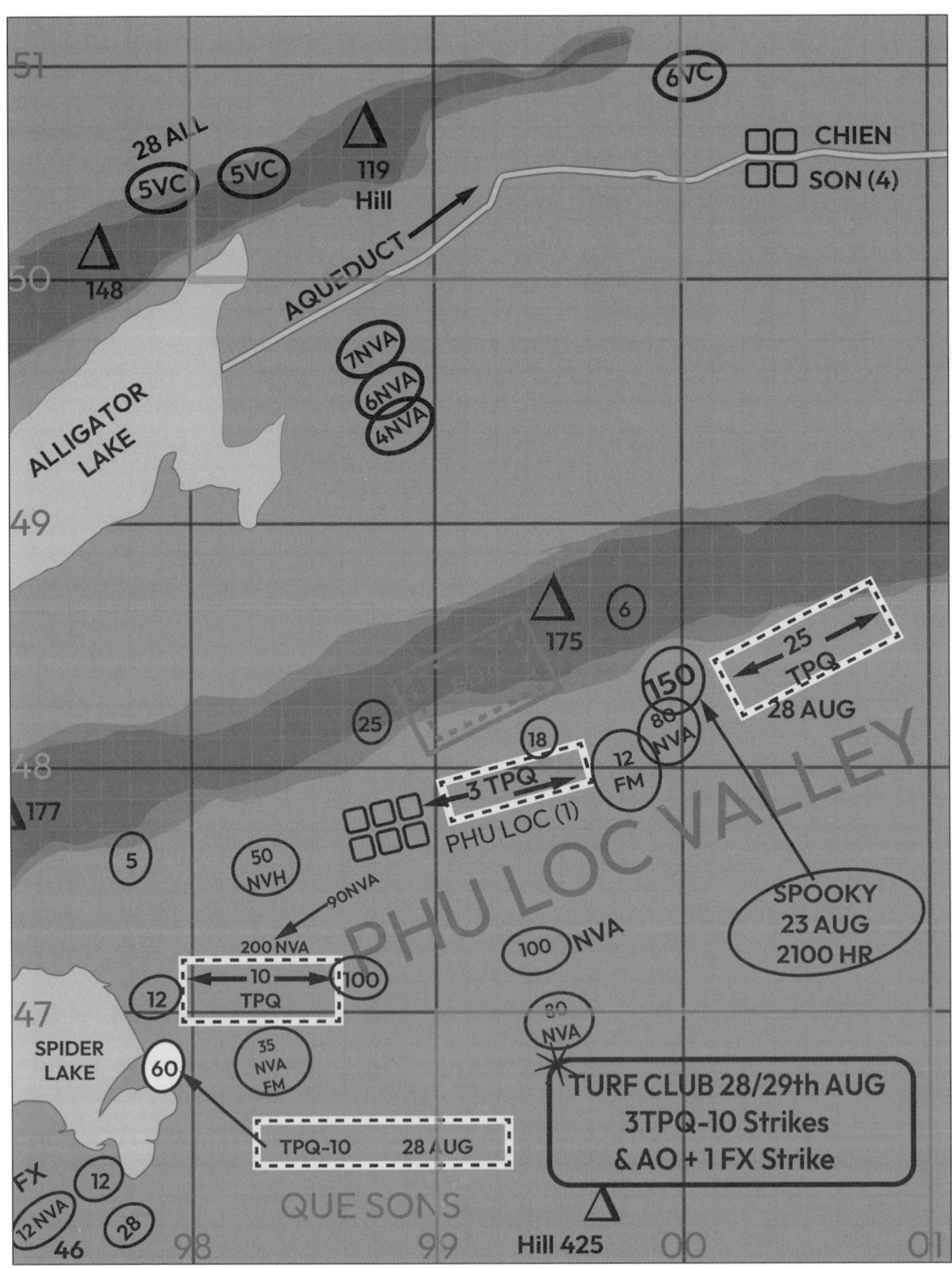

Team *Turf Club*'s BDA plan. (M. Fallon and W. Denham)

he did not want to walk into an ambush going uphill, so they went off-trail to the southeast towards the summit of 175. Hill 425 could not see them now, so he called Diaz and asked how it looked. Sergeant Diaz checked the entire finger of 175 and said they looked clear. Pfeiffer did not go to the old infantry position on the summit but moved 200 meters to the west, stopping on top. He called *Turf Club* and hit them with a mirror flash to mark his position and asked them to talk him into the first target box. The first BDA rectangle was on the south side of Hill 175. *Turf Club* talked him into the bombing site. Besides large, fresh bomb craters, they found slim indications of the previous night's aerial assault. *Turf Club* directed them to each of the next three target-box sites with no real results.[35]

They were downstream from Spider Lake when *Turf Club* asked them to check a trail towards the lake. They found the trail lined on both sides with holes sized for the protection of 2–3 men, but no enemy use was indicated. The BDA found nothing, which was not surprising, as the NVA always policed up their dead, wounded, and all gear during the night; with the Que Sons so close there was nothing but bomb craters to count. Now in the afternoon, Pfeiffer turned the patrol around and headed back. He decided to go through a small set of hooches west of Phu Loc (1). They would take a quick look to check them out. The patrol made point-blank contact, at the outskirts, with two VC in a spider hole. *Turf Club* shot one, and Pfeiffer reached into the hole and small tunnel behind it, physically pulling out the second wounded enemy.[36] Then Dennis Swick took a .45 pistol and went into the tunnel, which turned out to be a dead end. He came out with a little food but nothing else.[37]

Shortly after coming out of the tunnel, Pfeiffer split the patrol into two security and two search elements. Grossman and Haney were sent out the furthest to become the east security element, with Haney down the trail 10 meters laying prone and facing out.[38] While the patrol was searching the remainder of the hamlet, a round of artillery could be heard whistling the air and then impacting. Pfeiffer grabbed the handset from Bowers, his primary radio operator, who was humping the PRC-25. He was on the radio with the *Pace Avenue* Fire Direction Center in An Hoa, immediately calling a check-fire. Grossman came running up the trail saying Haney was down.[39] He was not moving. Doc Sanders stopped treating the prisoner and ran up the trail to Haney who was bleeding from the back of the neck. He had not moved. His helmet and flak jacket were on, and he had a hole the size of a quarter leaking blood out the back of his neck.[40] Doc applied pressure but could not stop the internal bleeding, even though the external bleeding slowed. Doc was afraid to administer morphine. Haney passed out with low blood pressure and was barely breathing. Doc told Pfeiffer he needed an emergency medevac NOW! Pfeiffer called *Turf Club* who radioed directly to the An Hoa airfield. This was not exactly the normal procedure, but it was the fastest way to get a medevac bird. They moved everyone out to a rice paddy, set security, and a bird was inbound in under five minutes.

When it landed, they loaded Haney as an emergency medevac.[41] There were already routine medevacs from An Hoa on the bird in transit. With a quick decision, Pfeiffer waved the entire patrol onto the bird, making this his team's extract. In doing so, however, he overloaded the bird. With both rotor heads of the CH-46 fully turning but not engaged to lift yet, dust was up everywhere. The crew chief was yelling at the lieutenant over the sound of the engines that they were overloaded. Pfeiffer insisted. Swick and Lowery were collar dragging the wounded VC toward the ramp when the crew chief yelled at the lieutenant, no way, they were too overloaded. Pfeiffer waved Swick off and told him to leave the VC, drop him, and get to the bird.[42] Pfeiffer waited just off the ramp and jumped on as Swick dove on as the bird was pulling out. The overloaded bird slowly struggled for altitude and then went straight and fast to the Naval Support Activity (NSA) Hospital, where Haney was offloaded straight to the emergency room for surgery. The other walking wounded got off. Haney was alive but the doctors could not do much with the piece of 105 artillery shell shrapnel that had entered the back of his neck and lodged in the back of his cerebellum.[43] He died that night at the NSA hospital.[44] That piece of iron went through a one-inch gap between his flak jacket and helmet.[45] The medevac bird took the patrol to LZ 401 at 1st Recon as their day was complete.[46] Pfeiffer told his Marines to go to chow and come back to the LZ in 30 minutes. They walked up the hill to the mess hall, hot, tired, angry, and dejected. They went to the head of the line via the privilege granted to all returning patrols, got their chow, and went outside to eat together away from everyone else. Nobody talked, nobody really ate. That patrol had been Robert Haney's first.[47]

While the team was at chow, Pfeiffer went into the S-3 bunker just uphill from the LZ. He was tired, hot, mad, and pissed off about the friendly 105-mm artillery fire out of An Hoa Combat Base on his patrol, in his haven, that he had not cleared. One of his Marines was at NSA now dying![48] He was still loudly protesting to Porpotage and the 11th Marines' artillery liaison officer when the S-3, Major J. P. Cole, walked over and calmy told Pfeiffer they would take a hard look at the friendly fire incident. The air officer had gotten him a bird to take the patrol back to Hill 119 before total darkness.[49] He and his Marines were needed for the defense of Hill 119 that night. With an "Aye aye, sir," but still hot under the collar, Pfeiffer walked out of the bunker and jogged to the LZ, waving at his dirty group of Marines back from chow to get up and get ready for the CH-46 now approaching the LZ. Swick handed Pfeiffer a can of large K-ration-sized peaches he had fingered from the mess hall.[50] Once on board the aircraft, Pfeiffer poked two holes in the top of the can and drained the sweet, thick syrup. He had not eaten since 0430 in his bunker. They were back on the hill as the sun disappeared west over On Tue Slope. Pfeiffer walked slowly off the LZ, the last man through the wire. He saw Diaz at the NOD and told him he had the hill. He went to his bunker and laid on his cot. Not able to find sleep, he mentally walked through the patrol planning, the fire-support planning, and the patrol execution. The failed coordination and randomness of the friendly fire single round would not leave his mind. About noon on 30 August, the hill learned Haney had not made it. The lieutenant called them together, every Marine at the mortar pit. He told them, but he had no words to explain or justify the loss.[51] Their last few days on the OP had included a few uneventful sightings. They were all ready to go back to Camp Reasoner and get off the hot hill with no shade and closed-in bunkers that were hotter on the inside than out. All the Marines slept on top of the bunkers thinking of their lost brother Robert Haney. Coming up to replace them on 4 September was 2nd Platoon.[52]

This was also Pfeiffer's last duty. A week after his return found him on the stage in the Staff Noncommissioned Officers/Officers Club at Camp Reasoner receiving his 1st Recon plaque from Lieutenant Colonel Mickelson. The colonel's words that evening spoke to Pfeiffer's bush credentials as well as his loyalty to, and taking care of, his Marines.[53]

Pfeiffer departed the next morning for his flight to Okinawa en route back to the United States. He was a changed man. Lieutenant Bob Pfeiffer would carry the loss of Robert Haney for the rest of his life. Bob died in 2019.

CHAPTER II

Business is Slow on 119, September 1969

In Hanoi, Ho Chi Minh had been in poor health. He died on 2 September 1969. Radio Hanoi announced the death on 4 September.[1] On 24 September, the Central Committee elected Ton Duc Thang as President of the Democratic Republic of Vietnam, or North Vietnam.[2] In the United States, the Draft Lottery announced that men born on 14 September and celebrating their 19th through to 26th birthdays would be given the highest priority for military service, Class 1A.[3] On 16 September, President Nixon announced another withdrawal of troops. The Marines' share would be 18,400 and would come from the 3rd Marine Division.[4]

At III Marine Amphibious Force, the command's new orders and policies authorized Afro haircuts and the use of the raised fist as a greeting among black Marines.[5] Meanwhile, the 1st Marine Division conducted rice-denial operations during the harvest month of September in an effort to deny the North Vietnamese Army/Viet Cong (NVA/VC) from directly harvesting rice and taxing the villagers. Patrols were focused on the lowland rice fields in each of the regimental zones. The Vietnamese provincial election was on 28 September.[6] The division made Marines available to assist provincial forces in providing security for polling locations.

At 1st Recon Battalion, Camp Reasoner was a busy place with seven companies providing teams to patrol. The battalions' companies, A through E, Alpha 5th Recon, and 1st Force Recon with its six platoons were kept busy.[7] Lieutenant Colonel Mickelson continued to focus on training and the basics of patrolling. Recon Indoctrination Course 9-69 kicked off with him addressing the newly joined Marines and Corpsmen on 2 September. Pre-SCUBA 8-69 kicked off a week later. In staff changes, Captain C. A. Delateur assumed command of Alpha Company and Major William Bill H. Bond became the battalion's operations officer (S-3).[8] Both had previous Vietnam tours with experience in the grunts and Recon. On 16 September, Major General O. R. Simpson, commanding general of the 1st Marine Division, came down Hill 327 to the battalion area and presented seven Bronze Stars to personnel of 1st Recon.[9] Mickelson took care of his people, seriously, ensuring, where awards were merited, that the division recognized the Marines and Corpsmen. On 22 September, 1st Lieutenant J. C. Creg Howland, the experienced patrol leader back from the hospital, became the battalion's intelligence officer (S-2).[10] He was responsible for not only debriefing patrols and preparing patrol reports, but also for liaison with Division G-2 and participating in the process of where patrols were to go and with what type of missions.

Headed to the observation post (OP), on 4 September at 0900, was Delta's 2nd Platoon; two CH-46s landed in the saddle landing zone for Hill 119. Second Lieutenant Klein and Sergeant

Gawlaki were returning to the OP at the head of the platoon.[11] The significant change was the size of the haven.

While every hill commander had recommended the haven be expanded to allow security patrols more freedom of movement, Klein's new haven was 200 meters less to the east. The big change, however, was the northern boundary had shrunk and pulled in by 500 meters.[12] They had lost tactical control of Route 537 across their northern front. More significantly, the hamlet of Tho Son was now outside their haven and therefore out of their control for free firing and access. This had to be a politically drawn line influenced by the South Vietnamese District Chief and his military commander. When Klein had asked, nobody on the battalion staff, at the lieutenant level, could answer as to who had made the change to the smaller-size haven. Klein asked his company commander, 1st Lieutenant A. T. Bouts, who told him to forget about it and not make waves.[13] Klein knew Bouts had never been to Hill 119 and did not understand the tactical situation. Klein was coming up with a full platoon of 23 Marines in addition to his platoon sergeant, corpsmen, and an attached dog handler and dog. His mission remained the same: "Conduct both reconnaissance and surveillance operations within his assigned haven to detect NVA/VC troop movement and to interdict with supporting arms both Arty and air."[14]

Klein and the OP would keep the same callsign, *Spillway*, and coordinate their Arty with *Veal Stew-South* at An Hoa. Activity was light. On 6 September, at 0745, they observed four VC, wearing black "PJs" and carrying rifles, moving into Tho Son hamlet, which they no longer controlled. There was an OV-10 up over Go Noi Island, so they contacted the aerial observer (AO), who brought aboard a fixed-wing strike; two F-4s conducted a bombing run on the hamlet.

The VC went into a bunker. The AO gave the attack aircraft two bunkers destroyed and one secondary fire.[15] The OP could confirm the fire. On the 7th, the morning wire patrol smelled death and investigated the downhill trail south toward the lake. Two hundred meters down the trail, in a fighting hole on the Hill 148 side, they found a body. According to "Doc" Semararo, the bloated body was approximately two weeks old. They left it as it might have been booby-trapped. Early that night, they observed one VC moving in Tho Son. They got two helicopter gunships to make strafing runs, resulting in a secondary explosion. The gunships took heavy green tracer small-arms fire from behind the hamlet close to the river. The OP reported it to the gunships, who were outbound, and wrote up a spot report for Battalion.[16] In their ten days on the hill, 2nd Platoon had only two sightings totaling five VC. They had conducted two figure-8 patrols covering both sides of their haven. It had been quiet. Klein reported his recommendation for a larger haven to patrol into Tho Son hamlet along with a recommendation to bulldoze the empty hamlet because it was full of bunkers.[17] Second Platoon was due to flip out on 14 September.

Lieutenant Jim Unsworth and 1st Platoon of Delta Company arrived at 0900 on the 14th. Jim had Staff Sergeant Ommondson, Hospital Corpsmen Third Class Jensen and Vineyard, and 22 Reconnaissance Marines.[18] Their Operations Order #820-69 maintained the same mission of interdicting enemy movement with supporting arms, but, to Unsworth's dismay, it reduced the haven size again.[19] Their box was down to 1,200 meters by 1,300 meters. He felt penned in and at the mercy of the clearance gods. The OP still had part of the abandoned railroad in the north but not Tho Son hamlet. They kept part of the aqueduct in the south but not the dam at Alligator Lake. They could still do wire patrols but anything out of their haven had to be precoordinated with Battalion. The OP callsign, thus their callsign, had changed to *Rummage*. Echo Battery at An Hoa was now *Asparagus-South*.[20] On 22 September, a walk-off patrol went down to check out the abandoned railroad berm to the north. They discovered seven bunkers dug into the berm. They destroyed them with Composition B high explosive and returned to the hill. It was a quiet ten days with only three sightings of a total of 23 NVA/VC and one fire mission, the effects of which could not be observed.[21] Unsworth felt the NVA knew the OP and how far it could observe and just walked around it at night. He also knew Tho Son hamlet was a VC-controlled hamlet with a bunker complex inside that should be destroyed.[22] He was departing on the 24th and a new lieutenant, who replaced Bob Pfeiffer, would be coming up. Second Lieutenant "Butch" Waddill was the new 3rd Platoon commander. Sergeant Diaz remained the platoon sergeant and "Doc" Sanders remained as both had hill experience.[23] Waddill would have to learn from scratch about securing the OP. The callsign remained *Rummage*, and the mission, with the smaller haven, remained the same.[24]

Meanwhile, on the night of 25 September at the Alpha Company OP on Dong Den mountain (Hill 868), which overlooked Elephant Valley, 1st Lieutenant "Chip" Gregson's Team *Impressive* had some excitement. There was sustained noise and movement, like a probing of their wire across the landing zone. They responded with small arms. The next morning, upon investigation, they found they had killed a small female black bear.[25]

On Delta Company's OP, Waddill and "The 3rd Herd" were on Hill 119 for 15 days. They had only four sightings totaling 28 enemy.[26] They utilized the hill's 60-mm mortar and M60 machine guns in attempts to flush out or engage the enemy, with no observed results. They had difficulty getting fire missions due to slow clearance times which allowed the enemy to move away from observation. Their flip out on 9 October did not happen till the end of the day at 1800.[27]

CHAPTER 12

Surveillance and Reconnaissance Center, and Integrated Observation Device, October 1969

The Illinois National Guard was called out on 9 October 1969 to put down the riots organized by the Weather Underground. Called the "Days of Rage," they were protesting the trial of the "Chicago Seven," charged with inciting violence at the 1968 Democratic National Convention in Chicago.[1]

In an effort to convince the Soviets to put pressure on the North Vietnamese, on 10 October, President Nixon issued "Top Secret" orders to the Joint Chiefs to start Operation *Giant Lance.* The operation sent a squadron of B-52s armed with nuclear weapons towards the Soviet Union on 27 October. The bombers turned back before entering Soviet airspace.[2] And, on 12 October, anti-war protesters invaded Fort Dix, New Jersey; they were met by 1,000 military police who drove them off base with tear gas.[3] That was followed by the "Moratorium to End the War in Vietnam," on Wednesday, 15 October, which was a series of demonstrations across the United States. In Washington, D.C., alone, the estimate was 250,000 protesters.[4]

In Da Nang, at Camp Horn, Lieutenant General Herman Nickerson was the new III Marine Amphibious Force (III MAF) commanding general. III MAF was the senior operational command in I Corps tactical zone at the time. In October, in order to coordinate reconnaissance efforts between multiple units and locations across the entirety of I Corps territory, including the demilitarized zone, Laotian border, spurs of the Ho Chi Minh Trail, and Thuong Duc corridor, Nickerson created a new agency, the Surveillance and Reconnaissance Center (SRC).[5] Stood up at III MAF headquarters at Camp Horn, the SRC reported to Nickerson through the MAF G-2 (intelligence). It had tasking authority over 1st and 3rd Force Reconnaissance Companies and coordination authority over all reconnaissance assets in I Corps, including the Army's XXIV Corps. Conveniently located near the Horn Direct Air Support Center (H-DASC), the SRC facilitated coordination for both insertion and extraction aviation packages. General Nickerson was considered the "Godfather of Marine Reconnaissance" by many Recon Marines. The SRC concept and functions remain today within the structure of the Marine Expeditionary Force.

At 1st Marine Division, the normal command changes took place at both 1st Recon Battalion and at 1st Force Recon Company. At Battalion, Lieutenant Colonel "Mick" Mickelson rotated back to the continental U.S. on 7 October. Taking his place was another Korean War veteran and friend—Lieutenant Colonel J. J. Grace. While the soft-spoken Grace was not as outgoing as "Mick,"[6] he was old school and believed in the process and the chain of command. He had the trust of Major General O. R. Simpson, the division commander, earned during the Korean War, where he had served with Echo Company, 2nd Battalion, 5th Marines, in heavy combat against the Chinese. At 1st Force Recon, Major William H. "Bill" Bond relieved the innovative Major Simmons.[7] Having just served as the Recon Battalion operations officer (S-3), he was up to speed on day one. This, coupled with the experienced patrol leader, 1st Lieutenant W. E. Wayne Rollings, as his Force Company S-3, meant Force Recon was in good shape. Moving into Battalion S-3 was the energetic Captain D. C. "The Rocket" MacCaskill.

The battalion continued with its established training regime with Recon Indoctrination Course (RIC) 10-69 commencing on 7 October and Pre-SCUBA 9-69 beginning on 12 October. The battalion detached 5th Force Recon Company while maintaining their teams and moving them over to Company A, 5th Reconnaissance Battalion, which had already been attached to 1st Recon Battalion.[8] The result was that the battalion maintained seven patrolling companies.

October 1 found 6th Platoon of First Force Recon securing a landing zone (LZ) deep in the Que Son Mountains on Hill 953, Hon Nui Tau. They provided pathfinder and helo terminal guidance for 1st Battalion, 7th Marines (1/7).[9] Known as *First Team*, 1/7 would hold the mountain and move south down the ridgeline into the pass between Que Son village and Antenna Valley, searching for the North Vietnamese Army (NVA) who were avoiding contact until a time and place of their choosing. At 1st Recon Battalion, the second-tour-experienced master diver Sergeant J. L. Blum took over the SCUBA locker.

He was now running pre-SCUBA class 9-69, which was comprised of 13 Marines, including two officers—1st Lieutenants Jack Holly and Charlie Kershaw. Meanwhile, the exceptionally large RIC class had 52 students, including nine new members of Delta Company.[10] Notably, Hospitalman Thurman G. Mullins and Hospital Corpsman Third Class J. D. Fears would join Delta Company after successful completion of RIC.

On Hill 119, first timer 2nd Lieutenant "Butch" Waddill had assumed command of the hill on 24 September.[11] His operation order had scheduled his return as 4 October, but that got extended until the 9th. During his two-week stay, they were operating out of the smaller haven. It had been remarkably quiet; monsoon season was in full throat. It rained all day and blew cold at night, followed by fog in the morning. His platoon, callsign *Rummage,* had only four enemy sightings in 15 days on the OP. They had fired no artillery fire missions due in part to low activity but also the slow clearance process through *Asparagus-South* at An Hoa.[12]

Coming up to the hill next was the experienced hill commander of 2nd Platoon, 1st Lieutenant Ed Klein; he was coming up for the third time. His platoon was the last insert of the day on 8 October.[13] This gave the two platoons a full 24 hours of turnover as 3rd Platoon did not depart till 1800 on 9 October.[14] Klein had the experienced platoon sergeant Gawlaki along with the Hospital Corpsman Third Class Semararo with him.

The first week on the hill was rainy and slow; there were no sightings.[15] Klein was running two listening posts each night, and the morning wire patrol. Gawlaki said the NVA knew the hill and were moving in their blind spots. He wanted to run a patrol to the east towards the trail leading to the railroad bridge to Go Noi Island. Klein would radio to get permission but wanted Gawlaki to stay close to the hill. For training reasons, Gawlaki had Corporal McCommons lead the patrol to gain additional experience. Gawlaki would birddog the seven-man team, which departed at 0530 out the east gate. They proceeded east, dropping off-trail to avoid booby traps by walking sidehill. It was slow but safe. They moved due east and, as the sun came up, they could easily see the entire Chien Son village and all the way to Route 1. They established a clandestine observation post (OP) 200 meters above the valley floor. At 0730, they observed four Viet Cong (VC) coming out of Chien Son (4) and moving quickly to the southeast in the streambed. They were wearing black-and-white "PJs" and carrying three packs, but only one rifle. Being too far away to accurately engage, McCommons moved the team in the enemy's direction. The VC spotted the patrol, dropped the packs, and ran back into the village. The team moved down to the streambed and recovered the three packs which were filled with 100 pounds of rice.[16] Searching the well-populated village outside the haven was not possible for a seven-man team. Gawlaki told the patrol leader to take the packs and a sample of rice and move back up the hill.

On 18 October, at 2100, the night-observation device (NOD) detected a large group of NVA. They were down on Route 537 in front of the OP, moving from west to east on the road in a double column. They wore dark utilities and were carrying packs, rifles, and other gear. The column was spread out over 300 meters. When trying to call a fire mission, *Rummage* learned from *Asparagus-South* that the artillery direction center was in a check-fire due to *Spooky* being in the air. Switching frequencies, *Rummage* radioed *Spooky* with the target and its location. The AC-47D circled the target, firing its deadly Gatling guns, for over an hour until it was out of ammunition. Departing the area, it reported there were bodies on the trail. Utilizing flares from *Spooky*, and the NOD, the hill was able to confirm the bodies along Route 537 below the hill.[17] Following *Spooky*'s departure, Klein called a fire mission on the same target, trying to get anyone coming to their aid or support. After achieving good coverage, he called for a ceasefire. He did keep harassment and interdiction fires going on the target area and both directions on the road coming into the kill zone.[18] Klein and Gawlaki talked after the excitement. They both thought a bomb-damage assessment patrol, at first light, was needed. The purpose of the patrol was to check out the area and search for survivors and equipment. Klein called Battalion and got permission to check the area.

At first light, a nine-man patrol led by Gawlaki moved off the hill. He had briefed them that they would establish a security team east and west on Route 537 and have a search team for the area. They knew exactly where they were going. The Marines were excited as they departed the saddle LZ and headed north down the main trail. About seven hundred meters outside of the OP, the trail met the abandoned railroad line with its two trails, one on each side. Gawlaki had briefed this danger area before they departed. After crossing the berm and heading down the steep north side that dropped off, the deuce point man hit a trip wire across the descending trail. The large explosion of the surprise firing device, as the battalion called them, could be heard on the OP. Five were down; when Gawlaki called the corpsman up, nobody came. "Doc" Semararo had moved forward earlier in the walk-off and was down next to the trail. Gawlaki had five down and four up. He put Lance Corporal LaRue out below them for security and called the lieutenant to get him to start a medevac. By the time he had checked the first three down, he knew it was an emergency situation. He called the lieutenant again to raise the medevac level to emergency. Two of the wounded Marines were struggling to breathe. The other three, including the Doc, who was now at work trying to save the two emergencies, had been knocked down by the blast and had small shrapnel wounds. In under ten minutes, a bird that had been refueling at An Hoa was inbound. Gawlaki popped green smoke on the dry hillside above the railroad berm as the bird came straight in from the west. The Marines loaded all five wounded.[19] The bird pulled out and headed directly to the naval hospital LZ in order to discharge the two emergencies. With only three other tired Marines, Gawlaki headed back up the hill on what was the worst day of his second tour. This was supposed to be the platoon's flip day. Klein would let the next platoon observe the kill zone or check out Route 537. He told his team to pack up and get ready to flip. It was 19 October.[20]

Upon returning to Camp Reasoner, Klein sought out 1st Lieutenant Bouts, the company commander, and volunteered to move up to executive officer (XO) and take over the office.[21] With newly joined officers, Bouts had flexibility and concurred that would be the best for Klein.

October 20 found Team *War Cloud* being inserted on a specific mission to find a large enemy food cache.[22] They were chasing a lead from a recent interrogation. *War Cloud* from Alpha Company was using *Rummage* on Hill 119 as a radio relay. First Lieutenant "Chip" Gregson had chosen his platoon's most experienced team, led by Corporal McAfee, which proved to be a wise decision. On the patrol's third day, 23 October, while walking a trail, *War Cloud* made point-to-point contact with six NVA wearing dark-green utilities and carrying AK-47s; one enemy was carrying an M16 and wearing a headband.[23] The contact resulted in killing the NVA's point man while Gregson went down with a AK-47 round in a heel. The team pulled back with the point man covering as McAfee got the emergency extract started. They quickly found an LZ. While "Doc" Literas worked on the lieutenant, *War Cloud* got an aerial observer (AO) on station. The AO ran six flights of fixed-wing all around the LZ, knocking back the enemy, while the emergency extract CH-46 came in to get the team.[24] Gregson went straight to the Naval Support Activity Hospital in Da Nang and, two days later, was in the naval hospital on Guam where he underwent a successful surgery. He would be out of action for three months. Returning in January to become the Delta Company XO, he continued his recovery while remaining on light duty.[25]

Introduction of the Secret Integrated Observation Device

The Integrated Observation Device (IOD) was a combination of three existing pieces of equipment. Its purpose was to facilitate target location with an accuracy of within five meters and one mil in azimuth out to a range of 30 kilometers.[26] By eliminating the cumbersome adjustment process of bracketing a target, short and long, to find the correct firing solution, the IOD created the opportunity to allow immediate massed fire-for-effect with artillery or naval gun fire. The VC and NVA had mastered the skill of avoiding fire by moving quickly, when the first round was heard or seen, into preprepared bunkers and spider holes dug specifically to avoid above-ground shrapnel by an exploding high-explosive round. If the Marines could skip the adjustment process and shoot accurate massed fires at a precise target location, then the enemy would be caught in the open outside its bunkers and suffer the consequences.

The IOD combined Kollmorgen ship's binoculars, with a NOD and a laser range finder, all on one tripod.[27] This now "Classified Secret" integrated device created a level of accuracy in target acquisition that allowed for first round hits. This was made possible by surveying a specific location for the tripod. The survey was done with the same site-survey equipment that was employed to lay in each piece of artillery on the gun line. Then, using the accuracy of a laser shot at the target, a range was established from the tripod and azimuth. Given this data,

Integrated Observation Device, developed by Office of Naval Research, 1969. (DoD fair use rights, DoD Photo A372433)

it was a simple matter of a polar plot from the tripod to the target. Solving the mathematical triangle from the gun line to target was done in the Fire Direction Center (FDC). This was a new capability and a game changer in target-location accuracy. The 400-pound tripod-mounted IOD unit cabled to its large battery box, to power the laser, cost a quarter of a million dollars in 1968. The integration effort was a product of the Marine Corps SPEED (Special Procedures for Expediting Equipment Development) Program with the integration engineering provided by the Office of Naval Research.[28] This six-month effort culminated in October 1969 with ten IODs being delivered to the 11th Marines at the Northern Artillery Cantonment (NAC) outside Da Nang. The Marines kept six units and sent four to the Army's Americal Division in southern I Corps.

With the IOD's arrival in country, the 11th Marines formed a specialized unit within their Regimental S-2 shop for IOD forward observers (FO), radio operators, and maintenance crew.[29] Mr. Al Smith, the Tech Representative from RCA Services Division who was charged with maintaining the new laser range finders, set up shop at NAC.[30] The 11th Marines set up a one-week school on IOD use and level-one maintenance at Fire Support Base (FSB) Ryder for FOs and radio operators. The school was run by 1st Lieutenant Gary Hughes and Gunnery Sergeant Stan Kiester.[31] The 11th Marines, in conjunction with Division G-2 and 1st Recon Battalion, selected the six locations for the IODs. The first two would be deployed to OPs on Hill 119 and

425 because of the previous success of observation and the known high volume of enemy traffic between the Que Son Mountains and the Go Noi Island stronghold. The remaining IODs would deploy to Hills 65, 190, 250, and 270 all around the Da Nang Trace for those OPs watching current infiltration routes.[32] Hill 190, with its location on the south side of the Song Cu De, could observe Da Nang Bay and Namo Bridge to its east, and up Elephant Valley to its northwest. From Hill 270, they could observe west into Happy Valley, Mortar Valley, Sherwood Forest, and the northern slope of Charlie Ridge. Hill 250 observed the Thuong Duc Corridor and northern Arizona Territory, as did Hill 65. Hill 425, on the north shoulder of the Que Sons, observed to the northeast the entire Phu Loc Valley, and Spider Lake directly below it, as well as Alligator Lake to its northwest. While Hill 119 was situated to observe both the Arizona Territory and Go Noi Island/Dodge City to the north, it could also see the Phu Loc Valley, the two lakes, and Hill 425. At FSB Ryder, they observed the eastern slopes of the Que Son Mountains and the pass. The 11th Marines trained new FOs with the equipment at Ryder. Safety was a concern. If a Marine looked directly into the laser when it was fired, it could affect his vision or blind him. Therefore, firing procedures and commands were developed; for each time an FO was going to lase, he would loudly call out a preparatory command: "Standby to Lase;" "Ready;" "Lasing" (as he hit the button to do so).[33] The laser went out to the target and showed the distance, in meters, in a digital readout displayed on the black box. While looking down at the circular metal ring on the tripod, the observer could read the compass direction, in mils, to the target from the IOD tripod. The distance and mils were transmitted to the FDC for conversion and passing the data to the guns to fire. Now a trained observer, in good daylight and weather, could see 30 kilometers, laser for an accurate range approximately ten kilometers, and see at night out to four kilometers. With each of the IODs surveyed at their hill tower, the new artillery standard operating procedures for IOD fire missions were fire-for-effect on the first salvo.

On 19 October, 1st Lieutenant Gary Hughes, an experienced FO, and a survey team from 11th Marines' Survey Platoon, flew out to Hill 119.[34] They were there to select the location for the IOD tripod and hammer a stake to mark the point. They would also do an assessment on the OP to determine if it needed physical improvement, such as a tower, platform, or protection from the elements. At Hill 119, the existing central observation deck, where the Recon NOD was located on a tripod, was a flat deck on top of the central hill bunker. They surveyed the point, and spray painted the survey mark on the plywood deck on the roof of the bunker. They also said they wanted to build an elevated deck or short tower with sides and a roof. They said this would allow them to see from a higher position, but the real reason was protection from the rain and sun. Giving the Arty team the central observation deck and bunker below it, the hill commander said, "Knock yourself out." He figured they were creating a target! He moved all his spotting equipment out to the perimeter bunkers and the radios to a newly built communications bunker on the south-central trench line. On day one of the IOD site survey, the two units started to split the difference on how each organization viewed the hill. To the Recon Marines, who first came clandestinely and then developed the permanent OP, the hill always had a low silhouette with bunkers and a perimeter trench line designed for security and defense of the hill from attack. The bunkers were close to the ground for a reason. Their hill was overshadowed by Hills 148 and 175, both of which could rain rocket-propelled grenade or mortar fire on 119 from the advantage of higher terrain. The Recon Marines had security of the hill as their primary thought. On the other hand, the FOs with the 11th Marines were focused on observation and raining artillery shells down on the enemy from a distance. The site-survey lead, a warrant officer, said his engineering team would be up the next week to build the tower. That happened over the next four days, so the tower was ready when the IOD itself and its first FO team arrived. First Lieutenant Hughes and six enlisted Marines arrived on 23 October. They had a new tower and a clean bunker waiting for the installation of the observation device.

Second Lieutenant Chuck Overton had arrived as the new hill commander on the morning of the 19th.[35] He had been prebriefed by his company commander, 1st Lieutenant A. T. Bouts, about the Arty guys coming up to take over forward-observation duties. Bouts had stressed his job as hill commander was security of the hill and that he should support the FO team, who would be tenants. Bouts wanted good relations and directly emphasized that fact to Overton. Indeed, Overton's Operation Order #906-69 read as follows: "Mission: Conduct reconnaissance and surveillance within your assigned Haven to detect possible NVA/VC troop movement or arms infiltration with special emphasis to be prepared to call and adjust air/Arty on targets of opportunity."[36]

Overton had been polite to the 11th Marines team (as instructed by Bouts) and had given them an observation deck and bunker the Recon Marines had built. The 11th Marines' construction personnel departed on a late-afternoon helo, so Overton had the hill and his mission to himself. Overton had already proven himself on snap-in patrols with Staff Sergeant Ommondson. He was smart and aggressive, but this was his first trip to the hill. He was fortunate to have Staff Sergeant Keen as his platoon sergeant, a hill veteran, as was half the platoon. He was pleased to have every man in the platoon make the trip to the hill. This would provide him with time to talk individually with all 24 Marines plus the two "Docs," Hospital Corpsmen Third Class Vineyard and Avenel. He was glad to have Rex, Scout Dog #A327, and his handler, Sergeant Drye.[37] All the IODs were being emplaced in the last two weeks of October. They would go online and begin operating in November. For now, Overton would run his hill. The first night, at about 2030, the entire hill could see lights moving northwest in Thon Bon (1) hamlet. Overton called *Asparagus-South* and got a fire mission going. The bunkers agreed there were 11 lights. With the impact of the first rounds, all 11 went out.[38] It was thought the hamlet or group of thatched huts had been empty for months.

On 22 October, the comms bunker called Overton over to listen to the emergency extraction going on for Team *Big Flower,* a Charlie Company team. They had three Recon killed-in-actions and one wounded. The seven-man team was now in a partial LZ, with air support, but bad weather in the mountains was preventing either extraction of the team or insertion of the reaction force flying above the clouds.[39] All the Hill 119 Marines could do was listen to the green radio-speaker box and pray for their brothers.

Earlier in the afternoon, *Big Flower* had made point-to-point contact on a trail. They had been in a two-hour firefight while withdrawing to their LZ. The reaction force got into an adjacent LZ 30 meters away at 0045. In the dark, trying to move fast off the LZ towards *Big Flower,* the reaction-force point man hit a surprise firing device. The reaction force now had three wounded. A larger, second reaction force was inserted an hour later. They were able to consolidate all the

Marines in the primary LZ and, with overwhelming air support by both fixed-wing aircraft and gunships, they were able to execute the emergency extract. The new patrol leader for *Big Flower* had been Overton's friend, 2nd Lieutenant K. A. Kubik, who was now dead along with Private First Class T. C. Robinson and the team's corpsman, Hospitalman R. W. Yates. The team leader, Sergeant M. Jones, was gravely wounded. The three wounded from the reaction team had been lucky, escaping with only shrapnel wounds. The booby trap they hit was aimed up trail to catch someone running into the LZ, not coming off it.[40]

On the morning of 24 October, the OP watched a Marine infantry unit moving east on Route 537 from the old CH-53 crash site northwest of their hill. The infantry callsign, *Average Mike,* started taking long-range small arms and machine-gun fire from Thon Bon (1) hamlet. *Rummage* had an on-call target registered on the hostile hamlet. They called the target and got good coverage which shut down the harassing fire.[41] The infantry unit stopped and set in at about 0930, forming a blocking position west of the hamlet. At about 1730, the OP spotted *Average Mike*'s enemy approximately fourteen hundred meters away next to the Song Ba Ren with 12 packs and rifles.[42] The OP passed the information on to *Aroma Charlie*, another infantry unit, who stated they were in contact and pushing the VC south. The Recon Marines were fine watching rather than sweeping on-line towards the enemy.

On 26 October, after the morning wire check and coffee, Overton was using the BC-Scope (ballistic coefficient scope). He picked up 40-plus NVA/VC doing a river crossing east of the first southern railroad bridge. They all had rifles and were moving from the island south across the Song Chien Son into dense brush. Overton called *Asparagus-South* to shoot a fire mission but was told it was too close to the South Korean (RoK) Marines' boundary to shoot, so he radioed Battalion rear and requested they use a landline to call the DASC to prosecute this lucrative target. Twenty minutes later, an OV-10 aircraft came out from Marble Mountain Air Facility. *Hostage Egor* came on station and the hill vectored him on to the target. *Egor* expended all its ordnance and was relieved on station by *Hostage Jim*, which found bunkers and camouflaged hooches on the south bank. Both the AO and the OP saw the enemy drop their packs and rifle in the bunkers and move further south towards the village of Chien Son (1). *Hostage Jim* was relieved on station by *Hostage Bill* (pilot Bill Paulson). *Bill* tried going to the southern artillery unit *Ipswich*, however the target area was not in an area they were allowed to shoot. The AO (Steve Tace) in the back seat of *Hostage Bill* then tried both *Sunrise* and *Pony Boy* with negative clearances. The only units that could shoot in this area were the RoK Marines and they said they had a friendly patrol moving in that direction. Three OV-10s and the OP, with eyes on the enemy for over four hours, could not get permission to fire on the enemy.[43] The enemy was taking advantage of the boundary between Allied units as a seam that allowed them to move freely.

Since they could not get firing clearance, Staff Sergeant Keen suggested running a patrol out and setting a night ambush on the edge of their own haven. At 1900, with light fading in the west, a six-Marine patrol pushed off the hill to the north. Forty-five minutes later, as the point man was moving on the trail, at the abandoned west–east rail berm, he hit a booby trap. It detonated five feet in front of him on the trail, the concussion knocking him down.[44] With their position compromised, Overton had them return to the hill. In the communications bunker debriefing the patrol members, they said there had been no wire but a depression in the trail that allowed for a pressure detonation. They had been extremely lucky. From the gray smoke, size, and sound, the Marines thought it was a US M26 hand grenade that had been booby-trapped.

On the 27th, at around 0915, *Hostage Echo* called the hill asking for targets. The OP gave them the hostile hamlet Thon Bon (1). *Echo* worked over the area with "Willie Pete" (white phosphorous) rockets and 7.62-mm machine guns with unobserved results. While *Echo* was working the hamlet, the OP observed three VC to the east near the RoK boundary. They briefed *Echo* who called for an artillery mission but was denied clearance. The VC, with packs and rifles, walked into the populated village of Chien Son (1). That evening at sundown, the hill observed three NVA in green utilities out by the crashed CH-53. They had *Hostage Christian* on station who engaged with rockets and machine guns, killing all three. *Hostage Bill* arrived with two helo gunships looking for work. *Christian* talked them into bunkers near their engagement which *Bill* and the gunbirds worked over, destroying two bunkers.[45]

The last two days on the hill, the boat traffic picked up. Firing at moving boats with artillery is a challenge. They wished they had their artillery all week, but it was supporting a higher-priority unit in contact in the Arizona Territory. October 29 was flip day.[46] It would be a fast turnover with 2nd Lieutenant Durwood Waddill bringing 1st Platoon, Delta Company, up to the hill.[47] It was Butch's second trip.

CHAPTER 13

194th Marine Corps Birthday, November 1969

President Richard Nixon addressed the nation on live television on 3 November 1969. He announced his plan to end American involvement in the Vietnam War. He explained his plan for "Vietnamization" and the complete withdrawal of U.S. ground combat forces. He said they would be replaced by South Vietnamese forces.[1]

Seymore Hersh, who contributed to the Dispatch News Service, broke the story of the My Lai Massacre on 12 November. The Army was completing an investigation to determine if Lieutenant William Calley deliberately murdered at least 109 Vietnamese civilians in March 1968.[2] On 15 November, in Washington, D.C., 500,000 protesters staged the largest peace march in American history.[3] On 30 November, Senator Henry Bellman (Republican, Oklahoma) introduced legislation, that failed to pass, in the Senate to prohibit trials of soldiers who kill Vietnamese.[4]

Inside the Marine Corps, the 9th Marine Amphibious Brigade was deactivated on 7 November.[5] On 10 November, the United States Marine Corps commemorated the establishment of the Continental Marines with its 194th birthday. Additionally, Marine Aircraft Group 36 completed the redeployment of helicopters and observation aircraft from Phu Bai, Vietnam, to Futenma, Okinawa, Japan, on 20 November.[6]

Back in Da Nang, during the month of November, the 11th Marines had fired 169,609 rounds on 17,213 fire missions.[7] Colonel Don D. Ezell, the commanding officer of the 11th Marine Regiment, was laser focused on the number of kills attributed to his artillery.[8] Deploying the Integrated Observation Device (IOD) with its laser range finder for the first time dramatically increased the number of enemy killed by artillery. In November, sightings by the six IOD teams on observation posts (OP), including Hill 119, resulted in the deaths of 463 North Vietnamese Army/Viet Cong (NVA/VC); 72 percent of the enemy casualties credited to artillery and 42 percent of all enemy casualties reported. All told, artillery accounted for 639 of the 1,098 confirmed kills within the 1st Marine Division in November.[9] The aggressive Ezell was chasing statistical kills and rewarding (time off, R&Rs, promotions) his forward observer (FO) teams for increased kills using the just-fielded new technology. He was providing the division and Saigon the statistical measurement they were demanding on daily, weekly, and monthly totals of enemy killed. During the Vietnam War, one of the primary measures of effectiveness (MoE) imposed on the fighting forces was the number of enemy killed in action (EKIA).

This was a top-down policy from Secretary of Defense McNamara who, with his industrial background, demanded statistical measures of effectiveness that could be monitored over a long period of time. The number of EKIA became the primary MoE for every unit, from the smallest to the largest, and was used as a yardstick to judge their performance. It was used by McNamara and the president as a yardstick to judge the country's performance in the war.[10] Enemy casualty counts were demanded by the chain of command for every operation. One result was that an inflationary trend started and was compounded by every level rolling up the enemy wounded and killed each day, week, and month. Reporting enemy confirmed, and probable deaths and casualties, evolved over time from a science to an art. It became a game of lies and deception to placate higher command and their commanders.[11] Not only did inflating the numbers make you and your unit look good, but it was also a means of gaining an advantage for your unit. Thus, inflating the numbers was rationalized by many commanders and personnel who were in reporting positions. In a war with limited supporting resources, prioritization went to units in contact who were in the worst situation. If two units were in the shit, the unit fighting 100 enemy got the prioritization over the one fighting ten. With multiple units having troops in contact, the priority of fire support went to the unit deemed most in trouble. Commanders, FOs, and air controllers all inflated numbers to gain support for their team during the fight, and then, after the fight, had to answer the bomb-damage assessment (BDA) question, "How did you do? Report your EKIAs and EWIAs." The system was broken, and the inflation led to senior commanders declaring they were winning the war based on these great statistics. Problematically, the communist leadership in Hanoi was not using casualties as their MoE. They were playing an entirely different game with a different set of rules. They were playing the long game and were focused on getting the United States to withdraw all its forces and aid. As we now know, they were successful in doing so as reflected by the Paris Peace Accords in 1973. This allowed them to focus solely on their South Vietnamese enemy, which they defeated in 1975.

***

November would be the first operational month for the six Marine IODs. Although operated by 11th Marines FOs, there would be dual reporting by both the OP reporting up their chain of command, be it infantry or reconnaissance, and the FO reporting a fire mission up the artillery chain of command. The process of dual reporting remained throughout the war. Deconfliction or numbers sorting and credits for kills would be sorted out by higher headquarters. One could ask, did the dual reporting inadvertently inflate the numbers?

In a change in procedures, the aggressive Colonel Ezell established a new and innovative quick-fire procedure with 1st Reconnaissance Battalion and 1st Force Recon Company. It would facilitate a more flexible and rapid response to calls-for-fire by their Recon Teams. Each team was assigned a battery in direct support. The team now had a quick-fire communications frequency that connected them directly to their supporting battery. This saved time and cut out multiple staff levels in the clearance process for patrolling teams. Unfortunately, it did not apply to fixed OPs.[12]

Lieutenant Colonel J. J. Grace continued to command 1st Recon Battalion. Major W. H. Bill Bond, at 1st Force Recon Company, would change operational reporting and tasking by moving over and reporting directly to III Marine Amphibious Force through the Surveillance and Reconnaissance Center.[13] On 1 November, the second-tour, Ranger-qualified Captain Thomas W. Martin took over Delta Company as 1st Lieutenant A. T. Bouts rotated home. November 3 saw

Major General O. R. Simpson, the division commander, at a Camp Reasoner awards ceremony, presenting the battalion a Navy Unit Commendation. More important than the unit award, he recognized the actions of Hospital Corpsman Third Class C. A. Viento with the Silver Star in front of his patrolling peers.[14] Training continued with the graduation of Recon Indoctrination Course (RIC) 11-69 and the commencement of RIC 12-69 a week later. The end of the month saw a string of visitors to Camp Reasoner, including the Deputy Secretary of Defense, The Honorable Mr. David Packard.[15] The Stanford University electrical engineer was one of the founders of Hewlett-Packard Corporation. He was now helping to lead the enormous Department of Defense with the same data-analysis techniques he employed in the private sector.

Up on Hill 119 was 1st Platoon, Delta Company. The hill commander was 2nd Lieutenant "Butch" Waddill.[16] They were averaging just one sighting a day and, due to slow artillery clearance procedures, Butch was doing better utilizing aerial observers (AO). On 29 October, at 1848, the OP spotted 40 enemy moving south by crossing the southern bridge from Go Noi Island. They observed a four-man team pushing a cart. Waddill called *Hostage Nape*, the OV-10, and got on the radio with the backseat AO, *Cowpoke One-Zero* (1st Lieutenant G. G. "Jerry" Spolter). The OV-10 tried to engage with organic ordnance of rockets and mini-gun fire. The mini-gun sight was misaligned and, as a result, they missed the target. Worse yet, the rockets misfired. The enemy moved into Chien Son (1) as darkness fell. *Hostage Nape*, now low on fuel, returned to Marble Mountain Air Facility.[17] Little did Spolter realize that, in three months' time, he would be out of the air, having volunteered and extended his tour for another six months, for duty with 1st Recon, snooping and pooping on the ground again and serving in the same Delta Company that manned the OP he was supporting from the air.[18]

On 1 November, at 1430, Team *Rummage* observed five NVA on Go Noi Island directly north of them. They were wearing khaki uniforms and pith helmets. They had packs, rifles, and a mortar.[19] They stopped and started digging in defensive positions. Waddill got going on both radios. Calling *Asparagus-Mike* on frequency 39.35, he got an artillery fire mission coming out of An Hoa. While they were firing, he contacted *Hostage Golf* on another radio frequency and got him moving towards Go Noi. With *Golf*'s arrival overhead, Waddill turned off the Arty and let him work the area with his rockets and mini-guns. With ordnance expended and low on fuel, *Hostage Golf* departed.[20] When the aircraft stopped firing, the same five NVA got up and started running away. *Rummage* got *Asparagus* back up and fired the same data, immediate fire-for-effect, three times with good coverage of the area, the enemy going back underground. *Hostage Baker* came on scene and took over. He had a flight of fixed-wing aircraft to run on the bunker complex. *Baker* ran the fixed-wing which hit the bunkers with bombs. Much to the fast-mover's disappointment, besides destroyed bunkers, no other results could be reported by the AO or the OP.[21] While catching a nap at 2030 on 2 November, the hill started taking serious incoming fire.[22] In shorts and shower shoes, Waddill sprinted down the trench line to the new communications bunker. Platoon Sergeant Diaz had identified the rounds by sound and sight as being friendly 155-mm artillery coming out of Fire Support Base (FSB) Ross, which was located to their southeast. Waddill was on the radio to his Fire Direction Center, *Asparagus-Mike*, in An Hoa, calling for a check-fire, while Diaz was on another radio calling the Combat Operations Center at FSB Ross for the 155s to cease fire. The hill took eight 155 rounds, with shrapnel covering the hill, but no direct impacts inside the wire.[23] They never knew who got through on the radio for the ceasefire or if it was the end of misdirected harassment and interdiction fires. Waddill radioed Battalion, callsign *Reward Money*, and asked to speak directly with the 11th Marines' liaison officer (LNO). Forty minutes later, the Arty LNO radioed. Butch had calmed down. He explained the incoming 155 rounds and asked that it be checked out. The LNO said he would send the report over to NAC (Northern Artillery Cantonment), home of the 11th Marines.

On 4 November, at 1445, the OP observed eight suspects in green utilities and bush covers, with heavy packs and rifles, just northwest of the hill in Thon Bon (1) hamlet. They observed this potential enemy patrol talking with Vietnamese civilians. The hamlet was in a restricted area for civilians, so Waddill called *Asparagus-Mike* for a fire mission. It took some time but when the call came back to the hill, the fire mission had not received clearance. When checking through the larger fires deconfliction process, it was determined this sighting was a South Korean (RoK) patrol outside their area.[24] Waddill looked down with his 7 × 50s. They could be Koreans and, yes, they were five kilometers west of their boundary on Route 537. Something was not right.

On 5 November, the 11th Marines' resupply helicopter landed, and Corporal Mark Bayuk got off with his pack and reported into Lieutenant Hughes for duty with the IOD team.[25] Little did he know that he would have hill duty for five months, going from hill new guy to the longest-serving Marine on Hill 119.

On 6 November, the OP was watching the Korean Marines pushing a company along the Go Noi Island railroad berm. At 1130, the OP saw 11 NVA in khakis and rifles running away from the Koreans towards the west of the island. Waddill tried for a fire mission but was denied due to the Koreans being in the area.[26] Hughes, the IOD team leader, tried for a fire mission but was also refused.[27] The boundary between the two Allied units continued to be difficult to coordinate. The lack of coordination between friendly units proved to be an advantage the NVA used every day.

Delta Company's flip was scheduled for the 9th. On 7 November, Waddill got a radio call from his new company commander whom he had not yet met. He was informed that his platoon would be extended one day, and that 2nd Platoon, with a new lieutenant, would be out on the 9th and the two platoons would do a 24-hour turnover.[28] Captain Martin was also coming for his first visit to the Delta Company OP with the new platoon commander, 2nd Lieutenant Stamm.[29] Waddill remembered to suggest to the captain that he bring an extra cot to the hill as they had no guest cots. He did not tell them just how cold it was. With a direct breeze off the East China Sea, and rain showers at least twice daily, the hill was wet and cold, bone-chillingly cold. On the 9th at noon, two CH-46s brought the company commander, Stamm, 17 Marines, and a corpsman.[30] This was Hospital Corpsman Third Class Thurman Mullins's first of many trips to Hill 119.[31] On the evening of 9 November, it would prove to be crowded in each bunker as Marines from the two platoons caught up on all the latest news that 18-year-old Marines talk about: women, music, women, sports, women, and playing cards. In the officers' bunker, Waddill, having finished his second hill flip, was briefing, or at least bringing them up to speed, Captain Martin, and Lieutenant Stamm on his thoughts about the hill. He had never met either officer so he figured he would just stick to the facts. The hill needed to add another strand of concertina wire to the two it already had. It also needed a new set of pioneering equipment and more sandbags. The FO team had just arrived and were still getting orientated. Waddill had left them alone and really did not understand the command relationship. He was the hill commander, but they were not attached to him, as was customary in the infantry. They were tenants, as if the hill were a base. He informed the captain to let him work on the issue. Taking the officers outside and looking to the north, he explained Go Noi Island was an enemy stronghold. Looking below the hill, both hamlets were VC hamlets. To the northeast, the southern railroad bridge was close to the boundary with the RoK Marines, therefore gaining artillery clearance along the railroad berm on Go Noi Island was time consuming and had only a 50 percent chance of approval. The north–south berm was also an NVA infiltration route, used every night, and was well fortified. The two valleys to his south were enemy valleys and fertile rice-growing areas, while, just five kilometers south, the Que Son Mountains loomed over them. Lastly, he pointed out that both Hills 148 and 175 offered the enemy the ability to provide direct fire with rocket-propelled grenades downhill onto the OP. He wryly said, "Welcome, gentlemen, to Hill 119!"

The next morning, 10 November, was the Marine Corps' birthday, and Waddill's platoon was getting off the hill. On their return, the main topic of discussion was not whether there would be a birthday cake in the mess hall but how big. Waiting for the birds at the LZ, the Marines were bullshitting and horse playing, as Marines do to kill time. They waited on LZs for half their careers, the "Old Salts" would say. Or they would say, "Time to Spare? Fly Marine Air." The birds arrived at 1000, and the entire platoon was back at Camp Reasoner by 1030.[32] They were just in time for the noon meal, which did have large, white sheet cakes with the Marine Corps' emblem in icing and "194th Birthday." First Platoon would have its cake.

Captain Martin told Waddill he liked his ideas from the prior evening's discussion and requested he write them up for him and make a list of pioneer gear to submit as a requisition to supply.[33] That is how it worked. You have an idea; you write it up. Waddill did not mind. He knew with the captain's signature they might just get most of the requested gear and supplies.

At 0800 on 10 November, the 1st Marine Division was doing a division-wide change of callsigns and frequencies. This was done randomly for communications security fairly often. Just to confuse the Marines, and the enemy, the hill and 2nd Platoon's new callsign would be *Asparagus*, while their artillery support, who had been *Asparagus-Mike*, changed to *Report Card-Mike*. The 1st Recon Battalion became *Defend*.[34] All the radio nets changed frequencies. In the communications bunker, both platoon radiomen covered the change of all the radios and frequencies and updated the quick-reference cardboard C-ration wallboards in the bunkers with the unit's name, radio net, and callsigns. There were more radio networks than the hill had radios, so quick references were needed to change frequencies to call a different unit. There were strict radio protocols for what could be said and not said on different networks. Recon Battalion Operations had a network. Artillery had a call-for-fire network. The S-4 had a logistics network to pass request for provisions. Second Lieutenant Stamm observed on the 10th that his platoon sergeant, Gawlaki, was a hill veteran and had already made the bunker assignments. After the company commander and other platoon had departed, Stamm went to the communications bunker and sat in the corner just listening. He wanted to understand everything that was going on. This bunker was a key for the hill's defense and offense for anything off hill. After two hours, he got up and walked the perimeter, visiting all six of the hill's defensive bunkers and just talking to the Marines. This two-week flip was a good time for him to get to know every Marine in his new platoon. He intended to do individual interviews and update his green platoon commander's notebook, but that was not for this slow walk around. After a C-ration lunch of beans and weenies with Sergeants Gawlaki and Harvey, his other sergeant, he excused himself. He headed up to what the Marines called "The Tower" as he needed to meet the Marines who manned this new IOD and see how it worked. Captain Martin had reinforced directly to him that he was responsible for this classified piece of equipment and that it should be destroyed before it fell into the hands of the enemy. For that, he needed to see it and determine the destruction plan. Stamm met the FO team of observers and radio operators from 11th Marines. They were headed up by a sergeant. He got a briefing and demonstration of the IOD. It was impressive. He asked about a destruction plan and got the deer-in-headlights look, so he told them he would figure one out and they could all agree. The 11th Marines did not want to think about destroying their quarter-of-a-million-dollar, 400-pound, baby.

Back in his bunker, he made coffee. It was raining. He called for Gawlaki and Harvey, offering them coffee, which they declined. When he offered cigarettes, they accepted. He presented the "Destroy the IOD" challenge to them. The two sergeants looked at each other as if the lieutenant was a rock. He said what? At the same time they both said, "Thermite grenades, sir." Stamm had never seen a thermite grenade or seen one work. Harvey, who had been a seagoing Marine in a ship's detachment, explained that thermite grenades were standard issue for seagoing detachments as one of their missions was to destroy classified communications gear on a ship, if required. He explained that one set the grenade on top of whatever you wanted destroyed, pulled the pin, stood back, and it would pop and then burn at extremely high heat through whatever it was on. The key was to put it on the top. He said they could set up a demo. The lieutenant suggested not doing it in the rain. This time it was Gawlaki, "Sir, the grenade is just like us sergeants, it does not know it is raining." Stamm told them to set it up with something metal and invite the artillery sergeant and anyone else who might want to see it. Stamm knew Marines loved to see things blow up and, in his mind, this fit that category. Harvey went to the ammunition bunker and found two thermite grenades and got four wooden ammo boxes and two green metal .50-cal ammunition cans. He got Lance Corporals LaRue and Iantorno, briefed them on the plan, and told them to set up a wooden stage with the cans and place them in the center of the LZ. He also told them to find a metal engineer stake to put on top of the two ammo cans.

In the rain, everyone on the hill showed up. Gawlaki had to send two junior Marines, Privates First Class Rangel and Manypenny, back to Echo Bunker to cover the east gate and ridgeline trail as everyone else was on the westside LZ to see the show. Harvey narrated but let his two-man working party of LaRue and Iantorno each pull a pin and set the two thermite grenades on top of the pile in the middle of the LZ. The Marines stepped back, grenade spoons flew, and both grenades popped with a bright-white light and sparks and started their eating of the metal below them. It was over in four minutes and both grenades were still hot and smoking on the LZ. The engineer stake was cut into three pieces, both metal ammo cans melted, and the wood burned through. Only the dirt stopped the grenades. The sergeants were proud of the demo, and the lieutenant had a solution. Three thermite grenades would be in a wooden box prepositioned inside the tower well next to the IOD's tripod: one grenade each for the large metal-and-glass ship's binos, the night-observation device (NOD), and the top of the laser range finder. Sergeant

"Froggy" Hernadez, from 11th Marines, was not sure about the plan as he was worried about destroying the expensive IOD.[35] Stamm told him to check with his rear, but for now, as the hill commander, it was his responsibility. If they ever needed to execute the plan it would be him making the call and that would only happen if they were abandoning the hill or being overrun. Stamm told the sergeant neither was on his dance card. "What's a dance card, Sir?" Stamm told him not to worry, the destroyed IOD would be on him. Stamm was pleased with the solution. He would brief the captain and the other lieutenants in Delta Company who were hill commanders about the IOD-destruction plan.

The hill had its regular complement of weapons with one new addition. Somebody had traded for a 61-mm mortar.[36] It was old but believed to be functional. The mortar was a Soviet design, which enabled it to fire both its ammo and U.S. 60-mm rounds from the same tube. Stamm told Gawlaki that, on the first non-rain day, they would have mortar training and test fire both mortars.

On 11 November, the IOD team called Stamm to the tower and showed him a group of 11 NVA/VC 4,000 meters away on the northeast corner of Go Noi Island. Through the ship's binos, he could clearly see they were hanging out and swimming in a pond. They were wearing dark uniforms, and one rifle could be seen. The team tried to call a fire mission but got negative clearance as the location was east of the rail berm and inside the Korean zone.[37] On the 12th, about 0930, Sergeant Harvey put his head in the lieutenant's bunker and said, "Hey, sir, you might want to check out this large group of NVA that Alpha Bunker has sighted." There was a healthy competition between bunkers for sightings, and between the Recon Marines and IOD team. Harvey had walked over and quietly told the lieutenant because he wanted to call the fire mission instead of the IOD team. They proceeded to the top of Alpha Bunker and Corporal Moran handed a pair of 7 × 50 binos to the lieutenant while Harvey pointed northwest. You did not need binos as marching out of Thon Bon (1) hamlet and moving south on the high-speed two-foot-wide trail, was a column of NVA. They were wearing a mixture of uniforms. The center group clearly had packs and rifles. Moran said his count was 100 and counting. All the movement at Alpha Bunker had been noticed by the tower watch 100 feet behind and above them. As soon as they swung the "Big Eyes," which was the Marines' nickname for the IOD, they saw the lucrative target. The watch FO, Corporal Mark Bayuk, started their fire mission. Harvey complained quietly to the lieutenant who congratulated him on the sighting, but that it was the FOs' job, so let them do it and just sit back and watch. The enemy column was strung out between Thon Bon (1) and the old, vacant, bombed-out Thon Bon (2) which was at the start of the north slope of Hill 148. The FOs got a fire mission with excellent coverage and a spread on the trail between the two hamlets. When the first round hit, the entire enemy column went to ground and disappeared.[38] Gawlaki explained to the lieutenant and anyone else listening on top of Alpha Bunker that the trail had spider holes and bunkers on both sides all along it just for the purpose of avoiding artillery fire. When the dust and smoke of the fire mission cleared, nobody was on the trail and nobody observed any enemy. An OV-10 working Dodge City saw the fire mission and flew over. *Hostage Golf* checked out the area after the check-fire. He told the hill he could see nothing but that a platoon from 5th Marines was patrolling east from Liberty Road on Route 537 and he would vector them into the area. Alpha Bunker watched the Thon Bon trail for the rest of the day and saw neither enemy nor Marine infantry.

On 13 November, midafternoon, Alpha Bunker had been watching an infantry unit sweeping north of Route 537 in the vicinity of the burned-out CH-53. They had pushed the enemy towards the Song Ba Ren either to trap them or force them to cross. In the summer, one could walk across the sandbar, but now, in the rainy season, the water was high and fast. Alpha Bunker told the tower, who started counting and got to 53 NVA. They also clearly saw a light machine gun besides the standard packs and rifles. They monitored a fire mission the infantry was calling and took over the adjustments once it was clear of the unit. An AO came overhead so they ceased fire and let the aircraft take over the fire-support coordination as they had a better view and had fixed-wing inbound. The fixed-wing aircraft dropped its ordnance and was gone after two passes in under two minutes. The tower had seen an NVA dragging a body, as had the AO. When the fixed-wing cleared, the AO gave the BDA of one confirmed kill to the fast movers.[39] The remaining 52 NVA were underground. On 14 November, at dusk, the hill observed NVA crossing the sandbar at Song Ba Ren north of the downed CH-53. Big Eyes counted 70 NVA moving in small groups carrying boxes, with packs and rifles. They called a fire mission but could not observe results due to darkness.[40]

Waddill had told Stamm to watch for boats moving on the Song Chiem Son directly behind Tho Son hamlet below the hill, and that they should watch at night. Stamm got his first boat observation on 15 November, at dusk, with two boats moving west on the river with three people in each. The river was a free-fire zone. Stamm got a fire mission and adjusted on target. He could not observe due to darkness and the height of the riverbanks. The next night, the Recon Marines in Alpha Bunker spotted a fire in Thon Bon (1). With the NOD on the roof, they could see one VC working around the fire. They called *Report Card-Mike* and got a fire mission on the hamlet. The fire went out, however a secondary fire started as result of the artillery.[41]

On 16 November, the IOD officially went operational.[42] Their callsign was *Lynch Law Eight-Three*. It was sundown and their first target was directly north of the OP on Go Noi Island. Three VC wearing black "PJs" were moving east checking out a communications wire on the trail. *Lynch Law Eight-Three* called their first fire mission with excellent coverage and reported two confirmed enemy killed.[43] On 17 November, as the sun set, *Lynch Law* spotted five VC wearing black PJs. They all carried rifles except the middle man was carrying a light machine gun. One had a pack. They were crossing the sandbar on the Song Ba Ren river. Stamm was in the tower, amazed at how clear a picture and such detail one could see in the ship's binoculars. *Lynch Law* called a fire mission. They reported to *Report Card-Mike* excellent coverage of the target. But, since it had gotten dark, they could not report a result to *Mike*.[44] November 19, at 0745, they observed three NVA/VC. One was wearing green utilities and carrying a pack and rifle. The other two were sitting and eating next to a fire on the riverbank. The fire mission covered the target, and they claimed three confirmed kills. The IOD's next fire mission came at 1530. The sighted enemy was 11 kilometers, or 11,000 meters, to the northwest in *Dodge City*. There were five NVA/VC wearing black PJs. One was wearing green cammies and had a rifle. The other four were putting something in the ground. *Lynch Law* called and adjusted the fire mission. They claimed three confirmed kills and two probables.[45] The Recon Marines in Alpha Bunker did not believe the claim but neither did they have ship's binos. Stamm's operation order had said they would depart on 18 November, however, on the 18th, he got a radio call extending them to the

20th.[46] Stamm let Gawlaki know to pass the news to the Marines, who really did not mind. On the 20th, Stamm had 3rd Platoon stage their gear at the LZ to await the arrival of 1st Platoon led by 2nd Lieutenant "Chuck" Overton.[47]

With the Recon Marines departing, the 11th Marines' FO team remained. The FO tours on the hill were scheduled for five weeks on and one week off.[48]

After what seemed a long wait for the "3rd Herd," at 1400, they saw two CH-46s racing each other and flying fast and low straight at Hill 119 at 200 feet. They both broke into opposite turns after buzzing the hill with the lead bird making a tight 360 and flaring his landing, back wheels touching down first as he lowered the nose and then the ramp. Half of 1st Platoon came trotting off, Overton being last man. The second bird landed just after the first departed the LZ. They would have the standard one-hour turnover.

The hill had changed since Overton's previous trip. The tower now dominated the center of the hill. Stamm's Marines had dug a second mortar pit and repositioned the ammunition bunker between the two pits. Overton's callsign remained *Asparagus* and the FO team in the tower remained *Lynch Law Eight-Three*. They both got artillery from *Report Card-Mike* in An Hoa. The 1st Recon Battalion's callsign remained *Defend*. Overton's mission remained the same, as stated in the canned written statement, "to conduct recon and surveillance in his haven with special emphasis to call and adjust Arty/air on all targets of opportunity."[49] The haven remained the same small block 1,200 × 1,300 meters around Hill 119.[50]

After talking with Stamm and getting settled into his bunker, Overton walked the perimeter, checking each bunker and his Marines. The perimeter trench line was shallow with a rock bottom. Before sundown, he would go up to the tower and get a brief and a demonstration of the IOD. Stamm had told him about the thermite grenades, and he wanted to see where they were. He also wanted to see how the laser range finder worked. He got Staff Sergeant Keen and had him go over the safety procedures and the commands for lasing and told him to educate the hill with his drill-instructor voice and stature; he wanted no lased eyes on his watch. Overton and Captain Martin had discussed the duties between Recon and Arty FOs on the hill. The FOs were there to observe and call fire missions. Therefore, Martin had said, let them have everything outside the haven to observe and shoot. However, inside the haven, close to the hill, they needed Overton's clearance just as if they were shooting into anyone else's tactical area of responsibility.[51] Overton would then determine if he were going to engage with his organic weapons or clear the fire mission for the FOs to shoot. It was a simple, straightforward, division of responsibilities that followed doctrine. Overton would talk through the responsibilities with the Arty FO team.

A new addition for this trip was the experimental XM174.[52] It was a crew-served 40-mm grenade launcher. Nobody had seen it fire. In the morning, Overton told Keen they would fire every weapon on the hill, including the new grenade launcher. After seeing it fired, he would have to determine where to place it. He also had a new sniper in the platoon. He would talk with the Marine and Keen to figure out how they could best employ him.

All Marines like to fire weapons. Starting in the morning, Keen walked to each bunker, and they fired all the personal weapons in the bunker. Overton observed. That afternoon they fired all the crew-served weapons on the hill. It was a good day. The Marines agreed the highlight was the XM174. In automatic, it put twelve 40-mm grenades, in short order, in a spread driven by the sitting operator who was swiveling the barrel on the tripod. The collective decision was to employ it in Bravo Bunker. Three enemy avenues of approach, ending in the LZ, were straight west of the bunker. Bravo got the XM174, and they got to clean it that night. Overton told Keen there would be a 100 percent weapons inspection the next morning at 1000.

Life settled into a normal hill routine. The FOs in the tower yelling out, "Standby to Lase" and "Lasing" commands became routine sounds on the hill along with Armed Forces Vietnam radio network during the daytime. No transistor radio music was allowed at night. The Recon Marines focused on weapons training with daily firing and cross training on the machine guns and mortars, both of which were not taught to Recon Marines as they were infantry weapons. Overton also tasked each bunker with a section of the trench line, leading into its bunker in two directions, to be deepened. They could dig or they could fill sandbags and build up the trench, their choice. He wanted the trench two-feet deep before they departed. They were scheduled to flip on 1 December.

Overton needed the fire-mission statistics for his debrief back at Recon Battalion. He had Keen collect the stats for him from the FO team. *Lynch Law Eight-Three*, whose callsign had changed to *Vesper Bells* on 27 November, had 39 sightings of 185 total NVA/VC in 11 days. They had fired 37 artillery fire missions, resulting in 61 enemy kills.[53] Team *Asparagus* had no enemy or friendly contacts. It had been a rainy, cold, dark, and quiet flip for Overton and 1st Platoon. Coming back up would be 2nd Lieutenant Waddill and the 3rd Platoon of Delta Company.[54]

CHAPTER 14

Christmas Gifts, December 1969

In the United States, on 1 December 1969, the first draft lottery since 1942, and the first in peacetime, was held.[1] In a rare matchup, the top two college football teams met on 6 December in Fayetteville where the top-ranked Texas Longhorns defeated the second-ranked Arkansas Razorbacks 15 to 14. President Nixon was in attendance, as was future president George H. W. Bush.[2] And, on 15 December, Nixon announced Phase III of the U.S. troop withdrawal from Vietnam of another 50,000 personnel, to be completed by 15 April 1970.[3]

In Vietnam, on 15 December 1969, Major General Edwin B. Wheeler, who had been back in Vietnam since June, serving as Deputy Commanding General, XXIV Corps, succeeded Major General Simpson as commander of the 1st Marine Division.[4] Major General Wheeler knew that, with the announced withdrawal of troops, his division, which comprised four infantry regiments, had to cover the same territory with three regiments, and then two regiments, over the duration of the 1970 phased drawdown. He had had time to think about a plan, an economy-of-force plan where infantry defended, and Reconnaissance went on the offense. A major part of that plan was to increase the size of reconnaissance areas and activities, the number of teams in the field, and area covered, as well as their aggressiveness. The 1st Recon Battalion was commanded by Lieutenant Colonel John J. Grace, a Korean war veteran and quiet professional. Under Grace, and with Simpson's guidance, the battalion had performed classic reconnaissance patrolling with a focus of attention on gathering intelligence, patrolling, and looking to determine enemy locations. The patrols used the *Keyhole* concept. A Recon team would be inserted and would move clandestinely to multiple observation points and quietly observe enemy lines of communication and infiltration routes between their base areas and the Da Nang Vital Zone, which the 1st Marine Division had a mission of protecting. The reconnaissance concept of operations suited the personality of the battalion's commander, and the battalion acted accordingly on the majority of its patrols, which tried to remain undetected while collecting information on its foe.

Wheeler was going to change Recon Battalion's methods of operation and mission. He believed he needed a new leader to implement the new mission. Grace was due to rotate out of command in mid-1970. With that in mind, the general sent for another Korean War veteran with a polar-opposite personality. Lieutenant Colonel William C. Drumright commanded the 2nd Battalion, 26th Marines (2/26). The battalion had come off the Special Landing Force (SLF) mission and had conducted an admin landing in November 1969 at Red Beaches 1 and 2 close to Nam O Bridge in Da Nang Bay. The SLF was both the III Marine Amphibious Force's (III MAF) and CINCPAC's (Commander-in-Chief, Pacific) strategic reserve. Once ashore, they chopped to the 1st Marine Division and had taken over security of the northern sector of the Da Nang Vital Area. The area included Hai Van Pass road and rail security, ESSO Plant security and Nam O Bridge, Route 1, and rail-bridge security over the Song Cu De.[5] The new division commander personally knew Drumright and the aggressive personality and leadership style which had earned him the nickname "Wild Bill." Drumright had the reconnaissance credentials, having swam the Han River as a corporal in freezing sleet with then Captain Kenny Houghton, capturing the main bridge into Seoul and enabling the 1st Marine Division to move across the bridge to begin taking the Korean capital.[6]

In the first week of December, during turnover to take command of 1st Division, Wheeler had Drumright over one afternoon and outlined what he was thinking, including expanded reconnaissance operations, covering more ground, and going on the offensive with supporting arms. He told Drumright to think it over and come back with his thoughts and confirm his desire to become the commanding officer of the 1st Reconnaissance Battalion.[7]

Drumright knew the general was a serious warrior and meant what he said. He also knew from commanding 2/26 that the individual-replacement policy adapted by the Marine Corps operating in Vietnam meant a unit was subject to turnover every day and, as a result, unit training suffered. The bill was being paid by inexperienced Marines in the rice paddies with newcomers making new-guy mistakes. Drumright knew it was so bad the Marines did not want to talk to new guys, and it took six months to gain field experience to prevent yourself from stepping on a booby trap or going the wrong direction in a firefight. Recon teams were five to eight Marines and a corpsman on patrol. It was one thing to hide and look or snoop and poop as the Marines called it. It was a different challenge to go out and seek contact and seek to bloody the enemy with a small force. Training and leadership would be the key to survival. Drumright thought about the challenge for two days and produced a plan and a list of requests. He would submit it to Major General Wheeler and, if the commanding general agreed, then Drumright would be his Marine to implement. At the appointment, he knew it would have to be short and concise, but that he would have to explain and justify his thoughts. Drumright confirmed with the general that he wanted *Sting Ray* patrols.[8] Wheeler vehemently agreed that he wanted to find the enemy in their base areas and bloody them. He wanted to disrupt his adversary, General Binh, the commander of the 2nd North Vietnamese Army (NVA) Division before they started to infiltrate into the Da Nang Vital Area. Drumright told the general to do that he needed experienced patrol leaders that could not only read a map but could call in supporting arms via use of artillery and air strikes. The general concurred and asked him to make his point. Drumright said that, under the individual-replacement program, assigning Marines to 1st Recon off the plane, on day one, would take six months to train them to be effective patrol leaders (PL); they did not have time to do that. He stated that lieutenants have the map-reading skills and supporting-arms theory from The Basic School (TBS) and, once in country at the six-month point, or halfway through their 13-month tour of duty in the grunts, they get reassigned as an individual replacement to a staff job just as they had learned how to map and shoot in the field. He said he wanted handpicked lieutenant Patrol Leaders with six-months experience in the grunts. He wanted authority to hire and fire.[9] General Wheeler asked what else he needed. Drumright, building up a head of steam, said:

> I need the division's priority of air support to change from we-will-get-to-you to Recon-gets-air-first! If one of my boys starts a fight, he has to know he gets priority artillery and air before the infantry. He does not have a platoon of thirty Marines to absorb an attack. He cannot wait. And I need aircraft dedicated on the Air Tasking Order from the Wing. An insertion and extraction package that comes to work every day, seven days a week. Not that the 7th Marines has a big company helo lift so Recon will have to wait until tomorrow. If we are going to increase the number of teams in the field, I have to be able to get them in and out.

When asked to continue, Drumright, now pushing it, said he wanted the basic daily food allowance increased if the teams were going to be "running and gunning." They would not be eating three hot meals on patrol like every one of the clerks did on Division Hill. Wheeler said he would work on it, but the change of command was 15 December, so he told Drumright to go back and run 2/26 and let him get his feet on the ground.[10]

Drumright went back to 2/26 but was already thinking. Both he and Wheeler knew he was not a staff officer and, when his six months' command was over, Drumright did not want to count tennis shoes or be a watch officer on Hill 327, the Division Hill. Wheeler assumed command on 15 December. He hit the deck running since he had already been in country since June as XXIV Corps deputy.

In December, at Recon Battalion, Lieutenant Colonel Grace had settled into command. Captain Thomas Martin was at Delta Company and Major J. M. Mattiace had just arrived as the S-3, having taken over from Captain MacCaskill who became the experienced assistant operations officer (S-3A) for continuity. Training continued with the commencement of Recon Indoctrination Course 13-69 and Pre-SCUBA 10-69.[11] On 6 December, Lieutenant General Buse, Commanding General Fleet Marine Force, Pacific, visited Camp Reasoner and was given operations briefs, viewed a static display of a Recon Team and equipment and then was given a live demonstration of the ladder and Special Patrol Insertion/Extraction (SPIE) rig apparatus attached to two CH-46s on LZ 401.[12] It served as a rehearsal, for, on 16 December, the new commanding general of 1st Division escorted, to Camp Reasoner, Lieutenant General LaVelle, U.S. Air Force, the director of the Defense Communications Project Group (later renamed Advanced Research Project Group). They reviewed the same briefs and another "dog and pony show" of the ladder and SPIE rigs attached to CH-46s flying Recon Marines off LZ 401 and out over Da Nang Bay as an example of an emergency extraction.[13] Given separate and more detailed briefs, but watching the same show, was Colonel Dzialo USMC, the incoming G-2 section (intelligence) of III MAF who would have some influence over future taskings. Two days later, Major General Wheeler was back, in his fourth day of command and second visit to the Reconnaissance Battalion. On this trip down Hill 327 he met the battalion staff and the company commanders. He was then briefed by the commanding officer in the S-3 bunker on a detailed laydown of locations and missions of current Recon teams operating within the division's tactical area of responsibility. The last visitor of the month received a short welcome brief and then, in the outdoor amphitheater, talked off the cuff to the assembled officers and enlisted Marines. CINCPAC, Admiral John S. McCain Jr., simply thanked the Marines and Corpsmen for their efforts.[14] Softly spoken, but easily heard, the admiral was talked about with awe by the Recon Marines and Corpsmen that evening, men who were not easily impressed.[15] During the month of December, the battalion ran 65 patrols and had 340 sightings of 2,738 enemy.[16]

***

Lieutenant "Butch" Waddill and 3rd Platoon arrived on Hill 119 at 0930 hours on 1 December in two CH-46s.[17] It was clear and cold. This was Waddill's third trip to the hill. His callsign remained *Asparagus*. The Integrated Observation Device (IOD) had a new lieutenant, by the name of Russell, to run the six-Marine forward-observer (FO) team, callsign *Vesper Bells*.[18] The Arty Marines now lived in a large, expanded bunker directly below the tower. Sergeant Herman Diaz, Waddill's platoon sergeant, remained with him along with 22 other Marines and two corpsmen, Hospital Corpsmen Third Class Sanders and Laski.[19]

One of Waddill's new Marines was Private First Class Eugene Marshall. Some of the Marines called him "Pepper" as he was black.[20] This was to distinguish him from the other Private First Class Marshall in the company, who they called "Salt" since he was white. Gene was smart. Coming out of boot camp/Infantry Training Regiment, due to his high-test scores, he was sent to Communications–Electronics School. A case of pneumonia and a naval hospital visit cost him an electronics-maintenance school seat and he ended up as a field-radio operator. Arriving in Vietnam, due to a shortage of radio operators in 1st Recon Battalion, he was assigned to Delta Company.[21] This was his first trip to Hill 119.[22] Gene Marshall spent seven years in the Marine Corps. He served on the aircraft carrier USS *Hancock* during the evacuation of Saigon and as the staff sergeant radio chief for 3rd Battalion, 9th Marines. Returning stateside and stationed at Quantico, he made the hard decision to get out of the Marine Corps to remain in his home state.[23] He changed his name to the family name Stockton and took over the family farm. In order to raise cash to run the farm, he joined both the Virginia Highway Patrol and the Virginia Army National Guard.[24] His Marine Corps training allowed him to succeed in both organizations. Gene Stockton retired after 38 years as a trooper in the Virginia Highway Patrol as Director of Training. Likewise, in the Virginia Guard, he rose to assistant adjutant general of the State of Virginia, retiring as a brigadier general.[25]

On Hill 119, Waddill told Diaz to get the troops settled in; training would commence the next day. He sought out Lieutenant Russell and asked him to walk with him for a short, private conversation. Waddill wanted to ensure they were on the same page. He explained to the new lieutenant that he was the hill commander and, as a result, would be responsible for security and his haven. He wanted Russell to have the haven marked on all the FOs' maps. His job was inside the haven. Outside the haven, Russell was to do his job and call fire missions. They had a clear boundary and responsibilities. This was his first-time meeting Russell, and he wanted no crossed wires. Russell did not say anything except "Okay" at the end and walked off. Waddill would withhold judgment for now.[26]

The first week settled into a routine. *Vesper Bells* was calling fire missions. *Asparagus* were running two listening posts nightly, one 360 wire check every morning, and a daily walk-off patrol that varied in direction, departure time, and length. On 7 December, the patrol was sent west over to Hill 148. Corporal Swick led the six-man patrol with Lance Corporal Lowery on point.[27] On the southwest military crest of 148, he picked up footprints. They were a mix of sandals and boot prints in dried mud on a moderately used three-foot-wide trail running east to west around the crest. They were not new, but they were not washed away in the rains, so a week to two weeks old was their guess.[28] Clearly somebody was observing Hill 119.

It was now foggy late at night and, until the sun could get up and burn it off, they waited. Waddill changed the 0400–0700 watch to 50 percent alert as anyone could walk all the way to either the east or west gate and not be seen in the fog. Their callsign changed from *Asparagus* to *Durham* at 0800 on 14 December.[29] On the evening of 15 December, Waddill had Marshall and the other radio operators work up the statistics from their daily spot reports to be sent to Battalion, callsign *Defend*. For their 15 days on the hill, *Vesper Bells* (IOD FOs) had 60 sightings, totaling 223 North Vietnamese Army/Viet Cong (NVA/VC) and three children. They called 35 fire missions resulting in 46 enemy kills.[30] At 1000 on 16 December, the "3rd Herd" was helicopter borne for Camp Reasoner.

Arriving was 2nd Platoon with their new platoon commander, 2nd Lieutenant Garry Parks.[31] He had graduated and was commissioned from The Citadel, the Military College of South Carolina, on 31 May 1969. On 1 June, in The Citadel's chapel, in a military wedding, he married the love of his life, Earlene.[32] That week, they drove Earlene's blue Volkswagen Bug to Quantico together to begin a career as a Marine Corps couple and family. They found a small apartment right outside the back gate to Camp Barrett, the home of TBS.[33] Garry became a student in Mike Company, class 12-69, graduating on 5 November.[34] He, along with 40 other classmates, went directly to Vietnam after their 30-day leave. Arriving in Da Nang on 11 December, he and four of his TBS classmates all found themselves assigned as replacement lieutenants in 1st Reconnaissance Battalion. Second Lieutenants Tom McAdams, Garry Parks, and Parker Miller all ended up in Delta Company,[35] while "Big John" Murphy went to Alpha Company, and former enlisted Marine, Tom Barrows, went to Alpha Company, 5th Recon. Captain Martin interviewed all three of the new Delta Company arrivals. Parks was immediately assigned to 2nd Platoon. McAdams and Miller would have to wait as Delta was currently short of Marines. After three weeks of sitting, North Georgia Military College graduate Miller heard on the grapevine from Murphy that there was an opening coming in Alpha Company. He went to Captain Martin and volunteered. He was transferred to Alpha Company, 1st Recon. Miller patrolled with Alpha Company for six-and-a-half months.[36] Rather than go to a staff job, he volunteered to go to the grunts and was reassigned to Hotel Company, 2nd Battalion, 5th Marines, where, in two-and-a-half-months, he picked up two Purple Hearts. Recovering from the second wound, he was transferred to Okinawa where he finished his 13-month overseas tour.[37] Miller had always wanted to fly. Returning to the States, he applied for flight training and was accepted. His orders were changed to Pensacola, Florida, where he earned his wings as a naval aviator. After getting his wings, he requested, and got, attack helicopters. He flew Cobras for the next 17 years. He became a career aviator, retiring from the Office of Legislative Affairs on Capitol Hill as a colonel.[38]

Back on Hill 119, on the morning of 16 December, 2nd Platoon, Delta Company, or D-2, arrived via helicopter. This was 2nd Lieutenant Parks's first trip to the hill. He had the experienced Sergeant Gawlaki as his platoon sergeant. "Doc" Mullins was making his second trip to the hill and had brought extra medical supplies as he expected to be treating the local villagers. Scout Dog, Camp (#A539), and his handler, Sergeant Brookins, had also been to the hill before.[39] Parks was looking forward to spending time with each of his 18 Marines. He had brought along a new Marine Corps-issued green memorandum pocket-size notebook to create his platoon commander's notebook, which would have a couple of pages on each Marine's background, education, skills, and family. Parks would complete his notebook on this flip by recording each Marine's details after he interviewed them. The lieutenant was serious and detailed.[40] His notebook would help guide him and his Marines. He had been prebriefed by Captain Martin and the other platoon commanders on hill duty. He let Gawlaki get the Marines settled into their bunkers as he went looking for Lieutenant Russell, the artillery officer in charge of the IOD. Their first meeting was low key. They exchanged where they were from. Parks wanted the callsign and was informed the IOD team was *War Cloud*, and they were firing through *Rice Krispies-Mike* artillery at An Hoa.[41] Most missions were 105-mm, but they could get 155s and 8" guns, if needed, from other firebases within range. Parks told Russell he was the hill commander and his callsign was *Durham*. Russell was making stew and did not seem to want to be disturbed, nor did he offer any stew, so Parks departed, stating he would like a demonstration of the IOD later that day.[42] He went to his bunker to get settled in, dropping his pack and determining where the candles and flashlight were.

About noon, there was activity in the observation tower, so Parks climbed the steps. Corporal Mark Bayuk, one of the IOD FOs, had sighted two bunkers and had received permission to fire on them. He showed Parks where they were out on Go Noi Island and explained the entire island was a free-fire zone.[43] Parks stayed and listened while the fire mission was called in. After 30 minutes of waiting, Bayuk offered that sometimes they did not get approval for small missions on bunkers, especially if it was during lunch hour. Parks asked why; Bayuk responded, off-handed, "Sir, the gun crews got to eat, and they like the mess hall versus eating C-rats behind the gun line." Parks departed for his own lunch of C-rations.

At 1415, Bayuk yelled off the tower, asking Parks if he wanted to see some VC. Parks still wanted to see the IOD in action, so he returned to the tower where he was shown three VC five kilometers out on the northwest piece of Go Noi. He was amazed to be able to see the details of the VC in the "Big Eyes." Bayuk gave commands to the hill, "Ready to lase," "Lasing," as Parks watched the digital lights on the laser box indicate they were 5,320 meters out at 292 mils of 6400 mils registered circle provided the azimuth for resection at the artillery battery. Parks, watching in the ship's bino, could see the "PJs" were black and he could clearly see the VC were carrying packs and rifles. Bayuk was on the radio with *Rice Krispies-Mike.* With real enemy, he got service immediately and was firing a battery-one fire-for-effect (six rounds fired at once, landing at the same time) with no adjustment. With the IOD, there was no need to adjust fire. His rounds were on target. Parks actually saw two enemy getting hit with shrapnel or blast before the smoke obstructed his view. Bayuk confirmed two EKIAs (enemy, killed in action).[44] Parks had gotten his IOD demo. Casually, he asked where Lieutenant Russell was. Bayuk said he was in his bunker doing whatever lieutenants do.[45] Nodding without comment, and leaving the tower, Parks walked the perimeter before it got dark so he would be familiar with it prior to his first night on the hill. He took his time, noting how shallow the trench lines were. He also checked every crew-served weapon and its gun card. He also looked over both Hill 148 and 175 from each of the bunkers with his binos. Seeing the closeness of both hills, he was pleased with Gawlaki's initiative with the 57-mm recoilless rifle he had scrounged.[46] That night in his bunker, Parks asked the sergeant about the weapon. Gawlaki explained the World War II/Korean War-vintage recoilless rifle was being supplied to the Army of the Republic of Vietnam (ARVN) by the U.S. as an infantry/antitank weapon. No longer viable against newer tanks, it was still good against the NVA's PT-76 tank. The sergeant was honest and said he had traded for the weapon in "Dog Patch." He added ammunition was not a problem since it was in the U.S. inventory that was being provided to the ARVN. As a result, it could actually be ordered in the system. Parks wanted to hear Gawlaki's opinion of the weapon. The platoon sergeant said it was accurate and, when in the direct-fire mode, could reach out to both Hills 148 and 175. The manual said the effective range was 450 meters, but its max range was listed at four kilometers. Gawlaki added that the wooden ammunition boxes, with four rounds each, were a great size for making furniture. Parks seemed satisfied and said they'd shoot it in the morning, figure out where to put it, and who should man it.[47]

December 17 began with fog, so Parks told Gawlaki to wait until the afternoon to run the wire patrol; after that, they would shoot the recoilless rifle. About 1530, Gawlaki had Privates First Class Rangel and Thompson set the weapon up halfway between Bravo and Alpha Bunkers, but behind the tower and above the trench. He had them point it west towards Hill 148 directly across the saddle landing zone (LZ). When Parks arrived and gave the go ahead, Gawlaki, using his best rifle-range commands, cleared the back-blast area, then told Thompson to load for Rangel. On the command "Fire," Rangel pulled the trigger. Even with the loud explosion and dust, everyone could see the round as it went towards the Hill 148 summit and clean over it. Nobody saw the impact and Parks was worried about firing into the 5th Marines area without clearance. He was going to stop the firing, but Gawlaki assured him they could hit the east facing side of the hill with the next round.[48] They did that halfway up, about 225 meters from them. It put a divot in the soft dirt. Parks told them to fire one more round to try to hit the high-speed trail going up towards the summit. The third round was off the trail by about a foot but was a satisfactory shot. He told Gawlaki to put the weapon in the ammunition bunker and get a count of how many 57-mm rounds they had, by type.

The hill settled into a daily routine with the IOD team doing their thing—fire missions—and the Recon Marines running patrols, within their haven, daily and each night. On the third day, the weekly IOD resupply helo, which the air wing called *Mission Nine-Nine*, the main purpose of which was battery resupply for the laser range finder, landed.[49] It arrived with a new lance corporal for the Arty team. To Parks's surprise, walking onto the bird was Lieutenant Russell. Sergeant "Froggy" Hernandez was now the noncommissioned officer in charge (NCOIC) of the IOD Team, which meant the competent Corporal Bayuk would be doing the real firing.[50]

December 23, in the late morning, the one-armed woman and three other women brought a young Vietnamese woman in a bamboo-pole parachute stretcher to just outside the observation post (OP). A security detail, plus Parks and Doc Mullins, went out and met the women. They were seeking medical treatment for the woman who was clearly in pain. She had shrapnel in the buttocks and a suspected broken pelvis.[51] Parks had Gawlaki call for a medevac but explained through broken English and Vietnamese, as there was no translator, that this hill was not a hospital for treatment or medevacs, and that they were in a restricted zone. He got a lot of nodding and smiling but Parks knew what he said would not be complied with as long as the hill did its humanitarian duty and evacuated wounded and sick Vietnamese. They sent the party back to the hamlet below and kept the wounded woman, a suspected VC, on the side of the LZ. It took two hours before a bird came out and picked her up.

On mid-morning of Christmas Day, a large group, consisting of 25 Vietnamese women and children, departed Tho Son hamlet at the north base of the hill and start walking towards the hill. The tower notified Parks who came up and looked through the Big Eyes. The group was carrying signs and at least one large banner on two bamboo poles.[52] He did not want this large group close to the hill or near the LZ. He decided to meet the delegation and determine what they wanted. He told Gawlaki he would have hill security while he, along with his second team and Doc Mullins, would find out what the Vietnamese wanted. Language translation was always an issue. Corporal Bayuk from the IOD team had picked up more Vietnamese than the other Marines and he volunteered to go with Parks to help with the translation.[53] The detail departed the west gate and went down the main north trail towards the hamlet. They met the Vietnamese group just inside the abandoned railroad berm in a wide-open field. The old one-armed woman and an elderly man led the villagers. With them, they had a young girl who could speak some English. They had come to present Christmas gifts of wreaths of flowers and rice cakes to the hill. They also wanted the U.S. to go home and end the war. Of the three banners, one, three feet high and 20 feet wide, mounted on two poles, read, in English, "TRUE PEACE IN SOUTH VIETNAM."

The villagers were friendly, all smiles and bows. They were wishing merry Christmas and peace on earth. They also brought a large wooden white cross and erected it on the side of the hill.

After lots of smiles and bowing, Parks told Bayuk to politely tell them they must leave and take everything, including the cross, with them. Bayuk recommended the lieutenant accept some rice cakes as a goodwill gesture.[54] Parks accepted the rice cakes. He informed the villagers they could come no closer to the hill than the railroad berm. The rest of the area around the hill was off limits. He wished them a merry Christmas and urged them to return to their hamlet. The Marines waved goodbye as they departed; the Vietnamese group turned and returned to their hamlet.[55]

On 26 December, between 1900 and 2130, Alpha Bunker reported hearing Vietnamese and broken English being broadcast through a speaker system down towards Thon Bon (1). Both Parks and Gawlaki came over to the bunker and listened. They also heard Vietnamese rock-and-roll music.[56] Thon Bon (1) was an uninhabited small hamlet. Somebody was having a party. Not being able to pinpoint the music and announcements, they took no action but listened for two and a half hours until the sounds ceased. On 27 December, at 1530, one wounded NVA/VC walked alone up the main trail towards the OP. He was wearing gray utilities and was clearly unarmed and struggling to walk. Parks sent a security team and Doc Mullins outside the LZ wire to evaluate the individual. Doc recommended a medevac, so Parks requested it from Battalion. While searching the suspect, they found no ID card, but they did find an exceptionally large sum of cash.[57]

The suspect was deemed to be a priority and was flown to the Naval Support Activity Hospital. On 29 December, Delta-2 was scheduled for their flip off the hill. For their 13-day stay, IOD Team *War Cloud* had 24 sightings of 143 NVA/VC with 23 fire missions, resulting in 27 enemy confirmed killed by artillery.[58] The Recon platoon had a relative quiet stay serving as security and a medevac station for the local villagers and VC to get medical treatment. Parks, Gawlaki, and Doc Mullins were outbound on two green CH-46 Sea Knight helicopters provided by their friends at HMM 364, the *Purple Fox* squadron. Delta-2 would spend the New Year at Camp Reasoner; the Marines were already talking about a party at the "Stagger Back Inn."

Coming up to Hill 119 was the 1st Platoon led by 2nd Lieutenant Butch Waddill.[59] They arrived by helo for a one-hour turnover before 2nd Platoon departed. This was Waddill's fourth trip to the hill. Parks told him there was no IOD officer and that the NCOIC, Sergeant "Froggy" Hernandez, was lazy.[60] He did tell him that Bayuk had his shit together and knew how to call fire missions. Waddill thanked Parks for the insight, they shook hands, and Parks walked down to catch the inbound bird at the LZ.

Waddill was not a happy camper. He had joined the Marines to fight his country's enemies. The former enlisted Marine and Montana smokejumper did not feel he was contributing to the fight running the *Keyhole* patrols the battalion leadership favored. When he first arrived, Captain G. R. Willson, the company commander, worked with Waddill and taught him that he had the freedom to make tactical decisions.[61] Willson's replacement, 1st Lieutenant A. T. Bouts, was all about Bouts. He and Waddill barely talked. Bouts's replacement, Captain Martin, was a talker, but he never said anything. Butch was fed up with the lack of action he had seen since coming to Vietnam. Before he came up for this flip, he had gone to the company office and filled out the Administrative Action Form (AA Form) formally requesting reassignment to the grunts, specifically 5th Marines.[62] The 5th Marines were the most decorated regiment in the Marine Corps and had a fighting tradition. They were based at An Hoa Combat Base. He could go there and see some action. He signed the AA Form and gave it to Lieutenant Klein, the executive officer of Delta Company. Klein said he was a fool for doing it. Waddill knew Klein was a rear-echelon motherfucker, so he just looked at him and said, "Ed, your job is to process it, not comment to me as I clearly do not need your two cents," while walking out the company office and slamming the screen door to make his point. Captain Martin knew the division policy was to move officers at their six-month point. If Waddill wanted to go to the grunts, who was he to deny that? Martin endorsed the request favorably and it went to the battalion adjutant that day.[63]

On the hill, after throwing his pack in his bunker, which he had actually dug, Waddill walked the perimeter to check each of the six bunkers. He found Staff Sergeant Mushett, his platoon sergeant, and told him to get the six EE-8 hand-cranked field telephones and put them on a communications-wire string, with one in each bunker and control in the comm bunker.[64] Now, instead of yelling or sending a runner, the hill would have a crank comm system for its defensive perimeter. He also told Mushett they would shoot all the crew-served weapons in the morning and then clean them in the afternoon. About 1440, Mushett said the tower was shooting a fire mission to the east on some NVA.

Waddill climbed the tower steps to find Bayuk on the radio arguing with the *Rice Krispies-Mike* fire-direction officer over a negative clearance to shoot. Waddill asked what the problem was and Bayuk explained it was hard to gain clearance east of the railroad tracks on Go Noi as it was Korean territory. "I can clearly see the NVA, and I should be able to shoot at them."

The lieutenant asked which way they were moving. Bayuk said south. Waddill told him to wait an hour and look southeast towards Chien Son (4); "I will bet you a Ham and Limas you will see the same NVA, and you can shoot over there." Bayuk took the bet. Nothing to lose except a can of ham and lima beans, which he hated. It wasn't an hour but at 1640 Bayuk saw the same six NVA right where Waddill said they would be. Bayuk was happy to lose the bet as he did get clearance and was able to shoot the fire mission. He got excellent coverage but could see no results due to the enemy melting into the tree line next to the trail. He walked over and tossed Waddill a can.[65] Waddill went to his bunker to make dinner. Most Marines disliked the C-rat meal and called them "Ham and Mothers," short for motherfuckers, which was a reference to the stale, whole light-green lima beans in each can. Waddill liked them, or had learned how to cook them, so was never in short supply as the Marines routinely discarded their cans. As Waddill prepared his meal, he listened to Bayuk calling four more fire missions over the next two hours. Parks had been correct in his assessment of this Marine, not to mention that he paid his debts.

The next morning it was foggy. The Marines were restless as they had been told they were going to be able to exercise their weapons. About 0900, the fog burned off and Staff Sergeant Mushett had the hill on 100 percent watch in their bunkers. He wanted to check out the new comm system. He was going to control fire from the comm bunker. Waddill got his coffee and sat on the sandbagged wall outside where he could see each bunker and also hear Mushett and Franklin on the phone system issuing firing commands to each bunker. After each bunker had fired, Waddill told Mushett to go fire the 60-mm and 61-mm mortars. He gave them some targets in the draws leading up to the hill and wanted to drop the mortar rounds deep into each draw, which was also an unobserved avenue of approach for an enemy coming at the hill. He told Mushett that, when they were done, he could fire the XM174. Mushett suggested letting Franklin do it. Truth was Mushett had fired it before and did not want to clean it. The honor fell to Sergeant Franklin who was next in seniority. By far, the 40-mm automatic grenade launcher was the Marines' favorite weapon to fire because it was unbelievable to see the string of 12 grenades descending onto one or more targets. Franklin knew whoever fired the 174 cleaned it but, in his mind, it was worth it for the thrill of firing such a lethal weapon. That day the IOD team, *War Cloud*, called four fire missions. Waddill was summoned to the tower for the third mission as they had 50 NVA wearing green utilities with packs and rifles in an organized river crossing at sundown. Bayuk got clearance immediately with that target and got excellent coverage. When the dust cleared, Bayuk counted 22 bodies on the sandbar. He also got one exceptionally large secondary explosion. Obviously, he hit the enemy ammunition cache on the bank of the Song Chiem Son.[66] On 31 December, *War Cloud* had four fire-mission attempts but only got clearance for the last one, at 1715, on five VC wearing black PJs, carrying rifles, and moving southwest on a trail out to Goi Noi Island which was in the free-fire zone, thereby enabling the quick clearance. Bayuk got excellent coverage of the target, but nobody could observe any enemy due to the high vegetation on both sides of the trail.[67]

It was tradition on New Year's Eve to fire weapons into the sky at midnight. This was against policy, but it was also a hard one for senior leadership in the rear with the gear to prevent. Waddill, having been a young Marine himself, knew his men wanted to do it, so he called Mushett and his three team leaders, Franklin, and Corporals Reinecks and Miller, into his bunker. Waddill, in a profoundly serious tone, told the four Marines it was against policy for Marines to initiate fire at midnight and he would not tolerate it. He asked if they understood as they would have to pass the word and enforce the policy. He looked each in the eye as they nodded. He then said it was his responsibility to defend the OP and to train his Marines in its defense. The last command a hill commander would give when close to being overrun was to fire the final protective fire or FPF. FPFs were interlocking bands of fire across the front of the next bunker down the line as you could shoot in front of a bunker to your left or right better than one shooting straight down. He said they would go to 100 percent watch at 2345, as if anyone on the hill would be sleeping, and that, at the appropriate time, and on his command only, he expected to test the finest FPF he had ever witnessed. Did they understand? All four in unison said, "Yes, sir!"[68] Waddill made himself a large coffee and cocoa mix in his metal canteen cup and went out to the parapet outside his bunker and started watching at 2345. At about 2359 he could see across Go Noi Island; well to the north, red tracers were going into the air. He could not hear them. At midnight, he saw Hill 55, about eleven kilometers due north, go off. He knew he was safe. Waddill yelled to the comm bunker, "Get on the 88s and, Marines, fire the final protective fires!" Instantaneously, and without waiting for the 88 comm-wire call, the hill erupted with every Marine firing his weapon in the air. Red tracers everywhere. Looking out over Go Noi Island, he could see some green tracers (NVA tracer ammo) going up. Mushett and Franklin came by his bunker and wished him a happy New Year. He said, "Welcome to 1970, gents, the Year of the Dog!"[69]

CHAPTER 15

Battalion Commander Down, January 1970

III Marine Amphibious Force (III MAF) remained responsible for the defense of the five northernmost provinces of South Vietnam.[1] This area was designated as the I Corps Tactical Zone. Marine Lieutenant General Herman Nickerson commanded an organization that included 50,000 Army troops from XXIV Corps, as well as 55,000 Marines and sailors.[2] Beginning in 1969, the number of Marines was reduced from their original strength of 79,000 due to "Vietnamization" and Operation *Keystone Bluejay*, which was the military's name for President Nixon's drawdown.[3] The 6,000 South Koreans of the 2nd RoK Marine Brigade, while not under operational control, were coordinated by III MAF, from their Hoi An enclave on the coast just south of Da Nang.[4] During this period, large-scale combat had become infrequent with the North Vietnamese Army (NVA) pulling back and waiting on the peace process while simultaneously engaging in hostilities of their choice (e.g., ambushes, small skirmishes, rocket and mortar attacks, and booby traps). These activities served to inflict the most ravaging toll upon Marines in terms of casualties.

New at the 1st Marine Division was Major General Edwin B. Wheeler, who found himself with a smaller division than in prior years. Division strength had been reduced by one infantry regiment but still included 28,000 Marines and Corpsmen.[5] He was tied to the defense of the logistics hub for I Corps: Da Nang. He would be called upon to defend the same area with less forces. To his credit, he knew the area well. As a result, Wheeler would employ some economy-of-force assignments with his infantry while tightening the outer rocket belt of Da Nang's defense. To keep his counterpart, General Binh of Front 4, off guard, he planned to change the mission of the 1st Reconnaissance Battalion. His intent was to take the fight to Binh in his base areas by putting Recon on the offense using *Sting Ray* instead of *Keyhole* patrolling. Wheeler had firsthand experience with Reconnaissance being on the offense. He had been a platoon commander in 1942 with the 1st Raider Battalion on Tulagi during World War II. On Guadalcanal, he was a company commander during the Edson's Ridge battle. Later, he led a composite raider company on a three-week long-range amphibious-reconnaissance patrol behind enemy lines to gain intelligence for the New Georgia campaign. Supported properly, he knew what Recon units could do as he had done it!

***

Camp Reasoner had long been the home of Reconnaissance units in Vietnam. In January 1970, 1st Reconnaissance Battalion was the primary occupant. In recognition of earlier successes and the change in mission, the battalion was at increased strength, consisting of five companies that provided teams for patrolling, with each company maintaining a permanent radio relay/observation post (OP). Also, its Headquarters and Service Company had a SCUBA locker that supported all SCUBA operations in I Corps including salvage, water rescue, and numerous bridge checks. Additionally, the camp was home to Alpha Company, 5th Recon. The battalion was led by a respected Korean War veteran, Lieutenant Colonel John J. Grace,[6] who had maintained the training ethos of his predecessor while stressing the Reconnaissance mission of obtaining intelligence by observation and surveillance, or classic *Keyhole* patrolling. He changed the name of the entry level class for new Marines and Corpsmen from "course" to "program" when Reconnaissance Indoctrination Program (RIP) 1-70 kicked off. New to the battalion was the executive officer (XO) Major Terry Turner as was the logistics officer (S-4), Captain C. J. Fitzgerald. At Delta Company, Captain Tom Martin had settled in and was enjoying the comforts of Camp Reasoner.[7] He formed a friendship with the battalion S-3 (operations), Major Mattiace.[8] As the year began, Martin's challenge was that he had too many lieutenants. He started with seven for five billets. He was challenged by seven personalities. Without a platoon assignment or any Marines, the newly arrived 2nd Lieutenant B. Parker Miller had volunteered to transfer to Alpha Company. Miller's departure started the new year's officer turnover in Delta Company. Martin's new XO, 1st Lieutenant "Chip" Gregson, had just returned from the hospital in Guam on 24 December.

The next day, Bob Hope's United Service Organizations (USO) show played the Freedom Hill outdoor amphitheater to 10,000-plus Marines, sailors, and soldiers. Gregson could hear the roar of the audience down the road less than two miles away while he listened to the show on Armed Forces Radio and got settled into the Delta Company officer's hut.[9] He was displacing, by seniority, Martin's like-minded XO, Fred Klein. Martin and Klein enjoyed the comforts of the rear and avoided going to the bush. Gregson was an experienced patrol leader on light duty, so Martin offered him up to his friend in the S-3 shop, trying for the major's good graces and creating space again for Klein.[10] Klein went on an in-country R&R and just hung out until the end of the month when the switch was made. He was a happy camper in the company XO slot which he had sought when it reopened. He had less than a month to do in-country. Klein was now a short-timer, and he acted like one. Most everyone in-country (meaning Vietnam) knew their projected rotation date was 13 months away when they arrived. Most Marines kept a calendar towards the end of their tour and checked off each day. Towards the end of a tour, many Marines could quote you the days, hours, and minutes they had left before their "Freedom Bird" home. A number of troops in the rear carried sticks under their arms similar to the old-school swagger sticks, except these were called short-timers' sticks. Each day they could whittle off a day, making their stick shorter. The closer to their rotation date, the shorter the stick, and the more they shied away from going to the field. It was called short-timers' attitude, not surprising for young troops, but not expected conduct for officers. Klein had a short timer's attitude, and everyone knew it.

***

On Hill 119, "Butch" Waddill of 1st Platoon did not know it but he would soon depart for the grunts as he was reassigned to 3rd Battalion, 5th Marines. This was fine by Martin as he found the older 2nd lieutenant pushy. He liked the new 2nd Platoon commander, 2nd Lieutenant Garry Parks, who had turned into a patrolling machine by running three patrols in January. Parks was adapting to the rigors of patrolling, while his newly arrived South Carolina friend, 2nd Lieutenant Tom McAdams, just seemed like a "good old boy" to Martin.[11] Fourth Platoon was led by the aggressive 2nd Lieutenant "Chuck" Overton, who was scheduled to flip up to Hill 119 on 11 January.

Meanwhile, on the hill, it was 1 January 1970 and, as the new year started, Waddill was bored, frustrated, and ready for a change. He would not let it affect him with his Marines. As he was good at communicating with his platoon, his firing of the hill's final protective fires as a New Year's celebration went over well.[12] He had pushed the weapons inspections down to his three team leaders after cleaning today. Enemy movement had picked up with five sightings that day by the Integrated Observation Device (IOD) Team *War Cloud* of 38 enemy working and moving around the southern railroad bridge to Go Noi Island. They had fired four fire missions and passed three of the movements over to *Prime Cut* on Hill 425 to observe and try for additional fire missions.[13] On 2 January, the IOD team had another five sightings, totaling 36 enemy. They called five fire missions resulting in five confirmed kills.[14] On that day, OP *Durham* was contacted by *Hostage King*, an OV-10 forward-observer aircraft, looking for work. The OP could only point the bird towards a raft on the Song Thu Bong. After observing the raft, *Hostage King* got reassigned to a higher-priority target out towards Thuong Duc special forces camp.

At noon on 3 January, Corporal Bayuk of the IOD team called Waddill to the tower. He was perplexed by over one hundred Vietnamese civilian men, women, and children 500 to 800 meters away on both sides of the abandoned railway berm. In Marine speak, they were just milling around. They were picking up grass and putting it in baskets and then dumping out the baskets.[15] Bayuk asked the lieutenant to take a look in the "Big Eyes." One could easily see green utilities worn underneath their white tops and black bottom "PJs."[16] *War Cloud* tried to call a fire mission with *Rice Krispies-Mike* who said no due to rules of engagement concerning the presence of women and children. Hence, the Marines were limited to observation only. Waddill called it in to Battalion at *Melody Time* and talked with Captain MacCaskill, the assistant operations officer (S-3A), explaining the situation. He knew MacCaskill was aggressive, so he was surprised to get, "Do not do anything, let me get back to you." An hour later, when MacCaskill called back, the group had split into two groups going to the unoccupied hamlets of Thon Bon (1) and Tho Son. As a result, no further action was taken. Waddill knew somebody inside the group of Vietnamese got a good close-up daylight look at Hill 119's defenses.[17] Over the next eight days, partially due to foul weather, activity was slow. Both sides hunkered down in cold driving rain. The IOD had nine sightings with nine fire missions and negative results due to vegetation, darkness, and low-lying ground fog.[18]

Coming up to the hill on 11 January was 4th Platoon, led by Chuck Overton. The prior evening in the Delta Company officers' hut, Chip Gregson, the experienced patrol leader, and XO of Delta, had a fairly long discussion with Overton on the hill's mission and tactics. Gregson, with the wisdom of one who had been recently wounded at close range by the enemy, was trying to provide some sage advice about booby traps and patrolling around a known hill in enemy territory—slow down and be cautious. Overton was nodding but Gregson did not believe he was listening.[19] The next day, 4th Platoon waited at LZ 401. Their insert had been bumped for the emergency extraction of Team *Pennywise.* Second Lieutenant Garry Parks, the patrol leader, had made point-to-point contact, killing the enemy point man, and grabbing a package of documents. They were back after 23 hours in the bush.[20] Overton waved to Parks as *Pennywise* trotted off the bird and 4th Platoon boarded both helicopters. They still got off early at 0900, arriving on Hill 119 at 0930 for the half-hour turn over. Waddill met Overton at the landing zone (LZ) and gave him some notes. First Platoon was off the hill by 1000.

Overton brought with him an experienced platoon. Sergeant Harvey remained his platoon sergeant; he and "Doc" Richardson both had prior stints on the hill. He also had two dogs for this flip, Champ, and Andy, handled by Sergeants Brookins and Matthews.[21] Dogs were fine in the winter with plenty of water available and they would do mostly nighttime duty at each end of the defensive oval perimeter. This freed up Marines for night patrols; Overton wanted to go hunting! Along with Overton was a new join to Delta Company, Gunnery Sergeant Terry Moore, who was coming up to learn the hill and ease his way back into patrolling.[22] Moore was a professional Recon Marine starting his third Recon tour in Vietnam. As a sergeant, he had served as an advisor assigned to the highly secretive and classified Military Assistance Command, Vietnam, Studies, and Observation Group (MACV–SOG) which was a cover name for the Special Operations Group headquartered in Saigon. His second tour was as a staff sergeant with 3rd Recon Battalion and then 3rd Force Recon Company. After a two-year break stateside, he volunteered for what he wanted to do: be with Reconnaissance Marines in combat. He was also smart enough to know everything changes month to month and year to year in combat and he had been gone long enough to know that changes would have occurred. Moore had told the lieutenant back at LZ 401 he was along for the ride; it was Overton's hill and Harvey's platoon but if the lieutenant wanted any help with the weapons, Moore was good to go. Overton reacted positively. "Gunny, you can start with the .50-cal machine gun and get us squared away."

Gunnery Sergeant Moore had also been given a tasker by the company commander, Captain Martin. He wanted a candid assessment of the hill's defenses and the enemy activity around it. Martin explained that, in the past three months, the reported enemy activity around Hill 119 had increased dramatically; it was the monsoon season so, in his mind, it should have decreased. He did not know if it really was more enemy movement or if it was the dramatically increased observation during both day and night by the technology associated with the secret IOD. Moore acknowledged his task and said he would not interfere with the hill's operations.[23] Moore had a week's notice before going to the OP, so he started his homework at the Delta Company Club, talking casually to Marines about Hill 119. To a man, they liked the hill. They thought it was not as dangerous as the bush, and not chickenshit like the rear at Camp Reasoner. Moore got a 180-degree view from the company XO, Lieutenant Gregson, who told Moore the hill was extremely dangerous.[24] The enemy tried to booby trap the OP inside its wire. The main infiltration routes from Base Area 116 in the Que Sons to Go Noi Island ran on both sides of the hill, and in fact, the shortest route was on the high-speed trail over the saddle that was 119's LZ. Bluntly, he pointed out that the OP was a thorn in the NVA's ass. Moore went to the S-3 shop and met with the ops chief, Master Sergeant Rene Regalot, and asked for the statistics on Hill 119. Regalot, another Recon professional, indicated that nobody had ever asked. He would have them worked up and get them to Moore. These two Marines implicitly trusted each other.[25] Next stop was the

S-2 (intelligence) hut where Moore met Staff Sergeant C. L. Wilson. Moore had used heat maps on his tour with MACV–SOG. He thought working them up may show him something. He held a class on Wilson with a 1:50,000 map sheet, placing a box around Hill 119, five kilometers by five kilometers with 119 in the center. Twenty-five square kilometers. He told Wilson to mark every booby trap by location with a "bt" and mark every sighting of the enemy with an "e" and every boat with a "b" to signify their respective locations over the past three months. Wilson liked the idea and said they could use it for all the OPs. Moore was fine with that as long as Wilson and his clerks did Hill 119 first. Wilson committed to having it in two days. While at S-2, Moore picked up a set of 1:50,000 maps for the 25 square kilometers around Hill 119.[26] He would laminate them himself after highlighting the key terrain. That night in his hooch, he marked all the north–south and east–west grid numbers with circles. He highlighted key terrain in yellow. With a roll of contact paper, which he had purchased in Okinawa, he got started. The lamination would protect the map from the rain and dirt.

That night, Staff Sergeant "Rabbit" Hare dropped in to get a free beer from Moore. Moore loved Hare like a brother. He had been with Moore on previous tours. If fact, he was Moore's point man on numerous patrols and they both hoped to continue that relationship but, for now, Hare was in Echo Company.[27] Hare asked what was going on. Moore said he was going up to Hill 119 and asked Hare if he knew anything about it, or whether he had been there? Hare said he had only seen the hill through the Big Eyes on Hill 425, which was the Echo Company OP.

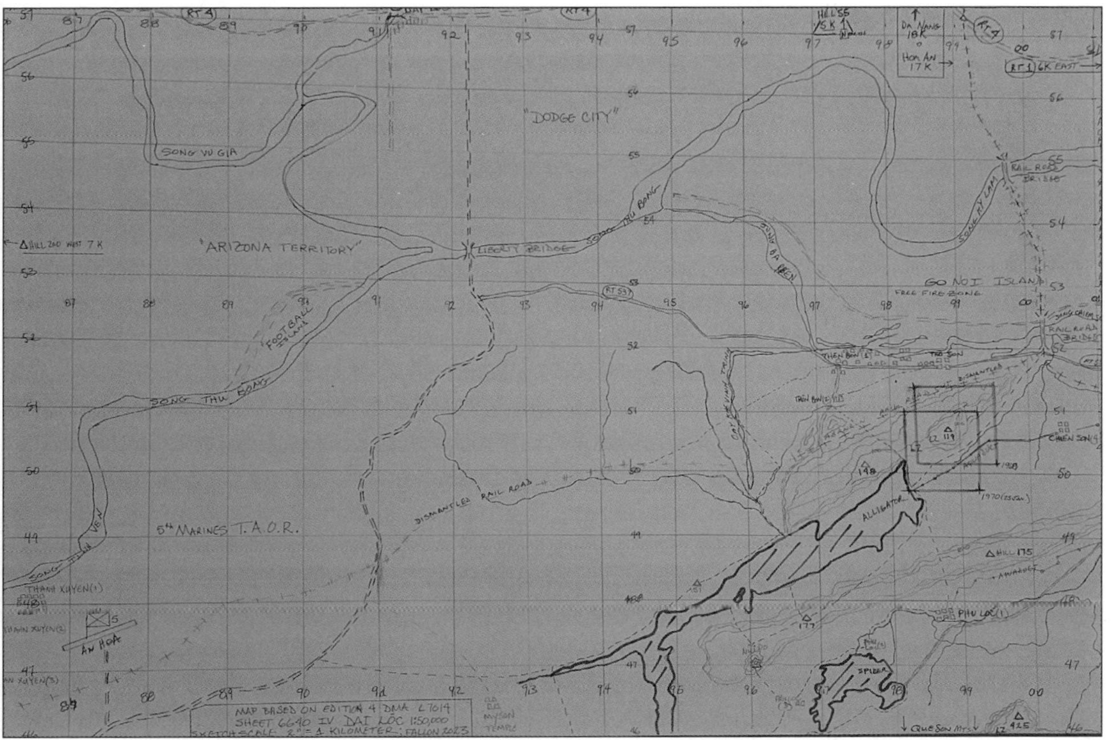

Two haven boxes sketched over Hill 119, 1970. (M. Fallon)

"Fine help you are!" Moore said, tossing him another can of beer before asking about the Big Eyes. Hare said he did not believe it until he had looked through them himself. Yes, you could count individuals, see colors, and count weapons. Hare added that when you did a walk-off patrol from the OP, the Big Eyes could watch both your front and back.[28] Moore had not thought of that and thanked Hare for the tactical tip.

Moore and Hare were working on the maps and visualizing the hill. What immediately jumped out at Moore were the two hills higher than 119, Hills 148 west-southwest one kilometer away and Hill 175 south-southeast at 1,400 meters. Both could shoot down on the lower, exposed Hill 119.

As the Marines continued their map study, they discovered that the hill was really just a finger with a trail on the ridgeline, or top of the finger. It had four draws that appeared on the map to be blind to the top. While the young Marines might have thought OP duty was easy, Gregson's words were ringing in the back of Moore's mind. He repeated it aloud to Hare: "The enemy was booby-trapping the Marines inside their own wire."[29]

Moore's gut told him the blind draws were being used to bring up booby traps. He told Hare that night he would have some scouting to do outside the wire. The next afternoon, Moore was sitting on his back steps cleaning his M16 when "Top" Regalot walked up. Regalot, true to his word, had two statistics charts on enemy sightings off Hill 119 for him.

Hill 119 Enemy Sightings, Pre-IOD v Post IOD

Pre-IOD / Post-IOD	NVA/VC sighted	Fire Missions	EKIA	Average
Pre: 19 October–10 November (21 days)[30]	200	12	1	1.2 sightings per day of 9.5 NVA/VC
Post: 9 November– 10 January (62 days)[31]	1,158	141	179	2.7 sightings per day of 18.6 NVA/VC

Moore looked at the charts, comparing before and after, and asked Regalot what he thought. The master sergeant was not one to mince words. He said that pre-IOD, clearly the hill was sleepy, laid back, and, for whatever reason, did not see the enemy walking past them. The enemy knew they were on the hill and knew how far they could observe so they just avoided them but continued their infiltration and rice-harvesting missions. Post-IOD, the hill's observation range had dramatically increased, which accounted for the increase in sightings, but the enemy did not know it! What they did know was that Hill 119 had become a killing machine. Looking at the numbers, Regalot said, in the past two months, the hill had killed on average three NVA every day, and its sister, Hill 425, had an even higher kill rate. Over the past three months, these two Recon OPs were the leading killers in the 1st Marine Division.[32]

Moore asked him how he knew that? Rene said he had run the numbers.

"Do you know what it means?" Moore asked.

"Well, if it were you or I, we would attack the fixed pimple and pop it."

"Guess you are going to take credit for this great analysis," Moore said, tossing Regalot a cold beer.

"Of course," Top said, and both laughed. They agreed the enemy had to react as the hill sat astride both main infiltration routes between Base Area 116 in the Que Sons and their stronghold for rice production on Go Noi Island. Additionally, the hill could now observe the main west-to-east infiltration route across the Arizona Territory to Go Noi Island. No doubt the enemy, through their village watch system, knew something had changed on Hill 119 and had to take action to counter it. Moore and Regalot figured the NVA had a number of options. They could just change their infiltration route. That was easy to say, but giving Hill 119 a wide berth added a day's hike. They could take the Gregson warning approach and booby trap them inside the wire. Or they could attack the hill. Moore needed a little time on the hill. He told Regalot about Wilson in S-2 doing heat maps. He asked his friend to sit on the statistics for two days so he could get up to the hill on 11 January. Regalot said it was Moore's initiative so nobody would be asking. He would get to Wilson, and they would not present the stats and heat maps to their principals until 12 January.[33] They drank to that. Moore was beginning to draw conclusions but knew he needed to walk the ground instead of making any recommendations two days before even seeing the hill in person. The next morning, Moore went to the S-3 bunker to review previous patrol reports and was told to walk back up the trail to Wilson in S-2 as he kept the past reports. Retracing his steps, he entered Wilson's S-2 hut and asked to review old reports. Wilson offered coffee and showed Moore the filing system. Moore focused in on the crew-served weapons each platoon was taking to the hill and jotted down the average by weapons. He had a rule of thumb for weapons and ammo—more was always better! The platoons had been averaging three M60s, so Moore made a note to add a fourth. He would talk to the lieutenant about keeping 2nd Platoon's XM174 40-mm grenade launcher as a loaner to them.[34] With the .50-caliber machine gun the lieutenant had talked about, that meant a crew-served weapon could be positioned on each of the six avenues of approach.

On the morning of 11 January, Moore felt good. He had prepared well and was looking forward to heading back to the field with Marines again. When they landed, Moore was the last man off the second bird. He recognized Staff Sergeant Mushett from 1st Platoon and walked over and talked with him for ten minutes. The two lieutenants were exchanging notes, and the troops were all headed to their bunkers. Moore asked Mushett where he had slept. The experienced staff noncommissioned officer (SNCO) said he stayed in the communications bunker. Because of the radios, it was dry and large. The only drawback was hearing radios squawk all night. Moore said he liked the idea, so they walked over and Mushett showed him a cot just inside the front blackout flap that served as a door. The 4th Platoon sergeant, Harvey, was getting the troops squared away. Moore walked over and climbed the steps to the tower. A lance corporal was on watch, said not much was going on, and started showing Moore the secret IOD. Moore looked through the Big Eyes and admitted to himself that Hare was not exaggerating. You could see a lot of detail. The lance corporal said he would yell for, or get, the gunny on the next fire mission. About 1230, Moore was at the .50-cal position accessing the gun when the tower yelled down for him to come up. He walked 20 feet over and climbed the stairs, thinking to himself that the tower was a rocket-propelled grenade (RPG) magnet, and not the place to be in a fight. The same lance corporal stepped away from the Big Eyes tripod to give Moore a look. He was looking north at a large area and did not see anything that jumped out. The Marine took Moore over to the waist-high north tower wall, pointed down the hill, and said, "Just past the dirt road and close to river, see the smoke?" Moore said he saw smoke. The Marine said there were Viet Cong (VC) in the grass around the smoke. Moore went back to the Big Eyes. He could clearly see the smoke and the grass moving but saw no people. Not to be deterred, the IOD team, *War Cloud*, called a fire mission.[35] Moore thought it was slow coming, but the forward observer (FO) explained, because he had called smoke or cooking fire, it was a lower-priority target for the Fire Direction Center. Moore watched the rounds impacting on top of the smoke. Six rounds, no adjustment. He liked that. Thanking the FO, he went back to the .50-cal. There were three additional fire missions that afternoon that Moore observed from the machine-gun position.[36] He broke down the weapon and cleaned it, then reset the headspace with a nickel he had brought with him for that purpose. Its width was perfect for the key headspace setting.[37] He later told Lieutenant Overton he was ready when the lieutenant and Sergeant Harvey wanted to start. Overton said they'd start in the morning. Moore heated a C-rat can of beans and weenies, and a small can of cheese which he added to the beans. Sitting on the trench-line berm watching the sun set in the west, Moore could see why the Marines liked to come to the hill. Three Marines to a bunker, reasonable watches, and a dry cot. He thought it would be easy to get lazy here. He turned in early. The radios across the bunker from him, with candles by each one, did not bother him as he dozed off.

Just after midnight, there was a stir and elevated conversation in the comm bunker. Moore had his trousers and boots on so he got up and checked. He was told by the duty watch that Champ, the scout dog, had alerted. Overton had already put the hill on alert. The first night most Marines had been up talking; Moore might have been the only one sleeping. He did not want to get in the way, so he walked over to the .50-cal position and took the tarp off the weapon and moved a box of ammunition over. He then sat, watched, and listened.

Harvey had gone down the trench line to Echo Bunker to talk with Sergeant Brookins, Champ's handler. Overton was in the tower with Sergeant Bayuk, the noncommissioned officer in charge (NCOIC) of the IOD team, looking through the night-observation device (NOD). He could hear Bayuk calling a fire mission and Overton telling him to check-fire as it was too close. About that time he heard the distinctive "bloop, bloop, bloop" of three M79 rounds being fired. Overton was leaning over the tower wall yelling for 60-mm illumination to the Marines on the mortar. It was all over in three minutes. Lieutenant Overton called for a quick huddle in the comm bunker while they wrote up the SALUTE (Size, Activity, Location, Unit, Time, and Equipment) report.[38] Both Bayuk and the lieutenant had seen five NVA in green utilities. They were crawling slowly up the northeast draw and were approximately twenty meters away from the wire when the M79 rounds were fired. With the first bloop, they turned around and walked slowly back down the draw in no rush, just away. Clearly the hill had been probed. In Moore's mind, the NVA had observed the change of platoons and were assessing the new unit on its first night. Why was another question. Overton wanted the area checked out. Moore said there was no need to go tonight as they saw them depart, so he volunteered for a wire check 360 in the morning. It would give him an opportunity to view the hill from the same direction as the enemy and allow him to look for weaknesses in the defense for his assessment for Captain Martin. Moore did not believe they would find anything where the probe was, but it was solid security to check your wire. You also checked the direction of your Claymore mines. The NVA liked to simply turn the mines around 180 degrees so when a Marine smashed the hellbox, the explosion came directly at him.

After the short meeting, Overton put the hill on 50 percent alert, so Moore volunteered to stay up since he had had three hours of sleep. At 0425, Moore was sitting looking south towards the Que Sons when he saw muzzle flashes. He walked over to the tower and asked them to swing the tripod around and look at Hill 175. Sure enough they confirmed muzzle flashes from the forward slope appearing to come towards them.[39] There was no sound and it was too far for small arms. However, it was enough to call a fire mission. *War Cloud* called *Rice Krispies-Mike* and got rounds out and on to the forward slope quickly. Moore watched the flashes of the Arty impacts from the south trench line. In the morning, he commented to Bayuk that his team had gotten that fire mission extremely fast. Bayuk told him that Hill 175 was an on-call target preregistered, and the battery was not firing for anyone else when they called last night.

January 12, at 0710, Moore led a seven-man patrol out the west gate to do the 360 wire check. They found nothing in the northeast draw where the probe had taken place. Moore found one weakness or blind spot in the hill's defenses on the southeast side with a secondary small draw that intersected the ridgeline 100 meters east of Echo Bunker. After the walk-off wire patrol, Moore visited with Bayuk in the tower and asked that he and his team focus southeast. He requested a systematic scan of the north slope of Hill 175 facing Hill 119. Bayuk acknowledged they had never done it, and they would get to it. At 1610, that afternoon, Bayuk picked up a construction site on the lower portion of Hill 175's north slope, about one kilometer south of the OP. He brought Moore up and showed him wood cuttings on the side of a trail. Early that night, *War Cloud* picked up lights in the supposedly empty Thon Bon (1). They called a fire mission, which caused the lights to go out. Overton hosted a late dinner in his bunker for Moore and Harvey to go over the upcoming days. Moore reported his concern for the gap in ground-firing coverage to the southeast and suggested they move an M60 machine gun to Delta Bunker. The gun could not shoot down the draw, but neither could anyone come out of it where it intersected the finger without the 60 cutting them in half. Overton agreed and Harvey departed to make it happen. Moore told Overton he was sure the enemy was on the forward slope of Hill 175 and that he would like to run a patrol over there to check it out. Overton said it was outside the haven, but he would ask Battalion. With the meeting finished, Overton went to the comm bunker and called *Melody Time* S-3A. About ten minutes later, Captain MacCaskill came on the net. Overton asked to meet on the secure encrypted net and switched radios. Overton asked for a 24-hour Recon haven Upper Left AT9850, Lower Right BT0148. It was a standard six-grid rectangle with Hill 175 almost centered. MacCaskill told him to plan it but do not go till he got the haven cleared and coordinated with Division, 11th Marines, and had notified the OP on Hill 425. Overton found Moore and Harvey at Delta Bunker with the M60, putting in aiming stakes on the parapet. Having them step out into the shallow trench, he said MacCaskill was agreeable and was getting clearances. Moore said he wanted five volunteers. Overton wanted to go but knew better. He would stay on the hill. The gung-ho Harvey volunteered on the spot. Moore told him it would not be a wire patrol but a full-on Recon patrol in uncovered terrain. Harvey said he would get four other volunteers and meet Moore back in the larger comm bunker in ten minutes. Moore went back and put together his patrol order by the book. He knew he would be judged.

In the comm bunker was Harvey and the four volunteers, plus an audience of four radio operators, Overton, and Bayuk from IOD. Moore had remembered "Rabbit" Hare's idea of having Big Eyes watch their front, thus the inclusion of Bayuk. Moore gave his patrol order, reading it from his notes and assigning patrol positions Harvey had recommended. He asked Bayuk to dedicate a radio to their patrol frequency in the tower and watch them after they crossed the aqueduct. Moore said to the Marines, "Make your preparations, a one-day patrol, ammo over food, and inspection at 0430." He asked Overton for comments. Overton reminded the Marines that the hill had their backs and expressed his desire to go. He asked them all if they had questions. With none, the meeting broke up well past midnight. Moore went to his cot to prepare his gear. He heard the radio call from Battalion come in saying the one-day haven had been cleared. At 0425, Moore moved from the comm bunker to the mortar pit. Harvey already had the team there and had inspected them. Moore had the Marines jump up and down for noise check, then he had both radios, callsign *Durham-Alpha,* do radio checks with *Durham* and *War Cloud.* He told the team to make a head call, drink a half canteen of water, and meet him in 15 minutes at Echo Bunker. There, Moore checked cammie face paint for shiny foreheads on each Marine. He had a burnt cork he used to make instant black smudge. The comm check had already been made so he told one of the watch Marines in Echo to walk back and tell the lieutenant, the tower, and the comm bunker that *Durham-Alpha* was Oscar Mike, on the move.

It was 0457 and still dark. Moore would be walking deuce point doing the navigation. He put Harvey as tail-end Charlie. Departing the east gate, Moore found the blind southeast draw and dropped into it. It was narrow and had thick growth at the top. They moved slowly down the draw in the cool night air. The sun was trying to rise over the East China Sea. The draw opened and they crossed a horizontal high-speed one-foot-wide trail that ran east–west and was unexpected. They were 200 feet above the valley floor and the scrub had opened up. On the floor, they could see in both directions along the wide high-speed floor trail running east–west. Moore quickened the pace as he wanted to be across this danger area before first light. They put security out crossing the trail, the aqueduct, and the far-side trail. As security went out, Harvey was coming up over the aqueduct. Moore pointed due south and headed across a dry rice paddy. He pushed the pace. They would take a break in the boulder field once they reached it. They stopped and called *War Cloud* and *Durham* with a position report. *War Cloud* said he could not see *Durham-Alpha,* but the crest of Hill 175 was clear. Moore thought that both reports were good news. His gut told him to summit now in the false dawn. With hand and arm signals, he got the team moving and pushed the pace straight uphill for 400 meters. They summited the ridgeline with the sunrise. They were east of the old infantry position on the top. Moore knew it would be booby-trapped. Just over the summit, he signaled for a 360 defense. They set up a clandestine OP. The team was in a good hide. Using the 7 × 50 binos, Moore shared the observation duties with each Marine, all laying prone, feet inboard and face and rifle outboard, the two radios in the center.

At 1330, Harvey spotted four enemy in black PJs in a draw below them to their north, towards Hill 119. He pointed to Moore, who could see them visually. Moore gave the saddle-up hand signal and then the two arms out at shoulder length putting the team on-line horizontally. The Marines had not seen that signal since boot camp but to a man they executed, standing up and walking on-line slowly and quietly downhill. When one of the NVA saw the Marines, Moore opened fire, as did the rest of the team after him. All four enemy dropped to the ground. There was no return fire. The team could see no movement. Harvey had a grenade out, but Moore waved him off, instead yelling "Chieu Hoi." One NVA put his hands in the air while still behind a big boulder. Moore yelled a second time, and he got to his knees behind the boulder, hands out. Moore pushed Harvey out to his left and another Marine to his right for security. Signaling the others to stay down, Moore got up and walked forward, M16 at his waist and pointed at the Chieu Hoi. Laying the Vietnamese face down, he zip-tied his wrists behind his back and pushed his head down, indicating he should remain down and in place. Moore checked the ravine. There were two bodies, no weapons, and the fourth enemy was gone.[40]

Moore signaled the team to center on him and the prisoner. He called *Durham* and asked to speak to the lieutenant. Overton came to the net and Moore said, "Six, we got one and we're coming in. Call for a chopper to come retrieve him, give us two hours, and tell *War Cloud* to watch our rear and to scope the dam." Putting the prisoner in between the two radio operators for movement, he told Harvey, who knew the area better than him, to take deuce point, trail walk back to the hill and stop when they were 100 meters away. Moore would walk tail end. If anyone came for them, it would be from the rear. Harvey took the team straight down the ravine through the boulder field to the closest trail parallel to the aqueduct and turned 90 degrees west. Then he headed straight towards the dam at the base of Alligator Lake. At the dam, they turned north and took the uphill trail to the saddle LZ. One hundred meters out, he stopped the team. Moore came forward, grabbed the prisoner by the collar and moved him forward past Harvey to the point position. If the VC had booby-trapped the trail then he would be first and would know where to look. He told Harvey that he was now tail end. The team moved up the trail toward the LZ. Moore was second behind the prisoner. He told the radio operator to call ahead and specifically tell Bravo Bunker, as they were coming in and would see the Vietnamese first, not to fire. They had made it back to the hill in an hour and 20 minutes. They were met at the LZ by a group of curious Marines wanting to see the prisoner and take photos. Moore told Harvey to give the prisoner water, sandbag his head, and sit him inside the first strand of wire with security. He also told him to send a fire team west of the LZ halfway up Hill 148 for security. Finished with instructions, he then turned and reported to Overton, who wanted to hear all about it. They went to the comm bunker and worked on a SALUTE spot report for *Melody Time.* The requested helo arrived about two hours later. It was a lone UH-1 Huey and would take the prisoner, who was about 35 years old with a high and tight haircut, to LZ 20 near Marble Mountain which serviced the III MAF prisoner-of-war (POW) compound which also housed the 3rd ITT (Interrogator Translator Team). The team would interview and then interrogate the prisoner to determine his unit, his job, and what he was doing on Hill 175. That night, the Hill 119 brain trust huddled again in Overton's bunker. Overton, Moore, Harvey, and Bayuk had coffee and talked over what they knew collectively. Bayuk said, in his view, the two northern hamlets were waystations where the NVA coming from the Que Sons met the VC guides for the follow-on journey to Go Noi Island. That made sense to them since the NVA were soldiers from North Vietnam and would need local guides. Moore was still concerned with hill defense. They had confirmed that Hill 175 was a threat. That left Hill 148. Moore proposed another walk-off to check out 148. Overton agreed and said he would start working on getting clearance for a haven around Hill 148. He radioed battalion and requested a four-grid-square haven around Hill 148 for 14 January. The clearance did not come back quickly as it had to be sent from Recon Battalion to Division and then 5th Marines in An Hoa. It was the tactical area of responsibility (TAOR) of the 5th Marines, who had it sub-leased to 2nd Battalion, 5th Marines, who patrolled the area. They would need to give it up for 24 hours to allow for the Recon patrol. Deconfliction by both terrain on the ground and specific times was a task, but everyone understood it prevented friend-on-friend fights. Standard deconfliction methods were assigning a space of ground and a time during which one specific unit was to control it. In this case, *Durham* wanted Hill 148 for 24 hours on 14 January.

Then *Durham*'s attention was diverted when, at around 1100, *War Cloud* called over to the comm bunker. They had Vietnamese walking slowly up the north trail. They were carrying a South Vietnamese flag to indicate they were friendly. Overton and Harvey had a standard operating procedure (SOP) for these visits. Harvey would take a security team along with Doc Richardson and a radio and go out and meet them at the railroad berm. Moore watched with interest from the roof of Alpha Bunker. He liked the procedures for meeting the Vietnamese. You did not know their intentions, so why let them get close to you? Meeting them downhill, 500 meters out, kept them away. The security team was bracketed with two M60 machine guns and two mortars ready to support them, while Big Eyes could watch the hamlets below for trouble. Harvey radioed the hill that Doc said one woman was severely wounded and in a parachute stretcher. All seven were military age, but without ID cards; he suspected all of them to be VC. Overton called it in and was told to detain and evacuate all seven.[41] Harvey searched them and brought them up, sitting outside the outer wire of the LZ. About an hour later, a CH-46 came out of Marble Mountain Air Facility (MMAF), radioing the hill to pick up the VC suspects. They arrived with military police on board who took control of all seven and took them to the III MAF POW compound for processing.

Meanwhile, inside the communications bunker, the Marines were listening carefully to the radio squawk-box speaker. It had Team *Spoonbill* (Delta Company, 3rd Platoon, 2nd team) on the radio. They had made point-to-point contact with 15 to 20 NVA in the Que Son Mountains.[42] They had downed the first three NVA and then broke contact. *Spoonbill* was now running and being pursued by the larger NVA unit. The Marines in the bunker recognized Corporal Dennis Swick, the team leader, urgently requesting an emergency extraction. *Pennywise* on Hill 425 was relaying the request back to *Melody Time*, the approval authority. After approval, the Direct Air Support Center (DASC) had to find the helos for the extract. An hour later, they were still being chased, with *Spoonbill* running down a ravine. They ran directly into and through a base camp that, fortunately, was empty. An OV-10, callsign *Hostage Turtle,* came on station, and started supporting the team. To find the team quickly, *Spoonbill* hit *Turtle* with a mirror flash and said the base camp and enemy pursuers were 300 meters south and up the draw from them. *Hostage Turtle,* in a slick move, rolled the OV-10 over and put two "Willie Pete" (white phosphorous) rockets into the base camp which *Spoonbill* said was on target. With that, *Turtle* or rather the aerial observer, callsign *Cowpoke,* in the back seat, had the first F-4 rolling in and dropping 250-pound bombs, followed by a second F-4 dropping more 250-pound bombs. That bought time. The CH-46 extract package of two troop-carrier helos flew from MMAF to LZ 401. There, a rope master from S-3 training ran out with the extract officer and attached the aluminum ladder to the ramp of the lead CH-46 while the battalion's air liaison officer (ALO) briefed the pilots on *Spoonbill's* situation, location, and radio frequency. It took ten minutes, and then they were off. The rope master would ride along to help the crew with the ladder, and the Recon Battalion extract officer served as Recon's representative with the pilots to advise them on the team's situation. All extract officers were seasoned patrol leaders with numerous patrols under their belts.

Flying south, the two CH-46s picked up two UH-1 gunships that had been vectored their way by the division DASC. The pilots talked with *Hostage Turtle* who said he would mark the enemy location with rockets and move out of the way, letting the two gunships make runs on either side of the extract helo. The extract helo had to come to a complete hover 100 feet above the team who were huddled in a creek bed with terrain on both sides higher than the helo. One gunship would hose down each finger while the CH-46 hovered and dropped the ladder. Then the team climbed onto the ladder two at a time, hooking in with snap-links for safety. Popping smoke when the patrol leader hooked on, as well as a radio confirmation with the extract bird, they were ready to pull out. Recon had had numerous incidents with a Marine being inadvertently left behind. These procedures had been designed to prevent that from happening. During the three minutes of hovering in one place, every NVA within sight was trained to shoot at the helo to knock it out of the sky. The Recon Marines loved the pilots and crews for putting their lives on the line to get them out of a shit sandwich. This extract was being flown by the *Purple Fox* squadron, whose motto was "Give A Shit." The extract officer was the experienced XO of Delta Company, Chip Gregson, who, returning to LZ 401 was surprised when the new 2nd Lieutenant McAdams got off the ladder with Team *Spoonbill.*[43] Since the team was from his platoon, he had decided to go on the patrol, birddogging and learning from Corporal Swick. McAdams admitted afterwards the ladder, which he had not had time to be trained on, scared the shit out him.[44]

Back on Hill 119, the clearance for the Hill 148 patrol had come through. Moore and Overton huddled. Moore said since it was late he could take the same team he had yesterday over to Hill 148, leaving Sergeant Harvey at the LZ with the seven VC suspects and the lieutenant on the hill. He said he could go over it and come back before nightfall. Overton approved. Moore told *Durham-Alpha* to saddle up. They did radio checks with *Durham* and *War Cloud.* Moore got on the radio while at the LZ and talked to Bayuk in the tower, asking for a look ahead. With a roger on radio, Moore took point himself and walked out the west gate across the LZ. He stopped, spreading out the team's dispersion on the LZ. He waved Harvey over to confirm something. Moore turned north and departed the LZ on the main trail for five feet and then took an immediate turn west and broke brush on a steep sidehill walk where the left foot was 12 inches higher than the right foot. Moore knew there would be no booby traps on such a slope. He took his time and patrolled over the 500 meters to about twenty feet below and outside the military crest of the old infantry position on the summit. He circled the entire crest from the outside, slowly walking and looking. About three-quarters around on the southwest slope, which was the unobservable position from Hill 119, they crossed a game trail heading down the reverse slope towards Alligator Lake, which was below them. On the game trail, he found fresh boot prints and one set of fresh sandal prints. Moore judged them to be less than 48 hours old. The grass was also matted down on both sides as if the enemy sat and waited there last night or this morning.[45] Moore thought the seven VC giving up that morning had been a distraction for the hill to allow an observer or two to lay prone on the side of the hill and observe operations on Hill 119. Moore now knew that, for the past three consecutive days, the hill had been probed and observed by the enemy. This was how they operated. The NVA were professionals. They were detailed planners based on specific intelligence they had developed. They would have the hill's defenses and gun positions down. Hence, this was an NVA unit planning a surprise for his OP. Moore had what he needed, time to head back to 119 and then talk with Overton.

Durham-Alpha saddled up and radioed they were coming in. Moore finished the 360 walk around Hill 148 on the side of the hill, the south side being very steep and falling off towards Alligator Lake—no trail walking. They cut over to the main north entrance and came in the LZ gate. After he thanked the team and explained the importance of sidehill, he told the Marines it was better to be uncomfortable than to fall prey to a booby trap where the walking was easy. He dismissed the team and then found Overton and invited himself to dinner. Overton asked if he wanted the brain trust, but Moore said he preferred a one-on-one meeting. Overton knew something must be up but waited for the Gunny to come over for dinner. Over a shared helmet of C-ration stew, made tolerable by Tabasco sauce, Moore shared his concerns about the hill, its defense, and the aggressive actions by the enemy which indicated they were planning something. He said for the past six months they just went around the hill but now that Big Eyes was impacting them they had shown renewed interest. He suggested they get on the secure radio and talk to the battalion. He said by now Master Sergeant Regalot and Staff Sergeant Wilson had briefed their bosses on the threat to Hill 119. Overton said the secure radio net was down, something about the KY encryption device having a wrong key. They could shackle a coded message but to say what? They were concerned. Best to focus on improving the hill's defenses. Moore recommended burning out some growth in the southeast draw. Overton liked that and knew the Marines would enjoy burning and blasting over digging and filling sandbags. On 15 January, the burn-and-blast working parties set out after the standard morning wire patrol. At 1505, *War Cloud* observed one VC in black PJs moving on a trail southeast of the OP and inside the Recon haven. Bayuk treated it like a fire mission except on his radio he called the comm bunker and asked for a 60-mm mortar mission. The mortar team ran to both mortar pits as Bayuk now simply yelled out of the tower the compass heading and distance. Both tubes dropped a Willie Pete round. Bayuk yelled for them to fire-for-effect. Each tube dropped three high-explosive rounds sequentially and had six rounds in the air before the first hit. The Marines were now excited, but Bayuk could see nothing due to thick foliage in the impact area.[46] Overton and Moore wondered what one VC was doing 300 meters away in the daylight?

Moore did not sleep well. His gut told him to keep working on the enemy situation outside the OP. He talked to Overton and asked if he could talk to SNCOs in the rear and have them work up a heat map for Hill 119 for the past five days. With a nod, Moore went to the comm bunker and called *Melody Time*, requesting the S-3 Chief. Regalot's voice was back at him instantly. Moore asked if he remembered the heat map Wilson made and to have him make one up for past five days, and for them both to show it to leadership. Top Regalot knew Moore would not ask if he did not think it was worth the effort. He would make it happen that day.[47]

That afternoon, 16 January, the battalion S-2 shop got a direct call from 3rd ITT. They said they had the POW interrogation report and were sending it to the Surveillance and Reconnaissance Center at III MAF and to Division G-2 but thought Recon Battalion would want a look. Not being able to talk on the unsecure phone, Staff Sergeant Wilson was all over it and told them he would send a driver over to pick it up. His fellow staff sergeant said not to bother, he'd deliver it after dropping off the G-2 copy at Division Hill in exchange for a beer at the SNCO club. Good to his word, the 3rd ITT staff NCO climbed the stairs into the S-2 hut inside Camp Reasoner. He handed Wilson a sealed envelope with the POW interrogation report. Wilson handed the envelope to the S-2, 1st Lieutenant J. C. Creg Howland. The ITT Marine asked Wilson if he wanted to read the report. Wilson said, "You can tell me at the club, and I have briefed the lieutenant that it's hot." With that, the two staff sergeants headed like cows to a barn to the First Recon SNCO/Officers Club, which was up the hill, for the cold one that had been promised.[48] Howland opened the sealed envelope which had a second sealed envelope inside, which was SOP for couriered classified documents. He logged the document-control numbers into the S-2 log. Opening the report, he was not surprised by what he read.

That afternoon, Top Regalot and Wilson had brought the three heat maps covering pre-IOD, IOD period, and then the past five days, for his review. This was just confirmation. The report said the POW captured on 13 January off Hill 119 was a member of the T89 Sapper Battalion. The battalion, one of two sapper battalions in the 2nd NVA Division, had the hill under observation in order to develop an attack plan.[49] Howland knew this approach was consistent with NVA doctrine. He put the report and the three heat maps in one folder. Grabbing his cover, he walked out of the S-2 shop and downhill on the trail to the S-3 bunker. Walking straight in through the blackout flaps he knew his way to the back left corner and through another flap into the S-3's space. "Major, you need to see this!" Major Mattiace took the report and read it, then looked at the three heat maps and said "So?" Howland said it indicated the NVA was going to hit Hill 119. Mattiace called for his Alpha and Chief. Both Captain MacCaskill and Master Sergeant Regalot came to his small space. Mattiace handed the documents over, saying that Howland thought 119 was going to get hit. Howland bit his lip as that was not his conclusion. Mattiace asked them what they thought.

MacCaskill did not want to commit so he deferred to Top Regalot who, knowing the situation, said "Sir, Gunnery Seargeant Moore is on the hill and the truth is this is his work. If Moore is concerned, then the command should be concerned."[50] MacCaskill piped up, "Sir, we should show this to the Old Man."

Mattiace did not like being interrupted. This was an interruption. "No shit, Sherlock!"

Grabbing his cover, he gathered everything together and stormed out of the S-3 bunker to climb the hill to the battalion commander's hut. The hut was at the top of the trail from the LZ, on stilts to make a level floor. The front porch was on the battalion road, with a screen door opening into the commander's office in the front half. The back half was sleeping quarters. It also had a back deck that overlooked LZ 401 and had a panoramic view of Da Nang Bay in the distance. Mattiace wanted to catch the colonel and brief him on the POW information before he headed to chow. He knocked on the screen door and kept walking in as Grace said "Enter." He knew not to talk; he just opened the envelope and handed Grace the classified interrogation report. Grace read the report. Not one to rush, he asked Mattiace to come back after dinner at 1830 with the S-2 and company commander for a pow-wow. He then asked for his driver to be sent in. As Mattiace departed, the driver, who had been sitting on the porch next to the only electric water cooler in Camp Reasoner, was already coming through the door. Grace asked the corporal to tell the sergeant major to join him for dinner and that he would be departing in 5 minutes. Five minutes later, walking out of his office, Sergeant Major Harold Skinner was standing in the center of the street. He snapped off a drill field salute with a "Good afternoon, sir." Walking up the hill to the Recon mess hall, Grace briefed Skinner on the Hill 119 situation. Then he asked for the sergeant major's thoughts.

"Well, sir, if the 'gooners' want to attack the hill, our Marines will kick their ass! But, it would not hurt to go up there and look at the defenses."

"Sergeant Major, that is exactly what I was thinking."

Both Grace and Skinner were Korean War vets. Both had fought the Chinese. Both knew the communist forces would try to make a propaganda statement with a massive attack to wipe out an entire hill. "Not on my watch!" Grace said to Skinner as they entered Gunnery Sergeant Paradise's mess hall.

Returning from dinner, at 1830, Grace came out of his sleeping space to his office to find his team ready for the pow-wow. Standing around the room were Major Mattiace (S-3), 1st Lieutenant Howland (S-2), Captain Martin (Delta Company's commanding officer), Skinner, and Master Sergeant Regalot.

The colonel's driver had pulled extra seats in from the porch. They all waited for the colonel to sit. As they sat, he asked for their thoughts. Regalot, being junior, got the nod to talk first. He repeated what he had told the S-3 earlier. "Gunnery Sergeant Moore was solid and if Moore was concerned, they should be concerned." Regalot had credibility with Grace as he was also a Korean War infantry veteran.[51] Lieutenant Howland provided background on the T89 Sapper Battalion, saying they were the elite troops of the 2nd Division. They were North Vietnamese and, after graduating from infantry training, they became school-trained sappers. Besides engineering, they were trained in reconnaissance and explosives. Captain Martin wanted to take credit. He told the colonel he had told Moore to do an assessment of the hill. Grace cut him off with a wave of his hand. Mattiace decided to ask the colonel what he thought. Grace said he believed the information was credible. He liked the heat maps and wanted to do them for all the OPs. He already knew Skinner's thoughts but wanted to give the sergeant major a chance. On cue, Skinner said, "Sir, believe we should go up to Hill 119 and take a look for ourselves." Grace smiled, turned to Mattiace, and requested he set up a trip. He asked for final thoughts; there were none since the decision had been made, so he told the men to inform Division G-2 and G-3 of their thoughts and plans for Hill 119. Grace knew the importance of keeping the division staff appraised.

On 17 January, Overton, at Moore's urging, sent another walk-off patrol to scout out Hill 175. Sergeant Harvey led this patrol. Eight hundred meters south of Hill 119, on the lowest part of Hill 175's north slope, the patrol found a partially constructed rocket site. This was an important development because, once completed, 122-mm rockets could be launched from the site. *Durham-Alpha* found three firing positions with two rocket positions in each. They were dug 10 inches in diameter and were 6–9 feet deep, oriented directly at Hill 119. Two of the sites were almost complete. The three sites were spread 25 meters apart and were 10 feet by 12 feet of cleared ground. Based on fresh grass and broken branches, the site was less than two days old and had been worked on the previous night. Harvey called in the grid, turned around and made for the OP. Overton radioed in the SALUTE report,[52] which just further confirmed what the hill had been reporting. The rocket site confirmed in Lieutenant Colonel Grace's mind that the hill would be attacked in a ground attack supported by rockets and mortars.

On the 18th, the S-3 huddled with his air officer on the best way to get up to Hill 119. They did not want to impact the daily operations of the Recon insert/extract package of two CH-46 and two gunships, so they decided to frag a separate mission for their battalion commander. The Air Tasking Order process normally took three days, but the ALO thought he could get it locked on in two days for the morning of the 20th. They decided to also visit Hill 425, Echo Company's OP and the 5th Marines Combat Operations Center in An Hoa, all three of which were south of Da Nang. The air officer started a roster and soon realized he would have to frag a CH-46 for the day. On the roster he had the colonel, sergeant major, S-3 rep, S-2 rep, Delta's commander, Echo's commander, and more strap hangers. He sent the air request in for 20 January for ten passengers in all-day round-robin flights throughout the Da Nang TAOR.

On 18 January at the OP, *War Cloud* was busy with separate sightings of 10, 7, 2, and 11 NVA/VC. They called three fire missions with six confirmed kills. The fourth fire mission was denied due to RoK Marines being too close to the grid called.[53] January 19 was a quiet day. *War Cloud* had only one sighting of five NVA wearing green utilities, carrying rifles, and moving on a trail into Thon Bon (1) hamlet below the hill. They called a fire mission with *Rice Krispies-Mike* at An Hoa. The unoccupied hamlet, Thon Bon (1), was an on-call target, so they got rounds out in under a minute. They shot a battery-one, all six guns shooting at the same time and at the same target for a total of six rounds. When the dust cleared, the hill could see two enemy on the trail not moving. *War Cloud* fired another battery-one and called a ceasefire due to darkness, thus giving the battery two confirmed kills.[54]

Overton had been given a heads up that the colonel was coming for a visit, so the 19th was a "Clean the Hill" and "Clean the Marine" day with both bunker and personnel inspections in the late afternoon. Overton held a meeting in the mortar pit for all hands except those on watch. He gave the Marines the game plan. The colonel and his staff were expected to be on the ground for 30 minutes in the morning. Overton would manage the colonel and the sergeant major. He asked Gunny Moore to take care of the S-3. He said others were coming and asked Sergeant Harvey to be ready to give tours. The Marines would remain in their bunkers. He would walk the colonel around the perimeter to each bunker and then they would go to the tower where Sergeant Bayuk would give a demonstration of the classified IOD. Then Overton, using the heat map Moore had made, would brief their concerns of enemy on Hills 148 and 175, while the colonel could look at both hills through the Big Eyes. Overton asked for questions; there were none. He was a hard charger, and he wanted to impress the battalion commander.

The sun broke early on 20 January. Overton was up and had already walked the entire perimeter, checking police of each bunker. He heated water and shaved. He was full of nervous energy. He checked the two-hole open-air shitter, which had been burned off the previous day, to ensure it had toilet paper.

The morning dragged on. *Melody Time* called and said there was no ETA, and they currently had no bird. The air officer had completed the roster, as was SOP for every bird departing LZ 401. The Recon S-3 shop kept a roster on who got on every bird. This inspection visit had the battalion commander and his sergeant major, plus the S-3 actual. As a reward, Howland had said Staff Sergeant Wilson should go since he did the work. Wilson wanted the day out of the office. Creg Howland, the experienced patrol leader, did not need another day flying around. Captain Thomas Martin was on board for a day in what he considered in the field with his CO. He would bring along 2nd Lieutenant Tom McAdams as he was due to take over the hill on 25 January and had never been.[55] The Echo Company commander, 1st Lieutenant J. L. Snow, was on the roster since the second stop was his Hill 425. A late addition that morning was a captain from Division G-2 plus two security Marines. The morning passed slowly on Hill 119 as the morning routine was interrupted and they simply waited on the VIP visit.

At Camp Reasoner, the air officer told everyone there was no bird until 1130. Lieutenant Colonel Grace climbed the hill with Sergeant Major Skinner; both went back to work, as did Major Mattiace. The division's G-2 captain went to the battalion S-2 shop and just hung out. At 1115, the group started to reassemble at LZ 401. Since it was the battalion commander and S-3's ride, the air officer was overseeing this pickup and quick pilot brief. The lone CH-46 approached at 1125 and landed. The pilot kept the rotors in neutral spinning as the ten Marines loaded. The air officer ran in first and up to the jump seat between the two pilots to brief them over the intercom on the three legs and desired time on the ground at each stop. The bird lifted out at 1134, circled west to avoid the airspace of Da Nang International and then climbed, heading south over Division Hill 327. Flying straight south they soon saw the bald and crowded Hill 55 and the command post of the 1st Marines. In 20 minutes, they were talking to Hill 119 LZ control and called for smoke. They identified green smoke and took the brief from the LZ. The bird came in from the north, flared and landed smoothly, dropping the ramp. Walking down the ramp, Grace met Overton, Moore, and Harvey. Yelling over the turning rotors and dusty air, Overton said he wanted to show the colonel something and he should follow him while the Gunny would take the rest of the visitors to the OP. Turning west, Overton led Grace, another officer, and Skinner off the LZ, through the outer wire, away from the OP and up the main trail. This was not the plan, but Harvey thought he should go with his platoon commander. All were kneeling and waiting for the bird and dust to clear the LZ. Gunny Moore led the S-3, Captain Martin, and the others east across the LZ and through the west gate next to Bravo Bunker. Everyone had waited for the dust and noise to settle. Now two groups of Marines moved in opposite directions off the LZ. Walking behind Moore, Martin and Mattiace, both talkers, were in a deep discussion. Gunny Moore walked the main body to the mortar pits.

Sergeant Mark Bayuk, the 11th Marines' NCOIC of the FO team, was in the tower with his radio operator. He was still scanning the area for enemy as he did on any other day. They all heard a loud explosion. Moore immediately recognized it as an M26 grenade. Bayuk swung the Big Eyes toward the noise to the west in time to see the lightbulb-shaped gray smoke cloud over the main trail and up to the crest of Hill 148. The smoke dissipated and Bayuk could see four Marines down about twenty meters up the main west trail.[56] He could see Sergeant Harvey, the fifth and last man in the west column, on one knee with his .45 drawn, scanning the area for enemy. Gunny Moore knew immediately it was a booby trap! He turned and yelled for Doc Richardson and ran out the west gate across the LZ and up the trail. Running past Harvey, he yelled at the sergeant to get security out and get a radio. As he arrived, three of the four down were stirring. Moore stopped and helped Skinner to one knee. Skinner said he was okay. Moore moved to the next Marine, an older captain who had rolled over holding his ankle. Moving forward, Moore rolled over Lieutenant Colonel Grace, who had been wearing his flak jacket. Had it been zipped up he would have been okay. But as was the habit with Marines, they wore their flak jacket all the time but left it unzipped for comfort and hoped for a breeze, except when the shelling or shooting started. Grace was peppered with shrapnel from his waist to his neck and he was bleeding badly. Moore started working on the colonel who waved him off and pointed to Overton face down on the trail just two feet in front of him. Doc Richardson arrived with his Unit One kit, Moore pointed the Doc to the colonel, and he moved to Overton. Overton was out. Blood from his lower left leg and his left arm was flowing. Moore pulled his belt off and placed a tourniquet on the leg above the thigh, ratcheting it down hard.

Running, Harvey was back, pushing two Marines past Moore and Overton for security. Moore yelled at them both, to walk, and to get the fuck off the trail. He told Harvey to call their bird or An Hoa tower and get an immediate emergency medevac. Overton was in shock; he had blood and shrapnel on the left side of his face. Moore got a compress bandage from Doc and applied it to Overton's eye, tying it off around his head. Moore yelled at Harvey to get a stretcher. Harvey replied that they didn't have any. Moore yelled to get a "fucking poncho!" Doc had stopped the colonel's bleeding and had moved over to help Moore with Overton. They both worked to stop the bleeding. The poncho arrived. Moore and Harvey folded it in half twice on the ground. Then they rolled Overton onto the poncho face up. Four Marines got a corner and carried the lieutenant down the trail and through the outer-wire defense to the landing zone.

Grace was up, and walking, helped by Sergeant Major Skinner to the LZ. Moore told Skinner to ride the medevac bird with his boss and Overton, who was an emergency medevac. Moore told Harvey to get on the radio and tell the pilots to go straight to the Naval Support Activity (NSA) Hospital. Harvey popped green smoke for the pilots before they called for it to see wind direction and they knew they were cleared hot. The CH-46 was coming fast and low out of An Hoa, straight in. The bird flared with the ramp already down. Ducking their heads, the four Marines carried the immobile Overton onto the bird and put him on the aluminum deck towards the front. They ran off as the sergeant major, with his arm around the battalion commander, walked up the ramp to a red nylon seat in the rear.[57] They both sat as the bird pulled out and flat hatted it straight to NSA. The surgeons said whoever worked on Overton saved his life. Overton lost half his left leg, half his left arm and his left eye as well as suffering brain damage, all caused by the surprise firing device.[58]

On 119, Major Mattiace and Captain Martin moved to the communication bunker and called the S-3 bunker at Camp Reasoner. He spoke with the S-3A, Captain MacCaskill, told him what had happened, and that he needed the air officer to frag another bird to get them. Ten minutes later, the new battalion XO, Major Terry Turner, was on the radio with Mattiace to get the information firsthand before he reported the incident up the hill to Division. Mattiace said Overton was an emergency medevac and the colonel had been a priority evac. Turner called on the landline from the S-3 bunker to the battalion aid station. Talking with the battalion surgeon, Navy Lieutenant L. J. McCarthy, he told him to call the NSA Hospital and get a status on the two officers. He called the adjutant shop next and told the new adjutant, Captain E. W. Sterling, to have the colonel's driver get his jeep and for him to meet Turner at the top of the trail next to the colonel's hut. On Hill 119, Captain Martin called Moore over and said the hill was his. He and the rest of the party would return to Camp Reasoner. Overhearing this, the older captain from Division G-2, who had a piece of shrapnel in his ankle said he was staying. He had come to do an enemy assessment and needed to get a better feel for his report. Martin looked at Major Mattiace who said a bird would be sent out the next day to pick him up. Mattiace looked at Martin and told him to write up a spot report and send it in for the record, no names, or billets, short and factual.[59] Martin looked at Moore who nodded that he would take care of it. The call came on the radio, and they heard it on the comm bunker speaker calling for smoke. Harvey, on the LZ with a backpack PRC-25, popped smoke and the pilots called yellow. Recon never broadcast what color they were popping as many times the NVA was listening and would also pop smoke trying to draw a bird into an LZ for an RPG ambush. The pilot always identified the color and if he called the wrong color or got two of the same color then they went around gaining altitude and started over to separate the good guys from the bad guys in the correct LZ.

Harvey confirmed yellow smoke as the birds started down. Mattiace, Martin, Lieutenant Snow from Echo Company, and 2nd Lieutenant Tom McAdams, with the two security Marines, headed for the LZ and their ride. The booby trap had gone off at noon. The emergency medevac departed at 1220 and the second bird with the rear-echelon motherfuckers (REMF) departed at 1245.[60] The hill was quiet but buzzing with hushed conversations. Moore knew it was better to keep the Marines busy rather than let them sit and stew and let their minds wander. He put the hill on 100 percent alert, not that anyone was sleeping, and called Sergeant Harvey over and said he wanted "Butch" to lead a large security patrol off the north side too check the railroad berm and Route 537. They could down a quick lunch, but he wanted them gone by 1315 and back before sundown. He also told Harvey they would do two-man listening posts that night, both east and west. Harvey should designate those Marines now and tell them to nap after lunch.

Moving to the tower, Moore checked in with Bayuk. He was fine and had not left the Big Eyes through the entire evolution. Moore wanted to hear what the sergeant saw. Bayuk said, when the colonel's bird departed, he saw Overton and four other Marines walking through the west wire headed to Hill 148, that the lieutenant was walking point on the main trail looking over his right shoulder talking to the Marine behind him. The third Marine was close and then there was a gap of at least 40 feet and the last two Marines. He thought the second to last was a big Marine and Harvey was tail end.[61] He then swung the Big Eyes in periscope fashion south to check the area and came around east to north and scanning Go Noi Island when he heard the explosion. All he could see was the gray smoke cloud rising and then the last Marine up on one knee with his weapon drawn. It was Harvey. Bayuk said it had to have been a booby trap as they were west of the outer wire fence and up the trail by 20 meters.[62] He asked Moore what the lieutenant was doing since that was not the plan. Moore said he did not know and had only heard the lieutenant say to the colonel he had something to show him. Obviously, the lieutenant had been talking and looking backwards walking up the main trail, not looking at the ground. It might have cost him his life.

Moore walked back down to Bravo Bunker and was sitting on top of it when Harvey plus six Marines came by at 1315 hours for their north walk-off patrol. Moore told them no trail walking today and got a "No shit" in return as they walked out to the LZ. *Durham-Alpha* moved down the north slope off-trail toward the railroad berm. This was an infantry style security patrol instead of a snoop-and-poop patrol. At 1345, in the tower, *War Cloud* spotted four VC in black PJs carrying rifles, moving from the west to east along a tree line next to paddies, about five kilometers to the northwest close to the Song Thu Bong. They called *Rice Krispies-Mike* and got an immediate no-adjust fire mission on target. They could not observe effects of the fire mission due to heavy foliage.[63] Fifteen minutes later, the hill heard a burst of sustained M16 fire from Tho Son hamlet below the hill. The radio squawked "*Durham* this is *Durham-Alpha*, we made contact with three NVA wearing green utilities carrying supplies on the trail moving west, one body, no documents, over."[64] The other two enemy had run towards the river. Moore told them not to pursue and to come home. *Durham-Alpha* acknowledged. When they were back on Hill 119, Sergeant Harvey found Moore in the comm bunker; he was asleep, so Harvey told the radio watch to let Moore know he was back when he got up. Moore said, "Butch, I know you're back, good job today."[65] After evening chow, Moore found Harvey and told him to go to sleep, that he had the night watch. Moore watched both two-man listening posts move out each end of the OP. Neither team was on the ridgeline trail. Each had a radio and were in position within 30 minutes. It was a long but quiet night on the hill.

Back at Camp Reasoner, "Doc" McCarthy reported to Major Turner that Overton was still in surgery, but they had stabilized him, and that Grace was out of surgery and had been put under while they were picking out so much shrapnel. He would be down for a while. Turner got the battalion driver and drove two-thirds up Hill 327 to the 1st Division underground command bunker. This 300-ton concrete bunker poured by the Seabees for 3rd Division now belonged to 1st Division. He walked through security and found the small chief of staff's office. Knocking on the door, he waited for the colonel's call before entering. He reported in and told the chief he was the XO of 1st Reconnaissance Battalion. He was reporting on the Hill 119 incident with his commander. The colonel listened quietly and said, "Come with me." They walked down the hall further inside the bunker to the commanding general's (CG) office. Outside, the chief told the general's aide that they needed five minutes with his boss. The aide got up from a small field desk on the side of the bunker hall, opened the door to the office and said "Sir, the chief needs five." Major General Wheeler looked up and said it was fine. The aide opened the door and ushered them in. Wheeler stood, came around his desk and remained standing, which meant the two officers would stand and it was his signal to the chief to make it short.

"Chief, what have you got?" the general asked.

"Major Turner here is the XO of 1st Recon," the chief said, giving the general the clue to the topic. "Sir, Lieutenant Colonel Grace was wounded today out on Hill 119 and is now at NSA Hospital.

"What else?" Wheeler asked.

"One of his lieutenants," Turner added, "a 2nd Lieutenant Charles Overton, is still in surgery and in bad shape."

"And what is the prognosis for John?"

"He is stable, but we have lost him for a while," the chief replied

"Okay," Wheeler said, "Major Turner, as of now, you are the acting commanding officer. Go back down the hill and keep the battalion going, you are dismissed. Sit down, Chief."

Wheeler looked at the chief of staff and said, "Okay, have the division surgeon get me a report tomorrow morning on both officers. He can bring it to me directly before the morning brief. If John is down, we will send him home to recuperate. John was wounded in Korea with Echo 2/5 and now he is wounded here with First Recon. We will move forward early with the Sting Ray plan for 1st Recon. Have the G-1 get us a list of all the infantry lieutenant colonels on staff to backfill Drumright at 2nd Battalion, 26th Marines as they rotate home soon."

The chief of staff stood and departed.

Major Turner's head was spinning while walking out to the jeep. He had been in-country seven days. Riding back down the short drive to Camp Reasoner, he knew he had to communicate with his new team. He told the driver to take him to the adjutant's shop, drop him off, and told him he could secure and get dinner. At the adjutant's office, he told Captain Sterling to have the entire staff and company commanders assemble in the S-1 (administration) conference room at 1900. He told Sterling the short version of the incident on 119 and that he was the acting commander. Sterling was also new, with only two weeks in-country, but this was his second tour in Vietnam. Turner told him he would continue to do his two jobs as adjutant and S-1 but add a third job, acting XO. "You keep the staff and admin going while I refocus on the command and operational side," he said. After talking with Sterling, Turner walked down the battalion road and then down the trail to the S-3 bunker where he found Major Mattiace. He asked him to come outside. The two majors walked down to the LZ. Turner told Mattiace that he had spoken with Wheeler and was acting. Mattiace asked for how long and Turner said he had no idea, but he did not believe Grace was coming back. He intended to go over in the morning and talk to Grace. He asked Mattiace to keep the daily operations going and to keep him informed of major events so he would not be blindsided by Division. Turner said there would be a staff meeting at 1900, and he would call on Mattiace first to tell the staff and commanders what had happened since he had been there.

At the meeting, Major Turner opened with "By now you all have heard that the CO [commanding officer] and Lieutenant Overton of Delta hit a booby trap this afternoon. It was touch and go on Overton, but he is out of surgery and stable. The colonel got hit pretty good. The CG has decided that I will be the acting commander. Major Mattiace, please tell us what happened." Mattiace said there was not much to tell. He had not seen the actual explosion, just heard it. It was obvious Overton hit a booby trap walking up the Hill 148 trail with the colonel. He told the staff they had been out to Hill 119 to survey the defenses as intel had indicated they were going to get attacked by the T89 Sapper Battalion. Turner then said, "I expect you all to continue to do your job as you have done, and I pledge to keep you all informed." He asked for questions, but there were none. The officers were stunned and a bit confused. It was over in less than fifteen minutes.

After the meeting, Mattiace asked Turner and Captains Martin and Sterling to remain behind. Mattiace said, "Our S-3A, Captain MacCaskill, will be rotating in seven days. We need a good replacement who is a proven patrol leader, and has the respect of all the patrol leaders, for his replacement." Turner asked if he had a recommendation. Mattiace turned to Martin who said, "First Lieutenant Gregson, who is just back from hospital, meets the criteria of experienced patrol leader and is respected. Currently he is my XO since he is on light duty. Lieutenant Klein was the XO, and I am over a lieutenant." Mattiace said he wanted to talk with Gregson first but liked the idea. Turner concurred. "How about just telling Sterling when you want to cut the battalion order and move him over?" That happened the next day, 21 January. It gave Captain MacCaskill and Gregson three days' turnover and would give MacCaskill a couple of days to check out.

On the morning of the 21st, Turner had the CO's driver take him and Sergeant Major Skinner to the NSA Hospital to visit Grace. In the hospital room, Turner told him he had met with the general and was acting and everything was being taken care of. Grace asked about Overton's condition as he was not being told by the hospital staff. Major Turner reported that he was in ICU, sedated and stable, but would need more surgeries. The plan was to give him a day or two to stabilize and then medically evacuate him to either Japan or Guam and then back to the States. He was clearly headed for a long recovery. Grace told his visitors that the assistant division commander (ADC) had visited him that morning to check on his condition but, in reality, to tell him they thought it best if he recovered at home. He had told the general he did not want to give up his command, that he would recover in-country and come back.[66] The ADC said it was not Grace's call, nor his, but he would share his request with the commanding general. However, the doctors said it would be at least thirty days before Grace could return to full duty. That sealed his fate. He was medically evacuated within two days, via Japan, to the United States and placed on convalescent leave to recover. Lieutenant Colonel J. J. Grace was promoted to colonel and then, in the early 1980s, served as the commanding officer of the 3rd Marines before retiring. Second Lieutenant Charles "Chuck" Overton was medically evacuated to Japan where he underwent three surgeries. He had lost his left eye, his left foot, and left hand. He was further evacuated to Philadelphia Naval Hospital and went through even more surgeries. He was promoted with his class to first lieutenant and, after more than a year of physical therapy, was medically retired at that rank.

On 21 January, after his morning brief, Major General Wheeler got the medical update on Grace needing at least thirty days to recover. That made his decision straightforward. He called in his G-1, G-3, division air officer, and the chief of staff. With four colonels standing in his office, he said he was changing Project *Sting Ray* from the planning stage to the operational stage. All except the chief of staff stared at him blankly. Wheeler said it would be an offensive economy-of-force operation using 1st Reconnaissance Battalion.

He wanted the battalion to cover more ground, with more teams, and be more aggressive. Recon was going to take the fight to his adversary, General Binh of Front 4, and the 2nd NVA Division.

Wheeler told the G-1 to get an in-country replacement saddled up and sent out to 2nd Battalion, 26th Marines' (2/26) forward command post in Hai Van Pass to start the turnover with Lieutenant Colonel Drumright. After executing the turnover, the plan was for Drumright to become the new commanding officer of 1st Recon Battalion. The G-1 departed to get those moves started. Wheeler had the other three colonels sit down. He also told the chief he needed to see Don Ezell, the commander of the 11th Marines (the division's artillery regiment) later, or the next morning after the morning brief if he had already departed for the Northern Artillery Cantonment. Telling the aide to get coffee, Wheeler explained to the sitting colonels what the *Sting Ray* Concept was and how it would work. Wheeler then clearly defined his priorities of support for the concept and therefore for Recon Battalion, who would be executing the concept. He reiterated that the Recon Marines' lives would depend on priority support from artillery, rotary wing, and fixed-wing aircraft, and, most importantly, on the emergency extraction helo packages, with their accompanying air support, in those cases when a Recon team was surrounded by the NVA. They needed to know the cavalry was coming to get them out of the jungle to save their skin. He stated this new prioritization of supporting assets had to be put into place in the division's planning cycles and in their execution at the Fire Support Coordination Center (FSCC) and DASC.[67] He said he would talk to the commanding officer of his artillery regiment to ensure staff and commanders were all aware of the change. Small Recon teams would get priority over larger infantry units when both were in simultaneous contact with the enemy. Asking for questions, the general got a request from the division air officer, a savvy pilot who was also the spy for the commanding general of the Marine Air Wing. "Sir, it might be good for you to socialize this concept and your priorities with the Wing CG." Wheeler agreed that he would talk with his warrior friend Major General Gay Thrash. To prove his point, he went straight into telling them that Gay was a great Marine warrior—a World War II aviator, who also flew in the Korean War, earning a Silver Star, and then being shot down and held as a prisoner for two years. Wheeler thought Thrash might have some ideas for improving support for the Recon teams. With that, the meeting ended.

Back at Hill 119, on 22 January, they received a radio call from a 2nd Battalion, 5th Marines, patrol. They had been patrolling east of Liberty Road to An Hoa and south of Route 537, moving towards Hill 119 when, west of and outside of Thon Bon (2), a deserted hamlet below Hill 148, found four mortar aiming stakes, about 2,500 meters out, pointed directly at Hill 119. The aiming stakes were freshly cut bamboo five feet high and 3–4 inches round.[68] This was another indicator the sappers were planning a combined-arms ground assault supported by mortars and rockets. Moore could see the enemy plan in his head: 122-mm rockets from the north slope of Hill 175 and 82-mm mortar shells from Thon Bon (2) in the opposite direction, with a ground assault up one of four draws.

The older LDO (limited duty officer) captain from G-2, who was slightly wounded in the Overton booby-trap incident, had spent the night of 20 January with Gunnery Sergeant Moore. He and Moore had pieced together the reconnaissance, observation, and attack plan of the T89 Sapper Battalion. When the captain returned to the rear on the 21st, he drove to Charlie 1st Medical Battalion, across from Freedom Hill, and had the piece of shrapnel dug out of his lower calf. He then drove over to see his friends at 3rd ITT and the POW compound near Marble Mountain. With the terrain and past events in his mind, he asked them to get the T89 POW Moore had captured. With the original interrogator, he told the prisoner he knew the plan to attack Doi Chiem Son hill west of Chien Son village. The prisoner nodded understanding. The original interrogation had used an American grid map and Hill 119 during the interrogation, both of which the Vietnamese prisoner had not seen before or understood. The experienced Korean War limited-duty intelligence officer gave his subject a cigarette. He then showed him a hand sketch of the Doi Chiem Son hill, Go Noi Island, and Chien Son village and had the fluent Vietnamese translator walk him through the terrain. He nodded understanding and said yes, they were going to attack the American lookout position, killing all 21 Americans defending it. It will be an important victory during Tet. The captain asked when the attack was scheduled? The prisoner said he did not know. In response, the captain said he could stay with the Americans, or they would turn him over to the South Vietnamese if he did not tell them. This was no veiled threat and seemed to work. The prisoner revealed he was the chief scout for T89 and that the Americans from Doi Chiem Son hill had killed his commanding officer and his operations officer. He was able to "Chieu Hoi" because the political officer had run away, leaving him. He said the attack would be soon, as they were scouting to find the best approach route for the sappers to the hill; he could not say when. This all fit together. The captain gave him another cigarette and departed after a solid three hours of quiet talk. The Americans could not keep him forever, but they also did not have to turn him over immediately. That night, the G-2 officer authored his report for his boss and the general. His conclusion was the T89 Sapper Battalion combined-arms assault on the hill was being planned for Tet 70! However, with the loss of the three key leaders and planners in the commanding officer, operations officer, and chief scout, it would not take place until those billets were filled. Those three replacements would have to come out of North Vietnam after sapper school and then come down the Ho Chi Minh Trail to the 2nd NVA Division in to Base Area 112. Then they would have to infiltrate into Go Noi Island, the operating home area of the sapper battalion. The G-2 estimate was that it had bought Hill 119 six months from Tet 70 until an August 1970 timeframe.[69]

When General Wheeler read the report, he took it as a confirmation of his *Sting Ray* plan for 1st Recon. Gunnery Sergeant Moore's aggressive patrolling had foiled the attack. The general was ready to institute *Sting Ray* operations, and he had the warriors to do it. The next morning, 23 January, the division's G-1 went back to the chief of staff and said that moving any of the in-country lieutenant colonels would cause an unwanted ripple effect, and any inbound would take at least a week to get up to speed, or longer to really get their feet on ground. The chief, impatient, asked what he recommended. The G-1 said he had talked with Lieutenant Colonel Drumright who had said he had a superior executive officer who was fully capable, knew the area, and that since the battalion was due to rotate in March to the U.S. and deactivate, he recommended Major Donald L. Humphrey take command of 2/26 and that he be backfilled with a major off the staff.[70] The chief asked what the regimental commander thought and was told he agreed. The chief said, "I'll inform the CG, you start the wheels in motion." That afternoon, the G-1 cut the orders for 27 January for both battalions to change leadership.

On Hill 119, it was a quiet 22–24 January. On the 25th, 3rd Platoon was due to flip to the hill with 2nd Lieutenant Tom McAdams. Major Mattiace and Captain Martin had a long talk about McAdams being the hill commander. Mattiace wanted Captain Martin or 1st Lieutenant Klein to go up for the flip and let McAdams birddog. Neither had any liking for the hill or the field. Martin deflected Major Mattiace with a "How about we leave Gunny Moore on the hill with McAdams?" Mattiace was fine with the compromise. McAdams would go up as hill commander, but Moore would stay for two more weeks as insurance. That night, Martin got on the radio with Moore. He thanked him for the great job he had done with the colonel's medevac and saving Overton's life. Then he said, "Gunny, I need you to stay up on the hill for this next flip." Martin was prepared to keep selling the idea, but Moore simply said, "Aye Aye!" Before getting off the secure net, Moore made the case for increasing the size of the Hill 119 haven. A larger haven would allow for the platoon to run security patrols to the overlooking hills. Martin did not like getting a request from the Gunny, but he could not deny it was smart tactics. Martin said he would talk with the S-3.[71]

On 24 January, Moore and Sergeant Bayuk were in the tower when the Recon radio watch called up and said Team *Razorbill* was on the company tactical net asking for *Durham-Alpha,* which was Moore. Moore walked down and grabbed the radio, calling his friend Staff Sergeant Mushett: "*Razorbill-Six*, this is *Durham-Alpha*, over." Mushett was the patrol leader for the first team of 1st Platoon, Delta Company. He and *Razorbill* had walked off the sister OP on Hill 425 six days earlier. Now he was south of Spider Lake moving out of the Que Sons. Mushett said, "We are Oscar Mike [on the move] and being followed and pushed by the NVA. Can you swing your Big Eyes over and watch?" Moore said he was on it. Climbing to the tower, he briefed Bayuk and then, using Bayuk's VHF radio, called on the *Hostage* network, "Any *Hostage* bird looking for work, dial up *Durham* on Hill 119." Not even a minute later, *Hostage Duke* came up on the net. Moore had him drop down to *Razorbill*'s net and ask to contact them. *Razorbill* said they had been moving all morning and were now looking for an LZ. The OV-10 came over and caught a mirror flash from *Razorbill.* He then identified a workable LZ on a small knoll 400 meters east. Mushett said he would move there. *Hostage Duke* departed, because of bingo fuel.[72] By 1130, Team *Razorbill* was on the knoll calling for their extract. They were out of water and had at least two cases of dehydration and exhaustion. Waiting in a 360 defense, the team could hear the enemy on three sides.[73] At noon, another *Hostage* OV-10 arrived with two gunships. The aerial observer (AO) in the back seat, *Cowpoke Three*, took over the fire-support coordination and extract for the team. While waiting for the extract package of two CH-46s, he ran both gunships at the foot of the hill and then got the artillery firing. Moore could watch his friend through the Big Eyes. The enemy stopped firing at the team and focused on firing at the gunships. The extract package arrived at 1445 with the bird coming in lower than the hill, straight across Spider Lake at 25 feet.[74] Moore watched it up close through the ship's binos, as "Doc" Schneider and another Marine helped the exhausted Marines to the extract bird. He saw Mushett with the radio on his back boarding last as the ramp came up and the bird departed. They took small-arms fire on the extract. *Razorbill* was headed for Camp Reasoner and the "Stagger Back Inn" later that night. Moore would have to wait to hear the whole story, but he was pleased his friend was out. It was 1500. Time to check the listening-post positions for the night and ensure everyone was ready for the flip in the morning. He did not have to pack his large Vietnamese rucksack as he was staying. The morning of 25 January came with 3rd Platoon arriving at 0930. By 1000, Sergeant Harvey was headed back with 4th Platoon to Camp Reasoner.[75]

Moore and Bayuk watched the two CH-46 departures as 3rd Platoon arrived. Gunny Moore walked down to the mortar pit, meeting Tom McAdams and his acting platoon sergeant, Corporal Holmes.

Moore said, "Lieutenant, let me show you your bunker while Holmes here gets the Marines settled in."

Holmes nodded and departed. Moore turned and walked the lieutenant over to his bunker. Holding the blackout flap open, he said, "Sir, when you're settled we should talk."

McAdams had been briefed in detail by Martin that, although he was the hill commander, he should listen to Gunny Moore. He had told him at least five times in the last 24 hours. McAdams was an easy going South Carolinian, but he knew instinctively he needed to listen to Moore. "Now is fine, can we sit here?" he offered.

Agreeing, Moore asked the lieutenant how many Marines he had brought to the hill. Thirteen was the answer.[76] Moore said the hill really should have 22 Marines for a solid defense.

"Well, lieutenant, your choices are to change the size, making a smaller perimeter or focus on watch schedules that help address the issue."

The lieutenant wisely asked what Moore would recommend. "Well, we are small, so getting smaller, besides a lot of digging work, just backs us into a smaller corner. I would recommend fewer Marines per position and reverse watch schedule."

McAdams said he would have to walk him through that. "We have six primary bunkers, normally they are three- to four-man positions. We can make them two-man positions in the nighttime with twelve Marines. We also have a radio watch of three to four. So we're out of Marines to cover slots."

Moore continued, "I can take a watch, and 'Doc' Bennett can either take a radio watch or man one of the two-man bunkers. Lieutenant, let the Doc pick what he wants to do on the hill, which leaves you and the artillery FO team as the only other manpower. They man the tower 24/7 and there are six of them between the FOs and radio operators. Let's ask them to help. The easiest watch time for security is during daylight hours. If we got two Arty Marines in the daytime, one for Bravo Bunker watching the Alligator Lake trail and one for Echo Bunker watching the east trail, that would be three Arty Marines on watch during the daytime: one in the tower and two on bunker duty. The result lets your twelve bunker Marines sleep during the day as we were expected to be up all night. It is doable if we just flip the day–night watch routine of the hill. We also do not have a sufficient force for security patrols which is fucked up. Recommend we still run a morning wire 360 patrol."

McAdams said it sounded good to him. He would tell Holmes. Moore said it was best to have a meeting with the Arty sergeant first to get his concurrence, then have his platoon sergeant and his three team leaders in to explain the night watch system. McAdams understood.

Moore then said, "Let me introduce you to Sergeant Bayuk, the NCOIC of the FO team. He has his shit together and he can also give you an IOD demo. After that, you should get him away from his Marines and just tell him we need him and his Marines for security."

McAdams suddenly remembered Captain Martin had asked him to tell Moore he had got his haven changed. For a minute, Moore was surprised and pleased. "Good timing," he replied, "as we need to give it to Bayuk as it represents the dividing line between his free-fire zone and your haven around this hill. Lieutenant, let me get my map and I will be right back."

Returning to the lieutenant's bunker, Moore spread out his 1:50,000 that had the current haven around Hill 119 clearly marked. McAdams confirmed he wanted or recommended adding

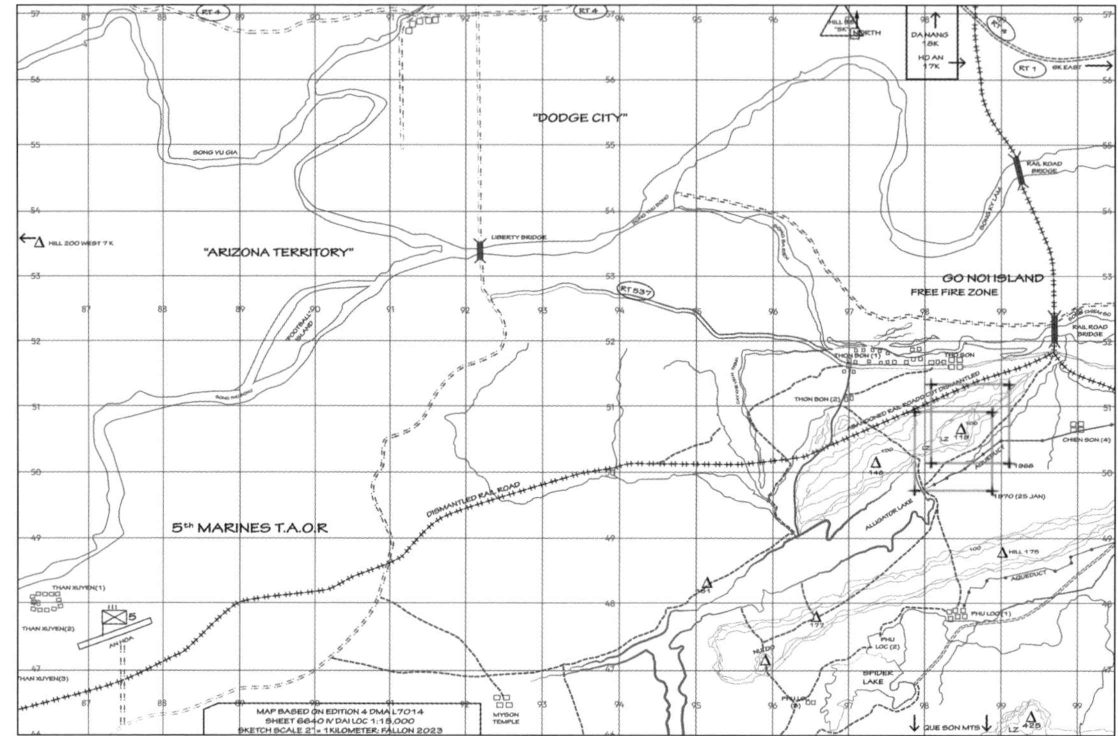

Enhanced sketch, Hill 119 area and haven. (M. Fallon and W. Denham)

Hills 175 and 148 to the Hill 119 haven. Moore agreed. McAdams pulled out his operations order and read the Upper Left grid square intersection AT9982510 and Lower Right AT993498. Moore drew the new box on the same map.[77]

He was clearly disappointed and said so. The new haven was smaller than the last, which was inadequate in size. It had neither Hills 175 nor 148 inside it. However, there was some good news in that it shifted the haven south 400 meters, giving ownership of the southeast draw to the hill and giving them the Alligator Lake dam and aqueduct trail. To the north, they lost the railroad berm ground, which would now fall into Bayuk's restricted area, the free-fire zone (FFZ).

McAdams asked Moore, "Hey, Gunny, I understand haven but what is a free-fire zone?"

Moore needed coffee, so he pivoted and said, "Let's get coffee and you ask Sergeant Bayuk that question during your demo, and we will discuss it up on the tower."

Walking to the comm bunker, Moore made up two C-rat coffee cups while the lieutenant put his gear away. Five minutes later, they were climbing the stairs to the tower, with their coffee, to get the demo.

McAdams was impressed with the secret IOD equipment, and its capabilities, as was everyone who got to see it up close. He said aloud to no one, "We will have to get Corporal Holmes up here to brief the laser safety concerns and the preparatory commands."

Sergeant Bayuk, now having been through six Recon flips, interceded, and said, "Lieutenant, our procedure is for you to bring your Marines up here and get a demo and safety brief. If they understand how it works, they will pay attention to laser safety. It will take fifteen minutes max, and I will send two of my guys out for security." Moore smiled.

McAdams asked, "When?"

"Normally after you're settled in, and everyone has had lunch."

The lieutenant said they would be there at 1300 and started down the stairs. Gunny Moore said, "Lieutenant, what about security watches?"

McAdams cursed and came back up to the tower platform. He held Moore's arm and said, "Sergeant, we need to talk security of the hill."

It was just the three of them. McAdams laid out the request. Bayuk asked to talk to his team and discuss further after the IOD laser demo and safety brief. Bayuk was smart and he knew this was a watch issue that would impact his Marines. He was responsible for a 24/7 observation-deck watch on the IOD which took one man in shifts to maintain focus. He also had a 24/7 radio watch on the Arty network which took a man. The Arty team was running a three-section, two-man watch system. Bayuk thought if he moved the radio monitoring to the Recon bunker and let Recon monitor the Arty net, it would free up one man each shift. Recon was asking for two men for daytime security. He could have less watchmen per shift for his team during routine times. Bayuk presented the counterproposal to McAdams and Moore after the safety demo. Moore smiled.

The lieutenant, buying time, asked, "Gunny, what do you think?"

Moore said one Recon radio man could easily monitor two nets if they both terminated in the comm bunker. It would take an extra radio on the net as the call-for-fire radio had to remain in the tower. Bayuk said he had an extra radio. So they set it up that way with the Arty admin/support radio now monitored in the comm bunker. It really made for better situational awareness in the comm bunker, but it also made for a noisier space as the Arty network was nonstop loud traffic. The flip was completed, and the short-handed platoon had a plan.

Moore had another thought to help address the shorthanded OP. That evening, when it was quiet, he called the rear and asked to speak to the S-3 chief. Master Sergeant Regalot came on the radio and asked, "What's up?" Moore said the haven was a shoebox, and they were undermanned at 13 Marines. They were an entire Recon team down. He suggested to Regalot that Battalion could task Delta Company to send a full team with a specific mission of a walk-off patrol in a regular-sized haven round the hill. Lastly, Moore said Mushett owed him after Mushett's last patrol, so working the SNCO chain through Gunny Radcliff at Delta Company could get Mushett's team assigned. Regalot got the last shot in before signing off. "You don't want much. Any other teams you want to frag for your personal use? Out!"[78]

***

Back in the Hai Van Pass, forward headquarters of the 2nd Battalion, 26th Marines, the turnover with Lieutenant Colonel Drumright's current XO was short, sweet, and completed by the 24th, but not official until the 27th. The new major had arrived to become XO. On 25 January, Drumright sat in on the division's morning staff meeting and was introduced by the commanding general himself as the new 1st Reconnaissance Battalion Commander. Major General Wheeler also added he expected everyone to give him their cooperation with the *Sting Ray* operations his battalion would be running. After the morning brief, Drumright then had an in-call with the general. Wheeler told Drumright he expected results soon and asked if he had any questions.

Drumright's only question was, "Sir, do I get my experienced lieutenants?"

The general said he had made it clear to the G-1 and chief and to let him personally know if it did not happen. "Wild Bill" Drumright had his marching orders! After being dismissed, he went outside the bunker and walked over to the division personnel officer, who worked for the G-1. Easier talking with a fellow lieutenant colonel than the colonel G-1. In the meeting, he stated his criteria for lieutenants. He wanted infantry (Military Occupational Specialty; 0302) 1st lieutenants with six months' combat experience in the grunts. He wanted volunteers, no forced transfers. He explained to the personnel officer that these lieutenants would become patrol leaders (PL). He needed officers who had proven themselves in-country reading a map and calling supporting arms. He expected to be manned well over the Table of Organization strength for lieutenants.[79] Returning to the division's bunker and the G-3 shop, he met with the G-3, division air officer, and the chief of fire-support coordination from the co-located FSCC. The 1st Marine Division Command Center was in a large underground concrete bunker dug into the north side of Hill 327. It housed the Command Center, the FSCC, and Division Air Office with direct links to the DASC next door. Drumright sat with the group of colonels and talked them through the *Sting Ray* concept, explaining his small Reconnaissance team of five to eight Marines/Corpsmen would clandestinely find suitable enemy targets. Similar to a small stingray that employs its barbed venomous tail on its prey, the Recon team would employ the powerful supporting arms of artillery, rotary wing attack aircraft and fixed-wing air strikes on the located enemy. For the concept to work, his team had to be good at calling supporting arms, thus the need for proven combat lieutenants. Since they were a small force against an enemy with superior force in every engagement, they needed to be the first priority for supporting arms. If a patrol leader called, he could not be put in line for support or second guessed by a staff officer in the rear looking at a map. When his teams called, Drumright, and by extension Major General Wheeler expected the teams to get the requested support.

There was pushback. It was the staff's job to prioritize competing demands. The infantry regiments and battalions also needed support. Drumright said he understood and reminded them he had just completed command of 2nd Battalion, 26th Marines. However, it was not a discussion or a debate. The commanding general had established the priority. Drumright stated he expected his teams to be supported and implied he would go directly to the general if they were not. The G-3 ended the meeting by telling the others that the division's priority for fires, meaning Arty, air, and naval gun fire would now go to Recon. The meeting ended.[80]

Drumright departed, moving down the side of Hill 327 and found the division's food services officer (FSO) in his office. He knew the Korean War LDO captain from both Korea and earlier dealings with him in Vietnam. Drumright stated that the general had authorized for 1st Recon a new basic daily food allowance (BDFA). This is an authorized budget amount per Marine per day for food. The unit received their BDFA based on the actual strength of the unit. The two men had a good dialog as Drumright explained his mess hall fed 1st Recon Battalion, which was one letter company over strength, and Alpha Company 5th Recon. He needed the higher BDFA authorized for the total number of Marines on his rolls and eating in his mess hall. Drumright had not seen his mess hall yet, but he was laying the groundwork. Soon it will become the best in the division. He got agreement from the FSO, who had more time in the Corps than Drumright. The FSO looked at his watch and told Drumright he owed him a beer and with that the two friends headed to the division Officers Club one street below the FSO's office on Division Hill, and one street up from Division Road. They entered the dark club; it was late afternoon, but the club was empty. It would be full by happy hour and remain so through dinner until midnight. The two officers went to the bar and the NCO barman asked their preference. The FSO asked for his usual Pabst Blue Ribbon beer; Drumright told the NCO to give him a shot of bourbon. When the drinks were brought over, Drumright threw his back, said "Get me two more" and threw down a fistful of MPCs (Military Payment Certificates), the in-country script printed to try to control the black market. Dollars were not authorized tender in Vietnam but were still everywhere. The two sat talking and reminiscing about Korea. Drumright was a functioning alcoholic. In the "Old Corps," this was not a detractor nor uncommon. Nor was an officer judged on alcoholism. The officer was judged on results, executing and fulfilling his mission. Drumright finished his third, thanked his friend for the food support for his warriors, and departed the club. He had two short blocks to walk downhill, and across the two-lane Division Road to the wooden guard shack and red metal gate pole across the entrance to 1st Reconnaissance Battalion. It had a weatherbeaten red wooden sign behind it announcing the unit, a skull and cross bones logo, and a slogan, "We have been where the Division goes." Drumright made himself a mental note the entrance needed to be redesigned to be more fitting for his battalion, in other words, a major upgrade.

The private on duty waited for the shadow to move into the one beam of light provided by a bulb strung above the wooden phone-booth-sized guard shack. He immediately recognized the silver oak leaves on both collars and snapped to attention with a Rifle Salute. Drumright acknowledged and asked which street went to the command post. The guard walked behind the gate, said "Follow me, sir," and, walking to his left, showed Drumright the street that did a hook down past the battalion aid station, heading downhill. The private told him he would see signs. Drumright walked on, the guard went to the shack, and hand cranked the double EE-8 phone. He got the duty NCO and reported a lieutenant colonel walking down the hill. Drumright had been there the day before. He found Major Terry Turner's office before the guard's chain of command could pass the word. Without knocking, he stepped on the porch and entered Turner's office through the screen door. Standing in front of Turner, he announced he was aboard in a loud voice. Turner, now standing, asked the colonel to sit. He said he would not but would rather turn in for the night and they would talk in the morning. Drumright, a farm boy from Tennessee, was an early riser. He told Turner he would have coffee with him at 0500 and then meet with him and the S-3, who was the other field-grade officer in the battalion, at 0600. He'd then bring the company commanders together at 0700 and the staff at 0800.

Walking out of Turner's office without another word, Drumright walked down the hill to find his personal Southeast Asia (SEA) hut. Each commanding officer had improved the Recon Battalion commander's hut. It was an entire SEA Hut with a front porch, one step up from the battalion street which ran in front of it on the south side. The hut's front door faced south, and it and the shaded porch looked up at Division Hill rising above it outside the Camp Reasoner compound. The hut ran south to north and was on stilts to accommodate the steep hill dropping off behind it down to LZ 401, followed by the rice paddies outside the wire. The large back porch was the width of the cabin and 10-feet deep with a substantial two-by-four rail around it. The back deck faced north and had 270-degree views of the Recon LZ below, the rice paddies, then the Force Logistics Command rear facing Route 1. Standing on the back deck, Drumright could see his old command's lights flickering in Hai Van Pass on the skyline. To the northeast, he could see at least twelve large ships at anchor in Da Nang Bay. He sat in one of the two chairs on the back deck and poured himself three fingers of whiskey. He sipped and thought, "It will begin tomorrow." He would lay down the law in the morning.

January 26, 1970, Lieutenant Colonel "Wild Bill" Drumright was up at 0400, approximately two hours before dawn. He'd slept well and felt energized. He walked to his desk and started making a list, the list he would use for each of his meetings that morning. About 0440, he heard heavy footsteps on the porch and three loud raps on the doorframe. At Drumwright's invite, Sergeant Major Skinner walked through the hatch with a "Welcome aboard, sir!" Skinner was bigger than Drumright, himself a large man. They shook hands. Drumright knew Skinner but they had never worked together. He was pleased Skinner, also a farm boy, had come over when he saw his light on. Skinner asked if he wanted coffee. Drumright replied with, "You know I do." Skinner got up, went to the door, and yelled at a Marine somewhere in the dark. Almost immediately, two steaming metal canteen cups with hot coffee were brought through the door by a Marine. "It was good to be King," thought Drumright.

That morning, he had the three meetings he had outlined with the XO the previous evening. Skinner sat with him in all three. Drumright outlined there was a new sheriff in town. The battalion was going on the offensive with the *Sting Ray* concept. He stated flatly they could get on "Wild Bill's Wagon Train" or leave the battalion. After the three meetings, he had two additional ones lined up before walking through his camp with Skinner. The first meeting was a short one with the new logistics officer (S-4), Captain Fitzgerald, and Gunnery Sergeant Paradise, his chief cook. Drumright informed them his Marines would eat like warriors. Starting the next day, there would be three full daily meals plus a healthy mid-rats at midnight. This was a major upgrade from two meals a day with no mid-rats. He further directed that all Marines could get coffee and ice cream 24/7. He also told them of their budget increase a higher BDFA per Marine. He was clear—great chow for his great warriors. The last morning meeting was with Captain Thomas Martin and his acting First Sergeant, Gunnery Sergeant Radcliff. Delta Company had just failed the division's major Personnel and Administrative Readiness Inspection, which assessed the company's ability to pay and promote its Marines.[81] The meeting was conducted with the Martin and Radcliff standing at attention. It lasted 45 seconds and was a one-way blast from Drumright. He would fire both of them if they did not pass the re-inspection in 30 days. His Marines would be paid properly! He did not ask for questions and dismissed them, calling them "Peckerhead" and shouting profanities at them as they departed his office. Afterward, he asked Skinner to talk with Radcliff, who was an 0369 (infantry unit leader), and determine why he was acting first sergeant, and if he would be better utilized in S-3 training. Drumright then grabbed his cover and stormed out to walk his domain.

On the same day, in Delta Company, 1st Lieutenant G. G. "Jerry" Spolter arrived and was posted as the new free-agent patrol leader. Spolter had extended his tour by six months for Recon. He was just back from 30 days' basket leave in San Francisco as part of the extension deal and was expecting to go to Alpha Company and become XO. He had cut a "deal" to come to Recon and work for Captain Delateur, the Alpha Company Commander. The basket leave, off-the-books leave, was the final incentive Delateur had used to lure him. Spolter's problem was the two officers he had cut the deal with, Delateur and Lieutenant Colonel Grace, had both been medevac'd while Spolter was on leave.[82] First Lieutenant Charlie Kershaw, a June 1968 graduate of Virginia Military Institute, was an experienced patrol leader and had assumed command of Alpha Company on 18 January. In a freak handball accident, Delateur got hit in the eye and had to go to Japan for specialized treatment.[83] Spolter was senior to Kershaw by over a year and had already been in-country for 13 months, and, therefore, could not slide into Alpha as the XO. The S-1 solved that issue by assigning him to a company with a captain commanding. Thus, the assignment to Delta Company even though Martin was fully staffed with lieutenants.

Spolter had graduated from The Basic School Class of 3-67 and had six months in the grunts with 3rd Battalion, 7th Marines, five of which were served as the S-5 (civil affairs) due to his fluency in Vietnamese. That was followed by seven months with VMO-2 as an AO calling artillery and air strikes. As *Cowpoke One-Zero* (his callsign), he had gotten to know Recon through supporting them. He had willingly extended for a paper-pushing job in the rear. Then, to his surprise, the Marine Corps and Captain Martin said, with all his experience, he could go straight to the bush.[84] It solved a small problem for Martin as well because Team *Spoonbill* was raw. Martin somehow missed that Spolter's last patrol in the infantry was 12 months prior. Martin bypassed any snap in or indoctrination for Spolter. He was immediately assigned to go out on patrol on 29 January. Sucking it up, Spolter would be joining Team *Spoonbill* for the patrol.[85] He had a young team with three lance corporals, three privates, and an experienced corpsman in Hospitalman Richardson. The patrol's eighth man would be a Kit Carson Scout (KCS #378) named Tan.[86] KCSs were former Chieu Hoi VC who had come over to the South Vietnamese side. After screening and training, the best ended up as scouts for U.S. units. Tan was most certainly not his real name, to protect him from VC reprisals on his family. Fortunately for Spolter, he had gone to the Army run Monterey Foreign Language Institute directly after The Basic School and taken the ten-month Vietnamese language course. Graduating from school, Spolter scored 4/4 for reading/writing, where 5/5 was native fluency. Speaking Vietnamese meant he and Tan understood each other. On patrol, it could be an immense advantage with the experienced scout.

Unbeknown to Spolter, that patrol would place him first among equals of lieutenants in Drumright's eyes. *Spoonbill's* patrol would last just 48 hours while making enemy contact twice.[87] They killed one NVA, seizing his pack. Going through the young enemy's wallet, Spolter found a picture of his family. It was a moment of realization that the young warriors, on both sides, held many of the same values.[88] One of Spolter's Marines, Private First Class Jones, suffered shrapnel wounds in the second contact with seven enemy. Spolter used two of his old mates from VMO-2, *Hostage Duke* and *Cowpoke-Six*. Additionally, he employed two AH-1 Cobra gunships, *Scarface One-Zero* and *One-Four* to keep the enemy at bay and off his back while buying time for an emergency ladder extract.[89] The aluminum ladder was fastened to the tail ramp of a CH-46 and lowered into small clearings where the helo could not land. It was a great ride once in the air, with the added relief of getting pulled out of an enemy situation where you were typically outnumbered. It was not a good ride coming out and through thick jungle to gain altitude while the Marines banged into tree limbs. It was a ride Spolter had not trained for or asked for but was grateful to take. During the extract, one flight of fixed-wing aircraft covered the departure zone, as the enemy closed in on *Spoonbill*. The team rode the ladder to An Hoa. Wild Bill Drumright had been on board the extract helo with a headset, listening to the choreographed extraction the former AO had managed. Spolter had organized the air assets, all culminating in the emergency ladder extract on 31 January.[90] It was Drumright's sixth day of command and Spolter's fourth day in Recon. It was the first emergency extract Drumright had ridden, listened to, and observed. He was strutting around the fuel pit at An Hoa, carrying a Thompson submachine gun, slapping every Marine he could find on the back.[91] He was ecstatic! Unwittingly, Spolter and Team *Spoonbill* had conducted the textbook example of a *Sting Ray* patrol!

The new battalion commander would often use *Spoonbill's* patrol as an example in the next two weeks, talking, selling, cajoling, and bullying the division staff, air wing staff, 11th Marines Artillery Regiment, and everyone he talked to within Camp Reasoner. Spolter was a marked man Drumright would use, although he could never get his name right; Drumright called him "Spollinger." Wild Bill, strutting with his Thompson submachine gun, loved this warrior example while Spolter despised the aggressive, bullying behavior the alcoholic Drumright used to whip his battalion into a different culture,[92] changing the modus operandi from classic snoop-and-poop *Keyhole* patrols gathering intelligence, to an aggressive *Sting Ray* patrol organization. Unknown to Spolter, that evening quietly drinking a cold Coke in the Delta Company officers' hut thinking, "What in the hell have I done?" he would be the Delta Company commander in 34 days.

Captain Martin failed the second administrative/pay inspection at the end of February, a mortal sin in Drumright's eyes.[93] He was gone four days later. Spolter, being a very senior 1st lieutenant and already in Delta Company, was an easy fit. Already on Drumright's "Warrior List," he was made the company commander on 4 March.[94] Drumright's encouraging words for Spolter assuming command were, "Peckerwood, I know you can fight but you got 30 days to fix my Marines' pay that BS artist Martin has failed twice. I will fire you next month if you do not pass the re-inspection."[95]

Sergeant Major Skinner protected Gunnery Sergeant Radcliff, moved him to S-3 training, and told him not to visit the SNCO/Officers club for three months in order to avoid Drumright. Skinner then moved the smart, very proficient, and professional Recon Marine Master Sergeant Rene Regalot into Delta Company's first sergeant slot.[96] The first sergeant was responsible to the commander for the administration and pay of his Marines as well as his senior-enlisted advisor. "Top," which was short for top sergeant, was what Spolter called Regalot out of respect. They made a great team. Regalot said he needed support and the platoon commanders' attention to canvas their platoon's record books for discrepancies. He and the clerks would fix them and work off the division inspector's prior two checklists; Spolter would sign all the documents that came his way. He was a charismatic and smart leader. He explained it all to the lieutenants over a beer in their hooch where he lived with them. He simply asked them to take care of their Marines. The lieutenants reviewed every Service Record Book. Three weeks of 18-hour days for Regalot and the clerks in March and the company office was ready for the re-inspection. On inspection day, Spolter personally got the coffee vat and donuts down from the mess hall. When the inspection team arrived for the third inspection of Delta Company's pay records, he told them they were ready, that he would let them and Regalot conduct the inspection, and he would get out of their way. That afternoon at 1530, the five inspectors entered Spolter's office with Top Regalot.[97] They said the debrief would be short. While they found minor items that needed to be taken care of administratively, there were no pay discrepancies. They explained the written-report-only grade was pass, since this was their third time at bat. However, verbally they stated if it had been the first time, it would have been marked as outstanding. Departing, they would out brief the battalion's S-1. After they departed, Spolter went out to the company office and told all the clerks, "Well done, well fucking done, Marines!" The beer that night at the Stagger Back Inn was on him! The inn happened to be the hut next to the office. He told Top and the clerks the office would be closed the next day; Top was to take the office to China Beach for the day!

***

Back on Hill 119, while the Recon platoon flip took place on 25 January, Sergeant Bayuk and FO Team *War Cloud* had a routine day. They called three fire missions on 21 enemy, declaring three confirmed kills and two probables to *Rice Krispies-Mike*.[98] The next day, the OP observed and listened on the radio as an AO, *Cowpoke Six*, was targeting a dud 500-pound bomb, close to the southern railroad bridge to the island, and suspected to be booby-trapped. The AO called a fire mission with good coverage of the target, but no secondary explosion was observed. The OP could not see the dud but noted its grid on their master map in the comm bunker. *War Cloud* then had four fire missions, reporting one secondary explosion and two confirmed enemy killed. On 27 January, at 2020, *War Cloud* spotted six of the enemy moving from the west to east into Tho Son hamlet below the hill in the FFZ. Bayuk would never catch them with an Arty mission. *Durham* Marines were in the mortar-pit training, so *War Cloud* called a 60-mm mortar-fire mission verbally over the tower wall. They got excellent coverage of the trail with six 60-mm high-explosive (HE) rounds from the two mortars.[99] To the Recon Marines' disappointment, *War Cloud* could not see the results due to darkness.

At 0600 on 28 January, *Durham* got a radio call from Team *Station Break* asking for a comm check on two radios. After the standard comm checks, *Station Break-Six* asked to speak with *Durham-Alpha*. Moore rolled over in his cot, stood up, and answered the radio call of the voice he knew. Mushett said, "I am inbound to *Durham* this morning with Team *Station Break.* Hope you have good coffee." Moore responded with, "The coffee is on." Top Regalot had worked some staff NCO magic. The OP did not have enough Marines for security patrols but now it would have a full-up team running patrols off the hill. Gunny Moore was anxious to see Staff Sergeant Mushett's haven.

Arriving at the Hill 119 LZ on a single CH-46, at 1030 hours, Mushett and *Station Break* walked off the bird.[100] Friendly inserts were a rare luxury in Recon. Mushett was the platoon sergeant for Lieutenant Garry Parks's 2nd Platoon, but he was also a seasoned patrol leader (PL). *Station Break* was team two of 2nd Platoon, or Delta 2-2. Corporal Miller was the team leader, and he had four other Marines and Hospitalman Schneider on the team. They were equipped for a standard patrol with two PRC-25s and one M79 besides their own M16s.[101] For this effort, Mushett would be the PL and Miller the assistant PL for the seven-man team.

Moore stayed out of the helo dust and met Mushett at the mortar pits. He said, "You are going to be here awhile so split up your team to bunkers with buddies. 'Doc' can huddle with Doc Bennett. Why don't you and Miller come with me for your coffee?" Good to his word, Moore actually had a regular metal coffee pot and ground-bean coffee. This was authentic, not freeze-dried C-rat instant coffee. Mushett wanted to know what was going on. Moore wanted to see Mushett's haven. He said, "Let's talk over coffee out in the trench. Then in an hour we will have a planning session with Lieutenant McAdams and Sergeant Bayuk of the IOD team." Mushett agreed, while Miller was happy with good coffee. "We are boxed in here with only thirteen Marines," Moore continued. "We realistically cannot run security patrols and, if we could, we got no space in the haven north and a straight drop to the aqueduct south. So I asked for a patrol team and, yes, I asked for you."

Mushett looked at Miller and said, "Knew it."

"So we are your security patrol," he said sarcastically.

"Absolutely not," replied Moore. "I have an idea I think you and the team will like for this patrol. Let me see your haven."

Mushett pulled out his green notebook and had the coordinates for Upper Left and Lower Right, as he was waiting to mark his map based on Moore's thoughts and had to get *Durham*'s haven marked and all the other approved boundaries. Moore took out his map; Mushett read the grids as Moore plotted them. Moore could not believe what he saw. It was not a standard six-grid-square rectangle but a large nine-square-kilometer Recon haven with Hill 119 dead center. Regalot had worked a coordination miracle for the patrol period of 28 January–6 February. *Station Break* owned the haven, but their patrol order, signed by Major Mattiace, said "to be coordinated with *Durham* and *War Cloud*."[102]

Moore put the map down. "You two are the PL and APL but if I were doing it, this is what I would do. There is no canopy here in this haven and nowhere to hide. This hill is under observation 24/7 by both the NVA sapper unit and by the VC in the enemy hamlets below the hill. If Marines walk off during the day, the enemy knows where they are headed before they get there. That would be ambush city. We know they move at night. We know they cannot see as good as we can at night, or as far. So why not sleep here during the day, relax with no watches and then, every night after sundown, move out to a selected ambush site. You can go hunting, we can watch your back with the big night-observation device, and you get direct-fire machine guns and indirect fire support from here on Hill 119 and from Arty in An Hoa." Miller was already smiling. "What do you think?"

Mushett said he liked the idea, but they would need help from Moore and the IOD team on where to set the ambushes.

Moore said, "No problem, we got heat maps for this place for the last three months showing enemy movement and trends. I think you can walk down there on any major trail and make contact. Moore continued, "You are so close; we will do this old school. Preplanned patrol route with check points. You and I will produce two thrust points so we can talk in the clear, saving the time to shackle. Okay, before lunch let's huddle with the lieutenant and the FO team and get everyone's buy in. Then over lunch the three of us can talk ambush sites and you can pick your site for tonight."

Thirty minutes later, they were sitting on the trench wall outside the lieutenant's bunker on the south side of the hill. Moore took over the meeting and introduced everyone. Buyak brought his primary radio operator and Mushett had Miller and their primary radio operator, Lance Corporal Moore, not Gunny Moore's son or brother as he pointed out with a chuckle. Moore said *Station Break* was on the hill because *Durham* was shorthanded. To prevent them from getting boxed in, *Station Break* would be running nightly ambushes off the hill and sleeping during the day. Every night there would be a new ambush site. He said he would be the planner, but that *Station Break* would have a veto. The routes off and back on the hill would be preplanned and off-trail. The FO team would have preplanned targets that they and *Station Break* would know. The NOD team would watch their backs. The lieutenant, as hill commander, would have overall command, and all radio calls would be *Station Break* to *Durham* to ensure tight coordination. Everybody liked it.

"I would like to talk one time to everyone on the hill before we go out tonight," Mushett said.

"Fine, in the mortar pit after your initial inspection. Marines, you have work to do," Lieutenant McAdams agreed.

Sergeant Bayuk wanted *Station Break*'s haven for his map. Moore and Mushett spent the next hour with the heat maps and selected a location for that night's ambush. They would set up on Route 537 one hundred meters east of Tho Son hamlet. The hamlet was a linkup place for the NVA marching in from the Que Sons to meet local VC guides. It was also a ferry terminal to get to Go Noi Island with many small bamboo docks on the river's edge. They selected two thrust points; one would be *Car* and the other would be *Cities*. They picked a route out and a route back. Moore said he could brief both Bayuk and McAdams while Mushett went off to give his team the new patrol order and then put them to bed as they would be up all night.

Early on the evening of 28 January, *Durham* got a call from *Laundryman-Echo*, the OP on Hill 425, five kilometers to their south, on the northern edge of the Que Son Mountains. *Laundryman* stated they had movement and flashes on the west side of Hill 148 overlooking Hill 119.[103] At 1915, Gunnery Sergeant Moore realized his worst fear: they took one incoming rocket-propelled grenade (RPG) round from Hill 148 that landed in the trash pit. Hill 119's 60-mm mortars responded with their on-call target for Hill 148, pumping 12 rounds of HE out of two tubes. Neither OP could observe the impacts beyond the flashes due to darkness and vegetation.[104] The Recon Marines were getting good at firing the mortars.

Now McAdams, Moore, Mushett, and Bayuk had a decision to make. Was the single RPG fired as harassment or was it fired as a ranging round, which would mean an attack later that night? No need to chase the lone RPG sniper, he was long gone. The leaders huddled in the comm bunker and discussed the options. Moore said if it were a ground attack, having seven additional fighters on the hill could just be the difference. He was thinking the NVA had taken a head count of defenders. Having the team out a little ways like a super listening post or ambush would give them warning if they picked the right direction. Having them 1,400 meters out would mean they would not be in the fight.

Mushett said, "We will do whatever the lieutenant wants," throwing the decision to the hill commander.

McAdams's entire life had been a slow southern approach to fishing—wait and see. He said there was no hurry for the night ambush, "Let's play defense tonight and beef us up."

"It's the right call," Moore said. "Doc Schneider can hole up with Doc Bennett. Let's put Miller and 'Little' Moore on the .50-cal. That frees me up. Let's put Collins, Eagle, and Bonini in the two mortar pits as ammo men and a reaction force. Mushett, you stay here with the lieutenant and me. That will give us the most flexibility."

They talked about the pros and cons of a listening post. Everyone was awake and super alert with the RPG attack, so they decided no listening posts. Bayuk said he had already called *Rice Krispies-Mike,* and the firing battery had laid their tubes on the Hill 148 registered target. He could adjust from there quickly. Everyone was ready. Let the NVA come tonight. Mushett went and told *Station Break* they were staying on the hill and what their duties would be. Hill 119 stayed on 100 percent alert all night.

In the morning, Moore saw Mushett and said, "Put your team to bed, you are going out tonight." He went to see McAdams and said he wanted to lead the morning wire check. McAdams said fine. Moore walked the trench line and volunteered Corporal Holmes, Lance Corporals Lowery, Calvery, and Wiley, and Private First Class Paul Freeman for wire check and told them to be ready in 30. As the sun came up, Moore pushed the wire patrol out the east gate and they dropped off the ridgeline immediately into the southeast draw. He did not want the Tho Son hamlet watchers to see them depart. They went down 200 meters with Holmes walking point. Moore had them come out of the draw and head west back up the hill from the draw towards the wire. He told Holmes to go up close, he wanted to check Claymore positioning and look for cut wires, both tricks of the sappers. Lastly, he spread out the distance between the Marines, as it was natural they had bunched up going downhill. Ready to move, he reminded Holmes "No trails, not even game trails, you look for booby traps and let Lowery at deuce point worry about 25 to 50 meters out, now move out." The wire check went on for three hours as Moore was simply being cautious and taking a thorough look at his defenses. They completed the 360 loop, coming back to the east gate and back in past Echo Bunker. Mushett was on top sunbathing, wearing his prized aviator-issue sunglasses. He commented to the tired wire patrol, who had now been up over eighteen hours, "Having fun, girls?"

Moore answered for the patrol, "Shut the fuck up, REMF!" Not much of a comeback but the Marines loved the banter.

Midday on 29 January, *War Cloud* called the *Durham* comm bunker. They had a large group of Vietnamese coming up the hill's main north public trail.[105] Moore got up from his cot and went over to McAdams's bunker and informed the lieutenant. He recommended a patrol be sent down to see what they wanted. McAdams said fine so Moore said he would do it. He asked Bayuk if he wanted to come since he was the best Vietnamese speaker on the hill. Moore got four Marines for security, one radio, and Doc Bennett, and headed out across the LZ and down the north hill. As always, Moore went off-trail. They met the Vietnamese civilians at the railroad berm. Speaking with the group of 21 woman and children led by the one-armed woman, the villagers wanted the bombing to stop in their area. Moore, through Bayuk, informed the villagers they were in a restricted area, and they should not be there, that they needed to leave and go back east to Chien Son village and tell the South Vietnamese Government about their request and demands.[106] They waited and watched as the villagers, in a gaggle, turned and went back down the trail to Tho Son hamlet. Tom McAdams had watched the hour-and-a-half-long evolution from the tower. He still did not fully understand the rules of engagement (RoE) and the FFZ for *War Cloud*. When the patrol got back to the hill, he asked Bayuk and Moore to join him on his back porch, the southern term for the trench line behind his bunker, to discuss FFZs. Sitting with coffee and taking Bayuk off the hook with the lieutenant, Moore said, "Let me try and explain FFZ and Sergeant Bayuk can correct me." Moore brought out his 1:50,000 map and spread it out on the parapet. He had, in black grease pencil, dotted lines that followed major north–south and east–west grid lines on his map. He had a blue box around Hills 119 and 425. Moore said this was to prevent blue-on-blue engagements (blue being the designated map color for Allied or friendly forces and red being the color for enemy map markings). The senior operational command, the 1st Marine Division, established what units owned what areas. They divided the map by zones defined by grid boundaries or easy-to-see terrain features like rivers or railroads. They then assigned friendly ownership to the land. That ownership was called a tactical area of responsibility (TAOR). The blue boxes were the Recon havens around their two OPs. He had a black dotted line following the trace of the north–south railroad. He said east of the line belonged to Korean forces. That was why it took a long time to get clearance to shoot there. Bayuk added that, sometimes, it was not worth trying. Moore then showed a dotted line around the Arizona Territory, Liberty Bridge, and An Hoa, defined by rivers and roads. He said that land belonged to the 5th Marines. He then pointed to the Dodge City area north of Go Noi Island and said that area belonged to the 1st Marines on Hill 55. Now, pointing to Go Noi Island, the area north and west of Hills 119 and 148. He said since no Allied forces were currently operating there, and no civilians lived there, the area was declared an FFZ. That meant if it moved you were allowed to shoot at it, quickly adding as long as it was within the RoE.

McAdams said he was tracking the FFZ but didn't understand the RoE caveat? Bayuk picked up the response since he made that call daily. Bayuk said there was a set of rules that required them to positively identify the target as enemy, friendly, or unknown before it was engaged with supporting arms. It is easy if someone is shooting at you, as then it's self-defense. It was also easy if they were wearing enemy uniforms or carrying rifles. You could judge their intent by what they wore or by their actions, like putting in a booby trap on a trail. Bayuk said the tricky part was Vietnamese in civilian garb. There you should determine what they were doing and were they allowed in that specific area. This was a judgment call by the observer on the assumed intent of the people being observed based on their actions and looks. Moore picked it up and said Recon had it easy compared to the grunts when they were on patrol. Recon operated in areas without a civilian population and within their own haven with no friendlies around. If you met someone on the trail, he was presumed to be the enemy, and you shot. The grunts and artillery had to work in areas co-located or interspersed with civilian populations, and with VC disguised as civilians intermixed with the population; Ho Chi Minh called it "Swimming with the population."

You could not shoot first. Many times the grunts were being ambushed or were the second party to fire due to the RoEs and the cautious behavior of their leaders. Moore said, "Lieutenant, it is a tough problem, which is why you get paid the big bucks as the hill commander. You make those type of calls based on the RoEs, who owns the area, your experience, and training. Like today with our visitors. We must determine the intentions of the Vietnamese. We are looking at people dressed as civilians, but they could easily be VC or NVA in black PJs. Today those twenty or so Vietnamese woman and children we met could have had two VC hiding among them. They could have shot the entire patrol. That is why we had two Marines drop off above us as overwatch security. Outside the group, as we were meeting, they covered for us. We could have been shot but the overwatch could get who shot us." McAdams's head was spinning, he said, "At The Basic School in Quantico they teach scenarios called, 'What now, Lieutenant?' I did not understand it then. This is one. Thank you, gents." He left the meeting and walked the trench line to think. This easily was a moral dilemma—protect your Marines or protect the civilians?

Early that evening, Mushett and his team were in the mortar pit for a cammie and sound inspection. He had them all jump up and down, calling them kangaroos. He was thinking of his upcoming R&R in Australia. The jumping and stomping, as the Marines were now hopping around like kangaroos, had Moore belly laughing. Mushett said, "Knock it off, girls!" They were ready. Lance Corporal Eagle was *Station Break*'s regular point man and led the way out. Mushett let Miller walk his normal deuce-point position as those two worked the point as a pair. He walked third, followed by the primary radio operator, then Doc, then secondary radio, and Private First Class Bonini walked tail. It was dark out past the east gate; off-trail, Eagle turned north and started down the preplanned route. They would weave through the scrub growth and move down to the abandoned railroad berm, their first danger area. Forty minutes later, they were at the berm. Security went out and they crossed individually and quickly. Now they moved northeast along a bamboo line towards Route 537. Finding the old French road, they crossed it, turning east, and looked for an ambush site. Miller found a spot that was two feet higher than the road, as it had sunk. Five meters back, five Marines on-line, in prone positions looking at the kill zone. The two radio operators were behind them facing the river as security. They called *Durham,* stating *Station Break* was at the baseball field, meaning the ambush site. The NOD could not see them. At about 2130, two soldiers walking east on the road, had AK-47s and cartridge belts. They walked into the kill zone. Mushett triggered the small-arms ambush. Five Marines fired. No return fire, two bodies lay on the road bleeding. Putting security out east and west on the road and the north riverside, Mushett and Miller moved in and searched the bodies. These were well-armed VC. The first was wearing green trousers and brown shirt. The second body had a Korean camouflage jacket on and green shorts. Both carried cartridge belts with AK magazines, and packs. They collected two assault rifles, two packs, and were starting to search the pockets when Miller saw five NVA/VC 25 meters down the road to the east towards the big railroad bridge to Go Noi. *Station Break* immediately engaged with small arms and their M79.[107] The enemy broke contact and moved back towards the bridge. Mushett was not going to chase them into an ambush. The team would move to a new location closer to Hill 119.

Saddling up, Mushett pointed Miller due south and uphill towards the OP. *Station Break* moved for five minutes and listened for five minutes. They had gone 300 meters uphill and were now moving 400 meters west next to a dike. They were not in a good position as they were below the abandoned railroad berm to the south and paralleling the irrigation dike. Time to get on the high

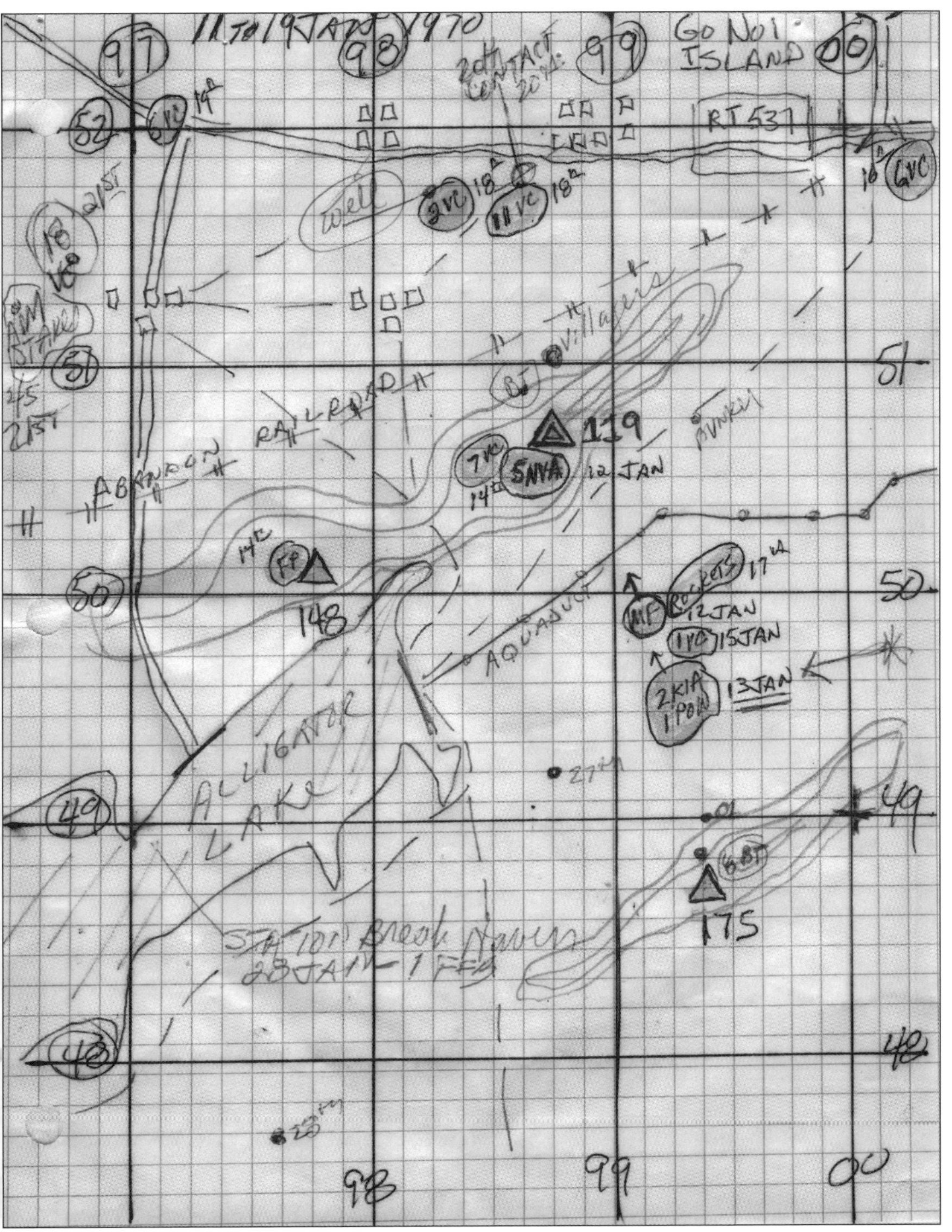

Original heat map of enemy sightings for 11–19 January 1970. (M. Fallon)

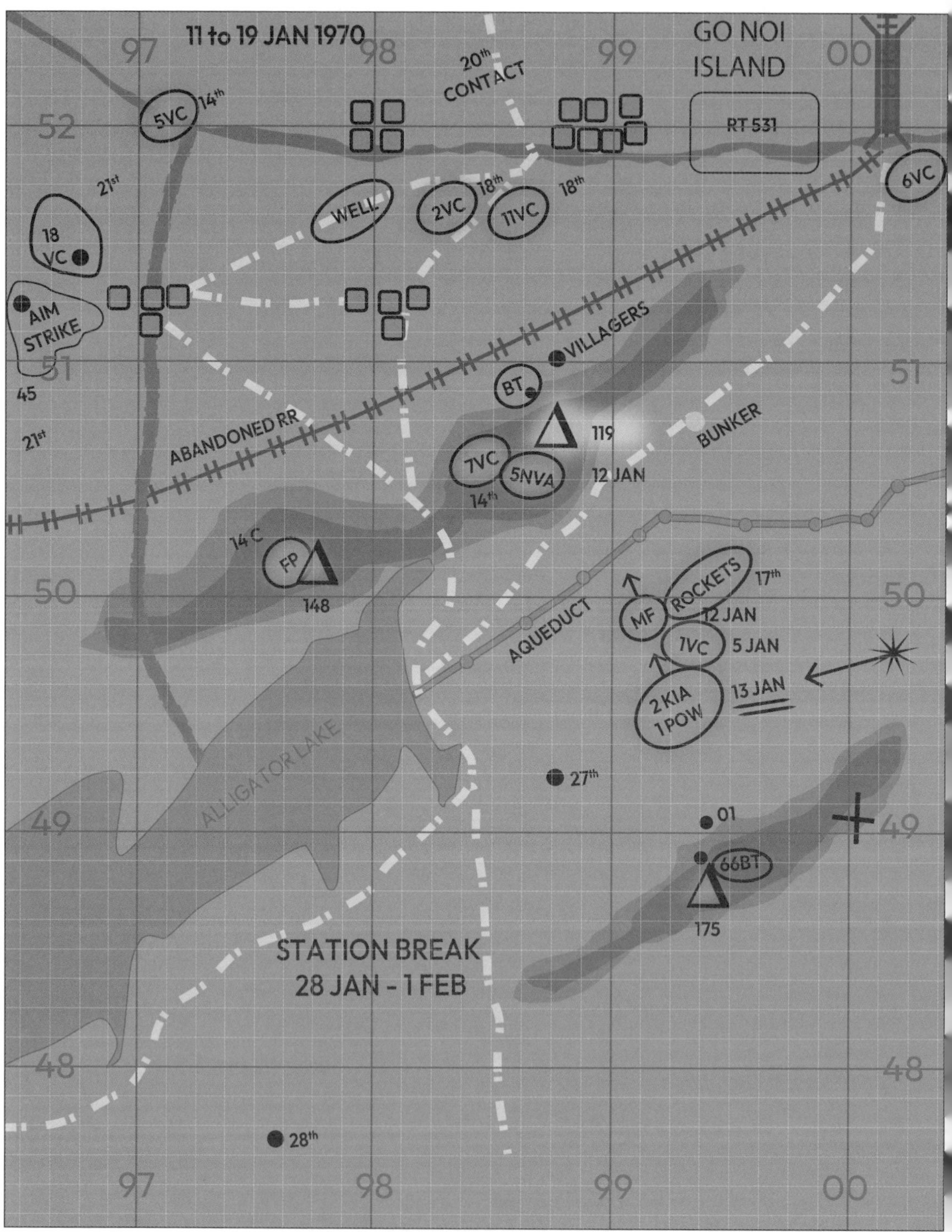

Enhanced sketch, Team *Station Break* patrol, 28 January–1 February 1970. (M. Fallon and W. Denham)

side of this danger area. They stopped and kneeled. It was 2220; they were startled, coming under small-arms fire. They could not see who was shooting at them from above on the berm. The enemy shots went high due to the steep downhill angle. It sounded like two AK-47s. *Station Break* was flat on the ground trying to get over being surprised and assessing their next move. Never a good feeling when you are ambushed! Mushett knew they needed to move. Before he could move the team, two Chi-com grenades came looping into their position. Now the entire team opened up on full auto, followed by the Marines throwing M26 grenades. The M79 was shooting high arch over the berm. The enemy was already gone, departing as they threw the Chinese grenades. They were gone behind the protection of the berm even before the Marines opened fire. Now moving between his prone Marines, Mushett found he had two men wounded, minor shrapnel from the Chi-coms; Corporal Miller and Doc Schneider had been hit but could move.[108]

Mushett told his radio operator, "Tell *Durham* we are coming back to the dugout." Since Miller was hit, Mushett moved up to deuce point and pointed Eagle due south and said, "Get over the berm quickly, stop and set up security, we're going to do this quickly." He raised his fist and gave the double pump, the double-time signal, and all were up and moving. Over the berm, they stopped and listened for 15 minutes. No sounds except an occasional noise drifting off the OP. Mushett had them up and moving; 20 minutes later they were 100 meters out of the east gate still on the steep northeast slope in scrub brush. Stopping, Eagle froze and pointed his M16, to his left; Mushett could make out four enemy, 200 meters further east silhouetted on the skyline. Mushett was in a draw, downhill from an unknown-size enemy group of at least four. He took the handset from his radio operator; whispering, he called *Durham*. Mushett told the OP to tell *War Cloud* to fire the eastern ridgeline on-call Arty target. They would stay put. *War Cloud* had a fire mission out in under thirty seconds. Bayuk had added 200 meters to the on-call just to make sure he was not shooting on *Station Break*.[109] *War Cloud* could not observer the impacts. *Durham* then put up 60-mm illumination. *Station Break* reported they could no longer see the enemy. This group had been in transit from the south to the north. They were a different group of enemy than the earlier engagement. Mushett wondered how the NVA/VC kept from shooting each other. The gunny had been correct on the enemy being everywhere around the OP. *Station Break* radioed *Durham* and said they would be on the move again once the illumination stopped. They were through the east gate in 15 minutes. The two wounded men went to the Doc's in Delta Bunker to get cleaned up. Mushett went to the comm bunker with the two AK-47s and two packs. The packs had rice and canned fish, but no documents or anything of value.[110] McAdams walked to Delta Bunker to check on Miller and Doc Schneider's wounds. They were from minor shrapnel, good for a Purple Heart, but nothing that prevented them from getting back to work. He would not need to call a medevac tonight. The two men were in a good mood. Mushett was amped up on adrenaline, so Moore let him talk through the entire patrol for everyone in the comm bunker to hear, along with McAdams and Bayuk. After hearing the story three times, and an hour later, Moore suggested they hit the sack as they were going out again tomorrow night. On 30 January, *War Cloud* had three routine fire missions on ten sighted NVA/VC, claiming five confirmed kills.[111]

After sundown, *Station Break* held its pre-patrol inspection in the mortar pits. Mushett's kangaroos were jumping about making fun of him. It was time to go. Tonight they were going to set up and ambush on the far west side of Hill 148. Only about 1,500 meters away, it was a blind spot the OP could not observe. They waited for total darkness and then slipped out of the west gate, skirting the north side of the LZ and sidehill above the trash pit. They went to the north side of Hill 148, 300 meters below the skyline. They were on a lateral game trail moving west when they made point-to-point contact with at least three NVA.[112] *Station Break* was in a column on the sidehill trail. Only Eagle and Miller engaged with M16s. The enemy did not fire. Two lay on the ground not moving. Mushett had seen a third soldier sprinting west around the curve of the hill. He told "Little" Moore to "Call your dad and get us some illumination." Mushett pushed Bonini and Collins up the trail, telling them to split up—top side, bottom side—for security. When the illumination came, Mushett and Miller moved up searching for the two bodies. They got two packs and two Russian 7.62-mm automatic pistols.[113] These two appeared to be VC by dress, but who knew. One wore black PJs that were dirty. The other wore green shorts and a black shirt. Mushett called *Durham* to tell them they had been compromised but they'd got two. McAdams told them to come back. It was only 2030, still a long night to get through. *Station Break* closed the distance by backtracking the same game trail in six minutes and were in through the west gate. Sitting in the comm bunker, Moore congratulated Mushett. Two night ambushes, four enemy killed, four weapons retrieved. "Get some sleep as you are on deck again tomorrow night."

Later that evening, around 2300, *War Cloud*, looking through the NOD, observed lights on the side trail between Hill 148 and Alligator Lake. They were blinking on and off like signal lights between Hills 148 and 177. The hills were on either side of Alligator Lake. *Station Break* was in the dugout, so the FO called *Rice Krispies-Mike* and, because he asked for area coverage, he got fire-cracker rounds.[114] He got excellent coverage of the north shore of Alligator Lake and south side of Hill 148. The signal lights ceased.[115] The next day, on 31 January, *War Cloud* had an enemy sighting northwest of Thon Bon (2) hamlet about two kilometers out. They counted 12 NVA/VC wearing a mix of black PJs and green utilities and carrying packs and rifles. They were moving in column to the northeast. *War Cloud* called a fire mission with solid coverage and could observe five bodies lying on the ground. They reported five confirmed kills to *Rice Krispies-Mike*.[116]

After dark, Mushett and his kangaroos were once again in the mortar pit preparing for inspection. Tonight's ambush was scheduled for the aqueduct trail south of the OP. After inspection and radio checks with *Durham*, *Station Break* moved out of the east gate. They dropped into the very steep narrow southeast draw. Eagle was glad to be going downhill. The team proceeded until reaching the small midhill east–west trail. Crossing it, they continued to the valley floor. To the east, they could see lights and cooking fires in Chien Son a kilometer away. This was a large village whose inhabitants farmed the valley. It was deemed a friendly village, but the NVA/VC always taxed them with a harvest tax. Hitting the valley floor, they crossed the danger area of the aqueduct and its dual parallel trails and then across two flooded rice paddies to the boulder field. They were wet from the knees down. This was close to where Moore, a month earlier, had killed the leadership of the T89 Sapper Battalion. Mushett found a sidehill cluster of boulders above the aqueduct and both trails about 200 feet away. He had boulders at his back. With the two radios centered, they got on-line, lying down double arms' distance apart. They were looking downhill, and it was uncomfortable to lie prone as you had to stork out your neck to see anything. As a result, everyone, on their own, was soon in the sitting position with a large boulder as a back stop. It was a good observation position but only a fair ambush site. Mushett called in their position from thrust-point *Car*, radioing Durham: "From, Cheve, down one and east two point three." Moore acknowledged. Moore had Bayuk try to find them with the NOD, but he could not see them. The rice paddies below them were flooded and had been fertilized with human waste and water buffalo dung. The night was quiet, starlit, and still. With no breeze, it smelled, and soon the mosquitoes found the Marines. Mushett had a plastic bottle of bug juice, what the Marines called insect repellant. He applied it generously on his face and neck, then reapplied his cammie stick. He passed the bottle down the line. *Station Break* swatted mosquitoes all night. In the morning, after sunrise but before the field workers arrived from Chien Son, Mushett had the team up and moving. They took the aqueduct trail west to the dam. At the dam, they picked up the clean high-speed trail north and up out of the draw towards their LZ in the saddle above. Mushett made Eagle go off-trail and break brush for the steepest and last 100 meters to the LZ. Soon they were through the west gate and at the mortar pit for a quick debrief.

It was 1 February. According to their operation orders, *Station Break* had been scheduled to stay on the hill patrolling until 6 February.[117] Moore had news for Mushett. "Pack your gear, you are scheduled for extract at 1030 today." Somebody up the chain of command wanted to debrief the team on their two contacts.[118] Moore pulled Mushett aside and told him to hide the two pistols and give them the rifles, four packs, and cartridge belts. "Keep all the AK magazines and give them as souvenirs and trading material to each *Station Break* member. If you give up the pistols you will never get them back! Then you decide who on your team gets the pistols." The two friends shook hands as the green smoke popped on the LZ. Mushett would never forget the three adrenaline-filled walk-off patrols from Hill 119. Later, in the S-2 hut at the battalion debrief, Sergeant J. A. Page had asked about the two pistols; Mushett said they remained in the kill zone. It was a short debrief.[119] When it was over, Page said, "Staff Sergeant, you and Corporal Miller need to be up to Division G-2 at 1300 for their debrief." At the division debrief, it was the LDO captain who had helped Moore on Hill 119. He pushed Mushett hard on the pistols. Pistols were an indicator to the intelligence community of enemy officers. He asked for ages of the two dead men and both Marines said they were older, but hard to tell. The captain wanted to know the length of hair and fingernails. Miller remembered long black hair and longer than normal fingernails. The captain did not believe Mushett did not have the pistols. He wanted a description of both. Mushett said two well-worn automatic Soviet 7.62s. The captain shared his thoughts that the two were VCI (Viet Cong Infrastructure), or political officers, or both. They were the enforcers, not field laborers, based on age, hair, and nails. The captain had his information. Mushett had told half-truths, as he did not have the pistols. He had given them to Corporal Miller and Doc Schneider.

On Hill 119, *War Cloud* shot five fire missions on 30–31 January, claiming ten confirmed kills.[120] The killing machine was grinding on. On 1 February, at about 1020 in the morning, the FOs spotted two enemy wearing a mix of black PJs close to the hill. The tower yelled to the comm bunker. McAdams came out and was waved up to the tower. He saw the two VC sitting cross-legged with packs off in the scrub brush north of the hill. They were watching the

OP. They were on the north side of the railroad cut directly below the hill but, with the haven shifting south, they were outside Recon's haven. Bayuk was happy to call a fire mission. He got good coverage of the targeted area but with the first rounds the pair went underground inside the berm, not to be seen again.[121] That evening, as the sun was dropping over the Arizona Territory, the IOD team spotted a large column of NVA moving from the north to the south. They were next to the Song Ba Ren, about three kilometers northwest of the OP and four kilometers due east of Liberty Bridge. Bayuk worked up his fire mission, asking for a battery-three zone and shift. He called it 70 NVA with packs and rifles. He got all 18 rounds and then repeated the fire-for-effect. The battery firing out of An Hoa was fast and on target. The smoke and dust were high. He got a secondary explosion with the second firing, so he fired the battery a third time. *War Cloud* called in 25 of the 70, as counted on the ground, confirmed kills.[122]

At 2120, both Alpha and Foxtrot Bunkers, on the north side of the OP, saw two enemy. Both bunkers engaged with hand grenades so as not to give away their machine-gun placements. After the explosions, while looking through the starlight scopes and the NOD, they could not see any enemy.[123] It had been a probe in Moore's mind, just assessing the defense. On 2 February, the action started at about 0900 in the morning, with *War Cloud* seeing another large column of NVA northwest near Cu Bon (3), the uninhabited hamlet on Route 537. They were wearing PJs, black bottoms, and white tops. Bayuk thought they were NVA trying to disguise themselves as farmers. Only problem for the enemy was that, with the fidelity of the Big Eyes, Bayuk was able to see rifles. At the 50 count, he initiated a fire mission with *Rice Krispies-Mike*.[124] They gave him negative clearance due to the battery being in check-fire. Check-fires happened for a variety of reasons, aircraft could be on the gun target line or there could be a safety issue on the gun line. He knew they liked to fire, and there was nothing he could do but watch the column move into the deserted hamlet. He also knew that *Rice Krispies-Mike* was co-located with 5th Marines' Combat Operations Center so the grunts would get the word. The hamlet was in the eastern sector of 2/5's tactical area.

That afternoon, just before 1600, the IOD spotted ten villagers with one small girl coming up the main north trail towards the OP. McAdams had his Marines, as per their SOP, send out a security team. The lieutenant went on this one with Bayuk along to interpret. At the meeting spot, they talked with the villagers. There were eight women and two incredibly old men. They said they represented the Chien Son Village Elders Committee. Wearing clean white tops, black bottom PJs, and straw coolie hats, they were very polite and formal. They were requesting permission to use the trail that split the saddle landing zone and went down to the Alligator Lake dam. They said it was their traditional trail, and it was the shortest and easiest route for the village to go fishing. The lieutenant, speaking through Bayuk, told a 12-year-old Vietnamese girl, who knew English fairly well, that this was a restricted area, and that the trail was closed. They could not use it. She interpreted for the delegation. Bayuk told them to turn around and return to Chien Son via Route 537 to the east.[125] The small security/greeting patrol got back to the OP for a dinner of C-rations. They had one more fire mission late that afternoon at sunset on Go Noi Island. The next three days were routine with fire missions and enemy movement onto and off Go Noi Island during both day and night.

On 6 February, at noon, *War Cloud* picked up a large delegation of civilian Vietnamese coming out of Tho Son hamlet and heading up the north slope. They were in civilian clothes, the traditional black-and-white PJs. Bayuk notified McAdams who deferred to Moore for the security patrol. Moore asked for volunteers. Every Marine volunteered, in part, because it broke the monotony of hill life. Moore told Corporal Holmes to pick seven, get Doc Bennett to join him and now regular translator Bayuk at the east gate next to Echo Bunker. The hill always met the Vietnamese from the LZ direction, but Moore did not like patterns. He would take the Marines out the east gate and walk off-trail down the steeper part of the hill. He taught Lance Corporals Lowery and Wiley how to walk a dual point in a column. It was safer due to increased dispersion, especially when a large group of Vietnamese were observing your route march down the hill. Arriving at the meeting spot next to the berm, they all exchanged greetings. Bayuk explained to Moore the delegation was there for Tet, the Vietnamese New Year, and wanted to give gifts and rice cakes. Moore wanted to reciprocate so he called on the radio for a runner to bring a new case of C-rations, 24 meals. He realized there were many more Vietnamese but that was the way it was. He later learned the Big Eyes had counted 45 Vietnamese. The delegation gave them rice cakes and gifts with many smiles and bows.

Then the delegation had letters and cards addressed for *Dublin City Three-Four*. Moore explained *Dublin City* was not on the hill, but they would get the letters and cards to them. *Dublin City Three-Four* was the third and fourth Recon teams of 2nd Platoon of Delta Company's normal callsign.[126] Obviously, Lieutenant Parks and "Doc" Mullins had made a good impression on the villagers with their kindness and medical care. Moore said he would deliver the mail. He wondered to himself how they would know the callsigns unless they were listening to radio traffic? There were five letters and six cards. After 3rd Platoon's flip on 8 February, at the S-2 debrief, the letters and cards were turned over and by day's end had made their way to ITT and then, once translated, over to Counter Intelligence. Parks and Mullins would never see the translated letters and cards.[127] The flip day for the IOD team was just another OP day. They were not going anywhere. The Recon Marines cleaned the hill, got on-line boot-camp style, and did a police call. The flip was tomorrow, 8 February. They were bored and happy to be departing. Gunnery Sergeant Moore was relieved to be leaving the dangerous hill after 28 days. He would be happy not to return. Coming up for his second trip was 2nd Lieutenant Parks and 2nd Platoon with Doc Mullins.[128]

CHAPTER 16

Lieutenant Colonel "Wild Bill" Drumright, 1–20 February 1970

The Chinese zodiac calendar began 6 February 1970 as the Year of the Metal Dog. On 21 February, the US National Security Advisor, Henry Kissinger, began secret sidebar peace talks with Le Doc Tho at a villa outside Paris.[1] At the same time, the regular peace talks continued in Paris between the three parties.

During the first two weeks of February at Camp Horn, Da Nang, the III Marine Amphibious Force (III MAF) Staff Working Group had been hosting XXIV Corps representatives. They were working on the turnover of I Corps' operational command between the two headquarters. With President Nixon's "Vietnamization," and the resulting draw down of Marine Forces in Vietnam, it meant that, in the spring of 1970, there would be more Army troops in I Corps tactical zone than Marines. With that change, the Army had insisted they become the senior operational command in the five northern provinces. This would be a role reversal where the previous senior III MAF would revert to, and report to, XXIV Corps. The decision was straight forward and what General Abrams, Commander of Military Assistance Command, Vietnam (MACV) in Saigon, had instructed.[2] The detail of the transition was being worked out by the functional working groups. All the groups had worked on the changeover, timelines, communications nets, etc. One issue remained—control of aircraft—and, in this matter, both the Army and the Marines shared a common concern at the notion of turning over control to the Air Force. During the second week, a compromise was proposed and would be briefed up both chains of command. The Marines and Army agreed to keep the current air command-and-control structure in place with the flip of senior headquarters. III MAF would retain operational control and tasking of the 1st Marine Aircraft Wing and XXIV Corps would retain operational control over the 101st Airborne Division's enormous helicopter fleet. The Marines would still provide an agreed number of fixed-wing sorties to the Air Force Component, Seventh Air Force. The only real change being proposed was a simple flip of the two current higher headquarters. On 19 February, at Camp Horn, Lieutenant General Herman Nickerson USMC and Lieutenant General Zais USA briefed General Abrams on the planned Army takeover of I Corps' Tactical Zone, with a proposed date of 9 March. Abrams approved the plan proposed by Nickerson that III MAF would become subordinate to XXIV Corps while continuing as the parent unit of the 1st Marine Division, 1st Marine Air Wing, and Force Logistics Command.[3] This approach would preserve the integrity of the Marine air–ground team in Vietnam.

At 1st Marine Division in February, the planning was all about the drawdown of strength and turning over positions while maintaining security of the Da Nang Vital Area. The 26th Marine

Regiment was designated to rotate out of country in March. They would begin turning over sections of the Da Nang Rocket Belt defense to the 1st Marine Regiment, who would expand to all 547 square miles of the inner-belt defense. The 26th Marines would be honored with the award of a Presidential Unit Citation for their defensive stand during the Khe Sanh siege as ordered by General Westmoreland in 1968. After receiving the award, they would board ships and planes and depart Da Nang, to be stood down at Camp Pendleton.[4]

***

Below Hill 327, 1st Marine Division headquarters, and across Division Road at Camp Reasoner, the Recon Battalion was in shock. First their quiet commander, Lieutenant Colonel J. J. Grace, had been booby-trapped and medevac'd on 20 January.[5] This event was followed shortly by his loud replacement on the 26th. Lieutenant Colonel "Wild Bill" Drumright had arrived with a mandate from the division commander, his boss.[6] The former Marine Raider, Major General Wheeler, had ordered Drumright, to go on the offensive[7] just as he had on Tulagi Guadalcanal, and New Georgia in World War II. Additional support came from Wheeler's boss, Nickerson, who was considered the "Godfather of Reconnaissance" in the Marine Corps. Drumright, with a Silver Star as a 2nd lieutenant in Korea, had commanded both an infantry battalion and the reconnaissance battalion under Wheeler in the 2nd Marine Division. Now commanding his fourth battalion under Wheeler, he knew what the old warrior wanted!

Down at the battalion, the Recon Marines were pleased with the mess hall doubling its meals served from two a day to four. When you went on patrol and lost three to ten pounds, it was good to be able to chow down when in the rear. Gunner Sergeant Paradise, Recon's chief cook, now had the backing and budget for him and his cooks to put on a feast. Somehow, they managed to trade captured weapons, received from the Recon teams, for steaks. He put on a steak fry every Sunday afternoon.

February 1 found Captain Thomas Martin in the Delta Company office drinking coffee and talking with Fred Klein, his executive officer (XO). First Lieutenant "Jerry" Spolter had been assigned by battalion, checked in, and pushed out on his first Recon patrol that last week of January.[8] On 3 February, 2nd Lieutenant M. O. Fallon checked into Recon Battalion after his duty as a platoon commander with 3rd Battalion, 26th Marines. Because of timing, and the fact he came from the 26th Marines, he was labeled by the current Recon officers as one of "Drumright's Boys." While he met the criteria, he had come from a different battalion and did not know the commander.

At Battalion, upon Drumright's arrival, he had Major Mattiace in the S-3 shop compile a list of all the battalion officers with the number of patrols they had completed and the last time they'd been on patrol.[9] Drumright's modus operandi was to fire the officers who avoided the bush while promoting the bush warriors. He had the S-1 (administration) start taking standard 4 × 4 polaroid mugshot photos of every officer. He had the logistics officer (S-4) build him a four-by-eight-foot photo board for his office wall. One private in the adjutant's shop now had a full-time job with the polaroid camera and the Dymo-Astro label maker printing the last name in black tape for every officer, and for keeping the board up to date. This board, which was an effective tool for a commander to visualize every officer in his organization, became the focal point of many discussions between the lieutenants in the battalion.[10] Soon, every officer in the battalion had his mug shot on the commander's wall with his last name below in black tape. Drumright had grease pencils and would make checks, Xs, and other annotations he understood but were the source of numerous rumors on the lieutenants' grapevine. If a company grade officer, captain, 1st, or 2nd lieutenant avoided going to the field or bush, that was grounds for Drumright to have him transferred out of the battalion. In Drumright's first week, ten officers were reassigned outside the battalion, including Lieutenant Klein; there was also an influx of seasoned lieutenants from the grunts.[11] These were gung-ho officers finishing their six months in the rice paddies who did not want a staff job, so they sought a transfer in order to stay operational in the field. These were precisely the warriors Drumright was seeking. These experienced new joins became known as "Drumright's Boys" or, his own Tennessee word, "Peckerwoods,"[12] which could be used as a compliment or derogatory term by the colonel depending on the situation. In forcefully stamping his aggressive personality on the battalion, Drumright instituted two daily routines. In the morning, he hosted a commanders and staff breakfast for all company commanders and principle staff members at a long rectangular table in the officers' section of the mess hall.[13] It allowed Drumright to eat the same chow as his Marines, and it put him visibly in front of the troops. Drumright would hold the morning meetings in front of the world. There he would berate the chosen officer who was not supporting his Marines to the level he saw fit. It became known among the lieutenants as "The Breakfast Club."[14] This was a club not worth joining, or participating in, for the weak of heart or those afraid of a public berating. In early February, besides the battalion staff, The Breakfast Club members were the following company commanders:[15]

Co. A: 1st Lieutenant C. W. Charlie Kershaw
Co. B: 1st Lieutenant S. H. Crane, (8 Feb) 1st Lieutenant A. J. Tony Pack
Co. C: Captain L. D. McVey
Co. D: Captain Thomas Martin
Co. E: 1st Lieutenant G. D. Banks
H&S Co.: Captain R. L. Wiltecut

The second Drumright meeting was informal, but nightly. A table had always been designated as the "Commander's Table" at the Staff Noncommissioned Officers/Officers Club on Camp Reasoner. The location of the table was an indicator of the commander's personality and leadership style. In 1969, Lieutenant Colonel "Mick" Mickelson, the outgoing and well-liked professional battalion commander, had his table in the center of the room,[16] a round table with wooden chairs equidistant from all corners of the club. Lieutenant Colonel J. J. Grace, the next battalion commander, was a quiet professional; not one for socializing, he had the table moved to the back corner of the room close to the exit.[17] He could quietly observe the lieutenants and SNCOs letting their hair down while not interfering with their stress-relief valve, and he could depart early without making ripples. His replacement, Drumright, moved the table to the front row, center stage![18] He had the sergeant major find a human skull. It was cleaned, lacquered, and buff shined. Placed in its mouth was a Ka-Bar knife. It was the centerpiece of the table. When Drumright arrived at night, he got a bottle of whiskey and a couple of shot glasses from the bar and moved to his table, yelling out to Peckerwoods he spotted and wanted a word with to join him.[19] Nobody sat at that table without invitation. There, Drumright would hold court.

Attended by rear-echelon motherfucker warriors he tolerated; Drumright more often invited the hero-of-the-day. That was whatever lieutenant had just returned from a patrol, having engaged the enemy and arriving via an emergency extraction. Emergency extractions meant, 90 percent of the time, you were shot out by the enemy after making contact, or you had a prisoner. They were adrenalin-producing, scary events. Drumright expected, demanded, cajoled, and then invited the lieutenant-of-the-day after his debrief and shower to join him at the club.

Like a moth to a light, there was a group of officers who were drawn to this aggressive commander. They tended to be college-fraternity boys or athletes, and jocks who had been center stage in high school and fared well in college. By nature, they were aggressive, outgoing, and attracted to the focus of attention. There was a second group of officers who were afraid of this wild man, this senior officer who yelled and sang songs about Valhalla. The remaining group of officers tended to think first. This cohort wanted and tried to be professional. They tended to be quiet and determined. Their view was that war was not a game. War was serious business. It was their job to protect their Marines' lives while accomplishing the mission.[20] The second and third groups started avoiding the club if Drumright was present and would relax in each company's officers' hut, enjoying their reel-to-reel tape deck and drinking beer from the small dormitory style refrigerator in every hut. They shared their stories and experiences with each other, trying to learn. They also decompressed from the "always on" mode of a patrol; it was time to get some sleep for two days before being fragged to go out again on patrol.

Operationally, Drumright wanted patrols to be led by lieutenants for their abilities to read a map and employ supporting arms. All enlisted patrol leaders now had to be reviewed and recertified. He had the S-3 (operations) shop produce a new additional week's training schedule for Recon Marines, post-Recon Indoctrination Program (RIP).[21] This program was to be executed at the company level, focusing on patrol-team-level skills instead of the RIP focus on individual training. It included actions after enemy contact such as immediate-action drills, communications, and antenna techniques, as well as advanced first aid. Drumright expected every team to go through the new training during its six-week cycle. It meant more work between patrols at Camp Reasoner. Finally, and what impacted every Marine the most, was an increase in operational tempo. The division had increased its requirement on the battalion from 24 to 30 teams on patrol daily plus maintaining the five observation posts (OP) over the enemy's major avenues of approach.[22] More teams out in the bush meant fewer days in the rear. When not in your training week, or your two-week OP cycle, a team could expect three weeks of patrolling by executing one patrol per week. The norm became two days between patrols to decompress, pick up a new frag order, and plan your next patrol.

General Wheeler's enemy counterpart, General Binh, commander of Front 4, and the 2nd North Vietnamese Army (NVA) Division, was busy in January and early February rebuilding and resupplying. He was preparing his battlespace for the spring Tet offensive as directed by his Central Committee and the Central Office for South Vietnam. He had an ongoing harvest and tax operation collecting rice in the lowlands. In his two main Base Areas, 112 and 116, he was bringing new replacements off the Ho Chi Minh Trail to backfill his battalions and regiments.[23] MACV intelligence estimated the trail traffic south had increased tenfold in December and January from the prior period of September–October.[24] Wheeler's plan was to disrupt Binh in his backyard. He had 1st Recon Battalion gearing up and beginning direct inserts of teams into both NVA base areas.

Purely by happenstance, Jerry Spolter was the first lieutenant to join the battalion one day after Drumright's arrival. Because of his seniority, he was assigned to Delta Company, who already had a captain commander. A week later, on 3 February 2nd Lieutenant M. O. Fallon arrived, having hitchhiked down the division road at the foot of Hill 327. The 3rd Battalion, 26th Marines' (3/26) rear was west of the division's headquarters area about a mile. With the Lima Company jeep deadlined after hitting a road mine near Hill 190, he had few options. However, the well-used gravel road, with military vehicles going in both directions, was an easy place to find a ride. He had turned in his M16 so, with his seabag and no weapon, he felt vulnerable as he walked downhill to the road, sticking his thumb out. The first six-by-six stopped. The driver was surprised when recognizing an officer and said, "Where do you need to go, sir? Fallon said 1st Recon and climbed aboard. The Marine said he drove right by it. Stopping at the Reasoner gate, Fallon thanked the Marine and, carrying his seabag, walked over to the guard, asking for the S-1 shop. Thirty minutes later, after talking with Captain Sterling, he was assigned to Delta Company as "Butch" Waddill's replacement, whose request to move to the grunts for his second six months had been honored. Butch was leaving because he was tired of working OPs and *Keyhole* patrols.[25] He wanted to mix it up with the enemy and thought by going to the grunts he may be able to get into some fighting. The irony was, had he stayed another month, he would have fit into Drumright's mold and may have thrived and seen the action he was seeking.

Butch's last patrol with Delta Company was with Team *Summer Breeze*.[26] It was a Drumright-type patrol, lasting only 26 hours. On 22/23 January, the enemy counter-recon team was on him from his late-afternoon insert, sweeping all night for the team hidden in a sidehill bramble. At noon, the team smelled cooking and fresh fish. They were close to a base camp. Pulling back and away from the draw, they were crossing a sidehill trail when they made contact with the point element of a large NVA unit coming downhill towards them. Butch pulled *Summer Breeze* back across a creek and up a finger. He was facing 30 NVA, that he could see. Calling an artillery mission, his next call was for an emergency extract. By 1430, they were in a 360 defense on a downhill finger with enemy moving all around them. The first OV-10 arrived. It was *Hostage Echo* who used his own rockets. He was relieved on station by another *Hostage* aircraft with *Cowpoke One*, followed by *Cowpoke Eight* who was running two gunships, *Scarface Five-Eight* and *Two-Seven.* They kept the large enemy force, estimated from the air at over one hundred, off the team's back. The extract CH-46, with ladder, arrived after a long two-hour siege. At 1635, the helo, hovering and taking small-arms fire from both higher ridgelines, began the extract. Waddill, with a PRC-25 on his back, was the last Marine to snap-link in on the aluminum ladder for the ride back to LZ 401.[27] Following that patrol, Waddill checked out of the battalion. There was a small informal going away in the Delta Company officers' hut. He had no exit interview from Captain Martin, which was fine by Butch.[28] In the turbulence of the dozen officer changes, he ended up talking to no one from Battalion upon his exit. Butch was assigned to 3rd Battalion, 5th Marines, and ended up in the Arizona Territory as a platoon commander. There, he chased ghosts in small engagements of the enemy's choosing and tried to avoid booby traps. Exactly what he had just left at Hill 119.

Back at Delta Company, Fallon, like the other new officers, was a volunteer for Recon, completing his grunt time as an infantry platoon commander. He had served in Hai Van Pass, Elephant Valley, Hill 190, The Claw, and Hill 124. He was learning by living and sleeping in the field. After The Basic School (TBS), he went through Recon Replacement School. The school in reality was a practical exercise in supporting arms. There he learned and practiced firing live artillery, naval gunfire, and calling air strikes in southern California. Fallon said it was the best school he ever went to as it taught him fire-support skills that he put into practice in combat less than a month after graduation by calling all three of the arms in support of his platoon in 3/26. In his first firefight, he was physically pushed by a Marine behind a dike who said, "Lieutenant, get on the radio and get us something, we will take care of these 'gooners.'" Fallon, like Spolter, met Drumright's criteria of experience in the field and ability to read a map and call supporting arms.

***

After Overton tripped the booby trap and was medevac'd on 20 January, Gunnery Sergeant Moore was the Hill 119 commander until the next Delta Company flip.[29] The newly-arrived 2nd Lieutenant Tom McAdams filled in and took the platoon up to the OP on 25 January, with Moore staying to back him up.[30] They stayed until 8 February, when 2nd Lieutenant Garry Parks took his 2nd Platoon up the hill.[31]

This was Parks's second trip to the hill. He had previously been on the hill during the last two weeks of December when, on Christmas Day, he had met a delegation of villagers from Tho Son hamlet led by the village elder, the one-armed woman. With Parks was his experienced platoon sergeant "Butch" Harvey. Moore was relieved to hear that 2nd Platoon was arriving with 22 Marines and two corpsmen. The hill also changed callsigns to *West Orange*.[32] They would have sufficient Marines to both defend and to actively patrol. It was a rushed flip driven by helicopter schedule instead of sound tactical handoff of a position to a new unit. Second Platoon arrived in two CH-46s at 1000 and McAdams and Moore were off with their platoon at 1100, headed for showers and steak from Paradise's mess hall at Camp Reasoner.[33]

Parks had Harvey assign bunkers while he went up and got a situational brief from the forward observer, Sergeant Mark Bayuk. In the afternoon, Parks met with Harvey to emplace the second .50-caliber machine gun they had scrounged for the hill. Parks wanted the second gun to replace the M60 in Charlie Bunker facing south toward the rocket site on the north face of Hill 175. The .50-cal had the range and punch to cover Hill 175, two kilometers southeast of the OP. He would move the M60 to another bunker. The hill now had six primary bunkers: two with .50-cals, three with M60s, and one with the 40-mm XM174 automatic grenade launcher.[34] Parks spent the next two days in live-fire training by teaching every Marine how to fire and load the .50-cals, and refresher training on how to employ the 60-mm mortar. With positions assigned and refresher training completed, he and Harvey talked walk-off patrols. On the afternoon of 10 February, they did a circular wire check. It was fortuitous as they discovered a booby trap on the side of the north trail down where they always met the villagers. It was a new M26 grenade with a trip wire. It was tied to an illumination round parachute from a 155-mm Arty round.

It was rigged so the person retrieving the parachute, a desired scrounge item, would trip the grenade. The patrol disarmed the booby trap, retrieving both the grenade and the parachute.[35] Parks called the five-man team to the pit and quietly counseled them that disarming the grenade was not the preferred solution. They did not know if the fuse had been fucked with or if it was a double booby trap. He said in future to just blow it in place, because the parachute was not worth the kind of injuries Overton and Lieutenant Colonel Grace had sustained while walking off Hill 119 on a trail.

On the 11th, the walk-off patrol checked out Hill 148 to the west. They only saw dated signs of the fight that had taken place there in January. On the 12th, they went east. They saw hundreds of Vietnamese working the fields outside the village of Chiem Son Dong (3) on Route 537. This area was controlled by the Marines from the Republic of South Korea with their brigade headquarters in the port town of Hoa An. The walk-off patrol on the morning of the 13th returned north, patrolling toward the closest small hamlet of Tho Son. Two hundred meters south of the hamlet, near a burial pagoda, Team *West Orange-Alpha* found a newly dug bunker, 5' × 5' × 4', situated directly under the pagoda. The bunker appeared to be unused. About 45 minutes later, they circled due west, parallel to Route 537 and found a trench line. It had fighting holes dispersed intermittently along the east–west high-speed trail. A second trench line appeared to have been recently worked. As the patrol turned south and headed back to the hill around noon, they found an 18-inch by 30-inch propaganda sign made of wood supported by four foot bamboo poles. One side of the sign read, "G.I. Neutralism will be appreciated," the other side read, "Refuse to fight and get killed."

The patrol left the sign where it was, fearing it could be booby-trapped. They continued west, patrolling beside the abandoned railroad bed headed towards An Hoa. After a kilometer they turned south and uphill to circle around and come up Hill 148 before returning to the OP. As they approached the west military crest of Hill 148, *West Orange-Alpha* found a booby-trapped M26 grenade on the side of the trail. With the pin pulled and spoon secured inside a C-ration can, the metal can was spiked into the ground. The team called their location in to *West Orange-Actual*, who told them to blow it in place and proceed back to the OP.[36] Although the patrol made no enemy contact on this daylight security patrol, they found indications of enemy construction efforts at every turn, all facing the OP or on trails routinely used by the Marines coming off the hill. Parks concluded the enemy was using the abandoned rail line as a simple navigation aide to move both east and west for the NVA who did not know the area. While the rail berm was a straight, elevated feature, it had two high-speed trails running parallel to, and below, it on both sides.[37] The following day, he would have *West Orange-Alpha* patrol east along the berm towards the old rail bridge to Go Noi Island.

The patrol pushed out at first light and moved slowly north and downhill, off-trail from the landing zone (LZ), until they intersected the berm. The team leader had coordinated with "Big Eyes" on the hill to watch their six, especially as they started to patrol east on the berm trail. They called in their checkpoints and moved very slowly as the sun rose in their face. After moving 600 meters looking into the sun, the patrol leader turned due south and moved up and over the low finger that led west to Hill 119. They were now moving downhill into Alligator Lake valley and would circle back around to the OP later that day. At around 1100, at grid coordinates

AT997507, they stumbled across a hidden rice cache as they were breaking brush off-trail. The cache contained approximately 350 pounds of rice in two vats, each measuring 34 inches by 36 inches. They took a one-pound sample and destroyed the rest of the rice. An hour-and-a-half later, now moving west back toward the OP, the team found an extraordinarily strong bunker built with railroad ties. Its entrance was small, two feet by two feet, and opened into one room 3.5 feet wide by four feet high. The bunker appeared to have been used within the past week. The team destroyed the bunker with grenades and headed back uphill to 119.[38]

For 15 February, Parks decided to switch the patrol from daytime walk-off to a night patrol and ambush. He asked Sergeant Harvey to put together a team and give them the day off to rest. He told Harvey to come back to his bunker and they would brainstorm a patrol route, set up checkpoints and preregistered fires. Parks knew the NVA were infiltrating past the OP and using the railroad berm and then tracks across the bridge to move in to Go Noi Island.[39] He and Harvey laid out a route that departed the hill headed north toward the abandoned railroad berm and then followed it east for a kilometer where the berm turned north toward the bridge. The turn was a good spot for an ambush looking in two directions. With the plan in place, the normal hill routine continued.

Harvey and patrol *West Orange-Alpha* pushed out 15 minutes after sunset with a little light to use to watch for booby traps while departing the OP. By 1845, they were on the railroad berm headed east. At 1904, Integrated Observation Device (IOD) Team *Hansworth* spotted nine Viet Cong/NVA moving from north to south. They were moving across a sandbar and were four kilometers west of the patrol. *Hansworth* called an artillery fire mission, resulting in five enemy kills.[40] Using the sound of the Arty as a distraction allowed *West Orange-Alpha* to pick up their pace. They reached the berm elbow heading north and set in the ambush position on the high side, ten feet off the berm trail. The team was in an "L" shape and had good fields of fire down the trail both south to north and east to west. They called in their position and waited. At 1920, they could see a squad of NVA coming down the tracks on top of the berm. They had AK-47s, and one had an M16. The team also saw enemy movement coming out of Tho Son hamlet headed their way. The enemy on the tracks stopped and set into a hasty ambush 100 meters prior to the berm L and Harvey's ambush. Harvey waited; nobody was moving except the Viet Cong (VC) coming out of the hamlet. Harvey thought the enemy must have seen the patrol depart the hill and this was a trap. He decided to move instead of being caught between two enemy forces. As they were moving south out of their ambush position at the L, contact was made with the enemy 100 meters west. They were on the low side of berm, so Harvey's fire went over their heads as the berm was protecting them. The enemy, firing uphill, shot high. Harvey withdrew the team south and up the finger, seeking higher ground as he called *Hansworth* on the radio and called for his preplanned target #2. Three minutes later, they had Arty fire on the berm elbow. Harvey adjusted fire, calling for a shift west 100 meters and fire-for-effect (FFE). He would use the FFE by the Arty battery out of An Hoa Combat Base to cover them and keep the enemy's heads down or in their bunkers. Harvey and *West Orange-Alpha* withdrew up the finger and back through the wire on the east end of Hill 119 by coming in the Echo Bunker gate.[41] They had not stopped their adversaries, except to send the message that the Marines were patrolling off the OP at night. Parks thought sending that message with a light contact was a good patrol effort. They also confirmed they were being observed coming and going; therefore, they needed to depart the OP after full darkness.[42]

On the 16th, *Hansworth* called two fire missions. One was at sundown on ten VC wearing black "PJs" and carrying packs and rifles. The effect of the fire mission was to kill five enemy who had been walking on the railroad berm. On 17 February, the IOD team called three more successful fire missions which resulted in five confirmed enemy kills. The 18th saw *Hansworth* shoot four fire missions, resulting in nine confirmed enemy down.[43]

On the 19th, Sergeant Harvey led a walk-off patrol to the southwest down to the Alligator Lake dam to check the trails and the intersection of the aqueduct that led east from the dam's lower face down the valley, along with the trails on both sides. There were large boulders in the draw. It was difficult terrain if you were not on a trail. Corporal Mike Carver was carrying the radio; Lance Corporal Iantorno, known to the platoon as "Big I" for his size, carried the M79 and 40 rounds (double the norm). Walking on the trail to make up for time, the patrol discovered fresh footprints running north to south, the same direction they were heading. Then they spotted wet green utilities and a pair of blue trousers on the side of the trail, somebody's laundry. *Alpha* reported the finds to *Actual.* It was midday, so Parks told *West Orange-Alpha,* via radio, to stay out and follow the leads. The team ate cold chow, filled their canteens, and pushed back out down past the laundry site, deeper into the boulder field. They would catch the enemy coming back for their laundry. They headed south but stayed off the trail toward the dam. They made good time going down the steep hill, crossing the aqueduct danger area and two trails, and heading southeast towards Hill 175.

About 1230, while kneeling for a security and listening pause, Carver smelled cooking and saw smoke coming out of the boulders as the ravine headed uphill. After checking the slight wind direction, Harvey had the team throw two CS (tear gas) grenades into the ravine. This flushed out three NVA wearing green utilities. They ran south and uphill on a trail toward the Hill 175 summit. *West Orange-Alpha* opened fire with their M16s. They observed one enemy fall. There was no return fire. After listening for ten minutes, they moved forward into the ravine to check out the small cave complex. They found two blood trails. The team searched the rest area; it was able to hold five or six men. They found evidence of a recent fire as the coals were still warm. They found four china plates, two metal dishes, and one spoon, an M26 grenade, one Chi-com grenade, one bandolier of ammunition, and a number of socks filled with rice, tobacco, and canned fish. Civilian clothes, including two pairs of blue trousers, two pinstriped shirts, were also found as were green utility uniforms and two hammocks.[44] This site was well hidden but close to the military crest of Hill 175, from which the enemy could observe Hill 119 to the north. During the one-way small-arms engagement, Big I slipped on a large boulder and fell five feet into the ravine. "Doc" Mullins went to his aid. It was apparent Big I was in pain and had a broken knee cap.[45] He could not walk. Harvey immediately called for a medevac. While it was getting approved, he sent four team members back down to the valley floor to look for and find a suitable one-bird landing zone. The rest of the team searched the small base camp and collected the enemy's gear. Forty-five minutes later, they got the call from the CH-46 and brought it into the zone for Iantorno's medevac. The well-liked Marine from Derwynn, Illinois, would be gone for over a month before returning to the platoon on light duty. Late that afternoon, Harvey, Doc

Mullins, and *West Orange-Alpha* turned around, and headed north back towards the OP. Lance Corporal "Boston" Ingemi grabbed Big I's M79 and 40-mm ammo while Harvey grabbed his H-harness and web belt/canteens to ensure his gear got to the rear. They brought the gear from the enemy camp back to the OP in the one NVA pack they had found.[46] Parks had *Hansworth* execute a fire mission on Hill 175 to cover the team's approach march back up the hill. The IOD team called two additional fire missions that afternoon, facing the northern Go Noi Island direction, with six confirmed kills.[47]

During this 12-day flip, Parks, 2nd Platoon, and *Team Hansworth* had 30 sightings by IOD or patrols, totaling 164 NVA/VC. *Hansworth* had called 26 fire missions, resulting in 58 confirmed enemy kills. Recon Team *West Orange-Alpha* had two enemy contacts resulting in one confirmed kill and two blood trails.[48] Parks's two-week stay was over on 20 February when he was replaced by Fallon and 1st Platoon.[49] This would be Fallon's first trip to the OP on Hill 119.

***

Meanwhile, Recon Battalions' operations intensified and continued following the new guidance from Division. Newly assigned to Delta from Headquarters and Service (H&S) Company, 2nd Lieutenant Chris L'Orange became Delta Company's 4th Platoon commander. For his first patrol, he would be taking Team *Chili Pepper* out on 13 February into the heart of Base Area 112.[50] His planned insert LZ was Hill 1031 high up on the jungled table-top terrain feature, the Ong Thu Slope. It was just east of the Song Vu Gia and Thuong Duc special forces camp. The camp would be the patrol's radio-relay site for this patrol. L'Orange was totally surprised that morning at LZ 401 when he was greeted by the battalion's new intelligence officer (S-2), Captain R. Cook. The captain informed him that he and three members of Division Public Affairs, an officer and camera team, were accompanying actor James Franciscus and would be joining them.[51] These five strap hangers would ride the insert bird to film and observe Recon in action. They were introduced to Mr. James G. Franciscus, who was decked out in brand-new cammies and boots with a large new bush hat and stood out as a FNG (fucking new guy) compared to the painted faces and worn boots of Team *Chili Pepper*. The public-affairs crew and celebrity went over and met the pilots next to the bird. Both were pissed off and said so to Captain Cook, but to no avail. The insert bird already had a wing strap hanger added to the five-man crew. With the Recon team of seven, and the VIP crew of five, it put the head count at 18 on the bird. Weight was the issue, with the insert going in at altitude on Hill 1031. The pilot could have overruled for safety but gave in to peer pressure or the camera.

Everyone got on board and the birds turned up and headed for the one-hour-long ride out west to the Thuong Duc corridor. Following the river west and gaining altitude, they identified the LZ on Hill 1031. It was an old well-known infantry fire-support base. The bird started its spiral down to land. At that time, the jungle below, on the helo's left side, lit up with massive, small arms and machine-gun fire. Green and red tracers arced at the bird. The CH-46 was coming down slowly and aborted the landing.[52] To get away, it needed to gain airspeed, dipping its nose and moving it closer to the jungle as it dove for the river to gain speed and fly west to the safety of the valley by putting distance between the bird and the hilltop LZ. Recon called this getting shot out of the zone. The bird took several hits; therefore, for mechanical reasons, it flew directly back to Marble Mountain Air Facility. The team and strap hangers all got off, switched to the chase bird, and went out for a second try on the alternative LZ. Every LZ on The Slope had NVA zone watchers. In this 100-square-kilometer area, there were only four LZs. In the second zone, they were also shot out.[53] Returning to An Hoa for fuel they tried a third time, but, due to darkness, could not find the third small alternative zone so flew back to LZ 401. Division Public Affairs was pleased with their film and Mr. Franciscus had a real war story. At least a month later, one of the *Chili Pepper* patrol members' sister mailed him a copy of a magazine article. It featured Franciscus and his brush with death on this exciting Reconnaissance Team insert.[54] Drumright met Team *Chili Pepper* at LZ 401 that evening. He was not pleased the team did not get in. He stated flatly they were going back the next day and would be the first mission in the morning.[55] The next morning, they did go in but were inserted down by the river and had to hump uphill to get to their haven.[56] Using the riverside LZ meant the NVA knew where the team started and would watch them the entire way and then choose to either avoid or come after them. The NVA were the home team; it would be their choice.

Back at Battalion on 14 February, The Honorable Mr. Paul W. McCloskey Jr., Representative from the 11th District of the State of California, visited 1st Recon Battalion and was provided with a brief on reconnaissance operations by S-3 Training.[57]

***

Meanwhile in Okinawa, Japan, Marines were trying to get in-country. They wanted a chance to prove themselves in combat, or they needed to get a combat tour on their record if they planned a career in the Marines. In 1968 and 1969, there were not enough Marines to fill the slots of two full divisions and a large air wing and logistics tail; now, in 1970, with the drawdown of forces, it was getting harder for officers to get in-country.

On Okinawa, the 3rd Marine Division had redeployed from Vietnam and was getting settled into the island's base camps. Two officers, having recently departed Vietnam with short tours, Lieutenants Porter "Hank" Rathmell and W. X. Lee, were ecstatic. Major George Rivers, the commanding officer of the 3rd Reconnaissance Battalion, recently redeployed from Quang Tri, Vietnam, to Camp Schwab, Okinawa, had worked his back-channel field-grade magic and the two lieutenants had orders to 1st Reconnaissance Battalion.[58] They were headed back to Vietnam and back to Recon! The two lieutenants had gone to the major when the 3rd Recon Battalion had redeployed with the 3rd Marine Division as part of the first phase of the Vietnamization drawdown plan. They had both been in-country less than six months and therefore were eligible to go back if they could get someone to accept them. Both had desires for careers in the Corps and for more trigger time. They had not only volunteered but had petitioned Rivers to release them. Rivers, a legendary Reconnaissance Marine, recognized some of himself in these two hard-charging lieutenants who had already proven themselves running long-range patrols on the demilitarized zone (DMZ) and along the Cua Viet River sand dunes and scrub brush against the NVA. He had made the call to fellow battalion commander "Wild Bill" Drumright at 1st Recon

Battalion.[59] Drumright was hiring patrol leaders and Rivers's word was the only endorsement these two needed.

It was 12 February 1970, and they had much to do in two days to checkout of 3rd Recon and report to Marine Corps Air Station (MCAS) Futenma on the morning of 14 February for a C-130 flight to Da Nang. They were going back. Besides packing their dress uniforms and civilian clothes in cardboard moving boxes, and turning those into the supply system for storage, they had to turn over their platoons, turn in their 782 gear (personal gear worn in the field and issued upon arrival at a unit), and their weapons to the 3rd Recon armory. The last act on the evening of 13 February was their going-away party with Major Rivers and the rest of the officers and senior staff noncommissioned officers of 3rd Reconnaissance Battalion,[60] most of whom would have traded places with them, including Rivers. That evening, they drank for their fallen comrades and for the future success of the Corps. They drank too much, but knew they had recovery time the next day in transit to Da Nang.

On the morning of the 14th, a Recon jeep took the two lieutenants and their seabags down the island to MCAS Futenma. When they checked in, they were told the morning flight was not going and they would have to wait for the afternoon flight. This hurry-up-and-wait served to confirm the old adage: Time to Spare? Fly Marine Air. They remained all day and spent that evening at the air station's transient bachelor officer quarters. That evening was steak night at the Officers Club where both enjoyed dinner, drank Coke, and crashed early. The next morning, the 15th, was another all-day wait for a late-afternoon C-130. While they were on orders, they were not a priority and had to wait for available spaces. Arriving after dark in Da Nang reoriented them to the nighttime sights, sounds, and smells of what, at the time, was the busiest airport in the world. The twin 10,000-foot concrete north–south runways of Da Nang International ran parallel to the river directly east. As they began the final approach, they could make out the blacked-out Monkey Mountain peninsula to the east of Da Nang Bay, with its spine prickling with radars, antennas, and air-defense missiles of the 1st LAAM (Light Anti-Air Missile) Battalion, their Hawk missiles pointed north and east. The Tactical Air Operations Center, callsign *Vice Squad*, manned by Marine Air Control Squadron-4, was a mile above the Air Force's Tactical Air Command Center, callsign *Panama*, which was also located on the Monkey Mountain spine. Little did Hank Rathmell know that, in his near future, he would be leading brand-new Recon Marines on their graduation patrols from RIP on Monkey Mountain's double-canopy jungle.[61] And yes, as anyone who ever set foot on Monkey Mountain knew, it was well named. Without natural predators on the peninsula, and isolated by the Da Nang River and city, the monkeys had multiplied and were overrunning the place.

With the landing of the C-130, the two lieutenants had to find a ride to Camp Reasoner. They checked in at the Marine personnel-processing terminal and were told the next scheduled transportation was in the morning. Rather than sleeping on wooden benches and waiting, they walked outside in the dark, looking at the busy airfield. They looked for any Marine with a truck or jeep. They found one with a 6 × 6 truck who was making a run to the 1st Marine Division headquarters on the northside of Hill 327. He said Recon base camp was across the road from Division. The two lieutenants arrived after a 30-minute ride due west from the airfield. En route, they departed the west gate of the airfield manned by Marines and entered a Vietnamese civilian shanty town around the intersection of the gate called "Four Corners" by Marines. It served as the commercial center for the village the Marines named "Dog Patch." Their driver told them if they needed anything it could be purchased in Dog Patch. Next on the two-lane macadam road west, on their left, he pointed out the large parking lot in front of the equally huge Freedom Hill PX (Post Exchange). He said there was also solid stuff to be had at the PX. And one could buy a new car (tax-free) from a round-eyed woman, with fringe benefits for each sale. The car could be purchased at Freedom Hill and then picked up at your local hometown dealership when you got home. After another mile-and-a-half, he pulled to a stop and said Camp Reasoner was on the right. They got out of the cab, retrieved their seabags from the back of the truck and walked over to the wooden guard shack, where a Marine put on a painted helmet liner and asked what they wanted. They informed him they were checking in. The sentry said everyone was asleep, but they could follow the road inside the camp around to the right past an aluminum butler building, which he said was supply, and the next building would be the mess hall with screened-in front porch. They could get something to eat. He continued that the new commander had come on board three weeks ago and had changed the mess hall rules from two meals a day to three squares plus mid-rats and that Gunnery Sergeant Paradise, the mess sergeant, was the best in the division. Recon Marines could eat 24/7! The two officers grabbed their seabags and walked the two blocks to the mess hall.

Walking up the steps and onto a screened porch, they left their bags and walked through double-hinged screen doors to the dining room. The two chow lines were on the far wall. They spotted a sergeant who said coffee was over to right and premade sandwiches were on the shelf, but he would cook up some eggs if they wanted them. After about an hour at breakfast, it was close to 0500 and Marines started showing up for chow. About 0530, Captain Sterling walked in and said he was the adjutant and if they came over to the S-1 shop at 0600 he would get their assignments, but it would go quicker if they handed over their original orders and officer-qualification records they had carried from Okinawa. He had been expecting them. They retrieved their orders and record books for the captain. It was 16 February.

Happy to finally be at Camp Reasoner, the two officers sat back and watched the beehive that was the Recon mess hall for breakfast. There were two lines, enlisted on the right and sergeants and above on the left. They also noticed that any Marine cammied up, indicating he was outbound on patrol, and had head-of-line privileges in either line. At 0605, the two departed, gathered their seabags and headed to S-1, which was about a ten-minute walk to the middle of the camp. Located on the north side of Hill 327 and on the low side of Division Road, the camp spread from the road down to the rice paddies below, where the first couple of paddies had been converted into an LZ, or LZ 401, callsign *Landing Zone Finch*. At S-1, the adjutant informed them that Rathmell was going to H&S to become the S-3 training officer, while Lee was assigned to Delta Company. Rathmell questioned the assignment, but the adjutant just said he could bring it up with Major Turner, the battalion's XO, at 0700 when he had an appointment. He said Lee also had an 0700 with the XO. The adjutant yelled for two Marines and he told them to split the lieutenants and take Rathmell to H&S Company office and Lee to Delta Company office. The two friends split up, saying they would meet at the XO's office at 0655. The adjutant also told them where the XO's office was located. After the short meeting with Major Turner at 0700, both assignments remained the same. Turner told Rathmell, because of his experience in Recon and because he was a Ranger School graduate, he was being assigned as the officer in command of the Reconnaissance Indoctrination Program. RIP was for every new first-tour junior Marine assigned to Recon and had to be completed if they were to remain. Turner also said that Major Rivers had prebriefed Lieutenant Colonel Drumright. Rathmell and Lee were both savvy enough to close their mouths and accept their assignments.[62] They departed the XO's office and headed back to their respective company offices. Lee walked back to the Delta Company office to retrieve his seabag. Now that it was daylight, he could read the red company sign in front of the office and found out the company commander was Captain T. Martin, the XO was 1st Lieutenant G. G. Spolter, and the first sergeant was C. C. Cannon. He stepped inside the office to be greeted by a clerk who handed him a check-in sheet, told him the captain would talk to him later in the morning, and that he should get settled in the Delta Company officers' hooch directly across the street. Lee grabbed his seabag and walked across the street to the Southeast Asia Hut. Up five stairs, screen door with strong spring pulled open, he entered the hut. It was empty. The hut was divided into individual spaces by four feet by eight feet plywood sheets with a center aisle. There seemed to be two empty cots, so he grabbed the one at the far end of the hut.

Second Lieutenant W. X. Lee was a former enlisted Marine or "mustang" in Marine Corps parlance. After graduating high school in Orange, California, and attending junior college, he had a draft status of 1A. Not wanting to be drafted into the Army with no choices, he enlisted in the Corps in February 1968. He was assigned to Platoon 334 for recruit training at Marine Corps Recruit Depot San Diego. Upon graduation, he moved north to Camp Pendleton for infantry training at the Infantry Training Regiment. Eight months later, making lance corporal fast, Lee, who clearly fit into the Marine Corps, was selected for the Enlisted Commissioning Program (ECP). In Quantico, Virginia, after completing the Officers Candidate School (OCS) in the 53rd OCS Class, he was commissioned a reserve 2nd lieutenant on 16 November 1968. Lee then joined TBS Echo Company, Class 5-69, for five months of infantry-platoon-commander training which was focused on Vietnam. Graduating in May 1969, he was disappointed that he was ordered, after leave and transit time, to 2nd Battalion, 27th Marines (2/27).[63] He was disappointed he was not going directly to Vietnam but happy to be back in California; he could visit his sweetheart on long weekends in San Jose. Stationed at Camp Las Pulgas, he joined Golf Company as a platoon commander. Fitting in well with the regiment and discipline of the Corps, Lee wanted to make it a career.[64] To do so, one must have combat in their record. He had been volunteering since being commissioned. Now at 2/27, he pushed again for an assignment to Vietnam. In mid-August, he got orders for the 3rd Marine Division in Vietnam. Moving through Staging Battalion, also at Camp Pendleton, and processing through Okinawa, he landed in Da Nang on 9 October 1969 and was processed through Marine Receiving and vectored the same day onto a C-130 and flown to Dong Ha, the 3rd Division's headquarters, and, subsequently assigned to the 3rd Reconnaissance Battalion. After interviews with the commander, Lieutenant Colonel Burritt, and the XO, Major "Fast Eddie" Badolato, he landed in Bravo Company as a platoon commander.[65] Lee immediately started running patrols in the eastern DMZ and in the sand dunes of the Cua Viet River area against the NVA. Lee and Rathmell, who were TBS classmates, both redeployed with 3rd Recon Battalion back to Okinawa as part of Operation

Keystone Cardinal on 20 November 1969.[66] The two lieutenants immediately started to figure out how they could get back in-country. Finally, they approached Major Rivers, put it in his hands, and had returned by mid-February 1970.[67]

After Lee claimed a cot, he dropped his seabag. With his check-in sheet in hand, he started the standard process of walking to every supporting organization and getting an initial saying one had been there, along the way dropping health records and gaining information and a weapon at the armory. Lee wanted a CAR-15. As a new guy, he settled for an M16 rifle, 16 magazines, and an M1911 .45-caliber pistol. He asked for more magazines and was told that was the Table of Equipment issue. Returning to the Delta Officers' hooch, he broke down both weapons on an empty footlocker and cleaned them. He felt better armed, even though this was the rear. About that time, the company runner knocked on the hatch and said the captain would see him in the company office. Lee, grabbing his cover, departed, walking across the street, and reported in to Captain Thomas Martin who put him at ease and told him to have a chair. He said he was terribly busy. He told Lee he was getting 3rd Platoon. His platoon sergeant was Sergeant Herman Diaz, a six-year sergeant who was competent in the field. Martin said Lee needed to get all over the platoon admin.[68] Then he said to expect a frag order for a patrol soon. Martin stated that since Lee was coming down from 3rd Recon, he would not need a break-in period or patrol, and to consider himself checked in. He said again how busy he was with the confounded admin horseshit and dismissed Lee. In under two minutes, Lee departed the captain's office which was a doorway through to First Sergeant Cannon and the company office. He met the first sergeant and asked for 3rd Platoon's Service Record Books (SRB). He was told that would take a bit of time; he could just talk to Sergeant Diaz. Not pleased, Lee said to have Diaz come find him in the officers' hooch. He departed, crossing the street, wondering what type of outfit Delta Company really was. Lee returned to the empty hooch and started to get organized in his cube, which already had a cot, footlocker, and an ammo box chair that fit a small plywood wall desk with two shelves. Better than the Korea-era canvas tent he had at 3rd Recon.

A little later, he heard three knocks on the screen door and met Sergeant Herman Diaz, his platoon sergeant.[69] After introductions, and desiring neutral ground, he suggested they go across the street where he had seen picnic tables and a brick grill. Seated, Lee opened with, "Before you brief me on the platoon and getting to know each other, I got to ask you, what is going on with the company office and why can't I see the Marines' SRBs?" Diaz offered that the company admin was fucked up and the Marines' pay was worse.[70] Lee made a mental note to personally check on every one of his Marines' pay and to ask when they were last paid when he interviewed each one. Diaz went on to say the company had failed a big Division admin/pay inspection in the last week of January and that the re-inspection was going to be next week.[71] That explained a lot about the 1st Shirt and the office. Lee found out Diaz had been in the Marine Corps for over six years, considered himself a career Marine and wanted to go to drill-instructor duty when he returned home. He said the Marines in the platoon were solid. Diaz said they'd had four lieutenants in five months. He just put it out there as a semi-challenge. Rather than be baited, Lee told Diaz he was former enlisted, had gone through the ECP and was coming in from 3rd Recon where he had been a platoon commander and patrol leader (PL). He added that he knew the terrain was different, the enemy was different, and that he was there to learn from the Marines of the platoon. He asked Diaz to describe each Marine's strengths and weaknesses. Lee was pleased to see him pull out a small green memorandum book that was issued by the supply system but sometimes hard to get. He told Diaz he needed one but would take notes on his stationery. They spent the next few hours going over the 22 Marines and two corpsmen of 3rd Platoon. Lee told Diaz that, over the next two days, he wanted to interview each Marine individually. Diaz said he could only interview those in the rear as one team was out on patrol and one team was getting ready to depart in the morning. Lee wanted to observe the outbound team's preparation and asked Diaz to let him know where and when to be there. He made it clear it was Diaz's show, he wanted to observe and learn, and that Diaz should introduce him so he could say a few words as to who he was and where he came from. About this time, late afternoon on the 16th, a runner approached Diaz and asked him if he knew where Lieutenant Lee was. After introductions, the Marine said he was from S-3 and the lieutenant was wanted in the S-3 shop. Lee thanked Diaz, who left him to supervise the outbound team, and, wondering what was up, departed with the guide for the S-3 shop.

CHAPTER 17

Team *Pal Joey*, 20–26 February 1970

Upon entering the S-3 (operations) bunker just up from LZ 401, 2nd Lieutenant W. X. Lee was ushered into the battalion's main Combat Operations Center (COC) and saw three officers huddled together. One looked up and a 1st lieutenant walked over and asked if he was Lee. With an affirmative from Lee, "Chip" Gregson introduced himself as the assistant operations officer (S-3A). He thanked him for walking down and asked if he was ready for a patrol. Lee said he was still checking in but was fine. Gregson handed him a typed one-page Battalion Operations Order, dated 15 February, with a departure date, in the Execution Paragraph, from LZ 401 on 18 February.[1] Lee said, "I was expecting to go out but thought the process was frag order as a warning order prior to the operations order." Gregson said he had given Captain Martin the frag order on the 14th and the operations order yesterday, just after he signed it by direction. Gregson saw the look in Lee's eye. He took back the order, numbered #0186-70, and made a pen change in paragraph 3, "Execution," by changing the departure to 19 February with a planned extract on the 23rd.[2] He gave it back to Lee and said that was the best he could do. He offered that Lee could draw maps for reference about his haven from the S-2 (intelligence) shop, the next Southeast Asia Hut up the hill. Lee thanked Gregson and departed for the S-2 to draw maps.

Walking back to his hooch, he read the order and noticed it had originally been given to Echo Company, 1st Platoon, Team 1, callsign *Pennywise*, but that had also been crossed out and changed to callsign *Pal Joey*, which Lee knew, from Sergeant Diaz that afternoon, was one of his teams. Lee found Diaz at evening chow. Over chow, he gave him the order to read. Diaz asked where the warning order was, adding that he was outbound in the morning with his team and that after chow he would send Lance Corporal McGowen, the senior member of *Pal Joey*, over to meet Lee at his hooch. He added that *Pal Joey* was shorthanded, with only five Marines, no corpsman and was not scheduled to go out but was supposed to have a week in the rear for training and rest. Lee acknowledged, asking when he could see Diaz's team, and that he would see McGowen in 30 minutes at the officers' hut. He had two days to meet the team, assess each member, provide a five-paragraph order, state his expectations, and set up an inspection and rehearsal of immediate actions.

Back in the hooch, Lee made the only decision he could—he would lead the patrol as the patrol leader, he would tell McGowen he was the assistant patrol leader and ask him to assign the other four Marines to be point man, tail-end Charlie and two radio operators. McGowen said he would carry the second radio, freeing up a Marine to carry the M79 in addition to his M16. Lee liked McGowen's thought process, told him to give the Marines a warning order and that he would issue the five-paragraph order to all the team members in the morning at 0800, and to plan for the entire team to spend the morning with him. He told McGowen he wanted a private place, indoors out of the rain and wind, stating, "No reason to be miserable in the rear." McGowen said the best place was the Delta Company club, the "Stagger Back Inn." The club's noncommissioned officer did not come in till noon since the club stayed open as late as a Marine was in there, or until the first sergeant shut it down. McGowen departed. Lee had the evening to put his maps together, do a map study of the area he was to patrol, and put together his gear, most of which he still lacked. His plan was to talk with the team after the five-paragraph order. Then he would determine how much experience each Marine had and to hear their ideas on the patrol and listen to their concerns. After lunch, he fully intended to run immediate-action (IA) drills, do an informal low-key inspection of their patrolling gear, and then set the schedule for his second preparation day. He worked late into the evening as he knew the next day would be his first impression with these five Marines that would set the tone for his platoon going forward.

A wise decision to go indoors, and the Stagger Back Inn had large tables to gather around, as it rained all morning. After McGowen introduced the other four Marines, Lee told them to sit so they could get to know each other. He said the smoking lamp was lit, tossed a pack of Marlboros on the table, and made a point about smoking them now as there was no smoking on his patrols. They went around the table, and he met Lance Corporal Wiley who was designated as point man; Lance Corporal Garza would run tail-end Charlie; Lance Corporal Kemp would be the M79 man; and Private First Class Freeman would be the primary radio operator.[3] It was Freeman's first patrol as primary radio operator, and Lee had the thought that he got the heavy radio because he was the junior man. Lee liked an experienced radio operator but accepted this thinking: Freeman will be carrying the radio, but I will be listening and talking on it. In part, this was because he needed to learn how 1st Recon did its radio procedures. After they got to know each other, Lee issued his five-paragraph order. He thought it was more detail then they were used to, but he was pleased to see all five taking notes. He passed them the radio frequencies, Primary 30.90, Alternate 44.25, and said that all Arty fire missions would go through callsign *Scandinavia* on 56.65.[4] He said he would be calling Arty, but they all needed all three frequencies in case someone was hit, and they had to stand in on the radio. He told them their primary radio relay was *Vesper Bells-Alpha.* He made a mental note to find out where *Alpha* was and to make a communications line-of-sight plan to the relay from the patrol area. Lee knew the team knew the mission but, for his comfort, he read the mission verbatim to the team: "Paragraph 2. MISSION: Conduct Reconnaissance and surveillance operations within your assigned Haven to detect possible VC/NVA [Viet Cong/North Vietnamese Army] troop movements or arms infiltration and be prepared to call and adjust air/Arty on all targets of opportunity."[5]

Under the execution paragraph, he told them they were departing the day after next, the 19th, by helo from LZ 401, and were scheduled for a five-day patrol with extract scheduled for the 23rd. He told them to plan for, and carry, two meals a day for seven days as the weather could delay their extract. He said his map recon and the weather indicated there was water in the area and they should carry at least four canteens, but did not have to go heavy on water as he planned to refill canteens. He told the two radio operators to go draw the team's shackle sheets. McGowen said he would do it, but Lee wanted Freeman to learn how; therefore, they both should go.

He also told them that, while at Communications getting the two PRC-25 radios, to draw an additional two PRC-93s. They wanted to know about the PRC-93s as they had not used them. Lee explained communications were their lifeline and the PRC-93 were survival radios that could beacon or talk to aircraft in a rescue situation. He further told them to pick up three Claymore mines and at least forty rounds for the M79. He wanted eight smoke grenades of at least three colors, and they each would carry two M26 frag grenades. McGowen explained they could not get the M26s until game day from the ammunition bunker next to the landing zone (LZ). Lee asked for questions but, since there were none, he dismissed the team for lunch and said he would meet them with their patrolling harness and weapons at 1300 to practice their IA drills. He said it would take a few hours, but they would have the rest of the afternoon and evening off. They could expect a full day of inspections and IA drills on the 18th.

The Marines caught a break on the afternoon of the 17th as the rain stopped. Lee took the team through routine IA drills of contact front, contact rear, ambush right, ambush left, and he stressed dispersion. They ended with Lee having McGowen go through their standard hand and arm signals. With that, the team got an early dismissal. Lee held McGowen back and told him he needed an ass pack for his harness and asked the best place to get one since supply was out. McGowen said the "Gook Shop" up the street past supply and next to the barbershop could usually find equipment. Lee walked up the street to the little Vietnamese shop selling souvenirs and other items. He was surprised to find this shop in the middle of the Reconnaissance base camp. They had a used ass pack which Lee purchased along with six magazines he would add to the 14 issued by the armory. The next day, 18 February, he inspected the team with all their gear and provided McGowen with a roll of black electrical tape, telling him to fix the noise issues on the gear. They then went to the test-firing range directly off LZ 401 and test fired and zeroed all their weapons. After firing their weapons, he dismissed them for lunch and said, "Clean your weapons for inspection at 1500 and then we will do IA drills and secure." The afternoon session went well and was rain free; Lee asked his Marines if they needed anything for the patrol and Freeman said he needed radio batteries and a few M16 magazines. Lee had missed both, but was pleased Freeman was honest; McGowen, a little embarrassed, said he would take care of it. Lee reminded them they had a 0430 wakeup call, to "go easy tonight," and he would see them in the morning. After a large dinner in the mess hall, Lee skipped the Officers Club on the camp for an early turn in. In the morning, he found his team outside the company office after a small breakfast. Together they walked to the LZ to draw grenades. It was drizzling rain on the walk down. The insert package of two CH-46s and two Cobra gunships arrived and shut down for the air briefing. The battalion air liaison officer was briefing the pilots on what teams were to be inserted where and what teams were to be extracted. Lee walked over and listened to the discussion by the pilots and the battalion S-3 shop where he noticed Chip Gregson, the S-3A, was listening intently. The weather was the big discussion point with all mountains socked in with a 400-foot ceiling. Since *Pal Joey* was going to be inserted into an old fire-support base (FSB) above 500 feet, they were scheduled for the afternoon. Lee went back and briefed the team to go back to their hut, rack out, rest, and to be back at the LZ at 1300. It was 0900 on the 19th. *Pal Joey*'s priority for insert ended up being delayed a day due to bad-weather issues, with extractions of teams that were two days beyond their planned extract day taking priority. With the cancelled insert, he walked back late that afternoon to the Delta Company officers' hut. There he met Mike Fallon, who was tired and wasted, having just got back from a midday emergency ladder extract. He and Team *Delicatessen* had made contact, killing seven NVA.

It had taken two aerial observers (AO) and four flights of fixed-wing for *Delicatessen* to break contact.[6] They had returned to LZ 401 at 1320, and, after the debriefing and a shower, Fallon was sitting with a towel wrapped around him, cleaning his weapon. Lee sensed he did not want to talk. Martin had told Fallon he was giving him a break by sending him out the next morning to Hill 119. Fallon wondered who was going to take the platoon up if he was still on patrol. He knew enough to keep his mouth shut. He crashed for the night and slept. The next morning he and 1st Platoon were on the LZ waiting for the flip. With the aviation ceiling again being low there and at Hill 119, they were given priority for insert and were off before 0900.[7] Lee and *Pal Joey* watched the platoon depart. They played the show-up-and-wait game for another day, making it two days of sitting on LZ 401.[8]

***

On the morning of 20 February at 0935, two CH-46s took 2nd Platoon back to Camp Reasoner.[9] The flip with 1st Platoon was a hot flip with blades turning on the helicopters as they sat on the LZ. Lieutenant Parks had prepared written notes and handed them to Fallon as they shook hands and Parks departed. The birds were on the LZ for just six minutes. As Fallon walked up the hill from the LZ, Sergeant Franklin, the platoon guide and one of his experienced patrol leaders, showed him to the officers' bunker. For this flip, Fallon would be alone in the bunker as the senior forward observer (FO) from 11th Marines was the newly promoted Sergeant Mark Bayuk, instead of the Arty officer the busy hill rated. As it turned out, Bayuk had been on the hill since 5 November after his graduation from the Integrated Observation Device (IOD) school over at FSB Ryder.[10] He had his shit together and Fallon actually thought the FO never left the observation deck.

Fallon's first order of business was to walk the lines with Franklin and Staff Sergeant Mushett to see what they had. Fallon was pleased with the gun positions and the fact Parks had left the two .50-caliber machine guns and the XM174 automatic 40-mm grenade launcher. With his three M60 machine guns, each of the six bunkers had a crew-served weapon. Not surprisingly, the positions were well policed; C-ration firing cards and wooden gun stakes were in each bunker. Garry Parks was a pro and, although they got no turnover time on the flip, the hill was in good shape thanks to him. Parks would go on to have a 32-year career in the Marine Corps, retiring as a lieutenant general.

Fallon, with 3rd Battalion, 26th Marines, had built out Hill 124, due west of Da Nang on the rocket belt, from scratch. What he did not like about Hill 119 was that two hills overlooked it. Hill 175 was two kilometers south, and worse, Hill 148's summit sat directly across the saddle which also served as the hill's LZ. It was one kilometer due west-southwest. Both hills not only looked down on Hill 119, but any direct-fire weapon would also be plunging fire on his Marines. Hill 119 was rocky. There was no real trench line to move between bunkers or to the exposed elevated plywood platform for the IOD. The Recon platoon's first mission was the security of the highly classified IOD. It was exposed and a rocket-propelled grenade (RPG) magnet in Fallon's mind. He told Mushett and Franklin to get the Marines assigned and settled into their bunkers. First Platoon was at strength with one officer, 17 enlisted Marines, two corpsmen, and had an attached dog named Champ with his handler.[11] That would put three Marines in each bunker with the corpsmen in the command post with Fallon on the radios. He instructed Mushett that, after chow, the Marines would live fire both the .50-cals and M60s. He wanted every Marine to learn how to fire these weapons and for Mushett and Franklin to put the best gunners on each weapon. Fallon sat outside his bunker on a sandbag wall and observed the platoon settle into its home for two weeks. The Marines liked the duty on the hill; they thought it was easy street. It was a good break from the stress and fatigue of patrolling with five other Marines/Corpsmen. Fallon knew it was dangerous to fall into a lull. He also knew they had to contribute by improving the hill's defenses on their watch. He made up his wish list. An hour later, he was on the radio and requested to switch to Battalion Tac Two. The second net was used for administrative matters and supply. He had a long message, and he wanted to not only get it sent, but he also wanted it hand delivered to 1st Lieutenant "Dog" Jones. Dog was the irrepressible battalion supply officer who knew how to make the system work and knew how to scrounge supplies for the Recon Marines he supported. Fallon wanted pioneer equipment—shovels, sledgehammers, and long crowbars—for digging or, really, for moving blown rock. He also requested 40 pounds of C4 explosives and 40 fuses, along with as much det cord as Dog could get. Fallon knew Marines liked to blow stuff up; if the price for blowing-up stuff was moving the rocks and dirt afterwards, it was a fair deal. He was going to try to deepen the shallow trench line connecting every bunker around the entire hill. Additionally, he ordered a full carpenter's kit, 40 boards (2' × 4' × 8'), engineer stakes, and five rolls of chain-link fence.

After the order was sent to battalion, the only question that came back was why there was a need for chain-link fence. Fallon later learned the question had not come from Dog, but from the battalion executive officer (XO), Major Terry Turner. The XO was not saying no, but wanted to know why the fence was needed? Rather than a long message, that evening, when it was quiet, Fallon asked for the S-3A, Chip Gregson, to call him on the secure radio. This radio, a PRC-77 with a KY-38 encryptor, allowed one to talk in the open, knowing the message was scrambled; even if intercepted or listened to by the NVA, it could not be deciphered. Fallon explained that the IOD, 20 feet above and on top of the FO's bunker, was exposed to downhill direct fire from Hill 148's front slope. Hence, an RPG fired from there could take out the platform. His plan was to build a chain-link fence barrier on the west side of the platform. Offset by 10 feet on the Hill 148 side, an RPG would have to hit the fence first; the explosion would spray the platform with shrapnel but leave it intact. The other three sides were shots from distance and the angle favored the platform. Gregson, who knew Hill 119 from his time as Delta Company XO, said he liked it and would explain and emphasize the chain-link was a priority resupply. It would take a week but, on the resupply bird six days later, the entire list was filled. The request came up at the staff meeting with Lieutenant Colonel Drumright, who was quoted as saying, "If that 'Peckerwood' Fallon wants to build a fence, then get him the materials!" Dog had his mission, and the materials were all delivered. Over time, the fence took different shapes and iterations; the recurring issue was sinking the fence post into the rock, which was next to impossible. Fallon had his fencing materials;

who knew if it would work or last? In the end, it never got fully erected on that flip. Blowing the rocks for the trench line took the next six days. It seemed only Fallon liked the fence concept.

With the resupply message sent and live-fire machine-gun training underway, Fallon climbed the steps to the tower platform of the IOD he was there to protect. He asked Bayuk, the lead FO, to explain the capabilities of the large tripod-mounted machine in the center of the platform. Bayuk began by showing the lieutenant the "Big Eyes," the ship's binoculars installed as the centerpiece of the metal tripod. The tripod legs stabilized the center shaft that could move through 360 degrees, similar to a submarine's periscope. He explained one could look out 30 kilometers. To demonstrate, he turned the Big Eyes northwest and focused on Hill 65 on the other side of the Song Thu Bon basin before turning them over to Fallon. He could see Charlie Ridge looming in the distance and, on the other side of the Arizona Territory, north of the river, he could pick out the brown, dusty hill easily. He saw Hill 65's building and could make out small figures moving around. He pulled out his 1:50,000 map sheet and found Hill 65 at grid AT880575 and measured back to Hill 119. It was 12 kilometers west and 8 kilometers north of 119. Bayuk then gave the command, "Ready to Lase," "Lasing." Fallon heard a whirring sound and then a metal box next to the Big Eyes shot out a red laser. A digital read out displayed red numbers in a black glass field—14,083 meters. The sergeant explained that, with a known distance from a known point, it was simple math to fire artillery on the polar plot for first-round hits. Fallon was impressed with the technology but asked Bayuk to yell for him on his next fire mission. The sergeant went on to explain that the tripod had been surveyed in to a ten-digit grid by the 11th Marines, same as that for the artillery tubes at An Hoa Combat Base. The result was that making calls-for-fire was now more science than art. He explained the kill ratio had jumped exponentially because of the IOD.[12]

Fallon climbed down and walked the perimeter. The Marines were into their midday meal routine at each bunker, making it their home for the next two weeks. About 1235, as Fallon was eating a beans-and-weenies can of C-rats he had just heated, he heard "Standby to Lase," and knew something was up. He walked over and climbed the back ladder closest to his bunker, over the waist-high sandbagged wall onto the platform. Bayuk explained he had three VC, wearing mixed black-and-white "PJs," moving south to north on a trail. As he stepped away to let Fallon take a look, he was on the fire-support radio calling in a fire mission, requesting a battery-one (six guns, one round each) fire-for-effect on the grid he had passed to the Fire Direction Center. Three minutes passed before they heard the radio call back, rounds out. Bayuk got back on the Big Eyes as Fallon grabbed a nearby set of 7 × 50 handheld binos to observe the impacts. The mission was 2,000 meters west-northwest; they watched six gray puffs of smoke hit the trail area. The tree line was thick next to the trail and, when the dust cleared, they could not see any enemy as they had ducked into the trees and, as Bayuk explained, predug bunkers or at least holes. The firing battery called and asked for results, and Bayuk replied on the radio, "Good coverage" of the target area, grading the shooting, but negative results due to surveillance being blocked by the tree line; he then ended the fire mission.[13]

The afternoon passed quickly as Fallon organized his bunker, placing candles and his red-lens flashlight within reaching distance of the small ammo-box desk and his cot. At 1620, Team *Hansworth,* the callsign for the IOD team, was busy again so Fallon climbed the back ladder to observe. They had sighted four VC, wearing mixed black-and-white PJs, carrying packs on a trail four kilometers to their northwest. The enemy was moving east to west. *Hansworth* called a fire mission and requested a spread battery with two fire-for-effect, immediately. When the gray smoke of the Arty impacts cleared, there were four bodies lying on the side of the trail. Bayuk turned the Big Eyes over to Fallon to confirm. *Hansworth* called in four confirmed enemy kills.[14] They would watch the bodies until sundown to see if anyone came to recover them; if so, he would fire again. Bayuk explained the bodies would be removed during darkness, which is what happened. He said on a noticeably clear evening, which it was not, they could see four to five kilometers with the big NOD (night-observation device), which was also on the spinnable tripod. This super starlight scope made observing the enemy infiltration routes a 24-hour-a-day job, thus the FO team of six observers and radio man lived in the tower and the sandbagged bunker it was built on. There was an open staircase to the tower on the west side but direct access from the bunker to the tower deck was a two-by-four ladder up the east side of the tower. On 21 February, *Hansworth* called two fire missions, resulting in two confirmed kills.[15] On the second day on the hill, Fallon instituted a fire-team wire check for each morning. This rotating duty had the Marines circle the hill, inside first, and then outside of the wire about twenty to one hundred meters, checking the wire for breaks, cuts, and confirming the Claymore mines were pointed outboard. They were also looking for booby traps.

***

Finally getting inserted at 0910 on 21 February, Team *Pal Joey* trotted off the hardpacked, large three-bird LZ of the old FSB.[16] They dropped, stopped, and got a comm check with the insert birds before they departed. Lee was concerned with communications but wanted to get off the open zone which could be observed from higher ground on two sides. The lieutenant's grapevine had told him the NVA were so frustrated with Recon that they were now using counter-recon teams with dogs. He had brought crystalized CS powder for that contingency. The lieutenants also said the counter effort used solo spotters to watch helicopter LZs; when they saw an insert they fired a single rifle shot as a signal. *Pal Joey* moved west off the LZ and into the double canopy jungle which was 60–70 feet high. Once out of sight, they stopped for 15 minutes and listened. It was so silent that it was even devoid of normal jungle sounds. Lee thought the insert birds had caused the native birds, of the feathered variety, to go quiet. He tried a radio check with *Vesper Bells-Alpha* but got no connection. He then tried a communication check with the other planned radio relay, *Puppet Show*; again, no joy. That made the next decision easy. When there was no comm, one moved to higher ground. He pointed west and signaled Wiley, the point man, to move out.

The movement through the secondary growth of thick vines, small bushes, and big boulders was slow going. They moved west for three hours and had made 300 meters by Lee's pace-count knotted shoelace tied to his belt. Wiley signaled a halt with raised fist as the team went to one knee and faced outboard. Lee liked the team's movement and actions thus far but remembered nobody was tired yet. As he moved forward, he saw why the point man had halted them. Perpendicular to them was a high-speed trail cutting across their front, running north–south. He signaled the team to come on-line parallel to the trail in a hasty ambush. They would wait and monitor. This was a good time for a communication check. They tried again to raise either radio relay with no luck. They had been out of comm for three hours. Lee did not want to make enemy contact without a communication link. It was decision time. If he continued west, it would be breaking brush and a slow go. If he took the trail north, it went uphill to higher ground, with the thought that comm was always better the higher one was. Decision made; he signaled Wiley to head up the trail to the north. Immediately, the team noticed footprints from bare feet on the trail. The prints were moving in the same direction they were moving but appeared a few weeks old. Hard to tell. Lee walked back to tail-end Charlie and informed him they would move at his pace backwards; Lee shifted positions to second from rear and would watch/cover his man to the rear. He signaled Wiley to move slowly out on the trail.

They had moved uphill for about thirty minutes, making 300 meters and gaining a little elevation. It was about this time that they heard an aircraft in the distance. Not wanting to be moving on the trail and not being able to hear first, Lee moved the team off the trail and set a hasty ambush. Soon he recognized the twin-engine sounds of an OV-10. It had been 4.5 hours since insert and they still had no communication; this may be a bird looking for them. Lee took the handset and tried calling the primary radio relay, *Vesper Bells-Alpha*. On his second attempt, *Cowpoke One-Zero* came up on the net and called the team. Lee acknowledged the call, reporting he'd no comm since insert, and he would continue to move to higher ground. *Cowpoke* said he would relay to *Vesper Bells* and he or his replacement would be back in four or five hours to check in. Not a good situation but, having made some time, it was prudent to get off the trail and break brush. Before starting, they took a water break which also served as time to listen and get their jungle hearing back before moving out. After 30 minutes, they moved out to the northwest, breaking brush, and almost immediately ran into a trail headed in their direction uphill. It was a northwest branch of the trail they had just left. Having listened for another 30 minutes, and hearing nothing, they got onto this trail, which was three-feet wide and hard packed. It was not visible from the air because of the double canopy.

At about 1500, the team came upon a thatched hooch just off the side of the trail. They checked it out. It was built off the ground; inside, it had two empty 5-gallon cans, for water, three wicker baskets, one metal serving tray, and a stove made out of wire. The thatched roof had a hole.[17] This waystation had not been used in two to three months. It was time to move off the trail to find a good place to harbor up for the night. They broke brush due north, covering about 150 meters. The best Lee could figure, the team was in the crotch of two high-speed trails forming a Y. He was approximately two hundred meters from each. It was already getting dark under the jungle canopy. They found a thicket, crawled in, and formed a 360 defense. While setting out one of their Claymore mines on the side facing the trail, now to their east, Kempe found three food packages and brought one back to Lee. He immediately recognized it as an NVA long-range patrol ration. He knew these rations from his 3rd Recon days and estimated them to be two to three days old as he could still smell a strong odor coming from inside the packages. The NVA had discarded them off one of the trails.

The Marines were hidden and camouflaged but had no real cover between two trails, both of which were obviously used by the NVA. Lee took stock of their situation. It was 1630 on Day 1. They were in a well-hidden harbor site for the night, but it had no cover. He liked the way the team had moved and assessed that Wiley was an excellent point man. He also liked the movements and actions of Kempe, the M79 man. With all three Claymores out and the hellboxes next to the radio in the center, he set the night rotation of radio watches and decided they would have two men on watch, each facing and listening toward one of the two trails. Watches would be two hours and he and Freeman would take the first and last watches. They planned to get up at dawn 100 percent alert, eat a light meal, listen 30 minutes after the camp was folded, and be ready to move. The night went quietly, but they still had no communications even though comm is best at night.

Thirty minutes after the morning snack, they were ready to move but first Lee huddled the team and said, "We have no comm, therefore we do not want to make contact. We will move for ten and listen for ten." He pointed Wiley to the east which would have them intersect the original north–south trail in about two or three hundred meters. At approximately 0730, after moving for 1.5 hours, the team came across numerous enemy harbor sites for sleeping on the ground, each about ten feet by four feet, on both sides of the well-used trail they were seeking. They observed two small fire pits in the center of the trail, consisting of wood debris and ash. The fire pits were 30 meters apart and each was marked with four bamboo sticks one inch in length in sets of two lying parallel to the trail. At 1000 on the 22nd, the team heard two single rifle shots, which sounded like an AK-47. The shots were spaced five minutes apart.[18] These were warning shots estimated to be 200 to 300 meters west of their current position, however the shots appeared to come from where they were yesterday. Lee had to assume the NVA knew *Pal Joey* was in the area, either from LZ spotters watching their insert, or from their freshly broken trail. And he still had no communication!

Lee moved the team just off the trail and assumed a hasty defense. He took his time to plot his exact position and weigh his options. About then, they heard the sound of the OV-10's engines in the distance. Before Lee could get the handset to his ear to try a radio call, he heard, to his immediate relief, "*Pal Joey*, *Pal Joey*, this is *Cowpoke One-Eight*, how do you read, over?"

Lee immediately answered in a whisper, "Loud and clear, *Cowpoke One-Eight*."

Cowpoke informed him they were scheduled for an extract that morning due to negative communications from the team. Lee acknowledged and asked *Cowpoke* to help him find an LZ for extract. Lee moved back to the trail, with Wiley for security, and hit *Cowpoke* with a single mirror flash. *Cowpoke* acknowledged and did three wider and wider orbits around their finger. He informed them the only LZ in the area was the old FSB to their southwest. Lee asked where the extract package was, and *Cowpoke* informed him they were to extract in about sixty "mikes" (minutes). There was no way to make the old FSB in 60 minutes, even if they used the trail going back to the insert LZ. This approach would have been particularly dangerous when knowing the NVA knew you were in the area. To do so was asking for a major ambush by the counter-recon teams who were the home team and knew that was the only LZ.

Lee told *Cowpoke One-Eight* that the FSB LZ was out, but he could get a ladder through an opening over the trail.

Cowpoke said, "Wait out," and he would talk to the "trucks" (CH-46s).

They heard the OV-10 depart the area. Lee started looking at his map and had Wiley go out and look for an opening for the ladder extract he had requested. Wiley came back and said there was a space southeast that went from double to single canopy of about twelve feet as it sloped off to the southeast. Lee had the team saddle up and move. While they were moving downslope, with an assumed enemy upslope northwest, *Cowpoke One-Eight* came back on line; Lee could not hear the engines but appreciated having communications. *Cowpoke* said negative to the ladder extract as the current insert/extract package had not been configured at LZ 401 with a ladder and that *Pal Joey* was not an emergency extract.

Lee's mind flashed to the old Basic School challenge, "What now, Lieutenant?"

"*Pal Joey*, this is *Cowpoke One-Eight*, trucks inbound in fifteen mikes, can you do a hoist extract? Pass Situation Report, and extract brief."

Lee moved the team to the opening and formed a 180-defense west, prepared the extract brief for the inbound CH-46s, which they could now hear, which meant the NVA could also. He still could not see the birds. Lee took the PRC-25 from Freemen, putting it on his back, telling Freeman to go up first and then, in reverse order of march, he established the individual hoist sequence. Each hoist would take two to three minutes, so, if everything were perfect, it would take 15 to 20 minutes to complete the hoist operation, all the while with the helo in a standing hover. Lee would go last with the radio.

The radio crackled with "*Pal Joey*, *Pal Joey*, this is *Purple Fox Two-Three* inbound, pass your situation, we're five out."

Lee passed that the enemy was to the west and uphill; they did not have an LZ, and they were on a side slope east 45-degree angle in 12-foot tree shrub. There were six packs. He had a signal mirror ready on their call. They heard the birds before they saw them. *Cowpoke One-Eight* asked for a flash now for him to orient to the west as the birds were coming in from east. Lee hit the OV-10 with a flash.

Purple Fox said, "Is that you, *Pal Joey*? Flash me!"

So Lee now started flashing east, hearing but not seeing the CH-46s. What Lee did not know was they were coming in at tree-top level up valley; within a minute they were eye-level horizonal to the east, he flashed, and *Purple Fox* said, "Pop smoke!"

Lee signaled Wiley, who popped a smoke.

The lead aircraft said, "I have yellow on my nose," and Lee confirmed.

The Marine pilot was a pro! He came straight on and hovered at 40 feet, came down to 30 feet, turned his nose outbound east and downhill, with the tail gunner's M60 facing west. The hoist was through the jungle growth and Freeman was on his way up. The next four hoists were made. Lee got on the hoist straddling the cable between his thighs. He then popped smoke indicating he was last man as well as telling them on the radio that he was on. He felt the nose of the CH-46 drop as the bird picked up speed. They were out![19] Lee rode the hoist into the bird. He looked at his watch; it had been 12 minutes from start to finish, a long time to hover in enemy territory but fast and efficient. He ducked and walked forward to the cockpit, put his head through and patted both pilots on the shoulder with a big thumbs up. Too loud to talk, he and the crew all had smiles, as did the five other Marines of *Pal Joey*. On the 30-minute ride back to LZ 401, Lee had time to reflect on the patrol. There were positives to each and every patrol member's actions. There obviously was a need for better communications planning, which was his job. He could not rely on the S-3 shop. He made a mental note to find out where all the radio relays were and determine their coverage before he went out again.

They landed at noon on 22 February.[20] It had been just 27 hours since they departed this same LZ, but to Lee it felt like 27 days. He would have to do better with his own sleep while on patrol. Lee had been briefed that the procedure upon debarking the team was to proceed to the S-2 hooch for debriefing. As they walked off the LZ, the Marine controlling the LZ with a radio on his back and two light wands walked over and yelled at Lee as the CH-46s lifted off for their next mission, telling him that he should go to S-3 to see the Alpha.

Lee told the team to go to S-2 and he would catch up. He walked towards the bunker thinking this would be interesting. Upon entering the dark bunker, he put his rifle on a hook in the

Corporal Ralph Witkin outside the main entrance to the S-3 operations bunker, summer 1970. (Ralph Witkin)

entryway, waiting for his eyes to adjust to the dark. He pushed aside the light-barrier flap and entered the heart of the 1st Recon Battalion COC. Upon seeing him, Gregson, the S-3A stood up, walked over, hit Lee's right shoulder with his left hand, handed him an operations order with his right, and said, "Get a good night's sleep, you're going out tomorrow! Come back after you debrief and eat lunch so we can chat. We are in the middle of a multi-team shuffle." He turned and returned to what he was doing.

Walking outside, Lee read Operations Order #0221-70 and saw it was dated 23 February at 1110, and he was going to be inserted on the 24th. Tomorrow was the 23rd. Turning around, he sought out Gregson for a clarification. Gregson said the order was in anticipation but, since they were back, it would be tomorrow, the 23rd, for *Pal Joey* to be re-inserted. At least this order had the company, platoon, and team listed properly as "D-3 Plt, 3rd team, *Pal Joey*."[21] They were to be inserted tomorrow and scheduled for five days on the ground, with extraction on 28 February. Gregson had just cut them a small huss, as the two patrols would equal the time of the original patrol, and they would get one night's sleep in their own cots with no watches. He would present it that way, knowing his Marines would simply say, "Yes, sir." But he also knew they would relish the night off. Lee caught up with the team at S-2, read the rough draft of the debrief, and added a few notes on trails they had seen. As they departed, he told the team they were going out in the morning and that they should clean up, get late lunch, clean their rifles, and he would see them and their rifles at 1500 to brief their five-paragraph order. He trudged up the hill to the Delta Company officers' hooch, opened the screen door and found the hut was empty.

Lee moved to his cube, pulled out his footlocker, and, sitting on his cot, quietly cleaned his rifle. After that, he ate a can of peaches he had saved, got up and departed for the S-2 shop to draw his maps for tomorrow, and then swung by Battalion communications, introduced himself and learned what he could before completing the 360 walk around Camp Reasoner to see Chip Gregson prior to meeting *Pal Joey* at 1500. He better not stroll as time was short. At S-2, he asked Staff Sergeant Wilson about his new haven. All he could say was nobody had been there in his memory. Lee walked back up the hill past the handball court to find the Comm Shack and seek out the communications officer, 1st Lieutenant M. J. Davies. Lee asked about comm in his next haven, showing Davies on the map. Davies looked at his propagation maps for *Vesper Bells-Alpha*, the designated radio relay, and said they should be okay in their haven. He also took the time to cut a specific length of black comm wire, the proper length for the battalion's primary frequency, 30.9 FM, wrapped it around a C-rat spoon and reminded Lee of how to string a directional antenna on the compass heading towards the *Alpha* relay. Lee had had mixed results with directional antennas as they were an art rather than a science, but the weight was minimal so he would hump it himself as a backup. This was a patrol lesson learned. Circling back down the hill, past the chapel and amphitheater, he went down the trail to the S-3 bunker to seek out Gregson, who immediately apologized for the quick handoff earlier. He explained the division was on the battalion's back to keep 30 teams in the field, so it was necessary to push *Pal Joey* back out. Gregson was not endorsing; he was just sharing. Lee asked Gregson if he knew anything about the next haven, but he did not, which was why *Pal Joey* was headed there. This haven was on G-2's list as an approach/infiltration route. Lee checked his watch, saw it was 1445, thanked the S-3A, and departed to meet *Pal Joey* at 1500 at the Stagger Back Inn. He grabbed his rifle from the hooch across the street and walked over to the inn, a high name for the Southeast Asia Hut.

Lee was pleased to see the team seated at the same table and, when he entered, they stood. He walked over to the bar, asked the tender to bring over six Cokes, and proceeded to the table. He gave the team their five-paragraph for the patrol the next day. Their mission was exactly the same as two days ago, except for the haven location, which was 10 kilometers east and north 14 kilometers from their previous patrol. There were no questions. The club was starting to get a few customers, so they went outside and formed a circle around Lee. After the extract, they were his team now and relaxed. He tossed McGowen his rifle and told the others to pass their rifle to the Marine on their right. He told them to inspect their teammate's rifle as hard as their drill instructor had inspected theirs while he inspected Wiley's weapon, which was immaculate. He gave them the clean-rifle speech and told them all to bring a rifle toothbrush on patrol; from now on they would clean their rifles outside, not breaking them down, every night in the harbor site as one of their habits. He had learned this trick patrolling the sandy area close to the Cua Viet River with Third Recon. He complimented the team on their IA drills and their performance on the previous patrol. Instead of IA drills, they would have a communications practical application. Telling McGowen and Freeman to get their PRC-25s for the class, Lee now realized this team was all grunts with no school-trained radio operators. When they returned, he told them to both put them on the battalion's primary frequency and get a comm check with radio relay (RR) *Vesper Bells-Alpha*. While they did that, Lee broke out the field-expedient directional antenna, his map, and compass. After explaining the directional antenna and aligning it on the azimuth to RR *Alpha*, he connected it to one of the radios and called *Alpha* for a comm check. From the clear sounds, they all could tell it was a stronger connection with *Alpha*. Thanking *Alpha* for the comm check, he signed *Pal Joey* off the net. He told the team he would be carrying the directional antenna rolled up inside his gas mask; if he were hit, one of them could retrieve it and use it if needed for better comm. He explained the lack of comm on the previous patrol was on him and that it would not happen again. Asking for questions, there was none but McGowen, the senior lance corporal on the team, spoke up and said, "Sir, we never heard of a field-expedient antenna." Lee said it was not on them, rather it was on the training system and if any of them had been to radio-operator school they would have known that. Mentally, Lee thought he would mention it to his friend Porter Rathmell, who was now running the Recon Indoctrination Program. It was a little after 1700. He reminded the team to get a good night's sleep, as the morning would be early, and he would see them at the LZ. Lee felt like it had been good day of prep for this patrol.

At dinner, Wilson from S-2 came by Lee's table and said he had gone back and checked on *Pal Joey*'s new haven. He said his old notes indicated this area belonged to the 38th NVA Regiment. Thanking him, Lee returned to Delta Company officers' hut, one block down the hill. Entering the hooch, he said hello and had a short conversation with Garry Parks, the 2nd Platoon commander, who had just come off Hill 119 on the 20th.[22] Parks asked about his short patrol, and he explained it was an extract because of lack of comms, and that he was going back out in the morning. Parks was headed to dinner and asked if Lee had eaten. Lee thanked him, saying he had work to do as Parks left for the mess hall. Lee moved into his space. He appreciated that some predecessor had built the small desk and chair from ammo crates. Lee broke out stationery and wrote his fiancé a short, reassuring letter that said he was in Da Nang and not to worry. She was in school back in his hometown of Los Gatos, California.[23] After that, he broke open a new case of C-rations and picked out two heavy cans to replace the two he had eaten on "No Comm

Patrol-1." With that, and the other officers out to the club, he turned off the overhead switch to the three bare lightbulbs, pulled on a sleeping shirt, and fell fast asleep.

Lee did not hear the others come in later. Next, he was awoken at 0430 by the company duty noncommissioned officer (NCO), calling for Lieutenant Lee through the back door. He thanked the NCO, grabbed a towel, and headed down the steps outside for a cold shave and shower in the dark. Dressing in a clean set of jungle cammies, he headed for early chow.

At the LZ, after they picked up their grenades, he circled the team away from the gaggle of six other teams getting ready for insert. He said they would institute a new habit of turning on both PRC-25s and having them do a comm check with RR *Alpha*. That completed, he told both operators to turn off the radios to save batteries and that they would turn them back on once airborne and headed for their insert. Battery life was always an issue. He made a mental note to ask his new friend, Davies the communications officer, how to test the emergency PRC-93 before the next patrol. The air officer called for the six team leaders as the pilots headed back to their birds after the morning insert/extract brief. They planned inserts and extracts for the same areas in order to save flying time. Lee heard that *Pal Joey* had made the afternoon lineup. He went back to the team and informed them to be back at the LZ by 1130. He would go back to lobby the air officer to be lead-off insert in the afternoon, as he wanted a few hours to get off the LZ before dark. The air officer said nobody else had asked so *Pal Joey* would be first. With a little extra time, Lee circled back to Comm and caught Davies walking out. After exchanging greetings, he asked what the procedure was for testing the PRC-93s. Davies said he knew the Wing Comm shop tested them because each pilot carried one, but no one had ever asked at Recon. He said he would talk to Wing Comm about getting the testing frequency so he could evaluate Recon's PRC-93s. Lee added that a battery tester might be a good addition for the -93 batteries. Davies said he had two days remaining in-country and was looking for a replacement. Lee assured him he was not qualified.

He headed to early noon chow to get a sandwich and some more coffee to prompt his internal system. He really wanted to take a dump here in the rear rather than having to stop just after insert when he should be doing a dozen other things. At 1130, *Pal Joey* was at LZ 401 ready to go. He told the team to crash, meaning lay down on their packs and rest. He found the Marine LZ controller who said the birds had gone to lunch and were due back any minute. The controller informed him *Pal Joey* was lead-off, to which Lee informed him he was *Pal Joey-Actual*, the patrol leader. In the bush with Recon, no rank insignia were worn. About then, the two CH-46s could be heard approaching from the east. The controller ran over and told Lee to saddle up as they would load, rotors turning, and, as soon as he knew which bird, he would tell him; he then ran to a second team who would be loaded on the chase bird. Lee saw the helos were from the *Purple Fox* Squadron. Based on his hoist extract and the talk among patrol leaders, they all respected the "Give A Shit" squadron.

The LZ controller pointed toward the lead bird as Lee trotted to the ramp. Turning, he counted his team on, then, jumping on the rear ramp last, he gave the crew chief a thumbs up. Lee went forward while the bird gained altitude. With his folded 1:50,000 map sheet and his haven outlined, he showed the pilot who looked and gave him a thumbs up. The pilot found the insert LZ. It was a steep sidehill slope with elephant grass. He indicated he would turn around, tail gate above LZ, but because the blades would be chopping the side of hill, it would be a jump off the ramp. Lee knew it was the selected LZ, now was not the time to argue, so he nodded as Wiley jumped and disappeared into six-foot-high elephant grass blowing sideways. Damn the blades. Lee gave the crew chief the thumbs-down signal to lower the bird and as it came down Lee jumped and hit a hard dirt surface, with Freeman almost landing on top of him. As Lee rolled sideways downhill, the bird was pulling out. All six on the ground, with no broken bones or sprained ankles.[24] They got a solid comm check with the insert bird and with *Vesper Bells-Alpha*.

Pal Joey regrouped on the downslope side of the LZ in the tall and razor-sharp elephant grass. Lee pointed Wiley, the point man, northeast as they moved. Entering 50-foot-high double canopy with a 12 foot first canopy and annoying scrub growth four to six feet off the jungle floor, they stopped and listened for 15 minutes. Their hearing restored from the high-pitched whine of the helo ride; they listened but heard nothing. They moved out, moving upslope, side slope, a difficult movement, for 15 minutes. They listened for five minutes and then repeated the pattern over the next two hours. Lee wanted to find an observation post (OP) to watch the valley and the river below. He was looking for a break in the canopy. At about 1430, they found a good OP, so they stopped and set up security. *Pal Joey* watched and checked out the valley floor with the 7 × 50 binos. After an hour, seeing nothing and determining it would take an entire rifle squad to defend their current position, he sent Wiley and McGowen out, with a radio, with instructions not to go more than one hundred meters and to find a defensible harbor site. They came back in ten minutes with a site they described as fair. The team saddled up and followed Wiley, the point man walking them into a bramble thicket on their hands and knees. They went with a 360 defense, and Lee indicated where the three Claymores were to be laid in. They had not seen or heard anybody since insert. He set a single watch rotation at sundown with one man on watch for one hour; he would take the first and last watch, giving the team seven hours to sleep. The night went well, and they made every comm check with *Vesper Bells-Alpha* calling out "*Pal Joey, Pal Joey*, if you're Alpha Sierra [all secure], click your handset twice." They had no issues that evening.

After morning chow, and peeing and pooping before snooping, the team packed their gear and pulled in the three Claymores. Lee had decided to find another OP closer to the valley floor and the river. He set Wiley due east and *Pal Joey* started to break brush. They patrolled east parallel to an east–west hard-packed three-foot-wide trail. They had time, so there was no need to trail walk, instead taking the slower, more difficult, but more secure, route. Breaking brush 15–25 meters above the trail, Lee was looking for his next OP to not only monitor the trail but to also see down into the valley.

Midmorning, they found a spot with broken overhead canopy that could monitor the valley. *Pal Joey* moved into a 360 defense and set up their middle-of-the-day clandestine OP with good observation, both north and east, so they could see parts of the valley. They were 20 feet off the east–west high-speed trail. Getting into the prone position, they put out three Claymores, two trailside and one covering uphill behind them. Lee broke out the 7 × 50s and scanned the valley floor. Seeing nothing, he knew it was good practice to change eyes, and it also built the team. He rotated observers every 15 minutes for the next three and a half hours. What he was coming to realize was they were still too high up. It was too late to move low and find a defensible position so, while he maintained the OP, he sent McGowen and Wiley with the secondary radio to find the night's harbor site. After 30 minutes, Lee was going to call the scouting party when he heard them coming back in. They said they had found some boulders uphill and northwest away from the trail. They pulled in the Claymores, saddled up, and moved out without a word being spoken, using only hand and arm signals.

The cluster of boulders was good on three sides with one open side. Lee told them to put all three mines out on the open side, on-line, and facing east. The team then backed into the boulders with each Marine finding one to use as a backrest. Lee set the same one-hour watch, with him taking the first and last, which would begin after sundown. It got dark fast in the double canopy and, when the sun dipped over the higher ridge line, it was dark and cold. The team members dug out sleeping shirts, putting them on under their cammie jackets in an effort to add extra insulation. The sky was clear, and the temperatures were dropping as Lee got the first comm check of his watch. Sitting against a boulder in the dark, Lee reviewed the first two days of this patrol. They had seen and heard nothing, but his skin was crawling, which told him the enemy was close. He could see in the valley that many of the paddies were close to harvest. He resolved tomorrow they would move down lower into the valley. He recalled there were three fingers running down into the valley. In the morning, he would break out the map and pick a route to get to a lower OP closer to the rice paddies. McGowen tapped him on the foot with his rifle; Lee's watch was over. He slid the radio over to McGowen with his foot. He must have slept well as the next thing he felt was his foot being tapped as someone was pushing the radio his way for the last watch of the night. Lee sat with the boulder against his back, shivered a little and listened to the morning jungle come alive. It was still dark, but the jungle was up for the new day with the bird sounds of sunrise. The team concluded morning chow and poop procedures with one guarding and one pooping in a cat hole. Lee pulled out the map, selecting the route to the finger, the center one of the three. The team pulled in the Claymores and then saddled up. *Pal Joey* was ready to move. Lee gave the hand signal to huddle up; before departing he wanted to tell the team they were going low, and it would be a danger zone. *Pal Joey* was going hunting, and he wanted every Marine ready.

Wiley headed out of the harbor site and went due east. Lee came up behind him and pointed him a shade more to the south, and indicated he should go down the sidehill. Shortly after starting, they came upon a high-speed trail. They put security out east and west, crossed it, and now headed due south downhill. The lower they moved, the easier it became as the overhead growth, now single canopy, was thinning out. They moved cautiously, crossing a second trail that ran northeast to southwest. Coming to the end of the single-canopy growth on the center finger of the valley, Lee started looking for an OP. They found a great one that had full visibility of the valley; the issue would be defensibility. It was sidehill with ground above on three sides, but the views were far better than the previous two OPs. Lee had the team put three Claymores uphill behind them, along with three team members for security. He, Wiley, and McGowen moved down and got out the 7 × 50 binos. Immediately, Wiley spotted VC in black PJs and straw hats, carrying large sacks and rifles on a trail out of the rice paddies to the southeast and heading northwest towards the mountains.[25] Lee started working up the grid coordinates for a fire mission. He told McGowen to switch the radio frequencies over to *Scandinavia*'s frequency and tell them to stand by for a fire mission. Lee knew he had one chance before the VC got under canopy where he would lose them. He got on the net and passed a grid 500 meters further up the trail just before it entered the tree line and asked for battery-one on his command. This meant that all six tubes of the 155-mm battery would fire on the same solution grid in spread at the trail tree line. Lee waited five minutes and then called "Fire!" It took 30 seconds before they heard the whistle of the six Arty rounds coming over their left shoulder. The shells were on target. Lee called a repeat fire-for-effect. Coverage of the target area was excellent, and they counted four dead VC laying in the rice paddy just off the trail where they had sought cover.[26] *Pal Joey* had drawn its first blood with Lee. They watched the bodies to ensure they were down. It was 1130. Their view was partially blocked east-southeast where the valley opened up. The only way to see it was to move lower. Lee gave the "circle-the-wagons" sign, and had the Claymores pulled in as they saddled up to move lower on the finger.

They took their time and moved down 200 meters, where they were out of canopy above them and in scrub. Finding a good viewing point, they repeated putting the mines upslope behind them, one on the animal trail on the spine of the finger, and one on each side slope. The observation was better down valley to the east while the defense site was less than desired. They were much lower than the previous two days and now closer to the valley. They were now sitting on a finger 25 meters above the valley floor. It was 1545 and the move lower was rewarded as they observed three NVA in green utilities, carrying large gray packs, and AK-47 rifles.[27] They were moving from southeast to northwest across an open rice-paddy dike. They were within small-arms range, so the team engaged with M16s, killing one. The other two made it to a hedge line that led into the canopy at the northern finger. They were gone and it was unwise to pursue them across an open rice paddy. Their position had been compromised. Lee gave the saddle-up sign and, with Claymores back in, they moved sidehill higher up the thin finger, looking for a more defensible position. Lee stopped and put the team in a 360-degree defense. They would take their evening meal here but after dark they would move to a nighttime position 75 to 100 meters further sidehill. This precaution was necessary in case the NVA had spotters watching them. The after-dark move would at least protect them from incoming mortars or rocket-propelled grenades the enemy would use if they were going to attack their last position. It was now 1845 and the sun was low in the west and would drop over the western ridge line within two or three minutes. They observed two VC in black PJs and straw hats carrying two large sacks on a yoke between them. They were rice sacks. They were moving from the east valley floor due west in to the foothills on a well-used trail. As the sun set, the two VC moved into the western scrub growth on the next finger to the team's north. The prudent move was no action. They saddled up after dark and moved to their harbor site, putting out Claymores for the 360 defense-of-the-wheel formation. They placed the radios in the hub with each Marine facing outward. They were ready for another cold night as they were exposed to the wind lower on the finger. There was no jungle to break the wind from the East China Sea blowing cold to the west.

As Lee took his first watch, he reviewed the day. The move from higher to lower had paid off with the engagement of the enemy. It had also made the team much more vulnerable. The NVA now knew a Marine Recon team was working in their rice-production valley. Tomorrow would be the key day as *Pal Joey* still had the initiative but not for much longer. The battalion commander, and thereby the staff, had been pressing the idea that prisoners produced more intelligence than spot reports of enemy movement east to west. *Pal Joey* may have an opportunity for a prisoner snatch off the trail at the foot of this finger. He would discuss the idea with the team in the morning. The night was uneventful, although he only dozed, going over the pros and cons for each option in the morning. The cautious approach would be to go back up high and observe. The bold approach was just to move at first light to the valley floor and ambush the trail. The middle approach was to move to yesterday's OP down low, close to the trail, and assess the valley for options. He liked having the large harvested dry rice paddies as an LZ. Much better than the insert LZ jumping in or hoisting out as had been done on the previous patrol. It was his job to think ahead, and the extract location was an essential decision in planning a patrol here in the jungle with few LZs. There were no LZs he knew of going back to high ground. There it was. *Pal Joey* would go low to the valley in the morning and assess.

Pal Joey went through the standard morning routine and was ready to move by 0630. Lee had the discussion with the team and said they would go low and close to yesterday's OP. He drew a diagram in the soil of the potential prisoner snatch. Freeman and McGowen with the radios would remain on the finger ten meters higher and provide overwatch. The four others would go down to the valley floor, Wiley off the trail to the east for security and Garza on the west side. Both would go on the high side in the brush and let potential enemy pass in either direction. Lee, who had played linebacker, and Kempe, who had played strong safety in high school football, were the designated tacklers. Large parties of NVA would be allowed to pass or would, as a last resort, be engaged with small arms. Small parties of one to three were the target. The team especially liked the fact that they had a large sit-down multibird-size landing zone. They moved out and were soon in the low OP in a 360-defense assessing the valley floor activity.

Around 0900, through scanning across the valley, the team observed five hooches in the foothills northwest of their position. This discovery must have been caused by the movement of two VC in black PJs repairing the thatched roof of a new bamboo-constructed elevated hooch. Lee requested an AO since they really could not see the activity across the valley but knew it needed to be checked out. *Hostage Egor* with *Cowpoke Six-Three* came on station about twenty minutes after the request.[28] Lee passed them the situation report and the grid. They flew over low and slow, and the two VC disappeared into a bunker. As the OV-10 rolled high, they called *Pal Joey*, stating they were correct, many hooches and bunkers. They had not seen any VC and were bingo fuel state. They would pass the information on to their replacement. Lee thanked them, knowing if there were higher priorities with grunts or a Recon team anywhere in the 1st Division's tactical area of responsibility, they would never get the second bird.

About 1030, the team observed two VC, in black PJs and straw hats, move into the rice paddy directly below and 20 meters west of their position. They started tilling the soil with hoes and clearing with a sickle. They were head down working up a sweat. This was their opportunity. Lee gave the rally signal to saddle up, along with a fist pumped into his hand, the signal they used to activate the prisoner snatch. Wiley moved out and, when they got to the low tip of the finger just above the paddies, they moved west through the scrub, Garza breaking off and moving east; the flankers were out and down. The two radio operators sat down, one observing uphill, the other observing the valley, 300 meters out. They were set. Lee and Kempe moved out. They crossed the dry rice paddy at a dead run, each making an airborne tackle. The tackles would make fellow

Recon Marine, Lieutenant Gump May, the legendary Pennsylvania high school football coach, proud! Both VC were down with the breath knocked out of them.

Lee and Kempe horse collared the two 90-pound-ish VC out of the paddies and up to the team's position on the finger. They taped the VCs' mouths closed, bound their hands, and then bagged their heads and laid them down flat. Lee was on the battalion primary radio to *Vesper Bells-Alpha* that *Pal Joey* had two prisoners and was requesting an immediate extract. While he was organizing the extract, Wiley reported there was movement and sound 200 meters southwest in the scrub growth, not on trails or paddies. It was the enemy searching for them. The NVA were on-line moving towards them through the scrub brush of the finger. Lee got the team on-line in the prone position. He initiated the engagement at 100 meters with all six M16 rifles firing on semi-automatic. The enemy dropped out of sight below the top of the finger for cover. They disengaged and moved away. Lee knew they would be back. He signaled the team to move out, pointing Wiley in the opposite direction and said, "Go over the top of the finger. Find a defensive position on the other side twenty-five meters down where we can skyline anybody coming over the finger after us."

The team moved out at a quick walk, not worrying about noise with Lee and Kempe horse collaring and walking the two taped and blindfolded prisoners. Wiley found a position and circled back 270 with the rest of team filling out the 360 defense, the radios, and prisoners in the center. Lee had to cold cock one of them who was trying to move and make noise. About ten minutes into the new position, their old position was fired on, with AK-47 rounds and green tracers flying over the finger. The shots were well over their heads at the new position 300 meters away on the other side of the finger. Lee called RR *Alpha* and asked for a status on extract; he was told they were next and was given the helo-extract-package FM frequency. He told *Alpha* he was switching frequency to the extract frequency, while McGowen was on *Scandinavia*'s working up an Arty fire mission. Lee contacted the extract package and was answered by *Scarface One-Zero* who wanted *Pal Joey*'s situation and LZ brief. *Scarface* was the gunship squadron's callsign. Lee said they were in contact and needed suppression on the other side of finger 300 meters out and he could hit them with a mirror flash when they arrived.

The two gunships sprinted ahead of the transport CH-46s, identified Lee's mirror flash, and started working out the other side of the finger in a racetrack pattern to the west. *Purple Fox Two-Three* came on the network next and said he was three mikes (minutes) out, coming in from the east low and wanted an LZ brief. Lee said they had enemy 300 meters west being worked out by *Scarface*, that their LZ was multibird hard-packed rice paddy to the east of the finger. He said they were moving now into the center of the paddy. There was no wind. The best LZ approach was from the east and the best exit was back out the same way. As they reached the center of the second dry rice paddy, the CH-46, at 50 feet and 200 mph, screamed by them and called pop smoke. Wiley popped smoke and *Purple Fox* called yellow and said they saw them. The pilot, having done a remarkable 180 flair turn, at speed, came in nose high, tail down, almost standing the bird vertically on its tail. This was an approach Lee had never seen but he appreciated the skill. In 20 seconds, the bird settled with ramp down ten feet past the team ducking their heads.

Lee threw his prisoner to the crew chief, turned, and helped Kempe manhandle the second man onto the ramp. Lee counted his five Marines running onto the ramp. All were on board in less than ten seconds. He gave the crew chief the thumbs up. The bird was already outbound east, 20 feet with a high-frequency screaming sound of rotor RPMs turning up for speed. The two prisoners were face down on the aluminum floor of the CH-46 at the feet of the six seated Marines of *Pal Joey*. It was 1200 on 26 February.[29]

Lee moved to the front of the bird, up to the jump seat between the two pilots, hitting both on the shoulder thanking them. Once again, *Purple Fox*'s airmanship was a magical circus of flying skills. First stop would be LZ 20 at the Marble Mountain Air Facility. It was just north of the north–south runway used by the Marine Helicopter Group, OV-10s, and O-1 Bird Dogs. LZ 20 was the landing zone for the III Marine Amphibious Force's Prisoner of War Compound where 3rd ITT (Interrogator Translator Team) would interrogate the prisoners. Once the interrogation was completed, they incarcerated them before turning them over to the South Vietnamese. Second stop would be LZ 401, home of 1st Recon, a 15-minute flight as they had to fly around Da Nang International and then three miles west to the north slopes of Hill 327. Thanking the pilots with a hand shake, as well as the crew chief and both door gunners, Lee was the last one off the ramp, trotting to catch up with his team. Unlike his last arrival from the bush, when he was unceremoniously summoned to the S-3 bunker, this time there was a gaggle of Marines from Delta Company and the S-3 shop to welcome them home at the edge of the LZ. Waiting at the back of the crowd was Chip Gregson, the S-3A, and Lee's 3rd Recon buddy, Porter Rathmell. Both were waiting to shake his hand. In the S-2 debriefing by Staff Sergeant C. L. Wilson, Lee and the team enjoyed a cold beer from the S-2 fridge. *Pal Joey* had been in the field for 72 hours with six enemy sightings for a total of 16 NVA/VC. The team had three enemy contacts with one confirmed NVA killed and two VC prisoners.[30] Lee was surprised to learn in the debriefing that, in the firefight after capturing the VC, Wiley had shot and killed a domestic water buffalo.[31] It was in the closest rice paddy with its nostrils flaring and was set to charge him at his eastern security position. Wilson paused and stated the buffalo kill was the most meaningful piece of information of the patrol because it put a dent in the plowing capability of the 38th NVA Regiment's Rice Production Unit. The team had also identified a rice-production camp and called an Arty fire mission which killed an additional four NVA.[32] It was midafternoon when Lee gave *Pal Joey* the afternoon off. He told them they would have a gift in the Stagger Back Inn at 1600. They were to enjoy their night off as, officially, they should still be on patrol. And, by the way, there will be a rifle inspection at 1100 tomorrow on the Company Street. He dismissed the team as they were yelling "Aruga, Aruga!" The team departed for the company area via a shortcut trail that avoided the center part of the camp. Sometimes Marines were very smart.

Lee walked directly up the hill to the main camp, found himself across from the handball court, turned left and walked uphill to the Delta Company officers' hooch. Coming in the back door, he was glad the hooch was empty as he wanted to decompress a little. Ever since boot camp in San Diego, cleaning his rifle always relaxed him. So, dirty as he was, he did what he was taught in boot camp. He sat on his footlocker, lit a Marlboro, and, in the quiet, broke down his M16 and cleaned it. When it was immaculate, he hung it on two posts above the small desk. He grabbed a towel and shower shoes and took them to the open shower in back. Stripping in the shower, his cammies and boots were filthy and wet. He would pay the Vietnamese mama-san to wash them and buff his boots. With a clean towel around his waist, and black plastic flip-flops on, he walked slowly back to the hooch, dropping the wet cammies and boots on the back stairs for mama-san. He remembered his promise to *Pal Joey*, so he pulled on UDT (Underwater Demolition Team) shorts. In flip-flops and shorts, he headed out the front door and across the street with a fistful of MPCs (military payment certificates). He entered the Stagger Back Inn and found the NCO-in-charge stocking the long cooler behind the plywood bar. Giving him the MPCs, he told the bartender that Team *Pal Joey* drank on him tonight. As he ascended the stairs to his hooch for the third time in an hour, he immediately crashed into his cot. It was 1630, and he had been up 18 hours with adrenaline pumping through him the last 12. Lee relaxed; deep sleep came fast.

CHAPTER 18

Hill 119, *West Orange*, and Team *Forefather*, 23 February–5 March 1970

On the morning of 23 February, the Hill 119 wire patrol found a booby-trapped M26 grenade in a draw 50 meters southeast of the observation post (OP).[1] The pin was partially pulled, and the grenade appeared to be an old one. They blew it in place and completed the wire patrol. That afternoon, *Hansworth* called Lieutenant Fallon to the platform to show him two boats in a flooded rice paddy about three hundred meters from the old railroad bridge to Go Noi Island. They called a fire mission with superior coverage of the boats, destroying both.[2] On the morning of the 23rd, Fallon called Sergeants Mushett and Franklin over for coffee and said it was time for night ambushes off the hill, that they should select a team and discuss locations, do their planning, and come back to him with a plan. Both sergeants had been to the hill before and knew the terrain. They recommended the Night Activity, or Nite Act, move west to Hill 148 and cover the trail coming up from Alligator Lake to the south. This was a well-known infiltration route from Base Area 116 in the Que Son Mountains to Go Noi Island. Late that afternoon, the patrol moved through the wire, stopped, rested, and listened 50 meters outside the wire; it was really a two-hour listening post before moving to the ambush site and setting in for the night. Franklin did not want anyone to observe him setting his linear ambush on the high side of the approaching south to north trail.

The evening passed. Waiting until well past sunrise, the patrol took a circuitous route west around the base of Hill 148 before turning east and heading back to the *West Orange* OP. At approximately 0900, moving 20 meters off the trail and parallel to it, they discovered two booby traps. Both were M26 grenades.[3] Both were well made, inside tin cans, water proofed with tar and each with a U.S. trip wire. They were covered with grass, with the trip wire running across the trail about two inches above the ground. Both traps were marked with three bamboo stakes 10 meters off the trail, pointing at 90 degrees, and both had one rock center trail on both sides of the trip wire, 10 meters away. Anyone walking the trail at night or not paying attention in daylight may miss one or, if seeing one, would not suspect the second trap a few meters up the trail leading directly over the saddle between Hills 148 and 119. Franklin's team called in the booby traps and gave notice to the hill they would be blown in place before coming back through the wire. The booby traps were within 200 meters of the large saddle landing zone (LZ). Fallon did not like being penned in by booby traps. The solution was to actively patrol further out from the OP. He needed a regular Recon box or haven around the OP, not the one-kilometer tight box given for the OP security platoon. In the grunts, he had been on both Hills 124 and 190 and activity patrolled three and four kilometers off the hill to push the enemy back from direct fire and/or booby-trap encirclement. Fallon got on the encrypted radio net with Gregson, the assistant operations officer (S-3A), and made his case. Gregson said to give him a day to work the coordination with 5th Marines and the Korean Marines in order to establish a larger regular Recon haven around Hill 119. Meanwhile, hill life followed its regular pace with *Hansworth* calling fire missions and the Recon platoon doing listening posts at night and wire walks in the sun checking for booby traps.

On the 25th, 1st Lieutenant Chip Gregson called Fallon on the secure net and passed him the news that his walk-off patrol request had been approved. Gregson explained he could not get clearance north of the *West Orange* OP due to an ongoing Korean Marine sweep, but he had succeeded in coordinating a standard Recon haven south of the hill between the two Recon OPs of Hill 119 and Charlie/Echo Companies' Hill 425, which was four kilometers due south. Fallon would have a four-by-three-kilometer box, or 12 square klicks, which encompassed both sides of Alligator Lake and the western end of the Phu Loc Valley, to include the Spider Lake dam. This would be a valley patrol in an open area. Gregson said he had the haven from 26 February–2 March. His callsign would be Team *Forefather*.[4] Fallon thanked Gregson and said the first beer was on him the next time he was at Camp Reasoner. The platoon commander called Mushett and Franklin over to his sandbagged porch overlooking the Phu Loc Valley and facing the northern slope of the Que Sons. He told them they had been given a haven between them and Hill 425. Fallon said that Mushett would take over as the hill commander and he would take Franklin and his regular team on the patrol. He described the big picture. Then he told Franklin to get his team in the mortar pit in an hour and for him and Mushett to come for the patrol order he would be giving to the entire team and both sergeants. He also told Franklin to have Sergeant Bayuk, from the Integrated Observation Device (IOD) team come to the meeting as there was coordination with Arty needed. They departed and Fallon sat on his ammo box and wrote out the three frag orders he would be giving and handing to his subordinates.

At 1300, the team was assembled along with the three leaders in the mortar pit. Fallon had to admit to himself that he had hill fever and was excited to get off for this patrol. He looked at the Marines and, spreading his arms, stated they would patrol over to Hill 425 and back between the two lakes where neither hill could observe. Fallon started with Mushett by informing him and the others that he would be the hill commander. He expected no change to their routine—two listening posts at night and one wire walk every morning. He told Bayuk that the two of them would register preplanned targets for this patrol tomorrow before he left. That got everyone's attention. Then Fallon told the team members—Franklin, Corporal Miller (the normal assistant patrol leader), Lance Corporal Weirick (the primary radio operator), Privates First Class Jackson and Evans, and Hospitalman Schneider—that the team would be moving at night and OPing during the day, which was not what Recon teams normally did in the jungle, but was what would keep them alive in the open countryside of the Phu Loc Valley with a large civilian population and a large North Vietnamese Army/Viet Cong (NVA/VC) presence gathering rice and moving through the valley at night. Before he forgot, he asked "Doc" Schneider to bring the new corpsman, "Doc" Avenel, by to see him that afternoon. Fallon wanted to impress on him he would be the hill corpsman working directly for Mushett and to ensure he was comfortable with his medical supplies on the hill.

Fallon looked at the team which he had patrolled with before. Franklin's team were experienced Recon Marines, but this patrol would resemble many of the grunt patrols Fallon had taken in the open valleys. With the grunts, he had had 30–40 Marines with machine-gun attachments on a day patrol or night ambush. He realized they would only be a seven-man team. Time to switch it up. He told them this was night movement and being quiet was a necessity. They were going out to recon, and use supporting arms from daytime clandestine OPs. He told the team it would be a standard five days for chow, go light on water, as they would fill canteens, but go heavy on ammunition. He said to prep their gear for quiet patrolling and gave them two rolls of black electrical tape to tape down rifle-sling swivels and other metal pieces. The black tape was not only good cammie, it also prevented metal-on-metal noise. They will have an inspection tomorrow followed by a test firing of their weapons. Fallon debated taking an M60 machine gun but that would leave one avenue of approach to the hill's defenses without a gun. He decided to take more ammo for the M16s and more 40mm for the M79. He told Franklin to cut three Claymore mines in half and to rig fuses for six wires and six hellboxes for the team's defensive command-detonated mines. Each patrol member would carry one, except Doc, who would be carrying his Unit One medical kit plus his M16. They would be taking two PRC-25 radios plus the PRC-93 survival radio Fallon always carried. He asked Team *Forefather* if there were any questions. Miller, a country boy, wanted to know if he should bring his fishing line. Fallon did not know if he was joking or serious, so he took it as an honest question and said no, explaining that might unnecessarily expose the team. He dismissed the Marines. Later, Franklin privately told Fallon that Marines from the hill had held swim call and fishing days at Alligator Lake. Fallon explained that if they were a rifle company and provided security for a few to rotate through to the lake it would make sense, but, on his watch, there would be no swim/fish call.

Bayuk was busy as *Hansworth* called three fire missions on the 25th.[5] Late that afternoon, Bayuk, with his map and notebook, found Fallon. They sat down and Fallon showed him where he wanted four preregistered targets. Hill 175 was obvious but when Fallon said Hill 177 between the two lakes, Bayuk knew this patrol was serious business. He had never seen a Recon team go there in his time on the hill since November 1969.[6]

The 26th was a quiet day on the hill. Only one fire mission and Team *Forefather* slept or played cards while resting in the bunkers. The team inspection and fam fire of weapons went well; everybody then went to their bunker to heat up a big meal of C-rations. The next five days would be cold chow. At 1845, *Forefather* gathered at the mortar pit, did comm checks on both radios with both *West Orange* (Hill 119) and *Vesper Bells* (Recon Battalion). Earlier in the afternoon, Fallon had used the secure net and called the commander of Hill 425, passed him his haven, and said all fire missions called by 425 in his haven must be personally cleared by him. He did not need 425 to see them move at night in their night-observation device (NOD) and think they were NVA; there would be no way for 425 to know friend from foe. Yes, Battalion had passed their haven to the artillery regiment and Division Fire Support Coordination Center, but he had been fired on by friendly Arty in the grunts, always due to insufficient coordination. He also put the Recon box on the map next to the Hill 119 IOD, with the same guidance. Any fire mission in the box would be controlled by *Forefather* or preapproved by *Forefather*.

Sometime after 1900, when the sun was completely down, *Forefather* moved out the east gate (not the obvious west LZ gate), knowing they would drop into the valley to the south after clearing the OP. Franklin walked point with Fallon at deuce point to control pace and to listen at night. He was the one with night experience. The remainder of the team got their distance as they departed around the boulders and scrub brush with Corporal Miller, also a good point man, walking tail-end Charlie. Fallon had told the team they would walk ten minutes and sit ten. They moved slowly and took 30 minutes to get to the first danger area, the high-speed east–west trail halfway down the finger. They sat for ten and listened but could only hear the Marines back on Hill 119. Franklin and Fallon moved across the trail, set up east–west security, and then moved the rest of the team across with Miller taking point; Fallon signaled for Franklin to move to the rear and let Miller walk point for the next hour. The largest danger area to cross was next. The team stopped and formed a hasty ambush 10 meters off the east–west trail/cement aqueduct trail that ran from the Alligator Lake dam northeast and parallel to the finger the Marine OP was on. The trail continued until the finger flattened out, then the trails and aqueduct ran due east for two kilometers to the village of Chien Son (4). It then connected Chien Son (3) and, two more kilometers, Chien Son (2) before running under the north–south railroad and jogging north to Chien Son (1).

They waited 30 minutes before putting out security and crossing the aqueduct to the south side of the small Chien Son Valley. They quickly began a gradual uphill walk into scrub brush headed directly for Hill 175. The plan was to move halfway up and find a defensible position from which to observe the valley. When they stopped, they were 400 meters due east of Alligator Lake. They could see the earthen dam at night, but not the trail they knew was below it, until it could be observed after sunrise. They went 360 with boulders above them and scrub growth below them. Fallon put 50 percent to sleep and set a watch that rotated one time before dawn. With the sun coming up, the team went to 100 percent and observed. They could easily see the Marines on Hill 119 as well as the Marines on Hill 425 well above them and three kilometers further south. They saw the villagers immediately in the east come out and begin working the rice paddies closest to Chien Son (4). The valley came to life with the dawn. About 0905, the team observed two NVA with rifles, wearing green utilities, moving northwest on a small trail toward the dam and the large boulder field directly below the dam.[7] He knew they had a small camp or waystation hidden in that field. These two were moving with purpose. Fallon decided to follow, they would be behind the two NVA who would be focused on the well-known Marine OP located to their right front. Team *Forefather* saddled up and moved onto the trail and, as Miller followed, Fallon told Franklin and Evans just to sit off-trail and provide security to their rear uphill. They followed for 300 meters down toward the dam but lost sight of the two NVA. Rather than go blind and split, the team stopped, reversed course, and were quickly back in the original night harbor site which was now a valley floor clandestine OP. They observed from there all day. With night approaching, they would move one kilometer southwest and uphill to find an ambush site near the summit of Hill 175. They found a one-foot-wide hard-packed high-speed trail leading toward the summit and took it. Close to the summit, they found an old infantry fighting position with old holes partially filled in, with a 360 perimeter. Fallon did not like it and stopped the team outside. They got the binos out and surveyed the position from ground level

20 feet out and picked up the first trip wire. Within five minutes they had found six wires and Miller found a pressure device on the trail five feet in front of the team. With close observation, all the booby traps, or self-firing devices (SFD), had markers of rock piled three high and bamboo pointed towards them. Any infantry unit running up hill to the summit in order to establish a defensive position, which was the infantry pattern, would definitely walk into a multiple SFD ambush. Fallon told Miller to put a M26 grenade on the pressure plate and blow it as the team backed down the trail.

After the explosion, the team moved off-trail sidehill southwest just below the military crest of the Hill 175 finger running back toward the lakes. This finger, with its crest trail, ran back west-southwest between the two lakes. After moving 500 meters, Fallon called *Hansworth* and fired the preregistered target on Hill 175. The fire mission detonated three additional SFDs. It was 2230. *Forefather* kept moving all night, following the 175 finger toward Spider Lake. At the false dawn, they moved over the top of finger and down a small draw 100 meters from the crest and found a position due north of Phu Loc (2) hamlet on the north shore of Spider Lake. They would OP the hamlet and the lake all that day. They watched the hamlet come awake on the morning of 28 February with smoke rising from cooking fires. It was cold and damp. The team was cold. Villagers, mostly women and children, moved to the rice paddies for the day's work. *Forefather* saw nothing until late afternoon. About 1500, they picked up small groups of NVA moving out of the Que Son Mountains on a trail directly below the cliff Hill 425 sat on. The Marine OP could not see NVA on the cliff-hugging trail from their position until they made the valley floor and moved into the hedgerows that neatly sectioned off every third or fourth rice paddy, as they dropped a foot each paddy to allow for natural irrigation. At 1525, Team *Forefather* picked up five NVA directly below their clandestine OP, moving into a tree line outside of Phu Loc (2).[8] The NVA were wearing green utilities and carrying heavy packs. Three had rifles and two carried submachine guns. One was carrying a brown box measuring 12" × 12" × 12". Brown Box NVA walked out to the middle of a dry field and left the box.[9] They then rejoined the others as they all moved further into the tree line. *Forefather* called a fire mission on the tree line with good coverage. After the mission, an aerial observer (AO) with *Hostage Egor* in an OV-10 arrived on station, took their brief, and worked over the area with his own ordnance. *Forefather* saw three enemy run from the tree line and suspected the other two were probable kills. *Hostage Egor* departed, and *Forefather* remained in their OP.

After sundown, at about 1805, the team picked up movement. It was another five NVA moving east on the same trail. They were dressed in green utilities, carrying packs and rifles at sling arms. They were relaxed; one was smoking. Another NVA was carrying a radio that was similar in size and appearance to a PRC-25.[10] The OP observed them, now meeting with three other NVA who came out of the trees where they had fled during the fire mission earlier that afternoon. The eight huddled, then one moved into the open field and retrieved the brown box left there by the earlier NVA patrol. Fallon had been thinking about the box. His only guess was it contained blasting caps, and they were keeping them separated from explosives. Why else leave a brown wooden box in the middle of the field? This NVA patrol then moved into a draw just off the trail, building a cooking fire. Approximately ten minutes later, three of the NVA departed the draw, moving southwest to skirt Spider Lake. These three were carrying rifles and the radio.

Forefather lost sight of them in the diminishing daylight as they moved back towards the Que Son Mountains. At that time, Fallon called another fire mission in the draw on the remaining five NVA near the cooking fire. The battery-two fire-for-effect shot 12 rounds, with good coverage of the draw, putting out the fire.[11] *Forefather* could not see into the draw to determine results, due to darkness falling and the angles of terrain. Fallon was excited about the radio but disappointed they had lost it. The radio team had to be linked to a headquarters unit. Team *Forefather* had a good defensible site, so they put out the Claymores and harbored in place for the night. It was a black night with low cloud cover, cold and windy. The team could only see a few meters, and because of the wind, they could only hear the wind which was blowing hard off the East China Sea and directly up the valley. They might as well sleep. Fallon was glad he had humped his sleeping shirt and one half of a poncho liner to wrap up in. He slept in the sitting position with his back on a big boulder.

The morning of 1 March, about 0710, Miller spotted four NVA moving west on the trail below the OP. The NVA were in green utilities carrying packs and rifles. They were moving west on the trail. Fallon called a fire mission but was not granted clearance. When he pushed the issue, stating it was his tactical area of responsibility, the delayed response came back that there was an aircraft on the gun target line. Fallon could hear no aircraft and had other thoughts, like was it breakfast in the Arty chow hall? He huddled with Franklin and Miller. They had been in the OP for over twenty-four hours; it was time to move. He wanted to check out the draw where the cooking fires came from. They made a plan to move down off the finger and come into the draw from the high side. They would leave Evans and Jackson with the second radio 100 meters above them; the team would drop into the draw and point man Miller and Lance Corporal Weirich would push all the way to the trail and post east–west security just off it.

At 1130, the team found the fire pit, and they also found a bunker, a reinforced hut, and a sleeping area. Fallon and Franklin searched the area and "Doc" Schneider provided local security. They also found three tunnels and fighting holes. This was a well-concealed waystation that could house 15–20 soldiers. The hooch contained two rice-grinding stones, a U.S. helmet, M16 bandoleer, as well as cooking and eating utensils. They also found the tail assembly from a 500-pound bomb. The coals in the fireplace were warm, indicating it had been used that morning. The hooch was 8' × 8' × 6'. The dirt walls were two feet thick, and it was dug down two feet below ground level. The roof was thatched bamboo and there was live secondary growth pulled over it and tied, to provide camouflage from over flights. Without the cooking smoke, seen on multiple days, the team would never have found the waystation. The bunker underground was 10' × 15' × 5' with a two inch bamboo roof covered with two feet of dirt. Two of the three tunnels were made from concrete sewer pipes four feet in diameter and 30 feet long, also covered with two feet of dirt.[12] These tunnels showed signs of being used, no doubt when artillery fire was close. While searching the tunnels, one NVA wearing green utilities and carrying a rifle approached on the trail from the west. Miller engaged with small arms and the enemy ran way to the west. Franklin and Doc Schneider threw M26 grenades in the tunnels while Fallon used two white-phosphorous grenades inside the hooch to start a fire. Using the fire as a cover, Fallon gathered the team and headed back up the draw to their high security team of Evans and Jackson. They did not stop but moved another 250 meters straight up to the crest of the hill. Calling a halt, *Forefather* went into a hasty 360 while he called a fire mission on the waystation below, with good coverage. Before Fallon could call for another fire-for-effect, *Hostage Egor* arrived on station. He contacted *Forefather* and Fallon gave him quick brief. The AO could easily see the dark smoke coming from the smoldering hooch. *Egor* made several passes using both rockets and guns on the draw with excellent coverage; the entire draw was completely burnt out. The hooch was burned down, and the tunnels appeared to have been hit by the OV-10's rockets. With the OV-10 scouting the ridgeline to the east, *Forefather* moved northeast, quickly moving off-trail through scrub growth parallel to the trail.

When the AO departed, the team pulled up for a listening break and drank canteen water, being thirsty from the morning and early afternoon activities. Fallon decided to move back to the Hill 175 area and monitor that hill from the south side. He would not go back to the old, booby-trapped infantry position near the summit, but wanted to monitor the trail that ran just below the summit from south to north towards Hill 119. They had covered 2,200 meters, in part thanks to air cover. Fallon knew when the OV-10 was over them the NVA were conditioned to run to their tunnels and bunkers, thereby allowing *Forefather* to move faster. Too quickly. While they were moving east below the summit of Hill 175, at 1730, they heard a spoon flying off and, as they dropped to the ground, an M26 grenade went over them and exploded. It missed the team and, due to the steep slope below them, no shrapnel came their way. The team got on-line, moved in the direction of the grenade, checked out the area, but found nothing. Whomever had thrown the grenade had taken off; the purpose was to slow them down.

Fallon pushed east as the sun was fading in the west. He told Miller to look for a good place to harbor for the night but hold up short of it as they would stop, observe it, and wait for darkness before moving in. They were walking in scattered scrub growth. Miller found a cluster of large boulders on the northeast side of Hill 175 a third of the way downslope. The team set up a hasty 360, got out the 7 × 50 binos and started a detailed survey of their upcoming harbor sight. While Fallon was getting a good azimuth to confirm their location, Franklin spotted three NVA/VC, about fourteen hundred meters to the team's northeast, wearing khaki shirts and walking into a hooch. Rather than call a fire mission, Fallon had Franklin call the IOD team on Hill 119 and let them fire up the hooch. Franklin talked *Hansworth* to the target and turned it over as it was getting dark. The fire mission hit the general area of the hooch, but it was too dark to see if it hit it. *Forefather* got up and moved down in to the boulders, They had big boulders above them and an open view of the valley below them. Fallon had the team put three Claymores above them on the other side of the large boulders. They formed a 360 defense with their feet in the center close to the two radios. They set the watch with two Marines awake on each one-hour watch, or three watch sections, which meant each watch would get at least two watches. Fallon was tired and asked Doc Schneider to sit the first watch with Evans and Jackson and be sure to wake him for his watch.

Five minutes after 0300, Doc kicked Fallon's boot, waking him. Doc had let the worn-out lieutenant sleep and took two watches. He was waking him because Franklin had alerted the entire team quietly when he saw, silhouetted above them, 12–15 NVA moving northeast down the finger toward the valley.[13] They could see rifles but, due to the darkness, could not see uniform colors or equipment. The enemy was moving slowly, and with purpose, as if looking or searching for the team. When they were 20 meters away, one member of *Forefather* coughed! With that, the enemy went on-line, spreading out. Fallon handed the three hellboxes for the mines over to Doc and picked up the radio handset. He did not want to talk a lot, so he whispered to *West Orange* over on Hill 119 for *Hansworth* to immediately call the preregistered fire mission for the Hill 175 summit. It seemed like a long time, the enemy had spread out above the boulders and stopped. Both sides were waiting and listening when Fallon heard the whistling sound of one Arty round go over their position. It went over the summit and impacted somewhere in the Phu Loc Valley, sounding like an echo. Fallon knew they were on the gun target line from An Hoa but felt better with the boulders above them. He whispered to *Hansworth* to drop 100 and fire-for-effect. Again they waited, and finally they heard the six rounds screaming their way, going over them, and impacting just over the summit but close enough to sound very loud. The enemy had gone to ground, not running. They were just on the other side of the boulders above the team. Fallon now whispered into the radio, "Drop 50, fire-for-effect." When *Ringbroom Mike*'s artillery mission was over *Forefather* could no longer hear or see any enemy. They were gone. Fallon knew there were booby traps on the former infantry position on the summit and did not want to move uphill from a secure location. He put the team on 100 percent alert and, thinking afterwards, as he sat up in the damp air, the team must have wondered at the 100 percent alert command as if anyone could sleep!

The team stayed in position until well after sunrise. Fallon told the team they would be heading back. With the first light, he ate sliced peaches, a can he had saved in the bottom of his ass pack, which he savored for the sweetness of the thick syrup. Now, with the Claymores pulled in, the team moved out of the boulders. He sent Evans and Jackson south and up towards the summit to set security while the rest of the team got on-line and checked out the area 20 meters above their nighttime harbor site. They found nothing. With that, Miller headed downhill off-trail towards the Alligator Lake dam and the aqueduct trails. The team spent the morning slowly scouting the trails below the dam. Fallon called *Hansworth* and asked the IOD team to watch their back trail, especially Hill 175 as they came uphill toward 119. The direct route back was due north to the saddle between Hills 148 and 119, where their LZ was located, but this was also the lazy way and a good place to get ambushed or, even worse, booby-trapped. Fallon pushed the team east just off the aqueduct trail for a kilometer. They would come up the steep southeast approach to the OP and come in the east gate through the wire with the sun at their back and looking for the booby-trap wires they all suspected might be across their path. At some point, you had to come to the trail to enter through the triple-concertina wire gate made of engineer stakes and barbed wire.

It was late morning on 2 March when they did the S-curved trail through the three layers of triple-concertina wire and were back at *West Orange*. Fallon gave the team the rest of the day off, said there would be a rifle inspection at sundown in the mortar pit, and they would stand their regular bunker watches with the rest of the platoon that evening. He went to his bunker to compile his notes to turn into the S-2 (intelligence) shop at their post flip debrief. *Forefather* had patrolled for 86 hours, with seven separate sightings of the enemy, totaling 32 NVA. They had uncovered and blown six booby traps in the vicinity of Hill 175. They discovered an NVA waystation close to Phu Loc (2) and Spider Lake where they destroyed its hooch and underground tunnels. The team had two enemy contacts resulting in no known results for either side.[14] It was obvious the enemy was moving every day and every night from the base area in the Que Sons past both lakes and over the fingers to Go Noi Island. It was also obvious the enemy knew where the Recon OPs on Hills 425 and 119 were located and what they could see and not see because of the terrain. Likewise, *Forefather*'s sighting of enemy in the open and moving were on trails that, due to terrain, were unobservable from the OPs.

***

While *Forefather* was out patrolling, the forward observer (FO), callsign *Hansworth,* had concentrated observing north toward the Go Noi Island free-fire zone. Their sightings totaled 17 enemy. They had fired four fire missions with *Ringbroom-Mike*, with unobserved results due to vegetation and terrain.[15] When the enemy heard an Arty round, they dived for premade holes and bunkers in every tree line off every trail. It often took a first-round direct hit to get results. Now with the IOD's precision, this was more likely if the FO gauged the enemy pace and fired in front of them with a six-round fire-for-effect instead of an adjustment round. Firing a one-round adjustment meant you were simply firing a warning shot telling them to dive for cover.

That evening, just past sundown at approximately 1910, *Hansworth* spotted 22 NVA, in green utilities and carrying packs, moving west on a trail next to, and 400 meters south of, the railroad bridge.[16] This was the rice harvest coming in from the Go Noi Island fields and moving back toward the base area. *Hansworth* called an immediate fire-for-effect with three batteries, or 18 rounds. They got excellent coverage of the railroad trail. Due to darkness, it was not possible to observe if they had hit the enemy. Even with the enhanced NOD, when it was a low ceiling or overcast, the effective observing range was cut down significantly. The next afternoon, *Hansworth* had one fire mission with unobserved effects due to terrain. The weather was downright shitting with a big storm moving in from the East China Sea. The next two days were bunker time, rain, and wind. If the enemy were out and moving, the OP could not see them, which meant they were moving past the OP in both directions.

Fallon called in Mushett, Franklin, and Bayuk to talk about the upcoming turnover of the hill, with 4th Platoon due up on 5 March. He wanted the hill to be well policed, but he also wanted a smooth turnover with solid gun cards for the six bunkers. He also wanted Mushett to make up a 60-mm mortar card with the four preregistered targets along with the azimuth and number of charge bags per round for each target. He also wanted a card on maximum illumination-round time. He explained it was their obligation to not only improve the hill but to improve the flip of platoons, which was far too short on time for a proper handoff. Fallon had met 2nd Lieutenant Chris L'Orange, the new 4th Platoon commander, only once in the Delta Company officers' hooch. He knew it would be Chris's first time on the hill. Fallon started a turnover logbook with hill notes he would hand off to L'Orange with preregistered targets and other information. He told Mushett and Franklin about the turnover logbook and asked for their input. Both had ideas so, instead of copying, he gave them the green cloth-covered book and said for each to write about their areas of responsibility on Hill 119, and to answer the question "What they would like to know if new to the hill?" He told Franklin to inventory all the ammunition by bunker and put it in the book, plus report on the amount of water in the hill's water bull. He actually had no idea how much was left. Water was not an issue in the winter, but it was in the summer. Since Recon was not trained in mortars, he told Mushett to write up a mortar page with diagram. Fallon said he would write up the danger areas and avenues of approach for the turnover book. On the morning of 5 March, the hill awoke covered in fog. There would be no flip unless it burned off. *West Orange* waited all day in the low cloud ceiling, listening on the radio for any progress of the insert/extract package. Finally, at 1500, they got word they were next. All their gear was already staged at the LZ. Miller, with a backpack radio, moved to the LZ to be hill LZ control, along with a five-Marine working party. They would help 4th Platoon offload as the birds turned on the LZ. The birds would go to An Hoa to do a hot refuel and be back to complete the flip in 30 minutes.

Fourth Platoon arrived at 1530 and took five minutes for L'Orange and 25 Marines plus "Doc" Hunt to offload.[17] Corporal Weese, his platoon sergeant, huddled with Mushett while Wiley, Franklin's old friend, huddled on logistics. Fallon walked L'Orange up the hill, pointing out the bunkers and their names, A through F. He showed him his bunker, telling him to drop his pack and together they went to the IOD platform, where Bayuk would quickly brief L'Orange on what he was observing that day. Fallon had told Bayuk to hold off the capabilities brief for later as, because of the quick turnover, this was just a tactical situational-awareness brief for L'Orange. When Bayuk was done, Fallon pointed out the enemy avenues of approach and pointed out the key terrain features: Hill 148 to the southwest, Alligator Lake, Hill 425 OP to the south, Hill 175 to the southeast, the railroad bridge to the northeast, Go Noi Island due north, and the Arizona Territory to the northwest which completed a 360-degree description. About then, they could see the two CH-46s coming in low and fast from An Hoa. Fallon and L'Orange shook hands and Fallon walked down the stairs off the IOD platform and jogged to the LZ. He would count his men on to the two birds and get on the second bird last with Franklin and *Forefather*, while Mushett was on the lead bird. It was 1548; the flip had taken 48 minutes from start to finish.[18] Fallon would talk to Gregson about trying to change the process to an overnight flip with both platoons being on the hill together for one night. The primary mission of the Recon platoon was to provide security for the classified "Secret" IOD on the OP. They needed a better turnover process.

CHAPTER 19

Sapper Probe, March 1970

Cash Box Top 100 had "Bridge Over Troubled Water" by Simon and Garfunkel as the number-one song on 1 March 1970. It would hold the position for the month. Popular in the USA, it was also popular with the troops in Vietnam on the Armed Forces Vietnam Network. On 5 March, President Nixon signed instruments of ratification, The Nuclear Non-Proliferation Treaty.[1] The U.S. Army charged 14 officers, including two general officers, with suppression of information about the 1968 My Lai massacre, and referred charges for court-martial on 17 March.[2] And, on 22 March, the U.S. Air Force used the first BLU-82 "Daisy Cutter" bomb, at the time the most powerful conventional weapon, on the North Vietnamese Army (NVA) operating in Long Tieng, Laos.[3]

***

At Camp Horn, namesake of a Marine engineering officer killed near Nam O Bridge early in the war, the turnover of the entire camp, from III Marine Amphibious Force (III MAF) to XXIV Corps, was in full swing. The MAF would move the week of 5 March across the city of Da Nang to Camp Hastings.[4] The camp was located on Route 1 across the two-lane highway from Red Beach on Da Nang Bay. XXIV Corps would move the same week from Phu Bai to Camp Horn. The official ceremony for XXIV Corps to assume command of I Corps' Tactical Zone took place on 9 March. Lieutenant General H. Nickerson USMC passed operational command of I Corps Tactical Zone to Lieutenant General M. Zais USA. At the same ceremony, he turned over III MAF command to Lieutenant General Keith McCutcheon USMC who would now work for General Zais.[5]

Meanwhile, on 11 March, the 1st Marine Division's communications officer established and activated the Division Reconnaissance Net. The purpose was to provide reconnaissance spot information to the Division G-2 (intelligence). Stations guarding the net included Division Combat Operations Center, Division G-2, 1st Recon Battalion, and 1st Force Recon Company.[6] On 19 March, the 26th Marine Regiment received a Presidential Unit Citation for their fighting at Khe Sanh a year earlier. The regiment then departed Da Nang to stand down at Camp Pendleton, California.[7] With the reduced responsibility for territory passed to XXIV Corps, but more likely due to the departure of Nickerson, both 1st and 3rd Force Reconnaissance Companies returned to the operational control of the 1st Marine Division.[8] The 1st Marine Regiment expanded its area of responsibility by assuming the area north of Da Nang from the 26th Marines. The critical highway and rail passage through Hai Van Pass was now also the 1st Division's boundary with the 101st Airborne Division to the north while, in the south, the Americal Division moved up to a boundary below Fire Support Base Ross. The 11th Marine Regiment reported that, in the first three months of operations, the six Integrated Observation Devices (IOD) fielded by them had accounted for 1,153 confirmed enemy killed, which represented over forty percent of the division's enemy kills.[9]

At 1st Reconnaissance Battalion, Lieutenant Colonel Drumright continued to hire and fire officers based on patrolling performance, or lack of patrolling. Captain Tom Martin had multiple Drumright sins. A lack of bush time coupled with a second failed Company Administrative/Pay Inspection, a cardinal sin, saw his relief and transfer on 3 March.[10] Martin, a career regular officer, would resign his commission after returning to the States. He entered the overseas construction business, eventually retiring outside of Boulder, Colorado.[11]

His unwitting replacement was the first "Drumright Boy." First Lieutenant "Jerry" Spolter, now on a six-month extension of his 13-month tour, assumed command of Delta Company.[12] Also leaving Delta Company in early March was 2nd Lieutenant Tom McAdams. On his last patrol in late February, during a ladder extraction, one of his Marines fell off the ladder, seriously injuring himself. It had been McAdams's responsibility to ensure each patrol member had a rope swiss seat and snap-link to snap in to the ladder to prevent falling off on emergency extracts. The speed and turbulence of a ladder extract made it next to impossible to just sit and hang on to the narrow aluminum ladder as blood circulation is cut off which results in the numbing of one's arms and legs. Drumright held McAdams responsible for the injury to one of his Marines.[13] McAdams was transferred to 2nd Battalion, 5th Marines, to become a platoon commander where, shortly after his arrival on 25 March, while providing security for a tank column on Liberty Road, he was ambushed. Multiple rocket-propelled grenades aimed at the tanks impacted near McAdams who lost both ear drums, suffered a brain concussion, and had large shrapnel wounds to his legs. Gravely wounded, Tom medevac'd through Da Nang Naval Support Activity Hospital back to Japan and on to Charleston Naval Hospital where he undertook a long recovery.[14] Transferred to Camp Lejeune for physical therapy, and on light duty, he was medically discharged. Tom went into the beer-and-wine-distribution industry and had a successful career in Greenville, South Carolina.[15]

At Camp Reasoner, the new "Breakfast Club" lineup had four of six changes in company command during March.[16]

Co. A: 1st Lieutenant Charlie Kershaw

Co. B: 1st Lieutenant Denny Storm relieved 1st Lieutenant Tony Pack, who rotated home

Co. C: Captain L. D. "Mac" McVey was killed in action on 2 March and was succeeded by 1st Lieutenant S. L. "Stumpy" Baker

Co. D: Captain Martin was relieved 3 March and succeeded by 1st Lieutenant G. G. "Jerry" Spolter

Co. E: 1st Lieutenant C.D. Banks was relieved by Captain F. S. Blair on 12 March

H&S Co.: Captain R. L. Wiltrout

The Charlie Company commander, "Mac" McVey, died when the jungle penetrator snapped, and he fell to his death. He had been going into the same area where, earlier that day, the jungle penetrator snapped on one of his platoon commanders, 2nd Lieutenant Skibbe, who fell to the ground and was initially thought to have survived the fall. Skibbe, already with an ankle wound and broken leg, had called in supporting arms that broke contact earlier that day and had supervised the medevac of a more seriously wounded Marine on the first jungle-penetrator lift. For saving that Marine's life and his actions during that patrol, in the face of a superior enemy, David W. Skibbe was awarded the Navy Cross.[17] He was declared missing in action when the battalion could not find him after numerous attempts in the following weeks.

While the battalion staff had stabilized with Captain Cook and 1st Lieutenant Creg Howland in the Intel shop, the Operations shop continued under Major Mattiace and 1st Lieutenant "Chip" Gregson. First Lieutenant Porter Rathmell now headed training and kicked off Recon Indoctrination Program 2-70 while Staff Sergeant Blum finished Pre-SCUBA 02-70.[18]

The officer replacements from the grunts continued to arrive. On 5 March, 1st Lieutenant Mike Hodgins arrived from Drumright's former unit, 2nd Battalion, 26th Marines, and was assigned to Charlie Company. "Mustang Mike" would go on to have a legendary Reconnaissance tour with multiple fire-support ambushes from the OP on Hill 425.[19] Second Lieutenant Paul Eglevsky, from West Hampton, New York, arrived on 20 March. The Basic School Class 8-69 graduate had five months in the grunts as a platoon commander with Fox Company, 2nd Battalion, 5th Marines.[20] Patrolling the Arizona Territory, while chasing Charlie and dodging booby traps, he met Drumright's criteria for joining the battalion. He was assigned to Delta Company as a platoon commander, moving Fallon to executive officer (XO) and free-agent patrol leader. Toward the end of the month, on 24 March, Major General Wheeler, the commanding general of 1st Division, brought his boss, Lieutenant General Keith McCutcheon, to Camp Reasoner for a briefing on battalion operations.[21]

In Delta Company, the new commanding officer (CO), Jerry Spolter, hated sitting through the Breakfast Club every morning.[22] His solution was to go to the field. Could combat in the bush be any worse than being berated in public? It had the added benefit of supporting Drumright's measure of lieutenants being in the field. Spolter became the CO on 4 March and had the great fortune of gaining Master Sergeant Rene Regalot, formally the S-3 (operations) chief, to come in and replace the fired first sergeant.[23] Regalot took over the office with Spolter's full backing. Spolter took the next frag order, #0246-70, for himself.[24] Regalot, having come from S-3, explained that #0246 meant this was the 246th patrol 1st Recon would run this year. It was signed, W. C. Gregson "by-direction." By-direction was the authority of the CO to provide orders in writing to the patrolling teams. Spolter would be taking out one of Garry Parks's teams from 2nd Platoon. Originally scheduled to leave on 5 March, Spolter got a pen change to 7 March to give him time to prepare himself and the team. Delta 2-2, or the second team of 2nd Platoon, was led by Corporal Wilson.[25] Team *Fig Newton* would be patrolling on the lower part of Charlie Ridge overlooking Happy Valley. Both were known NVA infiltration routes from the west to the rice fields of Happy Valley. On this patrol, Spolter met the effervescent Hospital Corpsman Third Class Thurman Mullins; they hit it off. Forty years later, "Doc" Mullins, now running Charlie Daniels's (of the Charlie Daniels's Band fame) farm in Tennessee, would name two of his horses after Recon Marine leaders. The horses were named General Parks and Lieutenant Spolter.[26] *Fig Newton* patrolled for five days, with signs and indicators of the enemy such as waystations and fighting holes, but with no enemy sightings.[27] Returning as the last extract on 12 March at 1830, all Spolter could think of was a shower and an excuse not to go to the Breakfast Club the next morning.[28]

Team *Fig Newton*, Delta Company street, prior to insertion. Spring 1970. (T. Mullins)

***

Lieutenant Chris L'Orange appreciated the handover of the Hill 119 logbook from Fallon as he surveyed his new domain. He had been new to the battalion 45 days earlier when Lieutenant Overton had hit the booby trap that ended his tour and career with an emergency medevac off Hill 119. The S-3A, Chip Gregson, the former Delta Company XO, had discussed and warned Overton of the booby traps around Hill 119. It was now 1600 with only a couple hours of daylight remaining. L'Orange had gotten the word to bring as many Marines as he could. He had brought 25 Marines and a corpsman, "Doc" Hunt. He had five corporals: Weese, Hayler, Wiley, Lawrence, and McAffee.[29] "The Five Corporals" were not a singing group. They were his platoon sergeant, platoon guide, and three team leaders. He had all five come up to the mortar pit. He wanted to get the defense organized for that evening. There was no better way than a live-fire exercise. There were six bunkers, each with a crew-served weapon, so he told the corporals they would go to bunkers A through E, on his command, and fire the resident weapons. He also passed the word he wanted two listening posts out the first night, one west and one east on the ridgeline. The live fire would start at 1700. Dismissing his corporals to allow them to get organized, he climbed the east ladder to the platform and, naturally, found Sergeant Bayuk, the IOD team leader and forward observer (FO). He got the brief from Bayuk and returned to his bunker to get himself organized before the live fire.

That evening, Bayuk had two fire missions which L'Orange went up to the platform to observe. The first, at 1830, was seven NVA due east, walking toward the hamlet of Chien Son (4). They had rifles and packs.[30] L'Orange was amazed that, even in the fading darkness, two kilometers away, they could see the details, even the color of green utilities.[31] The fire mission was denied because of negative clearance. Bayuk explained to the lieutenant that the north–south boundary between the Republic of Korea Brigade and the U.S. Marines ran along the north–south railroad and the bridge to Go Noi Island. That fire mission had to be cleared by both sides to ensure they weren't shooting on a friendly patrol or set-in ambush. Bayuk went on to say the NVA knew exactly where the boundary was and used it as a north–south corridor because it gave them more time to avoid artillery strikes.[32] That night, Chris, in his candlelit bunker, wrote a short letter to his parents, and looked at a bookshelf that included at least six Louis L'Amour paperbacks. He also found a tactical heat map of the area around the hill, started by Gunnery Sergeant Moore and updated by each hill commander ever since. It was a tactical sketch of the hill and the grid squares around it with prior enemy contacts and booby traps displayed. It at once showed a pattern. He took the map up to the platform and showed Bayuk, asking if he had one for earlier fire missions. He did not but said he would make one back two weeks and keep it going forward. By comparing the two heat maps they would be able to see where the enemy was moving and plan or expect what they should, or could, do as counter moves. While there, he asked about preplanned defensive fires. Bayuk showed him the defensive fires sketch and where each on-call fire mission was preregistered.[33]

The next night, 6 March, L'Orange was sitting on the sandbagged outer wall in front of his bunker drinking a coffee/cocoa blend he had just heated with a heat tab. He was pleased he had not gassed himself with the chemical tab. Corporal Wiley came over and said they had something in the starlight scope they had set up on top of Alpha Bunker. They had spotted three enemy crawling into the outer wire just 200 meters to the northeast; they were trying to belly crawl up a small draw under the wire. L'Orange had Bayuk call an on-call preregistered fire mission. As soon as the Arty howitzers were heard firing from An Hoa Combat Base, Wiley saw, through the scope, the three NVA get up and run to the south side of the finger. The six rounds were on target, hitting in the draw, but they only killed scrub growth. The probe was over.[34] L'Orange put the hill on 50 percent alert in every bunker. The rest of the evening was quiet. L'Orange did not sleep, rather he went bunker to bunker and had conversations with each of his Marines explaining they had been probed and why they had to remain vigilant.

The next morning, he sent a wire patrol out and they found the wire had been freshly cut in the draw through the first set of triple-concertina wire. The patrol restrung the wire and added three trip flares in the V at the base of the draw. L'Orange had the Alpha Bunker team add two

Claymore mines at the head of the draw. The draw also served as the hill's trash dump. The next week was quiet on Hill 119.

***

Before departing on patrol with *Fig Newton*, Spolter had told Lee to go down and see Gregson to get his next frag order. On 6 March, Lee visited Gregson who said the best he could do was a verbal warning order for 9 March to patrol in the Charlie Ridge area. The written order came at 0700 on 8 March for a 9 March insert.[35] Lee had already given Corporal Holmes a warning order for his team. Their callsign would be *Terrapin*. He put them through immediate-action drills and zeroed their rifles. He would inspect rifles late in the afternoon and give them the evening off. Lee would be taking Marines with whom he was familiar—Lance Corporals Garza and McGowen, Private First Class Paul Freemen, and Hospitalman Edison. Freeman, from Bethel, Washington, had been in-country since October 1969 after he had completed Reconnaissance School at Camp Horno on Camp Pendleton.[36] He was bush savvy and would walk point for *Terrapin*. Their helo insert was delayed all day, with them sitting next to the refueling point at An Hoa all afternoon. At 1645, they got the call to saddle up. Fifteen minutes later, they were getting off the CH-46 into a good one-bird landing zone (LZ) in two feet of elephant grass. Moving off the LZ at once into double-canopy thirty feet high, with secondary growth of eight feet, they were immediately in the dark jungle. Freeman stopped to let their eyes and hearing adjust. Waiting for the jungle sounds to return to their hearing, Lee did not like being inserted late as it gave him the difficult choice of moving in the dark through starlight-denied jungle with no visibility or harboring near his insert LZ. He chose the latter.

On the third day, while sitting in an OP, they saw one Viet Cong (VC) 800 meters away through their 7 × 50s. *Terrapin* called a fire mission but could not observe results.[37] Lee had let McGowen carry an M60 machine gun on a sling.[38] He was carrying 200 rounds of belt ammunition and Lee was carrying another 100 rounds of belted ammo. It turned out to be a mistake, because of the limited visibility. This was not the grunts in open rice paddies with 300-meter engagements. He would not repeat carrying the M60.

On the 13th, in a noon, clandestine observation post (OP), they sighted five enemy in black "PJs" 800 meters out. Three had AK-47s. Calling a fire mission with *Quizmaster-D*, they got poor coverage as the battery could not seem to adjust rounds properly.[39] On the 14th, while sitting in their OP on a finger, three enemy approached the team's position coming up a draw. They appeared to be NVA looking for something on the ground. Mushrooms? They were unarmed and barefoot. They wore green covers and blue shirts and khaki shorts. They stopped and then turned back down the draw. The team took no action as they were on the artillery battery's gun target line. Later, finding a good LZ, they were extracted the next day, 15 March, at noon.[40] In two days, Lee was scheduled to take 3rd Platoon up to Hill 119.[41] He was looking forward to having his entire platoon together for the first time as the platoon commander. It would give him time to talk with each of his Marines. Having been through boot camp himself, Lee knew it was up to him to develop communications with his men.

CHAPTER 20

The Raid, 10–14 March 1970

On 10 March, while both Spolter and Lee were on patrol, and L'Orange was on the hill, Gregson called Fallon to the S-3 bunker. Division G-2 wanted a raid on General Binh's forward headquarters communications unit. They had credible intelligence on its location. It was in the northern Que Son Mountains.[1] Gregson had only been given the general area. Looking at the map, it bordered the Phu Loc Valley. Gregson knew Fallon had just had Team *Forefather*[2] in the valley for an extended patrol and he had seen Fallon back in Camp Reasoner. It was that simple; the assistant operations officer (S-3A) said he had the mission and for him to develop a plan.

Fallon went to the S-2 shop, drew maps, and asked Captain Cook about the mission. Cook had not heard about it but would get more details from G-2. Not knowing the specific location but knowing it was in the mountains and underground, Fallon thought through the challenge. When he was in the grunts, they always went in high, landing on top of a hill, and patrolled down. They always found signs but few enemy unless it was a prepared ambush on a different hill. The enemy could hear and see the large Marine helicopters landing and avoided or prepared their battlespace carefully in advance. There were also landing zone (LZ) spotters watching all known LZs especially in the close-in Que Son Mountains. A communications center would have security. A plan was developing in Fallon's mind.

He walked back down the hill and found Gregson. He said, "I have two teams from 1st Platoon, but I need help and experience."

"Okay, what do you want?" Gregson asked.

"I want the RIP training cadre for the raid."

Gregson liked the idea but would have to get field-grade approval. Fallon said, "We also need a better idea where we are headed." Gregson said he understood.

Fallon went back to his hut that night. He knew tomorrow would be busy so he did what he could. He put together his patrolling kit which had been washed by mama-san. He filled it with canned peaches and filled his canteens. He cleaned his rifle and then spliced and laminated the map for the large haven of 18 square kilometers. After breakfast on the 11th, he walked back to the S-3 bunker where Gregson said he had the Recon Indoctrination Program (RIP) cadre and to be prepared to go tomorrow, the 12th. Division wanted to push the raid soon, afraid the comm unit would move.

In the S-3 training hut/office up the hill, Fallon found Gunnery Sergeant Terry Moore and said they needed to talk. Moore had heard there was a raid on. Fallon acknowledged and was starting to brief Moore when he said, "Let's get the others and all hear it all at once." Fallon took a cold Coke out of their fridge and watched the condensation on the side of the can as Moore left to round up the RIP trainers. Fallon knew and highly respected Moore, who had departed Delta Company and also taken the bush-savvy Staff Sergeant Mushett from Delta to become instructors in the RIP. The other two instructors were 2nd Lieutenant Porter Rathmell, the commander of RIP, and Moore's old point man, Staff Sergeant Hare.[3] Hare, called "Rabbit" by everyone, had a bowed right leg that sprung out 30 degrees below the knee. The rumor was he broke it in a parachute jump and never had it set. Who knew the truth, but it marked his gait a long distance off.

When they joined him, Fallon said, "We have little information but have been promised more." Somebody made a snide comment. Fallon continued, "The good news is we make the plan, we determine the support, and we execute the raid."

Fallon explained the idea that had formed in his mind. Marines always go in high and in the daytime. Therefore, go in low and at night! Moore immediately said, "I like it, but how do we get in?" Getting into the flow, Rabbit, who had come from Echo Company said, "The 'gooners' are used to seeing helicopters going into Hill 425. We go in midday like it is a flip and wait till it is dark and then walk off."

Having seen the cliffs on Hill 425 from the air and Hill 119 in the "Big Eyes," but never having been on the former, Fallon asked, "That is a huge drop, are we going to rappel?"

Mushett said he knew the trail from the observation post (OP) to the valley and explained that, leaving the OP, it started going uphill higher and south into the mountains but had a cross trail that dropped to the west into a downhill trail to Spider Lake.

Fallon said, "Great, get me to Spider Lake dam, or at least where we can see it or below the dam, and we can walk through the Phu Loc Valley to the east." They would conduct their approach march in the open valley at night, hoping for surprise. Moore started counting grid squares and said it is too far for one night's movement and still have sufficient time for actions on the objective, assuming it was found, during darkness.

Fallon asked, "What are our options?"

For the first time, Rathmell spoke. "Just make it a two-night operation. Movement to the assembly area on night one. Harbor up all day in the assembly area and on the second night hit the objective from below."

Moore said, "Sir, we need to assign responsibilities so we can start planning and organizing the patrol. Also, who else is coming?"

"Two of my teams, led by Sergeant Franklin and Corporal Mills," answered Fallon. Both Moore and Mushett smiled and said they knew both team leaders.

"We will have a command element, a security element, and an assault element. This will be my first raid so please make corrections."

He asked Rathmell and Moore to take an assault element. The two staff sergeants would each take a security element, and he would have the command element. "We will take five PRC-25s. Have one on the raid force frequency and one on battalion frequency. Each security element will have a radio as will the assault element. Let's meet after lunch at 1400 on the LZ, with weapons, for IA [immediate-action] drills. I still need to give the two Delta Company teams a patrol order."

"Sir, we need two corpsmen," Moore said.

"I will get two from Delta who will volunteer, should not be an issue."

"Before we start IA drills," Rathmell suggested, "we should spilt all the Marines into the four raid elements and, going forward, work not only IA drills but passing the word and rehearsals and inspections by raid element." All agreed as the planning session broke up.

Fallon walked up the hill, found Franklin in his hut and told him to get everyone in 1st Platoon (one team was on patrol) and have them at the inn in 30 minutes for a patrol order. "And tell 'Doc' Schneider I need to see him now in my hooch." Doc showed up in four minutes asking, "What's up, sir?" Fallon said he had a patrol order at the inn in 20 minutes and "Doc, we need a second corpsmen you trust to go with us." Fallon sat on his footlocker and wrote a standard patrol order. He then wrote, out of poor memory, a raid outline. Time was being crunched. He would give the patrol order to his two teams at the inn and then he would give what he was calling a raid outline at the LZ before IA drills. He decided to find Rathmell and Moore. Finding them both with Rabbit Hare in the S-3 training hooch, he entered and sat on an ammo box.

Moore asked, "What's up, Lieutenant?"

"Well, I have never run a raid, so while I am not concerned about moving at night, as I did that in the grunts all the time, I would appreciate your help."

"None of us have run a raid," Moore replied.

Rathmell offered he had run one in Ranger School. Rabbit could not let it pass, and said, "Sir, swamps of Florida against a lone building target called a radar site ain't a raid against a NVA [North Vietnamese Army] comm site!"[4]

"Gents, the floor is open," Fallon said.

"Best we get our act together before we meet the Marines for drills," Moore said.

"Okay, Gunny, what do you mean?"

"Well, sir, you named four elements but, besides the leaders, do you have any other thoughts?"

"The two Delta Company teams each have six Marines and are used to working as a team," Fallon replied. "So, for the two security elements we add the staff sergeant element leaders and take out their primary radio operators who come to the command element and their tail-end Charlies and M79 men who go to the assault element. That leaves each security element with five Marines, including one radio. The two primary radio operators and a corpsman are with me in the command element. That leaves the assault element, Rathmell, Moore, a corpsman, two tail-end Charlies, and two M79 men for a total of seven Marines. Gunny, is that sufficient for the assault element?"

"Yes, sir, which gives us three assault teams of two and a radioman."

"All right, I will split them on the LZ, and we will form in four elements and rehearse and move that way. For our movement off Hill 425, we will have Mushett and Mills's security element walk point since Mushett knows the trail. Let's call them 'Element M.' Bring the command element of four next in line."

"Sir, what's our call sign?" asked Hare.

"I have taken my regular, *Delicatessen*."[5] There was a collective groan.

Ignoring it, Fallon continued. "The assault element will move third in column, and we will call them Alpha, and Hare's security element with Sergeant Franklin will come off Hill 425 at the column's tail end. We will call them Hotel."

Hare said to the group, "I will walk drag and watch our rear."

Fallon said when they got to the valley floor that the point element would stop, put out security, and the entire column would move through them in a reverse Australian Peel[6] with Hare winding up as the point man. He said, "Franklin was with me and knows Phu Loc Valley."

"Sir, we will have to rehearse that one," Moore said. "After listening on the valley floor, the movement would be in a staggered column and the sequence would be Hotel Element, Command Element, Alpha Element and Mike Element."

Moore said he liked it, especially since Rabbit was on point. He explained that Rabbit had been his point man in MACV–SOG (Military Assistance Command, Vietnam–Studies and Observations Group).[7]

"Fallon, do we have a mission statement?" Rathmell asked.

"I have drafted this one for Gregson but would appreciate your input. It reads: 'Conduct reconnaissance and surveillance operations within your assigned haven and conduct a raid against an enemy radio station, in conjunction with a CI Team, and capture all radio equipment and crypto gear possible.'"

"What's CI?" Hare asked.

Fallon responded it was the Counter Intelligence Team, and they were supposed to tell them where the radio station was located.

"That would be nice, or we are just walking around the Que Sons on a super big Recon patrol," mused Moore.

"Any more questions?" Fallon asked, looking at his watch as he had to give a patrol order.

"This is a raid which means a planned withdrawal?" Rathmell asked.

"We are supposed to have an on-call helo package. We have two options depending on the location of the radio station. I do not think there will be an LZ at the underground site."

Moore interrupted and said, "Bring flashlights and red lens."

Fallon continued, "For extract we can go high in the Que Sons, humping uphill, or we can go out low into Phu Loc Valley using a rice paddy. We will plan for either and I will have Wilson in S-2 give me all known LZs previously used inside the haven. I need to go give the two teams the patrol order."

Mushett said he would like to tag along as Hare chimed in that he would also.

Fallon said no, which surprised the group. "I am not telling the teams it is a raid. If you come and we use that word, it will be all over the camp before dinner. I do not trust security here. It is a big patrol and that is all. You already know these Marines coming from Delta Company so you can meet them at 1400 on the LZ."

"Big Patrol," Hare repeated aloud, "Never been on one of those."

Fallon hustled back to the "Stagger Back Inn" to find the two teams, Franklin's and Mills's, plus two corpsmen, Schneider and Laski. Fallon felt much better after his last planning session with the training cadre. He gave the patrol order as if it would be a big patrol and potentially a mini-platoon patrol base. He told them to plan for four days' chow and go light on water. He told Weirich and Ravelo, the two primary radio operators, to draw five PRC-25s and four PRC-93s. To the questioning looks, Fallon said, "We are headed to the Que Sons where comm is hard" and left it at that. He then said "Six Claymores will do, three per team. Any questions?"

With that, he said they needed to be down at LZ 401 with harnesses and weapons for IA drills at 1400 and dismissed them.

It was 1345. Fallon went to his hooch, grabbed his M16 and H-harness and walked to find Wilson, who was also with Captain Cook and Lieutenant Howland. Fallon said to Wilson, "Staff Sergeant, could you give me every LZ previously used in our upcoming haven?" It was not a regular request, and he looked sideways. Cook said, "Do it."

Cook then ordered Fallon into his office. "An officer who is a Counter Intelligence officer and a Kit Carson Scout [KCS] will be coming with you. They know where your target is located. Supposedly, if you get them to Phu Loc (1) hamlet, they will know the way."

"Can they do rehearsals with us?" Fallon asked.

"You will meet them tomorrow morning on the LZ. The CI officer is a captain; however you are the raid commander. Do you understand?"

Fallon said yes but his mind was still back on meeting them in the morning. Departing, Wilson said he would track him down later with the LZ list. Howland smiled and said "Good luck" in a sarcastically cheerful voice. Walking down the dirt trail past the S-3 bunker to the LZ, Fallon could see the Marines milling around. He walked past the ammunition bunker and S-4 (logistics) Marines and past the Marine with a radio controlling the active LZ. He walked over to the side of the zero range indicating with his arm for his men to follow him. Away from eager ears, he said "Marines, please take your seats," which was the dirt side of the hill. He said this would be a platoon patrol order and a discussion, and that all comments and questions were welcome.

Fallon was tired, so he sat and pulled out his notebook. He said, "We will run a Platoon Patrol Base in the Que Son Mountains. Our mission will be to conduct R&S [reconnaissance and security] operations and to call supporting arms on suspected enemy." He looked up and surveyed the group. They knew something was up but were bored. "Four days, standard load, comm gear as given in the warning order this afternoon."

Ravelo raised his hand. Fallon nodded. "Sir, I could only get three, not four PRC-93s."

Fallon nodded and said okay. "We depart tomorrow at 1000 here on LZ 401. We will have an easy insert as we are going into Hill 425, Echo Company's OP in the Que Sons for a walk-off to our base. Comm will be through *Sunrise* on Hill 425, and Arty through *Rice Krispies-Mike* in An Hoa.[8] Any questions so far?" There were, but nobody asked.

"Marines, we are going in big because we are going into the heart of the NVA's base area in the Que Sons. For this patrol, we are going to break up into four groups or elements. Going forward, we will rehearse, move, and execute in these elements. You know the element leaders. I will have the Command Element, with Lance Corporal Weirich carrying a radio on battalion tactical frequency talking to *Sunrise*. Ravelo, you will join me with the second radio on our patrol frequency. You will be talking with the other patrol elements. Doc Schneider, you will join me. Staff Sergeant Mushett, who you all know from Delta Company, will be leading Mike Element, for Mushett or Mills, as, Corporal Mills, your team is with him minus your primary radioman, M79 man, and tail-end Charlie. Mike Element will have five Marines. Staff Sergeant Hare, formerly with Echo Company, will have your team, Franklin, minus your primary radioman, M79, and tail-end Charlie. That gives Hotel Element five Marines. Last, but not least, Lieutenant Rathmell, along with Gunnery Sergeant Moore, will lead Alpha Element. The two M79 men, and two tail-end Charlies will join Alpha Element along with "Doc" Laski, giving them a total of seven.[9] We will split up into our elements now. Take a head and water break, we start IA drills in ten minutes. Before breaking up, these are our helo stick assignments. Stick One will be the Command Element and Hotel Element. Stick Two will be Alpha and Mike Elements. Any questions? See you in ten."

Fallon called Moore over. "Gunny, for the IA drills, please take over and run the drills. Let's start with movement off Hill 425 with Mushett and Mike Element on point. Then let's do the reverse peel movement to take Hare from tail-end Charlie to point man. Then in that column formation, of Hotel, Command, Alpha, and Mike, let's do contact drills in all four cardinal directions. Also, please finish with a review of hand and arm signals. Let's use what you taught in Delta Company when you were with us. When you are done to your satisfaction, no rush here, let me speak."

"Aye, sir, when are you going to tell them it is a raid?"

"Gunny, I will not tell them until we are on Hill 425 tomorrow. The fewer people who know, the better."

Rathmell walked over to Fallon and said, "How's it going?"

"You tell me."

"We got a plan, but it would be nice to know where we are going."

"Yes. Tomorrow we will get two or three more joining us at the last minute, a CI captain who will bring along a Kit Carson Scout who knows the location of the radio site. They are supposed to know where we are going. You can tell our planning cell but, for now, I will just fold them in with me and the Command Element for movements. After that, they move to the Point Element and then the Assault Element based on location and time."

Rathmell smiled and asked, "Are you getting any help from the field grade of the battalion?"

"Surprisingly, no. I am dealing solely with Gregson and Cook who pushed it back on us." Rathmell said that was a good thing.

Moore was back. "Lieutenants, are you ready?" With a nod, Moore took over. He said loudly, "Staggered column formation, Marines, in this element order: Mike, Charlie, Alpha, Hotel."

The Marines spread out and, with dispersion, they spread the entire length of the LZ. Moore yelled to close it up. When it was closed up, he said, "For this first walk through we'll do it closed up to save my voice, Marines."

He had them walk through all the drills closed up, using his voice to direct and correct. When complete, he called them in and said, "Okay, Marines, now at full dispersion, no talking or voice commands, follow my hand and arm signals." Moving to the center of the LZ, "Follow my commands," he had them go through all six IA movements.

When that was over, and with everyone spread out, Moore walked over to Fallon and said, "Lieutenant, your turn. I recommend you walk them through a few drills but from your position in the column." Fallon was surprised but knew he was correct and needed to be rehearsed. Moore, in a loud voice, walking to his place with Rathmell, yelled out, "Marines we are live, follow the lieutenant's signals."

With that Fallon raised his arm and gave the "Forward, move out." They went through the drills again. When it was over, Fallon raised his arm and gave the "circle-the-wagons" signal. The Marines all formed up. He asked for questions. There were none.

He closed with "This is a classified platoon patrol base, so do not talk about it. See you all at 0930 tomorrow on the LZ." As soon as he said it, he was sorry he'd used the word "classified" as that would just start rumors.

The sun had set over Hill 327. Fallon stood at the side of the LZ's ammo bunker with the other raid leaders. He gave them a moment. One asked about going to dinner. Fallon said he was eating in his hut and staying away from areas where the senior leaders might corner him. He would skip the club tonight in order to get a good sleep if he could. All agreed and broke up. Fallon climbed the back short-cut trail through the Bravo Company area from the LZ to get to Delta Company's officers' hut, thus avoiding walking past the command bunkers, S-2 shop, and, specifically, the colonel's hut. He did not want guidance from above at this point.

Fallon slept fitfully, waking with thoughts of what he had missed in planning. Rising early, on 12 March, he went to the mess hall and ate a large breakfast alone. He was at the ammo bunker at 0915, where Sergeant Franklin had drawn all the grenades, giving Fallon the four M26s, two smoke, and two CS gas he had requested.

Moving to the LZ Control noncommissioned officer, he asked him the status of his birds for *Delicatessen*'s two-bird lift. He was told they would arrive at 1015. All the Marines were there and crashed out on the side of the hill. Fallon checked with the element leaders for any questions and to inform them of the 1015 lift. Looking up the hill, he saw Staff Sergeant Wilson walking down the trail towards the LZ, followed by a Vietnamese and a large Marine. He walked up and introduced the captain with no name and KCS Sergeant Vu.

Sergeant Vu nodded. He was under five feet, in utilities, carrying an ARVN (Army of the Republic of Vietnam) pack and an M16. He wore a black cropped bush hat. If the Vietnamese was small, the captain was large, big, six-foot-plus. He wore the old solid-green cammie utilities that were faded almost light green. No marking, no name, no USMC emblem. He carried a pump shotgun. The only way you would know he was a Marine was his herringbone utility cover with faded eagle, globe, and anchor above the brim. Fallon shook hands with them both. The captain took out a pack of cigarettes and offered one first to the KCS, who took one, and then Fallon, who declined. Fallon said they would be with him in the Command Element for the helo and approach march. They would move forward when the captain determined. They would break out maps on Hill 425 as they had time to kill up on the OP. Fallon explained they wanted to appear to the NVA observers as a normal midday OP flip. The captain nodded. Fallon said they were due to depart at 1015. With that, Wilson went back up the hill and the captain and KCS just sat down on the LZ; they, too, were used to waiting for helos.

The captain had brown, sunburned skin, a leathery face, and a world-class non-regulation handlebar mustache. He clearly was the oldest man on the LZ. He wore no rank insignia but neither did anyone else. Everyone was painted up in cammie paint except the two new arrivals. They would not need to cammie up until tonight when they walked off Hill 425.

The two CH-46s flew in low and fast for the LZ at 1014—time to go. Both helo sticks loaded. As he saw Rathmell count and load last on the Stick Two ramp, Fallon walked up the ramp, giving the crew chief a thumbs up. As the two birds lifted off, he walked up the floor inside the bird to the jump seat. Squatting, he pointed to his map, at Hill 425 and got a nod from the copilot. Insert confirmed, he went back and sat on a red nylon seat, closed his eyes, and vibrated in the loud internal helo noise for the 20-minute ride to Hill 425's LZ.[10]

Walking up the trail from the LZ, Fallon found Moore and asked him to split up the men into bunkers and tell them to rest; they would be there all day. There would be a meeting at sundown in the mortar pit and they would push out 15 minutes after sunset. Fallon wanted to get off the hill across the LZ and appear to observers to be walking uphill and into the Que Sons as the last light faded. That done, he told the captain he needed to speak to the hill commander and could they meet in 20 minutes. Nodding, the captain and KCS stopped at the first bunker, sat down, and started to make coffee. It was clear these two were not rear-echelon motherfuckers and had spent time in the bush together. Fallon was a little relieved they displayed bush savvy. Moving to the hill commander's bunker, he gave the lieutenant from Echo Company the big picture, providing him with his haven, radio frequencies, and, most important, checkpoints, thrust points, and a fire-support plan. OP *Sunrise* would be *Delicatessen*'s radio relay and fire-support/extract coordinator. It was important the hill commander understood what Fallon was doing and the support he was requesting. When he finished, he asked permission for his Marines to top off their canteens at *Sunrise*'s water buffalo. Then Fallon got the element leaders, and they walked down to the bunker closest to the LZ to meet with the CI captain and KCS.

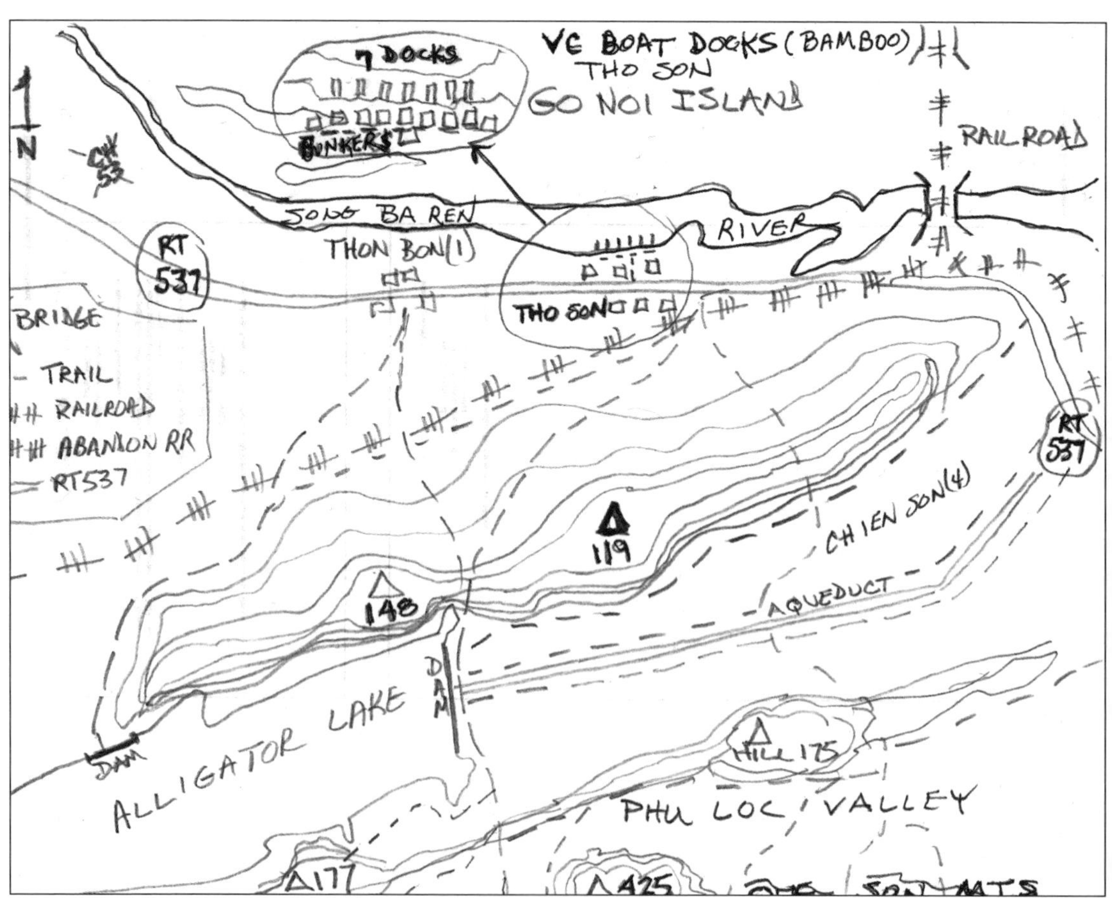

Sketch of Phu Loc Valley, north of Hill 425. (M. Fallon)

Fallon made the introductions, laid out the 1:50,000 map on the ground, and drew a valley sketch in the dirt.

He oriented the map to the terrain around them. He started by saying they were going after the radio site and specifically the radio equipment to which the KCS was going to lead them. He pointed to Hill 425 and said Staff Sergeant Mushett would lead them down to Spider Lake, where Staff Sergeant Hare and Sergeant Frankin would lead them to the outskirts of Phu Loc (1); they would bypass the village and head east to pick a draw to spend the next day's daylight hours in, hiding from villagers and the NVA. Tonight will be movement-to-the assembly-area in preparation for the raid the following night. At this point, the KCS, who knew a little English and had been following the briefing, stood, and walked over and pointed to a draw on the map; speaking in Vietnamese, he told the captain they should spend the night in this particular draw. The captain translated. At this point, Gunnery Sergeant Moore stood up, said no, and "No way" in Vietnamese, and said to the captain, that he, Moore, would pick the harbor site. He turned to the KCS and asked him where the radio site was[11] The Vietnamese said he could not read the American map, but he knew the trail cutting off the old French road in the Phu Loc Valley pointing below Hill 175. Moore talked to the captain who told the group of leaders that Sergeant Vu could not read maps but knew the area and would lead them to a cave complex in one of three draws he showed the team on the map. The captain trusted Vu and was sure if they got him on the old French road, in grid square BT00/48, the KCS would lead the Marines to the caves. The captain worried that it had been ten days, due to the slow intel processes, and the radio could have been moved. He said we would know in two nights. It was clear the Recon leaders, who did not know Sergeant Vu, did not trust him and it was just as clear the CI captain did. What was certain was that all their lives depended on it. Walking a draw uphill at night and into an enemy base camp that had its own security was an ambush waiting to happen unless the Marines had the element of surprise.

It was 12 March when the *Delicatessen* Marines spent the afternoon crashing out in the bunkers of OP *Sunrise*. After sunset, they met outside in the *Sunrise* mortar pit. This is when Fallon told the entire group they were going after a radio in a specific cave on the north-facing slope of the Que Sons. The radio was used for directional communications with Go Noi Island and Da Nang. He introduced the officer from Counter Intelligence and Sergeant Vu who would lead them to the cave. Fallon went over the schedule for the two-night raid with an expected extract on the third morning. He went over the sequence of movement for the first night and second night by each element in the column. He handed it off to Lieutenant Rathmell, the Assault Element commander, who explained they had three, two-man cave teams and they would hit the caves as close to the same time as possible. If there were more than three caves, then, after assaulting the first three, they would move up the draw. He explained they would be coming in from the side, not walking the trail up or down the draw. Sergeant Vu would walk point and get them to within one hundred meters and then the Assault Element would pick a side of the draw and get into position while Hare's Security Element would go high above the location; Mushett's element would already be left off below at the entrance to the draw. Fallon would follow the Assault Element and stay on the finger to maintain communications with *Sunrise* and all the elements. It was simple and straightforward. Fallon asked for questions. Getting none he said, "Marines, do your business now, hydrate, top off canteens, we push from the LZ in thirty minutes."

Both lieutenants from *Sunrise*, the Echo Platoon commander, and the Integrated Observation Device (IOD) team leader had attended the mortar-pit meeting. Afterward, Fallon and Rathmell met with them. They had no questions. The IOD team could watch the night movement through the night-observation device and would scout before and afterwards. Fallon reminded them it was his haven, and all fire missions would be approved by him off *Sunrise* for the entire period of the mission. The four lieutenants shook hands and broke up. Fallon went back and organized his maps again and went to top off his canteens. Then he found Mushett and asked if he had scoped out the route. He said he had used his 7 × 50s, as well as the ship's binos. He had it mapped in his mind. Then Fallon found Moore and told him to have the Marines line up in the south trench line, belly button to asshole tight, in order of march and do their jump sound check. With that completed, Fallon went back to the rear and asked Hare if he was ready at tail end. He then walked forward, physically touching, and nodding at each Marine, from the rear to the point, silently counting. When he got to Mushett at point, he had a count of 24.[12] He hit Mushett on the shoulder and nodded. Mushett moved out, Fallon let the five Marines in Mike Element go ahead and then got in the column. He let them gain space and dispersion. Both of his radio men followed and then Sergeant Vu and the CI captain, along with Doc Schneider, completed the Command Element. Moore was next, followed by Rathmell and the rest of the Assault Element. Franklin led the Hotel Element out and across the LZ as Rabbit Hare, the element leader, pulled tail-end Charlie. A *Sunrise* Marine closed their wire gate on the south side of the LZ. The big patrol snaked its way uphill and south into the Que Son Mountains. Reaching the second steep draw, Mushett sent Miller uphill ten meters, facing up and out, and said, "Stay there for security and fall in with Hare when he makes the turn." He and Hare had coordinated the turn and security. Fallon was surprised but knew it was a solid move and said nothing moving past them and into the draw.

Mushett had powered up the ridgeline fast, in the last vestiges of light, and wanted to get off it. Now, he put on the brakes and slowed down. They would make some noise on the steep downhill gravel but, moving slowly, he hoped to minimize it. The radio operators had made radio checks in the afternoon. Fallon had briefed no comm for the movement unless they had trouble or lost contact. No need to talk. He would call *Sunrise* once they were in the harbor site, but they would not do the routine hourly Recon check-in. Silence at night was the game.

Mushett took his time going down the draw. He stopped at its base. With everyone in the draw, he spent 15 minutes listening before turning northwest and heading towards the base of Spider Lake. He was moving off-trail to avoid any NVA who used the trails every night. At checkpoint three, about one hundred meters east of the dam's face and off-trail, Mushett moved aside, stopped, and started the reverse peel. Each Marine walked past him for a few meters and then stopped as the next Marine passed the Marine in front of him. Fallon stopped by Mushett and waved his element forward. He knelt with him as the Marines passed silently between the two of them. When Hare arrived and kept moving forward, Fallon followed and counted forward from Mushett, tapping each Marine's shoulder. When Hare reached the front of the column, Fallon had the 24 count. It had been dark in the draw, and they had made two large turns. As the valley opened up, it was lighter, but still dark. Hare moved out with Franklin now walking deuce point doing the navigation on this leg to Phu Loc (1). It was midnight when Fallon looked at

Aerial photo, Camp Reasoner, 1969. (E. Schwartz)

First Recon Delta Sign, Camp Reasoner. (M. Fallon)

"Best Fighting Men" sign, Camp Reasoner. (M. Fallon)

Camp Reasoner, front gate, 1st Recon sign, 1970. (E. Schwartz)

SCUBA locker front door. (M. Fallon)

Delta Company sign, in front of Company Office, Camp Reasoner. (M. Fallon)

The "Stagger Back Inn," Delta Company's enlisted club, 1970. (M. Fallon)

CH-46 taking off from LZ 401, and on bottom right, you can see the entrance to the ammo bunker with red "No Smoking" sign above it. (M. Fallon)

LZ 401, Camp Reasoner, 1970. (R. Fawcett)

Team *Fig Newton*, 2nd Team–2nd Platoon, Delta Company hooch, Camp Reasoner. (M. Fallon)

"Reenlist. Free Helicopter Rides" sign. Camp Reasoner. (M. Fallon)

Left to right: J. K. Murphy and M. O. Fallon, after Murphy's emergency extract. Fallon was the extract officer. LZ 401, fall 1970. (M. Fallon)

Lieutenant M. O. Fallon on LZ 401 waiting for insert. (M. Fallon)

Memorial listing the names of those who died, painted on side of the "Stagger Back Inn," 1970. (M. Fallon)

Team *Mission Impossible* outside S-3 training hooch, 1970. Standing, left to right: Unk; Staff Sergeant Beardslee; Gunnery Sergeant Terry Moore: Unk; Staff Sergeant Mushett. Kneeling, left to right: Lance Corporal Dan Nelson; Lance Corporal Sparks; Staff Sergeant Rodney Pupuhi; Captain F. S. Blair; Corporal Randall Manela; Corpsmen HM3 Hunt; Master Sergeant Rene Regalot. October 1970. (R. Regalot, colorized by W. Denham)

Motley crew, post-rappelling training, Delta Company street, spring 1970. Left to right: Lee, Fallon, L'Orange, May, and Spolter. (M. Fallon)

Fallon reading map on trail. (M. Fallon)

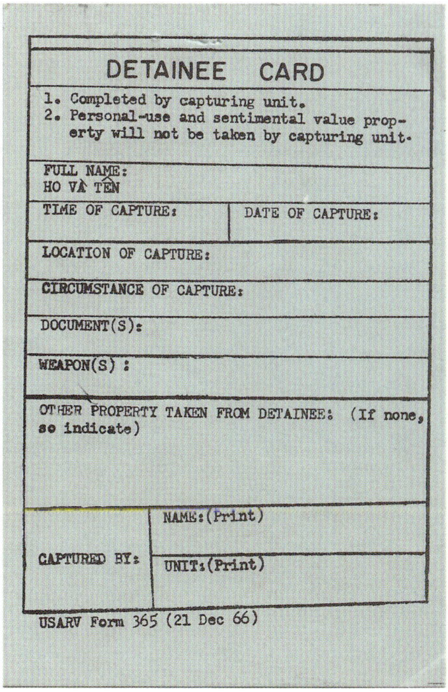

DETAINEE CARD

1. Completed by capturing unit.
2. Personal-use and sentimental value property will not be taken by capturing unit.

FULL NAME:
HO VÀ TÊN

TIME OF CAPTURE: | DATE OF CAPTURE:

LOCATION OF CAPTURE:

CIRCUMSTANCE OF CAPTURE:

DOCUMENT(S):

WEAPON(S):

OTHER PROPERTY TAKEN FROM DETAINEE: (If none, so indicate)

CAPTURED BY: NAME: (Print)
UNIT: (Print)

USARV Form 365 (21 Dec 66)

Detainee card. (M. Fallon)

Spolter's going-away party at the "Stagger Back Inn," 1 July 1970. Left to right: Lieutenants Spolter, Parks, Lee, Smith, and Master Sergeant Regalot. (R. Regalot)

Ladder training below a CH-46 with Marines snapped on. LZ 401, late 1969. (J. Unsworth)

Wild boar shot off the hill coming in for dinner, summer 1969. (E. Schwartz)

Sergeant Franklin and Lieutenant Fallon, in front of tower on Hill 119. (M. Fallon)

One-armed woman, village elder and Viet Cong Infrastructure, Tho Son hamlet, 1969. (T. Mullins)

Christmas visit to Hill 119 by villagers. (T. Mullins)

Villagers visiting Marines on the north slope, Christmas Day 1969. (T. Mullins)

Villagers visit, Christmas 1969. Front, standing, left to right: one-armed woman (village elder), girl translator, Lieutenant Parks. (T. Mullins)

Village peace protest, Hill 119. (T. Mullins)

Marines on Hill 119. Sitting second from right, "Doc" Schwartz, standing top left, Lieutenant Fallon, spring 1970. (E. Schwartz)

Hill 119, bunker, and trench line layout, 1970. (W. Denham)

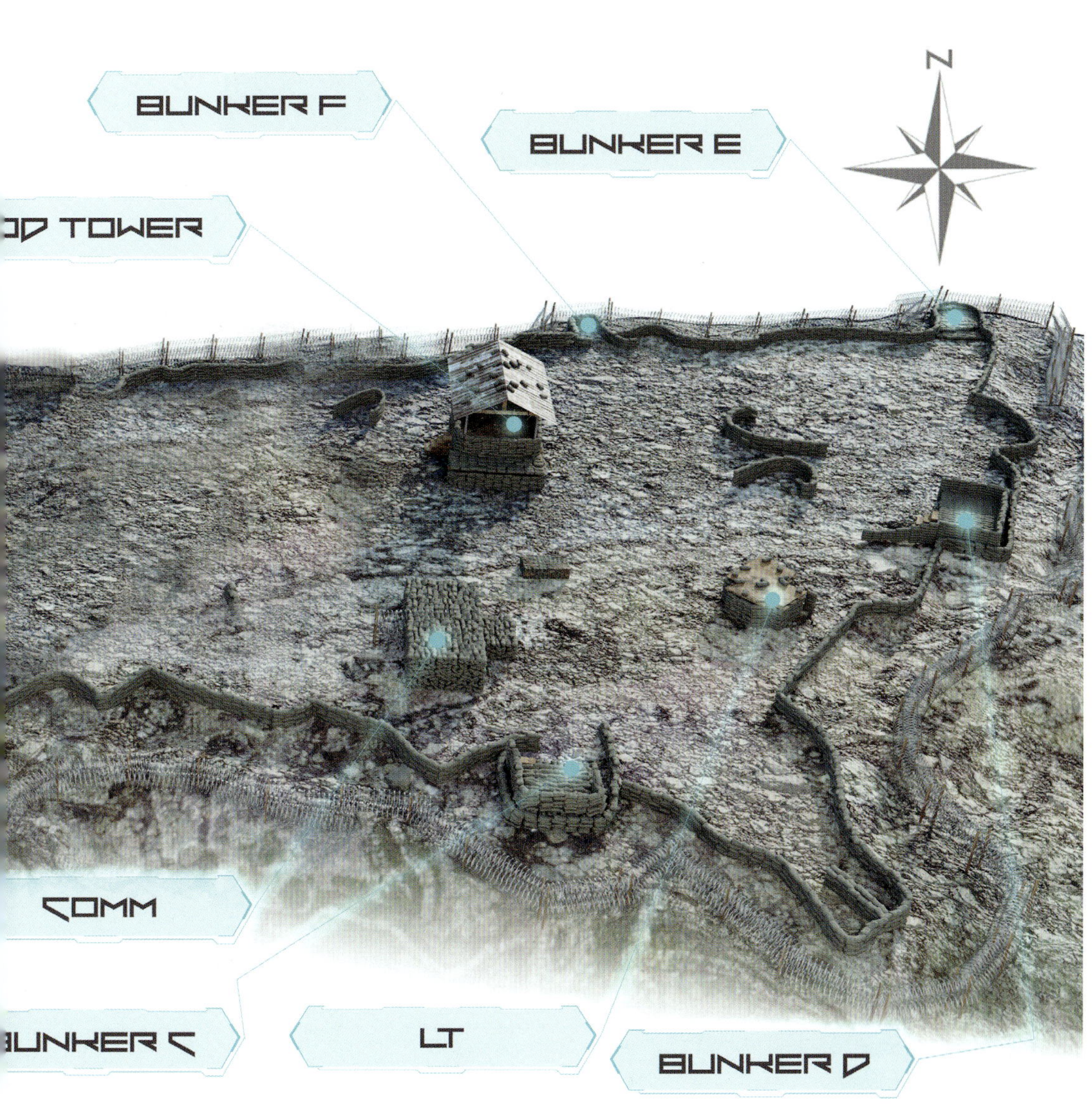

BUNKER F
BUNKER E
N
D TOWER
COMM
UNKER C
LT
BUNKER D

F-4 Phantom flying by Hill 119, at tree-top level. (J. Hackett)

Lieutenant Pfeiffer in prone position with a .50-cal machine gun. In background, tower with IOD, beyond it "People Sniffer radar." (J. Hackett)

Franklin and Ravelo with Hill 119's mascot puppy "Peckerwood," early 1970. (M. Fallon)

Scout Dog heading to bunker, left foreground "Doc" Mullins. (T. Mullins)

Hill 119 medical treatment of Viet Cong. (T. Mullins)

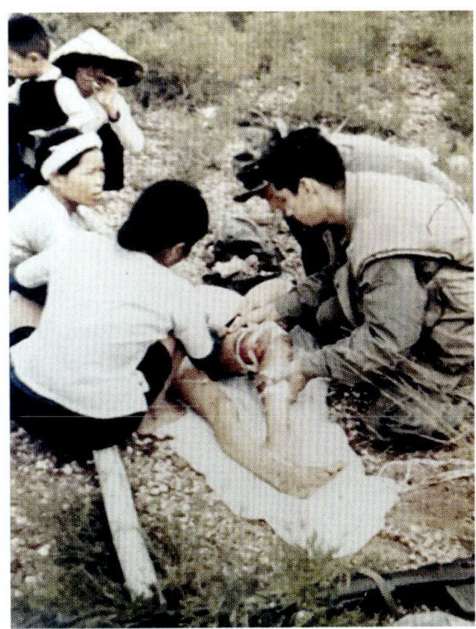

A Vietnamese in a parachute-bamboo stretcher being treated by "Taco" and "Doc" Mullins (behind Taco), January 1970. (T. Mullins)

Wounded Vietnamese being treated by "Doc" Mullins, sitting center, December 1969. (T. Mullins)

Wounded Chieu Hoi, with blown-off hand, being treated by "Doc" Schwartz, spring 1970. (E. Schwartz)

Chow time. Second from right, Sergeant James "Hack" Hackett and other lance corporals and privates first class. (J. Hackett)

"Doc" Mullins, with Alligator Lake in background. (T. Mullins)

Getting ready for a VIP visit, visiting barber, spring 1970. (T. Mullins)

A CH-53 on the Hill 119 LZ offloading Marines and supplies, late 1969. (J. Hackett)

Blowing up a booby-trap mine discovered just outside wire, 1969. (J. Hackett)

CH-46 landing with controller. (M. Fallon)

Integrated Observation Device tower. (M. Fallon)

"Heavies" (Senior Leaders) visit the hill, spring 1970. Left to right: Lieutenant Colonel Drumright, Corporal Iantorno, and Major General Wheeler, CG 1st Mar Div. (T. Mullins)

Two-hole outhouse with no house, spring 1970. Barrel #1 being burned, Barrel #2 in use. (E. Schwartz)

The Tennessee state flag flies over Hill 119, spring 1970. In the background is the railroad bridge to Go Noi Island. (E. Schwartz)

An aerial view of Hill 119, spring 1970. (E. Schwartz, colorized by W. Denham)

Fog lifting. Mortar pits overlooking Alligator Lake. (M. Fallon)

Marines on top of bunkers sunbathing, Hill 119, summer 1970. (E. Schwartz)

Team *Delicatessen*, helo crash, An Hoa. Far left one knee, Lieutenant Spolter extract officer; bottom center of three, Lieutenant P. Eglevsky Patrol Leader; standing far right, Sergeant Ravello, extract NCO. (P. Eglevsky)

Emergency ladder extract, Team *Pal Joey*, with Lieutenant Lee and the prisoner on the ladder, March 1970. (P. Freeman)

Que Sons, Nui Bu Nuo (Hill 905). Company Patrol Base *Gunsmoke*. Standing, left to right: Lieutenants Fallon, Murphy, and Anderson with 1st Platoon, Bravo Company, late 1970. (M. Fallon)

Flag flying over Hill 119, Que Son Mountains in background. (J. Hackett)

American flag over Hill 119, CH-53 delivering a Water Buffalo, fall 1969. (DoD public domain, Corporal W. P. Berger, colorized by W. Denham)

Mike Fallon and wife Sandy on the summit of Hill 119, March 2023. (M. Fallon)

his watch. They quickly found the old French road leading northeast from the dam towards Phu Loc (1). Franklin knew the road; he maneuvered Hare east of, and parallel to, the road as they moved out. In one kilometer, they were south of the hamlet and, as the road turned due east, so did the patrol. They had five more kilometers of night movement. After another kilometer, the road moved northeast towards the base of Hill 175. Here, Franklin had Hare move due east on the compass. In 300 meters, they had to cross the stream being fed by Spider Lake. It was broad and slow, providing irrigation for the rice paddies downstream to the east. Once across the water, the stream broke northeast with the road following on the other side. Franklin kept due east on the compass for another three hours.

They had covered three more kilometers. Gunny Moore came forward now during a listening pause. Time to turn south and find a daytime harbor site before first light. Moore pushed Hare out and assumed deuce point, looking at the options as the ground rose moving into the Que Sons. He did not want a wooded area as the villagers came every morning to cut and collect fire wood. He was looking for a boulder field that was difficult to move in. Humans avoided larger boulder fields. After 15 minutes of steady uphill climb, he found, off to his right, or back west a bit, the rock formation he was looking for. Hare had seen it too and, with a nod from Moore, he moved quickly and directly into the field, penetrating it for another 100 meters as he moved up hill. Moore caught him, said "Twenty meters," and started slowly looking clockwise for a 360 defense in the field with boulders 6–12-feet wide and high. Moore stopped and let each Marine pass, indicating by circle motion and pointing to the ground that was to be the 360 harbor site. The Marines circled and stopped. Hare went back out and with Franklin covered their trail and placed two Claymore mines. The Marines found boulders and got on the west side for shade. A watch schedule was set.

As the sun rose, Fallon called *Sunrise* with a position report.[13] They would stay put for 13 hours. With the daytime defenses set, the goal was to remain hidden from both the NVA and the local villagers. After a can of peaches, Fallon called the raid leaders to the center and, under a poncho liner for shade, asked the captain if Sergeant Vu knew where they were. Without translation, Vu said in English, "Yes." He pointed and gestured that they were two creek-bed draws from their target. In the dirt, Moore drew a sketch with a stick. He laid out the Phu Loc Valley and the creek west to east, then the Que Son mountains; he marked Hill 425 and then drew six draws north to south heading into the mountains. Moore put three small rocks to indicate the boulder field they were currently in. He gave the stick to Vu, who stood up and drew a line from the rock back out into the valley and then east for three draws, coming to a small draw. On the 1:50,000 map, Fallon pointed to Hill 322. The CI captain concurred and spoke Vietnamese with Vu for a minute, who simply said "Yes." The location surprised the Marines. Vu showed that there were three caves on the southwest side of the hill. The radio was in the largest cave. This location was much lower in elevation than was expected. Fallon said they would wait until 30 minutes after sunset and move back into the valley to head east. Order of march would change to Hotel Element with Hare on point along with Moore and the longtime point team, and Franklin covering the two at deuce point. The CI captain and Sergeant Vu would be moved to Hare's Hotel Element. The Assault Element and Rathmell would move second in the column followed by Command and then Mike Element in the rear. They would move out of the harbor site into the valley floor, off-trail, moving east in the foothills. The infiltration trails would be the south-to-north danger areas they would cross. There was a trail coming out of every draw headed north towards Go Noi Island, which was one night's march away. The day passed without incident with the Marines mostly sleeping.

After sunset, the Claymores were pulled in and the column leaders formed in the center, setting watches, and confirming the order of march as they pulled out of their defensive sectors. Fallon had Weirich tell *Sunrise* that *Delicatessen* was Oscar Mike (on the move). Ravello did the Recon two clicks of the handset on the raid frequency, ensuring those four radios were on frequency. Hare and Moore moved out. Fallon watched the longtime friends, and patrolling partners, work like two hunting dogs, moving, stopping, and listening in front. Franklin's job was to keep them in sight but stay back. The raid force was in a single column as Fallon did a head count leaving the boulder field. It was now 13 March and, at 2345, Hare froze, and Moore put up a balled fist to halt and freeze the force. Franklin passed the hand signal command back down the line. Fallon went to one knee looking forward; he was now 15 Marines back and could see nothing. After 15 minutes, Fallon walked slowly and quietly up seven Marines and laid down next to Rathmell who was in the prone position and on high alert. Fallon laid down and listened. He could see nothing in front, but he could hear a large enemy column moving at pace from the east to the west back into the Phu Loc Valley on the trail near the creek. The raid force laid still for 45 minutes and let the enemy force move back up valley. They were not the target.

After the enemy force passed, Vu and the captain moved forward and joined Hare and Moore at point. Vu now took point. It was obvious he knew where he was. He turned 90 degrees and headed up through the foothills straight for Hill 322. Now, ten minutes past midnight on the 14th, the point heard voices. The talking in Vietnamese was clear and approximately one hundred meters north and east of them and moving. Moore waited ten minutes after the last voice was heard. Vu moved into a draw west of the hill and started up the dry draw. Fifteen minutes in, Moore halted the column and walked back to where Fallon had remained in the line of march with Rathmell. Moore indicated this was a good place for Mushett to stop and cover the approach to the draw from the valley. Moore moved back up the draw; Fallon stayed put and would put Mushett in place when he arrived. Moore and Hare now went west and moved up out of the draw, found the game trail moving towards the spine of the finger, and moved quickly up the finger. Rathmell followed with the Assault Element, moving slowly and stealthily. Two hours later, Rathmell and Moore were overlooking a boulder-filled draw behind, or south of, Hill 322. Sergeant Vu was pointing out cave entrances as the Marines observed the area with 7 × 50 binos. At 0215, the Assault Element heard two voices and then two enemy moving in the streambed near the lowest cave. They were making noise, moving fast due north, down the streambed and away from the caves.

Rathmell waited no longer. The assault force of seven raiders moved on-line toward the three cave openings below the finger. It would be two Marines on each cave, with Doc Laski holding the radio Moore had been humping. Fallon waited on the finger and watched the three teams move to the caves. No firing occurred. Six long minutes later, Fallon saw Rathmell's three-red-lens flash, the signal for all clear. Leaving Hare high on the finger with his Security Element and the Command Element, he took Vu and the CI captain and walked down the rocky slope to the cave complex above the creek bed. Nobody was home. The two enemy they heard hastily departing at 0215 were the rear security. The complex had four caves, all with fire pits vented to disperse smoke before exiting through air holes. One pit had warm embers. The main cave, #4, was a split level with a front porch and large overhanging rock shelf above the porch. Cave #4 was 20 feet by 15 feet, and five feet high. Its entrance was four feet by four feet. The upper, and deeper, second room was ten feet by five feet, and four feet high. The room appeared to be for sleeping with woven mats on the ground. It had two air vents. There was a 20-foot-long tunnel, four-feet wide and ten-feet high, between Cave #4 and Cave #3. The latter was small, four feet by five feet and three-feet high. Its separate entrance was two feet by two feet. It had a fire pit for warmth and air vents. Cave #2 was separate with an entrance, measuring ten feet by ten feet, into one large room, 20 feet by 40 feet. It also had air vents and a fire pit, and a dug-out back room six-feet high and a 10-by-14-foot footprint. It had a large two-by-two-foot-high air vent big enough to crawl through. Cave #1 had a four-by-six-foot-wide entrance in the rock formation. The main room was five feet high and was 20 by 15 feet wide. It had eight-to-twelve-inch air vents all around the cave. All four main caves were solid rock formations with dug-out rooms, ledges, and benches.[14]

The raid force had security out below and above the caves. They were disappointed to find the dry hole with no radio equipment. There was a lot of gear to be collected, inventoried, or destroyed. The CI captain wanted everything except the food, which would be destroyed. The partial inventory included one M16 rifle, serial number 1291585, with nine magazines, and multiple grenades including M26s and Chi-coms, 15 pairs of clothing including NVA, black "PJs," civilian clothing, and personnel effects. The CI captain took the one wallet. Fifty pounds of rice and five pounds of canned fish were destroyed. Medical supplies, along with cooking and eating utensils, were inventoried. There were also four-pint bottles of kerosene, along with an assortment of hinges, wire, metal working tools, and a large assortment of small-arms ammunition, both U.S. and Chinese. They also found NVA helmets and cartridge belts, wood-cutting tools, and woven baskets.[15] It was clear the NVA had been there, and they had left carrying everything they could. The inventory was completed about first light. The gear was put in NVA and ARVN packs and distributed among the assault force.

Fallon conferred with the CI captain and got a nod of agreement that it was time to withdraw. Fallon had reported to *Sunrise* for relay to Battalion they had hit the target, and it was a dry hole with non-consequential equipment. Fallon wanted to get the four elements of the raid force back together before they incurred a chance contact with the enemy. The Que Sons were crawling with NVA in multiple dispersed base-camp areas like this four-cave complex. Fallon took the handset from Ravello, on the raid network, and asked for element actuals. When the three had checked in, he told Mushett to hold, as they would be coming to him from various directions. He told Hare to stay on the finger high ground and move east until it dropped into the valley and that he would delay for 30 minutes before departing. He was to go slow and be last in to the linkup. He told Rathmell to move straight east down the creek bed where they had heard the two NVA earlier. The Assault Element would be carrying the captured equipment. The Command Element would follow the Assault Element east down the creek bed. The CI captain and Vu were to rejoin the Command Element. With the plan in place, Fallon said Assault would depart in 15 minutes. Fifteen minutes later, Rathmell put Moore on point and began moving down the draw.

Two hours later, the Assault and Command Elements had linked up with Mushett and the eastern Security Element. At 1050, they heard M16 fire. Hare had come across one NVA in green utilities with a pack coming toward the finger when he was on the valley floor. He and Corporal Mills had both engaged and killed the soldier at 25 meters on the game trail.[16] They searched the body. He had a pack full of rice, which was scattered. Hare was disappointed not to find a souvenir weapon or NVA belt buckle. This was a junior rice humper. Hare called in and reported he would pick up the pace since they had fired their weapons. At 1100, while waiting on Hare's element, Private First Class Lee, in the harbor site, spotted seven NVA in green utilities carrying packs and moving from the west valley to the east on a rice-paddy dike. Fallon had Franklin and his team follow the NVA. When it was obvious they were moving fast to the east and into the Republic of Korea area outside *Delicatessen*'s haven, Fallon called him back and said to find a dry LZ outside their current boulder-field position. Hare was back. Franklin called in; he had an 800 × 300-meter hard-packed dirt grass LZ 700 meters from Fallon's position. Franklin was told to secure the LZ. Fallon called *Sunrise*, requesting the extract at the grid BT 045479. *Delicatessen* was on the move to the LZ.

It took an hour to cover the 700 meters and rejoin Frankin at the new LZ. It was 1400. At 1430, *Sunrise* called and said *Delicatessen*'s trucks (helos) were inbound.[17] The next call was from *Purple Fox Two-Four* calling for *Delicatessen*. Ravelo managed the LZ brief. It was a multibird zone so they requested two landing points and would pop two colored smokes. Rathmell popped smoke with Stick Two, as Ravelo popped smoke with Stick One. The birds identified one yellow and one green smoke. Fallon waited after counting his stick, and, standing off the ramp, watching Rathmell do the same. When Porter jumped on, Fallon walked up the ramp and gave the crew chief the thumbs up. Twenty minutes later, both birds landed at LZ 401. It was 1500, 14 March.[18] On the far side of Recon's LZ, Fallon called the raiders together and thanked them. He said the element leaders, plus Moore, Franklin, Mills, the two radio operators, along with himself, were to go up to S-2 hut for the debrief. He dismissed the Marines. The CI captain came over and said they would be leaving and walking directly up the hill to G-2, as it was quicker than waiting on the division motor pool. He asked for the recovered M16, which he took. He shook hands with Fallon, Rathmell, and Moore and he and Vu left up the hill. Gunny Moore said something to Vu in Vietnamese about next time and got a chuckle.[19] The element leaders departed for their debrief with Staff Sergeant Wilson in S-2. It had been 53 hours since they had departed LZ 401 on the "Dry Hole Raid."

CHAPTER 21

Pathfinder, 13–27 March 1970

Hill 119, 13 March, which Lieutenant L'Orange thought, but could not recall, was the "Ides of March." He sent out a walk-off patrol. As the patrol was starting to return at 1645, just outside Thon Bon (1) hamlet north of the hill, they spotted 10–12 North Vietnamese Army (NVA) wearing mixed uniforms and escorting a man in a blue suit, white shirt, and tie.[1] The soldiers had rifles and packs. The team moved east of the trail and set up a hasty linear ambush and waited. They waited for what seemed like a long time and were not sure they were on the same trail coming east out of the hamlet. Then they saw the enemy and sprung the ambush, all Marines firing small arms. Immediately, six enemy were down, the rest returning fire and breaking contact. The enemy retraced west up the trail. The patrol's flank security fired again hitting and dropping three more enemy. The Recon ambush had not waited long enough. Easy to say in hindsight but hard to do when you are outnumbered two to one. The team, *West Orange-Alpha*, set out security and checked the ambush kill zone. They were not going to chase the larger force and risk running into an ambush themselves. The found six bodies, and three large blood trails heading west on the main trail. They were disappointed the blue-suited man was not in the kill zone. He had escaped the hasty ambush. *West Orange-Alpha* gathered 12 packs, dumping out their rice contents along with the marijuana found in a large bag in one of the packs. They picked up the empty packs, cartridge belts, two Chi-com grenades, and one M26. The NVA had collected and taken all the rifles off the dead when they fled the field. The Marines recovered six wallets and a small batch of documents into one pack for S-2 (intelligence).[2] Then they called in to say they were departing and asked the Integrated Observation Device (IOD) team to watch their rear as they headed back up Hill 119. The IOD also called a fire mission on the ambush site, just for good measure, and to cover *West Orange-Alpha*'s return.

On 16 March, while the sun was setting in the west, Team *Hansworth* on the IOD spotted one Viet Cong (VC) coming out of Tho Son hamlet due north of the hill. It was after curfew so no villagers should have been moving in the fields or farming. The enemy was carrying a heavy pack. *Hansworth* knew he could not get a fire mission fast enough, so he notified L'Orange who decided to engage with a machine-gun ambush with the .50-caliber and one M60. They also shot some 60-mm mortar illumination rounds. The VC jumped into a thick tree line and a bunker. An aerial observer (AO) flying in the area saw the tracers and illumination and called *West Orange* to ask if he could help. It being a slow time, L'Orange had the OV-10 make two strafing runs. On each run, the aircraft took small-arms fire from the riverbanks and Go Noi Island.[3] That was to be expected. The pilot expended his ordnance so checked out; they could see it flying all the way back northeast to Marble Mountain as the sun went over the high Ong Thu Slope in the west.

The next day, 17 March, St. Patrick's Day, 4th Platoon was due to flip off the hill and were ready to do so. About noon, L'Orange was summoned to the radio bunker to get on the secure net, a PRC-77 with PRC-38 encryptor. Encrypting allowed one to speak and ensure the enemy, who listened to all radio traffic from the Que Son Mountains, would only hear static. It was Gregson from the S-3 (operations) shop saying 3rd Platoon would be inserted late; they were the last insert of the day as a higher-priority emergency extract was bumping them. Because the sun would be setting, and because Fallon had bitched about short turnovers coming out, 4th Platoon would spend the night with 3rd Platoon to do a proper turnover. Gregson said they would be on tomorrow's extract package as a priority. About 1715, they got the call from LZ 401 that 3rd Platoon was en route. It was a 20-minute flight and, just as Gregson had predicted, the sun was setting when 1st Lieutenant W. X. Lee and 3rd Platoon arrived at *West Orange*.[4] L'Orange had a working party ready to help and had his five corporals ready to serve as guides. He waited in the mortar pit for Lee to clear the landing zone (LZ) and come through the zig-zag wire route at the west gate next to Bravo Bunker. The two CH-46s departed south and headed east towards the sea. They would be at Marble Mountain in 15 minutes and on the chow line within thirty. Lee told his experienced platoon sergeant, Diaz, to break up the platoon. Everyone met, divided into bunker teams, and went to their bunkers for chow and gossip. The new platoon would have word on what was going on in the rear.

Lee did not believe they needed the overnight turnover but was not going to argue it with the S-3 shop.[5] L'Orange was the hill commander until he left. The two lieutenants went to their bunker's front porch. Lee threw his pack on the rack and came out. He told L'Orange he wanted to walk the perimeter before it got dark and left. L'Orange started dinner. The two lieutenants lived in the same hooch at Camp Reasoner, but the reality was you really had little time there between patrols. They did not know each other. Tonight and the next day, they could chat about the hill and about Delta Company and the battalion. Each wanted to know what the other thought and each admitted they were both new to 1st Recon. L'Orange knew Lee had been in 3rd Recon so had a perspective of that battalion and his experience running patrols along the demilitarized zone (DMZ) and Cua Viet river inlet. Lee wanted the dump on Hill 119 from L'Orange. Since that was tactical, L'Orange started there. Fourth Platoon had been on the hill since 5 March. During that time, they, *West Orange*, and IOD Team *Hansworth*, had had 12 enemy sightings of 59 NVA/VC. *Hansworth* had called ten fire missions with negative results, for a variety of reasons, including darkness, terrain, and a clearance issue.[6] L'Orange explained there were fire-support clearance issues with the 5th Marines patrolling to the west of the hill, and South Korean Marines patrolling to east, and that the Recon observation post (OP) on Hill 425 controlled most of the Phu Loc Valley to their south. They focused north toward Go Noi Island. The hill rated an Artillery lieutenant, but Sergeant Bayuk had led the IOD team for most of the five months he was on the hill; he rotated out on 7 March.[7] A Lieutenant Russell replaced him for four days. He departed on the artillery team resupply helicopter, leaving Corporal Aydt as the acting Arty noncommissioned officer in charge (NCOIC).[8] Some of the clearance issues could be attributed to turnover and the corporal not having the training and experience, nor his head in the game. Aydt had told L'Orange a new Arty lieutenant should be coming to the hill after he graduated from IOD school over on Fire Support Base (FSB) Ryder. L'Orange briefed Lee on the probe of the wire on their first night and the hasty ambush down by Thon Bon (1) killing six NVA.[9] He said that, besides Arty clearances, the challenge was the villagers from the two hamlets Thon Bon (1) to the northeast and, Tho Son 1,000 meters to the north. There also was the large village of Chien Son composed of four hamlets two kilometers to the east. The villagers were allowed in some rice fields to the east during daylight. Curfew had them in their huts at night. The two closest hamlets to the north were classified hostile in the G-5's Hamlet Evaluation System and considered controlled by Viet Cong Infrastructure. L'Orange showed Lee the heat map started by Gunnery Sergeant Moore that Fallon had given him. He had kept it updated and passed it on to Lee. He also briefed Lee on their "tenants," the IOD equipment and team for whom Recon was responsible for security. He said Bayuk had made a heat map of his fire missions. With his departure, the other four Arty Marines were lazy, claiming they could not cover all 24 hours. During the day, the IOD, which was supposed to be observing, did not always do so. He had not made an issue of it since his Recon Marines liked to observe during the day and were always up on the platform looking. The number of enemy sightings had statistically dropped off. L'Orange also told Lee the IOD lieutenant that had come out had chosen to sleep with Bayuk and spent most of the day in the bunker, saying he would observe at night. But truth was he slept all night and read books during the day.[10] They really had not talked. The last item surprised Lee. L'Orange said that, with the last Arty resupply, two ARVN (Army of the Republic of Vietnam) had come off the bird and joined the forward observer (FO) team. One a warrant officer was an FO for the 44th ARVN Artillery Battalion and the other his radio operator with a PRC-25. He said they were in the Arty bunker but were building a new one for themselves.

It was Lee's turn to update L'Orange. In his absence from Camp Reasoner, Drumright had fired Captain Thomas Martin over the pay/admin failure[11] and that 1st Lieutenant "Jerry" Spolter was the new Delta Company commander.[12] Also, that Master Sergeant Rene Regalot had been transferred from the S-3 shop to be the first sergeant. His friend, Porter Rathmell, had told him Regalot had his shit together. And, that he could expect to be handed a stack of his platoon's Service Record Book (SRB) to audit when he got to the rear. And, that Drumright was changing a lot of policies in the battalion, especially his expectations of what a patrol should do. The two lieutenants discussed the merits and risks of the aggressive patrolling Drumright wanted. The night passed slowly for L'Orange as he was ready to leave. Lee stayed up late, walking the perimeter, and listening to life on the hill.

The next morning, Lee asked L'Orange what was going on in the bunker on the southeast side of the hill furthest from the hilltop. L'Orange said, "Oh, that is the ARVN." Lee said, "I did not know there were ARVN on the hill before you told me." L'Orange said the warrant officer came in handy as an interpreter when they went down to the meeting spot to talk with the villagers. Lee asked where that was, so they went up to the platform and Chris pointed out the spot north and directly downhill that Garry Parks had established the previous Christmas as the point to meet villagers.[13] It was 500 meters down the north side of the hill in a clearing with a slight slope and a high-speed trail leading up to the OP. Out the other side of the clearing was a well-used trail to the hamlet of Tho Son, another 600 meters north. There was also a small trail from the clearing leading northwest to the hamlet of Thon Bon (1). Parks had set it up so that if the villagers wanted to talk, they came to the clearing and waited for a patrol to come down and meet them. The villagers were not allowed, for security reasons, any closer to the OP.

Lee was ready but he would have to wait all day before taking command of *West Orange*. He wanted to be in command, and it would come with 4th Platoon's departure on the 18th. They waited all day for the helos. Even being a so-called priority extract, the reality was it was routine and would be done at the end of the day. The birds showed at 1640.[14] At least 4th Platoon would get hot chow that night at the Recon mess hall. Lee had the hill at 1641, 18 March.[15]

***

At Camp Reasoner, Fallon had slept almost all day on 15 March after the 53-hour raid. On the morning of the 16th, a runner from S-3 knocked on the Delta Company officers' hut and said Fallon's presence was wanted in the S-3 bunker. Fallon dressed in clean cammies and shined boots, thanks to the Camp Reasoner mama-sans. What a luxury their service was, but also a security risk. The cold showers were welcome, as Fallon recalled, in the grunts, routinely going 45 days in the bush without clean uniforms or showers. Walking down the hill to the S-3 bunker, he thought it would be a routine patrol warning order. Entering the S-3 bunker, he looked for and found 1st Lieutenant "Chip" Gregson who said, "Well, stud, you are going out as a Pathfinder for 1st Battalion, 7th Marines [1/7]."[16] Fallon retorted with, "I have done my grunt time." Gregson said the leadership up the hill, meaning Division, wanted to exploit the cave complex *Delicatessen* had found. Fallon pointed out it was Sergeant Vu and Counter Intelligence (CI) who found it so why couldn't Vu and the CI captain be pathfinders? Gregson said something about Vu having gone to Tam Ka to see family and the captain had other business. Fallon would get the pathfinding mission, to leave on the 17th. Fallon had planned to go to the club for St. Patrick's day. Gregson said he was pressed for time, so he would get the order early tomorrow morning but could expect an admin insert with 1/7 midday. Fallon had a habit of keeping his maps, he did not know why, but, in this case, it saved getting new ones, as well as cutting and lamination. He went to the Delta Company office to tell Spolter, but he wasn't there. He asked the company runner to find Sergeant Franklin and have him report to the officers' hut ASAP, and not to worry about uniform. Franklin showed up 15 minutes later with wet hair, clean shaven, in shorts, flip-flops, and a cut-off 1st Marine Division-logoed green sweatshirt. Fallon suspected the shave had come after the word to report. Being the morning, Fallon gave him a cold Coke. Spolter arrived, got a Coke, and said carry on but he was there to find out what was up. Fallon gave Franklin his ammo-box chair with arms and pulled out his foot locker. Spolter stood. Fallon said, "We are going back to the cave complex we found the day before yesterday. We have a Pathfinder mission to lead 1st Battalion, 7th Marine Regiment into the Que Sons. We depart midday tomorrow, so no St. Pats Day for us. We will be with the grunts so no need for a corpsman and we can be small. You, me, Ravelo on radio, and pick two new Marines who were on *Delicatessen*. We can give them some point man and tail-end experience. We will have a patrol order and IA [immediate-action] drill this afternoon at 1400." With that, Franklin left.

"Nobody tells me anything around here!" Spolter said. "You got the Three Shop to do twenty-four-hour turnovers so Lee goes up tomorrow to the OP and will turn over with Chris, while I get to go to 'The Breakfast Club' with 'Wild Man' and later will have to go to his St. Pat's party."

"Skipper, that's why you get paid the big bucks."

Lee entered the hut, flopping on his cot. "What's up?" he asked.

"Fallon's got a Pathfinder," replied Spolter, while Fallon said, "The skipper has a case of the ass."

Spolter, unlike the other company commanders who lived separate from their lieutenants, remained living in the Delta Company officers' hut,[17] choosing to lead by example and camaraderie instead of being a senior 1st lieutenant and separating himself from what were his peers, except for billet. Jerry, the ultimate "California Boy," had a large California flag hanging on the wall in his corner space. Delta Company had become a California company with Spolter, Lee, L'Orange, and Fallon all hailing from the Golden State. Lieutenant McAdams, who had just departed for the grunts, and the 2nd Platoon commander, Garry Parks, were South Carolina Boys.[18] McAdams's new replacement, just joining from a 5th Marines tour, 2nd Lieutenant Paul Eglevsky, was from Long Island, New York.[19] Fallon broke out his green notebook and started writing a patrol order even though he did not yet have a frag order. He would give a normal order to his Marines as if it were a patrol. He had a fear that would come true with time, that *Delicatessen* would be walking point for a thousand Marines of 1/7.[20]

At 1400, on 16 March, Fallon walked down the five front steps of his hut and across the street to the "Stagger Back Inn." It was empty, except for Franklin, who had the others at a table. They stood as Fallon entered, he waved them down, handed Franklin some MPCs (military payment certificates), and said sodas all round. Franklin handed the fistful of MPCs to Private First Class Bonini without saying a word, Bonini got up and got five cold Cokes and left the money in a shoebox behind the bar. Fallon explained the Pathfinder mission. Then he said, "In reality, we will walk point for 1/7 and lead them back to the cave complex. We will go with standard equipment. Painted up. Expect shit from the grunts. I came from them, and they will give us shit. Just ignore them. In truth, they are jealous. Pack for three days, one PRC-25 radio, one PRC-93, standard ammo, light on water. We will be inserted into and out of a secure LZ with the grunts and, if we get extended, we will get supplies from them. Okay, Franklin, you are not point, and Ravelo has the radio, who is doing what?" With that Franklin said, "We have talked, and Stewart wants to walk point, which leaves Bonini walking tail end. I'll take the M79 and my M16, sir." Fallon asked if anyone had any questions. With none, they fell out on the company street for IA drills. This Pathfinder mission was a navigation test for Fallon as he would be responsible for leading the 1/7 to the cave complex.

On the street, *Delicatessen,* lined up: Stewart on point, Fallon deuce point/navigator, Ravelo radio, Franklin M79, and Bonini tail end. Fallon said same IA drills that Gunny Moore teaches, same arm and hand signals. They walked through four drills and were done in 15 minutes. Fallon called them together and said, "Remember, the grunts will taunt you, but don't sweat it. Go easy on the beer tonight as tomorrow we will be moving or humping with the grunts, nobody will fall out, you are Recon!" With that Franklin and Ravelo both gave a big "Aruga!"

Fallon stayed in that night to sleep, as did Lee, because both were going out in the morning. Spolter said he was avoiding the Recon club and Wild Bill's party and was going to the division's club for dinner, thereby also missing being spotted or grabbed by senior leadership at dinner.

The next morning, both Lee and Fallon were up early and went to early chow. They sat together and ate in silence, both in their own thoughts. Walking back to the hut, Lee asked Fallon about Hill 119. Fallon said, "What scares me is, it is a known fixed hill with higher hills around it. It is a dangerous place, more dangerous than the bush, but the troops love it as it is laid back, not like here in camp." Returning from breakfast, the two lieutenants stomped loudly up the stairs into the Delta officers' hut, flipping on the lights, knowing Spolter was trying to sleep. They got their weapons and personal rigs and headed down to the LZ. They made sure they slammed the screen door on the way out, leaving the lights on. On the LZ, they both drew grenades, already having their 21 magazines. Lee easily found his platoon and Sergeant Diaz as they were the largest group on the LZ. Fallon was early, without his team yet, so he found the LZ NCO to determine where *Delicatessen* was in the insert line-up. The birds had not arrived. Direct support of the grunts was a big deal, so it did not surprise Fallon to find out he was early in the insert flow and would be on the first southern lift after a northern insert and extract in Elephant Valley. Lee would spend the day on the LZ with his platoon. Fallon pulled out the new patrol order he had picked up in the S-3 shop 15 minutes earlier. Normally, he made notes and never took the classified battalion order with him. On this mission, he decided to take it in case he was asked to do something out of the ordinary or not in his order. He read the one-sentence mission statement. "2. MISSION: Conduct pathfinder operation to lead 7th MarRegt. To cave complex found on Operation DELICATESSEN of 12–14 Mar."[21]

He handed the order to Sergeant Franklin, sitting next to him, to read. Franklin returned Battalion Order #0313-70 signed "by direction W. G. Gregson"[22] and Fallon folded it and put it in a plastic battery bag. The LZ NCO yelled for *Delicatessen.* Fallon and his four Marines stood up from the crowd, indicating to the corporal they had heard him. He pointed to bird one, while Team *Prime Cut* had been called for bird two. Fallon trotted to the CH-46 and stopped and counted four up the ramp, giving the crew chief the thumbs up. The Recon Battalion air liaison officer had given him a grid, centered in the Phu Loc Valley and an FM frequency for 1/7. He had written both in black grease pencil on his map. As the bird pulled out of LZ 401, Fallon handed the map to the copilot as the pilot had the stick and was flying. The copilot copied both on his knee board, looked at Fallon's map and pointed to the letters LZ that Fallon had marked on the map. He gave Fallon a thumbs up. 1st Battalion, 7th Marines, had been helo lifted that morning into the Phu Loc Valley.[23] Twenty-five minutes later, looking out of the helo's side porthole with no glass, he saw yellow smoke swirl and a lot of Marines standing around. Going into a secure LZ was the easiest part of this mission. The best part would be leaving from a secure LZ upon completion of his mission. Fallon had *Delicatessen* looking like Recon—sleeves down, cammie paint on faces, ears and foreheads, bush covers, grenades and smokes on the H-harness, with swiss-seat rope tied on. He wanted the grunts to know who they were. After the bird left, a Marine walked over and said to follow him. He led the team off the LZ and down a small creek embankment about one hundred meters away. He took them to a group of Marines, most of whom were older, sitting on the ground. A Marine in the center looked up; not knowing specifically who it was but suspecting he was senior, Fallon came to the position of attention and quietly said, "Lieutenant Fallon and Team *Delicatessen* reporting as ordered, sir."

The older Marine smiled and said, "Gunny, take the team and get them settled. Fallon, sit down." The man had a big smile as he was having his own fun. He said, "Fallon, do you know who I am?" Caught off guard, Fallon said, "No, sir." He laughed, and said, "I am Charlie Cooper, CO of 1/7." Fallon was stunned and taken aback, getting up again to attention, but Lieutenant Colonel Cooper grabbed his arm and said, "Sit down and tell me how you have been doing." Fallon recognized the name but not the officer sitting in front of him, 25 pounds lighter with a drawn, gaunt face. He was one of his father's, Colonel E. B. "Doc" Fallon, Marine Corps compatriots. Cooper was a 1950 graduate of the Naval Academy and, as a 2nd lieutenant in Baker Company, 1st Battalion, 5th Marines, had earned the Silver Star in Korea. Cooper was known throughout the Corps for his leadership principles based on Shakespeare's famous line, "We few, we happy few, we band of brothers." In every unit Cooper commanded, he published a "Band of Brothers Leadership Principles" he expected his officers and NCOs to follow and care for their brother Marines. C. G. Cooper would retire after a 35-year career as a lieutenant general, Commander of Marine Forces Pacific.[24]

With his fun over, Cooper got down to business asking about Fallon's experiences in Vietnam. Fallon simply replied with "Five months as rifle-platoon commander in 3/26 and now three months in Recon, sir."

"Good," said Cooper. "We heard you found some caves we want to explore.

"Sergeant Vu, a Kit Carson Scout, led us to the caves, but they had been abandoned."

"Well, we are going there. Can you get us there?" Fallon responded that it was his mission, and he knew where the caves were located.

"Okay, Fallon, what's the plan?"

Taken aback a second time, Fallon decided to do what Gunny Moore did. He cleared a piece of dirt and, with a stick, drew a diagram of the Phu Loc Valley and the northern Que Sons. He pointed to the ground and said, "We are here and behind us to the northwest is Hill 175. We need to move four kilometers east and south. You may be able to make out Hill 322 to our southeast, pointing toward the Que Sons."

Getting up, Colonel Cooper said to his command group, "Let's get moving," and to Fallon, "You are with me until we turn south, then you and your boys go up front. We will talk about it as we walk. Please tell me how you went in on the raid we heard about."

As they walked, Fallon filled the colonel in on *Delicatessen*'s approach march, security positions, and assault. After three hours moving east in the Phu Loc Valley, the formation was 1,500 meters due north of Hill 322, which could be clearly seen. Every NVA in the Que Sons knew a Marine battalion was in the valley, as did every VC in Phu Loc village.

Cooper stopped the movement and called for an orders group. His company commanders appeared. He simply said, "Our objective is a cave complex in the draw on the south side of Hill 322. We will do two companies. C Company has security and D Company has the attack. Charlic Company, you have the flanks. You leave now and put a platoon on each finger, on east and west sides, overlooking Hill 322. When you are in position, Delta Company will take Hill 322." Speaking directly to the Delta Company commander, he continued, "I want the top of the hill before we go in. Charlie Company leave one platoon here in reserve. When Delta departs, Fallon will walk point for you and get you to your line of departure. After you have reached the hill, he will show you where the caves are located." The colonel asked for questions; there were none. Then he said, "Fallon, since you've been there, do you want to say anything?" Caught off guard again, Fallon said, "Well, sir, we spent two nights sneaking up on the cave complex with a Vietnamese guide and the NVA got out ten minutes ahead of us. With your battalion, I don't think there will be any enemy there. This cave complex is a waystation for overnighters, and there were no defensive positions around it." Cooper said, "Good point, Lieutenant, but we are the hammer. 2nd Battalion, 7th Marines, went into Hill 953 yesterday and they are the anvil.[25] Their mission is to seal off the south." With that, the orders group broke up.

Fallon found *Delicatessen* with the S-3 gunnery sergeant and told them what was going to happen. Within twenty minutes, a guide took them to the Delta Company command post (CP). The captain was not waiting to get moving. *Delicatessen* was pushed up to the point platoon and told to take point. The grunts were taking revenge on Recon who, in their book, had it easy. Stewart took point, Fallon grabbed him and said, "Take your time, just another bigger patrol." They moved slowly, slower than the grunt's normal pace.

After an hour, they were at the base of Hill 322. The Delta Company commander came forward and asked where the caves were. Fallon told him in the draw on the backside, or south side, of the hill. The skipper told his 1st Platoon commander, "Okay, take the hill." With an "Aye, aye," the commander called his squad leaders in and said, "We are taking the hill. It will be one up and two back, squad wedge formation, squads in columns, first squad point, third on my right." They were moving in under five minutes. Fallon had never used a wedge in the grunts but could easily see the flexibility it provided for the approach march, squads in columns were a solid formation. Team *Delicatessen* fell in behind the 1st Platoon commander and his radio operator directly behind the point squad to climb Hill 322. Thirty minutes later on the top, Fallon pointed out three cave entrances below and on the southeast side of the creek draw.[26] With a nod, *Delicatessen* took point, and one squad followed them down; they now had Marines above them on three sides. It only took 15 minutes to get to the caves. Predictably, they were empty. What had changed was evidence of a recent fire, freshly cooked rice, and newly cut firewood, which indicated use within the past 12 hours. *Delicatessen* sighted a fifth cave. The grunts would search the caves again.

The Pathfinder mission was complete. First Battalion, 7th Marines, would remain on the northern side of the Que Sons and Phu Loc Valley for another two weeks.[27] Fallon looked south at the massive Hill 953 overlooking them. It was 1430 on the 17th. *Delicatessen* took to the creek bed around Hill 322 and walked back out into the Phu Loc Valley. They took their time, not wanting the grunts to engage them, so they went slowly and walked high and in the open on rice-paddy dikes. Two hours later, they linked up with the battalion CP. Fallon wanted to check out with Cooper, but he was not there, so he spoke for about a minute with the S-3, Major R. E. Theer, and asked if he was released since he had shown them the caves. The major concurred and turned to more pressing matters. Fallon told Revelo to call *West Orange*, the Delta Company relay on Hill 119, and have them request an extract, giving Revelo the grid. Then he found the S-3 gunnery sergeant and asked where they could crash. An hour later, *West Orange* called and said they were not on today's schedule; it was late afternoon, and they would be put on tomorrow's extract schedule. It could be worse, at least tonight they were inside the lines of the 1st Battalion,

7th Marines; hopefully, they would not be mortared from the mountains. Sitting on the valley floor looking at the sun set over the Que Son Mountains, which in Vietnamese meant "Cinnamon Mountains," little did Fallon realize he would be spending a significant portion of the next eight months running patrols in the Cinnamon Mountains.

Delicatessen was extracted at 1100 the next morning, 18 March, and returned to LZ 401 for their Pathfinder debrief in S-2 (intelligence).[28] Fallon had had two shots at the radio station. Three weeks later, India Company, 3rd Battalion, 7th Marines, as part of the same operation, was helo lifted deep into the Que Sons one ridgeline south and east of the massive Hill 953. They had a Vietnamese Marine detachment with an enemy prisoner who said he could lead them to the radio station. The morning following the helo lift, India Company, in platoon column, patrolled down to a jungle-canopy-covered plateau on the south side and below Hill 953. On the plateau's north cliff face was a single cave covered from above by canopy with the cave entrance only visible from 20 feet away. The NVA had left as their security watched every trail into the plateau. India Company captured the exceptionally large radio transmitter, a gasoline generator, and backup batteries linked together in a series formation to provide power to the transmitter.[29] They also found a large cache of weapons and ammunition, including 122-mm rocket launchers and three 122-mm rockets.[30] In the trees outside the cave, they found multiple antennas strung in the canopies below the final layer of limbs, not visible from the air and hard to see from the ground. The Marines had followed the comm wire from the cave to the antennas that were directionally oriented, one to the northeast towards Go Noi Island and Da Nang, and one west towards the Thuong Duc Corridor and the Ho Chi Minh Trail into Laos.

***

At Camp Reasoner, 2nd Lieutenant Paul Eglevsky checked into Recon Battalion. He met Drumright's criteria of infantry experience with five months in the grunts. He was coming from 2nd Battalion, 5th Marines, where he had patrolled the Arizona Territory.[31] Spolter moved Eglevsky into Fallon's 1st Platoon, nominally making Fallon the company executive officer. "Top" Regalot had the office squared away and, with the pressure to keep teams in the field, he became a freelance patrol leader. Spolter had as many teams as he could field out on patrol. Garry Parks, with Team *Dublin City* from 2nd Platoon, had headed up Elephant Valley using the radio relay on Dong Den. It was an uneventful patrol from 23–27 March.[32]

Eglevsky took his first patrol out, Fallon's old Team *Delicatessen*. Spolter knew the experienced Sergeant Franklin, with the same team of Weirich, Ravelo, Evans, Bonini, and "Doc" Schneider would be a good break-in patrol. Nobody except Paul could say his last name, so he told the troops, "Call me 'Eagle.'"[33] *Delicatessen* was seen during insertion by NVA LZ spotters and followed by the enemy. Signal shots pushed the team. They moved for an hour-and-a-half, but the enemy had the high ground in boulders, and they almost walked into an L-shaped ambush, Eagle spotting it before it was triggered. *Delicatessen* engaged 25–30 NVA in green utilities and AK-47s.[34] *Hostage Egor* arrived and made a strafing run. The team re-engaged an enemy flanking effort, killing two NVA. *Egor* got multiple Arty missions from *Ringbroom-Mike* out of An Hoa Combat Base. They were shooting south towards Hill 462, getting good coverage. The NVA were wearing camouflage utilities, cammie paint on their faces, and wore bush covers. LZ observers, and this counter-recon team who had spotted *Delicatessen,* were making every attempt to wipe out the seven-man team. With the air cover, the team began breaking contact. *Hostage Hornet* arrived with two Cobra gunships from *Scarface. Hostage Egor* got all three aircraft in a racetrack providing covering fire and then a white smoke screen as *Delicatessen* broke contact and moved across a large draw and into triple canopy.[35] It was the Eagle's first day on his first patrol. Welcome to Recon, Lieutenant! They had multiple sightings of large groups of enemy on the move. During the entire patrol, the team heard signal shots as the counter-recon patrol was still looking for them. With their presence known, they were extracted after 96 hours, without incident, from a dry rice paddy.[36] Returning, the helos had to refuel at An Hoa and while doing so had a blade-to-blade strike, flipping one of the aircraft on its side. All Marines scrambled off and safely returning to Camp Reasoner on the chase bird.

The day prior, 26 March, Fallon was back in the bush with one of Parks's teams, *Fig Newton.*[37] It was a newly composited team with the freshly promoted Corporal "Big I" Iantorno as team leader. Private First Class "Nano" Villasina would run point. Elkins, Brandon, McAleese, and Hospital Corpsman Third Class Eric Schwartz rounded out the team. Fallon had Iantorno run the patrol to evaluate him in order to meet the new battalion policy for certifying patrol leaders. The insert LZ was an old 2,000-pound bomb crater. It was a poor LZ and the only one in the haven which was located in thick triple-canopy jungle. The team was west of the radio relay at Dong Den in extremely hilly, broken-up, jungle-filled terrain running downhill, high on the southern rim above Elephant Valley. The sidehills had been subject to commercial logging some 15–20 years earlier. There were old, felled logs laying in steep logging shoots running down to the river in Elephant Valley. Movement was extremely difficult cross-corridor with many detours to avoid logging waste piles. It was also clear there was no enemy present. After six exhausting days of movement, and having to double back, *Fig Newton* was extracted from its insert LZ on 31 March.[38]

Patrolling at the same time, Team *Chili Pepper* was led by their platoon commander, Chris L'Orange.[39] This was a big patrol as Sergeant Atkins's normal team was joined, not only by L'Orange, but by two ARVN officers who were learning reconnaissance patrolling from 1st Recon. They were Lieutenants Thanh and Tuan, making it a nine-man patrol.[40] During this patrol, the team discovered a series of five dispersed, but connected, camps running on both sides of two streams with a shallow finger between them. More than forty hooches made of thatch were counted. These hooches were unobservable from the air due to canopy in the jungle draws. The main camp included a hospital, class rooms, mess hut, and large kitchen. They had predug circular antiaircraft positions on the high ground. The base camp was empty but in good condition and had been recently used. Next to the classroom, three trees had been skinned with Vietnamese writing carved into each. The translation read: Tree 1—"Think Clean, Be Clean, Eat Clean, Drink Clean"; Tree 2—"Ready to Fight"; Tree 3—"Orders Outline, Security, Mission, Execution, Silence."[41]

Chili Pepper was extracted from a poor one-bird hover LZ made previously by a bomb blast. It had stumps three to four feet high and the pilot had to hover as the team did pull-ups on the ramp and into the aircraft to depart.[42]

***

At about 1310, on the 18th, Team *Hansworth* was working on a fire mission.[43] Lieutenant Lee climbed the stairs to the platform and met Corporal Aydt who was calling the mission. Lee asked him what he had, and he said he had two "gooks" in green utilities carrying packs and rifles. He swung the "Big Eyes" around and offered Lee a look. The fire mission was in process, and they were awaiting clearance to shoot. The enemy was due east about two kilometers walking north of the Chien Son (4) hamlet. The fire mission came, it was a battery-one (six rounds) coming out of An Hoa Combat Base. Lee heard the guns fire and seconds later saw the rounds impact with their gray/black smoke in the wet rice paddies. He heard Aydt on the radio call ceasefire and claim credit for one kill.[44] Lee asked him about the bomb-damage assessment (BDA), and he said, "You have to claim enemy results as that is how I am evaluated." Lee left the platform without comment but knew no enemy was killed on that fire mission.

Lee spent the next couple of days training his Marines on the machine guns on Hill 119. They were Recon Marines with no machine-gun training. Third Platoon had five M60 machine guns and one .50-caliber gun. Lee and Sergeant Diaz worked two full days, having every Marine learn to put the M60 into action. Five of the six perimeter defensive bunkers had an M60 with the sixth having the XM174 automatic 40-mm grenade launcher. The .50-cal was harder to master, so they finally decided Diaz would man it during defensive fires. Lee also held mortar school as he had a 60-mm mortar, a 61mm, and an 81mm. They needed to pick two Marines to man the mortar pit which was used to shoot illumination rounds. Third Platoon had brought five M79s so every M60 bunker also got an M79 40-mm "blooper" gun.[45] Lance Corporals Broe and Lowery had also brought their sniper rifles. Broe's rifle was right-handed, and Lowery's was left-handed. Both had gone to the in-country scout-sniper school run by the 1st Marine Division.[46]

Lee had been putting out two listening posts each night and doing a morning wire patrol around the hill but, after two days of training, it was time to settle in to a routine which would also allow for one walk-off patrol. On 21 March, the patrol left the hill at first light, directly behind the wire patrol and split off when they hit the first ravine after the east gate. They dropped into the ravine, not wanting to be seen, and headed north while the wire patrol continued east to west just outside the wire in sight for all below in the hamlet to see their daily routine. The walk-off patrol, *West Orange-Alpha*, dropped down 500 meters and then worked its way east, moving sidehill on the north side of the finger. They were breaking brush and moving slowly. When they were about eleven hundred meters northeast of the OP, they sighted an enemy camp in a ravine. They put security out above and below them and then dropped into the camp. It was an overnight or daytime resting place as the brush was cleared out 15 by 20 feet on the side of the ravine. They found rice, tobacco, utensils, clothing, and cammie material. There was a three-foot-wide trail leading downhill north out of the enemy harbor site.[47] They scattered the rice and kept the tobacco to give to their ARVN back on the hill. The patrol was back in the wire by early afternoon.

First Lieutenant Lee was a serious practitioner of warfare. The former enlisted Marine who had become an officer through the Enlisted Commissioning Program knew he had to work harder than the other officers and did so. In fact, he enjoyed being a Marine and planned to make it his career.[48] Sitting on the bunker wall that evening, his thoughts turned to the tactical situation on Hill 119. His team had found a fresh harbor site close to the OP. He took his mission to defend the classified IOD seriously. It had been raining havoc on the enemy since it was placed on this small hill astride the main infiltration routes of the 2nd NVA Division from Base Areas 112 and 118. The OP had excellent observation of the rice-basket Go Noi Island, now a free-fire zone with all the civilian population moved to strategic hamlets along Route 1 in the South Korean Marines' tactical area of responsibility. The Seabees had just finished a new bridge and eight miles of road connecting the friendly hamlet with Hoa An. Lee reflected on the heat map started by Gunnery Sergeant Moore. Gunny Moore spent two flips over a month's time on the hill in January and had thwarted an attack on the hill by the T89 Sapper Battalion. He had killed two of its planning officers and captured the third.[49] Then Fallon had a long walk-off patrol, Team *Forefather*, between the Hill 119 and Hill 425 OPs.[50] His additions to the heat map showed that Hill 175, overlooking them, was an enemy post watching Hill 119. L'Orange had been probed in his wire the first night he was on the hill.[51] To Lee, it was clear the enemy was watching the hill daily and planning. This hill was below, and watched by, higher hills to the west and south. It had six avenues of approach up draws that were unobservable until the enemy hit the wire. Lee reasoned the enemy was observing and plotting the hill's routine and would use it against them.

That night alone in his bunker, he wrote two letters, one to his parents and one to his love, both back in California.[52] He said nothing of substance but wanted to get them sent as he enjoyed getting letters from home. He thought all night about the challenge of defending his small hill. He would change the routine. Tomorrow, the wire patrol will go out in the morning but also again in the late afternoon and in different directions. He would push a night ambush up to Hill 148 and would ask for the boundary extension out to Hill 175, two kilometers south. Hill life was routine for the Marines—night watches and listening posts, sunbathing on top of bunkers during the days when it did not rain. Lee would break up the routine. He would push everyone on the hill. He was the commander responsible for security of the hill and his Marines. He would hold more live-fire training. Marines loved to fire weapons, and they had the ammo. He would also improve the trench line Fallon had started as it was still not deep enough. Lee understood firsthand the damage heavy shelling could inflict from his time on the DMZ. He had brought five pairs of 7 × 50 binoculars to the hill. He expected every bunker to man a watch and scope their sector every hour every day and night. He explained to his Marines that the IOD team was looking further out on Go Noi Island, the railroad bridge, and into the Arizona Territory. They were not watching the last two kilometers below the hill. That was their job. They were the security! The IOD was the offense, they were the defense. Lee liked football analogies as he believed his Marines could relate.

It was quiet for a few days. The IOD team from the 11th Marine Regiment had their routine and policies. Their new lieutenant arrived on 23 March, having just finished the IOD school for FOs on FSB Ryder. First Lieutenant P. R. Green focused on his Marines after arrival and stuck to himself.[53] Lee focused on his Marines and improving the hill's defenses.

On 24 March, it was a sunny day with good visibility. About 1100, there was excitement on the platform as Team *Hansworth* had sighted enemy out on Go Noi Island. They had spotted four enemy in green utilities carrying packs and rifles.[54] An AO was out looking for work, so the target was handed off to *Hostage Echo*, an OV-10 with his observer *Cowpoke*. They had fixed-wing on station. The Marines always enjoyed watching the coordination of an air strike with the planes sometimes at the same level as the hill as they jetted toward Go Noi Island to drop their ordnance. The air strikes were in many ways beautiful to watch if one was not on the receiving end. The hill turned out on this sunny day to watch the airshow. Lee got a pair of 7 × 50s and sat on the steps of the platform watching the island. He did not want to intrude or get in the way of Green running the show. After the strikes were over, Lee could hear on the tower squawk-box speaker *Hostage Echo*, the OV-10, asking *Hansworth* for a BDA as he needed to pass that info on to the departing fixed-wing aircraft. He heard the report of two confirmed kills with good coverage of the target area.[55] Lee could see the good coverage of area, but he had not seen bodies. The 200 power of the Big Eyes could see some things he could not. It was not his call, but he was of the opinion that Team *Hansworth* was inflating its figures to make themselves look good. That afternoon, *Hansworth* called an artillery fire mission on eight NVA on the riverbank of Go Noi Island. They got an immediate fire-for-effect and reported two kills with excellent coverage of the target.[56] Sergeant Diaz told Lee that all eight had gone underwater when the sound of the shells was still inbound and had not come up. That told Diaz they had an underwater entrance to a bunker on the side of the river. That evening, a weather front moved in, and it rained hard day and night on the 25th, 26th, and 27th. *Hansworth* called no fire missions, and the hill saw no enemy personnel out in the rain. At night, they could see less than ten feet with total cloud cover. Lee knew the enemy was moving but they could see nothing.

CHAPTER 22

The Shots, 28 March 1970

On 27 March, it was overcast with a low ceiling. A lone helo arrived with callsign *Sky Six*, the chaplain. It was Good Friday. The chaplain came off the bird and was escorted to the open .50-caliber machine-gun pit where the Marines had set up an altar made out of 81-mm mortar boxes. He placed his linen cloth over the ammo-box altar and provided a non-denominational service. He spoke of the sacrifices Jesus had made on that day. Every Marine on the hill attended.[1] Corporal Bob Grossman from Wisconsin recalled that, 45 minutes later, the *Sky Six* helo was inbound, picking up the chaplain, and taking him over to Hill 425 for their service.

That night, 1st Lieutenant W. X. Lee set out a night ambush. On 28 March, the weather broke. It was clear, warm, and dry with a slight breeze off the sea. The day would remain bright, and the temperature would rise to 80 degrees. The villagers were out in the fields early from every hamlet they could observe in all directions. The hill was active with Marines in shorts and flip-flops outside the bunkers, drying out wet poncho liners and cammies on the bunker roofs. The villagers were performing irrigation maintenance on their paddies east of the observation post (OP) near Chien Son (4). About 0930, with his coffee brewed in his canteen cup, Sergeant Herman Diaz, the experienced 3rd Platoon sergeant, perched himself on the .50-cal pit's sandbagged wall with his 7 × 50 binos. He started a systematic observation down the hill's north slope. He soon spotted Vietnamese below the hill slightly to the northwest. Diaz stopped and focused all his attention on them as they were in a restricted area, and they were too close to the OP. They were about 650 to 700 meters away. He could not tell if it was three or four as they were working and moving.[2] They were on the side of an old large, dry overgrown rice paddy with a bamboo tree line behind them close to the railroad berm. One of the group was going in and out of the tree line cutting long bamboo poles while the others on the main trail were digging out an old mortar crater by enlarging and deepening it. Diaz sat on the sandbag berm of the .50-cal pit for 25 or 30 minutes watching the activities below. He could clearly see the person in the tree line was a man wearing brown shorts, white shirt, and a coolie hat. After watching two others, he identified them as wearing black "PJ" bottoms and white tops, the traditional garb of women. The fourth individual, going back and forth to the tree line, was also in traditional women's garb.[3]

While Diaz was watching the suspected villagers, and trying to figure out what they were doing, Lee had been dealing with another group of villagers who had brought a wounded girl to the OP, north of the wire outside the landing zone (LZ). She had been brought to the hill by women for medical care. The girl had shrapnel in her thigh and needed treatment. Lee put out three Marines for security on higher ground above the corpsmen and told them to wait with

"Doc" for the medevac. He sent one Marine back for water. The corpsman, Hospitalman Glen Edison USN from Albuquerque, New Mexico, had just arrived in-country on 20 February after corpsman training and had been immediately assigned to 3rd Platoon. "Doc" Edison and the girl were staged 200 meters outside the LZ in the draw on the north side of the landing zone. The corpsman cleaned up the wound and comforted the scared girl and her mother.[4] Lee went back to the command/radio bunker and called a medevac for the girl. It would be a routine medevac and the last priority, so they expected to wait all morning for it to arrive.

Lee thought there was a lot of activity on the northside, all of which was within the hill's restricted haven. Outside, Corporal Grossman and Lance Corporal Broe came by and asked Diaz what was up.[5] Diaz pointed out the group of villagers milling around and digging. Broe went back to his bunker and got out his issued sniper rifle, an M40 Remington 700 with 3 × 9 power scope. He brought it up next to Diaz and spied on the villagers.[6] He asked Diaz if he could shoot the suspects. Diaz said no because he did not know what the Vietnamese were doing.[7] Broe said they should not be there. A recent graduate of the scout-sniper school, he was anxious to use his new rifle. At the school, each sniper's rifle is fitted to the specific Marine for eye relief and zeroing. All the Marines on the hill knew the Vietnamese were not allowed that close to the hill for security reasons. Further, the trail coming up to the saddle where the LZ was located was also a restricted area. The OP had a restricted area, its haven, around it that was a box on the map nobody was allowed inside of without permission from the hill.[8] It was the responsibility of the hill commander (Lee) and was there for security reasons.

The Integrated Observation Device (IOD) team's mission was outside the Recon haven as their mission was looking for targets in multiple free-fire zones, with special emphasis on Go Noi Island, some fourteen hundred meters north of the hill.[9] The IOD team had taken a cursory look at the villagers below the hill and moved on to observe, hopefully, bigger and better targets out on the island. The IOD team did not perceive the villagers as a threat and, besides, Sergeant Diaz was watching them, and it was in his haven.[10]

About this time, Lee noticed a group of his Marines looking down the north slope, so he walked over and climbed the stairs of the platform to take a look for himself. Broe had taken an M49 monocular spotting scope up to the tower. The M49 was a scope normally used by an assistant sniper to call shots or corrections for a sniper. Lee looked through the M49 and saw four Vietnamese near the bamboo hedge line in an area where they were not allowed. He knew they should not be there. So the question was, what to do about it? Could they be Viet Cong (VC) observing the hill? Could they be VC setting up a punji pit or a booby trap beside the trail? They could just be villagers harvesting bamboo. But why the digging? Lee could not figure out why they were digging in the crater which was now a hole next to the trail. Could it be a fighting position or the start of a protective bunker next to the trail? One person was cutting bamboo, one person was sitting with their legs in the hole and digging. Two people were walking around close to the others. No weapons were observed, so a direct engagement was not the appropriate approach, but neither could they stay there. Lee was on top step of the tower platform. He walked down the stairs to the .50-cal pit and asked Diaz if he wanted to work out the .50-cal on what he saw. Diaz said, "Sir, let's observe them for a while."[11] They watched the Vietnamese walk on the trail to the mortar hole, as one was digging, the others watched and then disappeared back into the tree line behind the digger. Lee asked Broe if he had ammo. Broe said it was in the bunker, so Lee told him to go get it.[12] Diaz said the villagers weren't threatening the hill. Lee agreed but said that they were in a prohibited restricted area and could be observing the hill. Broe came back with ammo and the bolt for the sniper rifle. Daniel Broe was a sniper. He wanted to shoot.[13] Lee asked for the rifle and ammunition. Broe inserted the bolt and gave him the rifle along with five rounds from the match box. Lee then told Broe to spot for him with the M49.[14] Lee walked back up the steps to the platform and placed the rifle on the platform wall for stability. He was now standing in the off-hand position on the third step with the sniper rifle. Lee told 1st Lieutenant P. R. Green, the officer in charge of the IOD team, "Green, I'm going to fire a warning shot to move the villagers."[15] Green was starting his fifth day as an IOD forward observer.

Lee then took the first shot. Broe, looking through the M49, called it out loud just like he would do at the rifle range: "Fifteen feet to the right and twenty feet short.[16] Green complained to Lee about the noise the rifle made. He was interrupting the platform's work. He was directly implying Lee should leave the platform. After the first shot, two of the Vietnamese who had not been working moved down the trail towards the Tho Son hamlet about one hundred feet, then one stopped and the other continued towards the hamlet. The Vietnamese man cutting bamboo came out of the hedge line. Lee now moved off the platform steps, per Green's request, to the ground halfway between the tower to the .50-cal pit and sat down. He ejected one round and loaded a second. Assuming a sitting position, elbows on his knees, rifle in his shoulder, he looked through the scope. Broe had moved to the platform and placed the scope on the wall to observe. Diaz, with the 7 × 50 binos, remained sitting on the bunker. Now most of the hill Marines, having heard the first shot, had moved over to the north side to watch. Lee pulled the trigger and fired the second shot.[17] He had moved his aim point toward the man in the bamboo. Again Broe called the shot, "Short ten and to the right twenty."[18] This was a difficult shot at a long distance. All Vietnamese had stopped, not moving, and were looking at the hill. Lee's goal with warning shots was to move the Vietnamese back towards Tho Son hamlet, away from the hill, and out of the restricted area. Lee pulled the bolt back, ejected the second round and loaded a third. One of the women on the trail reversed direction and had walked back toward the mortar-crater hole. The woman sitting in the hole was now waving her conical straw hat and yelling at the hill.[19] Lee sighted in again and squeezed off the third warning shot.[20] The woman who had returned was standing next to the hole with her back to the hill. She was talking with the now clearly visible one-armed elder woman from Tho Son who had been the one digging. As the shot was fired the standing woman moved and turned to face the hill. She moved towards the hill and into the fired round. Broe, spotting, called out, "You hit her!" "Where did I hit her?" Broe replied, "On the chest or shoulder, I saw red blood on the white shirt." Lee said, "Let's hope for her sake it's the shoulder."[21] The woman collapsed next to the hole.

In the bunker below the IOD tower, Lance Corporal Howard Miller of Headquarters Battery, 11th Marines, was busy playing monopoly with MacDonald and Callahan when Steel came running into the bunker. He said, "There has been a shooting."[22]

On the trail below, the woman furthest away from the fallen victim ran back to Tho Son. The man came out of the bamboo hedge line and, with the old woman, rolled the wounded woman over. After 15 minutes, four Vietnamese came up the trail from the hamlet carrying white and orange parachute silk. With two of the previously cut bamboo poles, they fashioned a stretcher and carried the woman toward Tho Son. Sergeant Diaz was watching and now referred to this as "The Ambulance."[23] The Marines on the hill watched as they carried her through the hamlet and east on Route 537 toward Chien Son (4) village and presumed help. They stopped halfway to the railroad bridge. After a short while they reversed course, and The Ambulance group of six or seven Vietnamese carried the stretcher back up the main trail towards the OP. The one-armed woman was carrying a South Vietnamese flag which was the signal requesting a meeting established by Lieutenant Parks. The normal meeting spot was at the bottom of the hill.[24] This was the signal they wanted to talk to the Marines. Lee told Corporal Gene McCommons to get together a security detail of four Marines, and the ARVN (Army of the Republic of Vietnam) Warrant Officer Thien to serve as an interpreter.[25] Lee and the detail moved out through the wire and down the hill to meet the delegation from the hamlet. The elderly one-armed woman and an elderly man led the delegation. They had brought the parachute make-do stretcher with the wounded woman to the meeting place. Lee sent a runner to get Doc Edison to join them.

When the corpsman arrived, he knelt down next to the stretcher on the ground, unfolded the parachute covering the woman, and turned her over, exposing a wound to her left chest. He examined her, checking for a pulse and checking the wound. Her eyes were cloudy. Standing up, he shook his head and walked away to continue tending to the young girl near the LZ. The woman was dead. Later, he said she appeared to have been dead for about a half hour.

Lee put security out while they talked to the delegation. He explained through the ARVN interpreter that the villagers had been in a restricted area and that the one-armed woman elder, and all the villagers of Tho Son hamlet, knew where the area was. He explained that the shot was meant as a warning shot to warn the villagers away, that it had been an accident. He expressed regret.[26] The village elders said the shot woman was pregnant, and that her husband had been killed two months prior, that she left two babies to feed. The elders wanted food to feed the babies as reparations for the life of the mother. The elderly one-armed woman was repeatedly demanding reparations for the dead woman. The delegation also demanded a shroud for the burial.[27] Lee sent word back up the hill to get two cases of C-rations and a full rain suit. Sergeant Diaz went to the platform and got a new gray two-piece rain suit, and told two Marines to each get a new case of C's and join him. They brought the two cases of rations, one case per child, and the rain suit to Lee who handed them to the elderly man saying these were the food reparations and the rain suit was a burial shroud, as interpreted by Warrant Officer Thien.[28] The villagers left with the body and moved back down the trail. They stopped outside Tho Son, just off the trail, and started digging a grave.

Sergeant Broadman and the IOD team took turns watching the woman being buried over the next two hours, northeast of the hill. She was not buried in a cemetery, which was the custom but, oddly, in a potter's grave just off the trail. The villagers used the new rain suit to serve as a shroud for the burial. The curious IOD team watched the burial on the "Big Eyes" and marked the grid of the grave.[29]

Pulling in security, and moving back up the hill, Lee walked with Diaz, telling him he assumed full responsibility for the shooting and would file a spot report on the incident when they got back. He also told Diaz to gather the Marines in the mortar pit and he would talk to them.[30] Upon arrival at the hill, Lee walked over towards the IOD platform; Green came down the steps and met him. Green was nervous, worried, and said, "You should not have done that!" In response, Lee told him he was responsible for security of the OP and that he assumed full responsibility for the woman's death.[31] He added he was going to file a spot report to the battalion. He told Green he need not fret, the incident was on him, and he accepted that totally. Green returned to the tower and filed his own radio report,[32] as did the ARVN forward observer to the 44th ARVN Artillery Battalion.[33] Lee went to the command/radio bunker to compile the spot report. He finished it and gave it to the operator, telling him to call it in to the battalion on the secure network. The report was received and recorded at the 1st Recon's Combat Operation Center, and it read:

> 281110Hr. VIC. AT984510 Team sighted 4 suspected VC/NVA wearing black PJ (bottoms) and white tops, hiding in tree line inside Team's haven. Team fired 3 warning shots and then 1 round struck suspects resulting in 1 probable KIA and 1 known WIA.[34] [Author's note, the known WIA and probable KIA were the same person.]

Lee then went to the mortar pit where the Recon Marines were gathering to address them.[35] The IOD team and ARVNs remained in the tower. They were upset and worried. Talking with his Marines, Lee told them it was a shame the Vietnamese woman had been killed. He said he had been firing warning shots to move the Vietnamese out of the restricted area and back to the hamlet, that there had been four Vietnamese in the tree line, cutting bamboo and digging next to the trail. He had been trying to warn them away from the tree line and the hill. He told the Marines he assumed full responsibility, it was solely on him, and that he did not regret the actions.[36] He then asked if any of them had questions or comments. Nobody did. Lee closed by saying if any of them wanted to talk about it, they could come by his bunker.[37] The Marines dispersed to their bunkers. None of them came by Lee's bunker to discuss the shooting. The Recon Marines understood the security challenges of the hill.

The Artillery Marines were concerned the woman's killing would blow back on them. The ARVN warrant officer was terribly upset.[38] He may have been playing both sides. He covered himself with a radio report of the shooting to his parent command, putting the killing of the woman solely on Lee. Hill life moved on.

At 1700, Green in the IOD tower sighted four NVA (North Vietnamese Army), wearing green utilities and carrying packs and rifles, moving from the west to east on a high-speed trail out on Goi Noi Island, 4½ kilometers to the north of the OP. *Hansworth* called an artillery fire mission from the 105 battery at An Hoa Combat Base. They called for and received an immediate fire-for-effect, battery three, which meant eighteen 105 rounds. They had excellent coverage of the target area and claimed two kills.[39]

Later that evening, Lee made the rounds, as was his evening habit, checking the bunkers, and stopped at the .50-cal pit where Sergeant Diaz was sitting. The experienced platoon sergeant was unusually quiet. Lee offered Diaz a cigarette and a light while he lit up himself. Quietly smoking and watching the sun recede, Lee asked Diaz what he thought. Diaz asked, "You mean about the woman?" "Yes." Diaz offered that he did not think it was necessary to shoot the woman.[40] There was no more conversation. When finished with the cigarette, Lee moved on to check the Marines sitting on top of Alpha Bunker. The two men never talked to each other about the incident again.

The hill was quiet the next day with the normal routine. On 30 March, at sundown, Green and his team called two fire missions east of the hill on the infiltration route along the railroad tracks, resulting in seven NVA claimed killed.[41] On the 31st, the sunrise was bright and clear off the East China Sea. Excellent observation conditions for the classified IOD that was having its cumulative effects on the NVA moving on and off their rice basket, Go Noi Island. Around noon, throughout the afternoon, and into the evening, Team *Hansworth* observed groups of NVA moving. During the afternoon, they called four fire missions claiming two kills. At 2045, Green called a fire mission just below the hill on what he called a cooking fire in Tho Son hamlet, 1,100 meters north. He reported excellent cover of the fire mission with the cooking fire extinguished.[42] Green's rules of engagement, allowing artillery fire in a free-fire zone, is what let him shoot the mission, but he had no idea who was sitting around the dinner cooking fire: VC, or Vietnamese villagers, or both?

Lieutenant Lee spent the afternoon preparing for the next day's flip with 2nd Platoon and Lieutenant Garry Parks. Lee had appreciated the heat map, so he updated it. He had Corporal Grossman take a full ammo inventory and put the results in the turnover logbook. Earlier, he had told Diaz that today there would be a major police call of the hill in prep for a clean hill flip. April 1, 1970, was another good weather day. They expected a midday flip and had staged all the gear they were taking off the hill on the saddle of the outer LZ. When it came, it came fast. The lead bird called at 1245 and said it would be a hot flip, blades turning, and the birds would remain as both platoons exchanged. Lee told Diaz to stage the entire platoon behind the water buffalo and form two helo sticks. Diaz would lead the first one on and Lee would be last man on the second bird. As the first bird landed, with Parks knowing it was a hot flip, he was the first man off. Lee waved him over, handed off the logbook and heat map and waited for the first bird to lift off. Yelling in Parks's ear, he told him he would need water resupply in a week and, although he had ordered it, the hill's mortar ammo, both 60-mm and 81-mm, was critically low on illumination rounds. The two lieutenants shook hands as the second CH-46 made its level approach to the saddle LZ. They could no longer hear each other, and the dust was at eye level, so Lee slapped Parks on the back and joined his stick of Marines to run onto the ramp of the turning bird. Hill 119 now belonged to 2nd Platoon and Parks. He had been here before.

CHAPTER 23

Prisoner Snatch, Emergency Extracts, *Bright Light* Mission, April 1970

President Nixon announced on 20 April the withdrawal of 150,000 troops from Vietnam as another step in turning the war over to the South Vietnamese.[1] Ten days later, he reversed that decision and announced the troop strength would not decrease and that the war would expand into Cambodia.[2]

***

On 18 April, the commanding general's helicopter crashed due to a mechanical issue. Major General E. B. Wheeler, the old raider, had not been taken out by the enemy but by fate. He had a compound fracture of his leg and was medevac'd to the Hospital Ship *Sanctuary* (AH-17) in Da Nang Harbor.[3] He refused to give up command, insisting he could return and command from the bunker command center on Hill 327 with a full leg cast. Despite his protestations, another raider, Major General Charles F. Widdecke, was flown out from Headquarters Marine Corps and, a week later, the change of command took place on 27 April.[4] Wheeler would be medevac'd to the States for his recovery and physical therapy. Widdecke was a Carlson's Raider as a lieutenant and was awarded a Silver Star for his actions on Eniwetok Atoll. Promoted to captain, and joining the retaking of Guam in 1944 as a company commander, he was awarded the Navy Cross while being wounded taking a ridgeline objective over a landing beach. In Korea, he commanded the 2nd Battalion, 1st Marines, before the armistice in 1954. His first tour of duty in Vietnam was as the commander of the 5th Marines landing in Da Nang with his regiment in 1966.[5]

At Camp Reasoner in April, Lieutenant Colonel Drumright was fully in command. The pace accelerated with the number of patrols in the field now continually exceeding 42. The 3rd Force Recon Company, with a reduced strength, was now attached to 1st Recon and had assumed the training mission for ARVN (Army of the Republic of Vietnam) and South Korean Marine Reconnaissance units.[6]

First Lieutenant Charlie Kershaw was moved from commanding officer of Alpha Company over to Headquarters and Service Company as S-3 (operations) training/SCUBA officer.[7] Kershaw was now officially a short-timer. With the "Vietnamization" drawdown, the battalion was assuming a more-robust SCUBA program conducting bridge checks on Route 1 and I Corps' bridges. That, along with water recoveries, had become a full-time daily mission. First Lieutenant R. L. "Bullet-Bob" Campbell assumed command of Alpha Company.[8] He had impressed Drumright. While "Jerry" Spolter continued to command Delta Company, Porter Rathmell completed training the Marines of Recon Indoctrination Program (RIP) 03-70 and, with his cadre, kicked off RIP 4-70 on 8 April. Additionally, Pre-SCUBA 03-70 also kicked off.[9]

The First Recon Staff Noncommissioned Officers/Officers Club on Camp Reasoner hosted a Philippine rock-and-roll band. Lieutenant Spolter, a rock-and-roll fan and guitar player, went to the club to watch the performance. The real performance that night was the battalion commander. He was a racist who verbally abused Orientals when drunk. This had begun with his hatred of the Chinese during the Korean War. Sitting at Drumright's front table with him was the six feet six Lieutenant John Huff, the Echo Company patrol leader, who had just finished another successful patrol. Drumright borrowed John's survival knife and threw it at the lead female singer, missing her but impacting and splitting the base drum behind her.[10] Spolter told himself he needed to escape Camp Reasoner and this insanity. He took the next Delta Company frag order from S-3 for himself. He would go to the field.[11]

On 23 April, Lieutenant General H. W. Buse, the commanding general of Fleet Marine Force, Pacific, along with his chief of staff, Brigadier General K. J. Houghton, visited the battalion and received an operational briefing and then a demonstration on reconnaissance capabilities by members of the ARVN RIP 02-70.[12] Houghton was pleased to see his former Recon mate from the Korean War leading the 1st Reconnaissance Battalion. On the last day of the month, Lieutenant Colonel W. G. Leftwich, the new commanding officer of 2nd Battalion, 1st Marines, visited Camp Reasoner for a capabilities and current ops brief.[13]

At the company level, on 1 April, 2nd Lieutenant Gump May checked into the battalion from the grunts, having served as a platoon commander for seven months with Bravo Company, 1st Battalion, 1st Marines. He had been working in the Hill 55 area, and south down Liberty Road in the Arizona Territory to An Hoa.[14] Despite his The Basic School (TBS) 5-69 Echo Company classmate and buddy, W. X. Lee, trying to get him assigned to Delta Company, Gump was assigned to Alpha Company. Charlie Kershaw showed him around the battalion and helped him get checked in.[15] Gump had been a college athlete and later a football coach at University of Virginia for another Recon lieutenant, "Pete" Gray. Because of his athletic experience, or because he was the new guy, he got the task to organize the 1st Recon Battalion track and field team for a III Marine Amphibious Force-wide Intermural Track Meet in April.[16] He pulled together Marines for the field meet held at Da Nang International Airport's track. Finally getting to the field, for his first patrol, callsign *Pickwick Papers*, Gump joined 1st Lieutenant J. K. Murphy and birddogged him.[17]

April 1 ended with Team *Delicatessen* being led by Staff Sergeant Mushett whose point man, Corporal Mills, hit a booby trap near the summit of Hill 726. With three wounded—Mills, radio operator Ravelo, and Mushett himself—the patrol was emergency extracted. They had been on the ground for two hours and 15 minutes. The extract was a superb bit of flying as the CH-46 pilot landed his back two wheels on a bomb crater lip for a tailgate extract while hovering the nose of the aircraft.[18]

On 3 and 4 April, Lieutenant Porter Rathmell and Gunnery Sergeant Moore took the entire RIP cadre, and class of 21 Marines and a corpsman, Hospitalman West, for a night river-crossing support mission. They were inserted by helo within the 3rd Battalion, 5th Marine's lines in order to set up rope safety lines and tow lines using seven IBS (Inflatable Boat Small) boats to ferry a company sized force of 110 infantry for a night river crossing. During the crossing, one Marine fell in the swift running river; Moore went in after him and pulled the drowning, unconscious Marine ashore. He was medevac'd.[19]

***

On 3 April, after a day off and returning from Hill 119, Lee was inserted at 0810 with Team *Pal Joey*.[20] This was Corporal Holmes's team along with "Doc" Edison. Private First Class Paul Freeman would walk point. Freeman quit Bethel High School in Spanaway, Washington, early in 1969 and joined the Marines. Finishing boot camp and Infantry Training Regiment on the west coast, he went to Recon school at Camp Horno, receiving a 0321 Recon Marine MOS (military occupation specialty) upon graduation. He found himself in Vietnam in October 1969.[21] After walking point all day, Freeman found a high-speed trail late in the afternoon. A Chi-com grenade was on the trail, which they avoided. The team moved away from the trail and harbored up for the night. The next day, instead of trail walking, Lee had the team move parallel to it and follow it. They did this for two days. That night in the harbor site they heard movement close to them of 2–4 enemy who then moved away. The morning of the 5th, they moved to the trail and found fresh footprints and a communications wire running along the trail. It was old U.S. black wire, which they followed[22] for three hours, eventually finding a base camp or waystation. At noon, they observed five wooden-framed hooches spread along the side of the trail. All five had underground bunkers reinforced by logs. The hooches had bamboo floors raised six inches off the ground and thatched roofs and sides. Each had a cooking stove vented to the outside. There was one trench above them 100 meters long, five-feet deep and three-feet wide for defense. Water was 50 meters below the string of huts and was a clear, fast-running stream one foot deep. The camp was empty. *Pal Joey* moved south on the trail for 30 minutes, finding another hooch.[23] They pulled off-trail and formed a 360-degree defense. There was one soldier on the front porch working on a pot. Lee planned a prisoner snatch, assigning jobs of security; the snatch would be himself and Lance Corporal Kempe, his Minnesota wilderness man.

The team got up and moved to within three meters of the enemy when he saw them, Lee said "Dung Lai" in Vietnamese, meaning halt. The soldier defecated on himself as Kempe punched him hard in the face and picked him up under his arm.[24] Freeman searched the hooch and found three AK-47s and a model EO754 field telephone.[25] Lee cut the wire and grabbed the phone. The hut had two cots, one chair, and was clean and well kept. The floor was inlaid with bamboo while the front porch was plywood, a foot off the ground. The hut also had a below-ground bunker with an open entrance six by four feet. In the rear, a cooking shed with stove had three 25-pound bags of rice, and four pots. On a clothesline they found a North Vietnamese Army (NVA) officers' belt with silver buckle and red star.[26] The team exited away from the camp to move to an extract landing zone (LZ). Turning around, they saw, further off the trail, another house with a plywood sides ten meters away. It had windows four feet off the ground and a trail back to the main path lined with bamboo to walk on. Looking to the south, *Pal Joey* saw three more hooches on the main trail which appeared heavily used. The team moved for the next hour, cross-country, with the gagged and blindfolded prisoner being carried by Kempe over his shoulders like a sack of potatoes to the extract LZ.[27] They arrived at 1400. They called their radio relay *Vesper Bells-Alpha* and requested an immediate ladder extract since they had a prisoner and only a thirty-by-thirty-foot opening in the jungle. The double canopy was 60 feet high. The team waited. Then they heard the extract bird before they saw it. Lee had his signal mirror out and flashed the lead gunship as it flew over the jungle opening. The transport birds circled back and dropped the ladder. When it hit the ground, Kempe tied the prisoner on and got on with him on the same rung, snapping his snap-link in. As the ladder rose, the rest of the team got on by twos: Wiley and Doc Edison; Patrick and Holmes; and Freeman and Lee, now with the radio on his back, who were the last two on the bottom rung. The bird continued to lift. The team hit trees coming up, fending the branches off with both legs and arms. Then they were out and airborne. The ladder drifted back behind and under the bird and the air was cool and refreshing. The ladder extract took place at 1710 and took *Pal Joey* and their prisoner to Thuong Duc special forces camp's short-landing strip. There, they got off the ladder and moved to the cabin for the long flight back to LZ 20 to drop off the prisoner. They then flew on to Camp Reasoner. Upon landing, the entire *Pal Joey* team climbed the hill to S-2 (intelligence) for the debrief. They had been in the bush for 57 hours when Captain Cook started his detailed debrief.[28] Cook later relayed to the team that the prisoner had been a lieutenant in the 8th Battalion of the 38th NVA Regiment. The reason he did not want to go out of the LZ was because he was afraid to fly over the large base camp and be shot down.[29] The comm wire that Lee cut led in the direction, the prisoner stated in his interrogation, of the large base camp.

Lee slept well that night after a cold shower. The next morning, 6 April, he wrote Bronze Star recommendations for his point man, Private First Class Paul Freeman, and his prisoner-grabbing mountain man, Lance Corporal Kempe.[30]

***

On 8 April, Lieutenant Chris L'Orange, the 4th Platoon commander, took his team, *Prime Cut*, west into double-canopy jungle.[31] This was Corporal Wiley's team. Along with four Marines, they had a new twist. They had two ARVN sergeants, who had just graduated from the ARVN RIP class, join the patrol for a total of eight pax. The insert went well, and they were patrolling by 1330. The terrain was difficult with steep boulders filled with draws. Many tangled "wait-a-minute" vines came out as they patrolled for two days, averaging 150 meters an hour while moving cross-compartment. On the morning of the second day, they found a well-used trail. Following it led to a hooch. While checking out the hut, they observed two NVA in green utilities carrying AK-47s coming up the trail.[32] *Prime Cut* engaged the enemy with small arms at close distance, killing the first, while the second escaped back down the trail at a dead run. Searching the body, they found a small notebook. They noted both soldiers were young, with clean uniforms and fresh haircuts, high and tight. Moving the body off the trail, keeping the notebook and AK-47, the team moved on down the trail leery of a potential ambush ahead. Thirty minutes later, they walked into an empty base camp. The cooking fires indicated they had been recently used. There were nine large, two-story hooches very well constructed and camouflaged from above in the double canopy. Each hut had an underground bunker reinforced with logs and a log door on hinges. Each structure was capable of sleeping 15–20 soldiers. On the sidehill above the huts was a training area with a triple-concertina wire fence running for 20 meters and woven ropes and pads used to get under and over the wire during training exercises. Each of the huts had left-over gear but it was clear no one was currently living there. After sketching a diagram of the base camp, L'Orange got the team moving, continuing south on the trail.[33] After another hour of cautious movement of approximately one hundred meters, they found another camp of seven hooches. These huts were built with cut three-inch logs. They were above ground, and each had an underground bunker. These huts appeared, from the log cuttings, to have been built in the past three months. The camp appeared to have been used within the past week or so. One hut was a dedicated kitchen with four cooking holes. There was a new set of bamboo steps leading up to an officer hut. Again, all the huts had left-over pieces of gear, uniforms, and spent shell casings. *Prime Cut* sketched the area and moved out.[34] The team moved off-trail and found a harbor site for the evening.

At 2030, they heard enemy movement east and north of their site. L'Orange called in an artillery mission and walked it closer with good defensive coverage. Shortly after the fire mission, an OV-10 came on station to support the team. The *Hostage* aircraft ran organic ordnance with good coverage on the next ridgeline. He departed station and the jungle went quiet and dark for two hours. At 2200, the team was awakened, receiving incoming direct fire, thought to be a recoilless rifle (RR) from the opposite ridgeline. The round impacted 50 meters east of the team. Another Recon team, *Pal Joey,* observed the back blast. At 2300, a second *Hostage* aircraft arrived along with a *Basketball* flare ship. They lit up the night and the OV-10 ran strafing, and rocket runs with its own ordnance for an hour. At midnight, it was all quiet. At 0200, L'Orange had the team up and moved. He knew the NVA would be coming for them in the morning. He moved the team west as the enemy had been to their east and north. He found a break in the jungle where he could see the stars. Fixing the jungle hole's grid coordinates, he called in his extract LZ, requesting an emergency ladder extract for early in the morning. *Prime Cut* set up a 360 defense at the ladder-sized extract site and waited for sunrise. They could now hear the enemy following them and moving to their south about one hundred fifty meters away, trying to cut them off. From 0300 to 0430 the team received three incoming RR rounds; the enemy was probing for them. The team was hugging the ground. L'Orange estimated the size of the RR to be comparable to a 106-mm shot. The rounds did not succeed in flushing *Prime Cut* from the thicket next to the small jungle opening. The RR squad on the opposite finger moved on in its search. The team stayed waiting, frozen in place. The sun rose and jungle life returned. At 0800, *Pal Joey* their radio relay called, said they were first, and to be prepared for a ladder extract. At 0820, the air package arrived with two Cobra gunships from *Scarface* and two CH-46s. L'Orange flashed the lead gunship with a mirror and, on the radio cue from the CH-46, Private First Class Hill popped green smoke. The 125-foot aluminum ladder came unrolling off the tail ramp as the bird hovered at 100 feet and started taking small-arms fire. The green tracer fire was directed at the aircraft. By the twos, *Prime Cut* climbed the ladder and snapped in. Last on was L'Orange, calling on the radio for lift off. As the bird lifted, the team engaged by firing from the ladder and throwing hand grenades as the enemy was now pouring heavy small-arms fire at the helicopter. All L'Orange could think of was the RR. They must have fired all their ammo at the team last night, as one round hitting the helo would spell their demise. *Prime Cut* rode the ladder to An Hoa and switched to inside the bird as it refueled. They were back at LZ 401 by 0930 with the entire team being debriefed by Gunnery Sergeant Ottinger in the S-2 shop.[35]

After L'Orange's extract, Lieutenant Lee and his team walked onto the same birds at LZ 401 for his insert on 11 April. He had Team *Terrapin* with Lance Corporals Grossman, Morey, McGowen, Packard, and the new Private First Class Wester. Their direct-support artillery battery would be *Ringbroom-Mike* out of An Hoa Combat Base.[36] Patrolling the Charlie Ridge area, communication was only available in the high ground. They patrolled difficult terrain for five days with no enemy sightings, only finding trails with bamboo-cut foot bridges placed over streams. *Terrapin* was extracted on 16 April at 1030[37] and was back in their Delta Company hooches by 1100, just in time for lunch in Gunnery Sergeant Paradise's mess hall.

***

On 12 April, the battalion had received a *Bright Light* mission. The mission was for a quick-reaction team to recover a downed pilot's body. First Lieutenant Charlie Kershaw was assigned the mission. Porter Rathmell approached both Lieutenant Colonel Drumright and Charlie in the S-3 (operations) bunker and said, "Charlie is short, let me take the mission." Drumright said, "Fine, but, Kershaw, you go as the insert/extract officer."[38] Both lieutenants suited up along with the training cadre to run the body recovery. After the crash site was located, the insert into a close LZ commenced, but the bird was shot out of the zone from a distant ridgeline. Circling back around, the *Bright Light* team decided to rappel directly onto the crash site, hoping to be ahead of the NVA. The bird went into the hover. Rathmell was the lead Marine out of the CH-46 hellhole into the dark canopy hole. He was on the ground by himself when the world opened up with small-arms fire from both ridge lines. The helo pilot wanted out, but the *Bright Light* team said not without Rathmell. The decision was made to pull Rathmell out by jungle penetrator as there was no close LZ. The bird lowered the jungle penetrator and Rathmell got on. The bird began pulling Rathmell up through the trees. He had cleared the 100-foot canopy of trees, and the winch had pulled him to the belly of the aircraft and hellhole, all the while, the aircraft is gaining altitude to escape the small-arms fire. Rathmell handed his M16 to Gunnery Sergeant Moore to use two hands to pull himself up and through the hellhole. It was then that the jungle penetrator snapped and Rathmell fell hundreds of feet back into the canopy.[39] He was met by small-arms fire and grenades when he hit the ground, fatally wounded. Kershaw and Moore had a 75-foot aluminum ladder on the tail ramp. It was too short in the 100-foot canopy to reach the ground. The helo package, low on fuel, departed and flew back to An Hoa for more gas and where the 75-foot ladder was traded out for the 125 footer. Returning to the crash site, they rappelled in as that was the fastest way to the ground. Kershaw, Moore, Hare and another Marine recovered Rathmell's body, placed it in a body bag, and waited for the 125-foot ladder. When it dropped, they got on with the body bag and snapped in for the ride back to An Hoa.[40] Porter died on that mission attempting to recover a pilot, whose body was not recovered in the end. First Lieutenant Earl Hailston, who knew Rathmell from their TBS Class (Echo Company 5-69), requested to be the body escort back to Pennsylvania.[41] Drumright denied the request, wanting to keep the productive patrol leader in the field. Hailston, a friend of the family, would write a difficult letter to Porter's father, John Rathmell, living in Williamsport, Pennsylvania. John was a World War II Marine officer who participated in the island campaign on Guadalcanal, New Guinea, Peleliu, and Okinawa. He resigned from the Corps after the war to run a successful business. The Rathmell name was carried forward by Porter's younger sister, Ann, who also became a Marine officer, following in her father's and brother's footsteps, and retired as a colonel.[42]

After patrol, Team *Dublin City* on LZ 401. Standing, left to right: Rowley, Woodhurst, Powell, Fallon. Kneeling, left to right: Thompson, Doc Schwartz, McLeese. April 1970. (M. Schwartz)

April 11 and 12 were busy days for Delta Company. On the 11th, two platoons had flipped on and off Hill 119 with Lieutenant Paul Eglevsky[43] replacing Lieutenant Garry Parks.[44] L'Orange's Team *Prime Cut* had returned by ladder while Lee's Team *Terrapin* had been inserted.[45] On 12 April, both Spolter and Fallon were inserted.[46]

Delta Company, with six officers, had four in the field with two just returned. Fallon was back in the bush with Team *Dublin City* from 2nd Platoon. Sergeant Rowley was the team leader and "Doc" Eric Schwartz the corpsman. They waited all day at An Hoa. The insert came late at 1600.[47] They were at the very edge of the artillery range fan. Fallon had marked on his map where the fan ended. He could still call fire missions further out but would lose accuracy. The next afternoon, *Dublin City* occupied a covered clandestine observation point (OP) overlooking Antenna Valley west of the Que Son Mountains. Antenna Valley was total Indian County. The valley belonged to the NVA. It was a rice basket, as well as the major infiltration route between the Thuong Duc corridor to the Que Son Mountains and enemy Base Area 116. At 1630, they observed five enemy in black "PJs" working with hoes in the rice paddies below. Fallon called *Ringbroom-Mike* and got an immediate fire mission. With the first adjustment round the enemy ran into the tree line and disappeared underground. The team fired one fire-for-effect but could not report any observed results. At 1705, they observed two enemy enter two stone huts at the side of a field. They called a fire mission, with negative results, as the huts were stone and, without a direct hit, the shrapnel bounced off. The next morning, at first light, 20 soldiers moved from the jungle's edge into the rice paddies, covering the two grid squares below. They wore mixed green utilities and black PJs. They worked each paddy in groups of two. *Dublin City* tried another fire mission on two thatched huts on the side of the field.[48] They got excellent coverage, destroying one hut and partially destroying the second. They had been in the clandestine OP for over twenty-four hours. Fallon got the team up and moved. They moved inside the tree line above the valley floor for a kilometer and found another clandestine OP with good fields of view south across the valley, immediately picking up a water buffalo herd mixed with cattle. One Vietnamese was tending the entire herd. Observing and counting, the Marines recorded 16 water buffalo and six cattle grazing.[49] This was enough beasts of burden to till the entire Antenna Valley floor. Fallon called a fire mission and was getting good coverage as the animals started to disperse when he received a ceasefire due to a higher-priority mission the battery had to support. The herd was rounded up and moved into a draw to the northeast of the valley and eventually moved out of sight. The next day was *Dublin City*'s extract day. Fallon moved the team close to the paddies and used a dry paddy on the valley's edge for their extract. They were extracted at 1500 on 15 April. During the debrief at S-2, the debriefer informed the team it was production season and the NVA were putting in the next rice crop. Fallon said he believed there was a base camp or large farm up the identified draw for the water buffalo and cattle. It should be a target as, without the buffalo, the NVA would be hard pressed to till the soil of Antenna Valley. He also noted to the debriefer that there were absolutely no women or children in the valley. It was devoid of anyone except the NVA workers.[50]

Spolter went out with Team *Fig Newton* again, with Corporal "Big I" Iantorno and "Doc" Mullins. They departed on 12 April.[51] The team patrolled along a riverbed for three kilometers over three days, monitoring from the tree line parallel to the river. They observed numerous footprints on the trails on both sides of the creek and trails branching off. They saw no enemy until the 14th when they observed one NVA crossing the river on a sandbar, heading away from them. They waited, hoping to see if he was part of a larger group. He had been alone. *Fig Newton* was extracted on 15 April as someone in the rear needed to talk with the company commander on a pressing matter.[52] The team did not mind the short patrol. Spolter was back, freeing Fallon, the titular executive officer of Delta, to go back out on patrol.

He grabbed the next frag order from S-3 and told Big I to take a day off because he would be taking *Fig Newton* out on 17 April.[53] Doc Mullins would take a break too. Fallon took Lance Corporal "Doggie" McBride, a trained First-Aid Marine, to carry the Unit One. "Gungy" Private First Class Mike Thornes would be joining the team. They were going out large, with an eight-man patrol, far west, well outside the artillery fan, two map sheets west of Thuong Duc Special Forces Camp, or forty kilometers away. *Vesper Bells-Alpha* on Ba Na would be their radio relay. They were inserted into a poor one-bird LZ, a sandbar on the side of the Song Cai. There was high ground on all sides. *Fig Newton* moved out of the open riverbed and quickly into the jungle, then stopped to listen and regain their senses. It was 0835 when they moved away from the insert LZ. They waited 30 minutes and then moved up river to the west inside the tree line. At 1000, they observed a cement bridge across the river. The bridge was constructed around six 'I' beams of steel that were 25 feet long and one foot thick.[54] The team observed the bridge and then moved to the road connecting to it. It was overgrown and not being used. Upstream from the bridge, the fields had been burned off as one would prepare to till the soil and plant. There were seven fields being prepared. There was a small lean-to next to each field. The fields were 50 × 50 meters each next to the river. Continuing west, the team observed a second cement bridge 15 feet wide and 10 across over a major tributary of the river. Moving west another 30 minutes, they found four old hooches with underground bunkers. Behind the last one was a new bunker being dug, the shovel stuck in fresh dirt. The team broke for midday rest and hydration in the shade and observed.

After an hour, Fallon got *Fig Newton* up and moved west parallel to the river in the tree line above the river. In the midafternoon, they heard animals and then spotted a farm. Moving to a better position, they began observing what was a working farm. The farm had two hooches, a barn, one pig pen, one chicken coop, four water buffalo pens, a drying rack for harvest, clotheslines with clothing hung to dry, plus a large outside table and one bunker.[55] The team observed for an hour with no sighting of people, only two large pigs and 10–15 free-range chickens running loose. The team moved into the farm area and started searching the first hooch, at which time they heard voices some distance away. The first hooch was 25' × 10' × 15', with a small attic used to dry harvest. There were at least ten corn fields between the farm next to the jungle and the river. The corn had been harvested and stored and the cornstalks burned. Inside the hooch, the team found clean, folded uniforms, green utilities and khakis, plus blue sweatshirts, a fireplace, cooking pots, three 10-pound bags of rice, and at least two hundred pounds of corn. This hut was for living in. The second hooch, with an elevated floor and roof, had no sides and was used for drying crops. There was a fenced, mixed vegetable garden, 50 feet by 50 feet. Near the river, the team found wet laundry on the bank, which was where the voices had come from.[56] Feeling they had been observed, Fallon backed the team into the jungle and requested an aerial observer (AO) through the radio relay. To establish communications, they had to put up a long whip antenna. It went up six feet above the radio. It also said, "Look at me." After they transmitted, they took down the antenna. Thirty-five minutes later, *Hostage Junkman* checked in with *Fig Newton*. Fallon hit *Junkman* with a mirror flash and talked him into a visual of the farm. Using organic ordnance of rockets and machine guns, *Junkman* worked over the farm, setting it on fire. Before departing, the AO in the backseat, *Cowpoke*, told the team there was a wide, high-speed trail on the other side of the river from them. The aircraft was close to bingo fuel and said, "*Fig Newton*, good farming and hunting" as he flew east. The farm was a unique sighting. Fallon called in a short spot report on an active farm with pigs, chicken, and corn.[57] Later, he wished he had saved it for the debrief. *Fig Newton* now faded back into the jungle and moved 500 meters up and sidehill into a thicket. Fallon liked to harbor at night on the side of a hill as people tended to walk on the top and bottom of hills as it was easier on them.

The next morning, the team moved back to the river valley and continued west close to the Laotian border. Early in the afternoon, the two tail-end Marines heard a truck engine shifting gears.[58] They stopped the team, which moved into a hasty defense and listened for an hour, hearing nothing. Fallon had been forward on deuce point focused forward and thinking of a midday break. His tail-end Charlie had heard the sound across the river where the AO had reported the wide trail. Fallon pulled *Fig Newton* back into the jungle but decided to stay low and listen, and harbor low that night trying to hear the truck. They heard nothing that afternoon or evening.

The next morning, they started to hear single rifle shots in the distance. Clearly some sort of signal. They heard ten shots over two hours. Then Thornes came forward and whispered, "Sir, they are hunting game." It made a lot of sense as the NVA, or farmers for the NVA, did not expect their foe to be in their back farmyard.

At about 1030 on 19 April, they heard an aircraft fly over but could not see it through the jungle canopy. Then they heard five shots at the aircraft as it continued west. *Fig Newton* had a preplanned extract at noon on the 19th; as they were so far west, fuel was an issue for the CH-46s.

Fallon had moved the team back down to the Song Cai and found a multibird sand-and-rock sandbar just upstream from a 90-degree bend in the river. The ridgelines would be nasty if manned with antiaircraft. They heard the "womp-womp" of the blades before they saw the birds.

They were coming fast when they called *Fig Newton* on the radio; Fallon said, "Just keep coming west up the river, we hear you."

Four minutes later, there appeared the two gunships who went into dual racetracks on each side of the river as one bird remained high. Big I popped a yellow smoke when the low CH-46 was inbound. It landed on the sandbar. Fallon had waited in the tree line, not wanting to expose the team on the open sandbar before the bird landed. Now they were racing in ankle-deep water and up the ramp with Fallon last on and giving the thumbs up. The bird lifted and stayed low along the river; "Unusual," thought Fallon. Two thousand meters later, the bird circled around, returned to the extract sandbar LZ, and landed, immediately turning off its engines. The crew chief reported a power failure, and they all had to get off the bird. This time, they sprinted the other way back to the jungle and set in a 180 defense. The chase bird came in and landed behind the original bird and immediately shut down its engines. Fallon could not believe it. It also reported a mechanical failure. Two CH-46s sitting on a sandbar in the middle of a river, both shut down. What a lucrative target for every NVA mortar man within hailing distance. Fallon jogged out and talked to both pilots. The two gunships were doing figure eights, drawing attention to the riverbed. All Fallon could think of was they were going to get mortared. The two aircraft were too much of a target to pass up. Fallon told the crews to leave the birds and come inside the jungle perimeter, they could cover the birds by ground fire if they had to. Both crews came across the sandbar and into the jungle. An OV-10 arrived immediately overhead and called *Fig Newton*, saying he had fixed-wing in two minutes, but only for two minutes. It would be one pass. Where did he want the ordnance? Fallon gave the AO the coordinates for the farm three kilometers downriver and told him to look for burnt corn fields. That was the best target they had. As the fixed-wing made their run, the Marines at the landing zone could hear small-arms fire chasing the fast movers. The two Navy birds were soon outbound.

It was 1315. Fallon had ten Marines from both aircrews. All had pistols. They discussed moving a .50-caliber machine gun into the jungle. Fallon said it would be better if they could hide rather than fight. The NVA would outnumber them. When a helo goes down and, in this case, two CH-46s, the Marine Air Wing scrambles everything they have to support them. The AO now above *Fig Newton* had fixed-wing flights stacked above them. Fallon told the AO, "Everybody knows we are here, start working the ridgelines on both sides of the river. Bomb the jungle." Fallon had turned over his secondary PRC-25 radio to the senior pilot mission commander. He had been having multiple conversations with the *Hostage* pilot on the mechanical issues while the *Cowpoke* AO in his back seat was talking with Fallon about running air strikes. Fallon, with 18 Marines on the ground, needed two more CH-46s for extraction.

It took over two hours, which was fast considering flight time alone was 1.5 hours one way. The 46s came out of Marble Mountain Air Facility, topped off with JP fuel at An Hoa, and headed west. When the lead recovery bird arrived, two additional pilots and two crew chiefs came off, while the ten downed crew members boarded. The lead bird departed. The two new pilots were test pilots; the Helicopter Group had made the decision to try to fly both birds out with nobody aboard except a pilot and crew chief in case it went down; if they had to set down it would only be a two-crew recovery. They had two broken birds, and the plan was to fly out before dark.

It was 1530 when the first bird turned up, revved, and departed; as it was outbound, the second broken bird turned up and it departed. Now, having spent the day on the river, *Fig Newton* was ready. The fourth CH-46 came in; the team was already running through the water for the sandbar. While the helo turned, Fallon counted seven Marines on and then he jumped on with a thumbs up for the crew chief. The long flight back down the Song Cai valley where it finally combines rivers at Thuong Duc was a welcome sight to see. They were all thinking they had been sitting ducks on the river sandbar. Fallon saw the Special Forces runway go by. They flew around the tennis courts and into An Hoa for a hot refuel. Next stop, LZ 401.[59] The entire team trudged up the hill to the S-2 hut for the debrief. Captain Cook took his time. *Fig Newton* wanted to talk about the extract as everyone's adrenaline was still running. Cook was not interested in Marine Air maintenance issues. He drilled down on the truck-engine noise. Cross-examining each Marine, he asked if it could have been a boat on the river. No. Could it have been a chain saw? No. Finally, in frustration, Corporal Wilson said, "Sir, I know how to drive a truck, it was a truck driver missing third gear and grinding a pound of metal that we heard." Satisfied, Cook told them Team *Trailer Park*, led by Sergeant Gunkel of Echo Company on 9 April, had reported the trail on the far side of the Song Cai as being 15 feet wide with tire marks in the sand. Cook now had two team reports ten days apart reporting vehicles next to the Song Cai.

It was late by the time the debrief was over; Fallon dismissed the team with a well done and beer on him at the "Stagger Back Inn." He walked uphill to the inn and told the bartender to run a tab for *Fig Newton*, but not all of Delta Company; he would cover it. Walking across the street and up the five steps to the Delta Company officers' hut, Fallon was tired. He opened the screen door to Spolter loudly singing an a cappella version of "Old Mic Fallon had a Farm" as Lee had a good belly laugh. As soon as Fallon heard the song, he knew the S-3 shop had told "Top" Regalot about the farm. They had a second verse with the correct number of pigs and chickens. Fallon sat down as Lee tossed him a beer from the hut refrigerator. He told them about the farm and the frustrating extract and coordinated air cover by a solid *Hostage* OV-10 with his *Cowpoke* running air strikes. Two days later, on 21 April, the Recon Marines learned an OV-10 *Hostage* bird from VMO-2 had been shot down by 37-mm antiaircraft fire. The pilot, Major Gene Wheeler, died with the bird; the AO, Captain "Chuck" Hatch, ejected and was rescued.[60]

***

Second Platoon and Parks fell into the daily routine of life on the hill. The routine for them was one walk-off patrol, *West Orange-Alpha*, during the day and two listening posts each night. *Hansworth*, the Integrated Observation Device (IOD) team, continued to do their thing calling for fire missions. Between the 1st and the 4th, they called six missions, sighting 21 NVA/Viet Cong and claiming six kills by artillery.[61]

On the night of 4 April, around 2305, Alpha Bunker heard movement 150 meters west in the draw near the LZ. Remembering he was low on illumination rounds on the hill, Parks had *Hansworth* call an Arty illumination mission. He also had Alpha and Bravo Bunkers engage the draw area with M79 high-explosive rounds. The movement stopped or went back down the draw. No further action or results due to darkness. Parks called both listening posts back inside the wire, figuring this might just be the first probe, and put the hill on 50 percent alert. Checking out the draw the next morning, they found broken brush and disturbed dirt. It had been a small group of enemy and definitely not animals. The same morning patrol did a 360 wire check. That afternoon, he told the platoon to rest. That evening, 5 April, Parks changed it up, with no listening posts, but a 50 percent alert for the night. It paid off at 0410 when they sighted one enemy sitting cross-legged 100 meters south-east, observing the OP.[62] The previous night's probe had been northwest; tonight was southeast. Behind the enemy scout, they could hear a large number of enemy moving in the draw, which they knew had no trail. Parks had *Hansworth* call an on-call Arty target 500 meters southeast of the hill and had them walk the rounds closer in. The OP was under the gun target line, so this was high stakes shooting and the reason to start 500 meters out. The rounds covered the target area. The movement stopped. The next morning, Parks sent a walk-off patrol, *West Orange-Alpha*, out the east gate and had them drop into the draw to check out the probe. They found nothing in the draw. Coming out of it, at the bottom they headed south to the aqueduct to check out the trails there. Crossing that complex danger area, they continued south towards Hill 175. Three hundred meters south of the aqueduct, in the boulder field before the hill gained elevation from the floor, they sighted a small trail and followed it into a cave and tunnel complex. The team stopped, got out their 7 × 50 binos and used them to search the complex. After ten minutes, they spotted a trip wire on the main trail. Checking it out, it was a M26 grenade in a can.[63] The area was old and unused, so the team blew the booby trap in place and started their hike back up to Hill 119.

Parks knew they were being watched and probed. He stuck with the same plan the night of 6 April, a 50 percent alert. Again on 6 April, he pushed a patrol out, this time in the opposite direction of yesterday's, toward the northwest. Late in the morning, *West Orange-Alpha* called into the hill asking for the actual, which was Parks. Coming to the radio, Parks listened to the report of a bunker complex on the north side of Hill 148 about a thousand meters from them. Parks cautioned that, since it was currently empty of enemy, it would be booby-trapped and told his team to slow down, take their time, and map the bunkers before turning around. Minutes later, the team called in. They had found a trip wire strung across the trail leading north on the downhill side of the bunkers. The bunkers were in an ambush position overlooking the abandoned railroad berm with trails running parallel to it. They were dug in, concealed three feet deep with two feet of overhead covered with grass growing on roofs. The bunkers appeared to have been recently occupied. While the Recon platoon on Hill 119 knew not to use the berm while patrolling, this was the 2nd Battalion, 5th Marines' tactical area, and they routinely pushed platoon patrols that far out from the Liberty Bridge road to An Hoa.

On 9 April, 1st Lieutenant P. R. Green departed Hill 119 for another IOD assignment on a different operating base.[64] He had not liked the Reconnaissance Marines and wanted to get assigned to a larger fire-support base with more creature comforts. On 11 April, Parks's platoon was scheduled for an early flip. Second Lieutenant Paul Eglevsky and Corporal Steward would be coming up with 18 Recon Marines and Hospital Corpsman Third Class Avenel to relieve 2nd Platoon for OP security.[65]

CHAPTER 24

Naval Investigative Service

Sometime during the 2nd Platoon tour of duty on Hill 119, the village elders from Tho Son hamlet had come to the hill meeting place with the flag.[1] Lieutenant Parks, with a security detail plus Warrant Officer Thien as interpreter, went down and met the villagers. They delivered to Parks two letters from the chief of Thanh Xuyen village which was located outside of An Hoa Combat Base and who, politically, also covered Tho Son hamlet.[2] Thien did a rough translation of the letters for Parks. The first letter was a request for building material for a new temple and school. The second letter was a complaint that the Marines on the Hill Nui Ue Dop (Hill 175) had shot a pregnant woman.[3] The Vietnamese letter had the wrong hill. Thien, still upset, explained to Parks the complaint should be against Hill 119. Parks told the delegation he would deliver the letters to the proper authorities. After Parks got back to his bunker, he dated the back of each envelope with when and where he had received them.[4]

South Vietnamese political pressure on the shooting started immediately. The Vietnamese would exert pressure on the Americans from the day of the shooting through both their political and military chains of command. The village elders from Tho Son hamlet and Thanh Xuyen village began the pressure campaign two days after the burial of the woman. She had two children, now orphans, and they wanted retribution beyond what had been provided by Lieutenant Lee on 28 March.[5] Their letter dated 30 March went by hand to Hill 119 and Parks and, simultaneously, a copy was sent from the Thanh Xuyen village to their district chief at Duy Xuyen. Thien, after orally translating the letters for Parks, pressed his boss at the 44th Artillery Battalion Fire Support Coordination Center and Lieutenant Green to take the position that the shooting was wrong.[6]

Thien, with Green, departed the hill by helo on 9 April, headed for the Northern Artillery Cantonment. Now in the rear, with a vehicle, he started making the rounds up the Vietnamese military chain of command to his battalion and then forwarded to the Quand Da Special Zone, who had the South Vietnamese Army responsibility for Duy Xuyen District. At the same time, the civilian District Committee sent another letter with the allegation along with a request to know what was going to be done.[7] The American response to both were, "We are investigating," and they were pointed to the Naval Investigating Service (NIS) Resident Agent (RA) in downtown Da Nang and his investigation. He had Vietnamese translators on staff and had opened a formal investigation. They were getting action. When Special Agents Gonzales and Fitzpatrick heard from Green, that they knew the location where the body was buried, the investigators had a real murder case where they could exhume a body.[8] Exhumation required a formal written request up both the Vietnamese military and civilian chains of commands.

Getting permission to dig up a grave had real meaning to the Vietnamese and showed real action on the part of the Americans. Those documents were produced, requesting permission, to be followed by a second set of documents requesting the Americans, in support of the investigation, do an autopsy. That led to a formal Vietnamese request for the results of the autopsy. In one sense, the Marine Corps' chain of command at the 1st Marine Division had painted themselves into a corner. They needed to go forward to show the Vietnamese they were taking their allegations seriously and that justice would prevail. Very predicably, the institution soon would have its Article 32, a preliminary hearing in civilian parlance, and move straight to a court-martial. They could tell the South Vietnamese Government and the Army of the Republic of Vietnam (ARVN) that justice would be imposed on Lee. The train had left the station and was headed straight for a general court-martial.

Having finished his observation post tour, on 11 April at 1300, Parks arrived at Camp Reasoner.[9] After the standard S-2 (intelligence) patrol debriefing, he showed the letters to 1st Lieutenant Spolter, the Delta Company commander.[10] Spolter had taken Vietnamese language at the Defense Language Institute in Monterey for ten months. He spoke and read Vietnamese well. After reading them and agreeing it was a serious allegation, they agreed that Parks would hand the letters to the battalion commander, thereby keeping the chain of custody on the letters simple.[11] Spolter was leaving on patrol in the morning and had to get himself and the team ready.[12] He was also avoiding Lieutenant Colonel "Wild Bill" Drumright. Spolter, as Lee's commanding officer, and the next officer in the chain of command, could have kept the letters and done a preliminary investigation into the allegation. However, he was a peer, and, because of the seriousness of the allegation, he chose to move the matter to the battalion level.

Parks, a Citadel graduate, knew the gravity of reporting the allegation as he walked down Battalion Street. He also thought it was the appropriate and proper next step. He knocked three times on the battalion commander's doorframe. After reporting in, he handed the letters to Drumright, explaining when and where he had received the letters and what he thought they said. Drumright told Parks he had done the correct thing to bring him the letters and dismissed him. The battalion commander had a choice to make. He could ignore the letters and destroy them, thereby taking care of his boys, or he could report them, taking care of the institution and, by default, himself. He did not know what to do, so he sent his driver to get the executive officer, Major Terry Turner. After explaining what he knew and showing Turner the letters, he asked for his opinion.

Turner said, "We really don't know what these letters say. It was translated verbally by an ARVN to Parks who told you what he thought they said. Why don't we have them officially translated?"

It seemed to them a middle ground. What Turner and Drumright could have done, and did not do, was conduct a preliminary investigation on an allegation against one of their Marines. The battalion commander could have appointed one of his two majors or five captains to look into the allegation. He also could have called in his S-5 civil affairs officer, Bill Lange, who spoke and read Vietnamese, to translate the letters or read them to Major Turner and himself. Lange had been Drumright's S-5 in 2nd Battalion, 26th Marines, and he trusted him, so he brought him to Recon. By getting the letters translated up at Division, he was ceding control of the informal inquiry to determine the facts on the ground. He also could have sent it back to the

Delta Company commander, who read Vietnamese, to investigate and report back. By doing so, he would have learned the pertinent fact that there was no dispute Lee had shot a woman. Lee had submitted a spot report.[13] They would have had an opportunity to review the rules of engagement and the location of the woman when she was shot. That also was never in dispute as had been reported the same day. These preliminary facts and a review of the Hamlet Evaluation System (HES) classification of Tho Son hamlet could lead one to believe she was a Viet Cong (VC) participating in an illegal activity in a restricted area. With those facts and information, the battalion commander would have the option of sending the allegation forward or managing the incident himself. Drumright, after reviewing the facts, could have counseled, or used lesser Uniform Code of Military Justice (UCMJ) tools available to him, with Lee and dismissed the letters as enemy propaganda. He and Turner did not conduct a preliminary investigation, reviewing the facts available to them in their own S-3 shop on one of his best performing lieutenants with three prisoners captured in the past two months (his number-one criteria!). They did not have any of the facts when they escalated the allegation to Division for help and translation. Drumright took his options off the table when he took the letters to Division. He decided to go to the division commander and his staff judge advocate (SJA).[14]

Drumright took the letters up the hill to the division staff for an official translation and the counsel of the SJA. The old football player had chosen to punt the ball instead of blocking for his running back. The first translated letter requesting building materials was sent by the chief of staff to the division's G-5 (civil affairs) section for consideration and action. After reviewing the official translation of the second accusation letter, Drumright attempted to go to his mentor and boss, the division commander. When the division's chief of staff heard what Drumright wanted, he denied entry to the general, saying he needed to preserve his options. Turning Drumright around in his office, he sent him to consult with Colonel Lucy, the SJA. Sharing the story and the letter with Lucy, Drumright asked him what he should do. Lucy was the legal advisor to the commanding general. It was his job to protect the general and the institution. Lucy advised Drumright that the prudent move would be to investigate the allegation. The Marine Corps was not the Army and the SJA did not want a Marine Corps' or the 1st Marine Division's version of the My Lai massacre. He said it was Drumright's decision, but he would support a formal investigation. The SJA, the senior lawyer in the 1st Division, and the commanding general's counsel, had told Drumright the matter needed to be formally investigated. On 16 April, Drumright handed the letters to the 1st Marine Division Criminal Investigation Division (CID), requesting they investigate. CID was already overwhelmed with marijuana investigations. They went back to the SJA shop and recommended handing off the investigation of an allegation of a potential murder to a more appropriate authority. The SJA then formally requested the NIS Da Nang RA conduct an investigation into the allegations that the Marines of Nui Ue Dop had shot a pregnant woman.[15]

The next day, 17 April, NIS RA L. A. Gonzales, Special Agent, opened a formal investigation on the allegations in the Vietnamese letter from the village chief of Xuyen Thanh, that Marines on Nui Ue Dop had shot a pregnant woman.[16] The letter was corroborated by an ARVN Warrant Officer Thien, a forward observer (FO) on Hill 119, who said he witnessed the shooting of the pregnant woman.[17]

The same afternoon, Special Agents Gonzales and Fitzpatrick visited Camp Reasoner. They interviewed Drumright and Turner together in Drumright's office. Major Turner stated that Parks had hand delivered two letters to Drumright on 11 April. The first requested building materials and was currently in G-5 for further action. The second—the investigators had both the original Vietnamese letter and the official translation—was dated 30 March 1970 from the chief of Xuyen Thanh village. It claimed the Marines on the hill had killed Ms. Le Thi Chia, a 32-year-old pregnant woman, while she was catching fish in a rice paddy. It also reported the shooting had been reported to the 44th ARVN Artillery Battalion on the day of the shooting.[18]

The same day in downtown Da Nang, at the NIS RA's office at #6 Yen Bai Street, Warrant Officer Nuynh Long Thien, ARVN, FO with the 44th Artillery Battalion was interviewed by NIS RA Gonzales and his certified Vietnamese interpreter. They took a sworn written statement from the eyewitness.[19] Thien stated Lieutenant Lee had shot the woman with a sniper rifle, thereby providing a name for the accused the letter had not provided.[20] Thien identified Lieutenant Green and Sergeant Boardman, of the American artillery team, that could give more specific details. Thien said he knew where the body was buried and could show the investigators. He also stated his radio operator, Corporal Nguyen Ban, ARVN 44th Arty, had also witnessed the killing. Continuing the investigation, four days later, on the morning of 21 April at the NIS RA Da Nang office, Green was interviewed.[21] He stated that he witnessed Lee shoot the victim with a sniper rifle. He also knew where the victim was buried. He also stated that all Lee wanted to do was warn the Vietnamese, and that Lee had filed a radio spot report that afternoon with 1st Recon Battalion.[22] Later that afternoon, ARVN Corporal Ban, radio operator, was interviewed by NIS RA Da Nang, corroborating what his boss had said.[23] The same day, Thien's commanding officer, Major Nguyen Ngoc Lien, Chief of Fire Support Coordination Center, Quand Da Special Zone, requested formal permission of Vietnamese authorities for the exhumation of the woman's body. The permission for exhumation would come from Lieutenant Colonel Cao Dien, Quang Nam Province chief. He would appoint representatives to form a joint investigation delegation. They were: Mr. Nguyen Kim Nguyen, clerk of District Court; Mr. Nguyen Thanh Phu, Chief of Police Judicial Section, Duy Xuyen District; Mr. Nguyen Phuc Thinh, Chief of Public Case Section, Duy Xuyen District; and Major Gordon, U.S. Army, Chief U.S. Advisory Team, Duy Xuyen District.[24] Duy Xuyen District was the parent South Vietnamese Government district above Thanh Xuyen village and Tho Son hamlet.

On 22 April, the NIS investigative party, with Warrant Officer Thien, flew by helo to Hill 119. The purpose of the trip was to specifically identify the location of the grave of the victim. Using the Integrated Observation Device (IOD), Sergeant Boardman and Lance Corporal Callahan, who were on the hill during the shooting and had witnessed the burial, showed both the location of the shooting and where the victim was buried to the investigation team. The NIS team recorded the grid coordinates and lased the exact distance from the IOD to both sites. It was 635 meters to the grave at 5,868 mils and a deflection of minus 51, while the victim had been shot at 720 meters at 5928 mills and a deflection of minus 41. NIS looked through the "Big Eyes" at both sites and took pictures, all from the safety of the tower.[25]

On 23 April, the exhumation party, composed of the NIS investigation team of the three special agents—Gonzales, Fitzpatrick, and Staff Sergeant Demario—plus a Navy/Marine Corps Graves Registration team, flew from LZ 401 to Duy Xuyen District Headquarters where they landed and picked up three Vietnamese representatives of the Joint Investigation Delegation to be present for the exhumation. The CH-46 then flew to Hill 119 and the exhumation party debarked.[26] Second Lieutenant Paul Eglevsky, of Delta Company and the current hill commander, had been prebriefed by battalion to provide a security patrol for the exhumation party and to ensure their safety. The exhumation party was to bring the body back for identification and to determine the cause of death for the ongoing NIS investigation.

Eglevsky had prebriefed his Marines and was ready when the helo arrived. He had spent six months as the platoon commander of 3rd Platoon, Fox Company, 2nd Battalion, 5th Marines, in the Arizona Territory.[27] He knew from experience the VC tactic of booby-trapping graves. They did this because graves, being on higher ground out of the wet rice paddies, were favorite places for Marines to set-up overnight. The "Eagle" himself would walk point on this security patrol as he had done with his platoon in the Arizona.[28] Immediately after the dust cleared from the helo, the patrol, in a tactically spread-out formation, snaked its way down the north side of Hill 119. One could see the fresh grave, dug three weeks earlier, from the hill, so navigation was not an issue. The Eagle moved slowly, using all his skill and experience. The Marines were just as happy to let the lieutenant walk point. Arriving close to the grave, Eglevsky moved forward, getting on his knees and searched over the grave and then, with a Ka-Bar, probed it for mines. Feeling it was secure, he posted the Marines in a 360-degree perimeter and turned over the site to the Graves Registration team. They dug and, at two-and-a-half feet, made contact with the shroud. Removing the dirt sufficiently, they lifted the body, which was wrapped and on a board, out of the grave to one side and photographed it. The gray rain suit was removed, and the body, wrapped in a parachute, was placed in a standard U.S. body bag and labeled. With the thumbs up from the Graves Registration team and the three NIS agents, Eglevsky headed back up the hill on a different route off-trail and back to the landing zone (LZ).[29] While en route, they called for the helo, which had gone to An Hoa for fuel and awaited their call. Picking up the exhumation party and body, the helo flew back to District HQ to drop off the Vietnamese reps, and then onto the Naval Support Activity (NSA) morgue where the body went to Graves Registration to await an autopsy.

The NIS special agent, Fitzgerald, shepherded a dual process of paperwork permissions through both the Navy Medical Command and the Vietnamese District approval process in order to obtain approval for the autopsy. This took a week. Meanwhile, on 24–25 April, the NIS investigating team interviewed the other four artillerymen from 11th Marines that were on Hill 119 about their recollections of the incident.[30]

On 25 April, Eglevsky and 1st Platoon would complete their flip, which had begun on 11 April, on Hill 119. During this period, Team *Hansworth* has called 17 fire missions and claimed 46 North Vietnamese Army/VC killed.[31] Lieutenant L'Orange and 4th Platoon were next in line to take over the hill.[32]

Back with the investigation, on 27 April, the Vietnamese District Chief signed a letter authorizing an autopsy of the victim. With the dual-approvals paperwork completed on 29 April, the body was moved from the morgue to an x-ray facility where a full body scan was done and sent to radiology. The body then went in for the autopsy, which was completed by Captain John W. Aussem, U.S. Army pathologist. The radiologist report said, "there were no bullets, no fragments, no metal detected in the body."[33] The captain's autopsy report stated that "due to the body's advanced state of decomposition, the cause of death could not be determined."[34] There was no report of pregnancy in the autopsy.

Additionally, on the 29th at Camp Reasoner, Major Turner provided NIS RA with a copy of the patrol report, including the spot report from Lee that was submitted on the shooting incident on 28 March.[35] That same day, the CID was informed by the III Marine Amphibious Force (III MAF) prisoner-of-war compound that they had a female inmate who had information about the atrocity on Hill 119. The detainee, named Ms. Do Thi Luc had been captured by 1st Recon off Hill 119 on 20 April. CID informed NIS, who went to the compound and, with an interpreter, interviewed Ms. Luc. She stated she was with the victim the day she was shot and was also present at the burial. Ms. Luc said the victim had been raped two to three weeks prior to her death. The investigator could not resolve the rape-allegation claim. NIS then took Ms. Luc from the compound to the NSA morgue. She was shown the rain suit and identified it as being the burial shroud. She then looked at the body. She identified the body as Li Thi Chin. When asked how she could be positive, she said it was because of her gold teeth placement. She was then returned, that afternoon, to the III MAF compound.[36]

April 30 was reinterment day. The victim's body was picked up at the morgue by the Graves Registration team. It was in a U.S. body bag and driven to LZ 401. There, the NIS agents, along with the graves team, flew out to Hill 119, landing at 0910. At 0920, a walk-off security patrol was provided by L'Orange, and 4th Platoon. They reversed the process and moved off the hill tactically and back to the original grave site 625 meters below the OP. The security team probed the former grave site for booby traps and then set up security. The graves team then reinterred the body. The reinterment party then returned to the Hill 119 LZ to await its helo ride to Da Nang.[37]

Lieutenant Lee's investigation by the NIS was now in full swing. On 4 May, a new letter, dated 24 April, arrived at NIS RA office in Da Nang from the Village Committee, registering another complaint on the shooting of 28 March and requesting a copy of the autopsy. It was translated and became part of the investigation.[38] A copy was also forwarded, via South Vietnamese channels, to the South Vietnamese Government in Saigon.

On 17 May, the Special Agents got around to interviewing Lee. He had been assigned a defense counsel from the division's SJA, Captain J. J. Hargrove. That day, Lee had been summoned up the hill by his defense counsel, who was using a conference room instead of his bull-pen office amid all the other defense counsels. At the SJA conference room, he was introduced to Special Agents Gonzales and Fitzpatrick who then read him his rights. Lee, after stating he understood his rights, was asked to make a statement on the alleged shooting of a woman on 28 March. Based on his counsel's advice, Lee told the Special Agents he would, but, at this time, would exercise his right to remain silent. Both agents stood and adjourned the session.[39] After the agents departed, Lee asked Captain Hargrove what his thoughts were. Hargrove said, "You are headed to an Article 32 and most likely a general court-martial, I strongly urge you to get civilian counsel."[40]

The very next day, 18 May, the formal Article 32 was initiated. An Article 32 of the UCMJ requires any service member accused of violating any punitive articles of the UCMJ to undergo a preliminary hearing. This hearing functions similarly to an arraignment or a pretrial hearing in a civilian court. Drumright, Lee's reporting officer, had signed the appointing order for Lieutenant Colonel J. P. King to conduct an Article 32 investigation into the allegations based on the preliminary report from NIS.[41] The purpose of an Article 32 is to determine if there is sufficient evidence to support the charges filed against the accused, and to give the accused an opportunity to respond.

Separately the same day, 18 May, in his defense counsel's conference room on Hill 327, Lee received a DD 458 charge sheet for a violation of Article 118, premeditated murder or felony murder.[42] It was signed by a certified legal sergeant in the SJA office of the 1st Marine Division for the SJA.[43] His assigned defense counsel, Captain Hargrove, explained that the common practice, Marine Corps-wide in legal offices, was to assign new and less experienced lawyers to the defense section first. When that defense lawyer becomes experienced, or shows his courtroom talent, he is then transferred to the prosecution side of the legal office. The experience then favors the institution. In his third meeting with Lee, Captain Hargrove reiterated once again that he was new and inexperienced, and he strongly advised him to obtain civilian counsel.[44]

In California, on the morning of 19 May, Lee's parents were reading the Sunday morning paper when they saw a Marine Corps sedan pulling into their driveway. Every family's worst nightmare flashed through their minds as the Marine Corps always notify the family of a death in person. Two uniformed Marine officers proceeded to their door and were welcomed into the living room. The good news was their son was alive. They were there to inform and provide the parents with a letter from the Commandant of the Marine Corps. The letter stated their son was the subject of an Article 32 investigation for an alleged charge of murder in Vietnam.[45] The next day, Lee's father called Headquarters Marine Corps to gain insight or get some direction on how to proceed. The legal authority at headquarters told him directly, "Sir, get civilian counsel because the Marine Corps will protect the institution and hang him."[46] On Tuesday, 22 May, Lee's father drove over to San Jose to engage the services of the law firm Hudson, Sylia, Rubnitz, DiNapoli, Hastings and Holden, the law firm that managed business cases for the company Lee's father worked for but also handled criminal defense cases. He met with Mr. DiNapoli and Mr. Hastings, securing their services with a retainer and asking them to travel to Vietnam to defend his son.[47] Following the legal meeting in San Jose, Lee's father drove to the Western Union office and sent a telegram to his son. Received by the Western Union office in downtown Da Nang, it was hand delivered the next day to Camp Reasoner and the Delta Company office as that was Lee's last address. Lieutenant Spolter signed for and received the yellow telegram, opening and reading it. He then realized it was not meant for him.[48] He took the telegram over to the Headquarters and Service Company office and handed it to Lee. The telegram simply read "Help is on the way!" Spolter asked Lee, "What does that mean?" "We will know soon," Lee replied[49] He now had government counsel and knew additional help, in the form of civilian counsel, was coming. He could also sleep at night because he knew what he had done was proper and he had accepted responsibility for his actions.[50] Naively, he believed in "The System." Only time would tell, as he began this slow, grinding legal process. He focused on learning and doing his new desk job. His company commander, Captain R. L. Wiltrout, had simply told him it was his job to ensure the unit diary was correct every Friday as that was the report that got the Marines paid. He was working out every day, which was the best part of each day. He no longer went to the Officers Club. Lee turned inward and focused on what he could control.

Unbeknown to Lee, both artillery teams, the U.S. and ARVN on Hill 119, were disturbed over the incident, but for different reasons. Warrant Officer Thien was pushing his government as hard as he could. This was an opportunity for him, regardless of the South Vietnam Government or VC position. He would be viewed in a positive light by both for pushing the incident. First Lieutenant Green had made a determination, in his mind, that Lee had acted inappropriately. His primary thoughts were to deflect the incident away from himself. Thus, on 23 May, Green went downtown and added a second sworn statement for the investigation at NIS' Da Nang office.[51] He wanted to add comments and his opinion to his first sworn statement. Making the second statement, he related that he considered Lee a good shot who could have missed the target if he intended. Green further stated the actions of the villagers did not even warrant a warning shot.[52]

In the United States, on 24 May, the *San Francisco Chronicle* headline read "Hanoi Charge Disputed: Marines Cleared in Slaying." This article was about the 15 April accusation against 1st Battalion, 5th Marines, in the Le Bac hamlet firefight. After reading the headline and losing the bureaucratic battle for requested support from the Marine Corps, the idea of using the media was planted in Lee's defense team in San Jose. DeNapoli and Hastings would go public, through the press in San Jose, where they knew the reporters. It was time for "Team Lee" to up the pressure on Headquarters Marine Corps and the Marines in-country. This was done without consulting their client over 7,485 miles away.[53] The San Jose counsels would use this public avenue through the *San Jose Mercury* and *San Jose News* throughout the Article 32 and to the general court-martial in an effort to influence the Marine Corps. There is no evidence it succeeded. On 25 May, the civilian defense team released the charges to both the *Mercury* and *News* newspapers. The *News* headline read "Los Gatos Charged in Vietnam Death" and the *Mercury* headline said "L.G. Marine charged with Murder in VIET." The local reader understood "L.G." meant Los Gatos. In part, the article read:

> Da Nang, Vietnam (AP) A young Marine officer has been charged with a premeditated murder in the death of a Vietnamese near Da Nang, March 28th, a Marine Spokesman said. The spokesman said 1st Lt. W.X. Lee, 24, of Los Gatos, a member of the 1st Marine Division reconnaissance battalion was serving at a Marine observation post 17 miles south of Da Nang when the incident occurred. An Article 32 investigation, similar to a civilian grand jury proceeding, has been convened to examine the charges against Lee.[54]

The headlines did not help the emotional state of the Lee family. It made his father angrier at the Marine Corps, an institution he had previously held in high esteem, and it put stress on his mother and his 19-year-old fiancée.[55]

On 25 May, NIS Special Agents Gonzales and Fitzpatrick flew back out to Hill 119 to take photos for the investigation and interview Lieutenant Parks.[56] They wanted to document the chain of custody with the Vietnamese accusation letters. They wanted to understand his role as the first recipient of the letters. Parks explained the two letters came to him on separate days and he wrote the date on the back of each envelope. He said he also had Warrant Officer Thien do a sketchy translation. Realizing the seriousness of the accusation, Parks stated he elected to keep the letters in the chain of command instead of turning them over to the staff intelligence debriefer at S-2, which was the standard practice with Vietnamese documents received from villagers, or captured.[57] Parks, at the time he received the letters, was the hill commander. He was responsible for security of the hill and security for the classified IOD and its "Secret" laser range finder. Neither agent asked Parks about his mission, his haven, the rules of engagement, or the free-fire zones near the hill.[58]

CHAPTER 25

Caucasian Enemy, May 1970

U.S. and South Vietnamese forces invaded Cambodia on 1 May 1970 in an effort to destroy the headquarters of the North Vietnamese in the "fishhook" region, and to cut their supply lines.[1] On 4 May, in protest over the Cambodian incursion, four students were shot and killed and nine were injured at Kent State University by Ohio National Guardsmen.[2] In New York City, on 20 May, a pro-war rally attracted 150,000 people, with a crowd that included workers and union members who supported the Nixon Administration's policies in the Vietnam War.[3] The National League of POW/MIA Families was incorporated on 27 May by family members of American servicemen who were listed as prisoners of war or missing in action. As of today, 1,574 from the Vietnam War period remain unaccounted for by the Department of Defense.[4] Their iconic black-and-white flag continues to be flown today.

***

Lieutenant General McCutcheon, commanding general of III Marine Amphibious Force, approved a request from 1st Marine Division to demolish the McNamara-imposed Da Nang Anti-Infiltration System (DAIS).[5] The cleared land strip with barbed-wire fences, minefields, and electronic sensors had been developed to stop enemy infiltration of the "rocket belt." Never fully funded, implemented, or manned, the DAIS was ineffective because it could not distinguish forest deer, farmers, and water buffalo from rocket-carrying enemy forces. This was the same challenge the Marines and commander of Hill 119 had below and around the hill in agricultural areas. The new commanding general, while constricting his forces around Da Nang on the rocket belt to prevent the North Vietnamese Army (NVA) from launching 122-mm rockets towards the vital airfield and port with fewer forces, tried to disrupt his counterpart General Binh's 2nd NVA Division. The disruptive force was 1st Reconnaissance Battalion, reinforced now with both 1st Force and 3rd Force Recon Companies. The plan devised by Major General Wheeler, the old raider, was understood and continued by Major General Widdecke, himself a Carlson's Raider of World War II.

***

On 3 May, Widdecke walked down Hill 327 from his underground bunker and across Division Road to Camp Reasoner to visit Lieutenant Colonel Drumright.[6] The general wanted to hear firsthand the plan to disrupt Binh and the NVA. He also witnessed a demonstration of reconnaissance capabilities. The lieutenants and Marines called the demos "dog and pony shows."

In warfare, the enemy always gets a vote or an opportunity to counter your plan. In 1970, with the announced American withdrawal, General Binh changed his plans and focus. He would rebuild, rearm, re-man with fresh recruits down the Ho Chi Minh Trail, and keep the pressure on the Marines through harassment attacks on different targets. As the Marines tightened their belt around Da Nang, the outlying combat bases, that were outside the belt, became lucrative targets. While these combat bases were well defended, there were no longer larger unit operations to push out from them and push the NVA back into its base areas. He could now stage within rocket range and close walking distance of the camps outside the rocket belt. On the night of 6 May, the Que Son District Headquarters south of Da Nang and Hoa An, defended by Popular Forces and Regional Forces (PF/RF) of South Vietnamese, had been put under siege. They received over two hundred 82-mm mortar rounds and rockets. It was followed by a ground assault led by sappers, followed by an infantry unit larger than a battalion. Simultaneously, the Marines at Fire Support Base (FSB) Ross were hit with 122-mm rockets and sappers. Hotel Company, 2nd Battalion, 5th Marines, supported the PF/RF's defense of the District HQ. The next day, when the dust settled, the cost was ten PF/RF killed and 27 NVA bodies in the village.[7] Binh had been looking for a soft target he could overrun and achieve a political victory. Despite the fact they failed on 6 May, his 89th Sapper Battalion would continue to look for soft targets.

The assistant division commander (ADC) was sent down to see the Marines' disruption plan.[8] Specifically, he wanted to learn how *Sting Ray* patrols were run and supported.[9] Drumright hosted Brigadier General William F. Doehler, the division's ADC, for drinks and dinner with his commanders and staff.[10] Drumright regaled them with stories of Valhalla, claiming in a loud yell, "Someday, we'll all be together in Valhalla!"[11]

General Binh would keep up the pressure. On 20 May, just after midnight, his soldiers awoke the entire Da Nang area with the lobbing of unguided 122-mm rockets into the city.[12] On 21 May, the XXIV Corps commander, now the senior commander in I Corps, Lieutenant General M. Zais USA, visited Camp Reasoner and was briefed on reconnaissance operations and received, complete with CH-46 rappelling, a dog and pony show.[13]

Early in the month, *Vesper Bells* (callsign for 1st Recon in May) received a tasker from XXIV Corps to support the 101st Airborne Division with SCUBA divers. *Vesper Bells-Divers*, led by 1st Lieutenant Charlie Kershaw, was launched by helicopter along with their diving tanks and gear.[14] Charlie had attended SCUBA School in November 1969 as an incentive for the three-month extension of his tour that he would complete in May 1970.[15] The divers flew north of Hai Van pass into the 101st area of operations to the Rao Trang stream. Conducting diving operations in 20 feet of water with a two-knot current and water visibility under six feet, they recovered a light observation helicopter. Hooking lift straps to it underwater, the Army airlifted the chopper from the stream to return it to Phu Bai airfield. It took the four divers, Kershaw, the SCUBA locker noncommissioned officer, Sergeant Blum, Corporal Jones, and Private First Class Burney seven hours in the water to complete the mission.[16]

In Delta Company on 1 May, Master Sergeant Regalot looked around the company office. He was in charge, but no officer was available to audit record books. Delta Company started the month with six officers on its rolls. Four were on patrol, including Spolter, his company commander. Mike Fallon was off to Subic Bay and SCUBA School for the entire month. His 3rd Platoon commander was now under investigation and on legal hold.[17] His 4th Platoon commander, Lieutenant L'Orange, was on Hill 119.[18] Spolter had departed on 28 April with 3rd Platoon's Team *Terrapin*.[19] Corporal Hunt was a new team leader and needed to be certified. As Lieutenant Lee was unavailable, Spolter took the patrol. *Terrapin* had the experienced Private First Class Paul Freemen walking point along with Lance Corporals Kempe and Wiley, "Doc" Edison, and tail-end was Private First Class Richardson.[20] On the previous patrol, they'd had sporadic comm. As backup on this patrol, they had three PRC-25s and Spolter carried a PRC-93 survival radio. They were out for six days. The worst event of the patrol was Spolter getting seriously jabbed in the eye with a stick while breaking brush and being evacuated and replaced by Staff Sergeant Mushett.[21]

Lieutenant Garry Parks had also gone out on 28 April with his team *Fig Newton*.[22] They were shot out of their first two attempted inserts. Their third landing zone (LZ) had to be outside of his haven on the floor of Elephant Valley. This patrol would be a long six days with Parks having to climb up the side of the valley to get comm with his radio relay *X-Ray* on Dong Den Mountain. When he went down into the valley to conduct surveillance, he would lose comm. It was a stressful patrol as nobody wanted to make contact with the enemy, especially with no communication, which was the survival link for supporting arms and extract. *Fig Newton* came out on 2 May on the second bird in the extract package that had pulled *Terrapin* and Corporal Hunt.[23] Having dismissed their teams, they walked up to S-2 (intelligence) together for the debrief with Gunnery Sergeant Ottinger. Neither had much to report.

Also going out on 28 April was Lieutenant Paul "Eagle" Eglevsky who took the entire 1st Platoon to the northeast Que Son mountains to coordinate a three-team saturation patrol.[24] The Eagle was with *Pal Joey-Alpha*, with Sergeant Ireland, which was inserted into Hill 484. They were two kilometers east of the observation post (OP) on Hill 425, who would be their radio relay. Inserted at 0830, they were in contact by 0945 with two NVA. Engaging at a distance with small arms, they wounded one while the point man, Lance Corporal Evans, was in turn wounded. Letting the enemy run, *Pal Joey* moved back up to Hill 484 and called in a medevac. After getting Evans out, they continued the patrol. Meanwhile, at 0840, Corporal Stewart and *Pal Joey-Bravo* had been inserted on Hill 322 two-and-a-half kilometers east of their lieutenant. Hill 322 was a return to the area Fallon, Rathmell, and Moore had raided earlier. The third team, led by Corporal McCommons, had gone into Hill 705, 2,500 meters south of their lieutenant. While the teams were close to each other, as the crow flies, there was no way they could support each other due to the steep terrain. All three teams had numerous sightings, in the distance, while observing the lowland valleys north and east. In the mountains, the sightings were limited to ones and twos moving quickly. Fire support was tried, but ineffective, due to having to radio relay twice, coupled with long clearance times. *Pal Joey-Bravo* checked out the cave complex below Hill 322 that *Delicatessen* had hit and found it had not been re-used. They moved on to observe the Phu Loc Valley to the north. All three teams were extracted from three separate LZs at midday on 3 May after 123 hours on patrol.[25]

As Eglevsky was flying back, Parks was outbound with Team *Dublin City* back into Elephant Valley.[26] This time they were on the valley floor with no overhead cover. He felt exposed. The entire patrol believed they were being observed from either ridgeline of the steep valley. That said, the secondary growth was thick and provided camouflage, if not cover. They had line-of-sight communications with *X-Ray* and patrolled the road and river below *X-Ray*. The Marines called it "The Yellow Brick Road." No recent signs of enemy activity were observed on the valley floor. The patrol discovered a camouflaged 500-pound dud bomb and, later, an old 250-pound dud. *Dublin City* was extracted without incident on 6 May.[27] Garry Parks was a patrolling machine. In May he would have six inserts and six extracts, by helo, patrolling in the bush for 25 days of the month.

The insert and extract CH-46 helicopters were Recon's lifeline. A unique bond was developed between the Reconnaissance Battalion and the three CH-46 squadrons that flew their inserts and extracts: HMM 262 (Flying Tigers) callsign *Chatterbox*; HMM 263, *Peach Bush* and, HMM 364, *Purple Foxes*. The UH-1 Hueys and Cobra gunships were flown by HML 357, *Scarface*. And orbiting over them, coordinating supporting arms in OV-10s, the front-seat pilot *Hostage* and his back-seat aerial observer *Cowpoke* were from VMO-2. The aviation package all came together in the air to get the teams in the bush and out of trouble.

On 8 May, four new lieutenants checked into 1st Marine Division Personnel, having arrived early that morning from Okinawa. They were fresh out of The Basic School (TBS) 2-70 as Bravo Company classmates. All four infantry officers attended Ranger School after TBS. Because they were all Ranger School graduates, the division's personnel officer sent the four down for interviews at 1st Recon Battalion. The personnel officer, Captain E. W. Sterling, kept the two 1st lieutenants, Floom and Smith, and sent the 2nd lieutenants back up the hill.[28] Bob Fawcett and Mike Cross were both assigned to 2nd Battalion, 1st Marines, and became platoon commanders under Lieutenant Colonel W. G. Leftwich.[29] Both would come back to Recon Battalion on 6 October 1970, shortly after Leftwich had assumed command.[30] Fawcett could only recall one point made during an in-call with the ADC, Brigadier General Doehler. He asked the lieutenants what they knew about the My Lai massacre.[31] Both lieutenants said they had not heard of the incident. The general explained that the My Lai massacre had occurred in the Americal Division, which was the Army division just south of the Marines below Hoi An and FSB Ross. And, that an Army platoon had shot between 300 and 500 unarmed Vietnamese civilians in the hamlet of My Lai on 16 March 1968. Further, there had been a cover-up. The news of the My Lai massacre had just hit the papers a few months prior. The Marine Corps was reacting to ensure it would not happen to them. Part of that reaction was a lecture on the massacre by the ADC to every new officer who joined the division and direct guidance that it would not be tolerated.[32] As it turned out, Fawcett and Cross had been in the middle of the Florida swamps during Ranger School and had no access to newspapers or news. The ADC filled them in, making a specific point of talking about the Law of Land Warfare, which they both vaguely recalled was a class at TBS. Fawcett recalled the focus of the class was overseeing prisoners properly, and did not mention the killing of civilians.[33]

Delta Company would get new blood on 8 May with the assignment of both 1st Lieutenants Smith and Marv Floom. They walked into Spolter's office after coming over from Captain Sterling to Delta Company. Spolter, in welcoming the two new lieutenants, in his offhanded low-key approach, said, "Who wants to go to the field?" Floom raised his hand. Jerry said, "Great, what's your first name?" Stating it was Marv, Spolter said, "Marv, drop your gear in the officers' hut, return and see 'Top' Regalot." Calling for Regalot, Jerry introduced the company first sergeant, saying, "Lieutenant Floom will take 3rd Platoon to Hill 119 tomorrow,"[34] which Spolter was going to have to take. "Please get him geared and introduce him to Corporal McCommons who is the acting platoon sergeant." He then said to Smith, "Come in and tell me about both of you as you know each other well." Spolter learned in the next half hour from Smith that both officers had graduated from the Naval Academy with the class of '68 and had been selected to go to the Naval Post Graduate School in Monterey, Spolter's old stomping grounds. After a year there, they proceeded to Fort Benning and were together in the same Ranger School class. After Staging Battalion together, they had arrived last night at Da Nang International and were assigned this morning.[35] Spolter told Smith he would be going out soon, to find a rack with Floom, and help him get ready for his departure tomorrow. As Smith exited, Spolter yelled, "Get Floom and head up to supply and the armory before they close." Smith and Floom, who had been together daily for the past six years, would be split up on 9 May forever. Floom, being the new guy, would be moved over to Alpha Company at the end of May with Fallon's return to Delta. Smith would become the executive officer (XO) as he was senior to Fallon, who loved the bush.

Meanwhile, the Naval Investigative Service (NIS) had the Lee investigation in full swing. The day prior, on 8 May, they had interviewed and taken a sworn statement from Hospitalman Glen Edison while he was down the street at 1st Med Battalion. At 0700, on 9 May, they were at Camp Reasoner to take statements from the rest of 3rd Platoon who were scheduled to depart for Hill 119 after lunch.[36] They used the "Stagger Back Inn" and called in each Marine separately for their statement. Lastly, they took Lance Corporal Broe to the armory and had him draw his sniper rifle, which they confiscated for evidence.[37] Broe would go to the hill with his M16. Floom would still have the left-handed Lance Corporal Lowery on the hill as a sniper. On 10 May, Special Agents Gonzales and Fitzpatrick traveled to 1st Med Battalion to interview Lance Corporal John Kempe, who was recovering from malaria.[38] Kempe, from Betha, Minnesota, had completed eight years of formal schooling before enlisting in the Marine Corps in April 1969.[39] He arrived in Vietnam in November 1969 and was assigned to Delta Company. The woodsman from Minnesota adjusted to the bush better than most Marines. Kempe, in his statement, stated the shooting he witnessed took place the day before Easter Sunday. He recalled Lieutenant Lee firing the sniper rife and killing the woman.[40] After the burial late that afternoon, he related that the lieutenant met with 3rd Platoon and talked about the shooting. Lee said he took full responsibility, that he was sorry for the incident, and if anyone wanted to discuss it to come see him.[41] With the investigation progressing, Lee had been reassigned to Headquarters and Service Company and became its XO on 12 May.[42] The reason given was to have him available for the investigation and the legal system, and to give him time to work on his legal defense. On 13 May, NIS Special Agent Gonzales flew to Subic Bay Naval Station and conducted an interview with Sergeant Herman Diaz.[43] Diaz was attending SCUBA School along with Lieutenant Fallon who was still not aware of the shooting incident. Diaz was given the afternoon off and was interviewed at the NIS Resident Agent's office on Subic Bay Naval Base. He said he witnessed Lee shoot the woman.[44] In conclusion, he offered that Lee was a good shot and could have missed anything he wanted to miss.[45] Interestingly, also on 13 May, Radio Hanoi charged Marines with the slaying of 33 civilians in the hamlet of Le Bac. Le Bac was less than four kilometers northwest of Hill 119. The 1st Marine Division had already opened an investigation on 17 April based on the allegations springing out of a firefight occurring on 15 April between 1st Battalion, 5th Marines, and the Viet Cong (VC) in Le Bac hamlet. It had been reported by Lieutenant Colonel Cao Dien, district chief of the Duy Xuyen District, which was the same district and district chief of the Lee investigation.[46]

Lieutenant Marv Floom, now on Hill 119, was getting his first look at the enemy through the "Big Eyes" of the Integrated Observation Device (IOD) system. On the 10th, at 1845, he observed Team *Hansworth* call a fire mission on eastern Go Noi Island on ten NVA in green utilities.[47] They were coming out of a bunker complex. The immediate fire-for-effect mission was on target, killing one enemy and creating a secondary explosion. The next afternoon, *Hansworth* showed Floom 11 NVA sitting on the ground, again in eastern Go Noi, with packs and rifles. Floom was amazed at the clarity of the enlarged 200-power scope, the sunlight coming from the west easily highlighting the enemy on the ground to his east. A fire mission was called with *Hansworth* claiming four enemy kills. Floom could not see bodies after the mission as he heard *Hainsworth*'s post mission results radioed in.[48] Welcome to Vietnam, lieutenant, and the game of body counts. On 15 May, Floom experienced his first probe. The night-observation device had picked up a lone sapper low crawling under the wire and cutting the strands. Floom observed as Alpha Bunker fired down the draw.[49] He did not observe the enemy again. The morning wire patrol confirmed the wire had been cut. There was no other evidence that the enemy had been there. The patrol repaired the wire and returned to the hill.

On 20 May, Special Agents Gonzales and Fitzpatrick, using a helicopter fragged by 1st Recon, flew to Hill 119.[50] The purpose was to do a field-of-view (diameter of the picture seen through the rifle scope) analysis on the scope of the sniper rifle which was the suspected murder weapon. Flying with them to the hill were Lance Corporal Broe, the scout sniper whose rifle was used, Lieutenant Green, and Lieutenant Parks. The agents had all three sit in the same position Lee sat when he shot the woman. All three looked through the scope and stated that from their seated position they could see both the hole where the victim was shot and the grave. The agents also measured the distance between where the victim was shot and the grave using the "electronic observation device" and determined it to be 37 meters. "Electronic observation device" was an unclassified name for the classified IOD that the special agents used to measure distances from Hill 119 to both locations.[51] Observing all this was the new and current hill commander Marv Floom. His father, a Marine officer on Guam in 1944, set high standards. Marv exceeded his father's expectations, retiring as a colonel after 31 years in the Marine Corps and had a second career in the defense industry.[52]

Two days later, McCommon led a seven-man walk-off patrol to investigate Tho Son hamlet below. At 1500, the OP heard two muffled explosions. *West Orange-Alpha* had found a dry well just west of the hamlet along old Route 537. They suspected it was booby-trapped and had a tunnel leading out the bottom. McCommons and Lowery each pulled an M26 grenade and dropped them into the well. The grenades went off with the hard clay walls of the well directing the shrapnel up and out. Three of the *Alpha* patrol had received face and head shrapnel wounds.[53] Lance Corporal Grossman called *West Orange* and requested a medevac. It took an hour to work its way back to battalion and over to the medevac hot pad. *West Orange-Alpha* set up a perimeter in a dry rice paddy as the CH-46 arrived. McCommons and Lowery, along with Doc Edison, were medevac'd.

Grossman now led the four-Marine *West Orange-Alpha* patrol back up the hill.[54] Grossman explained what happened to Floom who was not pleased with the actions taken and the loss of three men to the hill defense on their last night on the hill. On 23 May, 3rd Platoon flipped off the hill in the morning with Lieutenant Parks and 2nd Platoon coming back up to the OP.[55]

Lieutenant L'Orange, returning from Hill 119 on 9 May, when Floom had arrived, was immediately turned around and put on patrol, taking his Team *Delicatessen* with Corporals Johnson and Weirich.[56] He would have seven Marines on this patrol with him. They were inserted into the heart of the Que Son Mountains on Hill 848. His radio relay was Hill 119, *West Orange*, which he had just left the day prior. His direct-support artillery battery was *Ringbroom-K*.[57] On their second day patrolling above a trail and stream in a draw heading east, they observed, from a close distance, eight enemy. They had mixed dress, with the point wearing black "PJs" with legs rolled up, followed by one in khaki uniform with a pistol, five in brown utilities with packs and rifles, and one woman in white PJs. They were too close to call a fire mission but L'Orange wanted a shot at getting the presumed officer with the pistol, so they followed. The enemy was on a trail going downstream and *Delicatessen* was off-trail going sidehill. They lost the enemy patrol after 500 meters as they could not keep the pace without giving away their position or firing from behind them and higher than the enemy into a boulder draw; they never had a clear field of fire. They stopped after losing sight of the patrol. However, it did lead them to a cave, 20 feet long, 10 feet wide, and 5 high with three entrances. Fresh footprints were noted. Moving above the cave, L'Orange started his clandestine OP near the summit of Hill 381 or Nui Khui Son, at 1100. At 1210, 12 May, the team observed 16 enemy, well dispersed, moving in groups of three north along a trail. Thirteen were wearing brown utilities and pith helmets with sweatbands. One was wearing blue utilities and another green utilities.[58] L'Orange, the Virginia Military Institute graduate, laughed to himself about the old saw: "Ten per cent never get the word on the uniform of the day."[59] Ten enemy had packs while eight of those carried AK-47s glistening with oil. This was a disciplined and professional group of NVA. Looking through his 7 × 50s, L'Orange was shocked to see a Caucasian in the patrol![60] He had no pack or weapon. He passed the binos to Weirich who recalled the man was well tanned.[61] L'Orange called *West Orange* and requested an aerial observer (AO). This was a high-value enemy patrol. They got an OV-10 diverted, with the aircraft on station almost immediately. As L'Orange was talking the bird into and over the Que Sons, Weirich reported that when he heard the aircraft so did the enemy and they immediately went to ground and out of sight into caves along the trail. The AO made one low pass; seeing nothing, he had to depart because of a low fuel state. They could no longer see the enemy patrol.

At 1400, from the same clandestine OP, *Delicatessen*'s gig was up. They observed enemy now moving uphill towards them. All were wearing pith helmets and had shrubbery on their backs for camouflage.[62] They were moving in leaps and bounds and dropping to the ground, appearing as a bush. The enemy had seen the team. *Delicatessen* engaged with M79 and small-arms fire, killing the closest three. On the radio with *West Orange*, they got another AO. Using the OV-10's onboard ordnance, they started holding back the enemy. The NVA had maneuvered and cut off L'Orange's obvious extraction LZ on top of Hill 381. L'Orange called for an emergency ladder extract when his count of the enemy bushes moving his way went over twenty.[63] This was one of General Binh's counter-recon teams. They were trying to wipe out an entire Marine Recon team to send a message. The two *Scarface* Cobra gunships arrived first and started working over the north slope of Hill 381 with their chain guns. Then the team heard the "woompa-woompa" sounds of the twin rotor CH-46 and saw two birds coming out of the east and straight for them. Only an hour-and-a-half had passed since *Delicatessen* had requested the emergency ladder extract. Lance Corporal Lujan popped smoke, and the aircraft identified green. The ladder descended and the presence of the gunships kept the NVA on the ground trying to look like bushes. The team got on the ladder by twos, hooking in with snap-links. The last two were L'Orange and Weirich with the radio. They had the E-ticket ride all the way back to LZ 401.[64] They would be in the mess hall for dinner on 12 May. L'Orange never heard back on the sighting of the Caucasian.[65] The rumor in Delta Company was that it was Private First Class Garwood, the Marine deserter. Many staff officers at Division had a hard time believing what Recon teams reported unless it fit their desired outcomes.

Parks was back out at the same time, having been inserted 10 May with Lance Corporal McCleese's *Dublin City*.[66] They patrolled for five days, finding numerous trails with waystations evenly spread but none used within the past month. They heard a single shot of rifle fire each morning, signaling the enemy knew *Dublin City* was patrolling their valley. They were extracted by CH-46 on 14 May and, for once, were first in the batting order for extraction, arriving back at LZ 401 by 0800 in time for a late breakfast.[67] They would share breakfast with the Marines from Camp Reasoner who pulled nighttime security above the division command post on Hill 327.

First Lieutenant Spolter had promised 1st Lieutenant Smith would get his first patrol on 11 May with Team *Prime Cut*. Corporal Wiley's team would be eight strong, including Hospital Corpsman Third Class Richardson. Their artillery support would be *Ringbroom-M* out of An Hoa Combat Base and radio relay would be through *Stone Pit*.[68] Upon insert, the aggressive Smith moved the team directly off the LZ. Most teams would be doing comm checks and listening for the enemy. Smith was an officer in a hurry. He moved the team into a shallow streambed. Thirty minutes after inserting, they found fresh footprints walking southwest in and along the streambed. One was barefoot, two wore sandals, and two wore NVA lug-bottom boots. Smith immediately followed the prints. The team wanted to go higher and observe. They followed the trail for an hour and then lost track of the enemy prints in the rain and a larger streambed downhill. Now lower, Smith found a trail moving in the same direction, south to southwest. The team was now trail walking. The trail crossed the stream where they found fighting holes covering the stream crossing, either for the NVA security or an ambush. This was a danger area for a small Recon team. Wiley wanted to back up and observe the crossing site. Smith did not. While crossing the stream on the trail, *Prime Cut* made point-to-point contact with two enemy.[69] *Prime Cut* opened with small arms as did the enemy who, in tiger-striped shorts, turned and ran around the curve on the trail. The team pursued cautiously, not wanting to run into an ambush. The enemy was gone. Had they OP'd or set an ambush at the streambed trail-crossing site they would have bagged at least two enemy. It was raining every afternoon this time of year. The next day, 12 May, at midday, Smith called *Stone Pit* and requested an emergency extract based on multiple enemy sightings in the area. The team had seen none. He was granted an extract, and the ladder package came out at 1845. *Prime Cut* was out, riding the ladder. The Marines were always pleased to be going back to Reasoner, but they did not understand why. Gunnery Sergeant Ottinger conducted the debrief of Smith alone.[70]

May 16 found patrolling machine Garry Parks outbound with callsign *Dublin City*, his third team, which was newly formed, and led by Lance Corporal Duenas.[71] Experienced corpsman Eric Schwartz was also on this seven-man patrol. They were going into the northern Que Son Mountains, three klicks west and two klicks south of Hill 425. However a large mountain masked the OP from them. The insert was at 1030 in the morning into a good multi-CH-46 zone created by bombs. It had large rocks and five feet of elephant grass. There was no canopy but a thick secondary growth of bushes, vines, and scattered bamboo thickets in the wide draw that led due north six kilometers into Alligator Lake. Parks moved off the LZ and tried for a comm check with *Sunrise* on Hill 425, with no success. Putting up a whip antenna, he was able to establish comm with *West Orange* on Hill 119. Having informed them he had intermittent comm, he took down the whip and sat to listen for 30 minutes before moving away from his LZ. The team moved out, breaking brush and moving north downslope in the large draw.

After two and a half hours, they came into another large bombed-out area. It had been a former base camp. They counted ten manmade caves dug on the side of draw. Each had a bunker/fighting position in front of it with reinforced logs and firing ports covering the stream bed.[72] The area had not been used since it was bombed some time ago. They moved out of the bombed-out open danger area, quickly continuing north into the wider valley. When the camouflage provided by the secondary growth stopped and the valley opened into old fields, Parks paused for a water break. He checked comm and got a solid copy with *Stone Pit*, which was on Ba Na Mountain to his northwest across the Arizona Territory. He considered his options as it was getting late. Best to turn around and move back into the secondary growth to find a secure harbor site for the night, but low enough for good line-of-sight communications. They had a peaceful night and the next morning, breaking brush, they headed back up the valley into the same draw towards their insert LZ. At 1430, they found a trail, hard packed, two feet wide, running north to south. It had tracks and appeared to have been used in the past two days. It also had two-wheel marks, or skid marks, heading up the draw.[73] Parks took them above the trail on the west side of the finger and decided to clandestinely observe it. Seeing nothing, that afternoon they moved further up sidehill and found boulders for a harbor site. The next day, they went back to the insert LZ and checked it out. Nobody had been there. With the patrolled draw completely empty of enemy, the team went due east up and over the finger into the next steep north–south draw. It took them all day of cross-compartment movement. They harbored high up in the new draw below the ridgeline of the finger.

The team patrolled the next day and found a good extract LZ in a bombed-out stream bed area 75 meters by 150 meters with no aerial obstacles. Parks put the LZ under observation and found a harbor site 400 meters away. They were due for extraction in the morning on 20 May. Up early and moving towards the LZ, they were confirmed on the morning extract schedule and the weather was good. Life was good. Sitting in a hasty 360 defense above their selected extract LZ, Parks's tail-end Charlie observed an NVA soldier 20 meters away. When the enemy solider raised his rifle and pointed it at Powell, the lance corporal shot him in the chest, with a three-round burst, killing him. The soldier was wearing green utilities, with the cutoff trousers, had a red patch on his shoulder, and was wearing a camouflage bush cover. He carried a pack as well as his rifle.[74] Parks immediately moved the team north and towards their extract LZ. They then observed a second NVA 35 meters away on a trail headed south. They engaged him with the

M79 and small-arms fire. Upon investigating that second site, they found blood trails. The enemy had left quickly, leaving behind three packs, a medical pack, clean utilities, a Russian watch, and a first-aid kit. Radioing *West Orange* on Hill 119, Parks reported he needed the extract sooner than later, as their position had been compromised. It was 0920. *West Orange* got the on-duty airborne OV-10 to swing over the Que Sons. The AO reported at least four enemy maneuvering above *Dublin City* on the ridgeline before the *Hostage* aircraft developed a mechanical issue and had to depart the scene. *West Orange* pressed Battalion, who could only say another extract was already in progress and they were scheduled next. After two hours that seemed like ten, they heard the birds before they saw them, then they heard the radio call from *Purple Fox Two-Three* calling *Dublin City*. Lance Corporal Campbell passed the LZ brief as the aircraft were inbound. The lead bird came up the draw, flying from the north to the south. Parks flashed the mirror and *Purple Fox* called for smoke as Campbell popped a green smoke which was immediately identified by the bird. In three minutes, they were trotting up the ramp, Parks jumping on last, giving the CH-46 crew chief the thumbs up to lift off. They were home 30 minutes later; the team would make lunch.[75] Not for Parks, who, upon disembarking the helo, was grabbed by LZ control. The corporal told him a special agent wanted to talk with him. Fitzgerald, having learned Parks was inbound, held up his fragged helicopter flight to Hill 119. He wanted to take Parks to Hill 119 for a rifle-scope field-of-view measurement. Parks asked when they would be back and was told that afternoon. Turning around, he boarded the outbound bird with Fitzgerald and Lance Corporal Broe, the sniper from 3rd Platoon.[76] They flew over to the Northern Artillery Cantonment (NAC) less than two miles west of Camp Reasoner and picked up Lieutenant Green, the former Hill 119 forward observer (FO). Then they flew to Hill 119, where the bird dropped them and left for fuel. Fitzgerald had all three Marines sit in the same approximate location Lieutenant Lee had been sitting when he shot the woman. Then with Broe's sniper rifle, all three looked through it and confirmed they could see the mortar crater 720 meters away, where the woman had been shot.[77] Parks was not sure what the relevance of this was but did not argue as the CH-46 returned within thirty minutes and took them all back to LZ 401. Fitzgerald took Green back to NAC in his jeep which had been parked at the east side of LZ 401.

On 23 May, it was L'Orange patrolling again. He had callsign *Chili Pepper* with Corporal Wiley's team and "Doc" Hunt.[78] They lifted off LZ 401 at 0900. Chris was taking two new Marines to break them in, for a large patrol count of nine. They were headed west. Their artillery support would be from *Scandinavia* firing out of NAC. Their radio relay would be Team *Cossack* from Alpha Company on a clandestine radio relay above and north of Charlie Ridge. Approaching their insert helo LZ from the southwest, the bird went into a hover 20 feet above the zone and was settling down when the ridgeline from the east opened up with heavy small-arms fire. Both door gunners engaged with their .50-caliber machine guns, one shooting an enemy out of a tree.[79] The insert officer, laying on the tail ramp, shot another enemy just off the LZ. The pilot pulled out of the zone as the gunships started making their strafing runs into the triple-canopy jungle around the LZ. The mission was aborted as that was the only LZ within or close to their haven and clearly had been set up for a helo ambush. They estimated the enemy at 20, all of whom were wearing dark-brown uniforms. *Chili Pepper* was gone for 1.8 hours and was back for lunch.[80] L'Orange seemed to get shot out of more LZs than his peers.

Next up to bat for Delta Company in May was Parks again, on his sixth insert of the month, going back up to Hill 119 and *West Orange* with his 2nd Platoon.[81] Garry knew the hill was dangerous. He was going up with every man he had plus two from the company office who wanted some bush time. He would have 26 Marines plus "Doc" Schwartz with him. This gave him sufficient troops to run a daily walk-off patrol, as well as nighttime activities. Second Platoon departed at 1000 from LZ 401 to relieve Lieutenant Floom with 3rd Platoon. Parks also took a scout dog and handler.[82] On their second night, 23 May at 2155, the listening post on the far side of the saddle LZ on Hill 148's front slope, observed one enemy slowly working his way up the northwest trash pit draw below Alpha Bunker. The listening post engaged with small-arms fire and withdrew back across the LZ.[83]

On the 24th before sundown, Team *Hansworth* on the IOD picked up enemy on east Go Noi. They fired a fire mission with *Serviceman* and got secondary explosions which attracted an OV-10. *Hostage Colt* came on station at 1755 and expended all its onboard ordnance, receiving multiple secondary explosions. He was relieved at 1835 by *Hostage Smoke* which also expended all its onboard rockets and machine guns in the same area before returning to base at 1920. The nightly airshow for Hill 119 was over. At 2000, the west listening post sighted one enemy who then fired on them. The post moved their position when their scout dog alerted. Again, the enemy fired first on the noise. The listening post returned small-arms fire at the muzzle flashes. Parks also had *West Orange-Bravo* out on a night ambush north of the hill next to the abandoned rail berm. *Bravo* saw two figures run over the top of the berm. They appeared as shadows as they were skylined. *Bravo* engaged with M79 rounds over the berm and called *West Orange* for illumination.[84] They believed the enemy was setting booby traps as they got a secondary explosion when they engaged. Parks knew the enemy was trying to booby trap the Marines on the hill, keeping them inside the wire. He was countering that with active patrolling day and night and multiple nighttime listening posts. Two nights later, on 26 May, as the two-man listening post was setting in west of the LZ, they heard the cans rattling and then a trip flare went off in the northeast draw below Alpha Bunker. They saw three enemy with rifles in the light of the trip flare and engaged with small arms. They had to be careful when shooting back down the draw below Alpha Bunker so as not to sway to the right and shoot the bunker itself. The Marines had the enemy in a cross fire, but the NVA were in defilade below in the draw. The listening post, having been compromised, was withdrawn as *Hansworth* followed up with an on-call target of six rounds. There were negative observations due to darkness and inability to see into the draw below. On the 28th, one "Chieu Hoi" walked up the main northern trail at 0830 in the morning, hands raised and gave himself up. He was dirty and hungry, wearing a white shirt and green shorts and was barefoot. A patrol went out and secured his arms, covered his eyes with an empty sandbag, and brought him to the LZ under guard. They gave him water. He was evacuated to Fire Support Base Baldy for processing by a passing CH-46 headed that way.[85] On the 29th, at 1940, Alpha Bunker took one incoming small-arms round from the railway berm 700 meters below. The lone sniper was gone but *Hansworth* fired an on-call target, for good measure, at the muzzle-flash location as the sunlight faded.

On 31 May, the IOD team picked up significant movement four kilometers out on Goi Noi Island. On two occasions, they set up artillery ambushes with *Ridge Beam Fox* battery firing from west to east and the 44th ARVN (Army of the Republic of Vietnam) battery firing from east to west. *Hansworth* was controlling the U.S. Battery, and the ARVN FO team was controlling their battery. When the dust cleared, both observers reported up their respective chains of command that they had 13 kills.[86] By the time the stats were rolled up and forwarded on through two separate reporting chains, it would read 26 total kills in Saigon. Body count was how the artillery batteries were evaluated. Body count was also Saigon's method of measuring progress in the war. However, it was not the measure of effectiveness for the North Vietnamese leadership. The North Vietnamese were not counting bodies. They were trying to convince the populations of the United States and South Vietnam that they were not going anywhere. They had a hundred years if they needed it.

CHAPTER 26

War: "At the Rear," "In the Bush," "On the Hill," June 1970

"War," the song by Edwin Starr, was released and went to the top of the charts as one of the protest songs that became a popular hit. It was also a hit in Vietnam with Armed Forces Vietnam Network playing it multiple times a day.[1] On Hill 119, when it came on the handheld transistor radios in each bunker, one could hear Marines singing along at the top of their voices: "War, what is it good for?"

On 3 June 1970, President Nixon officially announced the initial withdrawal of U.S. troops from Cambodia by declaring the objectives had been met.[2] The American withdrawal from Vietnam continued, as Military Assistance Command, Vietnam informed III Marine Amphibious Force (III MAF) its share would be 19,800 Marines. The Marines would withdraw components of Regimental Landing Teams 7, and 3rd and 4th Battalions, 11th Marines, including support troops, along with a slice of both rotary wing and fixed-wing aviation. This first withdrawal increment, called Operation *Keystone Robin-Alpha*, was to be completed by 1 October that year.[3] In order to maintain as large a force as possible against the enemy, III MAF kept both the infantry and aviation units, to be withdrawn, fully engaged through mid-September while the MAF staff did the withdrawal planning. Major General Charles F. Widdecke continued to command the 1st Marine Division and focus on keeping the 2nd North Vietnamese Army (NVA) Division away from the Da Nang Vital Area and withdrawal port and airfield for the Marines.

On 11 June, the T89 Sappers, and the V25 Main Force Battalion, hit the hamlet of Thanh My. It was on the road from National Route 1, halfway out to Fire Support Base Baldy. The village had been a South Vietnamese model village for the secure hamlet program. Marine, Combined Unit Pacification Program, or CUPP, Team 9 from Alpha Company, 1st Battalion, 7th Marines, lived in the hamlet along with Popular Force and Regional Force platoons.[4] The goal of the NVA was to make an example of the model village for those who sided with the South Vietnamese Government and the pacification program. The all-night pitched battle totally destroyed 135 houses in the village and killed 74 villagers, who were satchel-charged in at-home below-ground bunkers. Another 160 were wounded. CUPP Team 9 had four wounded. The NVA attack became known as the "Thanh My Massacre" for the atrocities committed on the woman and children of the hamlet by the North Vietnamese soldiers.[5]

***

First Reconnaissance Battalion's Lieutenant Colonel "Wild Bill" Drumright kept the teams in the field and on the offense.[6] The good flying weather meant he could keep up a crisp pace of inserts and extracts checking the major enemy avenues of approach—Elephant Valley, Charlie Ridge, and the Que Son Mountains—while sending a few teams deep to disrupt General Binh, who countered the Recon Marines' efforts with two tactics. The first was to employ dedicated landing zone (LZ) watchers by placing one NVA soldier in an observation position over each LZ in their base-camp areas. The watcher's job was to simply watch and warn when U.S. helicopters landed in that zone. Since they did not have radios, they relied on a series of single rifle shots to indicate a chopper had landed. Where possible, they would track the Recon team. The second tactic was the NVA's creation of counter-reconnaissance teams.[7] These 20-man units were highly trained in tracking, well-armed, and well-disciplined. Their mission was to find and eliminate an entire team. As the 1st Marine Division increased its reconnaissance efforts, General Binh increased his efforts to counter them.

The Delta Company, 1st Recon Battalion, lineup for June was strong. First Lieutenant Jerry Spolter remained the friendly skipper; he was now a short-timer with one month left to do before his wake-up call and the "Freedom Bird." His new executive officer (XO) was the aggressive hard charger, 1st Lieutenant Smith. First Lieutenant Paul "Eagle" Eglevsky had 1st Platoon, although he was at 1st Med Battalion as a patient recovering from malaria.[8] First Lieutenant Garry Parks had 2nd Platoon and was currently on Hill 119.[9] The returning Mike Fallon took over 3rd Platoon as Floom had been moved over to Alpha Company to become its XO. Both Smith and Floom were senior first lieutenants, Ranger School graduates and were being groomed to assume company command when their current commanders rotated home.[10] First Lieutenant Chris L'Orange remained the ever-steady 4th Platoon commander.

***

Lieutenant Fallon, with Team *Terrapin*, was on patrol from 2–6 June.[11] The seven-man patrol included "Big I" Iantorno, Corporals McAffee and Elkins, Lance Corporals Packard and Yedinak, and Private First Class Watson as tail end. The gunships worked over the insert LZ and reported killing one NVA, assumed to be the LZ watch, to the team.[12] The team, after insert, was then tracked for three days and spent its time avoiding a counter-recon team. They received one sniper round from distance on 3 June, trying to push them into a draw. Fallon countered by going uphill cross-country and lost the tracking team. They spent the rest of the time avoiding obvious trails and streambeds. The entire area had numerous trails used in all four directions. There was also an extremely large amount of trash, C-ration cans, plastic, and broken deuce gear in the area from a recent Army of the Republic of Vietnam multibattalion operation in the area. There was no indication of enemy units living in the area. *Terrapin* was extracted on 6 June.[13]

***

Lieutenant Garry Parks and "Doc" Eric Schwartz were busy the first six days of June. On 1 June, at 0045, Hill 119 was probed near Echo Bunker by one NVA. When he tripped a flare, he reversed course back down the draw into the night.[14] Later that day, in two separate fire missions, Team *Hansworth* spotted five and then six NVA on Goi Noi Island. Firing on both groups, they claimed two kills with each firing.[15] At 0700, on 3 June, three "Chieu Hois" came up the main northern trail to the hill with their hands raised. A security patrol went out and met them, searched them, and blindfolded them before bringing them up to the LZ. At the LZ, they had detainee cards filled out and an evacuation called. *Dimer Two-Six*, a Huey, picked them up at 0800 and took them to Fire Support Base Baldy for processing.[16]

At 1400, they observed a large group of NVA crossing the railroad bridge to Goi Noi Island. *Hostage Colt* was on station and ran a fixed-wing air strike. Team *Hansworth* followed with a fire mission from *Ridge Beam-Fox* using delayed fuses. Both fixed-wing and Arty had excellent coverage of the target area but negative observations from *Hostage Colt*. At 1800, *Hansworth* picked up four NVA with packs and rifles on the north side of Goi Noi Island, in the Dodge City area, six kilometers north of Hill 119.

On 4 June, *Hansworth* called three fire missions on three targets totaling ten NVA. They got excellent cover on all three missions on Goi Noi Island which resulted in five kills and one secondary explosion reported to *Ridge Beam*.[17] On 5 June, still firing *Ridge Beam-Fox*, *Hansworth* called a mission on three NVA sitting on the railroad bridge in the center section of Goi Noi Island. They got direct hits with an immediate fire-for-effect, reporting three kills.[18]

Parks, working on his notes for the debrief at Battalion, noted that, during the walk-off patrol to the hamlet of Tho Son below the hill, they only found six Vietnamese living there yet they had food supplies well out of proportion to the population; they had 250 pounds of rice, 150 pounds of beans, and 3,000 pounds of corn. The boat docks of Tho Son were also a warehouse and transshipment site for the NVA. Since the elderly villagers all had South Vietnamese ID Cards, the Marines could only report the food stuffs.[19] There were numerous well-used trails from the hamlet due north to the river along with multiple docks. This was a waystation for the movement of NVA and their supplies to and from Goi Noi Island and the mountain base camps. That night, Parks, Corporal Doan, and Corporal Grossman got 2nd Platoon ready to flip in the morning. Coming up to Hill 119 would be 1st Platoon with Paul Eglevsky.[20]

On Hill 119, 1st Platoon and Eglevsky were on duty as *West Orange*. They provided security for the Integrated Observation Device (IOD) Team. Eglevsky was still weak, having just recovered from malaria. He used his time in the rear to the best advantage by trading for a big searchlight which they brought to the hill, only to realize they had a power issue or, rather, a lack of power. He had also requisitioned and received 96 Claymore mines. He had a solid plan to replace the old mines around the hill with new ones.[21] Joining him for this two-week stay were five Republic of Korea (RoK) Marines who would patrol and stand watch with 1st Platoon.[22]

On 10 June, a combined USMC and RoK walk-off patrol northwest of Hill 119 chased a suspected Viet Cong (VC), in white shirt and blue shorts, who ran away from them. The patrol was moving rapidly and tripped a booby-trapped M26 grenade that injured two RoK Marines, causing one routine and one emergency medevac.[23] It was about this patrol as an example of both VC presence and booby traps that Parks testified about the next day in Lieutenant Lee's Article 32 hearing in the 1st Marine Division Courtroom.[24] Later that day on Hill 119, four Chieu Hoi approached the hill on the main trail. A patrol went out, searched, and blindfolded them. They were dressed in white shirts and green shorts with no equipment, and no documents or ID cards. They were evacuated by a passing helo to the Interrogator Translator Team at Fire Support Base Baldy.[25]

During their 14-day stay, 1st Platoon had 20 sightings of 75 enemy. They recovered and forwarded five Chieu Hois. *Hansworth* had 18 fire missions with 25 kills and six secondary explosions as a result of IOD observation.[26] They flipped off the hill at 0815 on 20 June and were replaced with 4th Platoon led by Chris L'Orange.[27]

***

In the bush, on 9 June, Team *Dublin City*, led by Fallon, headed to the northern Que Son Mountains. The eight-man patrol included McCleese, Villasana, Hall, Duenas, and Doc Schwartz, plus they were taking two recent graduates of the RoK Marine Recon training, Staff Sergeant Hwang and Lance Corporal Om.[28] The team was inserted into a 2,000-pound bomb crater one kilometer south and below Hill 484. *Dublin City* was in a small valley with a stream running northeast. With mountains above them on all sides, communications were nonexistent near the stream, which was flowing and fordable. To establish comm, the team had to move uphill and use a whip antenna. Recon teams did not like using a long whip antenna as it was easy to observe. There was negative canopy to use for camouflage. On 11 June, they found a cave complex of 15 small caves on a finger between two streams that flowed into the valley. It was littered with old mackerel cans and plastic trash. There was a small fire pit in each cave. It was a transit waystation for the high-speed trail running alongside the stream, heading northeast toward the Phu Loc Valley.[29]

On the 12th, *Dublin City* was sitting in a clandestine observation post (OP) when they spotted 20 to 25 NVA northeast of them moving down the trail towards Phu Luc. They could not raise *Ringbroom-K* on the radio as they watched the enemy depart the Que Son Mountains into a hedge line in the valley. The team was extracted from Hill 233 by CH-46 at 1100 on 13 June.[30]

Four days later, Fallon was back in the bush with Team *Pal Joey*.[31] This was Corporal Wiley's team; however, Fallon knew the area well and would be the patrol leader for this one and Wiley would serve as the assistant patrol leader. He walked deuce tail-end while Fallon walked deuce point and navigated. This was a tight team that worked well together in the field. Lance Corporal Paul Freeman was on point, followed by Fallon, then Lance Corporal Capps as primary radio operator, Lance Corporal Browning with the M79, Lance Corporal Richey as the secondary radioman, then Wiley, and tail-end Charlie Lance Corporal Garza.[32] They were going in on the south slope of Elephant Valley, 22 kilometers upriver from their radio relay *X-Ray* on Dong Den Mountain. It was triple-canopy virgin jungle full of wildlife, dark, and dripping wet, 24 hours a day. Even if it only rained in afternoon thunder showers, it dripped all day. It was also dark on the jungle floor. They were inserted at 1000 into a one-bird, 40 by 40-meter LZ, with six feet of elephant grass growing on the zone. Jumping off the tail ramp into elephant grass was always begging for a twisted or broken ankle. Fallon kept them at the LZ's edge after the CH-46 pulled out. Getting a solid communication check with *X-Ray*, he waited for all the jungle sounds to return. They waited an hour before moving south. It was quiet and eerie when they found the first punji pit.[33] The pit was four-by-four-feet square, six feet deep with 12 punji stakes 1–1½ inches in diameter and three feet high anchored in the floor. Punji stakes were normally dipped or smeared with human feces to cause infection if it penetrated a foot or leg after falling in. They found three more punji pits on the south side of the LZ. The pits were in incredibly good condition. What gave them away was a light-colored, well-woven palm branch covering the pit that seemed out of place on the damp, dark jungle floor.[34] Had they been running back into the LZ, it could have been a disaster. Because there were punji pits on all sides of the LZ, Fallon noted he did not want to come back here for extract and would find another option.

The next day 18 June, Team *Pal Joey* found a narrow trail and moved north on it, slowly trail walking. As the trail came to a finger, they could see hooches on both sides. Moving off-trail and enveloping the hooches from an angle, they found them unoccupied. When they got inside the area, they discovered it was an old base camp, a 300-meter-long oval on the finger comprising 12 hooches, each with an underground bunker; firing ports were found in each bunker, facing down the finger. In the bunkers, they found South Vietnamese beer bottles, but no beer, much to *Pal Joey*'s disappointment. The base camp was in good condition but had not been used in a long time.[35] Due to the triple canopy, the base camp could not be observed by passing aircraft. Moving out of the small camp, Freeman, walking point, slowly moved on a trail heading west, deeper into the dark jungle. Fallon could easily hear the sounds of jungle life which told him they were currently alone in the woods. At 1500, they found two large trees midtrail, with five small campfire sites next to the trees. All had been used within the past week, but none were warm. They appeared to have been used at different times by two to three individuals each. There were numerous snail shells around the area.[36] This was clearly a midday break location with the two trees dissipating any smoke made from the small fires before it exited 300 feet above.

Still moving west on the trail, they found a log fence on one side as an aid to prevent falling off a deep drop. The fence was 4–5 feet high and ran for 500 meters. As the ground was now dropping away, *Pal Joey* searched the area and found an old antiaircraft artillery (AAA) position. It had a view into the large valley as the finger dropped off. The position consisted of a predug circular trench five feet deep and six in diameter with a center dirt stage that contained wooden trestles. The trestles were off the ground and would allow a gun to be moved 360 degrees by the gunners in the trench. It was also notched for elected firing positions.[37] The position was serviceable but at least a year old. It was decision time. *Pal Joey* was either out of its haven, or remarkably close to being so, and it was 1610. Fallon decided to move back east off-trail and find a harbor site for the night where they could monitor the trail. They were 50 meters off the trail and could not see it when they found a lone hooch in a small clearing. It was incredibly old, decaying, and falling in on itself. This was not associated with the AAA position or the main trail. They moved away from it, found a bramble patch, went inside it, and formed a 360, including deployment of three Claymores for defense. It was raining hard, the sound drowning out all other noises. It was going to be a long, wet, cold night. Most Recon Marines did not carry rain suits or ponchos. Fallon carried one half of a poncho liner he used over his head and shoulders at night. Sleeping in wet utilities with boots on, the challenge was trying not to get trench foot or trench hands when the rains came.

Fallon had the team up at sunrise. Everyone was shivering. The best thing to do was get up and move to gain body warmth. They moved for six hours over two kilometers and found an OP spot they could look out onto the valley floor. It was 1245 hours on 19 June. It had stopped raining for now. The team could see north into Elephant Valley, the river, the old French Road, and the northern side of the valley. They heard a single rifle shot to their south. Approximating distance in triple-canopy jungle is guesswork. Fallon asked Wiley and Freeman how far away the shots were and got 700 meters and 1,500 meters. He was looking at the map; it could have been either. Five minutes passed and they heard a second shot from the same southerly direction. After five more minutes came the third shot; the final shot was five minutes later. These were timed signal shots, not game-hunting shots. Best to move, so *Pal Joey* got up and was moving east when they crossed an old trail. Looking down at it, it turned 90 degrees in about ten meters. They broke brush to the sharp turn to investigate and found four punji pits on the side of the trail directly at the turn. They were old but still dangerous. Although it had been raining, they needed water. They could drink black/green punji pit water or drop down to a stream. *Pal Joey* dropped off the finger's crest and went down to the stream and filled canteens. They found a trail next to the stream and followed it a short distance and found an old campfire site. Again, snail shells littered the area. It was fresh and had been used by two or three soldiers in the past week. Moving up to the other side of the creek, they were breaking brush uphill. They had to find a harbor site that would allow them to communicate with *X-Ray*. That meant they had to crest the finger and get on the side facing east toward their radio relay. It took two hours. They settled in. Thus far there had been no rain that afternoon. Night comes quickly in triple canopy as the sun angle is low in the sky and light does not penetrate the canopy's three layers. The filtered light meant it was always twilight on the damp jungle floor until sunset and then it is instantly dark, a deep black dark.

The next day they found another good OP site from which to monitor the valley floor. Fallon was napping at 1545, trying to rest his eyes from looking through the 7 × 50 binoculars. It was a good OP, and they were there all day. He was instantly startled awake as they took incoming AK-47 rounds being sprayed into their position.[38] What had happened to their security? It was two bursts of approximately fifteen rounds. Wiley saw one NVA running away to the west when he rolled over. The team had not fired. Fallon called an artillery fire mission 500 meters west of their position from *Serviceman-A* out of the Northern Artillery Cantonment.[39] They could not see the artillery impacts, only heard them. *Pal Joey* got up and found the NVA's trail with Freeman tracking him for 300 meters before they lost the trail due to rain and the oncoming darkness. *Pal Joey* had made a mistake and got away with it! Fallon believed everyone was asleep, including him, as the entire team had not slept the prior night due to the cold rain. Time to stop chasing the NVA and reverse direction. *Pal Joey* needed to find a harbor site and, more importantly, an extract LZ.

They harbored on the side of a hill overlooking a streambed. The extract would be from the streambed, the only break in the canopy they had found. That night, *X-Ray* told them the northern teams would go first for extract in the morning. The next morning, *Pal Joey* moved to the streambed. It had three-foot boulders and running water. It was the only break in the canopy. At 0835, they heard the birds flying in Elephant Valley. No sun, so no mirror flash. Fallon took the handset and told the pilot he would talk him in by sound, that he should fly west upriver, and when he saw them fly by he would have them turn south. Three minutes later, the two gunships flew by and Fallon, now talking too loudly, said "Mark, mark, turn south," stating they were on a southern streambed running north into the river. It took two tries until they found the correct creek. The bird flew in and spotted the team's smoke, calling the yellow. The pilot turned the bird around 180 degrees, now facing Elephant Valley, and backed down into a hover. One by one the Marines climbed onto a three-foot boulder midstream and leapt for the tail ramp. Fallon, now carrying the PRC-25, was last to jump and he missed. Not known for his jumping ability, he remounted the boulder and waited for the hovering ramp to lower, this time jumping and landing on his stomach on the ramp as Wiley and Freeman pulled him aboard.[40] The pilot was putting the bird's nose down to gain airspeed and exiting the streambed into the large valley. Fallon went forward and thanked both pilots for their great flying skill. They were out. It was 0935, 21 June, when they exited LZ 401, wet and tired.[41] *Pal Joey* had been surprised by a chance encounter with one or two enemy. Fallon had made simple mistakes and got away with it this time. He would talk to *Pal Joey* that afternoon, having each patrol member critique the good and bad on their patrol together. He had to do better, and they had to do better, as all their lives depended on it!

***

On the hill, 1st Lieutenant Chris L'Orange arrived for his fourth flip on 20 June, his callsign was *Pal Joey-Kilo*.[42] He knew how dangerous the hill was, and the set routine. He was an avid believer in walk-off patrols to push the security envelope of the hill further away from its classified IOD. He was bringing a full Recon platoon of 18 Marines and two corpsmen, "Doc" Richardson and "Doc" Hunt, to the OP. He also had his experienced platoon sergeant, Staff Sergeant Mushett, and three attached soldiers from the Army of the Republic of Vietnam (ARVN), Sergeant Dang Luc and Lance Corporals Nquyen Cong and Nquyen Tinh.[43] The next day, the *Hansworth* IOD team called three fire missions north of the OP upon a sighting of 17 total NVA, with reported results of five kills, one wounded, and a secondary explosion.[44] On the last fire mission of the evening, they also sank a small sampan departing the docks of the hamlet of Tho Son.

This was the VC-controlled hamlet directly below Hill 119, which only had six hooches along old French Route 537 but had at least seven docks on the river. It was the ferry depot for NVA to get to Go Noi Island. On 22 June, the hill received a surprise visitor: their company commander, 1st Lieutenant "Jerry" Spolter, flying out to spend time with his 4th Platoon and good friend L'Orange.[45] Spolter was short, meaning he would be returning home in less than two weeks. The trip out to the OP would also give him a chance to avoid the battalion commander at Camp Reasoner. Rather than sit on the hill, the high-energy Spolter asked L'Orange if he could accompany that day's walk-off patrol scheduled to go down to check out last night's activities in Tho Son.[46] The strong, hard-charging Sergeant Atkins would be leading the patrol and Spolter would be along for the ride, coupled with his ability to speak Vietnamese with the villagers.

The patrol pushed off with seven Marines, a corpsman, and Spolter. This was not a clandestine Recon patrol but rather a straight-up security patrol to check the hamlet. They walked the main trail down to the hamlet, arriving a little after 0900. It was no secret to the Vietnamese they were coming down to look at the hamlet. In a small clearing in the center of the hamlet, Sergeant Atkins was talking with two of the village elders. He did not like an answer from one elderly man so hit him with the butt of his rifle. Spolter reacted immediately and grabbed the rifle away from Atkins, having harsh words with the sergeant.[47] He then apologized in Vietnamese to the elderly man which surprised the four Vietnamese standing there and some of the other Marines on the patrol. Spolter would report the incident to L'Orange and let him handle it.[48] He could have taken the judicial route which would have ruined Atkins's career in the Marine Corps. Atkins showed remorse and apologized to the villagers before the patrol departed. Heading out of the hamlet to pick up a different route back, they saw a young Vietnamese man running away down Route 537 to the west. Surprising the Marines, Spolter began running after the man yelling in Vietnamese "Dung Lai, Dung Lai," trying to get him to stop.[49] Atkins was trying to get Spolter to stop chasing the man as it was a good way to run into an ambush or booby trap. The young Vietnamese man disappeared into a bamboo thicket. Now the nine-man patrol headed back up the hill so the company commander could catch a late-afternoon helicopter back to Camp Reasoner. Over the next few days, there was no activity for *Pal Joey-K* or *Hansworth*.

***

In the bush, on 24 June, Delta Company had two teams ready on LZ 401 for insertion. Team *Mink Coat* would be going high up Charlie Ridge, using Team *Station Break* as their radio relay. The second outbound team was Team *Bag Shaw,* from 3rd Platoon, with their newly assigned Lieutenant Fallon as patrol leader. He would be taking Lance Corporals Watson, Capps, Kempe and Yedinak, Privates First Class Kozakowski and Hille, and "Doc" Edison.[50] This patrol was going west of Thuong Duc. It ran for 96 hours with no sighting of the enemy and no evidence of enemy activity. They returned to LZ 401 at 0915, 28 June, for their short debrief.[51] Fallon told Watson to have the team take 24 hours off and then get them ready to go back to Hill 119 on 2 July.

***

On the hill, at 1130 on 25 June, 1st Recon Battalion Combat Operations Center (COC), callsign *Pal Joey*, called out to *Pal Joey-Kilo* (Hill 119), stating the 5th Marines had fresh intelligence indicating eight senior Viet Cong Infrastructure (VCI) were located in Tho Son hamlet for a coordination meeting.[52] The 5th Marines asked that, due to proximity of the OP, could Recon check out the report. Lieutenant L'Orange figured if Recon Battalion and 5th Marines were asking, he would lead the patrol.[53] He had seven Marines, and a corpsman saddle up. No sneaking up on the hamlet during daylight across the open dry hill slope. So L'Orange asked *Hansworth* to watch the hamlet with the "Big Eyes" for the VCI departing as they approached. L'Orange took Corporal Wiley's team, Doc Richardson, and ARVN Sergeant Luc, and walked the main high-speed trail from Hill 119 down to the eastern side of the hamlet. The hamlet was empty of the usual elderly Vietnamese and children. It was totally vacated, which was strange. This was a good indication the residents had departed to avoid the VCI, or they were underground with the VCI. Departing west on the dirt old Route 537, Corporal Lynch heard something in the last hooch. He went to check it out with security. They found one military age male Vietnamese and detained him. He must have been a lookout. He had a short high and tight haircut and wore the white shirt and black "PJ" pants worn by the locals, but this person, with no equipment on him nor the standard South Vietnamese ID card, was clearly NVA. During questioning, the detainee could not name the hamlet or village. L'Orange had the detainee's hands bound and, with his eyes covered, the patrol started back out of the hamlet and up to their OP.

They were moving towards the abandoned railway berm, a known danger area. They had to pick a path to cross it. They were on a small trail and the point man moved over the berm and established security on the south side. As deuce point approached the north side of the berm, a command-detonated Claymore mine exploded. Instantly, five Marines were down as the gray-brown cloud lifted above the trail mixed with a red smoke.[54] Lance Corporal Pino, on point and south of the berm, engaged with his M-16 a male running away to the west as the enemy faded into a hedgerow of bamboo just below the berm. The hill heard the explosion, saw the strange gray/brown/red smoke and was on the radio trying to get the patrol, with no answer. Mushett went to the tower and got on the Big Eyes. He saw Doc Richardson working on one Marine. Mushett immediately called 1st Recon COC and requested an emergency medevac. After five minutes, Lindley came up on the radio and said they had five down, including the actual, meaning the lieutenant. He suspected a U.S. Claymore mine, an M18 directional antipersonnel mine, which sprays hundreds of small steel balls at human height through a kill range of meters across a 40-degree arc. They are triggered by remote control as an ambush weapon. The lone enemy soldier had triggered the mine. The gray smoke was from the Claymore, the brown was berm dirt, while the red smoke was from a smoke grenade on one of the five wounded Marines that went off when hit.[55] Mushett considered leaving the hill with a reaction force but, realizing the patrol had nine members and the platoon had 20 members, he had to secure the hill first, as was the mission. He told Lindley to put out security to the north between them and the hamlet and leave the hill side open, as he would cover them with the .50-caliber machine gun. He also instructed the corporal to determine a good hasty LZ. A medevac bird had been immediately diverted out of An Hoa's hot refueling point and was already inbound. Besides L'Orange, Corporals Wiley and Lynch and Lance Corporals Salas and Curey were injured. Two Marines were emergency medevacs, meaning their wounds were life threatening, the lieutenant was a priority, and the last two were routine evacs.[56] The well-timed and well-placed mine had taken out the second through the sixth Marine in the column. The detainee, moving in the seventh position of the column, was not hit.

In the rear, with the word that L'Orange was a priority medevac headed to surgery, the S-3 (operations) shop in Camp Reasoner called Delta Company for a replacement. Lieutenant Parks was in the rear between patrols.[57] Spolter tapped Parks, telling him to grab his deuce gear, rifle, and head down to LZ 401, along with three clerks from the office. They would be going out late that afternoon to Hill 119. Later that afternoon, Spolter took the company jeep to 1st Med Battalion where he saw the two routine medevacs and learned the other three were already undergoing surgery on the hospital ship.[58] The next day, 26 June, Spolter drove over to Marble Mountain Air Facility, trying to get a helicopter out to the hospital ship. He was having no luck with the Marine helos who were all on other missions. Being creative, he utilized his Vietnamese and talked directly to a South Vietnamese pilot with a Vietnamese Air Force Huey, giving him an order. He got the pilot to fly out and land on the hospital ship without radio clearance; the pilot agreed to come back an hour later and pick him up.[59] Landing on the hospital ship, and being told he should not be there, did not slow Spolter down as he asked where he could find L'Orange. Working his way around and down into the bowels of the ship, he found his friend Chris recovering from surgery and awake. They talked. The first question L'Orange had was, "How are my Marines?" Spolter informed him that all five made it.[60] Three, including L'Orange, were headed home via medevac planes to the States and the two routine medevacs were scheduled to come back to Delta Company. After commandeering the Vietnamese helo for his hospital visit, Spolter would return to Camp Reasoner to write to the parents of the five men from Delta Company.[61] Normally, the first officer in the chain of command writes a personal letter to the relatives of wounded or killed Marines. Since L'Orange was a platoon commander being medevac'd, it fell to Spolter to write the letters. Jerry Spolter, a man who could turn a phrase, struggled with the letter to Chris's parents, probably because he was so close to him. The good news was he could report Chris was on the way home.[62] As it turned out, Chris would talk by phone with his parents from Japan before Jerry's letter arrived.[63] L'Orange would undergo another surgery on his lower leg and heel and return to full duty. The Virginia Military Institute graduate was assigned to the prestigious Marine Barracks, Washington. He would become a platoon commander and march in the weekly sunset parades. Later, he would resign his regular commission, attend law school, and establish a successful practice in the San Francisco Bay area.[64] The Claymore mine had not been positioned properly as hundreds of stainless-steel BBs went into the ground. Had it been placed to explode level and parallel to the ground, there would have been five dead Marines.

***

On the hill, on 27 June, *Hansworth* spotted ten NVA in dark utilities, with packs and rifles, between Alligator Lake and Spider Lake. Firing *Pearl Chest-Mike* with a 12-round time-on-target fire-for-effect, they hit the target and killed all ten NVA at 1830 as the sun was setting behind the lakes to the west.[65]

At 0730 the next morning, Lieutenant Garry Parks was summoned to the tower. Coming up the main trail to the hill with hands in the air were four Chieu Hois. One was wearing green utilities; the other three were wearing white shirts and brown shorts. A security patrol met all four searched them, bound their hands, and blindfolded them. Questioning them, they said their ages were 35, 32, 30, and 18. One claimed to be an NVA doctor. This was a medical unit from Go Noi Island escaping and switching sides.[66] A helicopter was dispatched to retrieve these high-value officer Chieu Hois and take them to LZ 20, which supported the III Marine Amphibious Force's prisoner-of-war compound, and where the interrogator-translator team would interrogate them before turning them over to the South Vietnamese forces.

On 28 June, *Hansworth* fired two fire missions, resulting in six enemy kills, all NVA in uniform. On the 29th, *Hansworth*'s Big Eyes spotted six NVA in uniform with rifles sitting around a fire preparing dinner. Once again, with a fixed target, they fired-for-effect immediately and killed all six as the rounds landed on top of their campsite.[67] On 30 June, the observations shifted to the east. While trying to gain clearance to fire through *Lung Point*, they could not work through the deconflictions with the RoK Marines in time to shoot at moving columns.

On 1 July, the IOD team had three fire missions, resulting in enemy being killed in all three for a total of ten NVA killed that day from Hill 119.[68] The OP was clearly impacting General Binh's infiltration routes to Go Noi Island. The question would be, what would he order the T89 Sappers to do? For these last two weeks in June, the hill's artillery calling had been lethal killing at least thirty-eight enemy.[69] Parks and the hard-hit 4th Platoon would rotate off the hill on 2 July.[70]

Replacing them was 3rd Platoon. This was Lieutenant Lee's former platoon returning to Hill 119 for the first time since March. Third Platoon was now commanded by 1st Lieutenant Mike Fallon, a result of the continuous Delta Company platoon-commander's shuffle.[71]

CHAPTER 27

Article 32 Hearing, Da Nang, June 1970

On 5 June 1970, the *San Jose News* headline read "L.G. Officer's defense from SJ."[1] The newspaper's headline stood for "Los Gatos officer's defense is from San Jose." The story was reporting that Messrs. DeNapoli and Hastings of San Jose were flying to Da Nang to defend Lieutenant W. X. Lee, from Los Gatos, in an upcoming preliminary hearing for the military, an Article 32 in the Uniformed Code of Military Justice (UCMJ). The hearing was similar to a civilian grand jury determining if there was sufficient evidence to prosecute. The completed classified Naval Investigative Service (NIS) investigation was signed by Special Agent E. J. Fitzpatrick on 6 June and submitted to the commanding general, 1st Marine Division.[2] The report stated it was in a pending status awaiting the results of the Article 32 and the submission of additional classified "Secret" attachments on the Rules of Engagement (RoE) and the Hamlet Evaluation System (HES) status concerning the Tho Son hamlet. The investigation concluded by saying that the subject of the investigation (Lee) was not to have access to the investigation unless it went to an Article 32 or a court-martial. The 15-page single-spaced typed investigation had 57 numbered paragraphs plus 47 attachments. The attachments included information from the autopsy on the exhumed body of the victim. The report contained details on the location of where the victim was shot, and where she was buried. It also included evidence on the confiscated murder weapon and its test firing, both at the sniper range and off Hill 119, at the same distance and location of the alleged murder shot. The last 17 attachments were witness statements disclosing, in substance, that Lee had shot the victim.[3] The partial investigation was now in the staff judge advocate's (SJA) hands for the general and Lieutenant Colonel Drumright, as the commanding officer, to review. They had to make a determination as to whether or not there was sufficient evidence presented to warrant further action. The NIS investigation spent a prodigious amount of energy and time to prove Lee had shot the victim. However, that was never in doubt, nor really an issue, as Lee had submitted a spot report on 28 March stating the woman had been killed.[4] The flawed NIS investigation addressed four of the five "Ws" head on—who, when, what, and where the woman had been killed. The investigators did not address the why.

The why would be wrapped up in the specific location of the four Vietnamese in the incident of 28 March, what they were doing in relation to Hill 119, and, the definitions of Viet Cong (VC), RoEs, restricted areas, havens, free-fire zones (FFZ), and each of those areas in relationship to Hill 119, answering the question, whether or not the area around Hill 119 was under North Vietnamese Army/VC control, based on evidence such as the number of fire missions or booby traps in the area. Finally, what was the status of the three hamlets below the hill in the classified and formally evaluated Hamlet Evaluation System (HES)? While both the SJA and Drumright/ Major Turner had been updated weekly on the investigation's status, it was not until 6 June that they had the written pending NIS report on Lee.[5] The chain-of-command had made up their collective minds prior to receiving and reading the NIS investigation. As evidenced on 16 May, on the advice of Colonel Lucy, the 1st Marine Division's SJA, Drumright had already requested a formal Article 32 before receiving or reading the NIS report.[6] Lucy, known in Marine Corps legal circles as "The White Fox," told Drumright he would make his best officer available for the Article 32. On 18 May, before receiving the NIS investigation, Drumright signed the letter appointing Lieutenant Colonel J. P. King, the deputy SJA, as the Article 32 Investigating Officer (IO) for an allegation of Article 118, premeditated murder.[7] Lucy and Drumright did not consider why the shot was fired or the underlying mission and security risk associated with the observation post (OP). Their singular consideration was preservation of the Marine Corps' institutional and hallowed reputation. Be damned Drumright's loud speeches about taking care of his boys. He had hung out one of his best boys to preserve himself and the institution. Lee was on his own at Camp Reasoner. His military defense counsel had told him he could not defend him alone. His advice was to get civilian counsel. Lee's father had done just that. Now Captain Hargrove was talking every night, by phone, with the two civilian counsellors in San Jose.

The defense team had to overcome three large obstacles just to present a solid defense. First, Hargrove had to explain and hold school quickly for DeNapoli and Hastings on how the UCMJ was its own code of law with its own precedents and processes; in short, a new rule book. Second, they were playing an away game in Vietnam. Third, they were out of time.

King scheduled the formal Article 32 hearing for 10 June. DeNapoli and Hastings requested government air to fly them to Vietnam, even stipulating they would fly space available. The Marine Corps' bureaucracy denied the request. Lee would now incur not only their legal fees, but also the cost of round-trip commercial air to and from Da Nang from San Francisco for both counsels for the hearing and, later, for the general court-martial.[8]

The morning of 7 June, Special Agent Gonzales traveled to the 1st Marine Division Scout Sniper School with the sniper rifle used by Lee. There, at the rifle range run by the chief instructor, Master Sergeant Robert Diaz, they test fired the weapon to enter the results into evidence. Besides running the sniper school, Diaz was a Marine Corps Distinguished Shooter. Gonzales had Diaz fire the weapon at the range to test for accuracy. Later that day, they both travelled to Hill 119 and Diaz re-enacted the shots taken by Lee. He aimed at the same mortar crater where the victim was shot 720 meters downhill from the OP. After taking 14 shots, with the same rifle and the same scope, the distinguished shooter could not hit the hole next to where the victim stood.[9] Earlier, the defense team had requested a flight to Hill 119 and were denied by the SJA. The defense attorneys took that denial to the AP Wire Service and claimed government interference and influence in the proceeding. Hargrove, upon hearing that morning the NIS investigators were going up the hill, talked the defense team onto the party flying out to Hill 119 on 7 June.[10] Having just arrived in Vietnam, DeNapoli and Hasting, along with Lee and Hargrove, met Gonzales at LZ 401 for the trip out to the hill on a CH-46. The trip was to allow the team to complete their investigation, a byproduct being the chance for the defense team to view the scene before the Article 32 hearing. Returning from Hill 119, jet lagged and tired, the defense team used the next two days to prepare their case.

***

At 0913 on 10 June 1970, Lieutenant Colonel King, the IO, called to order the Article 32 hearing.[11] He stated the convening authority was the commanding officer of the 1st Reconnaissance Battalion (Drumright). For the record, he stated he was the IO, that the accused was Lee, and his defense counsel was Captain J. J. Hargrove USMCR. The trial counsel was Lieutenant A. C. Rudy USN.[12] The hearing was held in the Main Court Room of the 1st Marine Division on Hill 327. It was an air-conditioned Quonset hut.[13] Besides his military appointed defense council, Lee had his two civilian attorneys to represent him. Recording, and later producing the verbatim transcripts, were Sergeant Anderson and Corporal McClevey.[14] The recorders were duly sworn in. Then the IO had the counsellors state their individual legal qualification for the record. King then pointed out his function was to determine the truth, and that Rudy was not his counsel, but was representing the government. The IO then informed Lee of the general nature of the charge in the case as it appeared on the charge sheet:

> ... is a Violation of the UCMJ, Article 118, is on or about 28 March 1970 and which is alleged that you did to wit: with premeditation, murder an unknown Vietnamese female by means of shooting her with a Remington 700 Sniper Rifle.[15]

He then asked Lee if he had the charge sheet and if he understood his rights, which he would explain, if needed. Hargrove stated they would waive their Article 31 rights. The IO then asked the government counsel for a list of witnesses because he thought he had them but did not. Sergeant Michael Einsidler, who was a senior trial clerk at SJA, served as the runner for the IO and the hearing to get witnesses when they were called, and to chase down documents. The IO sent the sergeant to get the list. Einsidler returned with the list of ten names and one billet description, company commander, and handed it to King who shared it with both counsels.[16] The list had seven government and four defense witnesses, two of which were represented by billet or rank. The tenth witness was listed as a sergeant and would turn out to be Diaz from the sniper school; the other billet was listed as the Delta Company commander. As it turned out, the company commander was not called to testify.[17] Having only arrived in-country three-and-a-half days earlier, the defense was still pulling together its case. The IO then asked the accused, for the record, "Do you understand your rights in this investigation?" Lee stood, and responded, "Yes, sir." The IO then told the government they may proceed. Lieutenant Rudy stated the government would like to call Sergeant Herman Diaz. Einsidler departed the room to get him.

Hargrove then said out loud to the bench, "Excuse me. May the accused have a chance to *voir dire* the investigating officer?"

To *voir dire* means "to speak truth." In a court, it refers to a process of determining whether the person subject to *voir dire* can serve fairly and impartially. A *voir dire* is not seen in Article 32 hearings, and rarely in the UCMJ, so this was a risk for the defense as the IO would be the person making the ruling. The IO responded to Captain Hargrove, "You may *voir dire*."[18]

Now, Hastings for the defense stood and started a well-thought-out dialog challenging the IO for cause in three areas. The first was that he is in the legal chain of command as the deputy SJA both before and after the Article 32. The challenge revolved around the fact that King's fitness for duty report was written by the SJA Colonel Lucy, and, that Lucy was serving as the counselor for Drumright, who was the convening authority. Hastings asked, "Did your boss, Colonel Lucy, talk to you about this case?" King stated he did not, except to say he would become the IO. The second area revolved around conversations King had with the NIS Resident Agent Gonzales during his investigation. Could they have influenced the IO? The third area was the fact that King had served as one of the IOs for the 1st Battalion, 7th Marines, who were subject to courts-martial over the killing of 16 women and children; how did that major legal event affect the legal climate in the 1st Marine Division? Hastings took his time, over a full 20 minutes, and outlined the three perceived conflicts of interest. He closed with the suggestion King should step down.

Lieutenant Colonel King called a recess at 0945 and announced he would consider the challenge thoughtfully, without talking or seeking counsel elsewhere. At 0955, King reconvened the hearing and said, "I have searched my conscience and announce the challenge for cause is not sustained."[19]

Rudy, the government counsel, called Sergeant Herman Diaz. Einsidler had him standing outside, so he came in and was shown the witness stand and sworn in. Then, as background, he stated he had been in the Marine Corps for six and a half years, in Recon three years, at 1st Recon for the past 12 months and was currently the platoon sergeant for 3rd Platoon, Delta Company. Rudy then asked Diaz about Hill 119, had he been there and what was the mission. Diaz responded he had been there many times and Recon's mission was to provide security for the Integrated Observation Device (IOD). Rudy asked if Diaz was present on 28 March for the incident, to which he responded, "Yes, sir." Then he had Diaz talk about the events he had observed through his 7 × 50 binos, from the time he had first observed the four Vietnamese working near the tree line, through the shooting, and the burial, and to do so in his own words. Hastings, on cross-examination, had Diaz explain the FFZ. Diaz said that, in order to defend the hill, they were free to fire out to 1,000 meters around the hill. He had inadvertently used FFZ for what he meant as a Recon haven. It was not corrected. The hill could always defend itself, but it was not an FFZ. The IO stated, for the record, that they needed to get a definition of FFZ. Diaz talked through the entire incident, which covered the daylight hours of 28 March. His testimony took most of the morning. He was formally warned not to discuss his testimony, or the case, and was dismissed.[20] The hearing took a lunch recess at 1120.

Throughout the inquiry, there was some confusion over definitions between witnesses and members of the inquiry on the meaning of haven, FFZ, restricted area, and RoE. All four were defined in classified annexes. The Recon and Artillery Marines all had hand-me-down verbal definitions that were honest but slightly off, which led to confusion.

After lunch, at 1308, the inquiry reconvened. The government then called Lance Corporal Daniel E. Broe. He stated he joined the Marines on 28 April 1969 and arrived at 1st Recon on 1 February 1970. He also stated he had been to sniper school at Camp Pendleton before coming over to the battalion. He was now one of the two snipers in 3rd Platoon. The government then talked Broe through his participation in the events of 28 March, by retrieving his sniper weapon, then later retrieving the bolt and ammunition which he provided to Lee. He also described calling the rifle shots with the M49 scope. When asked by the defense, he clearly recalled Lee stating he was firing warning shots to move the Vietnamese out of the restricted area. He quoted the lieutenant as saying, "I just want the rounds to fire warning shots." In Broe's testimony, by using the M49 scope, he identified the elderly one-armed woman as the female that had been digging with a hoe in the mortar hole.[21] The woman was one of the village elders from Tho Son hamlet. As an elder, she had frequented the hill, often bringing people for medical care, and other Vietnamese who complained about trail usage for access to Alligator Lake for fishing on the south side of Hill 119 from Tho Son. She was easily recognizable and known to every Marine who pulled duty on Hill 119. Broe was warned not to reveal testimony and then dismissed.

The government then called Lance Corporal John P. "Jack" Kempe of 3rd Platoon, Delta Company. He had joined the Marine Corps on 21 April 1969 and arrived at 1st Recon on 15 November 1969. On 28 March, he described being with Diaz and asking him what he was doing. Diaz responded he had some "gooks down in there" and gave Kempe the binoculars to look. Kempe had been one of the Marines going down to meet the villagers with Lee and Warrant Officer Thien, the South Vietnamese forward observer, who served as an interpreter. He described what happened at that meeting with the villagers when they brought the body to the hill. He stated the lieutenant had told the villagers he was sorry for the incident, but they had been in a restricted area, and they knew it. Kempe also collaborated on the talk Lee had with the entire platoon later that afternoon, where the lieutenant had said he was sorry for the outcome but that he had done the correct action in firing the warning shots. He also said he had filed a spot report with Battalion concerning the killing. He said he was solely responsible and offered that if anyone wanted to talk about it to come by his bunker.[22] At this point, the IO recessed the hearing at 1450 for a head call.

The hearing resumed at 1500 with the government calling Corporal Robert Grossman. Grossman had joined the Marine Corps in November 1968 and had come to Vietnam and Recon in June 1969. Rudy had Grossman describe what he had observed on 28 March with the shots fired. Grossman testified that the villagers had been told numerous times that the north front of Hill 119 was off limits, and they could not congregate there. He testified that, on 28 March, the four Vietnamese were in a restricted area known to them. He said, on his previous patrol off the hill, they hit a booby trap just north of where the Vietnamese were on 28 March. Two of the patrol members were injured and had to be medevac'd.[23] Grossman was duly warned and dismissed from the hearing.

The government then called Hospital Corpsman Second Class Glen E. Edison USN. He had been in the Navy two years and his previous assignment was the Naval Hospital in San Diego. He was currently the corpsman for 3rd Platoon. He described taking care of the young Vietnamese girl with the leg wound on the morning of 28 March. He also said he was called down to the meeting with the village elders and the woman in the stretcher. He examined her and said she was dead and had been so for about thirty minutes. He said her injury was a bullet hole in the upper right chest and volunteered that she had lost a lot of blood.[24]

Next, the government called 1st Lieutenant P. R. Green USMCR. Green belonged to the S-2 (IOD) Section of Headquarters Battery, 11th Marines. He stated he arrived on Hill 119 on 23 March directly from IOD School and remained there until 9 April. He further said he was in the tower and witnessed the shooting. He was upset by the incident. Before he could answer capabilities of the IOD, the two civilian attorneys had to step outside while the classified discussion occurred. He then gave the inquiry a classified briefing on the capabilities of the IOD. He discussed his classified RoE for firing in the FFZ to the north, which allowed him to shoot at any target he deemed hostile. Sergeant Einsidler recalled the two defense attorneys. Lieutenant Green now stated he had observed the four Vietnamese on 28 March and did not deem them hostile, however they were not his concern as they were in Lee's area of responsibility. He did recall Lee telling him he was going to fire warning shots to move the Vietnamese on. He added he was dismayed she was shot and it upset him. The government and the defense both cross-examined Green and then the IO asked some clarification questions concerning the RoEs. When his testimony was complete, he was warned and then dismissed.[25] The IO adjourned the hearing at 1930.

It had been a long day. Captain Hargrove took the two civilian defense counsel to the division mess hall before they retired to the transient officers' huts near the court room. Lee walked down Hill 327 across Division Road and back to his hut where he hydrated a long-ration for dinner.

The hearing was reopened the next morning, 11 June, at 0930. The government introduced three exhibits. Exhibit 12 was a page from the accused's record book showing he was a marksman with the M14.[26] Marines must qualify with a rifle to graduate from Boot Camp or The Basic School. Marines shoot a 500 meter known-distance course. In qualifying, there are three levels: Marksman, Sharpshooter, and Expert. Marksman is the lowest level of qualification with the rifle. The square Marksman shooting badge with three ovals of a target on it resembled a toilet seat, which is what the Marines call it. The defense countered the prosecution's claim that Lee could hit or miss anything he wanted to with this exhibit which showed Lee was a marksman with the rife. Exhibit 13 was the entire patrol debrief for Hill 119 for the two-week period that included the 28 March incident. Exhibit 14 was a III Marine Amphibious Force order concerning the Geneva Convention, prisoners of war, and civilian personnel in times of war. The defense counsel objected that the force order was not relevant to the incident. The IO overruled the objection, and it was entered into evidence.[27]

The government then called 2nd Lieutenant Garry L. Parks USMC. He was sworn in for his testimony. Parks had been in the Marine Corps for one year and seven days. That response to his time in service question was an example of how detailed and professional Garry Parks was as a Marine officer. He had been assigned to Delta Company, 1st Recon, as the 2nd Platoon commander for the past six months, during which time he had been to Hill 119 four times as the hill commander.[28] The government asked him what his mission was as hill commander. Parks answered in general, "The defense of Hill 119 OP and specifically the protection of our personnel, equipment, supplies, and more specifically the IOD on the hill."[29] They asked Parks to describe the haven to which he said was a 1,000-meter box around the hill as outlined in the hill operations order, by grid coordinates, from Battalion. That was the land inside the haven that the hill commander owned. The government handed him Exhibit 1, which was a photograph of the north side of Hill 119 and then Exhibit 15, which was a plastic overlay. Rudy asked him to draw the haven on the north side. Parks said, as he drew it, that is was only approximate as the grid coordinates would come from a map. There was a discussion on who owed the land outside the haven box and the response was 5th Marines, specifically 2nd Battalion, 5th Marines. Next there was a discussion on the RoEs which Parks described as being able to engage enemy identified as such with uniforms, packs, or rifles and/or people conducting aggressive acts such as booby-trap emplacements. The government then asked what Parks would do if he had Vietnamese in civilian clothes inside his haven but had no indication of them being enemy or not enemy. He answered by saying he had three courses of action. First, he could call Battalion and seek guidance from S-3 Operations. Second, he could send a patrol out to the people to determine what they were doing if it were tactically sound to do so. Third, he could fire mortar warning shots with "Willie Pete" (white phosphorous) smoke, a CS (tear gas) round, or fire warning shots with a direct-fire weapon such as a .50-caliber machine gun.[30] The defense then asked Parks if there had been an incident the day before, 10 June, near the hill? He responded yes and was asked to relate it. Parks said a walk-off patrol north of the hill had hit a booby trap and two Republic of Korea Marines were wounded and had to be medevac'd. The defense entered Exhibit 16, which was Parks's patrol report for Hill 119 for the period of 21 May–6 June.[31] He asked if the hill had received incoming fire. Parks responded, "Yes, sir." He was then asked to read paragraph 5, the synopsis of the patrol report. He read it aloud; the patrol had 20 sightings of 57 NVA/VC, four "Chieu Hois," and one incoming round.[32] He was then asked to describe what he would do if he had Vietnamese inside his haven. He said, if the person was designated NVA/VC, or was performing some hostile act of aggression, then he had to make a decision to fire or not fire. He was asked, if there were Vietnamese dressed in civilian clothes observing the hill, what would he do? He said, "I would fire warning shots to warn them away or get them to move." After Parks's testimony, he was duly warned and dismissed.[33]

The defense counsel, Hastings, summarized a number of hypothetical situations concerning Vietnamese around the hill and what Parks said he would do in each. Hastings summarized the responses all boiled down to it being a judgment call for the hill commander.[34]

Rudy then drew the IO's attention back to Exhibit 13, a marked picture and stated he wanted to draw to King's attention that, during the 28 March incident, the Vietnamese were inside the haven.[35] At that point, the IO called a recess for a coffee break at 1015. The hearing was called back into session at 1030, where the government stated that, at this time, they had nothing further.

The IO nodded to the defense where Hargrove called Corporal Randy Lowery, who was duly sworn in. He stated he was with 3rd Platoon, Delta Company. He was asked where he was on 28 March, and he responded on Hill 119 and that Lee had asked him to bring in the medevac bird for "Doc" Edison, so he got a PRC-25 radio and his weapon and went east on the ridgeline, outside the wire, where Doc had the wounded girl. He would control the medevac chopper in a hasty landing zone (LZ) directly on the east ridgeline. The defense asked Lowery how many times he had been to the OP.

Lowery said, "Nine times, sir."

He was asked to mark the restricted movement area north of the OP on the photo, which he did. He was then asked if he ever saw Vietnamese working the fields in that area. He said the fields were overgrown and he had never seen them being worked. He was asked why Lee had fired the rifle? He said, "The Vietnamese were in an area where you could not see what they were doing. They could have been setting booby traps, so the lieutenant was trying to move them into the open."

Next, Hastings asked Lowery how many patrols he had run off Hill 119. He responded with 30 to 35 patrols. He was asked to state what encounters he had with the enemy on those patrols.

Lowery said, "We have had contacts but mostly booby traps."

Hastings then asked if there were booby traps near the tree line the Vietnamese were working on 28 March? He said "Yes, sir" and pointed to the location on the photos. The photos were marked with numbers 1 through 3.

Lowery explained, "Sir, a booby trap at the number 3 being a 155 Arty round booby-trapped with trip wire while the other two numbers were M26 grenade booby traps."

Hastings asked Lowery had he ever seen warning shots fired from the hill? He responded yes, that in December the captain had them fire the M60 machine gun to move the villagers away from the hill. (Author's note, this would have been Captain Tom Martin, Delta Company commander at that time.)[36] He was asked how close were the rounds from the M60 fired; he stated 2–3 meters. Finally, Lowery was asked if any patrols had hit booby traps and injured Marines? He said yes, that on 17 or 19 May they walked off and both Doc Edison and Corporal McCommon were wounded with a booby trap near a dry well in the village below the hill. They both were medevac'd.[37] The witness was duly warned and dismissed.

The defense now called Captain Gary P. Burns USMC from Division G-5, Civil Affairs. He was the civic-action officer for the 1st Marine Division. He had had the billet for the past five months and had been in-country for 18 months. His duties included getting materials for civil-affairs projects and keeping the statistics in the classified HES. The two civilian attorneys stepped out. Burns's testimony was classified secret and concerned the different threat ratings of the villages and the hamlet below Hill 119. The HES was a Vietnam-wide rating system run by Military Assistance Command, Vietnam to classify every hamlet and village as to who physically controlled it, the South Vietnamese Government, or the VC. Burns testified that the residents of Xuyen Thanh village, with a population of 1,018 spread through multiple hamlets, were VC sympathizers and that Tho Son and Thon Bon hamlets directly below Hill 119 were VC-controlled. He also showed the hearing the boundaries of the villages and district. He further stated that the boundaries had changed with the movement of the Vietnamese population east to the protected hamlets along Route 1.[38] The witness was warned and withdrawn from the courtroom.

It was 1140 and the IO recessed the hearing for lunch. The entire defense team and Lee walked to the division mess hall for lunch. The hearing resumed at 1310.

The defense called Master Sergeant Robert Diaz, USMC. He was sworn in and told the hearing he had been in the Marine Corps for 23 years. The past 15 years were on the Marine Corps Rifle Team. He was currently the chief instructor for the 1st Division's sniper school, and, that he was proud to be a Distinguished Shooter for the Marine Corps. It was stipulated and agreed to by both parties that he was an expert witness. The witness explained the process of zeroing a specific rifle to a specific shooter. Zeroing the rifle for that shooter on the range provides each shooter with his DOPE (data on previous engagement) for that weapon. For the sniper rifle, it was done at 500 meters. Special Agent Gonzales had recovered Lance Corporal Broe's sniper rifle from Broe earlier in the investigation at Camp Reasoner. On 7 June, Gonzales had that same rifle at the division range for Diaz to shoot for the government and defense counsels to observe. He fired five shots at 500 meters with the same DOPE that was set for Broe. Then the entire delegation flew to Hill 119, whereupon Hernandez reenacted the shots Lee had taken, he first shot standing from the stairs to the tower and the second and third shots from a sitting position at the same spot next to the .50-cal pit. Using the same weapon and aiming at the same mortar hole, Diaz fired 14 shots, missing and adjusting through the sight and using Kentucky windage. He missed the mortar hole on each shot. Now in the Article 32 hearing, the defense asked Diaz if a shooter, who qualified as an M14 "rifle marksman" using that same sniper weapon from 700 meters at the same target, could hit the target? He said, "It would be very unusual to hit the target."[39] The master sergeant was thanked and dismissed.

The hearing recessed at 1400 and reconvened at 1435. At that time, the government called 1st Lieutenant Arthur P. Gray USMCR who was the assistant operations officer (S-3A) of Recon Battalion while his prior billet had been the tactical plans officer in the S-3 Section. It was the tactical plans officer's job to draft the mission orders for a patrol or an OP. He was asked about his connection to Hill 119 by government counsel. Gray responded, "I wrote the Operations Order for the hill's Observation Post." They then asked him for the definition of haven. "Pete" Gray responded that it was a fire-support coordination measure, using a designated space on the ground, during a specific time frame, the duration of which the Recon commander owned the area. The commander therefore had to approve all firing inside his own haven. It was a safety measure to protect friendly units from friendly fire. Therefore, the haven that is designated in the operations order is owned by the hill commander. The area directly outside the haven was controlled by 5th Marines and that area was currently delegated to 2nd Battalion, 5th Marines. Gray explained these were tactical areas of operations in which units could operate freely. The government then had Gray draw the Hill 119 haven on the photo[40] before he was dismissed.

Pete Gray died one month later rappelling from a CH-46, on 19 July, while rehearsing for a rappelling demonstration on LZ 401 for a future visit by a dignitary.[41] His rappelling rope got tangled and snared in his waist snap-link connecting him to the CH-46 by rope which dragged him through rice paddies where he hit his neck and head on a hard paddy dike. It was a tragic loss for his family and the Marine Corps. He was a University of Virginia academic and athletic star and had already shown brilliant performance as a Marine lieutenant in the field.[42] His selection as the battalion's tactical plans officer meant he had a bright future. Gray was the Article 32 hearing's last witness.

The IO moved directly to closing arguments.[43] Navy Lieutenant Rudy's closing was a short statement. He stated that, from the witness and documentation, there did not appear to be evidence of premeditation, but "I do feel there has been evidence of criminality in the record of testimony." He then rested for the government.[44]

Hastings then started the defense's closing argument, reminding the hearing that he and DiNapoli had traveled almost eight thousand miles to defend their client. He then stated there had been no evidence of premeditated murder. He further stated there was no evidence for manslaughter or negligent homicide. He pointed out that the hill commander, Lieutenant Lee, was responsible for protecting his people, his position, and the equipment in a combat situation; that he had made a judgment call; that he was protecting a critical OP with a device so highly classified it could not be talked about it in an open hearing; that every witness had stated Hill 119 was in hostile territory; that the G-5 testified the hamlet below the hill was VC-controlled and at night was an outright VC hamlet. Hastings asked the rhetorical question: What evidence has the government presented that this is a criminal homicide? He stated the woman who was killed was in a VC-controlled area that was restricted to civilians. All the witnesses said she had been killed in the restricted area, that warning shots were used in the past and Lee, and everyone on the hill, believed he was firing warning shots. At the time, there was no farming or fishing in the area. What were the Vietnamese doing that day digging holes and cutting bamboo? Could they have been gathering information or intelligence on the gun and wire placement for the OP or could they have been laying booby traps? As characterized by Captain Burns, the woman could have been VC or a VC sympathizer. Hastings closed with, "This was not a criminal act in nature, this was a judgment call by a Commanding Officer in a hostile situation! This hearing shows the charges should be dismissed!"

The hearing closed at 1930 on 11 June.[45]

Although listed on the original witness list, the commanding officer of Delta Company, 1st Lieutenant Jerry Spolter, was not called.[46] That evening, Hastings and DiNapoli went directly to Da Nang International Airport to start their journey back to San Jose. All the witnesses returned to their duties. The Marines of 3rd Platoon went back out on patrol and, in time, returned to Hill 119. Lee walked down Hill 327 back to his duties in Headquarters and Service Company to await the slow wheels of justice to determine his fate. Mentally, he and his defense team were already preparing for a general court-martial.

In California, Hastings and DiNapoli continued with press releases trying to influence the next decision in the process. On 11 June, in the *San Jose News*, the headline read "Marine Defense claim delay" and, on 12 June, the *San Jose Mercury* headline read, "Viet Murder Defense Hits roadblock."[47]

On 19 June, Lieutenant Colonel King sent "Interim Report on Art. 32 for 1Lt W.X. Lee" by letter to Lieutenant Colonel Drumright with the status of the investigation. In it he recommended a reduction in the charges to a single specification in violation of UCMJ Article 119, Involuntary Manslaughter, and that the accused be tried at a general court-martial for that offense.[48] Drumright would have three weeks to think on the Lee case. He now knew what the formal investigation would recommend when he received it, along with the verbatim testimony. He could agree and simply forward the investigation, which is what Colonel Lucy, the SJA and, by implication, what the division commander wanted. They wanted to be able to report to the South Vietnamese Government and military and, of more import to them, the press, that a complete investigation of the incident occurred, and the results were a general court-martial, because the Marine Corps was not the Army; they investigated serious allegations rather than cover-up incidents as represented in the My Lai massacre.

The institution wanted a general court-martial for appearances.

Lee was simply not as important as the good reputation of the Marine Corps. Drumright would knuckle under to command pressure for appearances and bet on the river card that, in a court-martial, Lee would be acquitted. Lee was on his own! It would take the two recorders three weeks to transcribe the verbatim testimony of the Article 32 hearing. The report came to 167 single-spaced typewritten pages, without the seven classified annexes and 21 exhibits.[49]

CHAPTER 28

Teams *Bad Actor*, *Segment*, and *Allen Town*, July 1970

As July 1970 began, two significant events occurred on the Fourth of July. In Washington, D.C., Bob Hope and Billy Graham hosted a celebration of the nation's 194th birthday, which gathered a crowd of over four hundred thousand to the Washington Monument Mall to listen to the live entertainment. There was a small anti-war protest in Lafayette Park.[1] That evening in Asbury Park, New Jersey, there was a major civil disturbance and race riots. It began seven days of rioting, looting, and destruction in the small seaside town.[2]

In-country, XXIV Corps, in a preemptory operation to disrupt North Vietnamese Army (NVA) logistics towards the A Shau Valley, tried to clandestinely build a fire-support base (FSB) on the eastern shoulder to support further moves west into the valley. The construction from March–July was watched by NVA reconnaissance units. The NVA planned and moved supplies in and around the FSB, preparing the battlefield before they launched their mortar attack on 1 July that began the siege of FSB Ripcord. The siege lasted 23 days as the 2nd Battalion, 506th Regiment, 101st Airborne Division withstood daily rocket and mortar attacks. The NVA committed two divisions to the siege. The battalion was withdrawn on the 23 July, followed by B-52 carpet bombing of the FSB and the A Shau Valley. The siege and battle would turn out to be the last large ground set-piece action of the war between U.S. forces and the NVA. The division commander claimed it prevented the buildup of NVA forces for Tet 1971 in I Corps. President Nixon had Military Assistance Command, Vietnam (MACV) withhold casualty figures and details of the siege from the U.S. press as he was trying to control information provided to the anti-war movement in the United States.[3]

Meanwhile, at III Marine Amphibious Force (III MAF), they were coordinating the drawdown and making plans with XXIV Corps for Army and Army of the Republic of Vietnam (ARVN) units to take over Marine bases and positions throughout northern South Vietnam. The 1st Marine Division launched multibattalion search-and-destroy operations against the 2nd NVA Division. Called Operation *Barron Green*, the 5th Marines began, on 15 July, to deny the NVA the harvest of the ripe corn crop in the northern Arizona Territory, while Operation *Lyon Valley*, by the 5th Marines, was to prevent the 38th NVA Regiment from entering the Arizona Territory.[4] The 7th Marines began Operation *Pickens Forest* on 16 July by moving company sized units into enemy areas in Antenna Valley and the Que Son Mountains. *Pickens Forest* lasted until 24 August and accounted for 99 enemy killed.[5] The low enemy body count clearly indicated the 2nd NVA Division had pulled back and was waiting for the announced American withdrawal. At the Central Committee level of North Vietnam, its strategy would be to wait for the Americans to go home and then defeat the South Vietnamese Army. The 1st Battalion, 5th Marines, under Lieutenant Colonel "Mic" Trainor was relocated to protect the division command post and the immediate tactical area of responsibility around Division Ridge. They maintained a company-size heliborne Pacifier Force later renamed the division's quick-reaction force.[6]

***

At the 1st Reconnaissance Battalion during July, Lieutenant Colonel "Wild Bill" Drumright continued to push his "Boys" using *Sting Ray* missions to make contact with the enemy. The concept had been developed by 1st Force Recon in 1966 along the demilitarized zone, effectively utilizing supporting arms against large NVA formations. Marine Captain "Bing" West, after patrolling with 1st Force Recon, wrote the Marine Corps' training manual *Small Unit Action in Vietnam.* Later, he authored a study at the Rand Corporation entitled, *The Strike Teams: Tactical Performance and Strategic Potential.* Widely studied within the Marine Corps and used by Lieutenant General Nickerson and other small-unit advocates in Vietnam, it never gained traction with the senior Army leadership at MACV which favored air mobility in large unit operations. The 1st Recon Battalion now had a classified standard operating procedure (SOP), Battalion Order PO3000.4 entitled "SOP for Sting Ray/Clandestine Long-range Patrolling Operations."[7]

Utilizing dedicated helo assets and direct-support artillery batteries for Recon teams, Drumright was taking the fight to the enemy. He was maintaining between 32 and 42 teams in the bush. They were continuously covering the avenues of approach into the Da Nang Vital Area.[8] He was also selling his battalion's capabilities through operational briefs and demonstrations of capabilities known by the Marines as "dog and pony shows." The shows were an unnecessary burden on the over-committed battalion and took air and recon assets away from the primary mission. The demonstrations were conducted by the training cadre of the S-3 (operations) shop. On 19 July, during a rehearsal for a dog and pony show, 1st Lieutenant "Pete" Gray, a Rhodes Scholar nominee, and University of Virgina football captain, was killed unnecessarily when he was dragged by the rappelling rope attached to a CH-46 through the hard, dry rice paddy dikes below Hill 327 and Landing Zone (LZ) 401.[9] This training incident and non-battle casualty should never have happened, as the show for VIPs was not a wartime necessity. Gray's death fell directly on Drumright's shoulders as he was trying to impress his superiors. The dog and pony shows were subsequently terminated, at least for a while.

In Delta Company, on 2 July, Lieutenant Paul Eglevsky departed on emergency leave for the United States due to a death in his family. Since he had completed nine months in Vietnam, he was short-toured with orders and emergency leave en route home. He had served six months in the 5th Marines and had completed six patrols, and two observation-post (OP) flips, in his three months with the 1st Recon Battalion.[10]

On the same day, 2 July, 1st Lieutenant Fallon flew up to Hill 119 with an understrength 3rd Platoon of 15 Marines and a corpsman.[11] His callsign was *Pal Joey-Kilo*. To compensate, Fallon took 100 new Claymore mines and a 106-mm recoilless rifle and ammunition to defend the hill. One of his Marines had traded four captured AK-47s with an Army unit for the 106 rifle. On 4 July, 1st Lieutenant "Jerry" Spolter caught his "Freedom Bird" out of Da Nang after 19 months in-country. Initially serving with 3rd Battalion, 7th Marines, as a platoon commander

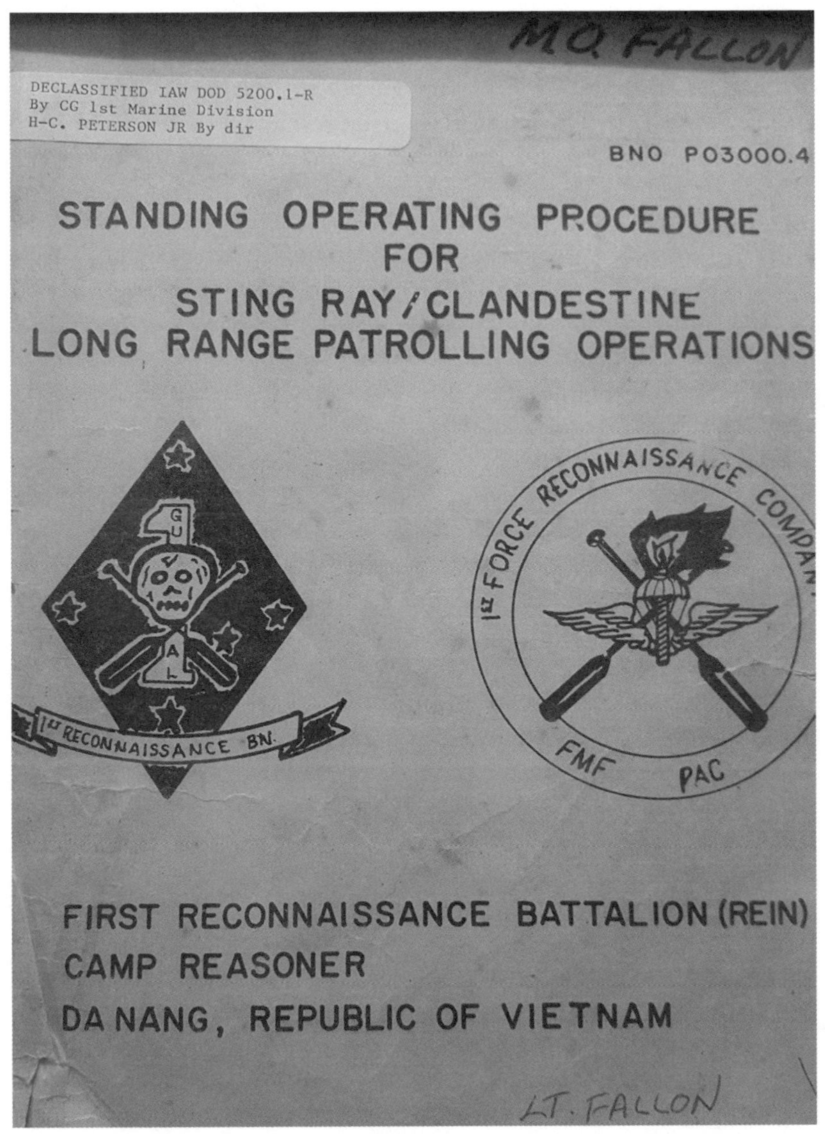
M.O. FALLON

DECLASSIFIED IAW DOD 5200.1-R
By CG 1st Marine Division
H-C. PETERSON JR By dir

BNO P03000.4

STANDING OPERATING PROCEDURE
FOR
STING RAY/CLANDESTINE
LONG RANGE PATROLLING OPERATIONS

1st RECONNAISSANCE BN.

1st FORCE RECONNAISSANCE COMPANY
FMF PAC

FIRST RECONNAISSANCE BATTALION (REIN)
CAMP REASONER
DA NANG, REPUBLIC OF VIETNAM

LT. FALLON

SOP for *Sting Ray* patrols, cover sheet of battalion order, 1970. (M. Fallon)

and later S-5 Civil Affairs Officer, he transferred at six months to VMO-2, becoming an aerial observer (AO), callsign *Cowpoke One-Zero.* Spolter finished his Vietnam service with six months at 1st Recon Battalion as a patrol leader and the company commander of Delta Company.[12] He was Drumright's first "Happy Warrior" even though he could not abide his alcoholic battalion commander's bullying behavior. Upon arrival in California, he moved from active duty to the reserves in order to attend law school. Spolter would have a successful career in law and become an international arbiter working from his office on Fisherman's Wharf, San Francisco. First Lieutenant Smith moved up from executive officer and assumed command of Delta Company.[13]

On the hill, back at Delta Company's OP, on 11 July at sundown, Lance Corporal Broe, on top of Alpha Bunker, observed eight NVA with packs and rifles northwest of the OP moving into the deserted hamlet of Thon Bon (2).[14] The enemy was setting up near a bunker in the old hamlet. Broe notified Fallon, and Integrated Observation Device (IOD) team *Empire State* who now observed the enemy through the "Big Eyes." *Empire State* called a fire mission with *Pearl Chest-Mike* at 2150 and got the first six rounds at 2151. Now utilizing the infrared searchlight Eglevsky had brought to the hill on the previous flip, they could see the target clearly and fired multiple fire-for-effect missions with the last rounds completed at 2230. They had full coverage, resulting in four enemy killed and two secondary explosions.[15] They observed the other four enemy running to the west. *Empire State* called a second fire mission on those enemy soldiers with *Pearl Chest-Mike* at 2215, getting first rounds at 2245 with end of mission at 2250. They claimed two kills and one probable. The hill tried using the infrared searchlight for the bomb-damage assessment, but the distance of 2,500 meters proved a challenge to do so. On 13 July, the IOD team sighted three enemy at 0640 in the morning on the forward slope of Hill 148, one kilometer west. They called a fire mission, resulting in two enemy killed, observed lying on the side of the hill.[16] Fallon considered a patrol over to Hill 148 to search the bodies but decided the prudent move was to stay close to the hill due to being shorthanded.

On the 16th, the sun set at 1920. At 2120, in the dark, the hill observed an OV-10, *Hostage Junkman* flown by Major Carlson with his *Cowpoke* AO, Lieutenant Hatch, flying over Go Noi Island and taking a large amount of antiaircraft ground fire. The IOD team requested a fire mission but could not get clearance, as the AO had control of that area. Fallon tried to raise the *Hostage* aircraft on the radio but failed to connect before the bird departed north.

At 2130 on 16 July, Hill 119 supported and helped coordinate Recon Team *Donahue*'s extract out of the Phu Loc Valley. *Empire State* called a fire mission on the extract LZ, after the team was out, shooting 32 rounds from *Moose Peak-A*. They got one exceptionally large secondary explosion from the fire mission. On 18 July, the platoon flipped out. During their 16-day period on the OP, the IOD team, *Empire State*, had called 13 fire missions on sightings of 48 total enemy, claiming 22 kills, one probable, and two secondary explosions.[17] Coming up to Hill 119 would be the newly joined 1st Lieutenant Taylor with Delta Company's 4th Platoon.[18] Taylor was taking Chris L'Orange's place in the company following his medevac.

***

On 7 July, 1st Lieutenant Earl Hailston took Team *Bad Actor* into the bush. He had four Marines plus two Korean Marine corporals, Park and Lee, for the patrol.[19] They were going south of Antenna Valley, near the coal mines in support of the 7th Marines' Operation *Pickens Forest*, to report enemy moving across the river into the valley where the 7th Marines were conducting a multibattalion sweep to deny the NVA the rice harvest.[20] They were inserted at noon on 7 July and had two quiet days, with signs of enemy everywhere, but no sightings. Slowly trail walking, Team *Bad Actor* was hunting. At 0800 on 9 July, they rounded a turn and got the jump on one NVA. Hailston shouted "Dung Lai, Chieu Hoi" as they grabbed the soldier. The soldier was wearing a gray flannel shirt and shorts. He had an AK-47 and a heavily loaded H-harness and cartridge belt. He had been sitting on the ground, resting, with the rifle and cartridge belt grounded. The NVA, now a prisoner, started laughing and talking.[21] The team tried to silence him by covering his mouth and rifle butting him in the chest and shoulder, but he wouldn't cooperate, continuing to make noise. The team then fired a warning shot over his head to quiet him. Moving to the top of a nearby hill, they established communications with *Pal Joey-K*, the radio relay on Hill 119. Hailston requested an AO for support. He also requested an immediate extract for the team, which was SOP upon capturing a prisoner.

Fallon, on Hill 119 working three radio nets,[22] got an AO diverted and then explained the situation to Battalion, adding that *Bad Actor* was also in contact and needed an immediate extract via ladder. At 0820, the team's tail-end Charlie observed five NVA, in gray uniforms and armed with AK-47s, pursuing them.[23] Now on a narrow trail on the spine of a steep, rocky finger, *Bad Actor* stopped and engaged the enemy with small-arms fire. With the team distracted by the firefight, the prisoner attempted to escape. The enemy solider shoved the closest Marine's rifle to the side as he dove off the trail, rolling downhill. The team's point man shot the escapee, who now laid in the draw on the ground, not moving. At the same time, the team's assistant patrol leader, Sergeant Norton, shot the leading enemy pursuer on the narrow trail, killing him.[24] Trying to break contact and reach the military crest of the hill, Hailston had the team place a Claymore on the narrow trail facing downhill and, after backing over to the other side of the hill, set it off on the pursuers coming up the trail. This bought them needed time to break contact.

Following the explosion, *Bad Actor*, now on a high-speed trail, ran down the backside of the hill, evading the enemy who were still pursuing them. They ran across a deep draw and up another hill. In the dense jungle, observation was limited to a few feet blocked by growth as the trail went around another tree or turn. Moving up the third hill, they could see at least fifteen enemy now on the crest of the original hill. In an organized pursuit, the enemy began down the trail, following the Recon team. This was an elite counter-recon team chasing them with the mission to wipe them out. Reaching the top of the hill, Hailston set a 360-degree defense around a small jungle clearing sufficient for a ladder extract. The jungle canopy rose to 80 feet on all sides except within the small clearing. The diverted OV-10 aircraft, *Hostage Bill*, piloted by Captain Bill Paulson with AO 1st Lieutenant Steve Tace (*Cowpoke Three-Two*),[25] arrived over the team at 0830 and had difficulty locating them due to the deep jungle canopy.

Hailston, using a signal mirror, hit the bird with a mirror flash of the sun to establish positive ID of the team's location. *Hostage Bill* began working over the first hill and steep draw between the NVA and the Marines with his onboard ordnance. Hailston's mirror flash to the aircraft had established the friendly hill that the aviation assets would try to seal off from the pursuing NVA. Tace had fixed-wing inbound. *Cowpoke Three-Two* put the multiple flights of F-4s in the air stack prioritized by how much time on station each flight could afford while waiting for his call. By the twos, for the next 45 minutes, Tace ran three flights of F-4s at "Danger Close," meaning 250 meters or less to *Bad Actor*'s hilltop position. Hailston could see the aluminum cannisters of napalm tumble off the aircraft after release. The Marine aviators were on target in the steep draw, as the flames and heat could be felt by each of the eight members of *Bad Actor* hugging the ground on top of the hill. The heat rolled over them. The Recon Marines then watched the 500-pound Mk.82 bombs with Mk.15 "Snake Eye" tail retarders (four fins that opened up to slow their descent so the low-flying aircraft could escape the shrapnel pattern). The team could hear the whining sound of the shrapnel flying over their heads. The faster movers put "snake" and "nape" on the north, northeast, and northwest sides of the extract hill. The AO followed the fixed-wing with two helicopter gunships, *Scarface-One* (Captain Gary Thiry) and *Scarface-Three*, to finish the isolation of the LZ with their last strafing runs. He immediately had *Hostage Bill* roll the OV-10 over in a vertical dive and, with a "Willie-Pete" (white phosphorous) rocket, mark the uphill trail for the gunships. The gunships started working the trail in the draw and all around the hill at 0900, making single passes, keeping the NVAs' heads down and focused on the gunbirds, until the two CH-46s from HMM 262, callsign *Chatterbox*, arrived for the extract at 0915. The low-flying CH-46 came to a hover and rolled the 125-foot ladder off its tail ramp into the small hole in the jungle canopy. The crew chief was the pilot's eyes, looking down at the ladder to correct the altitude of the hover. The crew chief kept talking to the pilot, who hovered the bird while taking small-arms fire. Both of the birds' .50-caliber machine guns were working over their side of the jungle. The ladder had to thread the needle through the jungle canopy to the small clearing.

On the ground, the two RoK Marines climbed the ladder followed by the Marines in twos, the rest of Team *Bad Actor*. Hailston, being the last and low man on the ladder to snap in with his snap-link, signaled to pull out. He popped yellow smoke indicating visually they were all on as he yelled on the PRC-25 radio to the extract officer from Recon Battalion who was on board the bird. The ladder rose vertically off the small hilltop clearing under heavy small-arms fire. *Bad Actor*, to a man, now sitting on the ladder, unleashed a magazine of ammunition on fully automatic towards the edges of the small clearing. The helo pilot held the hover for four minutes while the CH-46 absorbed the AK-47 fire. Now the CH-46 pilot had to pull the ladder, along with the team's weight, straight up in a hover another 100 feet. If he dipped the nose and went for air speed, he would drag the Marines through the double-canopy trees, breaking them and/or the ladder. The crew chief would tell the pilot when the ladder had cleared the top of the canopy. Once above the jungle, as the CH-46 gained speed, the ladder swayed back behind and below the CH-46. Two minutes earlier, the Marines were hot, sweaty, and worried; now they felt the cool breeze created by the aircraft's forward speed. They were now cold, relieved, and happy to be out. The ladder ride was a great view as the aircraft gained altitude above three thousand feet and effective small-arms range. They flew north over Antenna Valley, the Que Son Mountains and settled down at the An Hoa Combat Base's short airfield. Now hovering again and coming down slowly, Hailston was first man off, unsnapping his link, while the ladder continued to descend, each Marine unsnapping as his body hit the ground. The Marines transferred to the inside of the bird while the Recon ropemaster/ladder noncommissioned officer and CH-46 crew chief rolled the ladder back up, covering the entire back ramp. *Bad Actor* had been on the ground for 45 hours, having killed two enemy and bringing back one AK-47, a pack, and captured documents. By 1030, 9 July, Gunnery Sergeant Ottinger was debriefing the team at the battalion's S-2 (intelligence) shop.[26]

After that patrol, and with the disestablishment of Echo Company coming 1 August, Lieutenant Hailston needed a job. Drumright had nominated him for an aide-de-camp billet at III MAF. Hailston would get cleaned up, shower, have a haircut from the Vietnamese camp barber, and put on a clean set of cammies from the hut mama-san. He took the company jeep to the III MAF headquarters for an interview with the senior aide, a major, and the chief of staff. After being vetted by them, he repeated the process, coming back another day to interview with the commanding general of III MAF, Lieutenant General Keith McCutcheon. The experienced patrol leader got the billet and served as the junior aide, tied to a desk working the general's schedule. It meant long hours and the opposite of being on patrol in the jungle eating cold C-rations. At III MAF, he dined with a table cloth and silverware. Hailston wanted to fly jets! Upon returning to the United States, he was assigned to Marine Corps Air Station Cherry Point where he waited for his school seat in the aviation pipeline. In flight school, he competed and earned his Gold Wings in jet aircraft, accumulating 3,105 flight hours over his career.[27] He would advance to lieutenant general, and command III Marine Expeditionary Force (III MEF) in Okinawa, the new name for III MAF. Later, he commanded Marine Forces Pacific and Marine Forces Central Command. He retired, having gone from private in boot camp to lieutenant general in Hawaii.

***

At the rear on 10 July, a letter summarizing the Article 32 Record of Investigation on Lieutenant Lee was completed by Lieutenant Colonel King, the deputy staff judge advocate (SJA), and hand delivered to Drumright. The letter presented the facts as King saw them and stated the formal Article 32 would recommend a general court-martial.[28] The letter was an aid for Drumright who had to make the decision. A copy was not provided to Lee. It would take the court reporters and clerks six more days to type the verbatim testimony for the final report.[29]

***

On 11 July, Staff Sergeant Mushett, the experienced platoon sergeant, and patrol leader, took Team *Segment,* which was Corporal Floyd's team, and an ARVN scout, Lance Corporal Truong, out on patrol.[30] The team was inserted at 0900 and started moving after their comm check with the radio relay on Ba Na Mountain. Movement was exceedingly difficult due to vines and secondary shrub brush. The team was averaging 30 meters an hour. They heard dogs barking and then Vietnamese talking. At 1030, the team point man saw one enemy who also saw him. The NVA ran the other way.

The team continued to move and found a large meadow of elephant grass 12–16 feet high. Working through the grass, the team found a fresh trail in the grass that was beaten down by an estimated 30–40 soldiers. Stopping and establishing communication with their radio relay, *Segment* began hearing numerous bird calls that sounded distinctly manmade. At 1700, they heard movement 40 meters away in the grass. Mushett called a fire mission on the other side of the elephant-grass meadow. The Arty battery was put in check-fire when an AO arrived on station in an OV-10, callsign *Hostage Six-Two* (1st Lieutenant Huffman).[31] The AO took over the fire support and told Mushett to get their heads down. He reported to Mushett that they had numerous enemy on three sides who were moving towards the team. Mushett called Ba Na and requested a ladder extract before nightfall, due to the deteriorating situation based on the AO's reports. The AO got two flights of Marine A-4s who made multiple runs. With each passing of the Skyhawks, Mushett would report that the aircraft were taking small-arms fire.

At 1835, *Segment* started hearing grenade explosions 30 meters south of them as the NVA were now sweeping the elephant-grass meadow searching for and attempting to flush the Recon team. At 1915, the fixed-wing departed, as did *Hostage Six-Two* as he was low on fuel. He was replaced on station by *Hostage-Lima*. The OV-10 began runs with its own guns to keep the enemy off the team while the extract helicopter package of two gunships and two CH-46s, one with a ladder, had been scrambled from Marble Mountain Air Facility. The OV-10 was also taking small-arms fire with each pass, while Team *Segment* laid prone, on-line, at the edge of the elephant grass with its four Claymore mines across its front. At 1925, the two gunships arrived and began working the area northeast of the team where the large enemy force was regrouping, as identified by the AO. The AO had the two gunships drop smoke 360 degrees around the tall elephant-grass extract point. The CH-46 with ladder arrived, Mushett popping two yellow smokes inside the smoke screen to give the crew chief a visual for the ladder. The ladder came down as the CH-46 began taking heavy small-arms fire from two sides, until the gunships started running suppression runs on both sides of the hovering bird. The five Marines and ARVN scout blew the four Claymores as the ladder was dropped. Two at a time, they went up the ladder, climbing to make room for their fellow Marines below. Mushett, with an arm around Lance Corporal "Doggie" McBride, his primary radioman, got on the ladder last, calling for the lift out on the radio. They were out at 1950. The AO had an on-call 175 artillery battery, *Night Scholar*, fire 30 high-explosive rounds on the meadow after the ladder cleared the ridgeline.[32] While the bird climbed to altitude, Mushett radioed the extract officer on the bird from Recon Battalion and requested no intermittent stop to get off the ladder, if the birds had fuel to fly back into LZ 401. The birds agreed as night was quickly approaching. Team *Segment* was lowered down on LZ 401 in the dark at 2025 hours with at least fifty fellow Recon Marines on the edge of the LZ to welcome them home. They had been out for an adrenaline-pumping ten hours and 45 minutes.[33]

***

On 16 July, Lieutenant Colonel King signed the Article 32 Report and delivered it to Drumright, recommending a general court-martial (GCM) with a single lesser charge of Article 119, Involuntary Manslaughter.[34] On the same day, Drumright signed a cover letter forwarding the Article 32 to the commanding general of the 1st Marine Division recommending the GCM, for a violation of Article 119.[35] That night, Captain J. J. Hargrove, Lieutenant Lee's military defense counsel, called Messrs Hastings and DiNapoli, Lee's civilian defense counsel, in San Jose to inform them of the GCM and to start working a strategy for defense of the accused. The defense's strategy was to demonstrate, unequivocally, that the area around Hill 119 was controlled completely by the enemy, and that the Marines on the hill were booby-trapped inside the wire by the NVA sappers and Viet Cong (VC) as an operational way to keep the Marines on the hill. This would allow the enemy to enjoy freedom of movement past the OP. And the four Vietnamese working below the OP on 28 March were Viet Cong gathering intelligence against the hill.

After coming off Hill 119 on 18 July, Lieutenant Fallon had four days at Camp Reasoner before his next patrol.[36] During this time, he talked with former fellow Delta Company platoon commander, W. X. Lee, about the enemy situation around the OP on Hill 119. He also went up Division Hill 327 and shared the enemy situation with Captain Hargrove. Their discussion was in the small conference room where Hargrove was building the defense plan, long distance, with his colleagues in California. On 22 July, an SJA memo from Colonel D. E. Holben, who had replaced Colonel Lucy as SJA to the commanding general of the 1st Marine Division, recommended a GCM with the lesser charge of Article 119.[37] The original Article 32 charge was a violation of Article 118, Murder-1. The investigating officers' recommendation that was changed to Article 119 was accepted as the charge for the GCM.[38]

***

Lieutenant Fallon received his next frag order on 21 July for an insert on 23 July. He would be leading Team *Allen Town*,[39] taking three of his 3rd Platoon Marines—Lance Corporals Broe, Capps, and Kozakowski—along with "Doc" Stewart. It was another special mission, as paragraph 2 of the Operation Order read: "Conduct Reconnaissance and surveillance operations within your assigned haven to detect possible NVA/VC troop movement or arms infiltration and be prepared to call and adjust air/Arty on all targets of opportunity. With special emphasis to provide security for SCAMP [Sensor Control and Management Platoon] people and maintain O.P. in support of Vietnamese Marine Corps operation."[40]

All artillery missions were to go through *Tacky Raffle-J* or *Tacky Raffle-L*. The patrol's radio relay was to be *Pal Joey-Tango* or *Sierra*. Attached to Team *Allen Town* were four Marines from the SCAMP platoon of the 1st Marine Division, G-2 Section. Additional special equipment to be carried would be 12 Claymore mines, an M60 machine gun, and four demolition kits.[41] Fallon was going out heavily armed to establish a clandestine OP overlooking the small valley the 258th Vietnamese Marine Brigade would be sweeping.[42] There was a ground-sensor string at the head of the valley on two trails out of the mountains of Base Area 112 headed to the Song Cai. The SCAMP team needed to be within line of sight to pick up the electronic readings from the sensors. The OP options west of Thuong Duc were limited by the requirement to be line of sight to the sensors and not in the direct path of the Vietnamese Marines' sweep. Team *Allen Town* would be working on the shoulder of the Song Cai valley.[43] There was jungle canopy 80–200 feet above the team. After a hover insertion into a small sidehill, one-bird landing spot, jumping into 12 feet of elephant grass, Fallon held the team up to gain communications with their primary radio relay, *Pal Joey-Tango* on FSB Hatchet. While being able to talk with the insert birds, the team needed to put up a whip antenna to gain comm with the radio relay, effectively waving a red flag over their position. As soon as comm was established, the antenna came down. Movement was difficult due to secondary growth and vines, the extra equipment, as well as the SCAMP Marines not being practiced in jungle movement.

They were inserted on 23 July at 1236. With the heavy load moving at approximately seventy-five meters an hour, it took a day-and-a-half to reach the selected clandestine OP. Fallon established a 360 defense on the side of the ridge. The radios and four black metal SCAMP readout boxes with their batteries were in the center with the SCAMP Marines. They could easily see north, east, and west. They could see the river and they could see the Vietnamese Marines in the valley. After the OP defense was set, Sergeant Daugherty had his SCAMP Marines test their readout boxes. There of the four were working and receiving from the sensor strings. Fallon had Broe and Capps take eight of their Claymore mines, putting them out to cover two avenues of approach in three layers of defense and string the wires at max length back to the hellboxes. The M60 was positioned to cover the one trail into the clandestine OP. That evening, 26 July, after sundown, the team observed and heard ten rockets, thought to be 122-mm, launched in groups of two and three at a time, flying from the valley floor and impacting around FSB Hatchet.[44] An artillery fire mission could not be called as the 122s was out of range of the 105 howitzers on FSB Hatchet. The rocket waves were fired 60 seconds apart. All the team could do was provide radio relay *Pal Joey-Tango* with an "Inbound rockets, heads up" to pass to the FSB so they got their heads down. The remainder of the night and next day were quiet.

On the evening of 27 July, at 2315, they observed three rockets launched at 15-second intervals, traveling northeast in the valley.[45] The OP could not observe impacts and could not call a fire mission due to Vietnamese Marines in close vicinity of the launch site. Fallon knew there were U.S. Marine advisors with the 258th Marine Brigade but he did not have the frequencies to radio them. It was an oversight!

Two days later, it was extract day. Before departing the clandestine OP at 0625, *Allen Town* heard two rockets go over their heads towards FSB Hatchet. *Tango* reported they impacted outside the wire.[46] Fallon moved the team all morning down the finger and found a small hover LZ in a rocky streambed. The extract package arrived at 1130 with the pilot hovering for at least five minutes while the nine Marines and Doc Stewart threw gear onto the bird and then climbed on. With the PRC-25 on his back, Fallon was last onto the CH-46 ramp. Flying out, he got a better view of the Song Giang Valley where the rockets were coming from. It was a frustrating patrol as the sensor strings got no actionable readouts to fire artillery on and the incoming rocket fire at FSB Hatchet had been outside the range of the Allied artillery supporting the Vietnamese Marines' operation. *Allen Town* had not seen the enemy or fired supporting arms at the enemy.[47]

***

Back on Hill 119, Lieutenant Taylor and 1st Platoon arrived 18 July via CH-53 to take over security for IOD team *Empire State* and the OP.[48] This was Taylor's first trip to the OP. He would rely on his three team leaders, Corporals Elkins, Floyd, and Doan, plus the experienced "Doc" Eric Schwartz. Additionally, he brought two ARVN Recon Marines, Corporal Bro, and Lance Corporal Khe attached to support walk-off patrolling.[49] Taylor also brought a helo sling-load pallet of 106-mm ammunition under the CH-53. On their first night on Hill 119, at 2300, Bravo Bunker picked up movement on the Alligator Lake trail. *Empire State* followed the bunker's lead and identified one NVA with a pack and rifle moving from the east back west below the lake dam. *Empire State* called a fire mission, firing the first rounds at 2305, and had rounds complete at 2310 from *Pearl Chest-Mike* out of An Hoa. There was excellent coverage of the target, resulting in one claimed enemy kill. On 21 July, the IOD team sank a boat with Arty fire as it was trying to cross from the Tho Son hamlet docks to Go Noi Island.[50] On the night of the 22nd, the OP again picked up movement on the heavily used trail below the Alligator Lake dam. Fire missions were difficult to get due to a 5th Marines company in contact in the Arizona

Territory and having priority of fire. Again, in the early evening hours of 25 July, *Empire State* observed a boat with three NVA/VC moving along the river to the north of the OP from east to west. They called a fire mission from *Pearl Chest-Mike* with excellent coverage resulting in one boat sunk and three claimed kills.[51]

On the 27th at 0330, the perimeter took incoming small-arms fire, and Alpha and Echo Bunkers observed one trip flare going off in the concertina wire on the north side of the hill. No enemy were observed by either bunker or the IOD team's night-observation device. Taylor had been asleep and suspected everyone else had been too. The trip flare was a good reminder they could be hit anytime.

On the 30th at 2330, Bravo Bunker heard movement on the trail coming up from Alligator Lake. Taylor used the opportunity to fire the 60-mm mortars in the draw and then had the mortar team continue firing harassment and interdiction fires on the south side of Hill 119.[52] That morning, on the 31st at 0900, two NVA slowly walked up the north main trail in the open. They were wearing blue shirts and blue shorts. Taylor sent out a patrol and the two enemy soldiers, with their hands up, Chieu Hoi'd. They were searched, had nothing, and were bound and blindfolded. They were given water as they sat outside the wire next to the saddle LZ for the OP. Later that day, a passing CH-46 moved the two blindfolded soldiers back to LZ 20 for interrogation. One Marine was also medevac'd for second-degree burns as a result of using C-4 plastic explosive to heat his stew in a metal helmet. He grabbed the helmet to take it off the fire and burned the palm of his left hand.[53] During this OP flip, *Empire State* had accounted for ten kills, three lights extinguished, two boats sunk, and one bunker destroyed. The enemy activity level in and around Hill 119 had fallen off. This was, in part, due to their efforts to harvest rice and corn instead of fighting during the harvest season. Taylor and 1st Platoon were extracted by one CH-53 at 1730 on 1 August.[54]

They were replaced by 2nd Platoon and Fallon since their platoon commander, Parks, was away at Embarkation School in Okinawa.[55] It was a nice break from Camp Reasoner and it earned Parks an additional military occupation specialty (MOS) as an embarkation officer (0431).[56] When he returned, Parks would pay for the new MOS by becoming the battalion's embarkation officer. As a result, he would be supervising the construction of wooden embark boxes and their inspections for the pack out of Charlie and Delta Companies' return to the United States by ship in September.[57]

CHAPTER 29

NVA Attack, Hill 119, 9 August 1970

It was a hot summer in August, both Stateside and in Vietnam. It was another summer of protest against the war in Vietnam. On August 7, a group associated with the Soledad Brothers attacked the Marin County (California) courthouse during a trial to demand the immediate release of George Jackson, the Black Power activist.[1] The Soledad Brothers, George Jackson, Fleeta Drumgo, and John Clutchette, gained prominence during the turbulent era of the Vietnam War and the Black Power movement, becoming symbols of political activism and prisoners' rights.

On the same day, the *San Jose Mercury* newspaper headline read "Marines Reduce Charges," referring to the Lieutenant W. X. Lee case in Vietnam. Mr. J. Philip DiNapoli, one of his defense attorneys, told the paper, "I feel he is being railroaded!"[2] Also on 7 August, the defense team received a telegram from Marine Corps Headquarters notifying them of the Article 32 results, recommending a general court-martial.[3] Both defense attorneys told the paper the government had failed during the Article 32 (grand-jury equivalent) to prove the victim was a non-combatant.[4]

On 24 August, Sterling Hall on the University of Wisconsin's Madison campus was hit with a car bomb. It was intended to destroy the Army Mathematics Research Center in the building. It missed its target but got national headlines protesting the war and achieving results.[5] On 29 August, the Chicano Moratorium, a peaceful protest against the Vietnam War of over twenty thousand Mexican–American antiwar activists in East Los Angeles, turned violent when the Los Angeles County Sheriff's Department entered Laguna Park, resulting in three deaths.[6]

In Vietnam, General Creighton Abrams continued leading the United States' Vietnamization Plan whereby the South Vietnamese Forces would assume increasing responsibilities for the pursuit of the war. In XXIV Corps, Lieutenant General James Sutherland, U.S. Army, now working from Camp Horn in Da Nang, was planning for the handover of I Corps' combat bases and logistics centers between the Army and the departing III Marine Amphibious Force's drawdown as part of the Operation *Keystone Robin-Alpha* phase.[7]

At the 1st Marine Division, Operation *Pickens Forest*, on 9 August, had the 3rd Battalion, 7th Marines, do a long helicopter insertion from LZ (landing zone) Ross far west to Fire Support Base (FSB) Hatchet above the Song Cai. The 7th Marines continued the operation through to 24 August.[8] On 31 August, their last-named operation, *Imperial Lake*, kicked off with a helo lift of 2nd Battalion into a group of preselected mountain-top LZs prepared by the 1st Reconnaissance Battalion.[9] Marines, from varying organizations, would continue in the Que Son Mountains for the rest of the year. The 7th Marines would start the withdrawal in earnest, turning over their FSBs in the Que Son Valley to the 5th Marines as they pulled out of An Hoa Combat Base and turned it over to the Army of the Republic of Vietnam (ARVN), with tenant units remaining (especially the useful helicopter forward arming and refueling point).[10] On 16 August, Operation *Lyon Valley* was kicked off by 2nd Battalion, 5th Marines, 11 kilometers southwest of An Hoa.[11]

At 1st Reconnaissance Battalion, on 1 August, Echo Company was deactivated.[12] Its Marines were transferred to other patrolling companies if they had less than nine months in-country. Those with nine months or more were short-toured and sent Stateside unless they volunteered to stay. One of Echo Company's most-experienced patrol leaders, the six-foot-six John Huff, opted to complete his 13-month tour and was moved over to Delta Company.[13] First Lieutenant Huff immediately joined Fallon, going up to learn Delta Company's observation post (OP) on Hill 119.[14]

A farewell dinner for Lieutenant Colonel Drumright was held on 6 August, at the Recon Battalion Staff Noncommissioned Officers/Officers Club. The guest of honor was Major General C. F. Widdecke, the 1st Marine Division's commanding general, who, along with the battalion staff and officers in the rear, wished the Recon commander farewell.[15] On 9 August, Drumright's 13-month tour was over as he rotated home and was assigned as the executive officer (XO), Headquarters Battalion, Headquarters Marine Corps. He would report into the first female Marine commanding the battalion, Colonel Hazel Benn.[16]

The interim commander off the division staff was Lieutenant Colonel E. J. Regan. His principal job was to reorganize the battalion in order to maintain the maximum number of patrolling teams while preparing for Charlie and Delta Companies' withdrawal in September.[17] Also rotating on 9 August was the battalion's XO, Major Terry Turner.[18]

Now, no officer in Lieutenant Lee's chain of command, from company to division commander, remained in-country, meaning their replacements had only the paper trail of the 28 March shooting incident and no understanding of the tactical situation on the ground.

The hard-charging Major D. D. "Dale" Dorman replaced Major Turner. Two VIPs visited the battalion, one on 15 August—Lieutenant General Fred Leek, commanding general Fleet Marine Force, Atlantic—and one on 22 August—Rear Admiral Ramage, Commander, Carrier Division 7 from *Yankee* Station. Both received operational briefings and a static display of one team and equipment outside the S-3 (operations) bunker.[19] Reflecting on the death of 1st Lieutenant "Pete" Gray, there was no rappelling or ladder-extract demonstration. It would only be a matter of time before the collective memory of the tragic loss was forgotten, due to the rotation of leadership, before the live demonstrations known as "dog and pony shows" would return.

Meanwhile, in Delta Company, the new commander, 1st Lieutenant Smith, was short of officers. He had Fallon, who had been Delta's utility fielder on patrol, and the new join from the grunts, Lieutenant Taylor, who was currently on Hill 119. The experienced and highly-thought-of John Hoff moved over with the disestablishment of Echo Company. Smith decided to send both Fallon and Hoff to the OP to replace Taylor, ostensively for Hoff to learn the hill. Both Hoff and Fallon believed it was overkill and either of them could oversee the hill. Smith stuck with his decision getting both strong-willed officers away and on OP duty. On 1 August, the two officers with 18 Marines and Corpsman Hunt were leaning on their packs on the LZ all day waiting for the CH-53 to arrive.[20] The larger aircraft had been requested to carry a heavy sling load of 106-mm ammunition and, therefore, was the aircraft and crew's last flight of the day. The Marines arrived at 1700 to the saddle LZ of the OP and would have a few hours of daylight to move into Hill

119's bunkers for their two-week flip. Only half of 2nd Platoon had previously been to the OP, so a training routine was in order, starting the next day. Their callsign was *Pal Joey-Kilo.* The forward observer (FO) team *Empire State* would call the artillery fire missions. The next day, 2 August, Fallon worked with the Integrated Observation Device (IOD) FO team to preregister the artillery defensive on-call targets with the artillery battery *Pearl Chest-Mike* firing out of An Hoa Combat Base. He wanted on-call targets on all the high ground around the OP, plus the three main avenues of approach up to the barren hill. By preregistering the targets, and numbering them for Hill 119, the direct-support artillery battery would have all the firing data worked up and saved, meaning when the hill called any of their six on-call targets, the fire support would respond faster. This was an all-day effort since the battery could only do preregistrations when not actually firing to support troops in contact from other units. At the same time, John Hoff worked with the Marines on every crew-served weapon on the hill—the M60 machine guns in the bunkers and the .50-caliber machine gun which Platoon Sergeant Horton would man. He spent extra time with the Marines on the 60-mm mortars as they were not trained mortarmen. Last, with Fallon's support, they fired the 106-mm recoilless rifle at a selected target on the adjacent Hill 148. First, they fired three .50-cal spotter rounds then the 106's high-explosive (HE) round. Corporal Sheppard hit the plunger, triggering the shot after Hoff had bellowed, "Fire the 106," a firing command every lieutenant had learned in The Basic School. Everyone on the hill watched the round hit the top of Hill 148 and skip west out of sight. Fallon worried the impact area was not in his area, but hoping luck would favor him—thinking little bullet, big area—and not impact nearby friendly troops.

At the end of the day, Fallon, not one for pep talks, called an all-hill meeting in the mortar pits except for one security man east and one west. His simple point to the gathered Marines was that the hill was overdue to get hit. It had been six months since Gunnery Sergeant Terry Moore had throttled the T89 Sapper Battalion by killing their commanding officer, XO, and capturing their recon officer directly off Hill 119. They had been scouting their attack approach route. Fallon told the Marines the hill was a lady which would lull you to sleep and then, when you least expected, take advantage of your relaxed guard. He asked Hoff to comment, to which Hoff simply said, "It's time for chow, Marines," ending the session. Over dinner on the lieutenants' bunker sandbagged front porch, Fallon and Hoff discussed the hill's defense and each of their roles during an attack. In the event of an attack, Fallon, as the hill commander, said he would man the radios, direct the FO team, and coordinate air support. For his part, Hoff would move to the mortar pit where he could observe four of the six bunkers and supervise the mortars, .50-cal, and 106. The evening was calm, still, hot, and quiet. With two lieutenants, they split the watch three ways with the platoon sergeant, hoping to get some sleep. August was the hottest month of the year in the An Hoa basin with an average temperature of 93 degrees, and the humidity always above ninety percent. The uniform for working parties on the hill was shorts and jungle boots.

On 3 August, Corporal Ravello and Lance Corporal Pinto approached Fallon suggesting a walk-off patrol to the Alligator Lake dam. Fallon, having already been on the hill four previous times, knew this was really a request for a swim call. He told them it was too early in their stay but did not say no, giving them hope for a future walk-off to the lake just 500 meters to the southwest. At 0935, the IOD team got their first sighting. Fallon suggested Hoff go to the tower, watch the IOD process, and check out the "Big Eyes." *Empire State* had two NVA (North Vietnamese Army) in dark utilities with packs and rifles west and slightly north of the hill at a distance of approximately twenty-five hundred meters. They demonstrated the laser range finder for Hoff, getting 2,508 meters on the second lase. They called a fire-for-effect with first rounds from *Pearl Chest-Mike* getting rounds on target in ten minutes. They got total coverage of the area and could see one body on the trail, reporting it to the battery.[21] Hoff came back and spoke with Fallon, asking why it was taking ten minutes to get rounds on target. Fallon said that on small targets of opportunity, the battery took its time but, when pushed on the radio, they had responded very quickly in the past. Hoff said, "Well, that radio dance is on you." Fallon enjoyed having another Recon lieutenant on the hill with whom he could talk. Normally, he talked options in tactics and hill defense with himself. It was somewhat of a relief to talk to another officer who had similar experiences.

At 1400, *Empire State* spotted four enemy in dark utilities and rifles moving west on Route 537, four kilometers to their northwest. Calling a fire mission, they were denied clearance, as this was inside the tactical area of responsibility of the 5th Marines. Fallon got on the radio to the 5th Marines Combat Operations Center and passed them the grid coordinates and enemy description so they could inform their S-2 (intelligence) shop as well as the unit operating on Route 537 between the enemy and Liberty Bridge further northwest. That evening at 2230, the IOD team, using the night-observation device (NOD), spotted four enemy south of the OP on the forward slope of Hill 175 across the small southern valley. They called the fire mission at 2230 and had to adjust the grid twice, while waiting to shoot, as the enemy was moving to the north towards Hill 119. At 2300, they got first rounds, firing two fire-for-effects from *Pearl Chest-Mike*. Coverage was on target, resulting in two kills and one secondary explosion. Two of the enemy were seen running east and out of the observable area.[22] On 4 August, at 0517, the IOD team spotted three enemy with rifles and shovels digging due south of the OP on the forward slope of Hill 175, 600 meters from the wire. They fired the first rounds at 0602 and ended mission at 0607. There were no results, due to darkness and foliage in the area.[23]

Over coffee, Fallon and Hoff talked about the enemy activity over on Hill 175. Hoff wondered, aloud, what it was or meant? Fallon opined that it was the launch area for rockets coming at the hill. It was also the same general area where Moore's walk-off patrol had killed and captured the sappers.[24] They discussed the merits of a walk-off patrol, the best timing, and worrying about leaving the hill shorthanded while the patrol was out or not having a sufficient reaction force if it got in trouble. Daytime patrolling in wide-open spaces was what the infantry did around the hill with platoons and companies. On 5 August, *Empire State* called three fire missions on the enemy, all within fifteen hundred meters of the OP. The combined results were four enemy personnel killed.[25]

The enemy was definitely watching and moving in small groups on all sides of the OP. Thus far, no pattern had developed or shown itself on the updated heat map kept in the lieutenants' bunker by all the previous hill commanders. The next morning, the IOD team fired a mission on three enemy with weapons northwest of the OP near the river, resulting in three kills. That evening, as the sun was setting, looking south, they observed three enemy standing in a boulder formation on the military crest of Hill 175. They were observing Hill 119 with binoculars.

Empire State called the on-call target for the crest of Hill 175, getting immediate rounds fired. There was fair artillery coverage of Hill 175, but negative results observed due to darkness and large boulders on the north slope.[26] On 7 August, the hill only observed one enemy all day. He was walking west of the vacant Thon Bon (2) hamlet west of the OP, wearing dark utilities and carrying a pack and rifle at sling arms. *Empire State* called a fire mission with excellent coverage and claimed the kill.

The following day, the IOD team called a fire mission in the morning and one in the late afternoon, resulting in two kills.[27] At 0155, 9 August, the NOD team sighted three enemy in the open on the north slope of Hill 148 directly across from the LZ. They called the on-call target with *Pearl Chest-Mike* with excellent and immediate coverage, killing all three.[28] They could see the bodies on the open front slope. That morning, with first light, Big Eyes could no longer see the bodies. The NVA had retrieved them sometime during the night. While the Marines' ethos left no Marine behind, or his body, it sometime meant extra casualties as the enemy ambushed or booby-trapped dead Marines. As a policy, the body of every Marine who died was repatriated to his hometown for burial by his family. Similarly, the NVA recovered their dead but for different reasons; it was to deny the Marines' intelligence gains and/or the moral victory of recovering enemy bodies on a battlefield. The NVA removed the dead by dragging them with grappling hooks back to their base area, usually one night's march, and burying them in shallow mass graves.[29]

The morning of 9 August broke clear, hot, and humid. Fallon had reversed the hill watch cycle, having the majority of Marines sleep during the day while enabling more listening posts and watches each night. He knew if they got hit it would be at night. During the day, it would get to 98 degrees with 94 percent humidity; no one stayed inside the bunkers with their small shooting ports and no air movement. All the Marines had lean-to shelters with a poncho to provide shade on the side of the bunker where they tried to sleep. Fallon was down to a pair of tiger-striped shorts, flip-flops, and aviator sunglasses as he made the midday walk around the perimeter trench line.

Hoff was asleep under a shade shelter on the south side of the lieutenants' bunker. Talking with the few Marines on watch, he had thought about the defense that night. Hill 119's defenses were an oval trench line four feet deep with double sandbags as parapets, making it five feet. It had taken over a year of blasting and digging by the Marines to get to that depth in the rock shale. There were six fixed bunkers on the perimeter trench. Each served as a home for three Marines to live, sleep, eat, and to provide protection from overhead shrapnel. However, each bunker also represented a rocket-propelled grenade (RPG) magnet as they were above ground and the trench line, easily seen from outside the perimeter and below the hill. The enemy surely had the six bunkers plotted for RPG fire or satchel charges if they got through the wire. Therefore, Hoff worked with each bunker team and created alternate firing positions in the trench line on each side of their bunker. He had them dig grenade sumps, ammunition shelves, and sitting benches for every position.[30]

That afternoon, at the 1700 daily meeting in the mortar pit, Fallon laid out that night's plan. As with every night, it had three parts: the surveillance piece, the listening-post placements, and the evening watches in the trench line, instead of bunkers. For the surveillance piece, since the moon would be in the first quarter that night, with 48.87 percent illumination, he requested two Marines from the *Empire State* FO team in the tower, one on the Big Eyes and the second on the NOD. He also put a starlight scope on the roof of Bravo Bunker looking west and one on Echo Bunker looking east. That night they would have three listening posts of two Marines each, one from each of the three Recon teams of the platoon. He told the team leaders to pick the two Marines and have them see him for their assigned locations. Fallon deferred to Hoff who spoke to the trench defense. He reminded the Marines that, when the hill was receiving incoming mortars, they should be inside the bunkers, however, if the fire was rockets or small-arms fire, they should be outside the bunkers in the trench line at their alternate firing positions. The lieutenants asked for questions; as usual, there were none. The meeting broke up at 1720 with all Marines headed to their bunkers to make evening chow. At 1800, Corporal Ravello, the first team leader, came around with Lance Corporal Pinto. He said they were the first team's listening post, but Pinto wanted to take an M60 machine gun out to their position. It certainly would confuse the enemy if the listening post had to use it; they would think it was a larger unit. However, these Marines were not machine gunners so Fallon worried they might have an early jam. He compromised and told them they could do it, but both had to take their M16s with a full load of 20 magazines. Ravello and Pinto had to cover a steep draw to the southeast 200 meters outside the wire. The second listening post would be due east on the ridgeline trail coming toward the OP. The third was also on the south side monitoring the hard-packed high-speed trail coming up from Alligator Lake to the saddle between Hills 148 and 119. Each post had a PRC-25 radio, individual H-harnesses with grenades, ammo, canteens, and their M16 rifles. All three departed after sundown, moving through gates and the three separate bands of triple-concertina wire. It took an hour before all three had reported they were in their positions.

At 2110, Listening Post 3 (LP-3), which was in the southeast draw, saw three enemy coming up the draw in dark uniforms. Pinto opened up directly down the draw with the M60. Ravello later said the enemy point man was stitched up the chest with the gun's 7.62 rounds and was dead. At the same time, LP-2 on the southwest draw spotted two enemy on the trail heading up to Hill 148 from the lake. They opened up with their M16s across the draw at 500 meters.

After two posts had fired, and compromised their location, Fallon called all three back in with the code words "Locker Room" over the radio. At the same time, Hoff walked around the trench line, telling each Marine the listening posts were coming in and there would be no outgoing fire. Fallon told *Empire State* on the landline from the Recon communications bunker to the tower, to fire both the Hill 175 and Hill 148 on-call targets because there were enemy on the forward north slopes of both hills. After Ravello and Pinto were back from LP-3, Hoff had the 60-mm mortar team work out the southeast draw with ten HE mortar rounds. It took the three listening posts less than fifteen minutes to come back, where it had taken over an hour to move quietly into position earlier that evening. No need for quiet when coming back in. The verbal challenge used by the Marines monitoring the gates was yelling out "Pete" with the response from each listening post being "Rose."

Everyone on the hill was awake. There was no need to pass the word for 100 percent alert. Pinto was moving among the Recon Marines retelling his story of stitching the "gooner" with the M60. Fallon had Lance Corporal Curry call in a detailed SALUTE report to Battalion.[31] At 2320, the *Empire State* NOD Marine sighted four enemy moving on the railroad berm just north of the bridge going onto Go Noi Island. The enemy stopped and built a small fire. The FO called *Pearl Chest-Mike* and got first rounds on target, extinguishing the fire.[32] Fallon made cocoa-coffee with five packets of sugar. He planned to stay up all night. Minutes later, at 2330, sitting on the porch of his bunker trench facing south, he saw, and then heard, the first of five RPGs being fired near simultaneously. They were coming straight at the hill. Fallon yelled "Incoming" as he dove into the trench. Hoff had heard them and was yelling for the Marines to man the trenches. All five RPGs came from the north slope of Hill 175 to their south. Fallon was on the landline to the tower calling for the on-call Arty target for Hill 175. All five RPG rounds impacted inside the wire on the south side of the OP, but short of the trench line, throwing shrapnel overhead. While this was going on, the Marines heard the "thump, thump, thump" of mortars. Five 61-mm mortar rounds impacted south and east of the OP's narrow ridgeline. Had the two southern listening posts been out, they would have been in the impact area. Hoff was now in the OP's mortar pit and had ten 60-mm mortar rounds out in a counter-fire toward the NVA launch site before the first round hit the deck. He had the second batch of ten rounds out, while *Empire State* had the Arty rounds impacting on Hill 175. Fallon called on the landline and told them to drop 300 and fire-for-effect again. Fallon had "Doc" Hunt make a round trip in the trench line checking for casualties, nothing serious. There were a few bumps and bruises from diving off the top of bunkers, where they'd slept for cool air, into their trench for protection.

Hoff now moved quickly through the trench line, pushing and putting every Marine into their alternate firing positions and moving every machine gun to its alternate position. The guns covered the three avenues of approach for a ground attack, two on the south and one on the northwest side up through the trash pit below the LZ. Fallon was on the battalion frequency giving a verbal report to the acting S-3, 1st Lieutenant F. M. McDonough.[33] On the secure radio, he requested McDonough, or the air officer, call on their landline over to the Da Nang Direct Air Support Center (DASC) and request some air support for *Pal Joey-Kilo* on Hill 119. The DASC was the senior Marine DASC responsible for the management and distribution of direct-air-support assets to Marine ground units within the division's tactical area of responsibility. It was co-located with the 1st Marine Division's Command Center.

Fallon was in the communication bunker when he heard the entire north side of the hill open up. It sounded just like the practice final-protective-fires (FPF) all Marines are taught. Jumping outside, he saw and heard M60 and M16 red tracers going out from the northern trench and green tracers in-coming from Hill 148, and the trash pit, flying high over the hill. He saw John Hoff, all six-foot-six of him, standing calmly in the mortar pit with a crate of 40-mm rounds, shooting the M79 "blooper," firing non-stop in the draw below the LZ.[34]

Fallon jogged down the trench line to check Bravo Bunker and the position covering the LZ. He could see numerous NVA crawling through the second set of wire toward the last wire, which was set 25 feet below Bravo and Alpha Bunkers. He grabbed Lance Corporal Diaz and Private First Class Jones, with their M60 machine gun, and had them shoot directly over the LZ wire to the north side of Hill 148. He did not understand why, since he could not observe the area, then he heard another pop of the 60-mm mortar. Hoff had the mortar crew firing illumination rounds. Knowing they would run out of illum, Fallon ran back to the communication bunker and radioed Battalion in the clear requesting *Basketball* immediately, and any other air they could get. Looking at the comm bunker clock, it was 2340, the ground attack on Hill 119 had only been going for ten minutes.[35] Calling *Empire State* on the landline, he directed the on-call targets for both Hills 148 and 175 to be fired again, stating the hill was in contact to the FO, who obviously knew that. The FO team was wisely off the tower and in the deep bunker below the tower with their radios and maps.

Hoff had coordinated three M60 machine guns on the northside trench line that put the NVA ground assault in a triangulated machine-gun crossfire. The enemy fire had ceased. Twenty-five NVA had gotten to within twenty meters of Alpha Bunker, crawling up through the trash pit. Ten enemy bodies lay in the final defensive wire.[36] Hoff yelled for a ceasefire a number of times before the adrenaline-pumped Marines stopped shooting. Fallon had Doc Hunt make the rounds and then walked over to the mortar pit to talk with Hoff. Both lieutenants knew another ground assault could come, and that the enemy would try to recover their bodies.

Low on illumination rounds, the Marines stopped putting up 60-mm illumination. The hill got quiet. Fallon passed the word to shut the fuck up, stop talking, and listen. There was a low moaning and scraping noise outside the perimeter. He walked over to the FO bunker and told them to get back in the tower and on the NOD. He waited as his night vision slowly came back. He wanted to view the north slope. Curry was calling from the comm bunker that Battalion wanted the *Six-Actual* (meaning the hill commander, not his radio operator). Fallon looked at Hoff who laughed and said he had the outside watch, "Just go calm down Battalion."

Fallon walked back into the comm bunker, losing his night vision as soon as he entered. Radioing Battalion, he told them it was quiet now, that there had been a ground assault, with a coordinated fire-support plan, firing both RPGs and mortars from a direction 180 degrees out from the ground assault. No casualties except shrapnel and scrapes.[37] They would have to wait until morning for more details, but would they please press the DASC for support? Going back outside to Hoff in the mortar pit, it was dark and quiet. He stumbled, almost falling into the pit, having lost his night vision in the comm bunker. Hoff, now sitting, had directed the 60-mm crew to break out more HE and illumination rounds from the hill's ammo bunker. He told Fallon that three more NVA had been shot in the trash pit while trying to drag bodies away and they continued to hear movement and noise below the pit in the draw.

Looking at Fallon he said, "Do you always fight the NVA in flip-flops and shorts?"

Fallon heard the radio speaker with a new voice calling "*Pal Joey-Kilo*, *Pal Joey-Kilo*, this is *Basketball*, over."

Fallon walked back to the bunker and, taking the handset from Curry responded, "*Basketball*, *Basketball*, this is *Pal-Joey-Kilo-6*, thanks for coming to the party. We will turn on a strobe light on your call and you can start dropping flares at will, over."

Basketball said, "*Pal-Joey*, strobe!" At which time, Curry took Fallon's strobe light and put it inside an upside-down helmet on top of the comm bunker. *Basketball* was the call sign for the Air Force C-130 or C-123 that dropped illumination flares that lit up a battlefield, making it appear as daylight. Fallon looked at the clock and it was 0030, 10 August. *Basketball* stayed on station flying an orbit at 5,000 feet, dropping flares, making it appear like total daylight until 0228.[38] While the sky was lit up, the *Pal Joey* Marines counted 21 bodies in the wire and trash pit. *Basketball* departed with a cheery thanks, that it had been nice supporting the Marines, as it flew north back to Da Nang International.

The remainder of the night was noise in the trash pit, or below it, followed by Marines shooting M79 rounds at the noise. Hoff and Fallon walked around and told the Marines not to fire the machine guns which had been repositioned or their M16s as it would just give away their positions. Instead, shoot the M79 blooper or throw grenades. There were no more ground assaults nor enemy rockets or mortar fire that night. The T89 Sapper Battalion had withdrawn. At first light, there were only eight NVA bodies remaining in the wire with drag tracks and blood trails down to Thon Bon (1) hamlet below the hill to the northwest 1,500 meters away.[39]

Over coffee, Fallon, Hoff, Horton, Doc Hunt, and Curry went through the sapper attack in order to write a detailed, accurate report. Fallon had sent a large patrol out to clear the bodies from the wire and search them. Not surprisingly, there were no weapons or documents. The sappers were in shorts with no shirts. The Marines attached a rappelling rope to the feet of the bodies and dragged the stench away from the OP to the south side of the railroad berm below the hill, knowing the NVA would police them up that night.

The body patrol led by Corporal Ravello was out all morning. When it returned, Fallon held a hill-wide meeting in the mortar pit. They had lost no Marines and sustained only a few shrapnel cuts. He told them they had done what Marines always do, they fought like the Marines before them. He said they survived and won that fight because they and the Recon Marines before them had prepared the hill's defense well. Hoff added he was proud of them, and they would all drink a beer together back at Reasoner. Before dismissing them, Fallon told the Marines to clean their weapons and take a nap that afternoon as nightfall would be coming. Talking with Horton, Fallon asked about the .50-cal machine gun's employment as he had not heard it during the fight. Horton said he fired one round, and the gun stopped, so he went to the trench line and supported Alpha Bunker's M60 by linking ammo and pointing out targets. Inspecting the gun, Hoff reported what both lieutenants already knew; the headspace on the gun was set wrong. The machine-gun jam was on them.

The NVA and VC had launched frequent harassing attacks against all six Marine IOD sites since their fielding in November 1969. The combined-arms indirect fire and ground assault on the Hill 119 was the most serious[40] attempt to knock out the lethal classified IODs. During 1970, IOD-directed fire missions counted for 40 percent of the enemy killed by artillery in the 1st Marine Division's tactical area of responsibility.[41]

August 10 was hot and quiet. There were no signs of the enemy or the villagers. The hill Marines cleaned their weapons, rested, and talked in small groups, retelling their part in the night's fight. That night, Fallon only sent out one listening post on the north slope of Hill 148 to watch the bodies and try to catch the NVA coming back. It was a four-man team. He thought the enemy would be back outside the wire, policing up their dead. At 2025, the listening-post team, *Pal Joey-Kilo-1*, spotted three enemy at the base of the trash pit 500 meters below the OP. They were using flashlights, which was unusual unless they were searching for dead or weapons. The Marines engaged with M16s, killing one.[42] They sighted another group of four down by the railroad berm in the vicinity of the dead bodies. They took no action due to reduced visibility and because

Fallon had already passed the word for them to return. They were pulling in their Claymore mines when the artillery started to land near the railroad berm. *Empire State* was also shooting on them. The listening post came across the LZ and was back inside the wire 15 minutes later.

At 2130, Bravo Bunker picked up a flashlight to their southwest, 800 meters below them. The light was stationary just below the Alligator Lake dam. It was out by the time the bunker told the tower to check it out. The enemy was moving around the OP cleaning up from the previous night. The two lieutenants wished they had more manpower on the hill to defend it and to put out three or four good night ambushes. It was not to be of course, as the priority mission was defending the hill's classified IOD, which meant they were tied to the OP. At 2145, Alpha Bunker's starlight scope picked up two enemy below the hill moving east on the trail, they skylined on the railroad berm and were gone behind it. At 2245, the NOD team picked up four lights at the base of the hill near the bodies. The lights were flashlights. *Empire State* tried to call a fire mission but were denied clearance.[43] There were no further activities that night. When the sun rose, Big Eyes scoped out the area below the hill and saw no NVA bodies. They had been cleaned up during the night and were gone. It was another hot, humid day. The air was not moving. All the Marines were sunbathing on top of their bunkers still talking about the NVA attack. They were not used to defending a hill. They were normally on the offense going into the NVA base camps, taking the fight to them with surprise, and fighting on their terms. These Marines were not used to having the fight come to them on the NVA's terms.

For the night of 11 August, *Pal Joey-Kilo* had two listening posts out, one on the north side and one on the south side of the finger OP. At 2245, the northern one spotted two enemy with lights moving northeast of their position and then due north 200 meters below and away from them. They then saw one enemy 25 meters from their west and another 75 meters to their east. They then heard movement 25–30 meters to their south, above them. The Marines opened fire on the closest enemy to their west while withdrawing to the OP, coming in through the LZ gate. Corporal Oliver came to the comm bunker and reported everything they had seen.[44] He also said the enemy saw them come back in and would not expect them to go back out. He asked to go back out. It was a large four-man listening post. The lieutenants expected he was correct so gave them the go ahead. They went back out and must have been silhouetted while crossing the LZ as, when they got close to their position on the northside below the OP, they started receiving small-arms fire, approximately fifty rounds from the northeast slope of Hill 148. They also sighted two additional enemy moving east towards the hamlet of Tho Son.[45] Fallon, calling Oliver on the radio, said Alpha and Echo Bunkers would lay down heavy fire to their north and they should return to the OP under the cover of the fire. Fallon had *Empire State* fire the on-call fire mission on Hill 148 and shift it north. Oliver came trotting back across the LZ as the first artillery rounds landed. The rest of the night was quiet.

The next morning, 2nd Platoon was due to flip out and go back to Camp Reasoner. Hoff would take them back and do the debriefing with the S-2. The Delta Company Commander Lieutenant Smith, had radioed out to *Pal Joey-Kilo* and told Fallon to remain on the hill, that he would bring up 3rd Platoon. He wanted to see the hill and view the area where the ground attack had been repelled. On 12 August, Hoff and 2nd Platoon had to wait all day as again it would be a CH-53 bringing up 3rd Platoon. They arrived at 1600.[46] It would be a hot flip since

Fallon was staying; the bird would remain while 3rd Platoon off loaded and 2nd Platoon trotted on. Fallon remained in the mortar pit, turning his back away from the LZ to avoid the large sandstorm caused by the CH-53's blades turning on the LZ. Sergeant Gunel, the new platoon sergeant, was first off. Fallon grabbed him and said three Marines each in Alpha, Bravo, and Echo Bunkers, two Marines in Charlie and Delta Bunker, and two corpsmen and himself in the comm bunker. The platoon was coming up short-handed for a solid defense.[47] He would talk with Smith about the proper number as it was his belief there were short-timers in the rear avoiding the hill. Smith came off the aircraft last as Fallon walked over and said, "Follow me," leading him to the lieutenant's bunker without comment. He showed Smith his cot and departed to let him settle in. Fallon found the platoon sergeant and said to give the Marines 15 minutes in their bunkers and then assemble in the mortar pit. Fallon wanted to set the night's defense and the tone with 3rd Platoon and did not want Smith's interference. Fallon went back to the officers' bunker and told Smith the Marines were meeting in the mortar pit, he would set the night defenses, and that Smith was welcome to attend. After the briefing, he would take Smith up to the tower where he could meet the IOD team and get a demo. Smith acknowledged with a simple, "Roger." Fallon, whose style of leadership was 180 degrees out from Smith's, walked back to the pit.

When the Marines were gathered, he welcomed them to Hill 119. He said their callsign would be *War Cloud-Kilo* and that their mission was a security mission for the classified IOD in the tower which was operated by the FOs from the 11th Marines;[48] their callsign was *Empire State Eight-Three*. They all would get a chance during this two-week flip to look through the Big Eyes. He also said each of them would get a chance for a walk-off patrol, a wire-check patrol, and nightly listening posts. He said they all had their bunker assignments, that the hill ran a reverse watch cycle with the primary watch being at night with 100 percent alerts at sundown and sunrise and 50 percent watch the rest of the night, and that tonight there would be two listening posts; Gunel and the three team leaders would pick the two-man teams who would then see him for locations, passwords, and radios within the hour. Fallon told them the sapper battalion had tried to overrun the hill three nights prior and the only thing that saved the hill was the excellent machine-gun work by the Marines. He asked, for a show of hands, how many Marines had ever fired a machine gun? Gunel and Corporal Wiley were the only two hands that raised. So, Fallon said, "Gunel, you will man the 50-cal. tonight and, Wiley, you will man the M60 from Alpha Bunker." He told the Marines there were gun cards with every gun showing their sectors of fire and that he would be around before nightfall to fam fire each gun and answer questions. Then tomorrow would be an all-day machine-gun training for every Marine to learn, firsthand, with live fire, how to operate the M60. He asked for questions; there were none. Fallon's final statement to the Marines was that he would be around after chow, and that if they wanted hot chow, to cook it before sundown as the smoking lamp and chow fire light was out after dark, no lights on the hill. Fallon noticed Smith had joined them sometime during the briefing, so he asked if he wanted to say anything. He waved it off with a hand signal. Fallon said, "Dismissed!"

Walking back to the officers' bunker, following his own guidance, Fallon broke out a can of meatball C-rations, opened it and put it on the C-rat can stove with a heat tab as he found a canned cheese to melt and add in for dinner. He was on the bunker's front porch. Smith joined him. Fallon suggested he get the IOD brief before dark so took him to the tower and did the introductions with the duty FO and returned to his dinner. Smith returned in 15 minutes to the porch and said, "Let's talk." Fallon deferred and asked if it could wait till after sundown as he had seven machine guns to fam fire before it got dark. Smith nodded as Fallon departed in his shorts and flip-flops. An hour-and-a-half later, after seven fam fires and two listening posts briefed, Fallon returned to the officers' bunker. Smith, on his cot, sat up. He wanted to hear about the ground attack, but he really wanted to establish himself as the Delta Company commander, so he talked, and Fallon listened. He told Fallon he was out of uniform and a poor example for his Marines, that he expected clean Marines in unform, meaning daily shaves and utilities worn. Fallon explained those were hard orders as the OP had one water buffalo with 400 gallons for drinking and weekly shaves to last two to three weeks. It was 95-plus degrees every day and hydration came first. Each Marine had one set of utilities they wore on patrol and listening posts and would not get cleaned as there was no mama-san laundry like at Camp Reasoner. Smith said he did not care; he wanted changes. Fallon countered with, "Well, Lieutenant, when you get two more water buffalos up here or pipe water up from the lake we can do that. But now I need to check lines," and departed, without further comment, in his tiger-striped shorts and flip-flops.

Fallon returned to the comm bunker two hours later after walking the lines and talking individually with every Marine. He knew "Doc" Edison was on radio watch. They got caught up and small talked. Fallon wanted to know from Edison what the status was with the Lieutenant Lee investigation. Edison told Fallon he had testified in the Article 32 back in June but had been warned not to discuss his testimony. Fallon said, "I respect that, just wanted to know what was going on." Edison said he heard on the grapevine that Lee was going to be court-martialed. Fallon asked what type and Edison said he did not know. He said both Lieutenants Parks and Gray had testified in the Article 32, so Fallon should ask them. Then he added to the news that Gray was now dead, and he should talk with Parks. Fallon thanked him and said he would. Edison explained Gray had died rehearsing for a dog and pony.

Fallon took the next radio watch and remained in the comm bunker until sunrise when he returned to the officers' bunker to put on his utilities and boots in a nod to Smith, who remained sleeping. Fallon was on the porch making coffee when Smith came out of the bunker sweating profusely, wet all over in his skivvies. He said it was hot in the bunker. Fallon just nodded and said, "Welcome to Hill 119." The hill was barren of shade except for the corrugated aluminum roof over the tower. Smith went back in the bunker and got dressed and came out to the porch and asked, "Where's the coffee?" Fallon said, "There is a rat-fucked case of C-rations, help yourself, as this is a self-serve hill." Smith found an accessory packet and using water in his canteen cup, made coffee. He told Fallon he was making changes in Delta Company, that Spolter had been easy on the men and that he was returning to Marine Corps' standards. Fallon simply asked when he was going to the rear. He said he had fragged his helicopter for this afternoon. Fallon asked about the Lee case and Smith replied, "I have no idea." Fallon reminded him he needed to be back for any trial. Smith got up and went to the tower where he spent the day waiting for his bird. When it came at 1430, he climbed down from the tower and said to Fallon, "I did not see any enemy." He walked to the LZ and got on the CH-46. Fallon had the hill again. He walked back to his bunker, changing back into tiger-striped shorts and flip-flops for the 97-degree afternoon.

The next few days, the hill Marines listened to Armed Forces Vietnam Network during the daytime while they repaired wire that had been cut by NVA and blown up in the ground assault on the night of 9/10 August. It was slow, hard work in the sun on the barren finger. The Marines wanted a swim call to rinse off after a hard day's work. Fallon explained to them in small groups they did not have enough Marines to guard the hill, put out security on two sides of the lake, and have a group swimming. It was not what they wanted to hear or believed. He finally just told them it was not going to happen.

On the 19th, early in the afternoon at 1330, *Empire State* fired a fire mission on an eight-by-eight-foot bunker they had been watching. It was west of the OP behind the deserted hamlet, Thon Bon (2). The bunker was destroyed and in the process they got a secondary explosion.[49] Pretty nifty shooting. At 1800, civilians from Tho Son below the hill to the north came up the main trail carrying four dead bodies. Fallon sent out a patrol led by Sergeant Gunel to meet the villagers halfway up the slope. Two ARVN accompanied the patrol to interpret. The villagers said the four had been near the bunker that had been destroyed earlier that afternoon. The four had mixed color "PJs" of working farmers. The ARVN said after they spoke with the villagers that these four were known VC.[50] Fallon radioed down to Gunel that the Marines wanted nothing to do with the bodies and told the villagers to depart and take the bodies with them. When the patrol returned, Fallon met them in the mortar pit with the ARVN and got a detailed report. The ARVN said the villagers wanted C-rations for the information and dead bodies. The ARVN had turned them down. Fallon said he would have given them a case of rations for each dead man's belongings. That was a large payment, but one that might deliver some intelligence. The opportunity had been lost. It was dark and the Marines would not be going into the hamlet that night. He told Gunel to get the two listening posts.

On the 19th, the FO fired two fire missions, resulting in one enemy killed and one secondary explosion. At dusk on the 20th, the OP picked up movement on the trail parallel to the aqueduct below the hill to the south. While *Empire State* worked up a fire mission, Fallon had Gunel and Wiley use the .50-cal to try to slow, or stop, the enemy moving east. The first sighting was three lights moving. They were extinguished with the first rounds of the .50-cal going south. The second sighting at 2110 was four enemy with packs and rifles moving east. The fire mission was on target, resulting in two probable kills.[51] Darkness and a cloudy sky cut down natural illumination and prevented clear observations. Later that night, just before midnight, the NOD picked up two enemy with packs and rifles crossing rice paddies to the northwest, one kilometer out. They did an immediate fire-for-effect on targeting data with good coverage. *Empire State* claimed one kill and one probable.[52]

The morning of 22 August was a hot, lazy summer day. Fallon was on his south-looking porch in a lawn chair finishing his fourth coffee when the tower yelled down they had one small Vietnamese person coming up the main trail. Fallon walked to the tower and took a look. He sent Wiley, Broe, and one of the ARVN out to meet the person. They brought him to the landing zone. He was a ten-year-old boy. He was given water, a can of C-ration peaches to eat, and a cigarette. The ARVN soldiers talked with him all morning. He appeared weak and terrified. He said an unknown number of VC were in his hamlet of Le Nam killing and terrorizing the villagers. He said the VC had killed both his parents.[53] The hamlet was west of the OP in the 5th Marines' tactical area of responsibility. Fallon notified both Recon Battalion and the 5th Marines Combat Operations Center at An Hoa about the detained boy and what he had reported. Since it was in the 5th Marines' area, they would send a patrol to the hamlet to check it out. Later that day, at 1405, a passing helicopter picked up the boy and took him to An Hoa and the 5th Marines for further questioning.

The next evening at sundown, the IOD team spotted three enemy with dark utilities, packs, and rifles entering a bunker to the west near the hamlet of Le Nam. They fired an artillery mission, destroying the bunker, and getting an exceptionally large secondary explosion. At noon on 25 August, outside Lo Thap (1) hamlet four kilometers west of the OP, the Big Eyes picked up five enemy in dark-green utilities carrying packs and rifles. They were moving north in the open in the direction of Route 537. The FOs called a fire mission through battery *Recline-F.* When the gray smoke cleared, the Big Eyes counted five bodies on the ground and not moving. At 2330, the NOD picked up two enemy on the south side of the abandoned hamlet Thon Bon (2) moving west into a tree line. *Empire State* called a fire mission, claiming two probable kills.[54] That fire mission started a large fire that burned all night in the dry scrub and brush. It burned all the next morning and burned itself out by midday. It was quiet and hot the rest of the week as 3rd Platoon waited for its flip off the hill on 29 August.

The flip came early in the day with a single CH-53 bringing out 1st Lieutenant Taylor and 1st Platoon.[55] There were no issues with the flip as Fallon handed Taylor the hill logbook and shook his hand. Fallon was happy to leave after 29 days on the hill. Little did he realize that, although he would be in-country five more months, this was his last time on Hill 119. In the 29 days he was the hill commander, the combined 11th Marines and 1st Recon Marines had accounted for 37 separate sightings of 213 NVA/VC and 46 enemy killed by artillery.[56] The hill had repulsed a large ground assault by the T89 Sapper Battalion, suffering six non-medevac wounded.[57]

After landing, Fallon dismissed the Marines and, taking Gunel and Wiley with him, walked up the wooden stairs from LZ 401 to the S-2 hooch near the top. Each of them got a cold can of Coke from the S-2 refrigerator as they started their lengthy debrief with Lance Corporal La Croix from the S-2 shop.[58] La Croix had been a clerk typist in the shop typing every patrol report, mostly at night, with carbon copies for distribution. He had done well and now knew the area well and was promoted to debriefer while wishing for his corporal's stripes. Fallon included in his report that the enemy was moving at will from south to north and back between the Que Son Mountains and Go Noi Island and that they were moving every night in the gap between the OP and the 5th Marines to the west below, and around Hill 148 on the west side. He recommended Hill 148 be manned and that ambushes should be set out west of the hill.

***

In the rear at Camp Reasoner, while Fallon was on the hill for the month of August, Delta Company continued to patrol. Lieutenant Garry Parks had returned from Embarkation School in Okinawa. The school was considered a good deal, as it gave one a break from the bush and the grind of four to five patrols a month. Upon his return, he learned he was transferred to

Headquarters and Service (H&S) Company to become the battalion's embarkation officer for the upcoming redeployment of Charlie and Delta Companies, by ship, during September.

Short on officers, 1st Lieutenant Smith took out a patrol. The patrol made contact with one enemy who fled. The team was ready to continue patrolling, but Smith called for, and received, a ladder extract. During the extract, a Marine fell off the ladder and, in the process, shot another Marine with a silenced .22-caliber pistol.[59] Fortunately, the Marine just suffered a flesh wound. Once back in the rear, the battalion XO performed an internal investigation into the patrol. Why did they have a silenced .22-cal on the patrol? Why the extract? How exactly did the Marine get shot? The investigation found Smith was carrying the pistol, responsible for it being on the patrol and for the negligent discharge. Smith was a company commander with no field experience due to his long training pipeline. Major Dale Dorman would send his recommendations to the battalion commander. Smith had to await the decision.

On 19 August, John Hoff received the warning order for his next patrol. He no longer has his experienced Echo Company patrolling team. He had to form and train a new team in four days. He was scheduled out on 23 August, with an appropriate, tongue in cheek, callsign for the six-foot-six lieutenant: *Big Flower*.[60] John thought somebody in the S-3 shop was pulling his leg. He picked experienced Maines: Sergeant Norton, Corporal Sparks, Lance Corporal Pinto (a solid point man), Lance Corporal Curry for primary radio, Private First Class Brooks, plus the experienced corpsman "Doc" Daniels. They had not patrolled together so immediate-action drills were the order of the day. They would be within the artillery fan and had 155-mm battery *Auditor-B* in direct support.

Hoff lobbied the air officer and got an early insert. On 23 August, at 0900, they were inserted into a good two-bird LZ consisting of three-foot-high elephant grass.[61] Upon insert, *Big Flower* moved to the edge of LZ where the secondary growth of bushes and vines grew 10–12 feet high. They stopped, got a communication check, and waited to let their hearing adjust to jungle life and sounds before moving out in a northeast direction. They were breaking brush and listening to determine if an LZ spotter had seen them.

Moving slowly and listening an hour after insertion, the team observed one enemy running down a finger 500 meters across a draw from them. The soldier had his rifle slung behind his back and was moving downhill for speed. Ten minutes later, the team observed a downed CH-46 helicopter. All the equipment and weapons had been removed. The team noted the grid and called in a spot report through radio relay *War Cloud-Mike* on Hill 425 on the northern side of Que Son Mountains.[62]

Two days later, moving along a high-speed trail which was hard packed and running parallel and above a stream 20 meters below, they observed a small base camp or waystation on the other side of the stream. Circling east, they observed the camp for 20 minutes and then moved in and conducted a search. It was 35 meters above, and on the east side of the stream and had four hooches. One of the hooches had a plastic roof. All had cover from the air. One had a cave under a boulder. The plastic-roofed hooch had comm wire to a tree and a horizontal wire between two trees: a directional antenna. The trash from canned food was less than twenty-four hours old. The team moved back across the stream and continued south on the high-speed trail. Two hours later, and 200 meters south, they found a single shallow grave just off the trail. The grave was six feet long and three wide. It had a one-foot-high mound on top with dirt covered by rocks. The grave was in a cleared square, eight feet by eight feet. The team inspected the grave and found a young woman sitting in the upright position two feet below the surface. Doc Daniels, inspecting the upper body, estimated she had been dead for three days.[63] They could not remove the body due to a lack of entrenching tools. The team moved out of the area and further south down the well-used hard-packed trail. They patrolled south down the trail for two days with no sighting of the enemy but small signs of recent use all along the trail. The team found a good multibird LZ, 75 × 75 meters wide, and monitored it from a distance, calling in a shackled grid through the radio relay for their morning extract on 27 August. *Big Flower* was extracted, without incident, at 0930 and back at LZ 401 by midmorning for their debrief with Captain Cook, the battalion's S-2. During the debrief, Cook stated Team *Blue Spruce* had made contact in that area on 20 August with eight enemy, two of whom were females. The team reported at least two enemy wounded. Cook stated the grave was a multibody grave resulting from the *Blue Spruce* contact.[64]

As August came to a close, Master Sergeant Rene Regalot was collaborating with every Marine in the company as to where they would be transferred in mid-September. Any Marine with nine months or more in-country, and desiring to return to the United States, would remain in Delta Company and return via ship. Those Marines with less than nine months, or desiring to extend their tours, would be transferred to other units mostly inside 1st Recon Battalion, which meant H&S, Alpha, or Bravo Company. Regalot would try to maintain team integrity but, similar to the disestablishment of Echo Company, this was the exception to individual transfers. Regalot himself would be returning to H&S where he would once again join the S-3 training cadre and the *Mission Impossible* team.[65] This was used for short-duration missions that required additional technical skills such as rappelling in for the insertion. Typical missions were *Bright Light* missions, going after downed pilots or a body recovery from a crash site. The team was also used for high-water river-crossing support for infantry units by employing rope guides and safety lines.

As August closed, the Delta Company commander, Smith, was under a preliminary investigation for his actions, or lack of thereof, on his last patrol. While the results of the investigation did not indicate purposeful negligence with intent, it did indicate failure to supervise and utilize proper safety standards and inspection procedures during the extract, specifically, the lack of snap-links to hook to the ladder. Nor did it explain the .22-cal pistol.[66] Major Dorman had recommended a soft relief of command and transfer to the infantry where he explained Smith could gain infantry experience.[67] Lieutenant Colonel Regan, the battalion commander approved the recommendation and the adjutant, 1st Lieutenant D. J. Jenkins, through normal procedures with Division Personnel, had orders cut for Smith to be assigned to 3rd Battalion, 5th Marines, where he would become a platoon commander.[68] Unfortunately, a month later while leading an infantry platoon in the western Arizona Territory, Smith was shot pursuing an NVA soldier. He died instantly from a single shot from an AK-47 to his upper chest.[69]

CHAPTER 30

General Court-Martial, 31 August–3 September 1970

Robert "Randy" Lowery was sipping his second cold beer in the only bar in Onaga, Kansas, population 628, when a gentleman in a suit and tie slid on to the bar stool next to him and nodded. "Are you Randy Lowery?" When Randy nodded, he was served a U.S. Federal Subpoena to appear in a general court-martial in Da Nang, Vietnam.[1] On 16 July, at 1000, 1st Lieutenant D. J. Jenkins, the battalion's adjutant, received 1st Lieutenant W. X. Lee's charge sheet (DD Form 458) for the commander of the battalion.[2] He provided Lee a copy that morning. On 22 July, Colonel D. E. Holben, who had replaced Colonel Lucy as the staff judge advocate (SJA) for the 1st Marine Division, in a detailed memo, recommended a general court-martial (GCM) of Lee to the commanding general. The memo recommended a reduced charge from violation of Article 118 to Article 119, Involuntary Manslaughter.[3] On 25 July, Major General C. F. Widdecke signed the endorsement referral-to-trial order.[4] Both the prosecution and the defense had to prepare for the trial. The SJA had to find a senior qualified judge for this politically sensitive trial, someone whose docket was open and could set a court date in the future that allowed time for preparation but also allowed for travel time for defense attorneys, and witnesses no longer in the general area of the Da Nang Vital Area complex. On 25 July, a certified trial judge, Commander Keith B. Lawrence, USN was notified he would be the presiding judge for the GCM; he set the date for 31 August and instructed counsels to block out one week for the trial. Everyone was informally notified there would be a trial, and it would start on the selected date.[5]

On 29 August, the commanding general signed the convening order.[6] Both the prosecution and defense, who were previously informed, now formally knew the trial would start 31 August. The SJA had to notify key witnesses that had rotated to new duty stations or were already discharged. For example, the prosecution wanted to call the 3rd Platoon sergeant, Herman Diaz, who was on leave in Chicago en route to his next duty station. They also wanted to call Corporal Randy Lowery who had rotated home in late June and been granted an early discharge. Now a civilian, Randy was down on the family farm outside Onaga, Kansas. Lowery was relaxing after returning from 13 months in the bush patrolling with 1st Recon Battalion. His platoon sergeant, Diaz, called him at home and told him they had both been subpoenaed to testify back in Vietnam, and, that a U.S. Marshal was looking for him to deliver the subpoena. If he did not want to go back, he should go hunting and not be available to have the subpoena delivered.[7] Lowry was already bored and did not have a job lined up. A few days later, Randy was sitting in the bar when the marshal walked in and served him. The government was providing the plane tickets and was paying per diem plus nine cents a mile. Randy decided to go back. He called Diaz in Chicago who had no choice but to go as he was still on active duty. They agreed to meet in a couple of days at San Francisco International Airport for their flight back to Vietnam.[8]

In San Jose, the defense team of Hastings and DiNapoli was making their plane reservations to get to Da Nang a couple of days prior to the trial to meet with Captain Hargrove, the defense counsel, and their client, Lee. In telephone conference calls, Hargrove and the defense team decided on three character witnesses: Lieutenant Colonel William Drumright, Major George Rivers, and Sergeant Major Skinner. Skinner was still the sergeant major at 1st Recon, so he was in-country and available. Drumright was in a leave status, having checked into Headquarters Marine Corps and gone back out on leave to Tennessee. He was notified and more than happy to put off a desk job working for a female Marine colonel.[9] He hopped the first flight he could get and was on his way back to Da Nang. Major Rivers was in Saigon with the Marine Advisory Unit to the Vietnamese Marine Corps. When notified, he went to his boss, Colonel Frank Tief, explaining Lee had been one of his Marines in 3rd Recon Battalion and that he needed to go and support him. He requested, and received, the time to travel for the GCM. Rivers took the daily Air America flight between Saigon and Da Nang and was the first to arrive.[10] When the witnesses arrived, they were billeted in the transient hooches of Headquarters Battalion, 1st Marine Division, on the north side of Hill 327.[11] This included Hastings and DiNapoli who would reside in the Transient Officers' huts and took their meals with Hargrove in the division's Officers Mess.

Sergeant Mike Einsidler was the 1st Marine Division's trial chief. His job was getting everything from the court room field day to insuring a pitcher of water was available for the judge. His duties were to support the trial judge, Commander Lawrence, to ensure the trial ran smoothly and on time. He spoke for the judge, as his runner, going to get witnesses ready to enter the court room, fetching evidence from an evidence locker, and doing everything Lawrence required of him.[12] He was not the court recorder for this trial, he was logistics.

The GCM was to be held in the 1st Marine Division's courtroom on Hill 327, known as Division Hill. The courtroom was plush for Vietnam in that it was an air-conditioned room inside a Quonset hut. The inside had been built out with plywood as a standard courtroom. It featured all the furniture of a courtroom, but built-in. The judge's bench was at one end opposite the main entrance on an elevated platform. Below it was a witness box with one chair and then the courtroom floor. The members of the jury sat along one wall in a jury box behind a four foot fence. Above the member's box, pinned to the wood-paneled wall, was an American flag.[13] Both the defense and prosecution had library tables with three chairs behind each. There was one row of chairs on the back wall for observers. This GCM was closed, so there were no observers. Outside, a wooden sidewalk with rails led to a nearby Southeast Asia Hut that served as a waiting room for witnesses.[14] Inside the court, the recorder was Staff Sergeant S. D. Ratliff who would be talking and repeating everything that was said in the courtroom into a dictaphone, to be transcribed later.[15] The prosecution or trial counsels were Captain J. H. Granger USMC and Lieutenant A. C. Rudy USN, who had represented the government in the Article 32 hearing.[16] The convening authority was Major General C. F. Widdecke, commanding general of the 1st Marine Division.[17] He had appointed the court president, meaning head juror, and all members, on 29 August and then modified the president and three members on 31 August.[18] The president was Colonel Louis S. Hollier USMC. A twenty-eight-year Marine, Hollier was a native of Bozeman, Montana. He attended Montana State University and the U.S. Naval Academy. His class of 1946 graduated a year early, in June 1945, due to World War II. Hollier served as an infantry officer during the Chosin Reservoir campaign in Korea and was currently on the 1st Division Staff. Another Korean War veteran, Major Jack K. Ringler, sat as a member. He served two tours with the History Division, Headquarters Marine Corps, and retired in 1973, taking a job teaching history at a junior college in Las Vegas, Nevada. The other members of the court were Lieutenant Colonel William F. Coffey USMCR, Major Albert G. Borlan USMC, Lieutenant Commander Ernest C. Yoes USN, Major Joseph A. Galizio USMC, Captain William J. Max USMC, and Captain Gary M. Boggess USMC.[19]

The judge called the court in session at 1025 hours on 31 August 1970.[20] Present in the courtroom besides the judge, the president, and seven court members were Lieutenant Rudy and Captain Granger, the trial counsels; Lee; and the following defense counsels: Captain Hargrove, Mr. Thomas C. Hastings, and Mr. J. Phillip DiNapoli.[21] Their legal credentials were read into the record of trial. The trial counsel stated the legal qualifications of the prosecution's team were correctly stated in the appointing order. The trial counsel announced the accused had not made a request, in writing, that membership of the court include enlisted personnel. Members of the court and defense counsel, who had not been previously sworn in, were sworn in. The accused was extended the right to challenge any member of the court for cause and to exercise one peremptory challenge against any member. Captain Hargrove challenged, for cause, Captain Gary Boggess. No context was stated by the defense, so the prosecution made an argument against the challenge. The judge upheld the challenge and Boggess was dismissed.[22] The defense had removed the junior Marine as he was a first-tour staff officer with no combat experience. With his removal, the jury consisted of seven members. The accused was then arraigned on the charges and specifications in the amended DD 458 Charge Sheet which became part of the record. The amended charge read:

> Violation of the Uniformed Code of Military Justice, Article 119. Specification: In that First Lieutenant W.X. Lee, U.S. Marine Corps Reserve, "D" Company, 1st Reconnaissance Battalion, 1st Marine Division (Reinforced), Fleet Marine Force, Fleet Post Office, San Francisco, California, 96602, on active duty, did at Hill 119, Quang Nam Province, Republic of Vietnam, on or about 28 March 1970, by culpable negligence, unlawfully kill an unknown Vietnamese female by means of shooting her with a Remington 700 Sniper Rifle with a 3x9 scope.[23]

For the record, the judge stated that Major General C. F. Widdecke was in command on the date of the reference for the trial. The judge than asked if the defense understood the charge and specification to which Hastings said yes. Commander Lawrence than asked the accused, "How do you plead?" Lee stood at the position of attention and said, "Not guilty, sir."[24]

Rudy for the prosecution then made his opening statement, that the government would prove their case with eyewitnesses to the killing of the unarmed Vietnamese woman. He then called his first witness, Lance Corporal Daniel Broe, a key prosecution witness as it was his sniper rifle Lee had used for shooting the woman and he had observed the entire incident through the M49 scope. Broe was also the Marine who made the verbal shooting adjustment calls to Lee by watching the impacts of each of the three rounds through the spotter scope. Broe testified that, earlier that morning, using his 3 × 9 scope, he had counted four Vietnamese moving in and out of the bamboo thicket and the high-speed trail next to it. In the thicket itself, a man had been cutting long bamboo poles and bringing them out to the trail. Broe stated the one-armed woman was sitting in a hole. He thought it might be an old mortar crater, and she was digging with a hoe. She was talking with a woman who was standing close to the hole. And a fourth person, a woman, was standing on the trail 50 meters away towards the hamlet. Rudy asked how he knew they were women or men? Broe said by how they dressed. The women all had black "PJ" bottoms and white tops, while the man had a brown shirt and black PJ bottoms.

Rudy pushed and asked, "How can you be so sure?"

"Because I saw them in my rifle scope and then again with the M49 spotter scope."

Broe testified he had seen Lee shoot the woman. He had seen the impact of the third round produce a large red blood smear on the white blouse on her upper chest just before she had turned and fallen to the ground.[25] Broe was warned not to divulge his testimony, and he was dismissed, but told to stay available and let Einsidler know where he could be found.

The next witness the prosecution called was Corporal Kempe. Rudy asked Kempe if he had been on Hill 119 during the shooting incident. He said he had and that it was the day before Easter because the day before a chaplain had flown in and held an Easter service for the observation post (OP) Marines.[26] Rudy asked him where he was and to describe the events. Kempe said he saw Sergeant Diaz sitting near the .50-cal machine-gun pit watching something through his binoculars, so he went over and asked Diaz what he was doing.

Diaz told him, "I'm watching some 'gooks' down there, trying to figure out what they are doing." He offered the binos to Kempe to take a look.[27] He said Broe came over and wanted to shoot, but Diaz said no. Then Broe got his rifle anyway and came up and lay down next to Diaz.

Kempe asked him what he was doing, and Broe said, "I am just scoping them out through my scope."

A while later, he heard a shot and then saw Lee with the sniper rifle in the tower. He said the lieutenant left the tower and walked halfway towards the .50-cal pit and assumed a rifle-range sitting position with the rifle, zeroed in, and took a second shot. Broe called out that he was wide right and short. The lieutenant then loaded another round in the rifle, aimed in and shot. A Vietnamese woman standing next to a sitting woman then fell to the ground.[28]

Broe called out, "You hit her!"

Lee said aloud, "Damn, where?"

To that, Broe, who was looking through the M49 scope, said in the upper chest and "I could see red blood on her white blouse."[29]

Lee said, "Let's hope so for her sake."[30]

Hastings asked for clarifications on the use of the word "damn." Was it meaning "I wanted to hit her" or meaning an inflection like it was a mistake?

The prosecution objected to the question, the judge overruled and said, "Corporal, answer the question."

Kempe said it was as if it was a mistake.[31] "Lee later told us he was trying to warn the Vietnamese, not hit them."[32] Kempe was warned not to discuss his testimony and was dismissed.

Following Kempe, 1st Lieutenant P. R. Green was called. He said he had arrived on the hill on 23 March after finishing Integrated Observation Device (IOD) School.[33] He explained his billet as the forward observer (FO) for the classified IOD, the capabilities of which were explained to the court members by Green in general, unclassified, terms. He stated his mission was to shoot artillery at enemy targets, in accordance with the Rules of Engagement (RoE).

"Who determines if the targets are enemy?" Hastings asked. "I do based on observation and what they are doing," Green replied.

"So it is a judgment call on your part?"

"Yes."[34]

Lieutenant Rudy asked Green to describe the incident. He stated he had seen a group of Vietnamese civilians at the base of the hill but had ignored them as they did not appear to be a threat and, besides, they were not in his area. "They were in Lee's haven and his issue since he was responsible for the defense of the hill."[35] He said he had asked Lee to leave the tower after the first shot because the noise bothered him. This was a weak excuse to move Lee out of the tower which was his and he did not want to be associated with the shooting. Green then said Lee moved to the ground, firing at the woman and killing her.[36] He stated he did not believe Lee should have shot the woman. On cross-examination from Hastings, Green acknowledged that Lee had told him before firing, "I'm firing warning shots to move the Vietnamese," or words to that effect.[37] Lieutenant Green was warned and dismissed.

The next prosecution witness was Sergeant Nguyen Ban, Army of the Republic of Vietnam (ARVN), along with certified interpreter, Nguyen Quan Trin. Ban was the Vietnamese radio operator for the Vietnamese FO, Warrant Officer Thien. He had been promoted from corporal to sergeant for the trial. He testified the accused had shot the woman. He did not understand why as she had just been standing at the base of the hill. He went on to say that it upset him and his FO and that they had reported the shooting by radio to the ARVN 44th Artillery Battalion, their higher headquarters.[38]

Next, the prosecution called 2nd Lieutenant Garry Parks. Rudy asked him his billet, how long he had been in-country, and how many times he had been to Hill 119. Parks said he was the 2nd Platoon commander with Delta Company and had been in-country for six months and had had four tours on 119 in the capacity as hill commander.[39] Rudy then asked about how to deal with civilians around or approaching the hill. Parks's testimony revolved around what different courses of action a hill commander had when presented with a situation of Vietnamese civilians in an unauthorized area. He summarized saying there were three approaches or actions:

1. Radio battalion and ask for guidance
2. Send a patrol to investigate after getting clearance
3. Fire warning shot with multiple weapons of choice.[40]

In cross-examination, Hastings asked Parks what his mission on the hill was. Parks responded first was to defend the hill and the OP. Second, to protect the Marines and equipment and, third, specifically safeguard the classified IOD from falling into enemy hands.[41] Hastings, in summary of Parks's testimony added, "How to oversee so-called civilians came down to judgment of the hill commander. Parks agreed and said, "Yes, sir, that sums it up."[42]

Hastings asked, "Do you know of any enemy activity around the hill?" Parks said, "Yes, sir, on 9 June, a security patrol off the hill, including two RoK [South Korean] Marines, had hit a booby trap and the two RoK Marines had to be medevac'd."[43] Hastings then asked Parks if his perimeter wire had ever been cut, to which he responded, "Yes, sir." Finally, Hastings handed Parks the patrol debrief report for 21 May–6 June while also providing a copy to the clerk as evidence submitted.[44] He asked Parks to read aloud the synopsis of the patrol which was for Hill 119 for that period. "The patrol was from 21 May to 6 June. It had one listening post take fire; 20 sightings of 57 VC/NVA; and one incident of incoming small arms fire to the hill. And, that Empire State [IOD Team] had called artillery missions resulting in 33 EKIAs [enemy killed in action]."[45]

Lieutenant Parks was warned and stepped down. That testimony ended the first day with the judge calling a recess until 0900 the next day, 1 September.

After dinner, the defense team met in Hargrove's borrowed conference room and went over the first day. They were pleased their challenge of Captain Boggess was upheld. They felt he was a desk officer or staff Marine with no combat experience. They were pleased with the composition of the jury. Two, if not three, Korean War veterans were members of the jury. Their case rested on the members understanding the hard judgment calls a commander must make in combat in order to accomplish his mission. In this case, Lee's mission was protecting his Marines, the classified IOD, and Hill 119 from the enemy.

The court opened on time, 1 September, with Lieutenant Rudy calling Hospitalman Glen E. Edison. The "Doc" explained he was the corpsman for 3rd Platoon and that day he had been treating a wounded Vietnamese child and waiting for a medevac Lee had called. Therefore, he had not witnessed the shooting.[46] He was present later that morning when the villagers brought the body back to the base of the hill, that he had gone down with Lee and examined the body of a woman and stated she had been shot in the upper chest, and she had been dead about thirty minutes.[47] The corpsman was warned and dismissed.

Next, the prosecution brought on Sergeant Steven S. Boardman, who was an FO with the 11th Marines on the hill. He explained he had watched through the IOD's "Big Eyes," which were large 200-power ship's binoculars. He watched while the villagers buried the woman at the base of the hill outside the hamlet of Tho Son. He had helped identify the specific location of the grave for the investigation and for the exhumation of the body.[48]

Next, the prosecution called Sergeant Herman Diaz, who was not in the waiting area. As a result, the judge called a recess and a lunch break. He sent Sergeant Einsidler out to find Diaz who had just arrived from the United States and was in the barber shop.

After the noon recess, the trial resumed with Diaz being called and sworn in.[49] He was the 3rd Platoon sergeant and a career Marine on his second tour. He explained he had first observed, with 7 × 50 binos, three or four Vietnamese working below the hill in the restricted area, and that he was trying to figure out what they were doing. He said one man was cutting long bamboo poles and another woman was digging in a hole, while others were just milling around the area. He watched them for over an hour.[50] Then Broe came to him and asked if he could use his sniper rifle to shoot them. He had said "No, we don't know what they are doing."[51] Later, when Lee came over, he asked Diaz if he wanted to work out the .50-caliber machine-gun to warn them. He had declined.[52] When asked, Diaz confirmed Lee had fired warning shots and had hit the woman. After the villagers brought the body up seeking compensation, he had brought two cases of C-rations down to the meeting and a new rain suit to use as a burial shroud. On the way back up the hill, the lieutenant had told him to gather the platoon in the mortar pit and he would talk with them.[53] He stated that, at the meeting, Lee told the Marines what had happened, that the Vietnamese were in a restricted area, and that he could not tell precisely what they were doing besides digging and cutting. He said they could have been setting a booby trap, or they could have been observing the hill's defenses and the positions of our machine guns as a reconnaissance for a future attack. He had been firing warning shots to move the villagers away from the hill. It was an accident that the woman got hit. He accepted full responsibility and would submit a spot report to Battalion on the incident. Lee added he thought he had done the right thing. In ending the mortar pit meeting with 3rd Platoon, Lee said if anyone wanted to discuss it further or talk about it they should come by his bunker.[54]

The prosecution during the trial had photographs of the hill and had the Marines identify locations on the photographs as to where events happened. With the platoon sergeant's testimony, they also introduced the OP patrol report for the period that 3rd Platoon had been on Hill 119.[55] It contained the spot report submitted by Lee that afternoon. It stated they had one killed in action and one probable wounded in action.[56] Hastings made the point that the fact the Vietnamese woman had been shot and killed was not at issue. Lee had reported it in accordance with Battalion procedures on 28 March. Sergeant Herman Diaz was warned not to discuss his testimony and dismissed, and that he was to remain in the area until the conclusion of the trial in case he may be recalled as a witness.

The prosecution now called Master Sergeant Robert Diaz, the noncommissioned officer in charge of the First Marine Division's Scout Sniper School.[57] He was a Marine Distinguished Shooter, having shot for the Marine Corps Team in competition, each of the past 15 years. Both the prosecution and defense agreed, and stipulated, that he was an expert witness on shooting. The prosecution explained the Naval Investigative Service investigation had taken Lance Corporal Broe's sniper rifle from the evidence locker and had Diaz shoot it with the same setting that Lee had used. Diaz did the shooting both on the division's sniper range and when they flew him out to Hill 119.[58] They had him shoot 15 rounds from the same weapon at the mortar hole where the woman was shot. The prosecution was trying to establish that the sniper rifle was accurate. On cross-examination, Hastings had Diaz admit he had not been able to hit the mortar hole at 765 meters, the same distance at which the woman was shot.[59] Hastings then entered a page from Lee's Officer's Qualification Record into evidence, noting for the members that Lee, in order to graduate from The Basic School, had only shot 209, which qualified him as a Marksman while most infantry officers qualified as Experts.[60] He then asked Diaz for his expert opinion; did he believe a Marine trained on the M14 and scoring Marksman on the rifle range could pick up a sniper rifle he had never shot and hit a target in three shots at 765 meters? He responded that it was very unlikely.[61] Diaz was dismissed.

The prosecution then recalled Lance Corporal Daniel Broe and asked him about the ammunition and his bolt for the weapon and if the DOPE (data on previous engagement) had been changed. He stated he had gotten the weapon out of its case in his bunker and brought it to the northside of the hill to use the spotting scope to see what Diaz was looking at. Using his 3 × 9-power scope on nine power, he identified one man and three women, one being the one-armed woman working and digging in the hole with a hoe. He then stated Lee asked him for the rifle and ammunition. He had to go back to the bunker to get the bolt and an open box of ammo. When he returned, he inserted the bolt and handed the lieutenant the rifle and five rounds, three of which were used in firing the shots.[62]

The last witness of the day was a surprise to both the witness and the defense. The prosecution called 1st Lieutenant Michael O. Fallon. He had been added to the witness list by the defense, but the prosecution decided to call him. Fallon was sworn in. Lieutenant Rudy asked him to explain his duties and experience on Hill 119. Fallon said he was a platoon commander with Delta Company and within those duties had taken different platoons to the hill four times, and that his most recent time on the hill was a double trip from 1–29 August as the hill commander.[63] Rudy then asked Fallon what he would do as the hill commander if he saw Vietnamese civilians near the hill. His response was that, in an ideal situation, he would send a patrol out to investigate, which was the answer for which Rudy was looking. However, Fallon continued that, many times, if you are shorthanded on the hill, you would not want to weaken your strength by sending out a patrol that you then might have to send a reaction force after to reinforce it if it got ambushed or sustained casualties. The other alternative was to fire warning shots. Rudy asked, "What weapon would you use?" Fallon stated it would depend on situation, location, time of day, but either a machine gun or a mortar shot would suffice. Rudy asked about a sniper rifle and Fallon responded if one were on the hill it would be appropriate, but that not every platoon had a sniper. Hastings declined to cross-examine but retained the right to do so, stating it was late in the day. At that time, the prosecution rested. It was after 1900; the judge declared a recess until 0900 the next day.

The next morning, the court resumed at 0902 with the judge asking if the defense was ready.[64] Captain Hargrove said they were. Hastings rose and requested to make a motion to the judge, which was granted. Hastings presented a motion for a finding of "Not guilty."[65] He did so on the grounds that the prosecution had not proven a violation of the Uniform Code of Military Justice, and that the incident had occurred in a combat situation where a commander had made a judgment call to protect his Marines and the classified equipment on the hill. The motion was denied by the judge,[66] who told the defense to proceed.

Standing, walking in front of his table, and facing the members of the court, Hastings now made the defense's opening statement. He said Lee was simply doing his job defending the hill, his Marines, and the equipment in enemy territory from the enemy activities engaged in actions against the hill.[67] Hastings planted the seeds of their defense before they called their first witness.

1st Lieutenant Thomas C. Baumgaertel USMC was called.[68] He was sworn in and stated he was with Division G-5, Civil Affairs. Hastings asked him if he were familiar with the Hamlet Evaluation System (HES) and could he explain the system. He said he was, and he could, but that it was a classified system; therefore, uncleared personnel needed to be cleared from the courtroom and the proceeding would have to be classified. Both the defense and the prosecution had side-bar conversations, and the judge called them both forward. The issue was Hastings and DiNapoli's lack of security clearances. The prosecution said it was a defense issue since it was their witness. The agreement was that the court would go into classified session with the two civilian attorneys stepping out with Captain Hargrove, for the defense, and the accused remaining. When the court reconvened in the classified session, Baumgaertel explained that the HES was a Military Assistance Command, Vietnam (MACV) Program to classify every hamlet in every province as to their status in the Pacification Program.[69] It represented the Government of Vietnam's status for loyalty and control. The system graded each hamlet based on their loyalty to the South Vietnamese Government or the Viet Cong Infrastructure. It was a rating of hamlets based on 18 factors judged by the Province Advisory Team and submitted to Saigon. Hamlets were given letter grades based on the factors: A, B, and C level were Secure Hamlets, D and E level were Contested Hamlets, and Viet Cong-controlled hamlets were labeled with the letters, "VC."[70] After the HES system was explained to the members of the court, Hargrove asked Baumgaertel to explain the village structure around Hill 119. Using the Dai Loc 1:50,000 map sheet, he said Hill 119 was in Zue Xuyen District and that the three hamlets below the north side of the hill all belonged to Xuyen Thanh Village.[71] The Government of South Vietnam had relocated the population of those hamlets east to the coastal highway where they could provide security.[72] During daylight hours, villagers could farm their fields but must return before curfew to the secure hamlet. Hargrove asked Baumgaertel to provide the scores or the letter grades for the hamlets closest to Hill 119, specifically those directly below the hill—Tho Son, Thon Bon (1) and (2). Baumgaertel responded, "Gentlemen, the classified answer is all three hamlets were VC hamlets in the HES system which meant that the Government of South Vietnam was not operating inside those hamlets, and they were controlled by the Viet Cong Infrastructure."[73] Baumgaertel was dismissed.

With the defense team returning after the HES brief, they called Gunnery Sergeant Robert A. Foley.[74] Foley was from 11th Marines S-2 and was a witness called to explain the classified nature of the IOD. Hastings and DiNapoli departed the courtroom again as it went back into a classified session. Foley explained the technology in the black-box laser range finder could lase a target out to 10,000 meters and was accurate to the meter.[75] The distance and technology were both classified "Secret." Hargrove asked what the procedure was to prevent it from falling into enemy hands. Foley stated that 1st Recon had come up with keeping two thermite grenades in an ammunition box next to or near the laser range finder and, if it was going to be captured, they were to destroy it first. The destruction procedure had been implemented on all six IOD hills. Captain Hargrove thanked the gunnery sergeant, who was dismissed.

With the full defense team now back in the courtroom, they moved on to the defense's character witnesses for Lieutenant Lee. The defense team had selected three witnesses who they believed, by their individual reputations, would have impact and influence on the views of the members of the jury. They selected known combat veterans, as the crux of their defense was about a judgment decision by a combat commander. First called was Sergeant Major Charles W. Skinner, 1st Recon Battalion's sergeant major.[76] Skinner was a warrior and veteran of three wars, having served in World War II, Korea, and now Vietnam. In most rooms, he was the largest man present. The former drill instructor always looked great in uniform and today was no different. When asked by Hastings for thoughts on Lee, Skinner turned in his chair and faced the members. He told the members that Lee was a former enlisted Marine or "Mustang." The lieutenant was hard, fair, and took care of his Marines, the type of leader young Marines looked up to. Lee had his Marines' respect because they knew he took care of them. He said he knew the lieutenant personally from observing his actions around Camp Reasoner, such as drilling his Marines on immediate actions upon contact, which they knew would save their lives. He had observed him often in the weight room and on the handball court. Skinner confided that, if he were going on patrol or a mission, he would want to have Lee lead the patrol. Hastings thanked the sergeant major, who was dismissed.[77]

Hastings called Lieutenant Colonel Willam C. Drumright USMC and asked him his opinion of Lee.[78] Drumright was also a Korean War veteran. He explained he had just given up command of 1st Recon Battalion and that, during his command time, Lee was one of his best lieutenants. In fact, he recalled multiple patrols where Lee had mixed it up with the North Vietnamese Army (NVA) and had always produced results, including prisoners.[79] On three occasions, he had captured prisoners, which brought the division valuable intelligence. Drumright said Lee was mission oriented and always got his mission completed. He ranked Lee as one of his best.[80] Hastings thanked Drumright.

When Drumright had concluded and was getting up, Captain James Granger for the prosecution said, "Wait, sir, we have a few more questions." Granger asked "Were you not the officer who recommended a general court-martial? Now you are telling us Lieutenant Lee is a great lieutenant. Which is it, sir?" Drumright, who never liked being challenged, had anticipated the question. He said, "Yes, both are correct. As a commander who receives a serious allegation, I am duty bound to investigate. We are not the Army! We had a serious allegation from the South Vietnamese Government and villagers, and we investigated it. Then, I am sure my fellow Marines and members of the court, will see it the way I do, Lieutenant Lee was defending his hill!"[81] Granger had made his point. Drumright had made his. Drumright was dismissed.

Hastings then called up Major Ernest R. "George" Rivers.[82] All of the Marines in the courtroom knew him or had heard of George Rivers. He was currently on his third Vietnam tour. The former Basic School company commander, wearing the tailored tight-fitting tiger-striped uniform, told everyone he was an advisor to the Vietnamese Marine Corps (whose Marines wore tiger-striped utilities). His was a billet only the best Marines were selected for and one who had experienced ground combat. Rivers had hopped the daily scheduled Air America C-46 passenger service known as the "Saigon Rocket," that departed Saigon at 0900 for Da Nang, in order to be at the trial. Hastings asked Rivers to explain how he knew Lee and to provide his opinion of him as a Marine. Rivers explained he had met then 2nd Lieutenant Lee when he checked into 3rd Reconnaissance Battalion in Quang Tri, Vietnam. Rogers had been the executive officer (XO) before becoming the commanding officer of the battalion. He explained Lee had been one of his two best patrol leaders in 3rd Recon. Lee had been patrolling on and in the demilitarized zone against hard-core NVA formations.[83] When 3rd Recon Battalion was withdrawn from Vietnam with the 3rd Marine Division, it went to Okinawa. Rivers, now the battalion commander, was immediately accosted by his two best lieutenants to get them back in the fight. They were volunteering for Vietnam again. Rivers knew it was best for them and for the Corps, so he made the phone calls to Headquarters Marine Corps to make it happen. He then called his fellow Recon battalion commander, Drumright and said, "I'm sending you my two best!"[84] Shortly thereafter, Lieutenants Lee and Rathmell were transferred from 3rd to 1st Recon Battalions. Continuing his dialog, Major Rivers said, "Now 1st Lieutenant Hank Rathmell is already dead here in Vietnam in a rescue attempt on a fallen Marine pilot and here we are with 1st Lieutenant Lee who was doing his duty defending his hill. I am here for Lieutenant Lee!"[85] Hastings thanked Major Rivers and reminded the members he had flown in from Saigon to testify. Granger knew it was best to get Rivers off the stand, so he had no questions. Rivers was dismissed.

Departing the courtroom and walking to the division's Officers Club, he caught up with his old friend, "Wild Bill" Drumright.[86] The defense had carefully selected their character witnesses as they wanted them to talk directly to the members of the jury, especially the Korean War veterans who knew combat was not black-and-white choices but filled with gray areas where commanders made decisions on partial information every day.

It was close to the end of the day, and the defense surprised the prosecution when they called their final witness, the accused, 1st Lieutenant W. X. Lee.[87] Hastings and DiNapoli had not wanted Lee to take the stand. Lee felt strongly that he should[88] as he felt he had done the proper actions as the hill commander so why not say so directly to the court? He had nothing to hide. They had all agreed to wait and make a game-time call.

Following the effect the strong words of the three character witnesses had on members of the court, Hastings saw the immediate merit in the straightforward way of Marines. He called Lee to take the stand. The accused was sworn in. Lee had a prepared statement, not on paper in front of him, but in his mind, that he had gone over more times than he knew.

Addressing the issue directly in Marine Corps fashion, Hastings asked Lee why was he shooting at the woman on 28 March? Lee turned, facing the members of the jury, looking each in the eye:

> As Commander of the Hill, I was responsible for its defense; it was my mission! The four Vietnamese below the hill were doing something in a restricted area close to our perimeter. They continued looking at our defenses. They were digging in the ground, causing me to ask: was it for a booby trap or a bunker? The most prudent action was to warn them. They needed to move out of the thicket and into the open and back to the hamlet. The sniper rifle was used to control the fire. I took the shots because I did not want my inexperienced sniper shooting.[89]

Lee also said, "Warning them was the best defensive action for the situation. I take full ownership of the decision and the action that day."[90]

Captain Granger and Lieutenant Ruby huddled at the persecution table and decided to let it stand for now. Hastings said, "Your Honor, the defense testimony for today is concluded." Commander Lawrence asked the prosecution how many witnesses they had for rebuttal. They responded, "At least two, sir."[91] It was 1905, Lawrence recessed the court until 0900, 3 September.

The defense team huddled for 15 minutes in Hargrove's conference room. They had no real idea how it was going. The members of the court were very attentive, and the president was taking notes. Lee reminded the defense team, "We had Fallon lined up to talk about the enemy around the hill when the prosecution called him. He got hit hard by the NVA on his last trip up to Hill 119.[92] We could call him back." Hargrove explained that tomorrow the prosecution would start with their rebuttal witnesses. He said, "Let's see what they say. After the prosecution closes, we will get surrebuttal, where we can call anyone we want." The defense meeting broke up. Hargrove was taking the two civilian attorneys to steak night at the O'Club. Lee declined the invitation to join them. He was drained. He walked back down Division Hill to his hooch at Camp Reasoner. He sat on his old hospital bed and broke out a long-range patrol ration, pouring half a canteen of water into the dehydrated chicken-and-rice plastic envelope.

The next morning, 3 September, at 0900, Judge Lawrence gaveled open the court and nodded to the prosecution. At this time, Rudy called Lieutenant Nguyen Thein ARVN to the stand.[93] Thein spoke and understood reasonable English. He had been promoted for the trial from warrant officer. He was sworn in. Rudy asked him his unit and to describe what had happened on 28 March on Hill 119. Thein stated he was an FO with the 44th Artillery Battalion of the ARVN.[94] He said he was in the observation tower that morning observing when, for no reason, Lee of Recon got a rifle and started shooting at civilians below the hill. Thein said he shot a woman for no reason. Later that day, the villagers brought the body to the hill for compensation. He said he had served as the interpreter for Lee and that Lee had given the villagers two cases of C-rations, one for each of her orphans. On cross-examination, the defense asked if Lee had told them they were in a restricted area. He said yes, but that did not matter as they were just civilians. Thein was emotional and stated the woman was a widow of two months and had been pregnant. She left two orphans. Lieutenant Thein was dismissed.

The prosecution then recalled 2nd Lieutenant Garry Parks.[95] The questions for him were now based on the RoE. They asked Parks what RoEs were and how he had received them. Parks stated they were on every patrol order as "Reference (d) 1stMarDivO P003000.2A (Rules of Engagement)." However, he had never seen the actual order. He said, "We got them verbally."[96] Parks explained that, fundamentally, it was the ability for self-defense. After that if you could identify the enemy by uniform or if they were carrying a rifle or war materiel, it was fair game to engage. He added that if people were in hostile areas or free-fire zones, one could engage. He said it became tricky when there was a civilian population living or working in an area. The prosecution asked if he had seen the RoEs written and he said not since The Basic School.[97] The prosecution introduced three orders into evidence in the general subject of how to treat civilians. The defense objected, but the judge overruled and allowed them into evidence. The first order was the 1968 "FMF Pac Order 1610.2A w/ Ch.1: Individual Responsibility." The second order was an extract from the 1949 "Geneva Convention Article 3 on POWs" republished by FMFPAC [Fleet Marine Force, Pacific]" in 1968 which had one page on treatment of civilian personnel. the third was an "MACV Directive of 2 March 1969 on Military Operations and the Minimizing Noncombatant Battle Casualties."[98] He asked Parks if he had ever seen these orders to which he responded, "No, sir."[99] Lieutenant Parks was thanked and dismissed. The prosecution failed to put into evidence "1st Marine Division Order, POO3000.2A (Rules of Engagement)," that appeared as a reference on the cover sheet of every 1st Recon Battalion Operations Order.

The prosecution now made a motion to introduce into evidence the testimony of 1st Lieutenant Arthur "Pete" Gray III, now deceased, as given at the Article 32 Investigation of this case.[100] After arguments by both sides, the judge allowed both the direct and cross-examination of Lieutenant Gray's testimony as given at the prior Article 32 to be read aloud verbatim into the record in the presence of all court members.[101] Gray had been the tactical plans officer in the battalion's S-3 shop. As such, he drafted all the operations orders for each team. He also drafted the orders for manning the OP and had drafted Lee's order and mission statement for the manning and defense of Hill 119.[102] Pete Gray's testimony focused on definitions of "Recon Haven," "Free Fire Zone," "Restricted Area," and "Tactical Area of Responsibility," and who had the authority to fire weapons in each area. The prosecution indicated that was their last piece of evidence.[103] The judge ordered a 15-minute break for a head call the president of the court had requested.

Back in session for the defense, Hastings stood and recalled 1st Lieutenant Michael Fallon for surrebuttal.[104] Hastings went straight to the enemy situation around Hill 119, asking Fallon to describe it. Fallon said Hill 119 was a cork in a bottle between the NVA's Base Area 116 in the Que Son Mountains and its island stronghold on Go Noi Island, 1,300 meters north of the OP. The NVA controlled the ground around the hill both day and night, as exemplified on his last two trips to the hill in August.[105] Hastings asked about booby traps and ambushes. Fallon recalled that there were numerous booby-trap incidents. Hastings asked for a few specific examples if he could recall any. Fallon said in January, the hill commander, 2nd Lieutenant Chuck Overton, was walking the landing zone trail with the then battalion commander, Lieutenant Colonel J. J. Grace, when he hit a booby trap.[106] It resulted in an emergency medevac for the lieutenant who lost half a leg, an arm, and one eye. Grace was a priority evac and was evacuated to Japan. He had to give up command. Another incident was 2nd Lieutenant Chris L'Orange of 4th Platoon, who was leading a walk-off patrol from Hill 119 in June. His patrol was ambushed with a command-detonated mine on the trail close to the railroad berm. They suffered five casualties and L'Orange had to be medevac'd back to the States.[107] Hastings asked Fallon to mark the location on a photo. After he did, Hastings stated to the members of the court that it was less than two hundred meters from where the Vietnamese were working on 28 March on the same high-speed trail. Hastings then asked if the hill had ever been attacked. Fallon said it had. Hastings asked if he could provide the court with a summary. The prosecution objected. Hastings argued the attack was an indication of enemy activity around the hill. Judge Lawrence overruled the objection and said to Fallon, "Make this a short summary." Fallon then described the combined-arms ground assault on the night of 9/10 August just a few weeks before.[108] The T89 Sapper Battalion had started with rocket-propelled grenades and mortars, followed closely by a ground attack on the hill. The enemy sappers were repulsed and suffered heavy casualties with at least twenty-five killed. He said eight sappers died hung up on the third and closest strand of wire to the hill, 20 feet below Alpha Bunker. Hastings asked from what direction the attack came from. Fallon said it was from the railroad berm northwest of the OP, then up the draw where the trash pit was located.[109]

"Would the sappers have reconnoitered the hill for its defense prior and could the VC have helped their recon by describing where the defenses were?" Hastings asked.

"Yes, sir," Fallon replied

Hastings then asked about the hamlets on the northern side of the hill. Could Fallon describe them? Fallon said there were three hamlets. To the northwest was Thon Bon (1) and (2); both of those were deserted hamlets used by the NVA to rest or to meet guides. Hastings asked for clarification regarding the guides. Fallon said the NVA were from North Vietnam, and they did not know their way around in the South. Therefore, they used local VC guides that met them and led them to where they needed to go on that day's march, or to their attack positions. Hastings then returned to the hamlets, asking about the third. Fallon said it was Tho Son, one kilometer directly north of the OP. He said it had been abandoned but, in the past six months, had been re-occupied by 8–10 women and children. Hastings asked if he knew about the HES system, but Fallon did not, so Hastings rephrased the question, asking, "How would you classify the villages' attitude toward the hill?" Fallon said they were known by everyone in Delta Company as hostile villages due to the continued, daily, sightings of enemy in the hamlets and because of the booby traps in the area that seemed to harm the Marines, but not local villagers. Hastings, in closing, asked, "What was the mission of Recon on the hill?" Fallon responded that it was to provide security for the hill, its Marines, and the IOD system. Lieutenant Rudy indicated to the judge he had no questions; with that Lieutenant Fallon was warned and dismissed from the court.

Hastings now recalled Corporal John P. Kempe.[110] He asked Kempe, "Have you ever found booby traps on patrol?" Kempe said he was on a patrol on either 17 or 19 May off the hill with Corporal McCommon and Doc Edison when they found a booby trap in a dry well in Tho Son hamlet. They threw two M26 grenades into the well to destroy it, but two of the patrol's Marines suffered shrapnel wounds from the secondary explosion.[111] Switching subjects, Hastings asked Kempe to describe what Lee had said to the platoon in the mortar pit on 28 March. Kempe said the lieutenant stated he was sorry for what happened, but he had done the proper thing as the Vietnamese were in a restricted zone behaving as if they were doing something to the trail, like putting in a booby trap. He said he accepted full responsibility and had filed a spot report, and that if any of the Marines wanted to talk about it, they could come by his bunker.[112] Hastings asked Kempe if he would go on patrol with Lee. He said, "Definitely," and that the lieutenant was an outstanding patrol leader and in fact had led a patrol he went on in April, after the shooting on the hill, where they grabbed a prisoner who turned out to be an NVA officer.[113] With that Corporal Kempe was dismissed. The judge asked if there were more witnesses. Both sides answered no. He called a morning recess for 20 minutes.

When they returned from the recess, the prosecution, now Captain Granger, made their argument and in final summation said Lee had deliberately shot and killed the civilian woman in violation of standing orders and his sworn duties.[114]

The defense, Hastings, then made a long statement arguing that Lee was doing his sworn duty and following his mission statement in protecting the hill.[115] The prosecution had failed to prove the woman was a civilian and in fact, he contended, she was VC conducting a reconnaissance of the hill and gaining gun-position locations to pass to the NVA in preparation for their attack of the hill, which had, as a matter of fact, they just heard had happened three weeks ago! In fact, Lee, as a combat commander, was prudent in that he was firing warning shots to move the villagers out into the open where they could be observed and push them away from the hill and out of the restricted area. As hill commander, he had made a judgment call on how to protect the hill, his Marines, and the equipment that was so classified it could not be talked about in open court. Lee was taking the same actions countless previous hill commanders had used to protect the hill from the enemy. The defense rested.

The prosecution, this time Lieutenant Rudy, got up and made a closing argument that Lee had violated the Geneva Convention, and everything the Marine Corps teaches, and had shot a civilian woman, killing her. He should be held accountable for his actions. Rudy closed.[116]

Judge Lawrence than instructed the members of the court, in accordance with paragraph 73 of the Marine Corps Manual, including elements of the offense, the presumption of innocence, reasonable doubt, and the burden of proof as required by Article 51(c).[117] He told the court it was now 1605. "I expect you to deliberate tonight. You may take time for dinner, but, in so doing, you are to cloister yourselves. Notify Sergeant Einsidler, who will remain outside the courtroom if you have questions or need to see me, or when you have reached a verdict."[118] Neither sides having anything further to offer, the court was closed.[119]

The Quonset hut courtroom was vacated except for the seven members of the jury. At 1710, the members did take a 30-minute break where some used the head, had a smoke break, or grabbed a quick bite to eat. The president, Colonel Hollier, had them all back by 1745. At 1810, he sent Einsidler to find the judge, who was waiting in the SJA main conference room.

"The members are ready, sir."

Einsidler then went to the prosecution offices and to the defense conference room, advising them to return to the courtroom.[120] At 1828, the judge called the court back in session. He stated, for the record, that all parties who had been present at adjournment were now present. In the open court, the judge asked the president if a verdict had been reached. Colonel Hollier said they had.

The president, reading from a short script announced, "That, in closed session and upon secret written ballot, the accused was found not guilty."[121]

Lee sat with his forehead on the table in front of him, not moving. A large weight had been lifted off him. He felt immense relief. He was a Marine again, not an accused second-class citizen. The defense team jumped up and were shaking hands and congratulating themselves.

Commander Lawrence simply said, "This court is adjourned."

It was 1837 on 3 September 1970.[122]

The judge, court reporter, and members all filed out of the Quonset hut and went their separate ways. Lee and the defense team walked up the boardwalk one level to the defense's conference room. There, Lee shook hands with each of his three counsel and thanked them. Hastings and DiNapoli were anxious to leave to try to catch a midnight commercial flight out of Da Nang. Captain Hargrove said he would take them to the airport. Hastings said he would send a telegram to Lee's parents. They shook hands again and all walked outside into the sticky, hot night. Hastings wasted no time in sending telegrams. The first was to Lee's parents. They received the good news at 0400 with a knock on the door from Western Union and the telegram that their son had been found not guilty.[123] Hastings also sent telegrams to the newspapers.

On 4 September, the *San Jose Times* headline declared "Gatos Officer Cleared." The article read, "Lt W.X. Lee was exonerated of a manslaughter charge involving a Vietnamese woman who was killed in a March 28 incident." It continued:

> ... that no information on the alleged murder was released by the Pentagon except a report that a Vietnamese civilian was killed during the course of a combat mission involving Lt Lee's patrol. Based on the information the defense attorneys claimed that Lee was being Railroaded, and that the woman he is accused of killing was a known Viet Cong Sympathizer.[124]

The *San Jose Mercury* headline was "Lt Lee Acquitted in Vietnam." The article led with "Lt Lee acquitted in Vietnam. The 7-man GCM Board cleared Lee after 45 minutes of deliberation, after the four-day trial. The defense argued that by firing three warning shots Lee was taking positive action to protect the security of the outpost."[125]

Lee was physically and mentally relieved as, alone, he slowly walked downhill from the courtroom and across Division Road. At the 1st Recon cement guard shack, with the painted eagle, globe, and anchor embellished above the door, he received a hand salute from the sentry. Returning the salute, he felt he was back in the Marine Corps! He stopped and talked with the guard, who was one of his Marines from Headquarters and Service (H&S) Company. Walking down the battalion street to his hut, he thought he wanted his old platoon back and to patrol again. Parks and Fallon were not in the hooch. They were at the club. He did not want to go there as it would be a scene; he just did not want to deal with that tonight. He removed his utility blouse, got a cold beer out of the small refrigerator, and went to the back wooden steps. Sitting, he took a long swig, lit a Marlboro cigarette, and just looked at the rice paddies below and the stars above. He was glad to still be a Marine! In the morning, he would get his platoon back.

Back at the SJA offices, the court recorder may have been the most pleased person; Staff Sergeant Radcliff and two other clerks did not have to type up the verbatim transcripts for the entire GCM! A verdict of "Not guilty" meant they only had to type a summary.[126] He would do it in the morning for Commander Lawrence's signature. The summary would end up being seven-pages long put into the Form DD 491 between two light-blue cardboard cover and back sheets that all GCMs received.[127] Commander Lawrence would sign two copies, one for the 1st Marine Division's records and one for Lee, who put his copy in a large plastic envelope and placed it in the bottom of his green foot locker. It stayed there for 53 years, never seeing sunlight, a record of the past.[128]

Sergeant Herman Diaz, who had come from Chicago to testify, had to find Randy Lowery, who had come back to testify and was never called as a witness. It took him over an hour to find Lowery. Now a civilian in jeans and a t-shirt, Lowery was down in the Delta Company, 3rd Platoon hut at Camp Reasoner, talking and drinking beer with his buddies. Diaz said, "I'm going to Saigon for some fun, do you want to come along?" Lowery said, "I have nothing going on, I am not going on patrol with these guys."[129] Diaz and Lowery needed a ride. It was after dark and curfew but that was not a problem for these Recon Marines. They simply got the Delta Company driver and jeep. Diaz, being a sergeant, made up a story that he had to get Lowery to the airport. They commandeered the jeep and departed Camp Reasoner. Driving east past Freedom Hill and "Dog Patch," they continued through the Four Corners intersection to the main gate of Da Nang International. Through the gate, they proceeded to the Air Force side of the runway where they wanted to catch one of the military flights to Saigon. They spent the night there in the terminal with others and got a morning flight to Saigon.

Diaz knew his way around Saigon from a previous tour there as an embassy guard.[130] Three days of partying and the two Marines were out of money. Time to catch a military flight back to Da Nang where they had commercial plane tickets back to the States. Diaz went on to have a successful career as a Marine, retiring as a master sergeant. After retiring, being fluent in Spanish, he then worked as a government contractor training South American armies in small arms.[131] Randy Lowery returned to Kansas where he used the GI Bill to attend barbers' college. He was a barber for 20 years until a bad skydiving landing wrenched his knee; the long days standing as a barber were finally too much for his back and legs. Back to college in criminal justice, he switched careers, working at a detention facility in Hutchinson, Kansas. Now retired, he enjoys woodworking and his family, wife, and two grown children.[132]

On 4 September, Lee went to see the battalion's adjutant, 1st Lieutenant D. J. Jenkins, and requested to be reassigned from H&S Company back to Delta Company. Jenkins told Lee he could not do that because the powers up the hill, meaning Division, wanted him out of the country ASAP. Not satisfied, Lee's next stop was the battalion XO, Major D. D. "Dale" Dorman, who told him it had come straight from the commanding general, to get Lee out of Vietnam.

He was concerned the Vietnamese would not be satisfied with the results of the GCM and that it was for his own good and that of the Marine Corps that Lee needed to go. Dorman told him, in fact, the G-1 at Division was expediating his orders and he should turn in his gear and get ready. The command wanted Lee out of country to prevent him from becoming a focal point of protest for the South Vietnamese. Whether this was true is speculation. Lee thought they just wanted him gone.[133]

Departing from Dorman's office, he walked across the battalion street to the sergeant major's office and banged loudly three times on the doorframe. The sergeant major yelled "Enter," and then stood up when he saw it was Lee, who extended his hand and simply said, "Thank you, Sergeant Major, for the kind words and white lies at my trial, it was greatly appreciated and meant a lot to me personally." Sergeant Major Skinner asked him if he knew where he was going and he said no, except they were shuffling him out of country soon. Walking back up the battalion street past the Delta Company office, he put his head in looking for Parks or Fallon; they were not there. Lee ducked back out of the office, not really wanting to talk to anyone. He returned to his hooch to organize his gear for turn in. It would not take long, and he did not have long. Late that afternoon, the clerk from S-1 (administration) brought Lee his orders and his flight-manifest slip. He had orders to Officers' Candidate School (OCS) in Quantico, Virginia. He was manifested to depart in less than 48 hours on the early morning flight, at 0200, on 7 September.[134] There was no going-away party or a plaque presentation that most senior noncommissioned officers and officers received when departing the battalion. It was a quiet jeep ride in the H&S Company jeep at 2300 on 6 September to check in for his flight later that night. Lieutenant W. X. Lee's tour in Vietnam was over. He travelled home via Okinawa.

He skipped taking leave en route to his new duty station at the OCS, where he was assigned as an S-3 trainer in the Physical Fitness Section. After checking in at OCS and working for a month, Lee took leave in December. Traveling back to California, he married the love of his life.[135] They had a military wedding, including a traditional sword arch. His former company commander, "Jerry" Spolter, now a civilian, reserve Marine, in law school, attended. Spolter had his hair trimmed slightly and put on his Dress Blue uniform to round out the last man in the sword arch.[136] Returning to Quantico immediately after the wedding, both Lee and his wife were working full time to earn sufficient money, while living in a subterranean, one-bedroom rental apartment. This was in order to pay the monthly installments on the large debt they incurred for his legal defense, as well as the travel expenses of both legal counsels.[137] It would take years to pay off the debt, by which time Lee was a senior captain and well on his way to a 32-year career as a Marine, retiring as a colonel. Never bitter at the Corps, as his former Marine father was, Lee was always thankful that a former lance corporal of the Marines without a college degree could overcome a GCM and retire as a colonel.[138] Lee and his wife now live outside Colorado Springs in the same neighborhood as their two children and three grandchildren.

***

In 2008, retired Colonel Broman C. Stinemetz, who commanded 1st Reconnaissance Battalion from January to July 1968, returned to Vietnam. On the tour, he climbed Hill 119. Returning to

Route 537 below the hill, he stopped in Tho Son hamlet and engaged an elderly man in talking about the "American War." Sitting under a tree sharing cold sodas, he asked the man if he knew the one-armed woman from Tho Son who had been one of the village elders? He said he did, and that, yes, she was a village elder. Continuing, the old man stated she had joined the Viet Minh to fight the French, where she lost the arm. In the American War, he stated she was a VC leader and had been the political officer for the entire village.[139] Five months before Lieutenant Lee's trial, on 28 March 1970, the woman who had been shot was standing next to the one-armed woman who had been digging a hole with a hoe.

CHAPTER 31

Lieutenant Colonel Leftwich Arrives, September 1970

In Washington, D.C., during September 1970, the U.S. Senate voted not to approve a resolution by Senators McGovern and Hatfield to force President Nixon to withdraw all American troops from Indochina by 31 December 1971.[1] The country was split between the prowar "Hawks" and the antiwar "Doves." A popular Capitol Hill bar opened at 329 Pennsylvania Avenue, S.E.; it was called the "Hawk & Dove," reflecting the split and spirit of the times. The bar was frequented by young Capitol Hill staffers whose offices were three blocks away, and by young Marines from Marine Barracks, Washington, D.C., located at 8th and I Streets, S.E.[2] Meanwhile, President Nixon had ordered 1,000 new FBI agents to be stationed at college campuses in response to anti-Vietnam War protests.[3]

The number one song on the Billboard Hot 100 was "War" by Edwin Starr. It was played often on the Armed Forces Vietnam Network but not as often as "We Got to Get Out of This Place" by the Animals which reflected the attitude of the troops in Vietnam, all of whom would sing along every time the song was played.

***

In Vietnam, the drawdown continued while, between 11–14 September, MACV–SOG (Military Assistance Command, Vietnam–Studies and Observations Group) conducted Operation *Tailwind*, a joint/Allied covert U.S. Special Forces Operation into Laos. Its purpose was to create a diversion for a Royal Lao Army operation against communist forces. Because of the distances to be flown, the heliborne forces were flown by three Marine CH-53s from HMH-463 (*Pegasus*) and escorted by 12 Cobra gunships (*Scarface*), the entire Marine squadron. Two CH-53s were shot down during the operation, with crews recovered immediately after being shot down. The force encountered heavy resistance from the North Vietnamese Army (NVA). They destroyed an enemy base camp and captured documents pertaining to the NVA logistical operations before being extracted by the Marine helicopters. The classified "Secret" mission went unreported by the media for more than 27 years.[4]

At 1st Marine Division, in September, they prepared for the 7th Marines' departure by withdrawing them incrementally to Da Nang for sea and airlift.[5] Their flag would depart on 1 October 1970.[6] The 5th Marines began Operation *Catawba Falls* which was a two-phased operation. In phase one, preparation was air strikes and artillery fires. The last piece of phase one was a helo lift of a composite artillery battery of four 105-mm howitzers and two 155s into Fire

Support Base (FSB) Dagger on Hill 1031, Ban Co Mountain, west of An Hoa. The second phase was a scheduled helicopter assault which both the Army of the Republic of Vietnam (ARVN) and NVA knew about in advance and assumed would be to the west in the Thuong Duc corridor, supported by FSB Dagger artillery units per previous operations. The major helicopter lift of 2nd Battalion and 3rd Battalion of the 5th Marines picked up troops in An Hoa Combat Base, Hill 65, and Hill 37. The move west was a helicopter feint, and the Marines were repositioned to the southeast on FSBs Ross, Baldy, and Ryder. It had been a well-planned leak and fake to cover the 7th Marines' withdrawal and the reoccupation of their key bases that were protecting the Que Son Valley and the strategic north–south National Highway 1.[7] The An Hoa Combat Base and runway would be turned over to the ARVNs.[8] The 5th Marines now took over the Que Son tactical area of responsibility formerly patrolled by the 7th Marines. Operation *Catawba Falls* ended at noon on 21 September with the last helo lift into FSB Ryder.[9] Colonel P. X. Kelly's 1st Marine Regiment maintained the defense around the Da Nang Rocket Belt.[10] Colonel Kelly continued his career, retiring as a General and the 28th Commandant of the Marine Corps.

***

At 1st Recon Battalion, it was a cross between a Mexican hat dance and musical chairs for all the personnel during the month of September. The entire battalion was being reorganized and downsized while at the same time receiving 30 percent of new personnel. This was done to remain operationally capable, for those who remained, and complying with Operation *Keystone Robin-Alpha*, the withdrawal of forces. Recon Battalion had already cadre Echo Company and was now sending two companies back to Camp Pendleton by ship in September.[11] All the battalion's short-timers were transferred to Charlie and Delta Companies for the voyage home, while those with less than nine months in-country, as well as the large cohort of Marines on extensions, were transferred to Headquarters and Service (H&S), Alpha, and Bravo Companies.[12] The new arrivals went to the three remaining companies. This mix master was done while maintaining 20-plus teams patrolling in the field. The result of this massive personnel shuffle touched every Marine and every patrolling team that remained in the battalion as it was trying to balance new arrivals with experienced Marines and Corpsmen in every team. The reorganization gave Alpha and Bravo Companies three platoons of three teams and a fourth platoon with four teams. This, along with OPCon Subunit 1 of 1st Force Recon, would provide a total of 24 teams available for direct support of 1st Marine Division.[13] Looking ahead, these teams operated in support of Operation *Imperial Lake* in the Que Son Mountains and Operation *Catawba Falls* near Nong Son and Thuong Duc. The battalion also provided teams to conduct pre-operation reconnaissance for the upcoming Operation *Dubois Square* in Elephant Valley.[14]

In the Que Son Mountains, there remained a strong NVA presence. Operation *Imperial Lake*, the last major operation of the war for the 1st Marine Division, was planned to drive the NVA out of the Que Sons. Intelligence sources still placed the following enemy units in the complex jungle mountains: General Binh's Front 4 Headquarters; three infantry battalions, the D3, R20, and V25; the 42nd Reconnaissance Battalion; and three Sapper Battalions—3D, T89, and T90,[15] although the T89 Battalion had to be reconstituted after its repulsed attack on Hill 119. The T89 sappers would have to wait for more trained sappers to graduate Sapper School in Song Tay,

North Vietnam, and then walk down the Ho Chin Minh Trail.[16] During August, in support of Operation *Imperial Lake*, 1st Platoon, Delta Company, 1st Recon, established three clandestine observation posts (OP) in the northern Que Sons. They were calling fire missions from the *Whiskey* battery's large 4.2-inch mortars of 3rd Battalion, 11th Marines, who had established a firebase on Hill 845.[17]

First Lieutenant Taylor arrived on Hill 119 on 29 August with 4th Platoon to relieve Fallon and 3rd Platoon.[18] His callsign was *War Cloud-Kilo*. It would be the last Reconnaissance callsign for Hill 119. Defending the OP, Taylor had an understrength platoon of 13 Marines and two corpsmen. On their third night, 31 August at 2145, the listening post west of the landing zone (LZ) heard movement southwest down the trail, 30 meters below them towards Alligator Lake. They engaged with two M26 grenades and small-arms fire and then withdrew back across the LZ to the perimeter. In the morning, the wire-check patrol found blood trails leading towards the lake.[19] Again, on the night of 2 September, the listening post on the north side of the hill was probed at 1955 by at least two enemy. The post engaged with M26 grenades and withdrew to the OP. Taylor covered the withdrawal with an on-call artillery mission on the north side of Hill 148. Later that evening, at 2105, the OP received another probe as two Chi-com grenades were thrown at the northwest perimeter, landing below Alpha Bunker in the trash pit. The hill engaged with M79s.[20] There was no indication of the enemy the next morning during the wire patrol around the hill.

Hill 119 had movement around it every night. Taylor was too shorthanded to actively patrol outside the hill and maintain a defense. He believed the probes were distractions to occupy the OP in order that larger units could move past. His platoon was withdrawn on 11 September. During their two-week stay, they had five enemy sightings totaling 20 enemy. They also had three direct probes of the OP at night. The Integrated Observation Device (IOD) team fired ten fire missions in support of *War Cloud-Kilo*, using batteries *Auditor-Bravo* and *Musk-Ox-Bravo* with four enemy kills.[21] The OP's reduced sightings were a reflection of the NVA's new strategy to wait for the Americans to leave.

On 11 September, in accordance with 1st Recon Battalion Operations Order # 1073-70, Taylor conducted a turnover of Observation Post Kilo, Hill 119, with the 11th Marine Regiment. He was to obtain written verification of the turnover. After conducting a joint inventory of the crew-served weapons and ammunition, which were left behind, Taylor received the signed receipt for the hill from the senior member of the 11th Marines IOD/forward observer (FO) team.[22]

On the same day, Bravo Company turned over the OP on Hill 250[23] and Charlie Company turned over Hill 425,[24] both to the 11th Marines. While the 11th Marines now assumed responsibility for the three IOD OPs (Hills 119, 250, and 425), the division tasked 5th Marines to provide security for the hills. One company from 3rd Battalion, 5th Marines was chopped OPCon (operational control transferred) to 11th Marines for security of the IODs.[25] The company command and a platoon remained at FSB Ryder with the security mission for Ryder. The company also had the mission of security for Hills 119, 250, and 425. They provided a platoon-minus of grunts for Hills 119 and 250 with a reinforced squad for the cliff fortress at Hill 425.[26] As Recon departed by chopper, the FO teams hoped the 5th Marines' security platoons would arrive before nightfall on each hill. The relief of the OP security mission for Recon freed up ten reconnaissance teams that could be applied to their primary mission of patrolling. First Recon continued to maintain the two mountain-top radio relays at Ba Na and Dong Den in support of their own operations to ensure solid communications with patrolling teams.

***

On 3 September, during a morning formation and awards ceremony at the Camp Reasoner amphitheater, Lieutenant General Keith McCutcheon, the commanding general of III Marine Amphibious Force (III MAF), and Brigadier General E. H. Simmons, the assistant division commander of 1st Division joined Lieutenant Colonel E. J. Regan to recognize 12 Recon Marines. During the ceremony, McCutcheon presented the Silver Star to 1st Lieutenant Gary C. Allord for actions as a patrol leader with Echo Company.[27] That morning, accompanying the commanding general, was Allord's friend, and fellow former Echo Company platoon commander, 1st Lieutenant Earl Hailston, now the III MAF commanding general's junior aide and, coincidentally, also a Silver Star recipient for his actions as a patrol leader in Echo Company.[28] Lieutenant Fallon missed the ceremony and his friends Allord and Hailston as he was sitting in the witness hut waiting to be called in the Lee general court-martial.[29] Also on 3 September, on paper, Fallon assumed command of Delta Company.[30] Since he knew most of the Delta Company Marines, he and Master Sergeant Regalot would oversee and coordinate which Marines would be rotating home with the company flag and which Marines would be transferred to Bravo Company to continue patrolling.

On the afternoon of 4 September, Lance Corporal Paul Freeman had just come back from two weeks on Hill 119 with 3rd Platoon.[31] He went to Freedom Hill with a couple of his platoon buddies. After stopping at the big PX and seeing nothing they wanted, they walked across the street to "Dog Patch" village. The Marines found a local bar with cold beer on the second dirt street off the main Freedom Hill hardball road.[32] Dog Patch was off limits for U.S. personnel. The local Vietnamese had children sitting on each intersection as lookouts so when military police (MP) came checking the area, the small shops on the main road and bars on the secondary roads were given a heads-up, providing time to hide the Marines who were availing themselves of what could be found in Dog Patch, which was everything from booze, to drugs, to women. Paul Freeman got drunk with his buddies. After dark, and after curfew, while walking back to Camp Reasoner, the small group of Recon Marines was spotted by an MP patrol. The Marines scattered off the road and into the rice paddies between Dog Patch and LZ 401 at Camp Reasoner. Freeman was the only one to get caught at Recon security post #4, trying to sneak back into camp.[33] The next day, 5 September, Lieutenant Lee, now back as the executive officer (XO) of H&S Company, was the place the MPs came with Freeman and turned him over with the Curfew Violation Report. Lee took the report and custody sheet by signing for Freeman, who was one of his former 3rd Platoon Marines from Delta Company. He immediately took Freeman to Master Sergeant Rene Regalot, the Delta Company first sergeant, to take it from there.[34] Freeman would now appear before the new company commander, 1st Lieutenant Fallon, for officer hours. The company level non-judicial punishment (NJP) took place the next morning in the Delta Company office.[35] Freeman, who was UA (unauthorized absence), out-of-bounds, and in a restricted area, could have been awarded a summary court, with jail time, or a reduction of rank, or he could have been fined and restricted a company at NJP. Fallon asked Freeman, standing at attention as Regalot read the charges, what he was doing and why. Freeman said he was celebrating being a short-timer and partying with his friends before rotating home in two weeks. Fallon chewed him out, an ass chewing Paul Freeman remembered 50 years later.[36] He was fined $45.00 and restricted to his hut, except for chow and chapel, until he rotated home. Fallon placed him on "Top" Regalot's daily working party and suggested to the master sergeant that Freeman burn the shitters during his last two weeks. After Freeman departed the office, Fallon handed the unsigned paperwork to Regalot and said, "Lose it."[37] Freeman had patrolled well for 12 months and two weeks. He had earned a break, which meant burning shitters his last two weeks in-country, not being reduced in rank and fined. No NJP ended up in Freeman's Service Record Book.[38]

On 10 September, Charlie and Delta Companies were stood down from tactical operations in accordance with *Keystone Robin Redeployment (Phase IV)* and were cadre preparing for their departure by ship.[39] Lieutenant Colonel Regan had completed his task of reorganizing 1st Recon Battalion from five patrolling companies to two while maintaining the capability to field up to thirty teams. This was done by overmanning the patrolling Alpha and Bravo Companies along with 1st Force Subunit 1. With his reorganization task complete, Regan returned to the division staff. His 30 days of command allowed for a relief in place and solid turnover of 2nd Battalion, 1st Marines, who were operating south of Da Nang, and freed up Lieutenant Colonel William Groom Leftwich to take command of 1st Recon Battalion on 13 September.[40] The next day, Fallon turned over Delta Company to 1st Lieutenant Taylor who would ride the ship and take the flag back to Camp Pendleton.[41] Twenty-seven Delta Marines transferred to Bravo Company for duty the same day. Fallon walked across Camp Reasoner to H&S Company and assumed command from Captain R. L. Wiltrout who was rotating home.[42]

***

Lieutenant Colonel Leftwich had studied his mission, a classic economy-of-force operation with limited assets. Upon assuming command, he provided written recommended changes to the 1st Marine Division's G-2 (intelligence) and G-3 (operations) on the employment of the Reconnaissance Battalion. This led to the 15 September 1970 republishing of "Appendix 1: Division Reconnaissance Employment Procedures to Annex B: Intelligence to Operations Order 301A-YR by the 1st Marine Division (-) (Rein)."[43] This document set forth the concept of operations, missions, and task, for the 1st Reconnaissance Battalion and detailed procedures for timely inserts and extractions of teams so as to minimize the jeopardy of team personnel.[44] It also minimized levels of operational teams in the field. Leftwich now had the order he had written for his battalion. He called in his staff and company commanders to explain how they would operate going forward. He had changed the scheme of maneuver on how he would employ his Recon teams. As an economy-of-force measure, the division expanded Recon's area of responsibility while they pulled the infantry units back into a tighter belt around Da Nang. To save time on insertion and extraction, which cost a team two days of a five-day patrol, Leftwich instituted platoon patrol bases (PPB).[45] PPBs were where a platoon would deploy with three to five teams to a clandestine center hill. There they conducted saturation *Sting Ray* patrols in a fan shape, in and out of the center hill or base. A fan *Sting Ray* patrol would walk off for 4–6 days and circle back to the base where it started for resupply of food, water, batteries, and ammo. They spent one night sleeping inside the patrol-base perimeter and would then push out on the next patrol. The PPB would operate 36 days in the field. A Recon team could run six patrols, thus, with four teams, the platoon could run 24 patrols off the PPB. This concept of operations saved 48 days dedicated to inserting and extracting which could be applied to patrolling. It was also the monsoon season, so the PPB concept put less strain on helicopter resources in bad weather. The concept was to deny the enemy an area or to interdict an infiltration route by saturation patrolling. The PPB was a concept Leftwich had used successfully with 2nd Battalion, 1st Marines, coupled with a strong intel pull developed by 1st Lieutenant Gil Robinson on where to place the patrol base.[46]

On 20 September, Charlie and Delta Companies embarked on Navy shipping in Da Nang Harbor and sailed for home.[47] On 23 September, Fallon was called in for a future-operations planning session with Leftwich and 1st Lieutenant F. M. McDonough, the battalion's S-3. The dialog examined freeing up more teams for patrolling. It would be more efficient if they could hand off perimeter security duty of the PPB to an infantry platoon. Additionally, if you added an 81-mm mortar section it could cover most of the Que Son Mountains and the PPB could be expanded to a company patrol base (CPB). The proposed concept would take the company office as radio operators and a second Recon platoon and turn the current Que Son PPB into a CPB. Leftwich said it was a good idea but would need support of the 5th Marines. He would fly out and sell the concept to the regimental commander, Colonel Clark V. Judge, who would have to give up assets.[48] It would take a couple of weeks to run the coordination for the establishment of the CPB. The next day, 24 September, Fallon changed command of H&S Company, handing it over to Captain F. S. ("Fair and Square") Blair.[49] He was reassigned as XO of Bravo Company to resume patrolling and await command with Lieutenant Allord's imminent rotation date.

***

Returning to the bush on 29 September, Fallon, now with Team *Pony Boy*, had six Marines on patrol plus, newly assigned from the grunts, 2nd Lieutenant Jim Burns to birddog and learn.[50] The patrol area was nine square kilometers, a big Recon haven located five kilometers west of the Dong Den radio relay. The mission was to determine if the NVA was using this high, jungle-covered, hilly plateau south of Elephant Valley. The morning helo insert was into the Upper Left corner of their patrolling box. It was a two-bird landing zone with ten feet of elephant grass. After jumping into the razor-sharp elephant grass, Fallon moved *Pony Boy* off the LZ as the birds departed. Lance Corporal Mattious, the team's primary radio operator, got a solid comm check from the team's relay, *X-Ray*, on top of Dong Den mountain. The team stopped and waited for the jungle sounds to return before moving into the secondary growth below the 100-foot single-canopy jungle. Sunlight was shaded and muted and movement was slowed by vines.

After an hour of weaving through brush vines heading south, the team picked up a high-speed trail coming from their west and turning south towards Hill 594. They stopped; the trail was running outside their haven but looked promising. Fallon talked to *X-Ray* on Dong Den. He wanted to expand the haven west and south, requesting six more grid squares. The team took a water/food break and waited an hour for the decision from Battalion, which had to check the area was not occupied by anyone else. Fallon knew it was not but was teaching Burns. When the approval came, he got Corporal Valdes walking point and pointed him south on the trail, telling him to take it slow as they were going up to check out Hill 594. They were now patrolling uphill and soon summitted a small hill. Fallon stopped the team and put in a 360 defense. This was not Hill 594, as they were still 600 meters north of it, but it was a defensible position. Sitting there, the team realized they were not the first to the hill. There was trash and old C-ration cans. The hill had been used in the past by a grunt unit.

After the break, they patrolled off-trail southwest, downslope, and found a thicket on the reverse side of the finger. Fallon had Valdes get on all fours and high crawl into the thicket. He came back six minutes later, all smiles. He led the team, everyone on all fours, crawling into and through the 20-foot-thick thicket wall. Breaking into a small clearing 12 feet by 10 feet, he stopped. There was thicket all around them. Fallon gave the hand signal to circle the wagons, pointed at a Claymore mine and signaled Lance Corporal Grady to put it on their back trail. It was late afternoon; they had been moving all day. This would be their night-harbor site. Placing the two radios in the center, everyone was sitting with their backs to the radios and packs, weapons across their thighs. Not a word had been spoken except on their insert comm check and hushed radio dialog to expand their patrol area. Now Fallon took out his map and pointed for Burns and Valdes to do the same. Each calculated where they were. All three wrote different six-digit grids in grease pencil on their own map. Fallon looked at the three answers. He knew he was below Hill 594 and west of it by his pace count from the insert LZ. He circled his grid and showed the other two. He handed it to the primary radio operator and indicated he needed to shackle it and pass the position report to their radio relay. Then he took the second radio and changed the frequency to their direct-support artillery battery, *Air Hose-Alpha*. He hand-signaled Burns to shackle the six-digit grid for Hill 594 and radio it into *Air Hose* as *Pony Boy*'s on-call target. He pointed to the Marines on the left side of the circle and gave the hand signal for them to eat. When they were finished, the right four would eat. He set the watches: two Marines awake for two-hour watches, rotated between the eight Marines. He put Burns on the first shift, and he would take the last shift in the morning.

Fallon pulled a green can of C-ration peaches from his ass pack. Using a P-38 opener, he slowly punched four holes in the top before sucking the sweet, thick syrup out of the can. He savored the taste. Opening the top and using the plastic spoon from his front left pocket, he slowly ate the peach halves stacked inside the can. This was dinner. Now it was time to listen to the jungle and get some rest. The jungle was alive with noise, which was good as it meant there was not a lot of other human activity around. The nighttime noises were different from the daytime. At night, there were insects buzzing along with fluorescent light on the jungle floor. During the daytime, there were birds talking and monkeys moving in packs. At nighttime, barking deer were sometimes heard communicating to each other. The deer were half the size of those in the States and made a low barking noise, not dog-like, but deeper. In the morning, they would head up to Hill 594 and check it out. Fallon reached in his ass pack and pulled out a plastic bottle of insect repellant. He applied it generously around his ankles where his pants-leg garters were. The jungle was always damp, and the blood-sucking leeches sought out the warmth of the human body, looking for a seam to crawl into and get to one's skin to suck blood. The leech would balloon up to four times its own size by sucking blood, becoming the size of a thumb. If you tried to pull a leech off, it would dig in its pincers, and they would break off under your skin and get infected. One had to encourage the leech to back out himself. This was done with heat. In the grunts, a cigarette touched to the back of the leech achieved this. There was no smoking on a Recon patrol, and no fires at night, so, therefore, no heat could be applied to back out the leeches. In the morning, there would be a leech check. If the leech was full, he would back out and lay there; you just flicked them off with your finger. You could put a dab of insect repellent on them, and they would back out. If the harbor site was high and dry, there were fewer leeches. If it was damp, or in a depression even a couple of inches deep, you tended to gain the attention of a herd of leeches. Pulling ten off in the morning was common. Leeches sought out warm dark places on each Marine. Wearing boot garters and keeping long sleeves down and utilities buttoned up at one's neck line, even in the heat, would help keep them at bay. Marines with leeches in their armpits were common. What you wanted to avoid was a leech up your asshole or on, or in, your penis. Since Recon Marines did not wear underwear, to avoid chafing, it was important to have the leeches' avenues to your dark body parts blocked off. Fallon handed Burns the bug repellent. Pulling his half poncho liner over his face, he listened to the nighttime noises and dozed.

Valdes shook Fallon's boot and handed him the radio handset; six hours had passed. It was his watch, the two hours before dawn. Fallon sat up and placed the radio handset on his shoulder where he could hear it if it squelched, or if *Pony Boy* was called. At dawn, it was still dark under the jungle canopy. Fallon, listening to the radio, could now hear *X-Ray* calling each team by name for their morning check in. "*Pony Boy*, *Pony Boy*, this is *X-Ray*, if you are Alpha Serria [all secure], press your handset twice." Fallon depressed the rubber send button twice, transmitting a two-squelch burst, indicating they were secure. There was no rush on patrol when clandestine. There was a standard morning routine that included a can of cold C-ration and then an opportunity for each Marine to relieve himself. If the team was in virgin territory, they would smash the C-rat cans and carry out the trash. If there were signs of previous infantry, ARVN, or NVA trash in the area, then a cat hole would be dug to bury the trash. An hour later, *Pony Boy* pulled in their two nighttime Claymore mines and crawled out of the thicket. Mattious called *X-Ray*: "*X-Ray*, *X-Ray*, *Pony Boy* is Oscar Mike [on the move]."

Heading due south, they slowly broke brush downhill and across the saddle leading up towards Hill 594. They were parallel to the trail and headed up hill. They would not walk up the trail, but Fallon wanted to check it in the saddle, so they turned 90 degrees east, put out security south and north, and Fallon, Burns, and Valdes walked over and looked at the trail. It was hard-packed and three feet wide in the saddle. Fallon showed Burns the footprints. Not new, but also not old. They backed away and resumed patrolling uphill parallel to the trail. They were halfway up the hill and ten feet off the trail when they found the first of six recently dug holes. The holes were ten feet deep, six feet long, and four wide. They were incomplete bunkers defending the northern approach to 594.[51] Fallon pointed west, away from the holes and trail, moving sidehill around to the west side of 594 looking for another trail. He found it on the west side. It did not have defenses and again was three feet wide and hard-packed. It was the main trail from the west. *Pony Boy* was again at the western boundary of the haven extension. They still had the eastern half of the haven to recon.

After listening for 15 minutes, *Pony Boy* got on the trail and moved east uphill, summitting 594 in 15 minutes of walking the trail. On the summit there was an intersection in three directions, with no trail heading due east. There was nothing on the small summit except the intersection. Turning south, they took the trail and went down a fat finger for 500 meters until they hit a steep cliff. The trail turned east at the cliff on level ground, and they followed it but spread out and slowed down, walking for five and listening for five. Trail walking or patrolling had its pluses and minuses. A Recon team could make good time and cover ground, but it could also lead to point man to point man contact with the enemy using the same trail. Experienced teams, looking for contact, used trails to their advantage and set ambushes on well-used ones. Trails were where a team could snatch a prisoner. A trail was where your team could walk into a fortified position and be ambushed. Trails were danger areas and were treated as such by Fallon. They moved east all day, with no indications of anyone using the trail. Pulling off the trail and going uphill into the bush, they found a sidehill bamboo thicket and would harbor up there for the night. It was a quiet night.

The next morning, the team was back on the trail continuing east until it turned north and headed downhill. Fallon kept the team heading east, off-trail now; in 300 meters, they broke out of the canopy and could look east and see all the way to the Bay of Da Nang. It was a panoramic view. Setting one Marine for security north, west, and south, *Pony Boy* set up a clandestine OP looking east. Three Claymores went out in front of each security Marine. They would stay put that afternoon and all night. That night, with a clear sky, they could see the lights of the harbor. In the morning, Fallon now realized this OP was scenic, but it was too high and too far from anything to be useful. Back to work, *Pony Boy* headed north where they found a draw they needed to cross to get to the next finger. It was steep, deep, and narrow. A bad place to get caught. He left three Marines, including Valdes and the secondary radio for security and covering fire of this danger area, and headed down the draw. They would cross this danger area and gain equal height on the far side, set in, and then call the other three over. The trail led down into the draw. At a small stream, it continued downhill and north. The water was clear and moving fast; they filled their canteens. Fallon crossed the stream and pointed at the point man to go sidehill east and up off the trail. Thirty minutes later, they could look across and see their fellow patrol members across the draw. They set security and, with an arm signal, the other three followed them across.

After joining up, *Pony Boy* crested the top of the finger and set in. The finger was narrow, six feet across with a game trail. They could see the next cross-compartment draw and a small hilltop below them to the northeast. The small hill had an opening that looked like it might be an LZ. They would OP where they were and watch the potential LZ for enemy activity. The LZ was low, about two hundred feet in elevation, but it was a jungle opening with 100-foot canopy on three sides. Their scheduled extract was the next day. It was a quiet night on the narrow finger. The next morning, *Pony Boy* called in the shackled grid for their extract LZ. Then they moved out for the LZ. It would take two hours to cross the draw and get to the LZ. Arriving, they found it was not particularly good. It was a one-bird, tail-ramp, two-back-wheels LZ, with a 20-degree downhill slope and only one approach from the southeast. It would be a hover extract, jumping to the ramp. Recon had tremendous faith in the pilots flying the helos, and their gunners. They would make it work. *Pony Boy* called *X-Ray* and said, they were in the dugout, meaning at the LZ. They waited. All the jungle sounds told Fallon they were alone. They waited all morning. The weather was good. *X-Ray* called and said they were next. *Pony Boy* heard the extract-package helo blades beating the thick moisture air with sounds of "Wamp-Wamp, Thump-Thump, Thump-Thump, Thump-Thump, Thump-Thump," before they could see them. Each type of helicopter had its own sounds. "Wamp-Wamp" were gunships; "Thump-Thump" were troop transports. Then two

Cobra gunships streaked past them. Fallon had his mirror out and flashed the second gunship as it passed and then saw the lead CH-46 and hit him with a flash. On the radio it was "*Pony Boy, Pony Boy,* this is *Purple Fox Two-Three,* if that is you flashing me, pop smoke." Valdes threw a yellow smoke in the middle of the LZ. The two CH-46s circled, one going up high and one starting its spiral down. *Purple Fox* called "Yellow," identifying the friendly smoke. Fallon grabbed the handset and said, "Roger, yellow, approach from southeast, exit southeast, 20 degree down sidehill, two-wheel ramp only, how copy, over?" *Purple Fox* simply said, "Piece of cake, *Pony Boy.*" And with that, the pilot swiveled the bird 180 degrees around at the 100-foot hover just over the jungle canopy and backed it in. The ramp was down, and the crew chief was standing on it talking the pilot in as he backed the bird in and lowered it into the LZ. The pilot was backing his aircraft and lowering it blindly, using the crew chief's eyes and dialog describing where to park the bird, two wheels down, the nose hanging out horizonal to the ground in the air as the bird hovered. A magnificent piece of flying. Fallon could see his good friend, Lieutenant "Butch" Harvey, the Recon extract officer, standing on the ramp, M16 pointed out, not looking at the team but scanning the jungle behind them. As the back two wheels touched, and the team moved out of the tree line at double time, *Pony Boy* had to come from the side as the back approach to the bird had no head room for the blades due to the slope of the LZ. Butch was on the ramp counting the Marines on. Fallon grabbed Burns and held him until second to last then let the 2nd lieutenant jump on. Fallon was on as Harvey grabbed his arm, the crew chief told the pilot, and the ramp was coming up as the bird nosed down, diving, and pulled away from the zone, gaining airspeed, and headed straight east. Fallon walked the center of the bird toward the front and across the jump seat, leaning into the cockpit. Yelling thanks, even though the two pilots could not hear him, he hit both on their shoulders as a way to thank them, giving them a thumbs up and big smile. As they landed at LZ 401, it was 1400 on 3 October.[52] *Pony Boy* had been in the bush for 102 hours. They had no sightings of the enemy and no enemy contacts. This told the S-2, Captain Cook, that the enemy was not using this secondary trail network into Da Nang. *Pony Boy* had successfully completed its mission.

That was Fallon's last small-team patrol as the next day he assumed command of Bravo Company from the rotating 1st Lieutenant Gary Allord.[53] After his 30 days of stateside leave, Allord was assigned another Reconnaissance billet as the officer in command of the Amphibious Reconnaissance School at Landing Force Training Command, Atlantic in Little Creek, Virginia. Allord, who earned a Silver Star as a patrol leader, was a regular officer with the potential for a great career ahead of him but resigned his commission within two years and begin a career in urban-redevelopment housing.

***

In support of Operation *Imperial Lake,*[54] on 5 October, Bravo Company established a PPB in the Que Son Mountains on LZ Vulture, callsign *Lynch Law.*[55] First Platoon, under 1st Lieutenant Jim "Big Train" Anderson, a Harvard graduate, flew out to the Que Son mountain-top LZ with four teams to begin saturation patrolling. Now renamed LZ Rainbow,[56] it would serve as the patrol base and soon be expanded to a CPB on Hill 845 (Nui Mat Rang) with the arrival of Fallon and First Sergeant Maurice Jacques. They brought along the company office to man six radio nets with the callsign *Gunsmoke*. Bravo Company's CPB was the northern half of the Que Son Mountains. This combined-arms task unit was used successfully to deny the NVA use of Base Area 116. During October, the ten teams operated off the CPB, known to the troops as "Bravo Big Top," for the large canvas tent Jacques had placed over two huge boulders to create the Recon Company command post and radio center. The teams accounted for 180 enemy sighted and 23 enemy being killed.[57]

***

On 6 October, 1st Lieutenants Bob Fawcett and Mike Cross, both Naval Academy and Ranger School graduates, checked in from 2nd Battalion, 1st Marines (2/1). Both had volunteered and submitted administrative-action forms requesting the transfer to Recon to remain in the bush, instead of a staff job during their second six months in Vietnam, and to continue to serve under their 2/1 Battalion commander, now commanding the Recon Battalion, Lieutenant Colonel Leftwich.[58] Both Fawcett and Cross were assigned to 1st Lieutenant Marv Floom's Alpha Company as Bravo Company was full. At Leftwich's urging, on 18 October, the 1st Marine Division ordered a change to Quick-Reaction Force (QRF) priorities.[59] Now a six-man Recon patrol deployed in the Que Son mountains could directly call in the QRF. The QRF, callsign *Sparrow Hawk*, was pre-staged with CH-46s and a 5th Marines rifle company sitting on the LZ on daily alert. From FSB Baldy, a five-minute flying time from the Que Sons, they could quickly exploit any contact or sighting made by Recon's saturation patrols.

To represent him, and ensure close coordination, Leftwich selected 1st Lieutenant Zach Johnson, a senior lieutenant he trusted from the 1st Force Recon subunit and placed him in the 5th Marines' Command Center as his personal representative.[60] This was done to understand Recon Team language and to expedite launches of the QRF. Previously, a Recon Team that wanted the QRF as reinforcement or exploitation had to radio its radio relay, which then radioed Recon Battalion at Camp Reasoner, who telephoned the Division Combat Operations Center (COC), which radioed out to 5th Marines Command Center, which called 2nd Battalion, which called Hotel Company. That was six hops for one request and, if approved, six hops back. Under the revised system, a Recon Team called the 5th Marines' COC directly and usually spoke to Johnson who lived in the COC, manning the radio 20 hours a day. Johnson would talk to the Regimental S-3 and, if approved, they notified the company on the LZ directly and passed them Recon's grid coordinates and frequency, while Johnson called the team back and started them preparing to receive and or guide the QRF to a nearby LZ in the Que Son Mountains.[61] The streamlined approach worked. The saturation patrolling coupled with the Recon Team/QRF tactics achieved increasing results in locating NVA positions, base camps, and engaging small enemy formations.[62]

***

On 21 October, Foxtrot Company, 2nd Battalion, 5th Marines (2/5), replaced Mike Company, 3rd Battalion, 5th Marines at LZ Rainbow as security for the large patrolling base. Hotel Company ("Horrible Hogs"), of 2/5 Marines, commanded by Captain John Moffett, formed the QRF, with 2nd Platoon led by the former Naval Academy boxer, Steve Fisher, spearheading the lead platoon of the QRF.[63] On the 21st, queued by a Recon team sighting of four enemy, Moffett deployed a platoon of the QRF, inserting four kilometers south of LZ Rainbow and the Recon CPB. They found 1,000 pounds of rice buried in urns. The following day, two platoons of Moffett's "Horrible Hogs" killed four NVA, captured one rifle, and another 700 pounds of rice discovered in a large bunker complex.[64] On 26 October, Fisher's 2nd Platoon, patrolling in the monsoon's 24-hour rain of Tropical Storm *Kate,* found an enemy communications wire. The wire, laid next to a trail, was followed by Fisher and the grunt platoon straight into a recently deserted battalion-size base camp.[65] Second Platoon, Hotel Company, spent three days searching the camp and caves, uncovering a substantial amount of food and ammunition as well as future booby-trap material.[66] Moffett and Hotel Company also found documents and NVA orders before destroying the camp and withdrawing to Fire Support Base Baldy.

Meanwhile on 26 October, two Recon teams, *Cayenne* and *Prime Cut,* patrolling north of LZ Rainbow on parallel fingers, wedged 15 NVA into a small-arms ambush, killing five, capturing weapons, ammunition, and equipment.[67]

At this time, Bravo Company, 1st Recon, had seven seasoned lieutenants from other Recon companies and the grunts in the September reorganization. The XO was the experienced Butch Harvey of Alexandria, Virginia, who was on an extension in-country from 3rd Recon. He served as one of two battalion insert/extract officers flying daily with the helicopter packages.[68] Out on LZ Rainbow with the CPB, Fallon had 1st Sergeant Maurice Jacques, with his 40 months in Vietnam, along with the other lieutenants and their platoons.[69] The six-foot-four 1st Lieutenant J. K. Murphy, coming over from Alpha Company, was a former teaching assistant at the University of South Carolina and a favorite with the Marines because of his humor and care for them. "JK" had ten months and 25 patrols under his belt. The equally imposing 1st Lieutenant John Hoff, with over thirty patrols under his belt, came by way of Echo and Delta Companies. The remaining lieutenants were 1st Lieutenants M. O. "Mo" Greene and Steve "ZZ" Zrenda, a standout athlete from the University of Connecticut, and 2nd Lieutenant Jim Burns, just arrived from the grunts.[70] Bravo Company could field 15 teams. The last two teams came from the company office, where Jacques had established a rule that, before a Marine was assigned to an office job in the rear, he needed a minimum of ten patrols. When the company started platoon and company patrol bases, everybody went to the field, with the exception of Jacques's rat-hunting company dog named Ranger.

During October and November, all 15 teams were in the Que Sons. Jacques padlocked the company office door in Camp Reasoner with a note tacked to the front door saying, "Bravo Company is gone to the Que Sons fighting Indians." As a drill instructor, Jacques had taught Marine Corps' history to recruits.[71] His note was a direct reference to Colonel Archibald Henderson, the fifth Commandant of the Marine Corps, who led the Marines in the Florida Indian Wars of the 1840s. He is said to have left for the campaign with the entire available Marine Corps. According to legend, Henderson left a note on his office door that read, "Have gone to Florida to fight Indians. Will be back when war is over. Signed, A. Henderson, Col Commandant."[72] Back in the triple-canopy jungle of the Que Sons, by the end of October, the Marines had killed 74 NVA and captured 34 weapons[73] in the Recon/QRF operational area, making Base Area 116 unusable to General Binh and his 2nd NVA Division who withdrew west of Thuong Duc to Base Area 112 to wait out the Americans.

CHAPTER 32

The Marine Withdrawal and Beyond

In the fall of 1970, Henry Kissinger was in Paris conducting secret peace talks with the North Vietnamese.[1] It would take three more years of Paris talks, bombing, negotiating, and bombing before North Vietnam signed the Peace Accords on 27 January 1973.[2] In South Vietnam, in the fall of 1970, the Nixon Administration officially announced it was withdrawing from Vietnam and was turning the war over to the South Vietnamese,[3] full-blown "Vietnamization."[4] As the Allies withdrew into tighter perimeters around exit airbases and ports, the enemy in the Central Office for South Vietnam changed guidance on how they would pursue the war. They would no longer throw soldiers, in large units, against the Americans as they had in Tet '68. They would shift to guerrilla tactics while focusing on building up their forces in established base areas and train for the next major offensive against the South Vietnamese after the Americans were gone.[5] This happened with the North Vietnamese spring offensive of 1972, now known as the Easter Offensive. Once again, as in 1968, the North Vietnamese Army (NVA) was defeated by the Army of the Republic of Vietnam (ARVN) and U.S. air power.[6] While less publicized, but no less important, was Marine Captain John Ripley blowing the National Route 1 Bridge at Dong Ha.[7] On 12 October 1970, President Nixon announced that U.S. troops would operate only for defensive purposes.[8] The result in the last half of 1970 and 1971, as the Americans tightened their belts, was reduced contacts and casualties on both sides. The Americans were now on the defense and the NVA would now only probe with sappers, ambush targets of opportunity, mortar, and rocket regularly to remind everyone they were still in the jungle waiting for the proper time to seize the initiative. They could wait for the Americas to leave and then win.

In I Corps, during October 1970, General Binh, with his Front 4 headquarters and 2nd NVA Division, was in a rebuilding, resupply, and training mode. At the operational level, the American withdrawal was already into Phase IV of Operation *Keystone Robin*. The U.S. Army's XXIV Corps would shift Army units to the north, assuming responsibility for the five northern provinces from the withdrawing Marines. Earlier on 9 March 1970, Lieutenant General Zais USA had taken over command of I Corps tactical area from the Marines at his XXIV Corps Headquarters in Da Nang.[9] This complex relief-in-place operation had the U.S. Army and ARVN taking over positions from the Marines who were rapidly withdrawing. III Marine Amphibious Force departed on 14 April 1971, being downsized and then replaced by the 3rd Marine Amphibious Brigade (MAB) until it departed in June 1971.[10]

On the ground, the 1st Marine Division began withdrawing its infantry regiments from Vietnam in 1970 and the last members of the 1st Marine Regiment, as the ground-combat element of 3rd

MAB, departed Da Nang on 28 June 1971, returning to the United States at Camp Pendleton, California.[11] The 1st Marine Aircraft Wing Headquarters would depart Da Nang and relocate to Marine Corps Air Station El Toro, California, on 14 April 1971[12] after leaving a helicopter group at Marble Mountain and a fixed-wing group at Da Nang. During the withdrawal, the 1st Reconnaissance Battalion covered the enemy's ground approaches to the Da Nang Vital Area as the division/wing team withdrew. First Recon Battalion would withdraw and return to Camp Pendleton after participating in the Vietnam War from March 1966–March 1971, while 1st Recon's Alpha Company (Rein.) would remain as part of 3rd MAB until 13 May 1971.[13]

As part of the overall withdrawal, Hill 119 ended its position as a Reconnaissance observation post (OP) and radio-relay perch on 11 September 1970.[14] It would remain an OP site for the 11th Marines' Integrated Observation Device (IOD) forward observer teams until 30 April 1971, when they withdrew the classified IOD equipment.[15] The number of enemy sightings had dropped dramatically due to the NVA waiting on the Americans to depart.

Both sides were hunkered down when Typhoon *Kate* made landfall in Vietnam on October 25, 1970, near Da Nang. Both the Da Nang and An Hoa river basins were deeply flooded. The water ran over top of the newly built Liberty Bridge. The helicopter group was dedicated to saving and moving flooded and stranded Vietnamese civilians to higher ground. The water rescues were aided by teams of Recon Marines working with the helicopter crews as rescue swimmers.[16] Together, they moved 11,000 civilians from flooded areas to safety.[17] By late October, enemy sightings had dropped dramatically due to Typhoon *Kate*.

On 8 March 1971, a combined engineering-assessment team with personnel from 1st Engineer Battalion, 1st Shore Party Battalion, and 11th Marines conducted trips to the OPs on Hills 119, 250, and 425 to reconnoiter the three hills and plan for the destruction of the positions on the hills.[18] Military Assistance Command, Vietnam policy was that if a position was not physically turned over to another U.S. or ARVN unit, that position would be destroyed and returned to its natural state so as not to become an asset or position for the NVA. On 11 March 1971, a combined engineer/shore-party team was helo lifted onto Hill 119 for the execution of the destruction plan. Two Case 450 tractors were lifted on to the hill to support the demolition of the tower, 12 bunkers, the perimeter trench line and nine rows of concertina wire. The demolition and ground clearance were accomplished by 15 March when the destruction team was lifted off the hill.[19] Hill 119 was barren and devoid of all building materials with the trash pit burned and then covered over with dirt in the northwest draw. The last two Marines off Hill 119 were the Helicopter Support Team from 1st Shore Party Battalion after the equipment had been lifted off. The hill became a bald scrape until nature began its takeover with scrub growth.

On 29 April 1971, Brigadier E. H. Simmons, the assistant brigade commander for 3rd MAB, flew out to the small mountaintop, Dong Den, (Hill 868) on the south shoulder of Elephant Valley. The last Recon radio-relay site was inspected, closed, and abandoned as the radio-relay personnel departed.[20] Later the same day, Reconnaissance teams *Lynch Law* and *Cayenne* were extracted by helicopter, becoming the last two to conduct Marine Reconnaissance operations in Vietnam.[21] Alpha Company was stood down operationally.[22] On 13 May, Major H. C. Cooper took the flag and headquarters element of Alpha Company (Rein.), 1st Recon Battalion, and departed Vietnam, thereby becoming the last Recon Marines out of Vietnam.[23]

During the withdrawal period, starting in late 1969 through the final withdrawal, the 1st Marine Division's infantry regiments and battalions tightened around Da Nang. They became rocket-belt guards with ever-decreasing enemy contacts. The enemy was waiting for their departure. The 1st Recon Battalion became the primary offensive weapon in the division's tactical area of responsibility with its *Sting Ray* patrols, platoon patrol bases, and OPs on infiltration routes. Recon's four OPs on Hills 119, 200, 250, and 425 generated the largest number of enemy kills in the 1st Marine Division.[24] All four OPs had impressive numbers of NVA kills.

***

All hill commanders struggled with their interactions with the civilian population around the hill. They had not been adequately trained to deal with civilians nor were the Rules of Engagement structured to deal with the population with whom the hill commanders routinely dealt. Additionally, there were language and cultural barriers to be overcome. A few Marines learned a couple hundred words of Vietnamese. More Vietnamese had learned a small amount of English. The interpreter was, many times, a Vietnamese grade-school child. The challenges of explaining restricted areas to the Vietnamese, whose family had used the land for centuries, was always a challenge. The main trail from Tho Son hamlet to Alligator Lake went directly over the saddle between Hills 119 and 148 and was closed to Vietnamese civilians. As a result, they had to walk an extra eight kilometers to get to their fishing lake. With the platoons turning over every two weeks, the corporate memory of the hill commanders was lacking. How to deal with the apparent civilian population approaching the hill was a challenge experienced by all commanders. At night, everyone, Marines and Vietnamese civilians, knew there was a curfew. Anyone out at night was assumed to be enemy. It was during the daytime, when the Vietnamese villagers were allowed in the fields, that determining friend from foe became a challenge; was this person or persons walking towards the hill a civilian or an enemy presenting themselves as a civilian? When dressed in traditional civilian clothing of black-and-white "PJs," how do you deal with a group of 2–30 civilians coming to the hill to protest, or to give gifts?

The hill was used by civilian Vietnamese, and some NVA/Viet Cong, as a place to get medical treatment and medical evacuation. The elderly village spokeswoman with one arm was known by sight to every Marine who served on the OP as she visited weekly protesting the closure of the Alligator Lake trail or seeking compensation for her hamlet.

***

Hill 119's story was not complete with the withdrawal of Marines and its razing in March 1971.[25] During June 1972, it was observed from the air by a former Recon Marine veteran of the hill, and, now Army soldier, Paul Freeman, on his second tour to Vietnam.[26] He observed the hill as a helo door gunner. He saw a bald, vacant hill below, which was almost nude, in his mind, compared to the previously trenched and sandbag-bunkered OP he helped to build and defend. Freeman knew the Da Nang area from his first tour so the Army warrant officer pilots would listen to him when he described different areas as friendly or hostile. One area Paul had firsthand knowledge of, as being hostile, was Go Noi Island. The island was owned by the NVA with its hidden antiaircraft-artillery firing sites dug into the railroad berm and the low finger just south of the island with its overlook of Hills 119 and 148. He had served on the ground on Hill 119 and knew the dangers.[27] From the air, the hill was abandoned but the enemy remained on Go Noi Island.

In August 1972, Freeman, flying as a door gunner, over Go Noi, observed the hill again and was shocked. Three NVA flags, planted on poles, were flying over Hill 119. When he was on the hill, the American flag and the Tennessee State flag flew over the hill. "Doc" Mullins from Tennessee raised the latter. The Army helo squadron took exception to the red NVA flags flying over the hill. The Cobras started gun runs to shoot up the flags. After the gun runs had saturated the hill with fire, one LOH-6, covered by the gunships, swooped down, the gunner grabbing two flags as highly prized souvenirs for the squadron.[28] The third flag had been destroyed. With the withdrawal of the Army and the Americans, the ARVN took over I Corps in late 1972.[29] The hill remained abandoned as the ARVN showed no interest in the former OP. Hill 119 remained unoccupied between August 1972–30 April 1975, when Saigon fell, and the war was over.

***

Fast forward 55 years and the hill remains unoccupied, rocky with scrub growth. The only change is a high-tension power line that bisects the finger the hill sits on 200 meters east of the old OP in the low eastern saddle. The hard-packed dirt trail from the hamlet of Tho Son on Route 537 over to Alligator Lake remains across the western saddle of the finger between Hill 119 and Hill 148. The trail is devoid of growth, showing regular use. Returning to Vietnam in 2017 and 2025, Fallon, and a few Recon Marines and Corpsmen, with their wives, climbed Hill 119 and found it unchanged.[30] It still possessed the same dominant view, in all directions, that made it a great OP. If Hill 119 could speak, it would tell the best and worst stories of both Americans and Vietnamese. Today, this small Cinnamon Hill rests in peaceful slumber, sitting, as it always has, just south of the railroad bridge to Go Noi Island and north of the Que Son Mountains.

APPENDIX I

Statistical Review, Hill 119

All the statistics for Tables A to G, herein, are derived from 1st Reconnaissance Battalion debriefings included in each patrol report. There were 48 debriefings, each covering one tour of duty. The numbers were consolidated by category, each represented in a table.[1] They cover the 600 days that 1st Reconnaissance Battalion was responsible for the observation post (OP). Hill 119 was occupied as a Reconnaissance OP on 19 January 1969.[2] It was established to support Operation *Taylor Common* to watch for the North Vietnamese Army on Go Noi Island while Task Force *Yankee*, built around the 5th Marines, swept the Arizona Territory and Thuong Duc corridors.[3] The Recon OP was commanded by a Reconnaissance platoon commander from Delta Company which continued to observe, 24 hours a day, seven days a week, until 11 September 1970,[4] or 600 continuous days and nights. A routine tour, or "flip" as the Marines called it, on the hill was two weeks, give or take a day depending on weather or helicopter availability. During the 600-day period, Hill 119 had 24 hill commanders covering 48 flips.[5] The commanders ranged in rank from captain to staff sergeant but were mostly 1st lieutenant platoon commanders from one of the four Delta Company platoons. Each officer would take his platoon to the OP for a tour. Lieutenants Fallon, Klien, Pfieffer, Unsworth, and Waddill each had four tours of duty on the hill. Lieutenant Parks had three-and-a-half tours; he replaced L'Orange when he was medevac'd. Lieutenants Overton and L'Orange each had two-and-a-half tours with both being medevac'd in the middle of their third. Lieutenants Eglevsky, Taylor, and Wietecha, along with Staff Sergeant Ommondson, had two flips each. Lieutenant Lee and ten others did one tour, and Gunnery Sergeant Moore commanded half a tour, replacing Overton when he was medevac'd.[6] For the commanders' names, and their corpsmen, when they served on Hill 119, see Appendix 2.

Table A provides the count for the number of tours per commander. Table A demonstrates there was minimal collective memory or experience for operating on the OP because of the continual rotation of hill commanders.

Below the hill, the Viet Cong Infrastructure (VCI) had one leader the entire period, the one-armed woman who met every hill commander.

Table A: Commanders' Tours of Duty		
Number of Tours	**Number of Commanders**	**Total**
4	5	20
3.5	1	3.5
3	0	0
2.5	2	5
2	4	8
1	11	11
.5	1	0.5
Total	**24**	**48**

Sixteen of the 24 hill commanders had only one or two tours to master the hill and its surrounding environment, including the hamlets below the hill that were controlled by the VC. All hill commanders did well with defense of the hill and offensive fire missions against the enemy. Their training, and experience patrolling served them well coordinating fire support to defend the hill.

Table B shows supporting arms by type and by number of times of employed. All told, the hill commanders used supporting arms 814 times, or 9.46 times a week, or 1.35 times a day.

Table B: Supporting Arms	
Supporting Arm	**Number of times employed**
Artillery Fire Mission	721
Aerial Observer/Forward Air Controller	32
Fixed-wing Air Strikes	41
Helo Gunships	12
Spooky	5
Basketball	2
Naval Gun Fire	1
Total	**814, or 9.46 a week, or 1.35 a day**

Hill 119 was probed by the enemy in order to keep the Marines on the hill and to cover for the planting of booby traps. The desired effect was to keep the Marines, or condition them, to stay on the OP and not patrol. This would allow the enemy freedom of movement between their base area in the Que Son Mountains and Go Noi Island, which was their stronghold and assembly area for attacks on the Da Nang Vital Area. Hill 119 was the cork in between. The enemy kept the hill on guard, through small-arms fire, mortar and rocket-propelled grenade attacks, and probes

62 times during the Recon OP's existence. The T89 Sapper Battalion organized twice to fully attack, via a ground assault, to wipe the Marines off the hill. Both attempts failed. The enemy made contact with the Recon Marines, on or around the hill, 65 times during the 600 days, or .755 times per week (see Table C).

Table C: Enemy Contact	
Enemy Contacts	**Number**
Walk-off patrols	24
Enemy probes/SAF	39
Spoiled attack	1
Ground assault	1
Total	**65, or .755 per week**

General Binh charged his T89th Sapper Battalion to contain and/or neutralize the Marines on Hill 119. The OP represented a roadblock for the movement of his troops and logistical supplies between his base camps in the Que Son Mountains and the assembly area on Go Noi. The NVA sappers opposing the Marines placed numerous booby traps to contain them. The Marines found, and blew in place 31 booby traps, along with one command-detonated mine ambushing a Recon patrol (see Table D).

Table D: Booby Traps	
Enemy Booby Traps	**Number**
Booby Traps	31
Command-detonated mine	1
Total	**32, or .372 per week**

To counter the enemy's strategy of booby-trapping, the Marines patrolled both day and night around Hill 119 in all directions. This was an effort to prevent the Sappers and their VC supporters and guides from placing deadly explosive devices. The aggressive Marine patrolling captured 55 NVA/VC or .639 per week (see Table E). Captured, detained, and "Chieu Hois" were all searched, blindfolded, and moved from the OP's landing zone (LZ) where they were flown to LZ 20 at the III Marine Amphibious Force's prison compound and interrogated by the 3rd Interrogator Translator Team for intelligence.

Table E: Captured Enemy	
Captured Enemy	**Number**
Prisoners from walk-off patrols	6
Detainees without ID cards	24
Chieu Hois	25
Total	**55, or .639 per week**

The Marines suffered 23 wounded, 18 to booby traps and five to a command-detonated mine. Allied South Korean (RoK) Marines had two wounded by booby trap (Table F).

Table F: Friendly Casualties	
Friendly Casualties	**Number**
Killed	1
Wounded: USMC 23/RoK 2	25
Non-Battle Casualties–18	
Total	**26, or .302 per week**

The number of enemy wounded is unknown. Like the Marines, the NVA always removed their wounded from the battlefield during the fight and/or the first night after a fight. We know they suffered large numbers simply by the number of hospitals the Marines uncovered. Underground hospitals were found in Marble Mountain under the giant Buddha statue, on Go Noi Island under the railroad berm, along with multiple hospitals in the Que Son Mountains, and one directly under Hill 845, LZ Vulture/Rainbow.[7]

In comparing friendly killed and enemy body count, which was McNamara's measure of effectiveness,[8] the Marines suffered one death from friendly artillery fire. General Binh suffered 1,089 NVA/VC killed by the OP and its patrols.

Hill 119's body count ratio was 1:1,089 (Table G).

Table G: Kills		
Body Count		
Category	**US/Allies**	**NVA/VC**
Arty		953
Air		76
Sniper		4
Ground Contact		56
Friendly Fire (Arty)	1	
Total	**1**	**1,089**

Enemy Boats

To infiltrate enemy soldiers past the OP on Hill 119 to Go Noi Island, the NVA had to cross the Song Ba Ren or Song Chiem Son. This meant a boat trip in the rainy season or wading and swimming in the dry season. The hamlet of Tho Son, 1,200 meters due north of Hill 119, had a population of 4–6 elderly Vietnamese and 11 boat docks on the river. The VCI hamlet served as a ferry terminal for shuttling NVA across the river and returning rice and other food stuffs south to the mountain sanctuaries.

The Marines recorded 111 small boats sunk by supporting arms during their 600 days on the OP.

APPENDIX 2

Hill Commanders by Tour[1]

Tour of Duty/ *Callsign*	Commander/ Plt Sgt	Plt	Corpsman/Scout Dog	# Enemy Sighted	Comments
1969					
19 Jan 1969 19–26 Jan	Capt Willson, CO Delta Co	3	HM2 Dagley	171	15 civilians; 2 sniper kills; 5 booby traps 11 boats sunk; Construction of defense started
Empire State	1Lt Lawrence	1	Scout Dog Coco		2 Off/40 Marines/1 Corpsman; Construction
26 Jan–2 Feb	1Lt Lawrence	1	Hanson/Rucker	187	9 civilians; 1 sniper kill;4 booby traps
Vesper Bells	SSgt Jones		Scout Dog		Construction continues
2 Feb–11 Feb	2Lt Wietecha	2	HM3 Schwartz	139	enemy probe of hill; 55 tons rice found
Rudder	Sgt Loper		Scout Dog		
11–25 Feb	2Lt Downey	3	Hanson/Rucker	632	enemy probe of hill
Mad Hatter	Cpl McQuade		Scout Dog		
24 Feb–9 Mar	2Lt Wietecha	2	O'Rourke	425	65 boats, 7 NVA flags
Aunt Mable	Sgt Smith				12 women, 2 boys visit hill, complaint about Arty
9–26 Mar	2Lt Unsworth	1	Kenner	461	20 civilians visit
Night Scholar	Sgt Peai		Scout Dog		

Tour of Duty/ *Callsign*	Commander/ Plt Sgt	Plt	Corpsman/Scout Dog	# Enemy Sighted	Comments
24 Mar–8 Apr	2Lt Mann	3	2 Corpsmen	364	6 civilians visit, *Pennywise* walk-off patrol
Grim Reaper	SSgt Jones		Scout Dog		
8–25 Apr	SSgt Hall	2	Dana	382	en probe; 42 civilians, 5 medevac; 14 boats
Hanover Sue	Sgt Gawlaki		Scout Dog		1 booby trap: 3 USMC wounded
25 Apr–13 May	2Lt Unsworth	1	Kenner/Jansen	527	17 civilians; 1 sniper kill; *Spooky* utilized
Bag Shaw	Sgt Peai				1 booby-trapped M26
13–27 May	2Lt Schanck	3	Rucker	285	2 enemy probes of hill
Segment	SSgt Jones		2 Engineers		Aerial observer with FX strike and NGF mission
27 May–12 June	2Lt Pfieffer	2	Dana	475	Enemy probe of hill
Barkeep	GySgt Hall				Ground contact with 9 NVA, 8 kills
12–24 June	2Lt Unsworth	1	Kenner/Jansen	115	Enemy probe of hill
Defend	Cpl Dagneault		Scout Dog		
24 June–4 July	2/Lt Pfieffer	3	Sanders	451	Enemy probe: 1 ground contact, 1 kill, *Spooky*
Mayfly	Sgt Cronk				
4–14 July	2Lt Klein	2	Dana/Daugherty	98	Enemy probe; 1 Chieu Hoi; CH-53 shot down
Beech Nut	Sgt Gwinn				14 civilians visit, 6 women, 13 children medical
14–26 July	1st Platoon Sergeant	1		317	*report missing, derived sighting 11th Marines records
26 July–5 Aug	2Lt Pfieffer	3	Sanders	51	Eng probe; no artillery support; 3 villagers; 1 evac

Tour of Duty/ *Callsign*	Commander/ Plt Sgt	Plt	Corpsman/Scout Dog	# Enemy Sighted	Comments
Parallel Bars	SSgt Keen		Dog Harvey Baby		
5–14 Aug	2Lt Klien	2	Semararo	0	5 Chieu Hoi; civilian visit, 1 baby, 1 medevac
Spillway	Sgt Gawlaki		Scout Dog		1 NOD introduced to hill
14–25 Aug	SSgt Ommondson	1	Vineyard	51	2 civilians; 60-mm mortar mission, 2 kills
Spillway	Sgt Franklin		Scout Dog Barron		
24 Aug–3 Sep	2Lt Pfeiffer	3	Lee/Sanders	30	1 contact, PFC Robert Haney, killed, friendly Arty
Spillway	Sgt Diaz				1 prisoner; Swick; Lowery; Grossman
3–14 Sept	2Lt Klein	2	Semararo	5	Enemy probe; aerial observer support
Spillway	Sgt Gawlaki		Scout Dog		
14–24 Sept	2Lt Unsworth	1	Jansen/Vineyard	23	1 Arty fire mission
Rummage	SSgt Ommondson				
24 Sept–9 Oct	2Lt Waddill	3	Sanders	28	Enemy probe, flushed with M60 MG; Swick
Rummage	Sgt Diaz				Lowery, Grossman; Swick
8–19 Oct	2Lt Klein	2	Semararo	208	*Spooky* utilized; 1 booby trap: 5 USMC wounded
Rummage	Sgt Gawlaki				Sgt Gawlaki, LCpl Iantorno
19–29 Oct	2Lt Overton	1	Vineyard/Avenel	72	1 booby trap blown; 2 boats sunk: SSgt Keen
Rummage	SSgt Keen		Scout Dog Rex		

Tour of Duty/ *Callsign*	Commander/ Plt Sgt	Plt	Corpsman/Scout Dog	# Enemy Sighted	Comments
Integrated	*Observation*		*Device*	(IOD) Starts	11th Marines, forward observer (FO) missions on Hill 119 as tenant
29 Oct–10 Nov	2Lt Waddill	3	Lee	128	Four boats sunk; Sgt Diaz, Cpl Swick, LCpl Lowery
Rummage	Sgt Diaz		Scout Dog Rex	5 Nov	Corporal Mark Bayuk, FO 11 Marines, joins IOD team
9–20 Nov	2Lt Stamm	2	Mullins	300	2 boats sunk; 2 civilian medevacs
Rummage	Sgt Gawlaki				Sgt Harvey; Iantorno
20 Nov–1 Dec	2Lt Overton	1	Vineyard/Avenel	185	2 boats sunk
Asparagus	SSgt Keen				
1–16 Dec	2Lt Waddill	3	Sanders/Laski	223	2 enemy probes;1 boat sunk; 3 children medical
Durham	Sgt Diaz				Lowery, Grossman; Swick; Marshall-2513908
16–29 Dec	2Lt Parks	2	Mullins	143	Vietnamese at hill for Christmas
Durham	Sgt Gawlaki		Scout Dog Champ		23 Dec Woman with shrapnel in hip medevac
1970					
29 Dec–11 Jan	2Lt Waddill	1	Avenel/Schneider	307	100 Civilians below hill mixed w/ NVA
Durham	SSgt Mushett		Scout Dog Ago		Sgt Franklin, LCpl Ravelo
11–25 Jan	2Lt Overton (20Jan medivac)	4	Richardson	102	Booby trap, 3 wounded: Lt Overton, LtCol Grace, +1, medivac
Durham	GySgt Moore		Dogs Andy Champs	Sgt Bayuk	Moore patrol, 2 kills,1 prisoner from T89 Sapper Bn
25 Jan–8 Feb	2Lt McAdams	3	Bennett	311	2 patrol contacts, 4 killed, 2 USMC wounded
Durham	GySgt Moore				Lowery, Freeman, Holmes
Station Break	SSgt Mushett		119 Walk-off patrol		WIA, Miller, "'Doc" Schneider; 2 kills

Tour of Duty/ *Callsign*	Commander/ Plt Sgt	Plt	Corpsman/Scout Dog	# Enemy Sighted	Comments
8–20 Feb	2Lt Parks	2	Mullins/ Richardson	104	2 patrol contacts, 1 kill, 2 booby traps blown
Durham	Sgt Harvey				Iantorno broken kneecap
20 Feb–5 Mar	2Lt Fallon	1	Avenel/Schneider	141	3 boats; 7 booby traps
West Orange	SSgt Mushett		Scout Dog		*Forefather*; 32 en; 6 booby traps; 3 tunnels
Forefather	2Lt Fallon		119 Walk-off patrol	Jackson	Franklin, Miller, Evans, Weirich, Schneider
5–19 Mar	2Lt L'Orange	4	Hunt	59	Enemy probe; 1 contact; 6 kills, 3 wounded
West Orange	Cpl Weese			7 Mar	Sgt Bayuk, FO, departs 11 Mar (longest on 119)
18 Mar–1 Apr	2Lt Lee	3	Edison/Bennett	49	1 kill, Viet woman, 28 Mar 1 air strike 24 Mar
West Orange	Sgt Diaz		4 USMC FOs	2 ARVN FOs	Grossman, Lowery, Broe, Kempe, Freeman
1–11 Apr	2Lt Parks	2	Schwartz	35	2 enemy probes; 2 booby traps; 2 155 duds
West Orange	Sgt Rowley				Sgt Ireland, Cpl Iantorno, PFC Thornes
11–25 Apr	2Lt Eglevsky	1	Avenel	90	Enemy probe; 1 civilian hill visit;
West Orange	Cpl Stewart				Bonini, Lujan, Kozakowski
25 Apr–9 May	2Lt L'Orange	4	Hunt/ Richardson	148	2 en probes; 1 prisoner, 3 detainees
West Orange	Sgt Adkins		1Lt Spolter walk-off		1 contact; 1 USMC wounded (PFC Reese)
9–23 May	1Lt Floom	3	Edison/Bennett	51	Enemy probe: 1 booby trap; 1 boat sunk
West Orange	Cpl McCommons				3 wounded, McCommons, Lowery, HN Edison

Tour of Duty/ *Callsign*	Commander/ Plt Sgt	Plt	Corpsman/Scout Dog	# Enemy Sighted	Comments
23 May–6 June	2Lt Parks	2/3	Schwartz	57	1 contact 7 enemy; 4 Chieu Hois; 6 en probes
West Orange	Sgt Rowley				Broe, Grossman, Thornes, Villasana
6–20 June	2Lt Eglevsky	1	Schneider	75	5 Chieu Hois; 4 boats, 2 booby traps
West Orange	Cpl Ravelo		5 RoK Marines		2 RoK wounded
20 June–2 July 25 June medevac	2Lt L'Orange/ Parks	4	Hunt/ Richardson	58	1 detainee; 4 Chieu Hois; 3 ARVN patrollers
Pal Joey-K	SSgt Mushett		L'Orange walk-off	25 June	Cmd Det Mine; 5 USMC wounded
2–18 July	1Lt Fallon	3	Edison	48	
Pal Joey-K	Sgt Halloway				Freeman, Broe, Kozakowski
18 July–1 Aug	1Lt Taylor	1	Schwartz	18	2 enemy probes; 2 Chieu Hois; 2 boats sunk
Pal Joey-K	Cpl Elkins		2 ARVN patrollers		Villasana, McNeese, McBride
1–14 Aug	1/Lt Fallon 1/Lt Hoff	2	Hunt	80	9 Aug, T89 Sapper ground attack; 25 kills
Pal Joey-K	Sgt Horton		1Lt Hoff, straphang		Cpl Oliver, Ravello, Sheppard
12–29 Aug	1Lt Fallon	3	Edison/Sather	36	1 detainee; 3 grd contacts; 5 kills
War Cloud-K	Sgt Gunel		1Lt D. Jones visit		LCpl Walton, Broe, Kempe, Kozakowski
29 Aug–11 Sep	1Lt Taylor	1	Schwartz/ Slaughter	20	3 contacts
War Cloud-K	Sgt Bingenheimer			11 Sept 1970	Hill 119 transferred 1st Recon to 11 Marines

APPENDIX 3

1st Reconnaissance Battalion Structure, Team Composition, Weapons, and Equipment[1]

In 1970, each patrolling company had three platoons of three teams and one platoon of four teams. Each team consisted of six Marines. Each patrolling company, on paper, or table of organization, was manned at 13 six-man teams. The second wartime plus-up was a fifth patrolling letter company. Echo Company was similarly structured to the other letter companies. The battalion had a total of 65 teams. Alpha Company, 5th Recon Battalion, whose role was to support the activated 26th Marine Regiment, was attached to the battalion with three platoons, for an additional 12 teams. As a result, the battalion commander had 77 Reconnaissance teams at his disposal.

Based on experience and the assigned mission, patrol composition over time was standardized. By 1969 and 1970, Marine Reconnaissance patrols were built around a Recon team. Patrols were comprised of 5–8 Marines and one corpsman. All teams were tailored to each assigned mission. Some special missions saw teams as large as 30 Marines. Permanent observation posts (OP) were manned by a platoon of three teams. The basic building block for each patrol mission was the six-man Recon team. The "Standard Operating Procedure for Sting Ray/Clandestine Long Range Patrolling Operations" for 1st Reconnaissance Battalion and 1st Force Recon Company, written in 1967 at Camp Reasoner, continually updated the processes and procedure for preparation and patrolling.[2]

Six-Man Patrol Composition

- Point Man
- Deuce Point/Patrol Leader (PL)
- Primary Radio Operator
- Corpsman / Marine First-Aid Man
- Secondary Radio Operator
- Tail-End Charlie/Assistant Patrol Leader (APL)

Composition and Duties

The basic six-man team was enlisted Recon Marines or Corpsmen that had graduated from a Reconnaissance Indoctrination Program. They lived together in the rear and the senior man was designated team leader (TL). PLs were selected by experience, merit, and training. A TL could also be a PL if he were qualified and had the experience. Officer PLs were platoon commanders with three or four teams. They normally rotated within their platoon by taking out different teams on different patrols. If an officer, or a senior enlisted Marine, not normally assigned to the team was the PL, then the team would be comprised of seven members. After the PL gave the patrol order, each patrol member had designated responsibilities in preparation for the patrol. The APL normally drew, and distributed, chow and ammunition for the entire patrol. The two radiomen drew radios and batteries sufficient to support the duration of the patrol. The corpsman/first-aid man drew a Unit One medical kit and the drugs they carried, as well as saline solution bags. The PL would coordinate with various external organizations in order to get maps, receive intelligence briefs, and assigned insert times from the S-3 Air Liaison shop, while the APL and/or enlisted TL organized the team to best accomplish their assigned mission.

Weapons and Equipment

Weapons and equipment carried were based on mission analysis, duration, estimated movement, and time of year. There was always a weight-to-capabilities trade off made with every load for every Marine. Average loads ranged from 50–100 pounds per Marine based on duration of patrol, season, and mission. More weight equals more capabilities equals more energy to carry. Mission analysis could require carrying specialized gear. If the mission was a wiretap, that gear must be carried. Selected patrols carried cameras.

Notional list of weapons and equipment:

- Rifle: Each man carried an M16A1 Rifle.
- Knife: Each man carried a bayonet or Ka-Bar knife.
- Ammunition: 20 magazines, 20-round capacity, each filled to 18 rounds so as not to damage or wear out the magazine spring. Each Marine's basic load was 360 rounds of ammo. The third round, 10th round, and 17th round were red tracers. This informed the Marine where he was in the magazine and also helped put him back on target, from elevation creep, when firing fully automatic. The PL also normally carried one full magazine of red tracers to be used for marking targets or direction.
- Grenades: Each patrol member carried six grenades, four M26 high explosive and two colored-smoke grenades for marking. PLs and APLs carried two CS (tear) gas grenades. Some PLs carried a thermite grenade. M33s, smaller firecracker grenades, when available, replaced the heavier M26. PLs could carry one canteen pouch with six firecracker grenades.
- Radio: Radiomen carried the PRC-25 or PRC-77 radio with KY-38 encryptor. PL carried a PRC-93 survival radio.
- Batteries: Based on planned duration of the patrol plus two.
- Antenna: Multiple radio antennas—short, whip and directional—plus a spool of comm wire and spoon to cut out a directional antenna.
- Shackle Sheets: Controlled communication booklet with one page for each calendar day providing encryption key by letters. A new shackle sheet took effect each day. Sensitive messages were supposed to be encrypted, "shackling" a message.

- Wiz Wheel: Another encryption device that had multiple wheels. Personnel with the same Wiz Wheel version could encrypt or de-encrypt messages.
- Thrust Points: Pre-established grid coordinates given a generic name like "Car." Then, as short hand on the radio if both sender and receiver had the thrust point, could pass a grid clandestinely by saying "From Ford up 1 kilometer and west one kilometer" to establish a position that needed to be passed quickly, with no time to encrypt with shackle sheets.
- Binoculars 7 × 50: Carried by PL.
- Maps: Carried by PL, APL, sometimes point man training in navigation.
- Signal Mirrors: Carried by PL and APL.
- Pencil flares: Carried by PL and APL for helping aircraft find teams in triple-canopy jungles.
- Strobe Light: Carried by PL.
- Flashlight: With red lens for PL and APL.
- Compass: Carried by PL and APL, as well as often by the point man. Most PLs also wore a wrist compass providing cardinal directions on their watch band.
- Unit One Medical Kit: Corpsmen/First-Aid Man. One to four saline bags.
- M79 Grenade Launcher: 20 rounds, carried by one Marine. With a round mix based on a map estimate of terrain. Flechette rounds for close quarters, thick jungle, or if M79 was point man based on terrain. High-explosive rounds, 10 or half of all rounds. Shotgun and CS gas, two to four rounds.
- Gas Mask: Each Marine carried his gas mask on his right hip.
- 2–4 Claymore Mines: Some teams cut claymores in half and carried six halves and six hellboxes, one per team member.
- Insertion/Extraction: All team members carried a Swiss seat, snap-links, D-rings, or H-harness, both for insert or extract by rope, ladder, or Special Purpose Insertion or Extraction (SPIE) Rig.
- Food: Each Marine carried a mix of long-range patrol rations (dehydrated rice and meat product), light weight until you add the water to hydrate them. Number was based on water availability. C-ration cans, picked by the Marine, per taste. Many patrols planned for two meals a day, one heavy, one light. No fires to warm. All meals consumed cold. Many carried fruit cans for the liquid energy provided by the sugar-filled syrup juice.
- Water: Canteens, between 4 and 16 plastic canteens based on season and availability of water. Water was heavy to carry. Water planning depended on season and availability of water. It also forced the team to lower ground to get water, which was not always tactically sound. Dehydration and heat exhaustion were typical outcomes for inexperienced teams in the summer.
- ½ poncho liner.
- One poncho: In winter. Many did not carry as you were wet anyway.
- Cammie paint: All.
- Bush cover: All.
- Cammie Utilities: One set the Marine wore. No underwear.
- Jungle boots: Socks optional.
- Sweatshirt or sleeping shirt: Monsoon months for warmth.

Glossary

AC-47 Callsign *Spooky*. The first fixed-wing gunship in Vietnam. It had three 7.62-mm Gatling guns that could pump out 6,000 rounds per minute.

AC-119G *Shadow*. Four Gatling guns instead of three. *Shadow* flew close air support and air-base-defense missions.

AC-119K *Stinger*. Added two 20-mm cannon to *Shadow*; *Stinger* concentrated on trucks on the Ho Chi Minh Trail.

AC-130 *Specter*. The premier gunship. In addition to Gatling guns, two 20-mm cannons and two 40-mm Bofors guns. It worked at night, enabled by infrared sensors, a low-level TV sensor, and a Black Crow sensor that detected electronic emissions.

Across-the-fence Codewords meaning across the South Vietnamese border into another country on your ground operation or your flight. Operations in neutral Laos were across-the-fence.

ADC Assistant Division Commander, usually a brigadier general.

AFVN Armed Forces Vietnam Network ran an in-country radio station.

AK-47 Soviet-designed assault rifle, designer Kalashnikov. Soviet/Chinese supplied and used extensively by the NVA and VC as their infantry assault rifle. 7.62 × 39-mm round.

Alligator Lake A man-made USAID project with multiple dams and aqueducts to irrigate both the An Hoa Basin and the Chien Son Valley rice fields. It was located 26 kilometers south of Da Nang and was physically in between Hills 148 and 119 to the north and Hills 177 and 175 to the south.

ALO Air Liaison Officer. A pilot on the ground unit's staff to coordinate air support for the ground unit.

AN/PPS-6 Korean War-era "People Sniffer Radar." That is a lightweight non-coherent pulse Doppler combat-surveillance radar operating in the X band.

ANGLICO Air Naval Gunfire Liaison Company was a Marine unit trained in supporting arms of air strikes, artillery, and naval gunfire. Equipped with U.S. radios, their teams were attached to Allied units to allow them to use U.S. supporting arms quickly and easily.

Antenna Valley A narrow valley running east to west through the Que Son Mountains connecting Que Son Valley/village with the Song Thu Bong Valley. Antenna Valley was a major infiltration route for the NVA between Base Area 112 in the west and Base Area 116 in the heart of the Que Son Mountains. The old French Route 536 ran through the valley from the river in the west through a

	pass to Que Son village where it connected to Route 535 that then connected to National Route 1 on the coast.
AO	Aerial Observer was a trained back-seat rider in an aircraft or helo that coordinated supporting arms for ground units. Normally flying in OV-10A Bronco or an O-1 Bird Dog.
APL	Assistant Patrol Leader
Article 32	A UCMJ article that initiates and completes a formal investigation. Similar function to a grand jury in determining whether to recommend criminal charges in the Uniformed Code of Military Justice.
Artillery/Arty	Large-caliber (105-mm, 155-mm, 8", 175-mm) rounds, tube, cannon, or howitzer launched. Operated by crews to provide fire support overhead at distance depending on charge size and caliber. Organized into platoons, batteries and battalions with a Regimental HQ supporting a Marine Division (or on a ship). The 11th Marine Regiment supported 1st Marine Division.
ARVN	Army of the Republic of Vietnam, meaning South Vietnamese Army.
ASRT	Air Support Radar Team manned the TPQ-10 close-air-support radar.
ATO	Air Tasking Order. The daily order resulting from the process of daily tasking which aircraft from what units, on which mission, would fly each day in response to requests for air support.
B-40	North Vietnamese designation of the first RPG-2 (Rocket Propelled Grenade-2) shoulder-fired rocket used by the NVA and VC.
Bac si	Doctor in Vietnamese, pronounced "Bok See."
Basketball	Callsign for a fixed-wing aircraft that drops high-intensity flares to light up the night sky.
Battalion	A unit organization of Headquarters and Service companies and four line companies, and specialized companies such as weapons. The 1st Reconnaissance Battalion had H&S and five line companies: A, B, C, D, and E.
Ben Hai	Song Ben Hai is a river in central Vietnam flowing west to east and in the Vietnam War was part of the demilitarized zone between North and South Vietnam.
BC-Scope	Ballistic Coefficient—Scope for artillery observation and precision adjustments. World War II, Korea, and Vietnam. 15 power. On a standing tripod.
BDA	Bomb-Damage Assessment.
Bien Dong	Vietnamese for East Sea considered part of the South China Sea by the Vietnamese.
Big Eyes	Slang for 200-power ship's binoculars on the IOD.
BLT	Battalion Landing Team. A reinforced infantry battalion composited with amphibious vehicles, artillery, reconnaissance, and engineering assets to go on board amphibious shipping. Structured to conduct amphibious landing.
Booby Trap	Nickname for a Surprise Firing Device (SFD) during the Vietnam War. Today an SFD is called an IED (Improvised Explosive Device). A bomb or explosive device used as an indiscriminate attack to destroy, incapacitate, harass, or distract. Set indiscriminately, to be tripped by an unknown suspect or can be command detonated.

Bright Light Generic mission name for a downed pilot rescue or body recovery mission.
Bug Juice Marines' name for insect repellent, also slang for sweet colored and flavored drink.
C-4 Plastic explosives in one-pound bars. Also used for cooking.
Callsign The short name of a unit used on the radio to identify the unit. For example, one of Recon Battalion's callsigns in late 1970 was *War Cloud.*
CAP Combined Action Program or Combined Action Platoon. Usually Marine rifle squad co-located with South Vietnamese security forces in a hamlet or village.
Charlie American slang for Cong, Viet Cong, or Viet Cong Infrastructure.
ChiCom Chinese Communist, or Chinese Communist grenade like a pineapple stick.
Chieu Hoi A Viet Cong or NVA who accepted amnesty and surrendered. The Vietnamese phrase is a combination of two verbs, to welcome and to return. Some Chieu Hois were used as U.S. scouts in a program called "Kit Carson."
CH-46 Sea Knight cargo transport helicopter, featuring a rear cargo-loading ramp, a top speed of 166 mph, and the ability to carry 4,000 pounds of cargo or 22 combat-equipped troops.
CH-53 Sea Stallion cargo helicopter. Heavy lift military transport helicopter. The CH-53A carries a crew of four. It can carry various payloads, including up to 38 fully equipped troops, 24 litters with medical attendants, an internal cargo load of 8,000 pounds, or an external load of 13,000 pounds on the single-point sling hook. The Marines in Vietnam used CH-53As and CH-53D models. Used for both logistics and troop transports, it had additional capability of long range and ability to fly at higher altitudes.
CI Counter Intelligence.
CID Criminal Investigation Division.
CG Commanding General.
Claymore Mine Command-detonated anti-personnel mine of C4 perched on a stand, firing ball bearings out in a defensive arc.
Close Air Support Aviation fires (guns, rockets, bombs) delivered at close range supporting a ground unit. "Danger Close" defined as 250 meters or less.
CO Commanding Officer. The most senior officer of a unit responsible for all things the unit does or fails to do.
COC Combat Operations Center.
Company A unit comprised of platoons normally commanded by a captain. The lowest level at which non-judicial punishment (NJP), or Article 15 of the UCMJ, can be meted out.
Concertina Wire Type of barbed wire or razor wire that is formed in large coils which can be expanded.
CONUS Continental United States.
CORDS Civilian Operations and Rural Development Support. Most American personnel engaged in the Pacification Program placed in one organization and aligning it under MACV Command structure. Paralleling the South Vietnamese Government-created Central Recovery Committee.

Cowpoke	Callsign for aerial observers flying with VMO-2 in 1969–70.
CP	Command Post. Headquarters for a military unit of any size.
CPB	Company Patrol Base. A defined piece of terrain defended by a company and its CP, from which small patrols conduct day and night patrolling. An economy-of-force measure to control through observation and patrolling a larger piece of terrain.
C-rations	Meal, Combat Individual. Field ration consisted of one canned entrée (one of a dozen varieties), canned fruit, a B-2 unit containing cheese, crackers, and candy. An accessory pack containing can opener (P-38 or "John Wayne"), a hot beverage mixed with cocoa, coffee, salt, sugar packets, plastic spoon, chewing gum, a packet of four cigarettes and several sheets of toilet paper. One C-ration per box, 12 boxes per carton. Also, "C-rat."
CS	Chlorobenzylidene Malononitrile and Chloroacetophenone. Tear Gas. Packaged in hand grenades, 40-mm rounds, canisters, rockets, and dried crystals.
DAIS	Da Nang Anti-Infiltration System. DAIS was a plowed trace around Da Nang, seeded with ground sensors to detect enemy infiltration. When a sensor string received an alert, an artillery battery fired on the grid. It was supposed to stop infiltration. It failed. The sensors were first generation and could not distinguish between animals, rain, and people (farmers or enemy).
Da Nang	The third largest city in Vietnam. The major logistics hub for I Corps comprises its port, harbor, protected bay, oil-storage facilities, and a large international airport. It was home to III MAF, XXIV Corps, 1st Marine Division, 1st Marine Aircraft Wing, Force Logistics Command, and 1st Reconnaissance Battalion.
DASC	Direct Air Support Center controls and coordinates tactical aircraft operations directly supporting ground troops.
Debrief	To interrogate someone, such as a patrol leader, usually upon return from a mission in order to obtain useful information and make a record of the patrol. Debriefs at 1st Recon were conducted by the S-2 shop directly after a patrol. They were then attached to the original operations order and filed for record.
De-de mau	Vietnamese for leaving or running out.
Dien Caid au	Vietnamese, Americanized "inky dow," meaning crazy or certifiably insane.
Dung Lai	Vietnamese, meaning halt, and pronounced, "Zum lie."
DMZ	Demilitarized Zone. The Vietnamese DMZ was a five-kilometer-wide area following the Ben Hai River at the 17th Parallel in Quang Tri Province. It was established as the dividing line between the two countries, North Vietnam and South Vietnam, on 22 July 1954 and remained until 2 July 1976. In 1954, Vietnam was officially divided into the two military gathering areas, which were intended to be sustained in the short term after the First Indochina War. During the American War (1955–1975) it became important as the battleground demarcation between communist North Vietnam and anti-communist South Vietnam. The zone *de jure* ceased to exist with the reunification of Vietnam in 1976.

Doc Term of affection for Navy corpsmen used by all Marines. A Navy corpsman knows he has earned the Marine unit's trust when they call him "Doc." From then on the Marines will protect their corpsman.

Dog Patch American slang for a Vietnamese village, Thon Phuo Truong, located just outside the west gate of Da Nang International Airport.

Dong Den Hill 868, 1st Recon radio relay site overlooking Elephant Valley and the Song Cu De.

DOPE Data On Previous Engagement. A marksmanship acronym to describe elevation and windage data on a prior engagement with one's rifle by recording the clicks on your sight for height and vertical distance left and right. Used by Marines when aligning their sights before operations or range firing. DOPE is used for sighting in your rifle.

DRV Democratic Republic of Vietnam (North Vietnam)

Deuce Point Second man in a patrol behind the point man. Normally responsible for navigation.

ECP Enlisted Commissioning Program

EE-8 Hand-cranked, battery powered field telephone for defensive positions connected by wire. Developed in World War II, used in Vietnam.

EGA Eagle, Globe and Anchor, or the Marine Corps Emblem.

EKIA Enemy Killed in Action

ETA Estimated Time of Arrival

Emergency Extraction When a patrol extraction is declared immediately (not scheduled) due to enemy pressure or wounded Marines. The patrol mission terminated; all efforts are used to remove the team from the field. Emergency extractions were usually a helicopter extract supported by a package of additional aircraft, both helo gunships and fixed-wing, providing protection for the extraction helicopter, many times using a ladder or SPIE Rig to get the team out.

Extraction Term used for a reconnaissance team leaving the patrol at a scheduled time and returning to the base camp. Extractions can be done by foot, truck, boat, or helicopter.

FAC Forward Air Controller. A trained and qualified Marine, many times a pilot, on the ground with the infantry to control close air strikes.

FAC-A Forward Air Controllers-Airborne. Pilots or back-seat aerial observers qualified to control air strikes.

FDC The Fire Direction Center converted a request for fire into firing quality data for the guns to shoot the fire mission.

FFZ Free-Fire Zone. A fire control measure. A specifically designated area into which any weapon system may fire without additional coordination with the establishing headquarters. This was a geographic area cleared of all friendly forces and civilians. It was a geographically designated area where Allied forces could fire on anything they observed assuming it was enemy. These areas had had the civilian population removed and were void any friendly units. Aircraft and artillery observation of movement or personnel in a FFZ could

	fire at will without going through the clearance process. Go Noi Island was a designated FFZ.
Finger	A geographic terrain feature smaller than a ridgeline.
Firecracker	A small M33 fragmentation grenade introduced in 1968 and used by Marine Recon teams.
Fire Team	A four-Marine unit, the basic building block of a squad. A Fire Team has a team leader, automatic rifleman, and two riflemen. Three Fire Teams in a Marine squad plus the squad leader total 13 Marines.
FLC	Force Logistics Command. Senior Marine logistics command in Vietnam, headquartered at Camp Haskins across Route 1 from Red Beach, Da Nang. The logistics support element for III MAF, commanded by a two-star general.
Flip	Slang term for the change-out day of a two-week tour of duty on a Reconnaissance observation post.
Flip-flop	Simultaneous helicopter patrol inserts and extract of another team. Also slang for plastic shower shoe.
FMF	Fleet Marine Force.
FMFPac	Fleet Marine Force, Pacific. The senior Marine Officer in the Pacific Theater of Operations.
FragO	Short for Fragmentation Order, a shortened version of an operations order (OPORD) in the military that is used to modify or change an existing order.
Freedom Hill	American name for large PX (Post eXchange) complex between the Da Nang Airport and Hill 327, Division Hill. It also had a large amphitheater stage at the base of the hill to seat thousands on the hillside for USO Shows.
Friendly Fire	Term used to describe friendly forces shooting at each other. May be deliberate, e.g., incorrectly identifying the target as the enemy, or accidentally as firing and missing the enemy and hitting friendlies in proximity. Also known as blue-on-blue which is derived from the map color of friendly forces.
Four Corners	Main intersection on Route 1 north, south, east, road to west gate of Da Nang International and west road to Freedom Hill and Hill 327. Main intersection of Dog Patch.
FNG	Fucking New Guy.
FO	Forward observer trained for artillery calling or spotting and 81-mm mortar calling and spotting.
FPF	Final Protective Fires. Preplanned fires of infantry weapons designed to interlock and protect the position as a final firing defense.
FSB	Fire Support Base. A base with artillery emplacements established to support infantry in its area. Many times on the top of a flattened-off mountain in the operational area.
FSCC	Fire Support Coordination Center.
GCM	General Court-Martial. The military's highest-level trial court. This court tries service members for the most serious crimes. Must be convened by the general commanding the unit of the accused.

Gooners A derogatory name used by Marines in reference to the VC or NVA.

Go Noi Island Located 20 kilometers south of Da Nang, was part of the An Hoa Basin river delta of the Song Thu Bon. Bounded on three sides by rivers and National Route 1 on the east, it was a fertile agricultural island with two growing seasons. A Viet Minh stronghold in the French War, it became a VC and NVA stronghold during the American War in Vietnam. It was a rice basket feeding an NVA division and a staging area one day's march from the Da Nang Vital Area.

GRUNT General Replacement Un-Trained, a World War I acronym describing drafts of young men sent to the front in France. Adopted term for infantry, depending on context can mean affection or be derogatory.

GSV Government of South Vietnam.

Gung ho Gung ho is an English term, with the current meaning of "overly enthusiastic or energetic." It originated during the Second Sino-Japanese War (1937–1945).

GVN Government of Vietnam, official U.S. acronym for the South Vietnamese Government

Hamlet Evaluation System (HES) A U.S.–MACV–CORDS-established system to evaluate all hamlets in South Vietnam. Arranged and analysis of information on all aspects of pacification, security, political, and socio-economic. Information provided by province and district advisors of CORDS program. Computerized system placed letter grade in specific categories. Hamlets fell into one of six letter categories:

- **A** Has security and GVN-controlled hamlet, infrastructure, public projects, and economy improving.
- **B** Has security, GVN-controlled, VCI threat exists.
- **C** Has security, GVN-controlled, infrequent VC harassment.
- **D** VC activities reduced, internal threat remains in form of tax collection and terrorism.
- **E** VC are effectively in control with infrastructure intact in parallel to GVN.
- **V** VC-controlled hamlet. No GVN officials or advisors may enter hamlet except on a military operation. Population willingly supports the enemy.

Harbor site A position of security established by Recon Teams in the field as a base to rest between daily or nightly missions.

Haven Designate grid coordinates zone of responsibility for a Reconnaissance team where the patrol leader was responsible for clearing all fires into the zone. Also known as a Reconnaissance Area of Operations.

HE High Explosive

Heat Map An analytical technique of marking similar events with a symbol on a map at the location to determine patterns over time. For example, mark the location of every booby trap around a camp.

Heavies Slang name for senior officers or enlisted personnel derived from the fact that some senior officers or enlisted personnel weighed more or were fat.

H&I Harassment and Interdiction fires. A category of artillery fires based on intelligence to harass and interdict enemy base areas and avenues of approach. Shot at random times.

Hill # Height of hill identified by a number was used to identify it on a map and became the de-facto name of that location.

Hill 119, Doi Chiem Son Observation post, radio relay manned by Delta Company, 1st Reconnaissance Battalion. Located 25 kilometers south of Da Nang, it overlooked the NVA/VC stronghold of Goi Noi Island. An original IOD location in October 1969.

Hill 200 Located northwest of An Hoa Combat Base. OP manned by Bravo Company, 1st Recon, it overlooked the Arizona Territory, Liberty Bridge, and An Hoa Basin.

Hill 327 West of Da Nang four kilometers, ridgeline was original home of 3rd Marine Division followed by 1st Marine Division. Sometimes called Division Ridge, the division's base camp was built on the natural defense curve of the northeast slope. First Reconnaissance Battalion's base, Camp Reasoner, was at the base of the hill between Division Road and LZ 401 and the rice paddies below.

Hill 425 Located 29 kilometers south of Da Nang, the hill was located on the northern shoulder of the Que Son mountains. It overlooked Spider Lake to its west and the Phu Loc Valley to its northeast. Home to Echo Company's OP, later Charlie Company's, and radio relay. An original IOD post.

HLZ Helicopter Landing Zone. Also referred to as LZ.

HML Helicopter Marine Light, a Marine helicopter squadron of Hueys and Cobra gunships.

HMM Helicopter Marine Medium, a squadron of CH-46 helicopters.

HMH Helicopter Marine Heavy, a squadron of CH-53 heavy helicopters.

Hoi An A Vietnamese town located 25 miles south of Da Nang. It was the Brigade HQ for the 2nd Republic of Korea (RoK) Marine Brigade and the center of its TAOR; a 180-degree area from National Route 1 to the East China Sea.

Hooch Slang name for Vietnamese thatched-roof, one-story small building or home. Also U.S. military nickname for a Southeast Asia or SEA Hut, a corrugated metal roof on plywood base and screen-sided building, usually elevated off the ground, with plywood floor. Used as offices and sleeping quarters in rear base camps like Camp Reasoner.

Hostage Pilots' callsign for OV-10 aircraft flying with VMO-2 in 1969 and 1970.

HQMC Headquarters Marine Corps.

H&S Headquarters and Service, either a company or battalion-size support unit.

HST Helicopter Support Team. Marines who ran an LZ supporting helicopters working the nets to lift external loads.

Huey UH-1 helicopter. Utility helicopter in multiple versions from medevac, command, observation, gunship. Flown by Army and Marine units.

IA Drills Immediate-action drills were patrol member rehearsals for immediate action by each member of the patrol when making contact with the enemy. Example, IA drill for contact front, making contact with an enemy to your front.

IBS Inflatable Boat Small. Rubber raft used for beach and river operations either paddled by six men or used with small outboard engine.

I Corps US Military Region I, located in northern South Vietnam, contained the DMZ and the five northern provinces—Quang Tri, Thua Thien, Quang Nam, Quang Tin, and Quang Ngai.

III MAF III Marine Amphibious Force, the senior Marine Headquarters in Vietnam, responsible for I Corps TAOR.

Illumination Round An artillery or mortar round packed with a parachute and flare, deploying and igniting at predetermined height in order to provide spot or area illumination of the battlefield at night.

IOD Integrated Observation Device. A classified "Secret" system that integrated three sub-systems onto one tripod: a pair of 200-power ship's binoculars ("Big Eyes"), night-observation device (see NOD) and a laser range finder. Its purpose was to improve observation both day and night as well as accuracy to facilitate calling immediate-adjustment supporting arms on a called target. Initially, ten IODs were built and deployed to Vietnam in late October 1969. It was a product of the Marine Corps, SPEED (Special Procurement for Expediting Equipment) program integrated by ONR (Office of Naval Research).

ITR Infantry Training Regiment. The Class A school for enlisted Marines teaches infantry skills and military occupations. ITR East located at Camp Lejeune and ITR west located at Camp Pendleton

ITT Interrogator Translator Team.

Ka-Bar Standard Marine fighting knife, issued to those for whom the .45-caliber pistol was Table of Organization weapon.

KCS Kit Carson Scout. A Chieu Hoi Viet Cong who changed sides to the South Vietnamese, went through scout training and served as a scout for U.S. units.

Keyhole A recon mission with a 4–6-man Recon team inserted for only observation and surveillance.

Khung Crazy, nuts, pronounced "Koom."

KIA Killed in Action

Klick Short abbreviation word for one kilometer, used on the radio to describe distances. "I am six klicks out" means six kilometers.

LAAW Light Anti-Armor Weapon. M-72, tube launched, single shot, disposable, 66-mm rocket, range 200 meters.

Ladder Aluminum 125-foot ladder connected to and dropped off the ramp of a CH-46 helicopter. Used to extract Recon team when there was not an LZ. The helicopter hovered and dropped the ladder into small clearing and the Recon Marines got on the ladder and were pulled out as external cargo. Sometimes called Extraction Ladder or Simmons Ladder, after Major Roger Simmons, the CO of 1st Force Recon who had one made for a CH-46 based on smaller ladders used by MACV–SOG on smaller helos.

LDO Limited Duty Officer, normally a former enlisted Marine used in specialty fields for their experience. In Vietnam, the intelligence and the administrative communities used LDOs.

LP Listening Post. A position manned by one or more Marines at night and located outside friendly lines near avenues of approach in order to provide early warning of enemy movement or approach.

LZ Landing Zone, also Ladder Zone, used for extraction of Recon team via ladder device.

M14 Select-fire infantry rifle with 7.62 × 51-mm round; 20-round magazine. Standard issue rifle prior to M16. Many remained in Vietnam as heavier caliber infantry option.

M16 Automatic, semi-automatic assault rifle with 5.56 × 45-mm round; 20-round magazine. Became Marine Corps' standard rifle in 1962 with the M16A1 version, replacing the M14.

M18 57-mm Recoilless Rifle. World War II/Korean War antitank, shoulder-fired or tripod mounted. Effective range 450 meters. Max range 4 kilometers. Breach loaded, single shot, man portable, crew served. Ammunition: high-explosive antitank, high explosive, white phosphorous. Issued out of war reserves stock to the ARVN.

M40 Sniper rifle modified by Marine Corps armorers, Remington 700, bolt-action rifle, 7.62 × 51-mm round.

M49 Telescope ocular, with tripod for prone-position spotting sniper shots. The M49 Spotting Scope, also known as the M49 Observation Telescope, is a multipurpose scope system used primarily for long-range marksmanship observation. It can also be used for observing the effects of artillery fires and other general purposes. The M49 is a fixed 20-power telescope with an eyepiece focus.

M60 7.62-mm lightweight, air-cooled, metallic-linked, belt-fed portable machine gun. Effective range of 1,200 yards and a cyclic rate of fire at 550 rounds per minute. Maximum sustained rate of fire per minute of 100 rounds. Standard issue to Marine infantry units. Bipod for walking patrols, tripod for fixed positions with pintels.

M79 40-mm grenade launcher, single shot, shoulder-fired, break-action to load. Fired several rounds including high explosive, CS gas, flechette. Called a "Blooper" by Marines because of the sound it made when fired. Maximum range of 400 meters. Each recon team carried one M79 on patrol for indirect fire.

MACV Military Assistance Command, Vietnam. Senior U.S. command in Vietnam, headquarters in Saigon.

MAF Marine Amphibious Force. III MAF was the senior Marine Corps headquarters in the Vietnam War located in Da Nang and commanded by a three-star general.

MAG Marine Aircraft Group normally commanded by a colonel. Comprises aircraft squadrons and support squadrons.

MAW Marine Air Wing normally commanded by a major general. Made up of MAGs.

MCRD Marine Corps Recruit Depot. MCRD East is Parris Island, South Carolina; MCRD West is San Diego, California. Place of initial entry level training for ten weeks where all enlisted recruits earn the title, U.S. Marine. Known as Boot Camp.

Magazine (Ammunition) Storage and feeding accessory for a weapon that is spring loaded to feed ammunition up and into a chamber to fire, e.g., .45-cal pistol, M14, and M16 rifles are magazine feed.

Medevac Medical evacuation of wounded. By helicopter trying to get the wounded person to a hospital within the golden hour, or within one hour of the wound, to save the life. Medevac helos, also called "Dust Off," saved lives that in previous wars would be KIA on the battlefield.

Mess Hall Marine term for dining facility.

Midnight Requisition Marine slang for borrowing or stealing an item usually from a well-stocked source that would not feel the loss.

MMAF Marble Mountain Air Facility was a Marine Corps airstrip north of Marble Mountain, located between Da Nang city and China Beach. It was home to Marine helicopters and observation planes.

Monsoon A wind from the southeast or south that brings heavy rainfall to southern Asia in the summer.

Mortars Crew-served weapon employed at company level (60-mm) and battalion (81-mm) used to fire high explosives, white phosphorous, or illumination rounds at high-angle trajectory. Ranging out to 4,600 yards. First Recon Battalion used mortars on OPs and patrol bases.

NAC Northern Artillery Cantonment. Home of the 11th Marines west of Da Nang International Airport and northwest of Hill 327.

NAD Naval Advisory Detachment, a sub-unit of MACV–SOG with a base in Da Nang for fast patrol boats.

Nasties Norwegian-built patrol boats, manned by the South Vietnamese Navy, used by Marine Recon for coastal operations, insertions, and extractions.

NCO Non-commissioned officer, enlisted grades E-4 and E-5, corporals and sergeants charged with exercising leadership of other lower enlisted personnel.

NCOIC Non-commissioned officer-in-charge.

Net Marine Corps slang for a single radio frequency and all stations networked on the same frequency.

NGF Naval gun fire. 5", 8" or 16" barrel size. Guns' size depends on which ship. Destroyers 5", cruisers 8" and battleships 16".

NIS Naval Investigative Service.

NIS RA Naval Investigative Service Resident Agent was a Special Agent in charge of an office that supported a group of Navy and Marine Corps Commands in their area. NIS RA Da Nang was the office that covered I Corps Tactical Zone in Vietnam.

NJP Non-judicial punishment, Article 15 of the Uniformed Code of Military Justice (UCMJ).

NOD Night-observation device using ambient light, 7-power, could see about two kilometers on a moonlit night.

NUC Navy Unit Commendation. First Reconnaissance Battalion was awarded an NUC for actions against enemy forces in 1967 and 1968.

NVA North Vietnamese Army. Officially PAVN, People's Army of North Vietnam.

O-1 Bird Dog Single engine, forward-air-control aircraft used to find and mark targets for strike flights. Low and slow, with a top speed of 115 mph. Carried smoke rockets but no armament.

O-2 Skymaster Also known as Oscar Deuce, a little bigger and a little faster than the O-1. It had two engines. It could be fitted with a pod for a 7.62-mm minigun.

OCS Officers' Candidate School. Located in Quantico, Virgina. During Vietnam, ten-week course duration. Where all officer candidates earn the title Marine Officer.

OIC Officer-in-charge of a unit, or location if it had more than one unit at the location.

OP Observation post. A location to observe the surrounding area for enemy and enemy movement, usually at distance.

OPCon Operational Control of a unit. When one unit is assigned to another unit to control it during an operation for a specific duration of time.

Operation *Pipestone Canyon* Multi-battalion operations run by the 1st Marine Regiment, ARVN 37th Ranger battalion and RoK, 1st Marine Battalion against Front 4 and 2nd NVA Division in Dodge City and Go Noi Island from 26 May to 7 November 1969.

Operation *Taylor Common* Multiple-battalion infantry operation run by Task Force *Yankee* and the 5th Marine Regiment and ARVN Ranger battalions from 6 December 1968–8 March 1969. Objectives in Phases I and II were to offensively go after Front 4 and 2nd NVA Division in Base Area 112 on the On Tue slope and west of Thong Duc. Phase 3 went after the NVA in the Arizona Territory, Dodge City, and Go Noi island.

OPORD Operations Order. A directive that a military leader issues to subordinate leaders to help initiate and coordinate a specific operation.

Oscar Mike Codewords for radio use meaning "on the move."

OV-10 Bronco Forward-air-control aircraft with twin turboprop, introduced in 1968, sturdier than O-1 and O-2. Four 7.62-mm machine guns and could carry rockets. Max speed of 281 mph.

Panama Callsign for the USAF TACC–NS (Tactical Air Control Center–North Sector). A Control Reporting Center (CRC) which controlled all fixed-wing aircraft over North Vietnam. Run by the 620th Tactical Control Squadron, USAF, located on Hill 621, Monkey Mountain, overlooking Da Nang Bay.

Patrol A tactical movement through an area by a small unit in an effort to gain information and or locate the enemy or show presence in an area as a means to control the area. Reconnaissance units used clandestine patrols to gain information through observation of the enemy.

Patrol Names Protocol A patrol was given a callsign or name to use on the radio, such as Team *Delicatessen*. The patrol leader was either the *Actual* or the *Six*. The radio operator usually just used the team's name when he transmitted. If anyone wanted to talk to the patrol leader, they would ask for *Delicatessen-Six* to come to the radio.

PAVN People's Army of North Vietnam, or North Vietnamese Army, or NVA.

Perimeter Distance around a given piece of ground or terrain such as a hill. Tactically speaking, the trace of a defensive line.

PF/RF Popular Force and Regional Force were South Vietnamese forces composed to fight and provide security at the village and hamlet level. They were local components of the ARVN.

PJs Pajamas, nickname for loose-fitting clothes worn by Vietnamese farmers and worn by VC.

PL Patrol Leader. Designate Marine who leads the patrol. The PL is based on experience and merit, not rank. PL is responsible for the mission and Marines on a patrol.

PLAF People's Liberation Armed Forces, or PAVN.

Platoon A small unit, usually infantry or reconnaissance, led by a lieutenant with small headquarters. Consisting of three subordinate units, squads in the infantry and teams in reconnaissance.

Point man Marine who walked first on a patrol, breaking brush, and watching for booby traps and the enemy. The most-dangerous and most-tiring position on a patrol.

Police or Police call To pick up trash in a specified area.

POSRep Position Report.

POW Prisoner of War.

PPB Platoon Patrol Base. A defined piece of terrain defended by a platoon and its CP, from which squad-size patrols conduct day and night patrolling. An economy-of-force measure to control through observation and patrolling a larger piece of terrain.

PRC-25 Portable Radio Communications-25, "Prick-25." AN/PRC-25, Army/Navy-Portable Radio Communication-25. Standard VHF radio carried by infantry and reconnaissance units in Vietnam.

PRC-47 Portable Radio Communications-47. AN/PRC-47 High Frequency Radio used for long-distance communications.

PRC-77 Portable Radio Communications-77. The replacement VHF radio for the PRC-25 was the AN/PRC-77 with KY-38 encrypted messages.

PRC-93 Portable Radio Communications-93. AN/PRC-93 was known as a survival radio. Handheld UHF AM transceiver. Intended for use by air–sea rescue units in the location and extraction of downed aircrew members or reconnaissance units.

Punji Pits Camouflaged hole with punji sticks.

Punji Sticks Sharpened bamboo sticks often tipped with poison, set in camouflaged hole for the purpose of penetrating U.S. boots and creating infection.

Que Son Huyen Que Son District. Southernmost district in Quang Tin Province. District is in the Que Son Valley from Hill 953 in the west to An Hoa city in the east.

Que Son Mountains Located 32 kilometers south of Da Nang, it is a west–east-running branch of the Annamite Mountain range that splits Laos and Vietnam north to south. It was a geographic dagger to the coast which the NVA used as a staging area and base camp. It also represented a natural geographic boundary between Quang Nam and Quang Tin provinces.

Quonset Hut Lightweight prefabricated structure of corrugated steel with a semicircular cross-section.

Radio Hanoi North Vietnamese radio station. English-speaking presenters that broadcast in the South with their propaganda messages, sometimes to specific units and specific individuals by name. Also played music.

Radio Relay An established post with radios and larger antennas whose purpose was to relay radio messages between two or more units. Marine Reconnaissance organizations established clandestine radio relays for short periods with one team as the relay and one team going deeper into enemy territory on the Laotian border. Semipermanent radio relays for specific operations, and permanent radio relays to service the TAOR. The 1st Reconnaissance Battalion's two primary permanent radio relays were Dong Den Mountain (Hill 868), overlooking Elephant Valley, and Ba Na Mountain, a former French summer-holiday resort west of Da Nang with the relay post on the first floor of a decaying French hotel.

Radio Watch A period of duty, 1–4 hours, where a Marine listens to a handset receiver for incoming radio traffic, then recording the messages and sending responses. In the field or in a command post, radio watches were maintained 24 hours, seven-days-a-week between units. Used for coordination and support request.

RAO Recon Area of Operations, was a TAOR for the Recon team, called "Haven" by Recon for short. The patrol leader owned the ground for coordination of movement and fire support inside the area.

Recon An act of conducting a physical reconnoitering or exploration of an area. A slang term or reference to a Reconnaissance team, platoon, company, or battalion.

Reconnaissance The act of inspecting or exploring a geographic area, especially one made to gather military intelligence in preparation of future operations.

Reconnaissance Battalion Composed of H&S Company and five letter companies, its primary mission was to conduct clandestine surveillance and intelligence gathering along with designate *Sting Ray* operations, raids, and other special mission. The 1st Reconnaissance Battalion supported 1st Marine Division from its base camp, Camp Reasoner.

REMF Rear Area Motherfucker. A person who hung out in the rear and avoided the bush. Also used as reference for rear-area staff.

Rocket Belt A description of the Da Nang Anti-Infiltration System consisting of plowed ground at the 122-mm rocket range. Keeping the NVA/VC outside the rocket belt meant a rocket launch from there did not have the range to impact the airport or seaport.

RoK Republic of Korea. South Korea provided the 2nd Korean Marine Brigade in Hoa An, allied with the United States during the Vietnam War.

Route 1 The national coast highway in Vietnam that ran from Hanoi in the north to Saigon in the south.

RPG Rocket-Propelled Grenade, see B-40 or RPG-2.

R&R Rest & Recreation. United States service personnel serving in the Vietnam War were entitled to seven days (R&R) leave during a tour of duty in Vietnam. R&R could be spent in one of several countries outside Vietnam. Married Marines got priority on Hawaii to meet their wife.

RTB Return To Base.

Rules of Engagement Published orders that set rules for behavior between combatants and combatants, and combatants and civilians. The RoE are the when, where, why, and how one is authorized to use weapons or supporting arms. In 1970, the 1st Marine Division RoEs were spelled out in Div Order P 003330.2A.

RVN Republic of Vietnam. Name for the South Vietnamese government.

SALUTE Report Size, Activity, Location, Unit/Uniform, Time, Equipment.

Sapper Soldiers trained in engineering, explosives, and reconnaissance. Specialized soldier and specialized unit in the North Vietnamese Army. Sappers were always Communist Party members for loyalty to the cause as sapper units worked alone away from the command. Trained for an extra three months after infantry training in North Vietnam at the Song Tay sapper academy before being sent south. Sappers were used as pathfinders through wire and obstacles to lead an attack on a base for the NVA. NVA divisions had one to three sapper battalions.

SCAMP Sensor Control And Management Platoon. A platoon under Division G-2 responsible for ground sensors and sensor readouts and analysis.

SCUBA Self-Contained Underwater Breathing Apparatus. SCUBA School for Vietnam Marines and Navy personnel was a four-week course conducted at the Naval Ship Repair Facility in Subic Bay, Philippines.

SFD Surprise firing device. Also known as a booby trap or, today, an IED (improvised explosive device).

Shackle Sheet Daily encryption pad where each calendar day was a new encryption sheet. People with the same pad and same day sheet could encode messages or shackle messages to each other.

SIGINT Acronym for Signals Intelligence. It is the collection of radio signals the enemy transmits. On Monkey Mountain, the USAF's Det- 2 of 6925 Security Group collected or intercepted signals over North Vietnam in HF and VHF.

SJA Staff Judge Advocate was the senior lawyer of a command, and his office was the SJA office within the command's headquarters. The office had a defense and prosecution section and a support section of clerks for trials.

SKS Rifle. An older rifle used by VC. Ten-round magazine, 7.62-mm round. SKS is semi-automatic, designed by Soviet small-arms designer Sergei Gavrilovich Simonov in 1945.

SLF Special Landing Force. An afloat Battalion Landing Team (BLT) that was III MEF/CINCPAC reserve force during the Vietnam War.

Snake and Nape "Snake" meant the tail fins to slow down a bomb to allow the delivery aircraft to drop from low level and get away without taking shrapnel from its own munitions. "Nape" was napalm canisters. A standard bombing loadout on Marine close air support was part 250-pound bombs and part napalm canisters, thus Snake and Nape bombing package.

SNCO Staff non-commissioned officer, enlisted grades E-6 to E-9. Gunnery Sergeant, Master and First Sergeant, Master Gunnery Sergeant, and Sergeant Major.

Sniper A trained expert-level military marksman issued with his own high-caliber rifle upon graduation from Sniper School. His billet is to scout and shoot at distance, providing overwatch for his assigned unit.

SOG Studies and Observations Group of MACV. Cover name for the highly classified Special Operations Group of MACV. A multiservice U.S. special-operations unit which conducted unconventional warfare throughout Southeast Asia.

SOP Standard Operating Procedures.

Spider Lake A manmade lake and USAID project with dam and irrigation aqueducts and channels for the Phu Loc Valley's rice paddies. Located 29 kilometers south of Da Nang, it was just north of and was overlooked by the Que Son Mountains and Recon OP Hill 425.

SPIE Rig Special Insertion Extraction Rig. Single, reinforced cargo strap 100 or 200 feet in length. Weighted at one end with eight D-Rings sewn into the strap. Attached to hellhole of a CH-46 helo, thrown to ground below for Recon Marines to attach themselves to and be extracted as external cargo at the weighted end and flown to a friendly LZ. Used for Emergency Extracts when no HLZ existed.

Spooky AC-47 aircraft developed by USAF. Transferred to RVN-AF in December 1969. Armed with three Gatling guns firing 7.62. Selectively, each gun could fire 50 or 100 rounds per minute. Three guns on one side could fire one bullet into every square yard of a football field in less than ten seconds. Every fifth round there was a red tracer. At night, it looked like three red lines coming out of the sky from 3,000 feet to the ground. It looked like dragon fire, hence the nickname "Puff, the Magic Dragon." The gunship carried 24,000 rounds of ammunition and 45 illumination flares.

Spot Report A six-line radio report template. A short report on your situation for conveying intelligence or information over the radio that is logged by date and time sent and received.

SRB Service Record Book. Book kept on every enlisted Marine to track his administration, pay, training, items issued.

SRC Surveillance and Reconnaissance Center. A coordination agency within III MAF whose function was to coordinate ground and air surveillance and reconnaissance efforts.

Sting Ray Recon mission and tactic where a Reconnaissance team employed supporting arms on enemy as primary function. Normally in the enemy's backyard. The 1st Recon Bn Order P03000.4, "Standard Operating Procedure for Sting Ray, and Clandestine Long Range Patrolling Operation."

Supporting Arms Generic term for any munition or fire that supports the infantry, such as mortars, artillery, aircraft strikes and naval gun fire.

Swiss seat A rope rappelling harness. An eight-foot strand of rappelling rope tied around one's legs and butt to make a harness seat to be attached to a rappelling rope. Used to rappel from cliffs or from helicopters.

TACC Tactical Air Command Center. A Marine Corps agency from which air operations and air-defense warning functions are directed. It normally is the senior agency of the MACCS (Marine Aviation Command and Control System) and also serves as the operational command post for a Marine Wing.

Tail-End Charlie Marine who walked or patrolled last in the formation of a patrol, walking backwards and responsible for covering the back trail and observing that a team was not followed.

TAOC Tactical Air Operations Center. Marine agency for real-time surveillance, direction, positive control, and navigational assistance for friendly aircraft. The TAOC performs real-time direction and control of all antiair-warfare operations, including manned interception and surface-to-air weapons. The TAOC in I Corps was on Monkey Mountain, callsign *Vice Squad*, and manned by MACS-4.

TAOR Tactical Area of Responsibility. A control-measure-designated geographic area owned by a unit that coordinates all fire and maneuver in its area.

TBS The Basic School. Located in Quantico, Virginia, it was a five-month course of infantry instruction for all Marine Corps 2nd lieutenants who must attend between commissioning and their first duty assignment. It prepared all 2nd lieutenants, regardless of specialty, to lead a rifle platoon.

Tet The name for the 12-day annual Lunar New Year, short for "Tet Nguyen Den," is Vietnam's most significant celebration. Across Vietnam during this time, families reunite and honor their ancestors while praying for prosperity in the new year. Occurring annually during February according to the lunar calendar.

TIC Troops in contact. A category indicating a small unit was engaged with the enemy with small arms.

ToT Time on target. A planning time for artillery or aircraft ordnance to hit a target. Used when firing or utilizing more than one asset to coordinate each time to impact at the same time on the same target from different ranges and locations.

TP Toilet Paper.

Tracer A direct-fire projectile, small arms or machine-gun bullet manufactured with a colored phosphorous coating so its trajectory, once fired, can be observed by the gunner to adjust his rounds more effectively onto target. U.S. small-arms tracers were red, while NVA/VC small-arms ammunition were green.

Tripwire A wire leading to a booby trap that serves as the firing trigger when tripped. Many times across trails, gaps in hedgerows, doors, or attached to objects or dead bodies to set off a SFDs.

UA Unauthorized Absence. AWOL (absence without leave) in Army.

UCMJ Uniformed Code of Military Justice is the foundation of the system of military justice of the armed forces of the United States. The UCMJ was established by the United States Congress in accordance with their constitutional authority, per Article I, Section 8 of the U.S. Constitution, which provides that "The Congress shall have Power … to make Rules for the Government and Regulation of the land and naval forces of the United States."

UDT Underwater Demolition Team.

UDT Shorts Tan swim trunks with cinch belt issued to SCUBA Divers and UDT swimmers.

Unit-One Medical kit designation of the Navy corpsman's medical kit containing first-aid supplies and surgical instruments.

USO United Services Organization. A leading charitable organization serving active-duty service members and military families.

VCI Vietnamese Communist Infrastructure or "Victor Charlie" were the South Vietnamese communist political organizations.

VC Viet Cong, short for VCI.

Vice Squad Callsign for the Marine TAOC (Tactical Air Operations Center) run by Marine Air Control Squadron-4. The callsign remains the squadron's callsign today, remembering its rich history controlling Marine, Navy, and Air Force fixed-wing aircraft over I Corps. The TAOC was located on Monkey Mountain overlooking Da Nang Bay.

Viet Cong Term used since late 1950s to describe insurgent forces in South Vietnam. The fighting wing of the NLF (National Liberation Front). Shortened version of "Viet Nam Cong San," or Vietnamese Communist.

Viet Minh Pronounced "Viet Ming." Often spelled "Vietminh." Short for "Viet Nam Doc Lap Dong Minh Hoi" which means the "League for the Independence of Vietnam." Formed in 1940 by Nationalist and Communist opposition to the French in the Indochina War, or French War as the Vietnamese called it, prior to the American War in Vietnam.

VMO Fixed-wing Marine Observation Squadron flying O-1 Birddogs and OV-10 Broncos. VMO-2 flew out of Da Nang and MMAF.

VNMC Vietnamese Marine Corps.

Warning Order A preliminary notice of an action or order that will take place in the future. A commander issues it to subordinate units as soon as they receive an order from a higher authority. The purpose of a warning order is to give subordinate units time to prepare for the action or order.

Water Bull Short for Water Buffalo, an animal of burden used to plow fields in Vietnam. Also Marine slang for a water trailer that was the source of water on OPs or locations without a well. M-149 Water Trailer, 400 gal.

WIA Wounded-in-Action.

Willie Pete Nickname for white phosphorus marking round, rocket, or grenade.

Wizz Wheel A circular device with wheels that allowed one to encrypt words by each letter to a random letter or number for a message. Having the same wheel and same day allowed for sender and receiver to encrypt messages.

WO Warrant Officer.

WP White phosphorus chemical used as a marking round for artillery, mortars, and aircraft. Or a type of hand grenade used for destroying equipment with high-intensity heat. Also called "Willie Pete" by Marines.

XM174 Experimental-174. A 40-mm automatic grenade launcher fed from an ammo can. Tripod-based grenade launcher based on M1919A4 machine gun and the M79 grenade launcher. It was a crew-served weapon. Drum canister with max capacity of 12 rounds. Capable of semi-automatic or automatic fire.

XO Executive Officer or second in command of a military unit. Normally responsible for the unit staff and the administrative/logistics functions of the unit.

782 Gear Shorthand for individual equipment a Marine wore in the field such as cartridge bet, shoulder harness, canteens. Form 782 was the 5 × 8 preprinted tracking and receipt card listing the gear issued to a Marine and held in Supply. A Marine signed for his gear and was expected to return it to Supply when his tour was complete.

Endnotes

Chapter 1

1 Memo for the record, JCS meeting, Chapman Papers, MCHC, at the 15 January 1969 meeting of the Joints Chiefs of Staff.

2 Charles R. Smith, *U.S. Marines in Vietnam, High Mobility and Standdown, 1969* (Washington, D.C.: History and Museums Division, Headquarters, U.S. Marine Corps, 1988), 6, 380.

3 Ibid., 82.

Chapter 2

1 Charles R. Smith, *U.S. Marines in Vietnam, High Mobility and Standdown, 1969* (Washington, D.C.: History and Museums Division, Headquarters, U.S. Marine Corps, 1988), 286.

2 Robert A. Simonsen, *Every Marine: 1968 Vietnam, A Battle for Go Noi Island* (Westminster, Maryland: Heritage Books, 2008), 135.

3 Smith, *U.S. Marines in Vietnam*, 175.

4 NIC Report 208/68, 26 February '68, NIC Field Exploitation Team, National Interrogation Center (NIC). The intelligence summary is taken from a declassified report of the NIC. It was the result of interrogation activities conducted under the joint auspices of the South Vietnamese, Central Intelligence Organization (CIO) and the US Central Intelligence Agency (CIA) with the participation of Detachment 6, 499th Special Activities Group (USAF) with interrogation conducted by NIC Field Exploitation Team in Da Nang, February 1968.

5 Jack Shulimson, et al, *U.S. Marines in Vietnam: The Defining Year, 1968* (Washington, D.C.: History & Museums Division Headquarters, U.S. Marine Corps, 1997), 328.

6 Simonsen, *Every Marine*, 137–38.

7 Shulimson, *U.S. Marines in Vietnam*, 338.

8 Simonsen, *Every Marine*, 139.

9 Ibid., 140.

10 GRUNT: General Replacement UN-Trained, referred to drafts of men headed to France in WWI for the Allies. A term of endearment applied to Marine infantry.

11 Simonsen, *Every Marine*, 144.

12 Shulimson, *U.S. Marines in Vietnam*, 343.

13 Ibid., 436.

14 Author was deployed with Lima Company, 3/26, as the lieutenant responsible for Hai Van Pass road security sector of National Route 1.

15 Smith, *U.S. Marines in Vietnam*, 84.

16 Operations Order # 442-68, Patrol: *Parallel Bars*, Bravo 3rd Plt, 25 June–1 July '68, Msg: Op immediate 1stMarDiv (Rein): 1st Recon Bn (Rein) SitRep # 176-68 250001H to 252400H.

17 Operations Order # 24-69, Patrol: *Empire State-A*, Delta 1st Plt, 10 Jan '69.

18 Smith, *U.S. Marines in Vietnam*, 182.

19 G. R. Willson, Lt. Col. (Ret.), https://valor.militarytimes.com/hero/24030.

20 Operations Order # 24-69.

21 Ibid.

22 Ibid.

23 Ibid.

24 Msg: Op immediate 1stMarDiv (Rein):1st Recon Bn (Rein) SitRep # 10-69; 100001H to 102400H.

25 Jim Unsworth, interviews with author, 15 Dec 2023–Aug 2024.

26 Operations Order # 23-69, Patrol: *Fig Newton*, Delta 1st Plt, 8–9 Jan '69.

27 Operations Order # 22-69, Patrol: *Vesper Bells*, Delta 1st Recon Bn, Co, 7–11 Jan '69.

28 Operations Order # 21-69, Patrol: *Paddy Shell*, Charlie 1st Recon Bn, 8–12 Jan '69.

29 Operations Order # 39-69, Patrol: *War Cloud*, Charlie 1st Recon Bn, 15–16 Jan '69.

30 Operations Order # 52-69, Patrol: *Empire State*, Delta 1st Plt, 19–26 Jan '69.

31 Ibid.

32 Ibid.

33 Author's personal experience digging on Hill 119.
34 Operations Order # 52-69.
35 Ibid.
36 Ibid.
37 Ibid.
38 Ibid.
39 Ibid.
40 Operations Order # 72-69, Patrol: *Vesper Bells*, Delta 1st Plt, 26 Jan–2 Feb '69.
41 Operations Order # 52-69.
42 Ibid.
43 Operations Order # 72-69.
44 Ibid.
45 Ibid.
46 Smith, *U.S. Marines in Vietnam*, 91.
47 Ibid.
48 Ibid.
49 Operations Order # 72-69.
50 Ibid.
51 Ibid.
52 Ibid.
53 Ibid.

Chapter 3

1 United States Marine Corps, Command Chronologies for III MAF, FMF, Feb '69, 11.
2 1st Reconnaissance Battalion, Command Chronology, Feb 1969, dated 2 March 1969.
3 Operations Order # 39-69, Patrol: *War Cloud*, Charlie 1st Recon Bn, 15–16 Jan '69.
4 Art Weber, interview with author, 10 Mar 2024.
5 Operations Order # 39-69.
6 Art Weber, 10 Mar 2024.
7 Ibid.
8 1st Reconnaissance Battalion, Command Chronology, Feb 1969, dated 2 March 1969.
9 Ibid.
10 Ibid.
11 Operations Order # 90-69, Patrol: *Rudder*, Delta Plt, 2–11 Feb '69.
12 Ibid.
13 Ibid.
14 Ibid.
15 Jim Unsworth, interviews with author, 15 Dec 2023–Aug 2024.
16 Operations Order # 90-69.
17 Ibid.
18 Ibid.
19 Ibid.
20 Ibid.
21 Operations Order # 110-69, Patrol: *Mad Hatter*, Delta Plt, 11–25 Feb '69.
22 Ibid.
23 Ibid.
24 Ibid.
25 Ibid.
26 Ibid.
27 Ibid.
28 Ibid.
29 Ibid.
30 Ibid.
31 Ibid.
32 Ibid.
33 Ibid.
34 Ibid.
35 Ibid.
36 Ibid.
37 Operations Order # 148-69, Patrol: *Aunt Mable*, Delta 2nd Plt, 24 Feb–9 Mar '69.

Chapter 4

1 Operation Order # 148-69, Patrol: *Aunt Mable*, Delta 2nd Plt, 24 Feb–9 Mar '69.
2 Ibid.
3 Ibid.
4 Ibid.
5 Ibid.
6 Operations Order # 184-69, Patrol: *Night Scholar*, Delta 1st Plt, 9–26 Mar '69.

Chapter 5

1 Richard D. Coffelt, *The Coffelt Database of Vietnam casualties*, at www.coffeltdatabase.org.
2 John T. Correll, "The Shadow War in Cambodia," *Air Force Magazine*, Jan 2018.
3 Charles R. Smith, *U.S. Marines in Vietnam, High Mobility and Standdown, 1969* (Washington, D.C.: History and Museums Division, Headquarters, U.S. Marine Corps, 1988), 355.
4 Ibid.
5 1st Recon Bn Command Chronology, Mar '69.
6 Ibid.
7 Jim Unsworth, interviews with author, 15 Dec 2023–Aug 2024.
8 Operations Order # 184-69, Patrol: *Night Scholar*, Delta 1st Plt, 9–26 Mar '69.

9 Ibid.
10 Ibid.
11 Jim Unsworth, 15 Dec 2023–Aug 2024.
12 Operations Order # 184-69.
13 Ibid.
14 Andy Unsworth, interview with author, 25 Feb 2023; Jim Unsworth, 15 Dec 2023–Aug 2024.
15 Ibid.
16 Operations Order # 184-6.
17 Ibid.
18 Jim Unsworth, 15 Dec 2023–Aug 2024.
19 Operations Order # 184-69.
20 Ibid.
21 Ibid.
22 Ibid.
23 Ibid.
24 Ibid.
25 Ibid.
26 Operations Order # 231-69, Patrol: *Grim Reaper*; Delta 3rd Plt, 24 Mar–8 Apr '69.
27 Ibid.
28 Ibid.
29 Ibid.
30 Ibid.
31 Ibid.
32 Operations Order # 270-69, Patrol: *Pennywise*, Delta 1st Recon Bn, 5 Apr '69.
33 Operations Order # 231-69.
34 Operations Order # 270-69.
35 Operations Order # 231-69.
36 Operations Order # 270-69.
37 Operations Order # 231-69.
38 John Mann, interviews with author, 15 Dec 2023 and Aug 2024.
39 1st Recon Bn Command Chronology, May '69.
40 John Mann, 15 Dec 2023 and Aug 2024.

Chapter 6

1 "Vietnamization," 3 April 1969, *On This Day*, at www.onthisday.com/events/date/1969/april.
2 "Anti-war demonstrations," 5 April 1969, *On This Day*, at www.onthisday.com/events/date/1969/april.
3 Charles R. Smith, *U.S. Marines in Vietnam, High Mobility and Standdown, 1969* (Washington, D.C.: History and Museums Division, Headquarters, U.S. Marine Corps, 1988), 355.
4 Ibid.
5 1st Recon Bn Command Chronology, April 1969.
6 Ibid.
7 Art Weber, interview with author, 10 Mar 2024.
8 1st Recon Bn Command Chronology, April 1969.
9 Operations Order # 287-69, Patrol: *Hanover Sue*, Delta 1st Recon Bn, 8–25 Apr '69.
10 Operations Order # 231-69, Patrol: *Grim Reaper*, Delta 3rd Plt, 24 Mar–8 Apr '69.
11 Jim Unsworth, interviews with author, 15 Dec 2023–Aug 2024.
12 Operations Order # 287-69
13 Ibid.
14 Ibid.
15 Ibid.
16 Ibid.
17 Ibid.
18 Ibid.
19 Ibid.
20 Ibid.
21 Ibid.
22 Ibid.
23 Ibid.
24 Ibid.
25 Ibid.
26 Ibid.
27 Operations Order # 352-69, Patrol: *Bag Shaw*, Delta 1st Plt, 24 Apr–13 May '69.
28 Ibid.
29 Jim Unsworth, 15 Dec 2023–Aug 2024.
30 Operations Order # 352-69.
31 Ibid.
32 Ibid.
33 Ibid.
34 Ibid.
35 Ibid.

Chapter 7

1 "6 May," *On This Day*, at www.onthisday.com/events/date/may.
2 Charles R. Smith, *U.S. Marines in Vietnam, High Mobility and Standdown, 1969* (Washington, D.C.: History and Museums Division, Headquarters, U.S. Marine Corps, 1988), 355.
3 "20 May," *On This Day*, at www.onthisday.com/events/date/may.
4 Smith, *U.S. Marines in Vietnam*, 175.
5 Ibid., 337.
6 Ibid., 187.
7 1st Recon Bn Command Chronology, May '69.
8 Ibid; Art Weber, interview with author, 10 Mar 2024.

9 1st Recon Bn Command Chronology, May '69.
10 Ibid.
11 Operations Order # 352-69, Patrol: *Bag Shaw*, Delta 1st Plt, 24 Apr–13 May '69.
12 Operations Order # 401-69, Patrol: *Segment*, Delta 3rd Plt, 13–27 May '69.
13 Jim Unsworth, interviews with author, 15 Dec 2023–Aug 2024.
14 Operations Order # 401-69.
15 Ibid.
16 Ibid.
17 Ibid.
18 Ibid.
19 Ibid.
20 Ibid.
21 Operations Order # 453-69, Patrol: *Barkeep*, Delta 2nd Plt, 27 May–12 June '69.
22 Ibid.
23 Ibid.
24 Ibid.
25 Ibid.
26 An OV-10a Bronco a twin engine aircraft from Marine Observation Squadron Two (VMO-2).
27 Ibid.
28 Ibid.
29 Ibid.
30 Ibid.
31 Jim Unsworth, 15 Dec 2023–Aug 2024.
32 Operations Order # 453-69.
33 Ibid.
34 Jim Unsworth, 15 Dec 2023–Aug 2024.
35 Operations Order # 453-69.
36 Ibid.
37 Jim Unsworth, 15 Dec 2023–Aug 2024.

Chapter 8

1 Charles R. Smith, *U.S. Marines in Vietnam, High Mobility and Standdown, 1969* (Washington, D.C.: History and Museums Division, Headquarters, U.S. Marine Corps, 1988), 355.
2 Ibid.
3 Ibid., 178.
4 1st Recon Bn Command Chronology, June '69.
5 Smith, *U.S. Marines in Vietnam*, Chapter 11.
6 Operations Order # 484-69, Patrol: *Senator*, Echo Plt, 5–19 June '69.
7 Ibid.
8 Ibid.
9 Jim Unsworth, interviews with author, 15 Dec 2023–Aug 2024.
10 Ibid.
11 Ibid.
12 Operations Order # 453-69, Patrol: *Barkeep*, Delta 2nd Plt, 27 May–12 June '69.
13 Operations Order # 506-69, Patrol: *Delivery Boy/ Defend*, Delta 1st Plt, 12–24 June '69.
14 Jim Unsworth, 15 Dec 2023–Aug 2024.
15 Operations Order # 484-69, Patrol: *Senator*, Echo Plt, 5–19 June '69.
16 Ibid.
17 Operations Order # 506-69.
18 Ibid.
19 Jim Unsworth, 15 Dec 2023–Aug 2024.
20 Operations Order # 527-69, Patrol: *May Fly*, Delta 3rd Plt, 21 June '69.
21 "Snake"—Mk.82 Snake Eye, a general-purpose 500-pound bomb fitted with a tail-retarding device to slow the bomb's descent so a low-flying aircraft is not caught in the ensuing explosion. "Nape" canister-filled napalm, the incendiary consisting of a gelling agent and a volatile petrochemical like diesel.
22 Ibid.
23 Operations Order # 506-69.
24 Operations Order # 453-69.
25 Smith, *U.S. Marines in Vietnam*, 178.
26 Operations Order # 453-69.
27 Ibid.
28 Ibid.
29 Ibid.
30 Ibid.
31 Ibid.
32 Ibid.
33 Ibid.
34 Ibid.
35 Ibid.

Chapter 9

1 "20 July 1969," *National Archives*, at www.archives.gov/publications/prologue/2003/summer/20.
2 "25 July 1969," *This Day in History*, at www.history.com/this-day-in-history/the-nixon-doctrine-is-announced.
3 Ibid.
4 Charles R. Smith, *U.S. Marines in Vietnam, High Mobility and Standdown, 1969* (Washington, D.C.: History and Museums Division, Headquarters, U.S. Marine Corps, 1988), 178, 356.

5 Ibid.
6 Ibid., 178, 183.
7 Ibid.
8 1st Recon Bn Command Chronology, July 1969.
9 Ibid.
10 Art Weber, interview with author, 2 Aug 1969.
11 1st Recon Bn Command Chronology, July 1969
12 Jim Hackett, interview with author, 14 Dec 2023.
13 Ibid.
14 Ibid.
15 Ibid.
16 Operations Order # 586-69, Patrol: *Beech Nut*, Delta 2nd Plt, 4–14 July '69.
17 Ibid.
18 Ibid.
19 Ibid.
20 Ibid.
21 Ibid.
22 Ibid.
23 Smith, *U.S. Marines in Vietnam*, 178, 182.
24 Operations Order # 586-69.
25 Ibid.
26 Ibid.
27 Ibid.
28 Ibid.
29 Ibid.
30 Operations Order # 620-69, Patrol: *Beech Nut*, Delta, 1st Plt, 14–26 July, OP Hill 119, 1st Recon Bn, Da Nang, RVN, 120745H Jun 1969.
31 1st Recon Bn Command Chronology, July '69.
32 Ibid.
33 Jim Hackett, 14 Dec 2023.
34 Operations Order # 655-69, Patrol: *Parallel Bars,* Delta 3rd Plt, 26 Jul–5 Aug, 1st Recon Bn, Da Nang, RVN, 210815H July 1969 (1Lt Pfeiffer, Hill 119 OP, ISO Op *Pipestone Canyon*).
35 Ibid.
36 Ibid.
37 Ibid.
38 Ibid.
39 Ibid.
40 Ibid.
41 Ibid.
42 Ibid.

Chapter 10

1 "August 1968," *On This Day*, at www.onthisday.com/events/date/1968/august.
2 Charles R. Smith, *U.S. Marines in Vietnam, High Mobility and Standdown, 1969* (Washington, D.C.: History and Museums Division, Headquarters, U.S. Marine Corps, 1988), 178, 356.
3 Ibid. 187.
4 Ibid. 188.
5 1st Recon Bn Command Chronology, Aug '69.
6 Ibid.
7 Operations Order # 688-69, Patrol: *Spillway*, Delta 2nd Plt, 4–14 Aug '69.
8 Ibid.
9 Ibid.
10 Ibid.
11 Ibid.
12 Operations Order # 728-69, Patrol: *Spillway*, Delta 1st Plt, 15–25 Aug '69.
13 John "Jack" Holly, interviews with author, 2023 and March 2024.
14 Ibid.
15 Operations Order # 728-69.
16 Ibid.
17 Ibid.
18 Operations Order # 753-69, Patrol: *Road Test*, Bravo 1st Plt, 22–25 Aug '69.
19 Operations Order # 728-69.
20 Operations Order # 754-69, Patrol: *Spillway*, Delta 3rd Plt, 23 Aug–4 Sept '69.
21 Ibid.
22 Ibid.
23 Ibid.
24 Ibid.
25 Ibid.
26 Ibid.
27 Ibid.
28 Operations Order # 741-69, Patrol: *Turf Club*, Echo 3rd Plt, 21–31 Aug '69.
29 Ibid.
30 Operations Order # 754-69, Patrol: *Spillway*, Delta 3rd Plt, 23 Aug–4 Sept '69.
31 Operations Order # 741-69.
32 Ibid.
33 Operations Order # 754-69.
34 Ibid.
35 Ibid.
36 Dennis Swick, interview with author, Feb 2024.
37 Ibid.
38 Robert Grossman, interview with author, 29 Feb 2024.
39 Ibid.
40 Ibid; Dennis Swick, Feb 2024.

41 Operations Order # 754-69.
42 Dennis Swick, Feb 2024.
43 Ibid.
44 Operations Order # 754-69.
45 Dennis Swick, Feb 2024.
46 Operations Order # 754-69.
47 Ibid.
48 Jim Unsworth, interviews with author, 15 Dec 2023–Aug 2024.
49 Robert Grossman, 29 Feb 2024.
50 Dennis Swick, Feb 2024.
51 Ibid.
52 Operations Order # 787-69, Patrol: Spillway, Delta 2nd Plt, 4–14 Sept '69.
53 Jim Unsworth, 15 Dec 2023–Aug 2024.

Chapter 11

1 "4 Sept '69," www.history.com. https://www.history.com/this-day-in-history/september-4/radio-hanoi-announces-the-death-of-ho-chi-minh. See also Charles R. Smith, *U.S. Marines in Vietnam, High Mobility and Standdown, 1969* (Washington, D.C.: History and Museums Division, Headquarters, U.S. Marine Corps, 1988), 356.
2 "Ton Duc Thang," Historic Figures, BBC, at www.bbc.co.uk/history/historic_figures. https://www.britannica.com/biography/Ton-Duc-Thang. See also "Ton Duc Thang, Leader in Vietnam Since 1969." *The New York Times*. 30 March 1980. https://www.nytimes.com/1980/03/30/archives/ton-duc-thang-leader-in-vietnam-since-1969.html; and Truong Nhu Tang, David Chanoff, Doan van Toai, *A Viet Cong Memoir*, Vintage Books, 1986, 262–63.
3 "Draft Lottery Is Held for 1970—19–26-Year Olds Born on Sept. 14 head Callup List," *Pittsburgh Post-Gazette*, 3 December 1969, 1.
4 Charles R. Smith, *U.S. Marines in Vietnam, High Mobility and Standdown, 1969* (Washington, D.C.: History and Museums Division, Headquarters, U.S. Marine Corps, 1988), 356.
5 Ibid; "End Color Line, Marines Told," *Pittsburgh Post-Gazette*, 3 September 1969, 1.
6 1st Recon Bn Command Chronology, Sept '69.
7 Ibid.
8 Ibid.
9 Ibid.
10 Ibid.
11 Operations Order # 787-69, Patrol: *Spillway*, Delta 2nd Plt, 4–14 Sept '69.
12 Ibid.
13 Jim Unsworth, interviews with author, 15 Dec 2023–Aug 2024.
14 Operations Order # 787-69.
15 Ibid.
16 Ibid.
17 Ibid.
18 Operations Order # 820-69, Patrol: *Rummage*, Delta 1st Plt, 14–24 Sept '69.
19 Ibid.
20 Ibid.
21 Ibid.
22 Jim Unsworth, 15 Dec 2023–Aug 2024.
23 Operations Order # 849-69, Patrol: *Rummage*, Delta 3rd Plt, 24 Sept–9 Oct '69.
24 Ibid.
25 Operations Order # 844-69, Patrol: *Impressive*, Alpha 1st Recon Bn, 22 Sept–3 Oct '69.
26 Operations Order # 849-69.
27 Ibid.

Chapter 12

1 "Guard Called to Quell Chicago Riots," *Pittsburgh Post-Gazette*, 10 October 1969, 1.
2 Jeremi Suri, "The Nukes of October: Richard Nixon's Secret Plan to Bring Peace to Vietnam," *WIRED* magazine, 25 February 2008.
3 "MPs Repulse Invasion at Ft. Dix," *Pittsburgh Post-Gazette,* 13 October 1969, 1.
4 David L. Anderson, *The Columbia Guide to the Vietnam War* (New York: Columbia University Press, 2002), 143.
5 Charles R. Smith, *U.S. Marines in Vietnam, High Mobility and Standdown, 1969* (Washington, D.C.: History and Museums Division, Headquarters, U.S. Marine Corps, 1988), 252.
6 1st Recon Bn Command Chronology, Oct '69.
7 Ibid.
8 Ibid.
9 1st Recon. Bn Command Chronology, Oct '69.
10 Ibid.
11 Operations Order # 849-69, Patrol: *Rummage*, Delta 3rd Plt, 24 Sept–9 Oct '69.
12 Ibid.
13 Operations Order # 873-69, Patrol: *Rummage*, Delta 2nd Plt, 8–19 Oct '69.
14 Operations Order # 849-69.
15 Operations Order # 873-69.
16 Ibid.

17 Ibid.
18 Ibid.
19 Ibid.
20 Ibid.
21 Jim Unsworth, interviews with author, 15 Dec 2023–Aug 2024.
22 Operations Order #902-69, Patrol: *War Cloud*, Alpha Co 3rd Plt, 20–23 Oct '69, 1st Recon Bn, Da Nang, RVN, 161100H Oct 1969 (1Lt W. C. Gregson, WIA).
23 Ibid.
24 Ibid.
25 W. C. Gregson, interview with author, Mar 2024.
26 Smith, *U.S. Marines in Vietnam*, 248.
27 Ibid.
28 Ibid.
29 11th Marines Command Chronology # 0155-69, 1–31 Oct '69.
30 Mark Bayuk, interviews with author, Sept 2023 and Apr 2024.
31 Ibid.
32 Smith, *U.S. Marines in Vietnam*, 248–49.
33 Mark Bayuk, Sept 2023 and Apr 2024.
34 11th Marines Command Chronology # 0155-69; Mark Bayuk, Sept 2023 and Apr 2024.
35 Operations Order # 906-69, Patrol: *Rummage*, Delta 1st Plt, 19–29 Oct '69.
36 Ibid.
37 Ibid.
38 Ibid.
39 Operations Order # 910-69, Patrol: *Big Flower*, Charlie 2nd Plt, 21–23 Oct '69.
40 Ibid.
41 Operations Order # 906-69.
42 Ibid.
43 Ibid.
44 Ibid.
45 Ibid.
46 Ibid.
47 Operations Order # 929-69, Patrol: *Rummage*, Delta 1st Plt, 29 Oct–10 Nov '69.

Chapter 13

1 "Nixon Bars Running Out Now: Sticking To Own Viet Timetable," *Pittsburgh Press*, 4 November 1969, 1.
2 Seymour M. Hersh, "Officer Murdered 109, Army Charges," *Detroit Free Press*, 13 November 1969, 1.
3 Ron Young. *Crossing Boundaries in the Americas, Vietnam, and the Middle East: A Memoir* (2014), 95.
4 "Stop Trials of GIs for VIET Killings," *UPI Wire*, 29/30 November 1969. Senator Henry Bellman (R-OK) introduces legislation in the Senate to prohibit trials of GIs who kill Vietnamese.
5 Charles R. Smith, *U.S. Marines in Vietnam, High Mobility and Standdown, 1969* (Washington, D.C.: History and Museums Division, Headquarters, U.S. Marine Corps, 1988), 356.
6 Ibid., 357.
7 11th Marines Command Chronology # 0155-69, 1–31 Oct '69.
8 Ibid., 1.
9 Ibid., 5.
10 Sam Adams, *War of Numbers, An Intelligence Memoir of the Vietnam War's Uncounted Enemy* (Lebanon, New Hampshire: Steerforth Press, 1994), 215. This is the definitive account of this approach.
11 Ibid.
12 11th Marines Command Chronology # 0155-69.
13 1st Recon Bn Command Chronology, Nov '69.
14 Ibid.
15 Ibid.
16 Operations Order # 929-69, Patrol: *Rummage*, Delta 1st Plt, 29 Oct–10 Nov '69.
17 Ibid.
18 G. G. "Jerry" Spolter, interviews with author, 2024.
19 Operations Order # 929-69.
20 Ibid.
21 Ibid.
22 Ibid.
23 Ibid.
24 Ibid.
25 Mark Bayuk, correspondence with author, Sept 2023–April 2024.
26 Operations Order # 929-69.
27 Mark Bayuk, Sept 2023–April 2024.
28 Operations Order # 929-69.
29 Thomas Martin, interview with author, 10 Dec 2023.
30 Operations Order # 952-69, Patrol: *Rummage/Asparagus*, Delta 3rd Plt, 9–20 Nov '69.
31 Thurman Mullins, interview with author, Oct 2023.
32 Operations Order # 929-69.
33 Thomas Martin, 10 Dec 2023.
34 Operations Order # 952-69, Patrol: *Rummage/Asparagus*, Delta 3rd Plt, 9–20 Nov '69.
35 Mark Bayuk, Sept 2023–April 2024.

36 Operations Order # 952-69, Patrol: *Rummage/ Asparagus*, Delta 3rd Plt, 9–20 Nov '69.
37 Ibid.
38 Ibid.
39 Ibid.
40 Ibid.
41 Ibid.
42 11th Marines Command Chronology # 0155-69.
43 Operations Order # 952-69.
44 Ibid.
45 Ibid.
46 Ibid.
47 Operations Order # 989-69, Patrol: *Asparagus*, Delta 1st Plt, 20 Nov–1 Dec '69.
48 Mark Bayuk, Sept 2023–April 2024.
49 Operations Order # 989-69.
50 Ibid.
51 Thomas Martin, 10 Dec 2023.
52 Operations Order # 989-69.
53 Ibid.
54 Operations Order # 1016-69, Patrol: *Asparagus*, Delta 3rd Plt, 1–16 Dec '69.

Chapter 14

1 Charles R. Smith, *U.S. Marines in Vietnam, High Mobility and Standdown, 1969* (Washington, D.C.: History and Museums Division, Headquarters, U.S. Marine Corps, 1988), 357.
2 "Texas Nips Arkansas, 15–14," *Pittsburgh Press*, 7 December 1969, 4; and Dan Jenkins "Texas by an eyelash," *Sports Illustrated*, 15 December 1969, 20.
3 Smith, *U.S. Marines in Vietnam*, 357.
4 Ibid.
5 Author's personal notes, Hai Van Pass, November 1969.
6 W. C. "Bill" Drumright, interview with author, May 2001.
7 Ibid.
8 Ibid.
9 Michael C. Hodgins, *Reluctant Warrior: A Marine's True Story of Duty and Heroism in Vietnam* (New York: Ballantine Books, 1996), Introduction.
10 W. C. "Bill" Drumright, May 2001.
11 1st Recon Bn Command Chronology, Dec '69.
12 Ibid.
13 Ibid.
14 Ibid.
15 Eugene "Gene" Marshall, interview with author, 26–27 Feb 2024.
16 1st Recon Bn Command Chronology, Dec '69.
17 Operations Order # 1016-69, Patrol: *Asparagus*, Delta 3rd Plt, 1–16 Dec '69.
18 Mark Bayuk, correspondence with author, Sept 2023–April 2024.
19 Operations Order # 1016-69.
20 Eugene "Gene" Marshall, 26–27 Feb 2024.
21 Ibid.
22 Operations Order # 1016-69.
23 Eugene "Gene" Marshall, 26–27 Feb 2024.
24 Ibid.
25 Ibid.
26 Durwood "Butch" Waddill, interview with author, 11 May 2016.
27 Dennis Swick, interview with author, Feb 2024.
28 Operations Order # 1016-69.
29 Ibid.
30 Ibid.
31 Operations Order # 1069-69, Patrol: *Durham*, Delta 2nd Plt, 16–29 Dec '69.
32 Earlene Parks (Garry's wife), correspondence with author, Jan–Mar 2024.
33 Ibid.
34 Garry Parks, correspondence with author, 1981–2002.
35 B. Parker Miller, interview with author, 18–20 Feb 2024.
36 1st Recon Bn Command Chronology, Dec 1969.
37 B. Parker Miller, 18–20 Feb 2024.
38 Ibid.
39 Operations Order # 1069-69.
40 Author's knowledge from living in the cot next to Parks in Delta Co officers' hut, Camp Reasoner, 1970.
41 Operations Order # 1069-69.
42 Garry Parks, 1981–2002.
43 Mark Bayuk, Sept 2023–April 2024.
44 Operations Order # 1069-69.
45 Mark Bayuk, Sept 2023–Apr 2024.
46 Operations Order # 1069-69.
47 Garry Parks, 1981–2002.
48 Ibid.
49 Mark Bayuk, correspondence Sept 2023–Apr 2024.
50 Ibid.
51 Thurman Mullins, correspondence with author, Feb–Oct 2023.
52 Ibid.
53 Mark Bayuk, Sept 2023–Apr 2024.
54 Ibid.
55 Thurman Mullins, Feb–Oct 2023.

56 Operations Order # 1069-69.
57 Ibid.
58 Ibid.
59 Operations Order # 1096-69, Patrol: *Durham*, Delta 1st Plt, 29 Dec–11 Jan '70.
60 Mark Bayuk, Sept 2023–Apr 2024.
61 Durwood "Butch" Waddill, interview with author, 11 May 2016.
62 Ibid.
63 Thomas Martin, inbterview with author, 10 Dec 2023.
64 Operations Order # 1096-69.
65 Mark Bayuk, Sept 2023–Apr 2024.
66 Operations Order # 1096-69.
67 Ibid.
68 Durwood "Butch" Waddill, 11 May 2016.
69 Ibid.

Chapter 15

1 For an insightful study of III MAF as a headquarters, see Michael Morris's *Corps Competency? III Marine Amphibious Force Headquarters in Vietnam*, University Press of Kansas, 2024.
2 Graham A. Cosmas and Lt. Col. Terrence P. Murray, USMC, *U.S. Marines in Vietnam: Vietnamization and Redeployment 1970–1971* (Washington, D.C.: History & Museum Division Headquarters, U.S. Marine Corps, 1986).
3 Ibid.
4 Ibid.
5 Ibid.
6 1st Recon Bn Command Chronology, Jan '70.
7 Ibid.
8 Thomas Martin, interview with author, 10 Dec 2023.
9 W. C. "Chip" Gregson, interview with author, Mar 2024.
10 Thomas Martin, 10 Dec 2023.
11 Ibid.
12 Durwood "Butch" Waddill, interview with author, 11 May 2016.
13 Operations Order # 1096-69, Patrol: *Durham*, Delta 1st Plt, 29 Dec–11 Jan '70.
14 Ibid.
15 Ibid.
16 Mark Bayuk, interview with author, Sept 2023–Apr 2024.
17 Durwood "Butch" Waddill, 11 May 2016.
18 Operations Order # 1096-69.
19 W. C. "Chip" Gregson, Mar 2024.
20 Operations Order # 0036-70, Patrol: *Pennywise*, Delta 2nd Plt, 10–12 Jan '70.
21 Operations Order # 0040-70, Patrol: *Durham*, Delta 4th Plt, 11–25 Jan '70.
22 Ibid.
23 Thomas Martin, 10 Dec 2023.
24 W. C. "Chip" Gregson, March 2024.
25 Rene Regalot, interviews with author, 2020–24.
26 Ibid.
27 W. "Rabbit" Hare, interview with author, Jul 2020.
28 Ibid.
29 W. C. "Chip," Gregson, March 2024.
30 Statistics derived from Operations Order # 906-69, Patrol: *Rummage*, Delta 1st Plt, 19–29 Oct '69; and Operations Order # 929-69, Patrol: *Rummage*, Delta 1st Plt, 29 Oct–10 Nov '69.
31 Statistics derived from Operations Order # 952-69, Patrol: *Rummage/Asparagus*, Delta 3rd Plt, 9–20 Nov '69; Operations Order # 989-69, Patrol: *Asparagus*, Delta 1st Plt, 20 Nov–1 Dec '69; Operations Order # 1016-69, Patrol: *Asparagus*, Delta 3rd Plt, 1–16 Dec '69; Operations Order # 1069-69, Patrol: *Durham*, Delta 2nd Plt, 16–29 Dec '69; and Operations Order # 1096-69, Patrol: *Durham*, Delta 1st Plt, 29 Dec–11 Jan '70.
32 Rene Regalot, 2020–24.
33 Ibid.
34 Operations Order # 0040-70.
35 Ibid.
36 Ibid.
37 The headspace is the amount of play ("room") a cartridge has in the chamber. A nickel is a good field expedient to set the headspace on a 50-cal.
38 Ibid.
39 Ibid.
40 Ibid.
41 Ibid.
42 Operations Order # 0048-70, Patrol: *Spoonbill*, Delta 3rd Plt, 12–14 Jan '70.
43 Ibid.
44 Tom McAdams, interview with author, 21 Feb and 19 Mar 2024.
45 Operations Order # 0040-70.
46 Mark Bayuk, Sept 2023–Apr 2024.
47 Rene Regalot, 2020–24.
48 Ibid.
49 J. J. Grace, interview with Mark Bayuk, 1989.
50 Rene Regalot, 2020–2024.
51 Ibid.

52 Operation Order # 0040-70.
53 Ibid.
54 Ibid.
55 Tom McAdams, 21 Feb and 19 Mar 2024.
56 Mark Bayuk, Sept 2023–Apr 2024.
57 Ibid; Frank Thomas, interview with author, Feb 2024.
58 Thomas Martin, 10 Dec 2023.
59 Operation Order # 0040-70.
60 Ibid.
61 Mark Bayuk, correspondence with author, Sept 2023–April 2024.
62 Ibid.
63 Operations Order # 0040-70.
64 Ibid.
65 Sergeant "Butch" Harvey of Delta Company should not be confused with Lieutenant "Butch" Harvey of 3rd Recon and later Bravo Company, 1st Recon. Both superior Marines, the latter was killed on 18 November 1970 as the extract officer on the Team *Rush Act* extract that also killed the battalion commander, Lieutenant Colonel William G. Leftwich.
66 J. J. Grace, 1989.
67 W. C. "Wild Bill" Drumright, interview with author, May 2001.
68 Operations Order # 0040-70.
69 Author's personal notes, counterintelligence debrief, February 1970, Camp Reasoner, RVN.
70 2nd Bn Command Chronology, January 1970.
71 Thomas Martin, 10 Dec 2023.
72 Only enough fuel to get home, called "Bingo."
73 Operations Order # 0074-70, Patrol: *Razorbill*, Delta 1st Plt, 1st Team, 19–24 Jan, 1st Recon Bn, Da Nang, RVN; 171225H Jan '70 (SSgt Mushett, insert Hill 425, emergency extract under fire Phu Loc #1).
74 Ibid.
75 Operations Order # 0040-70.
76 Operations Order # 0094-70, Patrol: *Durham*, Delta 3rd Plt, 25 Jan–8 Feb '70.
77 Ibid.
78 Rene Regalot, 2020–2024.
79 W. C "Wild Bill" Drumright, May 2001.
80 Ibid.
81 Rene Regalot, 2020–24.
82 G. G. "Jerry" Spolter, interviews with author, 2023–24.
83 C. W. Charlie, interviews with the author, 2023–July 2024.
84 Thomas Martin, 10 Dec 2023.
85 Operations Order # 0105-70, Patrol: *Spoonbill*, Delta 4th Plt, 29–31 Jan '70.
86 Ibid.
87 Ibid.
88 G. G. "Jerry" Spolter, 2023–24.
89 Operations Order # 0105-70.
90 Ibid.
91 G. G. "Jerry" Spolter, 2023–24.
92 Ibid.
93 Rene Regalot, 2020–24.
94 1st Reconnaissance Battalion Command Chronology, Mar 1970.
95 Rene Regalot, 2020–24.
96 Ibid.
97 Ibid.
98 Operations Order # 0094-70.
99 Ibid.
100 Operations Order # 0099-70, Patrol: *Station Break*, Delta 2nd Plt, 28 Jan–1 Feb '70.
101 Ibid.
102 Ibid.
103 Operations Order # 0094-70, Patrol: *Durham*, Delta 3rd Plt, 25 Jan–8 Feb '70.
104 Ibid.
105 Ibid.
106 Mark Bayuk, Sep 2023–Apr 2024.
107 Operations Order # 0099-70.
108 Ibid.
109 Ibid.
110 Ibid.
111 Operations Order # 0094-70.
112 Operations Order # 0099-70.
113 Ibid.
114 A round that contained just over one hundred small explosives that released over the target, hit the ground and bounced before exploding. "Artillery Ammo," *1st Battalion, 83rd Artillery*, accessed 20 March 2025, at https://www.1stbn83rdartyvietnam.com/Artillery_Info/Ammo_Artillery/Artillery_Ammo.htm.
115 Operations Order # 0094-70.
116 Ibid.
117 Operations Order # 0099-70.
118 Ibid.
119 Ibid.
120 Operations Order # 0094-70.
121 Ibid.
122 Ibid.
123 Ibid.
124 Ibid.

125 Ibid.
126 Ibid.
127 Ibid.
128 Operations Order # 0143-70, Patrol: *Durham*, Delta 2nd Plt, 8–20 Feb '70.

Chapter 16

1 "21 Feb 1970," *On This Day*, at https://www.history.com/this-day-in-history/kissinger-begins-secret-negotiations-with-north-vietnamese.
2 Graham A. Cosmas and Lt. Col. Terrence P. Murray, USMC, *U.S. Marines in Vietnam: Vietnamization and Redeployment 1970–1971* (Washington, D.C.: History & Museum Division Headquarters, U.S. Marine Corps, 1986), 16–17.
3 Ibid.
4 Ibid., 443.
5 Operations Order # 0040-70, Patrol: *Durham*, Delta 4th Plt, 11–25 Jan '70.
6 1st Recon Bn Command Chronology, Jan '70.
7 W. C. "Bill" Drumright, interview with author, May 2001.
8 Operations Order # 0105-70, Patrol: *Spoonbill*, Delta 4th Plt, 29–31 Jan '70.
9 Steven "Stumpy" Baker, interviews with author, Feb–Apr 2024.
10 G. G. "Jerry" Spolter, interviews with author, 2024.
11 Steven "Stumpy" Baker, Feb–Apr 2024.
12 W. C. "Bill" Drumright, May 2001.
13 C. W. "Charlie" Kershaw, interview with author, 2023–Jul 2024.
14 Steven "Stumpy" Baker, Feb–Apr 2024.
15 1st Recon Bn Command Chronology, Feb '70.
16 C. W. "Charlie" Kershaw, 2023–July 2024.
17 Thomas Martin, interview with author, 10 Dec 2023.
18 Steven "Stumpy" Baker, Feb–Apr 2024.
19 William "Bill" Lange, interview with author, 18–19 Sept 2024.
20 G. G. "Jerry" Spolter, 2024.
21 Rene Regalot, interviews with author, 2020–24.
22 Ibid.
23 Cosmas and Murray, *U.S. Marines in Vietnam*, 5.
24 Ibid., 442.
25 Waddill "Butch" Durwood, interview with author, 11 May 2016.
26 Operations Order # 0082-70, Patrol: *Summer Breeze*, Delta 1st Plt, 22–23 Jan '70.
27 Ibid.
28 Waddill "Butch" Durwood, 11 May 2016.
29 Operations Order # 0040-70.
30 Operations Order # 0094-70, Patrol: *Durham*, Delta 3rd Plt, 25 Jan–8 Feb '70.
31 Operations Order # 0143-70, Patrol: *Durham*, Delta 2nd Plt, 8–20 Feb '70.
32 Operations Order # 0143-70.
33 Operations Order # 0094-70.
34 Operations Order # 0143-70.
35 Ibid.
36 Ibid.
37 Garry L. Parks, interviews with author, 1981–2002.
38 Operations Order # 0143-70.
39 Garry L. Parks, 1981–2002.
40 Operations Order # 0143-70.
41 Ibid.
42 Garry L. Parks, 1981–2002.
43 Operations Order # 0143-70.
44 Ibid.
45 Thurman Mullins, interviews with author, Feb–Oct 2023.
46 Ibid.
47 Operations Order # 0143-70.
48 Ibid.
49 Operations Order # 0201-70, Patrol: *West Orange*, Delta 1st Plt, 20 Feb–5 Mar '70.
50 Operations Order # 0191-70, Patrol: *Chili Pepper*, Delta 4th Plt, 25 Feb–1 Mar '70.
51 1st Recon Bn Command Chronology, Feb 1970.
52 Chris H. L'Orange, interviews with author, 2023–24.
53 Ibid.
54 Ibid.
55 Ibid.
56 Operations Order # 0191-70.
57 1st Recon Bn Command Chronology, Feb 1970.
58 George E. Rivers, interviews with author, 18–19 Sep 2024.
59 Ibid.
60 W. X. Lee, interviews with author, 1998–2024.
61 1st Recon Bn Command Chronology, Oct '70.
62 W. X. Lee, 1998–2024.
63 Ibid.
64 Ibid.
65 Ibid.
66 3rd Recon Bn Command Chronology, Nov 1969.
67 George E. Rivers, 18–19 Sep 2024.
68 Rene Regalot, 2020–24.
69 Herman Diaz, interview with author, Oct–Nov 1988.
70 Ibid; Rene Regalot, 2020–24.

71 Ibid.

Chapter 17

1 Operations Order # 0186-70, Patrol: *Pal Joey*, Delta 3rd Plt, 21–22 Feb '70.
2 Ibid.
3 Ibid.
4 Ibid.
5 Ibid.
6 Operations Order # 0184-70, Patrol: *Delicatessen*, Delta 3rd Plt, 15–19 Feb '70.
7 Operations Order # 0201-70, Patrol: *West Orange*, Delta 1st Plt, 20 Feb–5 Mar '70.
8 Operations Order # 0186-70.
9 Operations Order # 0143-70, Patrol: *Durham*, Delta 2nd Plt, 8–20 Feb '70.
10 Mark Bayuk, interviews with author, Sep 2023–Apr 2024.
11 Operations Order # 0201-70.
12 Mark Bayuk, Sep 2023–Apr 2024.
13 Operations Order # 0201-70.
14 Ibid.
15 Ibid.
16 Operations Order # 0186-70.
17 Ibid.
18 Ibid.
19 Ibid.
20 Operations Order # 0221-70, Patrol: *Pal Joey*, Delta 3rd Plt, 23–26 Feb '70.
21 Ibid.
22 Operations Order # 0143-70.
23 Mrs. W. X. Lee, interviews with author, 2024.
24 Operations Order # 0221-70.
25 Ibid.
26 Ibid.
27 Ibid.
28 Ibid.
29 Ibid.
30 Ibid.
31 Dennis Swick, interview with author, Feb 2024.
32 Operations Order # 0221-70.

Chapter 18

1 Operations Order # 0201-70, Patrol: *West Orange*, Delta 1st Plt, 20 Feb–5 Mar '70.
2 Ibid.
3 Ibid.
4 Operations Order # 0219-70, Patrol: *Forefather*, Delta 1st Plt, 26 Feb–2 Mar '70.
5 Operations Order # 0201-70.
6 Mark Bayuk, interviews with author, Sep 2023–April 2024.
7 Operations Order # 0219-70.
8 Ibid.
9 Ibid.
10 Ibid.
11 Ibid.
12 Ibid.
13 Ibid.
14 Ibid.
15 Operations Order # 0201-70.
16 Ibid.
17 Operations Order # 0242-70, Patrol: *West Orange*, Delta 4th Plt, 5–19 Mar '70.
18 Operations Order # 0201-70.

Chapter 19

1 "Nuclear Arms Ban In Effect," *Pittsburgh Post-Gazette*, 6 March 1970, 2.
2 "2 Generals Face Massacre Trial"—Charges Filed Against 14 Army Officers," *Pittsburgh Post-Gazette*, 18 March 1970, 1.
3 Kenneth Conboy and James Morrison, *Shadow War: The CIA's Secret War in Laos* (Boulder, Colorado: Paladin Press, 1995), 256.
4 Graham A. Cosmas and Lt. Col. Terrence P. Murray, USMC, *U.S. Marines in Vietnam: Vietnamization and Redeployment 1970–1971* (Washington, D.C.: History & Museum Division Headquarters, U.S. Marine Corps, 1986), 443.
5 Ibid.
6 1st Marine Division Command Chronology, 1–31 Mar '70.
7 Cosmas and Murray, *U.S. Marines in Vietnam*, 443.
8 1st Recon Bn Command Chronology, Mar 1970.
9 11th Marines Command Chronology, 1–31 Mar '70.
10 Rene Regalot, interviews with author, 2020–24.
11 Thomas Martin, interview with author, 10 Dec 2023.
12 1st Recon Bn Command Chronology, Mar '70.
13 Thomas McAdams, interviews with author, 21 Feb and 19 Mar 2024.
14 Ibid.
15 B. Parker Miller, interviews with author, 18–20 Feb 2024.

16 1st Recon Bn Command Chronology, Mar '70.
17 Michael Dan Kellum, *American Heroes: Grunts, Pilots and "Docs," Book II* (Longview, Texas: Navarro-Hill Publishing Group, 2011), 120.
18 1st Recon Bn Command Chronology, Mar '70.
19 Michael C. Hodgins, *Reluctant Warrior: A Marine's True Story of Duty and Heroism in Vietnam* (New York: Ballantine Books, 1996).
20 Paul Eglevsky, interviews with author, Feb 2024.
21 1st Recon Bn Command Chronology, Mar '70.
22 G. G. "Jerry" Spolter, interviews with author, 24 February 2024.
23 Ibid.
24 Operations Order # 0246-70, Patrol: *Fig Newton*, Delta 2nd Plt, 7–12 Mar '70.
25 Ibid.
26 Thurman Mullins, interviews with author, Feb–Oct 2023.
27 Operations Order # 0246-70.
28 G. G. "Jerry" Spolter, 2024.
29 Operations Order # 0242-70, Patrol: *West Orange*, Delta 4th Plt, 5–19 Mar '70.
30 Ibid.
31 Chris H. L'Orange, interviews with author, 2023–24.
32 Mark Bayuk, interviews with author, Sep 2023–Apr 2024.
33 Ibid.
34 Operations Order # 0242-70.
35 Operations Order # 0265-70, Patrol: *Terrapin*, Delta, 3rd Plt, 9–15 Mar '70.
36 Paul Freeman, interviews with author, 2022–24.
37 Operations Order # 0265-70.
38 Ibid.
39 Ibid.
40 Ibid.
41 Operations Order # 0305-70, Patrol: *West Orange*, Delta 3rd Plt, 17 Mar–1 Apr '70.

Chapter 20

1 Operations Order # 0259-70, Patrol: *Delicatessen*, Delta 1st Plt, 12–14 Mar '70.
2 Operations Order # 0219-70, Patrol: *Fore Father*, Delta 1st Plt, 26 Feb–2 Mar '70.
3 W. Rabbit, interview with author, Jul 2020.
4 Ibid.
5 Operations Order # 0259-70.
6 An Australian Peel is a combat withdrawal suited for a small formation facing a larger one. It involves members of the formation providing covering fire while one member pulls back to another position and then covers the next member to move.
7 W. Rabbit, July 2020.
8 Operations Order # 0259-70.
9 Ibid.
10 Ibid.
11 W. Rabbit, July 2020.
12 Operations Order # 0259-70.
13 Ibid.
14 Ibid.
15 Ibid.
16 Ibid.
17 Ibid.
18 Ibid.
19 W. Rabbit, July 2020.

Chapter 21

1 Operations Order # 0242-70, Patrol: *West Orange*, Delta 4th Plt, 5–19 Mar '70.
2 Ibid.
3 Ibid.
4 Operations Order # 0305-70, Patrol: *West Orange*, Delta 3rd Plt, 17 Mar–1 Apr '70.
5 W. X. Lee, interviews with author, 1998–2024.
6 Operations Order # 0242-70.
7 Mark Bayuk, interviews with author, Sept 2023–April 2024.
8 Ibid.
9 Operations Order # 0242-70.
10 Mark Bayuk, Sep 2023–April 2024.
11 Rene Regalot, interviews with author, 2020–24.
12 1st Recon Bn Command Chronology, Mar '70.
13 H. C. "Chris" L'Orange, interviews with author, 2023–24.
14 Operations Order # 0242-70.
15 Operations Order # 0305-70, Patrol: *West Orange*, Delta 3rd Plt, 17 Mar–1 Apr '70.
16 Operations Order # 0313-70, Patrol: *Delicatessen*, Delta 1st Plt, 17–18 Mar '70.
17 G. G. "Jerry Spolter," interviews with author, 2024.
18 Thomas McAdams, interviews with author, 21 Feb and 19 Mar 2024.
19 Paul Eglevsky, interviews with author, Feb 2024.
20 Operations Order # 0313-70, Patrol: *Delicatessen*, Delta,1st Plt 17–18 Mar '70.
21 Ibid.
22 Ibid.
23 1st Bn Command Chronology, March 1970.

24 Charles G. Cooper, LtGen USMC (Ret.), *Cheers and Tears: A Marine's Story of Combat in Peace and War* (Wesley Press, 2002).
25 Ibid., 175–76.
26 Operations Order # 0313-70.
27 Cooper, *Cheers and Tears*, 176–78.
28 Operations Order # 0313-70.
29 Graham A. Cosmas and Lt. Col. Terrence P. Murray, USMC, *U.S. Marines in Vietnam: Vietnamization and Redeployment 1970–1971* (Washington, D.C.: History & Museum Division Headquarters, U.S. Marine Corps, 1986), 53.
30 Ibid.
31 Paul Eglevsky, Feb 2024.
32 Operations Order # 0280-70, Patrol: *Dublin City*, Delta 2nd Plt, 13–17 Mar '70.
33 Paul Eglevsky, Feb 2024.
34 Operations Order # 0325-70, Patrol: *Delicatessen*, Delta 3rd Plt, 23–27 Mar '70.
35 Ibid.
36 Ibid.
37 Operations Order # 0332-70, Patrol: *Fig Newton*, Delta 1st Plt, 26–31 Mar '70.
38 Ibid.
39 Operations Order # 03xx-70, Patrol: *Chili Pepper*, Delta 4th Plt, 27–31 Mar '70.
40 Ibid.
41 Ibid.
42 Ibid.
43 Operations Order # 0305-70, Patrol: *West Orange*, Delta 3rd Plt, 17 Mar–1 Apr '70.
44 Ibid.
45 Ibid.
46 Written statement, LCpl Broe, "NIS Report of Investigation to SJA, 1st MarDiv, alleged murder of Vietnamese civilian by 1Lt W. X. Lee, 1st Recon Bn.," by E. J. Fitzpatrick, Resident Agent NIS Da Nang, 6 June 1970. The written statement by Broe is an attachment in NIS report. Have moved the second quote marker to show entire title of the report; Randy Lowery, interview with author, 29 Jan 2023 and 23 Feb 2024.
47 Operations Order # 0305-70.
48 W. X. Lee, interviews with author, 1998–2024.
49 Operations Order # 0040-70, Patrol: *Durham*, Delta 4th Plt, 11–25 Jan '70.
50 Operations Order # 0219-70, Patrol: *Forefather*, Delta 1st Plt, 26 Feb–2 Mar '70.
51 Operations Order # 0242-70.
52 Mrs. W. X. Lee, interviews with author, 2024.
53 Written statement, Lt Green, "NIS Report of Investigation," to SJA, E. J. Fitzpatrick.
54 Ibid.
55 Ibid.
56 Ibid.

Chapter 22

1 Robert "Bob" Grossman, interview with author, 29 Feb 2024.
2 Herman Diaz, Sgt, written statement attachment to "NIS Report of Investigation," to SJA, E. J. Fitzpatrick.
3 Ibid.
4 Glen Edison, HM2, written statement, attachment to "NIS Report of Investigation," to SJA, E. J. Fitzpatrick.
5 Robert "Bob" Grossman, written statement, attachment to "NIS Report of Investigation," to SJA, E. J. Fitzpatrick; Daniel E. Broe, LCpl, written statement, attachment to "NIS Report of Investigation," to SJA, E. J. Fitzpatrick.
6 Ibid.
7 Herman Diaz.
8 Operations Order # 0305-70, Patrol: *West Orange*, Delta 3rd Plt, 17 Mar–1 Apr '70.
9 P. R. Green, 1Lt, written statement, attachment to "NIS Report of Investigation," to SJA, E. J. Fitzpatrick.
10 Ibid.
11 Herman Diaz.
12 Daniel E. Broe.
13 Herman Diaz
14 Daniel E. Broe.
15 Herman Diaz.
16 Daniel E. Broe; Herman Diaz; Robert "Bob" Grossman; Daniel E. Broe.
17 Ibid.
18 Robert "Bob" Grossman.
19 Ibid; Daniel E. Broe.
20 Ibid.
21 Ibid.
22 Howard Miller, LCpl, written statement, attachment to "NIS Report of Investigation" to SJA, E. J. Fitzpatrick.
23 Herman Diaz.
24 Ibid.
25 Eugene "Gene" McCommons; written statement, attachment to "NIS Report of Investigation" to SJA, E. J. Fitzpatrick.

26 Eugene "Gene" McCommons.
27 Ibid.
28 Herman Diaz.
29 Boardman, Sgt, written statement, attachment to "NIS Report of Investigation" to SJA, E. J. Fitzpatrick.
30 Herman Diaz.
31 P. R. Green.
32 Ibid.
33 Thien, Warrant Officer, ARVN, written statement, official translation, attachment to "NIS Report of Investigation" to SJA, E. J. Fitzpatrick.
34 Operations Order # 0305-70.
35 Robert "Bob" Grossman.
36 Ibid.; Eugene "Gene" McCommons.
37 Ibid.
38 Thien.
39 Operations Order # 0305-70.
40 Herman Diaz.
41 Operations Order # 0305-70.
42 Ibid.

Chapter 23

1 "Nixon to Pull Out 150,000 by May '71," Bridgeport Telegram, Bridgeport, Connecticut, 21 April 1970. 1.
2 Denise M. Bostdorff, *The Presidency and the Rhetoric of Foreign Crisis* (Columbia, South Carolina: University of South Carolina, 1994), 92.
3 Graham A. Cosmas and Lt. Col. Terrence P. Murray, USMC, *U.S. Marines in Vietnam: Vietnamization and Redeployment 1970–1971* (Washington, D.C.: History & Museum Division Headquarters, U.S. Marine Corps, 1986), 443.
4 Ibid.
5 Ibid., 23.
6 1st Recon Bn Command Chronology, April 1970.
7 Ibid.
8 Ibid.
9 Ibid.
10 Steven "Stumpy" Baker, interview with author, Feb–Apr 2024; John Hoff, interview with author, 23 May 2024; William "Bill" Lange, interview with author, 18–19 Sept 2024; G. G. "Jerry" Spolter, interviews with author, 2024.
11 Operations Order # 0401-70, Patrol: *Fig Newton*; Delta 1st Recon Bn, 12–15 Apr '70.
12 1st Recon Bn Command Chronology, Apr. 1970.
13 Ibid.
14 Robert "Gump" May, interview with author, Oct 2023.
15 C. W. "Charlie" Kershaw, interviews with author, 2023–July 2024.
16 Robert "Gump" May, Oct 2023.
17 Operations Order # 0406-70, Patrol: *Pickwick Papers*, Alpha 1st Recon Bn, 14–19 Apr '70.
18 Operations Order # 0349-70, Patrol: *Delicatessen*, Delta 1st Plt, 1 Apr '70.
19 Operations Order # 0374-70, Patrol: *Flakey Snow*, H&S Co, S3 Trg, 3–4 Apr '70.
20 Operations Order # 0355-70, Patrol: *Pal Joey*, Delta 3rd Plt, 3–5 Apr '70.
21 Paul Freeman, interviews with author, 2022–24.
22 Operations Order # 0355-70.
23 Ibid.
24 Paul Freeman, 2022–24.
25 Operations Order # 0355-70.
26 Ibid.
27 Paul Freeman, 2022–24.
28 Operations Order # 0355-70.
29 Ibid.
30 Paul Freeman, 2022–24.
31 Operations Order # 0383-70, Patrol: *Prime Cut*, Delta 4th Plt, 8–11 Apr '70.
32 Ibid.
33 Ibid.
34 Ibid.
35 Ibid.
36 Operations Order # 0391-70, Patrol: *Terrapin*, Delta 3rd Plt, 11–16 Apr '70.
37 Ibid.
38 C. W. "Charlie" Kershaw, 2023–July 2024.
39 Ibid.
40 Ibid.
41 Earl B. Hailston, interview with author, Jan 2024.
42 Ibid.
43 Operations Order # 0393-70, Patrol: *West Orange*, Delta 1st Plt, 11–25 Apr '70.
44 Operations Order # 0352-70, Patrol: *West Orange*, Delta 2nd Plt, 1–11 Apr '70.
45 Operations Order # 0383-70, Patrol: *Prime Cut*, Delta 4th Plt, 8–11 Apr '70; Operations Order # 0391-70, Patrol: *Terrapin*, Delta 3rd Plt, 11–16 Apr '70.
46 Operations Order # 0400-70, Patrol: *Dublin City*, Delta 1st Recon Bn, 12–15 Apr. '70.
47 Ibid.
48 Ibid.
49 Ibid.

50 Ibid.
51 Operations Order # 0401-70, Patrol: *Fig Newton*, Delta 1st Recon Bn, 12–15 Apr ’70.
52 Ibid.
53 Operations Order # 0424-70, Patrol: *Fig Newton*, Delta 1st Recon Bn, 17–19 Apr ’70.
54 Ibid.
55 Ibid.
56 Ibid.
57 Ibid.
58 Ibid.
59 Ibid.
60 Mike McCollum, interviews with author, July–Aug 2024.
61 Operations Order # 0352-70.
62 Ibid.
63 Ibid.
64 P. R. Green, 1Lt, written statement, attachment to “NIS Report of Investigation” to SJA, E. J. Fitzpatrick.
65 Operations Order # 0393-70.

Chapter 24

1 Operations Order # 0352-70, Patrol: *West Orange*, Delta 2nd Plt, 1–11 Apr ’70.
2 Summary, “NIS Report of Investigation” to SJA, E. J. Fitzpatrick.
3 Translation of two letters in attachments; Summary, “NIS Report of Investigation.”.
4 G. G. “Jerry” Spolter, interviews with author, 2024.
5 Operations Order # 0305-70, Patrol: *West Orange*, Delta 3rd Plt, 17 Mar–1 Apr ’70.
6 Thien, Warrant Officer, translation of interview statement, “NIS Report of Investigation” to SJA, E. J. Fitzpatrick.
7 Translation of Vietnamese District Committee letter, NIS Report of Investigation, to SJA, 1st MarDiv alleged murder of Vietnamese civilian by 1Lt W. X. Lee, 1st Recon Bn, by E. J. Fitzpatrick, resident agent NIS Da Nang, 6 June 1970.
8 Summary, “NIS Report of Investigation.”
9 Operations Order # 0352-70.
10 G. G. “Jerry” Spolter, 2024.
11 Ibid.
12 Operations Order # 0401-70, Patrol: *Fig Newton*, Delta 1st Recon Bn, 12–15 Apr ’70.
13 Operations Order # 0305-70, Patrol: *West Orange*, Delta 3rd Plt, 17 Mar–1 Apr ’70.
14 Transcript, DD-457, record of the Article 32 investigation of charges against 1Lt W. X. Lee, 10 July 1970.
15 “NIS Report of Investigation”.
16 Ibid.
17 Thien.
18 Summary, “NIS Report of Investigation.”
19 Thien.
20 Ibid.
21 P. R. Green, 1Lt, written statement, attachment to “NIS Report of Investigation” to SJA, E. J. Fitzpatrick.
22 Ibid.
23 Ban, Cpl; attachment, translation of interview, “NIS Report of Investigation” to SJA, E. J. Fitzpatrick.
24 “NIS Report of Investigation.”.
25 Ibid.
26 Ibid.
27 Paul Eglevsky, interviews with author, Feb 2024.
28 Ibid.
29 Ibid.
30 “NIS Report of Investigation” to SJA, E. J. Fitzpatrick, 6 June 1970.
31 Operations Order # 0393-70, Patrol: *West Orange*, Delta 1st Plt, 11–25 Apr ’70.
32 Operations Order # 0452-70, Patrol: *West Orange*, Delta 4th Plt, 25 Apr–9 May ’70.
33 Autopsy report, attachment; “NIS Report of Investigation” to SJA, E. J. Fitzpatrick.
34 Ibid.
35 Operations Order # 0305-70
36 “NIS Report of Investigation,” 6 June 1970.
37 Ibid.
38 Village committee letter, translation, attachment, “NIS Report of Investigation,” by E. J. Fitzpatrick.
39 Summary, “NIS Report of Investigation.”.
40 W. X. Lee, interviews with author, 1998–2024.
41 DD-457, record of the Article 32 investigation of charges against 1Lt W. X. Lee, 10 July 1970.
42 DD-458, charge sheet of accused, 1Lt W. X. Lee signed by J. R. Taylor, 18 May 1970.
43 Ibid.
44 W. X. Lee, 1998–2024.
45 Mrs. W. X. Lee, interviews with author, 2024.
46 Ibid.
47 Ibid.
48 G. G. “Jerry” Spolter, 2024.
49 W. X. Lee, 1998–2024.
50 P. R. Green, 1Lt, written statement # 2, attachment, “NIS Report of Investigation” by E. J. Fitzpatrick.

51 Ibid.
52 W. X. Lee, 1998–2024.
53 Newspaper headlines, *San Jose Mercury,* and *San Jose News*, 25 May 1970.
54 Mrs. W. X. Lee, 2024.
55 "NIS Report of Investigation."
56 Ibid.
57 Ibid.
58 Ibid.

Chapter 25

1 "Nixon Stuns U.S. in Cambodia Thrust; 8,000 Yanks Sweep Across Border," *Wilmington (DE) Evening Journal*, 1 May 1970, 1.
2 "4 Killed, 10 Hurt at Kent State—Firing Erupts As Guardsmen Chase Crowd," *Pittsburgh Post Gazette*, 5 May 1970, 1.
3 "150,000 Parade for Nixon," *Daily News* (New York), 21 May 1970, 1–2.
4 "The National League of Families of American Prisoners & Missing in Southeast Asia," at www.pow-miafamilies.org.
5 Graham A. Cosmas and Lt. Col. Terrence P. Murray, USMC, *U.S. Marines in Vietnam: Vietnamization and Redeployment 1970–1971* (Washington, D.C.: History & Museum Division Headquarters, U.S. Marine Corps, 1986), 444.
6 1st Recon Bn Command Chronology, May 1970.
7 Cosmas and Murray, *U.S. Marines in Vietnam*, 444.
8 1st Recon Bn Command Chronology, May 1970.
9 "Standing Operating Procedure for Sting Ray/Clandestine Long Range Patrolling Operations," BnO P03000.4, 1 Oct 1967, 1st Recon Bn (REIN), Camp Reasoner, Da Nang, Republic of Vietnam.
10 1st Recon Bn Command Chronology, May 1970.
11 William "Bill" Lange, interview with author, 18–19 Sept 2024.
12 1st Marine Div Command Chronology, 1–30 May '70.
13 1st Recon Bn, Command Chronology, May 1970.
14 Operations Order # 0493-70, Patrol: *Vesper Bells Divers*, H&S Co SCUBA Locker, 3–6 May '70, 1st Recon Bn, Da Nang, RVN, 301235H Apr '70 (1Lt Kershaw).
15 Charlie W. Kershaw, interviews with author, 2023–July 2024.
16 Operations Order # 0493-70.
17 "NIS Report of Investigation" to SJA, E. J. Fitzpatrick.
18 Operations Order # 0452-70, Patrol: *West Orange*, Delta 4th Plt, 25 Apr–9 May '70.
19 Operations Order # 0468-70, Patrol: *Terrapin*, Delta Co 2nd Plt 28 Apr–2 May '70.
20 Ibid.
21 Paul Freeman, interviews with author, 2022–24; Glen Edison, HM2, written statement, attachment, "NIS Report of Investigation" by E. J. Fitzpatrick.
22 Operations Order # 0464-70, Patrol: *Fig Newton*, Delta Co 2nd Plt, 28 Apr–2 May '70.
23 Ibid.
24 Operations Order # 0466-70, Patrol: *Pal Joey*, Delta 1st Plt, 28 Apr–3 May '70.
25 Ibid.
26 Operation Order # 0487-70, Patrol: *Dublin City*, Delta Co 2nd Plt, 3–6 May '70.
27 Ibid.
28 Mike Cross, interview with author, 22 Feb 2024; Robert "Bob" Fawcett, interviews with author, 25 Feb and Apr 2024.
29 Ibid.
30 1st Recon Bn Command Chronology, Oct '70.
31 Robert "Bob" Fawcett, 25 Feb and Apr 2024.
32 Ibid.
33 Ibid.
34 Operations Order # 0517-70, Patrol: *West Orange*, Delta 3rd Plt, 9–23 May '70.
35 Robert "Bob" Fawcett, 25 Feb and Apr 2024.
36 "NIS Report of Investigation."
37 Ibid.
38 Ibid.
39 John P. Kempe, LCpl, written statement, attachment "NIS Report of Investigation" E. J. Fitzpatrick.
40 Ibid.
41 Ibid.
42 Officer Qualification Record (OQR), 1Lt W. X. Lee.
43 Herman Diaz, Sgt, written statement, attachment "NIS Report of Investigation" to SJA, E. J. Fitzpatrick.
44 "NIS Report of Investigation."
45 Ibid.
46 Cosmas and Murray, *U.S. Marines in Vietnam*, 348.
47 Operations Order # 0517-70.
48 Ibid.
49 Ibid.
50 "NIS Report of Investigation."
51 Ibid.
52 "Obituary, Marv Floom," at www.mountcastle.net/obituaries/Marvin-H-Floom?.
53 Operations Order # 0517-70.

54 Robert "Bob" Grossman, interview with author, 29 Feb 2024.
55 Operations Order # 0517-70.
56 Operations Order # 0504-70, Patrol: *Delicatessen*, Delta 4th Plt, 9–12 May '70.
57 Ibid.
58 Ibid.
59 H. C. "Chris" L'Orange, interviews with author, 2023–24.
60 Operations Order # 0504-70; H. C. 'Chris' L'Orange, 2023–24.
61 Operations Order # 0504-70.
62 Ibid.
63 Ibid.
64 Ibid.
65 H. C. "Chris" L'Orange, 2023–24.
66 Operations Order # 0514-70, Patrol: *Dublin City*, Delta Co, 10–14 May '70.
67 Ibid.
68 Operations Order # 0522-70, Patrol: *Prime Cut*, Delta Co, 11–12 May '70.
69 Ibid.
70 Ibid.
71 Operations Order # 0514-70.
72 Ibid.
73 Ibid.
74 Ibid.
75 Ibid.
76 "NIS Report of Investigation."
77 Ibid.
78 Operations Order # 0566-70, Patrol: *Chili Pepper*, Delta Co, 22 May '70.
79 Ibid.
80 Ibid.
81 Operations Order # 0585-70, Patrol: *West Orange*, Delta 4th Plt, 23 May–6 June '70.
82 Ibid.
83 Ibid.
84 Ibid.
85 Ibid.
86 Ibid.

Chapter 26

1 Edwin Starr, "War," *Psychedelic Shack*, song released 1 June '70, at https://classic.motown.com/story/edwin-starr-war/.
2 "Cambodian Objectives Achieved, Nixon Says," *Pittsburgh Post Gazette*, 5 May 1970, 1.
3 Graham A. Cosmas and Lt. Col. Terrence P. Murray, USMC, *U.S. Marines in Vietnam: Vietnamization and Redeployment 1970–1971* (Washington, D.C.: History & Museum Division Headquarters, U.S. Marine Corps, 1986), 59.
4 Ibid., 444.
5 Ibid.
6 1st Recon Bn Command Chronology, June 1970.
7 Cosmas and Murray, *U.S. Marines in Vietnam*, 309.
8 Operations Order # 0536-70, Patrol: *Summer Breeze*, Delta Co, 15–19 May '70.
9 Operations Order # 0585-70, Patrol: *West Orange*, Delta 4th Plt, 23 May–6 June '70.
10 Robert "Bob" Fawcett, interviews with author, 25 Feb and Apr 2024.
11 Operations Order # 0623-70, Patrol: *Terrapin*, Delta Co, 2–6 June '70
12 Ibid.
13 Ibid.
14 Operations Order # 0585-70
15 Ibid.
16 Ibid.
17 Ibid.
18 Ibid.
19 Ibid.
20 Operations Order # 0644-70, Patrol: *West Orange*, Delta 1st Plt, 6–20 June '70.
21 Paul Eglevsky, interviews with author, Feb 2024.
22 Operations Order # 0644-70.
23 Ibid.
24 Garry Parks, 1Lt, DD-457, Testimony, record of the Article 32 investigation of charges against 1Lt W. X. Lee, 10 July '70.
25 Operations Order # 0644-70.
26 Ibid.
27 Operations Order # 0710-70, Patrol: *Pal Joey*, Delta 4th Plt, 20 June–2 July '70.
28 Operations Order # 0658-70, Patrol: *Dublin City*, Delta Co, 9–13 June '70.
29 Ibid.
30 Ibid.
31 Operations Order # 0682-70, Patrol: *Pal Joey*, Delta Co, 17–21 June '70.
32 Ibid.
33 Ibid.
34 Ibid.
35 Ibid.
36 Ibid.
37 Ibid.
38 Ibid.

39 Ibid.
40 Paul Freeman, interviews with author, 2022–24.
41 Operations Order # 0682-70, Patrol: *Pal Joey*, Delta Co, 17–21 June '70.
42 Operations Order # 0710-70, Patrol: *Pal Joey*, Delta 4th Plt, 20 June–2 July '70.
43 Ibid.
44 Ibid.
45 H. C. "Chris" L'Orange, interviews with author, 2023–24.
46 Ibid.
47 G. G. "Jerry" Spolter, interviews with author, 2024.
48 Ibid.
49 H. C. "Chris" L'Orange, 2023–24.
50 Operations Order # 0724-70, Patrol: *Bag Shaw*, Delta Co, 24–28 June '70.
51 Ibid.
52 Operations Order # 0710-70, Patrol: *Pal Joey*, Delta 4th Plt, 20 June–2 July '70.
53 H. C. "Chris" L'Orange, 2023–24.
54 Operations Order # 0710-70.
55 Ibid; H. C. "Chris" L'Orange, 2023–24.
56 Operations Order # 0710-70.
57 Ibid.
58 G. G. "Jerry" Spolter, 2024.
59 Ibid.
60 H. C. "Chris" L'Orange, 2023–24; G. G. "Jerry" Spolter, 2024.
61 Ibid.
62 H. C. "Chris" L'Orange, 2023–24.
63 Ibid.
64 Ibid.
65 Operations Order # 0710-70.
66 Ibid.
67 Ibid.
68 Ibid.
69 Ibid.
70 Ibid.
71 Operations Order # 0782-70, Patrol: *Pal Joey-K*, Delta 3rd Plt, 2–18 July '70.

Chapter 27

1 "Defense from S.J.," *San Jose News*, 5 June 1970.
2 "NIS Report of Investigation" to SJA, E. J. Fitzpatrick.
3 Ibid.
4 Operations Order # 0305-70, Patrol: *West Orange*, Delta 3rd Plt, 17 Mar–1 Apr '70.
5 "NIS Report of Investigation."
6 W. C. Drumright, LtCol, letter, CO 1st Recon Bn to CG 1st Marine Div requesting Article 32 for 1Lt W. X. Lee dated 16 May 1970. Enclosure to Article 32 report dated 10 July 1970.
7 W. C. Drumright, LtCol, letter, CO 1st Recon Bn appointing LtCol James King as investigating officer for an Article 32 for alleged murder of Vietnamese civilian by 1Lt W. X. Lee dated 18 May 1970. Enclosure to Article 32 report dated 10 July 1970.
8 Mrs. W. X. Lee, interviews with author, 2024.
9 "NIS Report of Investigation."
10 Ibid.
11 Transcript; DD-457, record of the Article 32 investigation of charges against 1Lt W. X. Lee, 10 July 1970.
12 Ibid.
13 Michael Einsidler, interview with author, Feb 2024.
14 Transcript; DD-457, 10 July 1970.
15 DD-458; charge sheet of accused 1Lt W. X. Lee, signed by J. R. Taylor, 18 May '70.
16 Michael Einsidler, Feb 2024.
17 Transcript; DD-457, Record of the Article 32 Investigation of charges against 1Lt W.X. Lee, dtd. 16 July 1970, signed by LtCol King, USMC, investigating officer.
18 Ibid.
19 Ibid.
20 Ibid.
21 Ibid.
22 Ibid.
23 Ibid; Robert "Bob" Grossman, interview with author, 29 Feb 2024.
24 Transcript; DD-457, record of the Article 32 investigation of charges against 1Lt W.X. Lee, 10 July '70.
25 Ibid.
26 Ibid.
27 Ibid.
28 Garry L. Parks, interviews with author, 1981–2002.
29 Transcript; DD-457, record of the Article 32 investigation of charges against 1Lt W. X. Lee, 10 July '70.
30 Ibid.
31 Operations Order # 0585-70, Patrol: *West Orange*, Delta 4th Plt, 23 May–6 June '70.
32 Ibid.
33 Transcript; DD-457, record of the Article 32 investigation, 10 July '70.
34 Ibid.
35 Ibid.
36 1st Recon Bn Command Chronology, Dec '69.

37 Operations Order # 0517-70, Patrol: *West Orange*, Delta 3rd Plt, 9–23 May '70.
38 Transcript; DD-457, Record of the Article 32 Investigation, 10 July '70.
39 Ibid.
40 Ibid.
41 1st Recon Bn Command Chronology, July '70.
42 Robert "Gump" May, interview with author, Oct 2023.
43 Transcript; DD-457, record of the Article 32 investigation, 10 July '70.
44 Ibid.
45 Ibid.
46 Ibid.
47 "Marine Defense Delay Claimed," *San Jose News*, 11 June 1970; "Viet Murder Defense Hits Roadblock," *San Jose Mercury*, 12 June 1970.
48 James P. King, LtCol, Letter, interim report on "Article 32, Investigating Officers Report"; accused 1Lt W. X. Lee, investigating officer, Hq. Co. Hq. Bn. Letter, IO to CO, 1st Recon Bn, 19 June '70.
49 Transcript; DD-457, Record of the Article 32 investigation, 10 July '70.

Chapter 28

1 "400,000 in Capital Join in Honor America Day," *Chicago Tribune*, 5 July 1970, 1.
2 Martin Katrina, "The Asbury Park July Riots" blog, at https://blogs.library.duke.edu/rubenstein/2016/06/28/asbury-park-july-1970-riots/.
3 Michael P. Kelley, *Where We Were in Vietnam: A Comprehensive Guide to the Firebases, Military Installations, and Naval Vessels of the Vietnam War* (Central Point, Oregon: Hellgate Press, 2002), 442.
4 Graham A. Cosmas and Lt. Col. Terrence P. Murray, USMC, *U.S. Marines in Vietnam: Vietnamization and Redeployment 1970–1971* (Washington, D.C.: History & Museum Division Headquarters, U.S. Marine Corps, 1986), 445.
5 Ibid.
6 Ibid., 81.
7 Standard Operating Procedure (SOP), Battalion Order PO3000.4, "SOP for Sting Ray/Clandestine Long-Range Patrolling Operations," 1 Oct '67, with change '70.
8 W. C. "Chip," interview with author, Mar 2024.
9 Robert "Gump" May, interview with author, Oct 2023.
10 Paul Eglevsky, interviews with author, Feb 2024.
11 Operations Order # 0782-70, Patrol: *Pal Joey-K*, Delta 3rd Plt, 2–18 July '70.
12 G. G. "Jerry" Spolter, interviews with author, 2024.
13 1st Recon Btn Command Chronology, July 1970.
14 Operations Order # 0782-70, Patrol: *Pal Joey-K*, Delta 3rd Plt, 2–18 July '70.
15 Ibid.
16 Ibid.
17 Ibid.
18 Operations Order # 0867-70, Patrol: *Pal Joey-K*, Delta 1st Plt, 18 July–1 Aug '70.
19 Operations Order # 0793-70, Patrol: *Bad Actor*, Echo Co, 7–9 July '70.
20 Cosmas and Murray, *U.S. Marines in Vietnam*, 75–76.
21 Operations Order # 0793-70.
22 Operations Order # 0782-70.
23 Operations Order # 0793-70.
24 Ibid.
25 Flight Schedule, 9 July '70, VMO-2, MAG-11.
26 Operations Order # 0793-70.
27 Earl B. Hailston, interview with author, Jan 18–19 2024.
28 W. C. Drumright, LtCol, CO 1st Recon Bn, letter appointing LtCol James King as Investigating Officer for an Article 32 for alleged murder of Vietnamese civilian by 1Lt W. X. Lee dated 18 May 1970. Enclosure to Article 32 report dated 10 July 1970.
29 DD-457, record of the Article 32, 10 July 1970.
30 Operations Order # 0821-70, Patrol: *Segment*, Delta Co, 11 July '70.
31 Ibid.
32 Ibid.
33 Ibid.
34 DD-457, James P. King, LtCol, record of the Article 32 Investigation, 16 July '70.
35 W. C. Drumright, LtCol, CO 1st Recon Bn, letter to CG 1st Mar Div recommending GCM, 16 July 1970.
36 Operations Order # 0782-70.
37 Letter, SJA to CG 1st Mar Div recommending GCM, 22 July '70.
38 DD-457, Record of the Article 32 investigation, 16 July 1970.
39 Operations Order # 0860-70, Patrol: *Allen Town*, Delta Co, 23–29 July '70.
40 Ibid.
41 Ibid.

42 Cosmas and Murray, *U.S. Marines in Vietnam*, 68, 71–2.
43 Operations Order # 0860-70.
44 Ibid.
45 Ibid.
46 Ibid.
47 Ibid.
48 Operations Order # 0867-70.
49 Ibid.
50 Ibid.
51 Ibid.
52 Ibid.
53 Ibid.
54 Ibid.
55 Operations Order # 0907-70, Patrol: *Pal Joey-K*, Delta 3rd Plt, 1–14 Aug '70.
56 Garry L. Parks, interviews with author, 1981–2002.
57 Ibid; 1st Recon Bn Command Chronology, Sep 1970.

Chapter 29

1 Stephen Millies, "Long live the spirit of Jonathan Jackson," *Workers World Newspaper*, 8 August 2010; "Justice: A Bad Week for the Good Guys," *Time*, 17 August 1970.
2 "Marines Reduce Charges," *San Jose Mercury*, 7 August 1970.
3 Mrs. W. X. Lee, interviews with author, 10–12 February 2024.
4 "Marines Reduce Charges," *San Jose Mercury*, 7 August 1970.
5 Donald Pfarrer, "Bomb in Stolen Truck Caused explosion at UW," *The Milwaukee Journal*, 25 August 1970, 8.
6 "One Dead, 40 Hurt in East L.A. Riot," *Los Angeles Times*, 30 August 1970, A-1.
7 Graham A. Cosmas and Lt. Col. Terrence P. Murray, USMC, *U.S. Marines in Vietnam: Vietnamization and Redeployment 1970–1971* (Washington, D.C.: History & Museum Division Headquarters, U.S. Marine Corps, 1986), 58–59.
8 Ibid., 75–6, 91.
9 Ibid., 92–3.
10 Ibid., 95.
11 Ibid., 83.
12 1st Recon Bn Command Chronology, Aug '70.
13 John Hoff, interview with author, 23 May 2024.
14 Operations Order # 0907-70, Patrol: *Pal Joey-K*, Delta 3rd Plt, 1–14 Aug '70.
15 1st Recon Bn Command Chronology, Aug '70.
16 W. C. Drumright, interviews with author, Feb 1971 and May 2001.
17 1st Recon Bn Command Chronology, Aug '70.
18 Ibid.
19 Ibid.
20 Operations Order # 0907-70, Patrol: *Pal Joey-K*, Delta 3rd Plt, 1–14 Aug '70.
21 Ibid.
22 Ibid.
23 Ibid.
24 Operations Order # 0040-70, Patrol: *Durham*, Delta 4th Plt, 11–25 Jan '70.
25 Operations Order # 0907-70.
26 Ibid.
27 Ibid.
28 Ibid.
29 Michael Lee Lanning and Dan Cragg, *Inside the VC and the NVA* (New York: Fawcett Columbine, 1992), 144.
30 John Hoff, 23 May 2024.
31 Operations Order # 0907-70; SALUTE: Size, Activity, Location, Unit, Time, and Equipment.
32 Ibid.
33 1st Recon Bn Command Chronology, Aug 1970.
34 John Hoff, 23 May 2024.
35 Operations Order # 0907-70.
36 Ibid.
37 Ibid.
38 Ibid.
39 Ibid.
40 Cosmas and Murray, *U.S. Marines in Vietnam*, 302.
41 Ibid., 301–2.
42 Operations Order # 0907-70.
43 Ibid.
44 Ibid.
45 Ibid.
46 Ibid.
47 Operations Order # 0953-70, Patrol: *War Cloud-K*, Delta 2nd Plt, 12–29 Aug '70.
48 Ibid.
49 Ibid.
50 Ibid.
51 Ibid.
52 Ibid.
53 Ibid.
54 Ibid.
55 Operations Order # 1037-70, Patrol: *War Cloud-K*, Delta 4th Plt, 29 Aug–11 Sept '70.

56 Operations Order # 0907-70Operations Order # 0953-70.
57 Operations Order # 0907-70.
58 Operations Order # 0953-70.
59 Rene Regalot, interviews with author, 2020–24.
60 Operations Order # 0990-70, Patrol: *Big Flower*, Delta Co, 23–27 Aug '70.
61 Ibid.
62 Ibid.
63 Ibid.
64 Ibid.
65 Rene Regalot, 2020–24.
66 Ibid.
67 Robert "Bob" Fawcett, interviews with author, 25 Feb and Apr 2024.
68 1st Recon Bn Command Chronology, Aug 1970.
69 Robert "Bob" Fawcett, 25 Feb and Apr 2024.

Chapter 30

1 Randy Lowery, interviews with author, 29 Jan 2023 and 23 Feb 2024.
2 DD-458 charge sheet of accused 1Lt W. X. Lee, signed by J. R. Taylor, Capt Legal Officer, Hq Co, Hq Bn, 1st Mar Div, 18 May 1970.
3 SJA to CG 1st Mar Div, letter recommending GCM, 22 July '70.
4 DD-458, CG endorsement referral to trial, charge sheet of accused 1Lt. W. X. Lee, signed by J. R. Taylor, Capt Legal Officer, Hq Co, Hq. Bn, 1st Mar Div, signed by CG, 25 July '70, 3.
5 DD-491, summarized, record of trial of W. X. Lee, First Lieutenant by General Court-Martial Appointed by CG, 1st MarDiv (Rein) FMF tried at HQs, 1st Marine Division, Đà Nẵng, RVN, 31 Aug, 1, 2, 3 Sept 1970.
6 Letter, commanding general of the 1st Mar Div signs the convening order on general court-martial for 1Lt. W. X. Lee charged with a single violation of the Article 119, UCMJ, Involuntary Manslaughter. On 29 August 1970.
7 Robert Lowery, 29 Jan 2023 and 23 Feb 2024.
8 Ibid.
9 W. C. Drumright, interviews with author, Feb 1971 and May 2001.
10 George E. Rivers, interview with author, 18–19 Sept 2024.
11 Michael Einsidler, interview with author, Feb 2024.
12 "Convening Order for General Court-Martial, Ser. 24-70, dated, 29 Aug 1970; Michael Einsidler, Feb 2024.
13 Gary D. Solis, LtCol, USMC; *Marines and Military Law in Vietnam: Trial By Fire* (Washington, D.C.: History & Museums Division Headquarters, U.S. Marine Corps, 1989), 187.
14 Michael Einsidler, Feb 2024.
15 DD-491, summarized record of trial of Lee, W.X., First Lieutenant by General Court-Martial Appointed by CG, 1st MarDiv (Rein) FMF tried at HQ's 1st Marine Division, Da Nang, RVN, 31 Aug, 1, 2, 3 Sept 1970.
16 Letter, commanding general of the 1st Mar Div signs the convening order on general court-martial for 1Lt. Lee, 29 August 1970.
17 Ibid.
18 CG to Col U. E. Lees, letter convening order for general court-martial, Ser.24-70, 29 Aug 1970. Letter, CG to Colonel Louis S. Hollier Jr., U.S. Marine Corps, Hq Bn 1st Mar Div (Rein), FMF; "Modification to Convening Order for General Court-Martial," Ser: 24A-70, 31 Aug 1970.
19 DD-491, Summarized, Record of Trial of Lee, W.X., First Lieutenant by General Court-Martial Appointed by CG, 1st MarDiv (Rein) FMF tried at HQ's 1st Marine Division, Da Nang, RVN, 31 Aug, 1, 2, 3 Sept 1970, 2.
20 DD-491, summarized, record of trial, 1.
21 Ibid., 2.
22 Ibid., 3.
23 DD-458 charge sheet of accused 1Lt. W. X. Lee, signed by J. R. Taylor, May 1970, 2.
24 DD-491, summarized record of trial, 4.
25 Daniel E. Broe, LCPL, testimony followed sworn statement, DD-457, record of the Article 32 investigation of charges against 1Lt. W. X. Lee, 16 July 1970.
26 John P. Kempe, LCPL, DD-457, testimony followed sworn statement, record of the Article 32 investigation of charges, 16 July 1970.
27 Ibid.
28 Ibid.
29 Daniel E. Broe.
30 Ibid.
31 John P. Kempe.
32 Ibid.
33 P. R. Green, 1Lt, testimony followed sworn statement, DD-457, record of the Article 32 investigation of charges, 16 July 1970.

34 Ibid.
35 Ibid.
36 Ibid.
37 Ibid.
38 Nugyn Ban, Sgt, testimony followed sworn translation of statement, DD-457, record of the Article 32 investigation of charges, 16 July 1970.
39 Garry Parks, 2Lt, testimony followed sworn statement, DD-457, record of the Article 32 investigation of charges, 16 July 1970.
40 Garry L. Parks, interviews with author, 1981–2002; Garry Parks.
41 Ibid.
42 Garry L. Parks, 1981–2002.
43 Operations Order # 0644-70, Patrol: *West Orange*, Delta 1st Plt, 6–20 June '70.
44 Operations Order # 0585-70, Patrol: *West Orange*, Delta 4th Plt, 23 May–6 June '70.
45 Ibid.
46 Glen E. Edison, HM2, testimony followed sworn statement, DD-457, record of the Article 32 investigation of charges, 16 July 1970.
47 Ibid.
48 Steven S. Boardman, Sgt, testimony followed sworn statement, "NIS Report of Investigation" to SJA by E. J. Fitzpatrick, 6 June 1970.
49 DD-491, summarized, record of trial, 4.
50 Herman Diaz, Sgt, testimony followed sworn statement, DD-457, record of the Article 32 investigation of charges, 16 July 1970.
51 Ibid.
52 Ibid.
53 Ibid.
54 Ibid.
55 Operations Order # 0305-70, Patrol: *West Orange*, Delta 3rd Plt, 17 Mar–1 Apr '70.
56 Ibid.
57 DD-491, summarized, record of trial, 4.
58 Garry L. Parks, 1981–2002.
59 Robert Diaz, MSgt, testimony followed sworn statement, DD-457, record of the Article 32 investigation of charges, 16 July 1970.
60 Attachment, OQR, Lt. Lee, DD-491, summarized, record of trial, 11; rifle score 209, Marksman.
61 Robert Diaz.
62 Daniel E. Broe.
63 Operations Order # 0907-70, Patrol: *Pal Joey-K*, Delta 3rd Plt, 1–14 Aug '70; Operations Order # 0953-70, Patrol: *War Cloud-K*, Delta 2nd Plt, 12–29 Aug '70.
64 Presentation of defense case, DD-491, summarized, record of trial, 5.
65 Ibid.
66 Ibid.
67 Ibid.
68 Ibid.
69 Graham A. Cosmas and Lt. Col. Terrence P. Murray, USMC, *U.S. Marines in Vietnam: Vietnamization and Redeployment 1970–1971* (Washington, D.C.: History & Museum Division Headquarters, U.S. Marine Corps, 1986), 130.
70 Ibid., 130n.
71 Village locations: "Map: Dia Loc," 4-DMA Series L7014, sheet 6640IV, 1:50:000.
72 Ibid.
73 C. Broman, interviews with Snider and Stiteler, March 2008; W. C. "Bill" Drumright, Feb 1971 and May 2001; Garry L. Parks, 1981–2002.
74 DD-491, summarized, record of trial, 5.
75 Charles R. Smith, *U.S. Marines in Vietnam, High Mobility and Standdown, 1969* (Washington, D.C.: History and Museums Division, Headquarters, U.S. Marine Corps, 1988), 248.
76 DD-491, summarized, record of trial, 5.
77 W. C. "Bill" Drumright, Feb 1971 and May 2001.
78 DD-491, summarized, record of trial, 5.
79 W. C. "Bill" Drumright, Feb 1971 and May 2001.
80 Ibid.
81 Ibid.
82 DD-491, summarized, record of trial, 5.
83 George E. Rivers, 18–19 Sept 2024.
84 Ibid.
85 Ibid.
86 Ibid.
87 DD-491, summarized, record of trial, 5.
88 W. X. Lee, interviews with author, 1998–2024.
89 Ibid.
90 Ibid.
91 DD-491, summarized, record of trial, 5.
92 Operations Order # 0907-70.
93 DD-491, summarized, record of trial, 5.
94 Nugyen Thein, Lt, ARVN, testimony followed sworn statement, DD-457, record of the Article 32 investigation of charges, 16 July 1970.
95 DD-491, summarized, record of trial, 5.
96 Garry L. Parks, 1981–2002.
97 Ibid.
98 DD-491, summarized, record of trial, 5.
99 Garry L. Parks, 1981–2002.
100 DD-491, summarized, record of trial, 5.

101 Ibid.
102 Operations Order # 0305-70, Patrol: *West Orange*, Delta 3rd Plt, 17 Mar–1 Apr '70.
103 DD-491, summarized, record of trial, 5.
104 Ibid.
105 Operations Order # 0907-70; Operations Order # 0953-70, Patrol: *War Cloud-K*, Delta 2nd Plt, 12–29 Aug '70.
106 Operations Order # 0040-70, Patrol: *Durham*, Delta 4th Plt, 11–25 Jan '70.
107 Operations Order # 0710-70, Patrol: *Pal Joey*, Delta 4th Plt, 20 June–2 July '70.
108 Operations Order # 0907-70, Patrol: *Pal Joey-K*, Delta 3rd Plt, 1–14 Aug '70.
109 Ibid.
110 DD-491, summarized, record of trial, 5.
111 Operations Order # 0517-70, Patrol: *West Orange*, Delta 3rd Plt, 9–23 May '70.
112 John P. Kempe.
113 Operations Order # 0355-70, Patrol: *Pal Joey*, Delta 3rd Platoon, 3–5 Apr '70.
114 DD-491, summarized, record of trial, 6.
115 Ibid.
116 Ibid.
117 Ibid.
118 Michael Einsidler, interview with author, Feb 2024.
119 D-491, summarized, record of trial, 6.
120 Michael Einsidler, Feb 2024.
121 DD-491, summarized, record of trial, 6.
122 Ibid., 7.
123 Mrs. W. X. Lee, interviews with author, 2024.
124 "Gatos Officer Cleared," *The San Jose Times*, 4 Sept 1970.
125 "Lt. Lee Acquitted in Vietnam," *San Jose Mercury*, 4 Sept 1970.
126 Michael Einsidler, Feb 2024.
127 DD-491, summarized, record of trial.
128 W. X. Lee, 1998–2024.
129 Randy Lowery, 29 Jan 2023 and 23 Feb 2024.
130 Herman Diaz, interviews with author, Oct–Nov 1988.
131 Ibid.
132 Randy Lowery, 29 Jan 2023 and 23 Feb 2024.
133 W. X. Lee, 1998–2024.
134 Ibid.
135 Ibid.
136 G. G. "Jerry" Spolter, interview with author, 2024.
137 Mrs. W. X. Lee, 1998–2024.
138 W. X. Lee, 1998–2024.
139 C. Broman, Jan–July 1968.

Chapter 31

1 "Pullout-of-Troops Proposal Defeated By Senate, 55–39," *Pittsburgh Post-Gazette*, 4 September 1970, 1.
2 Author's notes and personal experience.
3 "Nixon orders 1000 FBI agents for college campus," *New York Times*, 25 September 1970, 42.
4 Jerry Lembcke, *CNN's Tailwind Tale: Inside Vietnam's Last Great Myth* (Lanham, Maryland: Rowman & Littlefield, 2003).
5 Graham A. Cosmas and Lt. Col. Terrence P. Murray, USMC, *U.S. Marines in Vietnam: Vietnamization and Redeployment 1970–1971* (Washington, D.C.: History & Museum Division Headquarters, U.S. Marine Corps, 1986), 445.
6 Ibid., 446.
7 Ibid., 97.
8 Ibid., 446.
9 Ibid., 99.
10 Ibid., map, "Realignment of Regiments," 98.
11 1st Recon Bn Command Chronology, September 1970.
12 Rene Regalot, interviews with author, 2020–24.
13 1st Recon Bn Command Chronology, September 1970.
14 Ibid.
15 Cosmas and Murray, *U.S. Marines in Vietnam*, 91.
16 Michael Lee Lanning and Dan Cragg, *Inside the VC and the NVA* (New York: Fawcett Columbine, 1992), 97.
17 Cosmas and Murray, *U.S. Marines in Vietnam*, 92.
18 Operations Order # 1037-70, Patrol: *War Cloud-K*, Delta 4th Plt, 29 Aug–11 Sept '70.
19 Ibid.
20 Ibid.
21 Ibid.
22 Operations Order # 1073-70.
23 Operations Order # 1071-70, Patrol: *War Cloud-B*, Bravo Co, 11 Sept '70, OP Hill 250, 1st Recon Bn, Da Nang, RVN, 121255H Sept '70 (turnover of Hill 250).
24 Operations Order # 1072-70, Patrol: *War Cloud-C*, Charlie Co 11 Sept '70, OP Hill 425, 1st Recon Bn, Da Nang, RVN, 121310HH Sept '70 (turnover of Hill 425).
25 Cosmas and Murray, *U.S. Marines in Vietnam*, 92.
26 Ibid.
27 1st Recon Bn Command Chronology, Sept 1970.
28 Earl B. Hailston, interview with author, Jan 2024.

29 DD-491, summarized, record of trial of Lee, W. X., First Lieutenant by General Court-Martial Appointed by CG, 1st MarDiv (Rein) FMF tried at HQ's 1st Marine Division, Da Nang, RVN, 31 Aug, 1, 2, 3 Sep 1970. 5.
30 1st Recon. Bn Command Chronology, Sept 1970.
31 Operations Order # 0953-70, Patrol: *War Cloud-K*, Delta 2nd Plt, 12–29 Aug '70.
32 Paul Freeman, interviews with author, 2022–24.
33 Ibid.
34 Rene Regalot, 2020–24.
35 Paul Freeman, 2022–24.
36 Ibid.
37 Rene Regalot, 2020–24.
38 Paul Freeman, 2022–24.
39 1st Recon Bn Command Chronology, Sept 1970.
40 Ibid.
41 Ibid.
42 Ibid.
43 1st Recon Bn Command Chronology, Sept 1970.
44 Ibid.
45 Battalion commander's meeting notes; author's green memo notebook, Sept 1970.
46 Robert "Bob" Fawcett, interviews with author, 25 Feb and Apr 2024.
47 1st Recon Bn Command Chronology, Sept 1970.
48 1st Recon Bn Command Chronology, Oct 1970.
49 1st Recon Bn Command Chronology, Sept 1970.
50 Operations Order # 1109-70, Patrol: *Pony Boy*, Bravo Co 3rd Plt, 29 Sept–3 Oct '70. 1st Recon Bn, Da Nang, RVN, 251415H Sep '70.
51 Ibid.
52 Ibid.
53 1st Recon Bn Command Chronology, Oct 1970.
54 Cosmas and Murray, *U.S. Marines in Vietnam*, 313–14.
55 1st Recon Bn Command Chronology, Oct 1970.
56 Cosmas and Murray, *U.S. Marines in Vietnam*, 111.
57 1st Recon. B Command Chronology, Oct 1970.
58 Robert "Bob" Fawcett, 25 Feb and Apr 2024; Michael Cross, interview with author, 22 Feb 2024.
59 1st Recon Bn Command Chronology, Oct 1970.
60 Interviews with Zach Johnson, 2016, 5 Mar 2023, 21 Oct 2023, and Feb 2024.
61 Ibid.
62 Cosmas and Murray, *U.S. Marines in Vietnam*, 106.
63 Steve Fisher, interviews with author, Aug 2024.
64 Cosmas and Murray, *U.S. Marines in Vietnam*, 111; 2nd Bn, 5th Mar Command Chronology, Oct 1970.
65 Cosmas and Murray, *U.S. Marines in Vietnam*, 112; Steve Fisher, Aug 2024.
66 Cosmas and Murray, *U.S. Marines in Vietnam*, 112.
67 Ibid.
68 Author's green memo notebook, Oct 1970.
69 Maurice A. Jacques and Bruce H. Norton, *Sergeant Major, U.S. Marines* (New York: Ivy, 1995), 333.
70 Author's green memo notebook, Oct 1970.
71 Jacques and Norton, *Sergeant Major, U.S. Marines*, Chapter 15.
72 Dob Burzynsk, "The Lore of the Corps: Gone to fight the Indians," *Times*, 13 February 2006.
73 Cosmas and Murray, *U.S. Marines in Vietnam*, 113.

Chapter 32

1 Stanley Karnow, *Vietnam: A History* (New York: Viking, 1983), 636.
2 Ibid., 654.
3 A. J. Langguth, *Our Vietnam: The War 1954–1975* (New York: Simon & Schuster, 2000), 548.
4 Graham A. Cosmas and Lt. Col. Terrence P. Murray, USMC, *U.S. Marines in Vietnam: Vietnamization and Redeployment 1970–1971* (Washington, D.C.: History & Museum Division Headquarters, U.S. Marine Corps, 1986), 179.
5 Ibid., 7.
6 Michael Lee Lanning and Dan Cragg, *Inside the VC and the NVA* (New York: Fawcett Columbine, 1992), 200.
7 Vicki Van Den Bout, "Ripley at the Bridge," *Leatherneck*, April 2022.
8 "October 12, 1970," *Richard Nixon Presidential Library and Museum*, at https://www.nixonlibrary.gov/research/almanac/october-12-1970.
9 Cosmas and Murray, *U.S. Marines in Vietnam*, 443.
10 Ibid., 448.
11 Ibid.
12 Ibid., 278.
13 Ibid., 314.
14 Operations Order # 1073-70, Patrol: *War Cloud-K*, Delta 4th Plt, 11 Sept '70.
15 11th Marines Command Chronology, 1–30 Apr 1971.
16 1st Recon Bn Command Chronology, Oct 1970.
17 Meritorious Unit Citation for MAG-16 for Typhoon *Kate* rescue operations saving Vietnamese, Oct 1970.
18 1st Eng Bn Command Chronology, 1–31 Mar 1971.
19 Ibid.
20 1st Recon Bn. Command Chronology, Apr. 1971

21 Ibid.
22 Ibid.
23 Recon Bn Command Chronology, May 1971.
24 Cosmas and Murray, *U.S. Marines in Vietnam*, 302.
25 1st Eng Bn Command Chronology, 1–31 Mar 1971.
26 Paul Freeman, interviews with author, 2022–24.
27 Operations Order # 0782-70, Patrol: *Pal Joey-K*, Delta 3rd Plt, 2–18 July '70.
28 Paul Freeman, 2022–24.
29 William Pearson, *Vietnam Studies: The War in the Northern Provinces* (Department of the Army, 1975).
30 Vietnam Battlefield Tours, a Marine-owned non-profit, takes veterans back to Vietnam, at www.vietnambatfieldtours.com.

Appendix 1

1 Hill 119 debriefs are contained as part of the 1st Recon Bn Operations Orders for the period. The Operations Orders are listed chronologically in the bibliography. They can also be found at The Vietnam Center and Sam Johnson Vietnam Archives at Texas Tech University, athttps://www.vietnam.ttu.edu/.
2 Operations Order # 52-69, Patrol: *Empire State*, Delta 1st Plt, 19–26 Jan '69.
3 Charles R. Smith, *U.S. Marines in Vietnam, High Mobility and Standdown, 1969* (Washington, D.C.: History and Museums Division, Headquarters, U.S. Marine Corps, 1988), 84.
4 Operations Order # 1073-70, Patrol: *War Cloud-K*, Delta 4th Plt, 11 Sept '70.
5 Hill commanders by name and by dates of their tour. See Appendix 2.
6 Ibid.
7 For a description of the medical support of the NVA from division to platoon, and from hospital to first aid man, see Michael Lee Lanning and Dan Cragg, *Inside the VC and the NVA* (New York: Fawcett Columbine, 1992), 154–55.
8 The definitive research work on McNamara's body count measure of effectiveness, see Sam Adams, *War of Numbers, An Intelligence Memoir of the Vietnam War's Uncounted Enemy* (Lebanon, New Hampshire: Steerforth Press, 1994).

Appendix 2

1 All the statistics shown herein are derived from 1st Recon Bn debriefings included in each patrol report. There were 48 debriefings, each covering one tour of duty. The numbers were consolidated by category, each represented in a table in the statistical review. All the patrol reports can be found in the Bibliography and were extracted from Texas Tech Vietnam Archives.

Appendix 3

1 Charles D. Melson, Paul Hannon, and Lee Johnson, *Marine Recon 1940–90* (Osprey Publishing, 1994), 16, 17.
2 "Standard Operating Procedure for Sting Ray/Clandestine Long Range Patrolling Operations," 1st Recon Bn, Camp Reasoner, Da Nang, Republic of Vietnam. BNO P3000.4, 1 Oct 1967 with changes.

Bibliography

Primary Sources

Interviews

All interviews with the author and formatted as: rank in Vietnam (rank at retirement/separation), and interview dates unless indicated by another interviewer's name.

Baker, Steven, "Stumpy" 1Lt (Capt), CO, Charlie Co., February–April 2024.

Bayuk, Mark, Cpl/Sgt, 11th Marines Forward Observer (FO), Hill 119, multiple emails, September 2023–April 2024.

Cross, Michael, 1Lt (Col, Ret.) patrol leader, Plt Cmdr, Alpha Co., 22 February 2024.

Diaz, Herman, Sgt (MSgt), Plt Sgt, 3rd Plt, Delta Co., patrol leader, Hill 119, October–November 1988 Camp Pendleton, CA, since deceased.

Drumright, W. C. "Bill," LtCol (Col, Ret.), 1st Recon Bn Cmdr, interview Hq Bn HQMC, February 1971, College Grove, Tennessee, May 2001, since deceased.

Eglevsky, Paul, 2Lt, patrol leader, Hill 119 Cmdr, Delta Co., three interviews, February 2024.

Einsidler, Michael, Sgt (Col, Ret.), Trial Clerk, SJA Section, 1st Mar Div, February 2024.

Evans, Bill, Sgt, Team Leader, Delta Co., Hill 119 veteran, email and interview, February 2023.

Fawcett, R. "Bob," 1Lt (Col, Ret.) patrol leader, Plt Cmdr, Alpha Co., emails, 25 February and April 2024.

Fisher, Steve, 1Lt, (Col, Ret.), Plt Cmdr, H Co, 2/5, email and multiple interviews, August 2024.

Floom, Marv, 1Lt, (Col, Ret.), patrol leader, Plt Cmdr, Co Cmdr, Alpha Co., at https://www.mountcastle.net/obituaries/obituary-listings?searchName=marv+floom&page=1.

Freeman, Paul, LCpl, patrol member, Hill 119, second tour with Army, email and multiple interviews, 2022–24.

Grace, J. J., LtCol (Col, Ret.), interview 1989, Arlington, VA, by Mark Bayuk since deceased.

Gregson, W. C. "Chip," 1Lt, (LtGen, Ret.), patrol leader, Plt Cmdr, Company Commander, S-3A, March 2024.

Gregson, W. C., 1Lt, (LtGen, Ret.), Oral History interview, Vietnam Commemoration Commission. https://www.vietnamwar50th.com/history_and_legacy/oral_history/gregson,-chip/.

Grossman, Robert, PFC, 3rd Plt, Delta Co., Hill 119 vet, 29 February 2024.

Hackett, Jim, Sgt, 11th Marines Counter Fire Radar, Hill 119 vet, 14 December 2023.

Hailston, Earl B., 1Lt, (LtGen, Ret.), patrol leader, Plt Cmdr, Echo Co., January 2024.

Hare, W. "Rabbit," SSgt (MSgt, Ret.), point man, patrol member, S-3 instructor, Echo and H&S Co., July 2020.

Hodgins, Mike, 1Lt, patrol leader, Plt Cmdr, C Co., January 2022. Deceased 2024.

Hoff, John, 1Lt, patrol leader, Echo and Delta Cos, Hill 119, 23 May 2024.

Holly, John "Jack," 1Lt, (Col, Ret.), patrol leader, B and C Cos, S-3 1st Force Recon Co., multiple interviews 2023–March 2024.

Howland, Greg, 1Lt, patrol leader, S-2 1st Recon Bn, interview August 2024.

Johnson, Zach, 1Lt, (Maj, Ret.) patrol leader, Plt Cmdr 1st Force Recon, LNO to 5 March, 21 October 2023, February 2024, trip to Vietnam with author to Camp Reasoner and Hill 119, 2016.

Kershaw, C. W. "Charlie," 1Lt (LtCol, Ret.) patrol leader, Alpha Co Cmdr, 2023–July 2024.

Lange, William, "Bill," 1Lt, S-5 with 2/26, S-5 with 1st Recon, 18–19 September 2024.

Lee, Wilson Xavier, 1Lt, patrol leader, Plt Cmdr, interviews 2020–24.

L'Orange, H. C. "Chris," 1Lt (Capt), patrol leader, Plt Cmdr, Hill Commander, Delta Co email, multiple interviews, 2023–24.
Lowery, Randy, Cpl, 3rd Plt, Delta, Hill 119, patrol member, sniper, 29 January 2023 and 23 February 2024.
Mann, John, 1Lt, patrol leader, Plt Cmdr, S-2, S-3A, CO Alpha Co., email/interview, 10 January 2024.
Marshall, Eugene, "Gene," PFC, radioman H&S Co., upon return to United States adopted family name Stockton, Eugene, BGen, VANG, 26–27 February 2024.
Martin, Thomas, Capt, Commanding Officer, Delta Co., '69–'70, Hill 119 visitor, 10 December 2023.
May, Robert, "Gump," 1Lt, patrol leader, Plt Cmdr, Alpha Co., October 2023.
McAdams, Thomas, 1Lt, patrol leader, 21 February and 19 March 2024.
McCullum, Mike, Capt, Aerial Observer, VMO-2, callsign *Cowpoke-One Three*, July–August 2024.
Miller, B. Parker, 1Lt, patrol leader, Alpha Co., 3 interviews, 18–20 February 2024.
Mullins, Thurman, HN, HM3, patrol member/corpsman, Hill 119 corpsman, interviews, email, photos, February–October 2023.
Parks, G. L. Garry, 1Lt (LtGen, Ret.), patrol leader, Plt Cmdr, Hill 119 Commander, Delta Co., multiple interviews 1981–2002, trip to Vietnam and Hill 119 with author, 2016.
Parks, Earlene (Garry's wife), multiple interviews, emails, and availability to Garry's records, January–March 2024.
Regalot, Rene, MSgt (MGySgt), patrol leader, S-3 instructor, 1st Sergeant Delta Co., interviews, 2020–24.
Rivers, George E., Maj (LtCol), Vietnamese Marine Corps Advisor, CO 3rd Recon, 18–19 September 2024.
Rowland, Ed, LCpl, patrol member, Alpha Co Return to Vietnam Hill 119, emails, interview, 2016.
Sanders, Steve, HN, Delta Co corpsman, Hill 119, January 2024.
Schneider, Michael, PFC, radioman Recon teams, H&S, B, and C Cos, 23 February 2024.
Schwartz, Eric, HN, Corpsman, Delta Co Hill 119 veteran, emails, photo, interview, 2010–24.
Snider, David, HN, Corpsman, Delta Co, Hill 119 visit, trip to Vietnam, 2016, emails, multiple interviews, 2016–24.
Spolter, G. G. "Jerry", 1Lt (Maj) patrol leader, Delta Co Commander, Hill 119, multiple interviews, 2024.
Spooner, Rick, Maj (Ret.), Marine, historian, proprietor of Globe & Laurel, interview, 6 October 2024.
Stinemetz, Broman C., LtCol (Col, Ret.), 1st Recon Bn Cmdr, January–July 1968, Tho Son hamlet, March 2008, interview by David Snider and Ed "Tex" Stiteler.
Stiteler, Ed, "Tex," Cpl, 3/7, return to Vietnam, 2022, visit Hill 119, emails, multiple interviews, 2022–24.
Swick, Dennis, LCpl, 3rd Plt, Delta Co., patrol member, Hill 119 veteran, email and interview, February 2024.
Thomas, Frank, SSgt, interview concerning Gunnery Sergeant Terry Moore, February 2024.
Unsworth, Andy, PFC (Capt, Ret.), rifleman 3/26, 3/5, 3rd MPs, 25 February 2023.
Unsworth, Jim, 1Lt, patrol leader, Plt Cmdr, Hill 119 Commander, Delta Co., multiple interviews, 15 December 2023–August 2024.
Waddill, Durwood, "Butch," 1Lt (LtCol, Ret.), patrol leader, Plt Cmdr, Delta Co., '69–'70, interview, 11 May 2016.
Wagner, Robert, LCpl (Col, Ret.), Embarkation Clerk, Hq Co., Hq Bn, 1st Mar Div, 1998–2000.
Walton, Darren, LCpl, patrol member, Hill 119 veteran, emails, and interviews, 2022–23.
Weber, Art, 1Lt (Col, Ret.), patrol leader, Plt Cmdr, S-3A, Alpha Co Cmdr, 10 March 2024.
Witkin, Ralph, LCpl, A Co., S-3 shop, 1969–1970, emails and interview, January 2025.
Zeigler, Edward, "MoPar Ed," 1Lt, Motor Transport Officer, 1st Recon, 24 September 2024.

Unpublished Government Legal Documents

All in author's possession.

Article 32, for 1Lt W. X. Lee transcript, 10 July 1970.
Convening Order for General Court-Martial, Ser.24–70, 29 Aug 1970.
DD-457, Record of the Article 32 Investigation of charges against 1Lt W. X. Lee, 16 July 1970.
DD-458 Charge Sheet of accused 1Lt W. X. Lee, signed by J. R. Taylor, Capt. Legal Officer, Hq Co Hq Bn 1st Mar Div, 18 May 1970.
DD-458, p. 3: CG Endorsement referral to trial, Charge Sheet of accused 1Lt W. X. Lee, signed by J. R. Taylor, Capt Legal Officer, Hq Co Hq Bn 1st Mar Div dtd. Signed 25 July 1970.

DD-491, Summarized, Record of Trial of Lee, Wilson Xavier, First Lieutenant, by General Court-Martial Appointed by CG, 1st Mar Div (Rein) FMF tried at HQ's 1st Marine Division, Da Nang, RVN, 31 Aug–1, 2, 3 Sep 1970.
General Court-Martial: Lee, W. X.; 1Lt; summary. 31 Aug, 1, 2, 3 Sep 1970.
Letter, CG to Col Louis S. Hollier Jr., U.S. Marine Corps, Hq Bn, 1st Mar Div (Rein.), FMF; Subj. Modification to Convening Order for General Court-Martial. Ser:24A-70, 31 Aug 1970.
Letter, CG to Col U. E. Lees, Convening Order for General Court-Martial, Ser.24–70, 29 Aug 1970.
Letter, CO 1st Recon Bn appointing LtCol James King as Investing Officer for an Article 32 for alleged murder of Vietnamese civilian by 1Lt W. X. Lee, 18 May 1970. Enclosure to Article 32 report, 10 July 1970.
Letter, CO 1st Recon Bn to CG 1st Mar Div recommending GCM, 16 July 1970.
Letter, CO 1st Recon Bn to CG 1st Mar Div requesting Article 32 for 1Lt W. X. Lee, 16 May 1970. Enclosure to Article 32, 10 July 1970.
Letter, interim Report on *Article 32, Investigating Officer's Report*; Accused 1Lt W. X. Lee, 1st Recon Bn; IO, LtCol James P. King, Hq Co Hq Bn Letter, IO to CO, 1st Recon Bn, 19 June 1970.
Letter, SJA to CG 1st Mar Div, recommending GCM, 22 July 1970.
Naval Investigative Service, Investigation into alleged charges on 1Lt W. X. Lee, 6 June 1970.
NIS Report of Investigation, to SJA, 1st Mar Div alleged murder of Vietnamese civilian by 1Lt W. X. Lee, 1st Recon Bn, by E. J. Fitzpatrick, Resident Agent NIS Da Nang, 6 June 1970.
OQR (Officer Qualification Record) 1Lt W. X. Lee.

Government Documents

NIC Field Exploitation Team. National Interrogation Center (NIC). NIC Report 208/68 dated 26/02/68. The intelligence summary is taken from a declassified report of the National Interrogation Center (NIC). 68. It was the result of interrogation activities conducted under the joint auspices of the Central Intelligence Organization (CIO) and the US Central Intelligence Agency (CIA) with the participation of Detachment 6, 6499th Special Activities Group (USAF) with interrogation conducted by NIC Field Exploitation Team in Da Nang, February 1968.

Command Chronologies, Operation Orders, and Patrol Reports

The Vietnam Center and Sam Johnson Vietnam Archive at Texas Tech University, https://www.vietnam.ttu.edu/, is the location for Command Chronologies, Operations Orders, and Patrol Reports.

1st Recon Battalion Command Chronologies

Command Chronology, May 1968, dated 2 June 1968.
Command Chronology, June 1968, dated 2 July 1968, LtCol B. C. Stinemetz.
Command Chronology, July 1968, dated 2 August 1968.
Command Chronology, August 1968, dated 2 September 1968, LtCol L. P. Sharon.
Command Chronology, October 1968, dated 2 November 1968.
Command Chronology, November 1968, dated 2 December 1968.
Command Chronology, December 1968, dated 2 January 1969.
Command Chronology, January 1969, dated 2 February 1969.
Command Chronology, February 1969, dated 2 March 1969, LtCol R. D. Mickelson.
Command Chronology, March 1969, dated 2 April 1969.
Command Chronology, April 1969, dated 2 May 1969.
Command Chronology, May 1969, dated 2 June 1969.
Command Chronology, June 1969, dated 2 July 1969.
Command Chronology, July 1969, dated 2 August 1969.
Command Chronology, August 1969, dated 2 September 1969.
Command Chronology, September 1969, dated 2 October 1969.
Command Chronology, October 1969, dated 2 November 1969, LtCol J. J. Grace, 8 October 1969.

Command Chronology, November 1969, dated 2 December 1969.
Command Chronology, December 1969, dated 2 January 1970.
Command Chronology, January 1970, dated 2 February 1970, LtCol W. C. Drumright, 25 January 1970.
Command Chronology, February 1970, dated 2 March 1970.
Command Chronology, March 1970, dated 2 April 1970.
Command Chronology, April 1970, dated 2 May 1970.
Command Chronology, May 1970, dated 2 June 1970.
Command Chronology, June 1970, dated 2 July 1970.
Command Chronology, July 1970, dated 2 August 1970.
Command Chronology, August 1970, dated 2 September 1970, LtCol E. J. Regan, 10 August 1970.
Command Chronology, September 1970, dated 1 October 1970, LtCol W. G. Leftwich, 13 September 1970.
Command Chronology, October 1970, dated 2 November 1970.
Command Chronology, November 1970, dated 2 December 1970, LtCol M. Trainor, 20 November 1970.
Command Chronology, December 1970, dated 2 January 1971.
Command Chronology, January 1971, dated 2 February 1971.
Command Chronology, February 1971, dated 2 March 1971.
Command Chronology, March 1971, dated 2 April 1971.
Command Chronology, April 1971, dated 2 May 1971.

3rd Reconnaissance Battalion (Rein.) Command Chronology

Command Chronology, November 1969, dated 2 December 1970.

1st Engineer Battalion (Rein.) Command Chronology

Command Chronology, 1–31 March 1971, dated 26 March 1971.

5th Marines Command Chronology

Command Chronology, 2nd Battalion, 5th Marines, October 1970, dated 15 November 1970.

7th Marines Command Chronology

Command Chronology 7th Marines # 3/5750-70, 1–31 March 1970, dated 17 April 1970 (Recon Pathfinder Mission ISO 1/7).
Command Chronology, 1st Battalion, 7 March 1–31 March 1970 3/RET/jfl/1500, dated 17 April 1970 (Recon Pathfinder Mission ISO 1/7).
Daily Journal: 1st Battalion, 7th Marines, Journal: 170001H–to 172400H, Place: Que Son, RVN.

11th Marines Command Chronology

Command Chronology, # 0155-69, 1–31 October 1969, dated 18 November 1969 (IOD statistics).
Command Chronology, # 0178-69, 1–30 November 1969, dated 17 December 1969 (IOD statistics).
Command Chronology, # 0039-70, 1–28 February 1970, dated 18 March 1970 (Arty, SPOT Report. Hill 119).
Command Chronology, # 0040-70, 1–31 March 1970, dated 19 April 1970 (Summary).
Command Chronology, # 0042-70, 1–30 May 1970, dated 19 June 1970 (Summary).
Command Chronology, 1–30 April 1971, dated 15 May 1971 (Summary).

1st Marine Division Command Chronologies

Command Chronology, 1–31 March 1970, dated 18 April 1970. (Comm Elec Section).

III MAF Command Chronologies

Command Chronology, III MAF, FMF, February 1969, DTG 25Mar69, Texas Tech University, Sam Johnson, Vietnam Center.

FMFPAC Command Chronology

Command Chronology, # 016074, Operations of U.S. Marine Forces, Vietnam, April 1970.
Command Chronology, # SO19090, Operations of U.S. Marine Forces, Vietnam, August 1970.
Command Chronology, # 160317, Operations of U.S. Marine Forces, Vietnam, January–February 1971.
Command Chronology, # 160511, Operations of U.S. Marine Forces, Vietnam, March–April 1971.

Dong Den: Operations Order and debriefings

Operations Order # 844-69, Patrol, *Impressive*, Alpha Co, 22 Sept–3 Oct 1969, Radio Relay, Dong Den, 1st Recon Bn, Da Nang, RVN, 190900H, Sep 1969 (1Lt Gregson).

Hill 119: Operations Orders include post-patrol debriefings

Operations Order # 24–69, Patrol: *Empire State-A*, Delta, 1st Platoon, OP Hill 119, 10 Jan 1969, 1st Recon Bn, Da Nang, RVN, 080900H Jan 1969 (Capt G. R. Willson site survey of Hill 119, for potential OP).

Operations Order # 52-69, Patrol: *Empire State*, Delta, 1st Platoon, OP Hill 119, 19–26 Jan 1969 1st Recon Bn, Da Nang, RVN, 180700H Jan 1969 (Capt G. R. Willson, establish and fortify OP Hill 119).

Operations Order # 72-69, Patrol: *Vesper Bells*, Delta, 1st Platoon, OP Hill 119, 26 Jan–02 Feb 1969, 1st Recon Bn, Da Nang, RVN, 280700H Jan 1969 (1Lt Lawrence continue to fortify OP Hill 119).

Operations Order # 90-69, Patrol: *Rudder*, Delta Co, Platoon, OP Hill 119, 02–11 Feb 1969, 1st Recon Bn, Da Nang, RVN, 111310H Feb 1969 (Lt Wietecha).

Operations Order # 110-69, Patrol: *Mad Hatter*, Delta Co, Platoon, OP Hill 119, 11–25 Feb 1969, 1st Recon Bn, Da Nang, RVN, 090930H Feb 1969 (Lt Downey, OP Hill 119, ISO Op *Taylor Common*).

Operations Order # 148-69, Patrol: *Aunt Mable*, Delta Co, 2nd Platoon, OP Hill 119, 24 Feb–9 Mar 1969, 1st Recon Bn, Da Nang, RVN, 221300H Feb 1969 (Lt Wietecha, OP Hill 119, 7 NVA flags, air strike).

Operations Order # 184-69, Patrol: *Night Scholar*, Delta Co, 1st Platoon, OP Hill 119, 9–26 Mar 1969, 1st Recon Bn, Da Nang, RVN 090945H Mar 1969 (Lt Jim Unsworth, OP Hill 119, ISO *Taylor Common*).

Operations Order # 231-69, Patrol: *Grim Reaper*, Delta Co, 3rd Platoon, OP Hill 119, 24 Mar–8 April 9–26 Mar 1969, 1st Recon Bn, Da Nang, RVN, 220900H Mar 1969 (Lt Mann, OP Hill 119).

Operations Order # 287-69, Patrol: *Hanover Sue*, Delta Co, OP Hill 119, 8–25 April 1969, 1st Recon Bn, Da Nang, RVN, 060930H April 1969 (SSgt Hall, Hill 119, 3 USMC WIA).

Operations Order # 352-69, Patrol: *Bag Shaw*, Delta Co, 1st Platoon, OP Hill 119, 24 Apr–13 May 1969, 1st Recon Bn, Da Nang, RVN, 220900H Apr 1969 (Lt Jim Unsworth).

Operations Order # 401-69, Patrol: *Segment*, Delta Co, 3rd Platoon, OP Hill 119, 13–27 May 1969, 1st Recon Bn, Da Nang, RVN, 100900H May 1969 (2Lt Schanck).

Operations Order # 453-69, Patrol: *Barkeep*, Delta Co, 2nd Platoon, OP Hill 119, 27 May–12 June 1969, 1st Recon Bn, Da Nang, RVN, 251015H May 1969 (1Lt Pfeiffer).

Operations Order # 506-69, Patrol: *Delivery Boy/Defend*, Delta 1st Plt, OP Hill 119, 12–24 Jun 1969, 1st Recon Bn, Da Nang, RVN, 090745H Jun 1969 (1Lt Unsworth).

Operations Order # 554-69, Patrol: *May Fly*, Delta 2nd Plt, OP Hill 119, 24 June–4 July1969, 1st Recon Bn, Da Nang, RVN, 090745H Jun 1969 (1Lt Pfeiffer).

Operations Order # 586-69, Patrol: *Beech Nut*, Delta 2nd Plt, OP Hill 119, 4–14 July 1969, 1st Recon Bn, Da Nang, RVN, 090745H Jun 1969 (1Lt Klien, Hill 119 OP, *Spooky-11* supports).

Operations Order # 655-69, Patrol: *Parallel Bars*, Delta 3rd Plt, 26 Jul–5 Aug 1st Recon Bn, Da Nang, RVN, 210815H July 1969 (1Lt Pfeiffer, Hill 119 OP, ISO Op Pipestone Canyon).

Operations Order # 688-69, Patrol: *Spillway*, Delta 2nd Plt, 4–14 Aug '69, OP Hill 119, 1st Recon Bn, Da Nang, RVN, 01 August 1969 (Lt Klein).

Operations Order # 728-69, Patrol: *Spillway*, Delta 1st Platoon, 15–25 Aug '69, OP Hill 119, 1st Recon Bn, Da Nang, RVN, 110800H Aug 1969 (SSgt Ommondson).

Operations Order # 741-69, Patrol: *Turf Club*, Echo Co 3rd Plt, 21–31 Aug '69, 1st Recon Bn Da Nang, RVN, 181130H Aug 1969 (3 TPQ-10 guided airstrikes Hill 425 OP: caused BDA Patrol off Hill 119, PFC Haney KIA).

Operations Order # 754-69, Patrol: *Spillway*, Delta 3rd Plt, 23 Aug–4 Sept '69, OP Hill 119, 1st Recon Bn, Da Nang, RVN, 211000H Sept 1969 (Lt Pfeiffer, PFC Robert Haney KIA).

Operations Order # 787-69, Patrol: *Spillway*, Delta 2nd Plt, 4–14 Sept '69, OP Hill 119, 1st Recon Bn, Da Nang, RVN, 310815H Aug 1969 (2Lt Klein, RZ Haven gets smaller).

Operations Order # 820-69, Patrol: *Rummage*, Delta 1st Plt, 14–24 Sept '69, OP Hill 119, 1st Recon Bn, Da Nang, RVN, 111130H Sept 1969 (1Lt Unsworth).

Operations Order # 849-69, Patrol: *Rummage*, Delta 3rd Plt, 24 Sept–9 Oct '69, OP Hill 119, 1st Recon Bn, Da Nang, RVN, 211139H Sept 1969 (1Lt Waddill/ Sgt H. Diaz).

Operations Order # 873-69, Patrol: *Rummage* Delta 2nd Plt, 8–19 Oct '69, OP Hill 119, 1st Recon Bn, Da Nang, RVN, 010815 Oct 1969 (Lt Klein, 5 USMC WIA, *Spooky* workout).

Operations Order # 906-69, Patrol: *Rummage*, Delta 1st Plt, 19–29 Oct '69, OP Hill 119, 1st Recon Bn, Da Nang, RVN, 171100H Oct 1969 (2Lt Overton).

Operations Order # 929-69, Patrol: *Rummage*, Delta 1st Platoon, 29 Oct–10 Nov '69, OP Hill 119, 1st Recon Bn, Da Nang, RVN, 261030H Oct 1969 (2Lt Waddill).

Operations Order # 952-69, Patrol: *Rummage/Asparagus*, Delta 3rd Plt, 9–20 Nov '69, OP Hill 119, 1st Recon Bn, Da Nang, RVN, 051030H Nov 1969 (2Lt Stamm, 2 civilian medevacs, HN Mullins).

Operations Order # 989-69, Patrol: *Asparagus*, Delta 1st Plt, 20 Nov–1 Dec '69, OP Hill 119, 1st Recon Bn, Da Nang, RVN, 191250 Nov 1969 (2Lt Overton).

Operations Order # 1016-69, Patrol: *Asparagus*, Delta 3rd Plt, 1–16 Dec '69, OP Hill 119, 1st Recon Bn, Da Nang, RVN, 281415H Nov 1969 (2Lt Waddill, Cpl Swick, PFC Marshall).

Operations Order # 1069-69, Patrol: *Durham*, Delta 2nd Plt, 16–29 Dec '69, OP Hill 119, 1st Recon Bn, Da Nang, RVN, 150900H Dec 1969 (2Lt Garry Parks, HM3 Mullins).

Operations Order # 1096-69, Patrol: *Durham*, Delta 1st Plt, 29 Dec–11 Jan '70, OP Hill 119, 1st Recon Bn, Da Nang, RVN, 271445H Dec 1969 (2Lt Butch Waddill).

Operations Order # 0040-70, Patrol: *Durham*, Delta, 4th Plt, 11–25 Jan '70, OP Hill 119, 1st Recon Bn, Da Nang, RVN, 271445H Dec 1969 (2Lt Chuck Overton, WIA; GySgt Terry Moore).

Operations Order # 0094-70, Patrol: *Durham*, Delta 3rd Plt, 25 Jan–8 Feb '70, OP Hill 119, 1st Recon Bn, Da Nang, RVN, 211030H Jan '70 (2Lt McAdams/GySgt Moore).

Operations Order # 0143-70, Patrol: *Durham*, Delta 2nd Plt, 8–20 Feb '70, OP Hill 119, 1st Recon Bn, Da Nang, RVN, 031555H Feb '70 (2Lt Garry Parks).

Operations Order # 0201-70, Patrol: *West Orange*, Delta 1st Plt, 20 Feb–5 Mar '70, OP Hill 119, 1st Recon Bn, Da Nang, RVN, 181425H Feb '70 (2Lt M. O. Fallon).

Operations Order # 0242-70, Patrol: *West Orange*, Delta 4th Plt, 5–19 Mar '70, OP Hill 119, 1st Recon Bn, Da Nang, RVN, 021110H March '70 (2Lt L'Orange).

Operations Order # 0305-70, Patrol: *West Orange*, Delta 3rd Plt, 17 Mar–1 Apr '70, OP Hill 119, 1st Recon Bn, Da Nang, RVN, 151242H March '70 (2Lt W. X. Lee).

Operations Order # 0352-70, Patrol: *West Orange*, Delta 2nd Plt, 1–11 Apr '70, OP Hill 119, 1st Recon Bn, Da Nang, RVN, 291215H March '70 (2Lt Garry Parks).

Operations Order # 0393-70, Patrol: *West Orange*, Delta 1st Plt, 11–25 Apr '70, OP Hill 119, 1st Recon Bn, Da Nang, RVN; 081515H April '70 (2Lt Eglevsky).

Operations Order # 0452-70, Patrol: *West Orange*, Delta 4th Plt, 25 April–9 May '70, OP Hill 119, 1st Recon Bn, Da Nang, RVN, 211335H April '70 (2Lt L'Orange).

Operations Order # 0517-70, Patrol: *West Orange*, Delta 3rd Plt, 9–23 May '70, OP Hill 119, 1st Recon Bn, Da Nang, RVN, 061415H May '70 (1Lt Marv Floom).

Operations Order # 0585-70, Patrol: *West Orange*, Delta 4th Plt, 23 May–6 Jun '70, OP Hill 119, 1st Recon Bn, Da Nang, RVN, 230825H May '70 (1Lt Garry Parks).

Operations Order # 0644-70, Patrol: *West Orange*, Delta 1st Plt, 6–20 Jun '70, OP Hill 119, 1st Recon Bn, Da Nang, RVN, 031110H June '70 (1Lt Eglevsky).

Operations Order # 0710-70, Patrol: *Pal Joey*, Delta 4th Plt, 20 Jun–2 July '70, OP Hill 119, 1st Recon Bn, Da Nang, RVN, 181537H June '70 (1Lt L'Orange/1Lt Parks).
Operations Order # 0782-70, Patrol: *Pal Joey-K*, Delta 3rd Plt, 2–18 July '70, OP Hill 119, 1st Recon Bn, Da Nang, RVN, 020953H July '70 (1Lt M. O. Fallon).
Operations Order # 0867-70, Patrol: *Pal Joey-K*, Delta 1st Plt, 18 Jul–1 Aug '70, OP Hill 119, 1st Recon Bn, Da Nang, RVN, 2 31458H July '70 (1Lt Taylor).
Operations Order # 0907-70, Patrol: *Pal Joey-K*, Delta 3rd Plt, 1–14 Aug '70, OP Hill 119, 1st Recon Bn, Da Nang, RVN, 011116H Aug '70 (1/Lt Fallon/1Lt Hoff).
Operations Order # 0953-70, Patrol: *War Cloud-K*, Delta 2nd Plt, 12–29 Aug '70, OP Hill 119, 1st Recon Bn, Da Nang, RVN, 291820H Aug '70 (1Lt Fallon).
Operations Order # 1037-70, Patrol: *War Cloud-K*, Delta 4th Plt, 29 Aug–11 Sep '70, OP Hill 119, 1st Recon Bn, Da Nang, RVN, 011347H Sep '70 (1Lt Taylor).
Operations Order # 1071-70, Patrol: *War Cloud-B*, Bravo Co, 11 Sep '70, OP Hill 250, 1st Recon Bn, Da Nang, RVN, 121255H Sep '70 (turnover of Hill 250).
Operations Order # 1072-70, Patrol: *War Cloud-C*, Charlie Co 11 Sep '70, OP Hill 425, 1st Recon Bn, Da Nang, RVN, 121310HH Sep '70 (turnover of Hill 425).
Operations Order # 1073-70, Patrol: *War Cloud-K*, Delta 4th Plt, 11 Sep '70, OP Hill 119, 1st Recon Bn, Da Nang, RVN, 121420H Sep '70 (1Lt Taylor turnover of Hill 119).

Hill 425: Operations Orders and debriefing

Operations Order # 422-68, Patrol: *Parallel Bars*, Bravo 3rd Plt, OP Hill 425; 25 June–01 July 1968; 1st Recon Bn, Da Nang, RVN, 230930H June 1968 (PL: Sgt Simko).
Operations Order # 484-69, Patrol: *Senator*, Echo Co, Platoon, OP Hill 425; 5–19 June 1969; 1st Recon Bn, Da Nang, RVN, 020800H June 1969 (1Lt Gary Allord).

Patrol Operations Orders and post patrol debriefings, 1st Recon

Operations Order # 18-69, Patrol: *War Cloud*, Charlie Co, 8–11 Jan '69; 1st Recon Bn, Da Nang, RVN, 111600H Jan 1969 (Lt Carpenter, Lt Brown).
Operations Order # 21-69, Patrol: *Paddy Shell*, Charlie Co, 8–12 Jan '69; 1st Recon Bn, Da Nang, RVN, 111315H Jan 1969 (Cpl Brunner, AAA site AT99/55).
Operations Order # 22-69, Patrol: *Vesper Bells*, Delta Co, 7–11 Jan '69; 1st Recon Bn, Da Nang, RVN, 061515H Jan 1969 (2Lt Mann, Dodge City; 4 USMC WIA; 1 POW).
Operations Order # 23-69, Patrol: *Fig Newton*; Delta 1st Platoon, 8–9 Jan '69; 1st Recon Bn, Da Nang, RVN, 080800H Jan 1969 (Dodge City, 23 NVA KIA, 2 USMC WIA).
Operations Order # 39-69, Patrol: *War Cloud*, Charlie Co, 15–16 Jan '69; 1st Recon Bn, Nang, RVN, 160800H Jan 1969 (Lt Carpenter).
Operations Order # 256-69, Patrol: *Millbrook*, Delta 1st Plt, 2nd Tm 31 Mar–4 April '69; 1st Recon Bn, Da Nang, RVN, 280800H Mar 1969 (Lt Unsworth).
Operations Order # 270-69, Patrol: *Pennywise*, Delta Co, 3rd Plt, 5–6 April '69, 1st Recon Bn, Da Nang, RVN, 311230H Mar 1969 (SSgt Jones walk-off Hill 119 to railroad bridge).
Operations Order # 484-69, Patrol: *Senator*, Echo Co, 2nd Platoon, 5–19 June 1969, 1st Recon Bn, Da Nang, RVN, 020800H Jun 1969 (1Lt Allord, Hill 425 OP).
Operations Order # 503-69, Patrol: *Panama Hat/Night Scholar*, Alpha Co 1st Plt, 3 Teams, 11–15 June 1969; 1st Recon Bn, Da Nang, RVN, 080330H June (1Lts Weber, Kershaw, Gregson).
Operations Order # 527-69, Patrol: *May Fly*, Delta 3rd Plt, 21 June 1969, 1st Recon Bn, Da Nang, RVN, 151100H Jun 1969 (2Lt Schanck, helo shot down, 8 USMC KIA).
Operations Order # 636-69, Patrol: *Summer Breeze*, Delta 1st Plt, 20–24 July '69, 1st Recon Bn, Da Nang, RVN, 160845 July 1969.
Operations Order # 741-69, Patrol: *Turf Club*, Echo Co 3rd Plt, 21–31 Aug '69, 1st Recon Bn, Da Nang, RVN, 181130H Aug 1969 (3 TPQ-10 guided airstrikes, caused BDA Patrol off Hill 119, PFC Haney KIA).

Operations Order # 753-69, Patrol: *Road Test*, Bravo 1st Plt, 3rd Team, 22–25 Aug '69, 1st Recon Bn Da Nang, RVN, 210930H Aug 1969 (1Lt Holly).

Operations Order # 844-69, Patrol: *Impressive*, Alpha Co 3rd Plt, 27 Sept–3 Oct '69, 1st Recon Bn, Da Nang, RVN, 190900H Sept 1969 (1Lt Gregson, Dong Den Radio Relay, Black Bear KIA).

Operations Order # 846-69, Patrol: *Wedding Ring*, Bravo Co 1st Plt, 3rd Team, 22–25 Sep '69, 1st Recon Bn, Da Nang, RVN, 191100H Sep 1969 (1Lt Jack Holly, 2 contacts, base camp, ladder extract).

Operations Order # 887-69, Patrol: *Station Break*; Delta 1st Plt, 11–14 Oct '69, 1st Recon Bn, Da Nang, RVN, 090800H Oct 1969 (Lt Overton span in patrol).

Operations Order # 902-69, Patrol: *War Cloud*, Alpha-3-3, 20–23 Oct '69, 1st Recon Bn, Da Nang, RVN, 161100H Oct 1969 (1Lt W. C. Gregson, WIA).

Operations Order # 910-69, Patrol: *Big Flower*, Charlie Co, 2nd Plt, 1st Team, 21–23 Oct '69, 1st Recon Bn, Da Nang, RVN, 181300H Oct 1969 (2Lt Kubik, 3 USMC KIA).

Operations Order # 0009-70, Patrol: *Flakey Snow*, Alpha 3rd Plt, 1st Team, 3–7 Jan '70, 1st Recon Bn, Da Nang, RVN, 301000H Dec '69 (2Lt B. Parker Miller).

Operations Order # 0036-70, Patrol: *Pennywise*, Delta 2nd Plt, 2nd Team, 10–11 Jan '70, 1st Recon Bn, Da Nang, RVN, 070820H Jan 1970 (2Lt Garry Parks).

Operations Order # 0048-70, Patrol: *Spoonbill*, Delta 3rd Plt, 2nd Team, 12–14 Jan '70, 1st Recon Bn, Da Nang, RVN, 081455H Jan 1970 (2Lt McAdams, emer. ladder extract).

Operations Order # 0063-70, Patrol: *Wage Earner*, Echo 2nd Plt, 1st Team, 19–21 Jan '70, 1st Recon Bn, Da Nang, RVN, 131000H Jan '70 (2Lt Gary Allord).

Operations Order # 0065-70, Patrol: *Terrapin*, Delta 3rd Plt, 1st Tm, 9–15 Mar '70, 1st Recon Bn, Da Nang, RVN, 080700H March '70 (1Lt W. X. Lee).

Operations Order # 0066-70, Patrol: *Terrapin*, Echo 4th Platoon, 3rd Team, 18–22 Jan '70, 1st Recon Bn, Da Nang, RVN, 161245H Jan '70 (2Lt John Hoff).

Operations Order # 0070-70, Patrol: *Veal Stew*, Echo 3rd Platoon, 3rd Team, 18–22 Jan '70, 1st Recon Bn, Da Nang, RVN, 190945H Jan '70 (2Lt Earl Hailston).

Operations Order # 0072-70, Patrol: *Aroma*, Alpha, 5th Recon, 20–24 Jan 1st Recon Bn, Da Nang, RVN, 171105H Jan '70 (2Lt Zach Johnson).

Operations Order # 0074-70, Patrol: *Razorbill*, Delta 1st Plt, 1st Team, 19–24 Jan 1st Recon Bn, Da Nang, RVN, 171225H Jan '70 (SSgt Mushett, insert Hill 425, emergency extract under fire Phu Loc # 1).

Operations Order # 0082-70, Patrol: *Summer Breeze*, Delta 1st Plt, 1st Team, 22–23 Jan '70, 1st Recon Bn, Da Nang, RVN, 181015H Jan '70 (2Lt Waddill, emer ladder extract).

Operations Order # 0092-70, Patrol: *Swampland*, Delta 2nd Plt, 3rd Team, 23–27 Jan '70, 1st Recon Bn, Da Nang, RVN, 201230H Jan '70 (2Lt Garry Parks).

Operations Order # 0099-70, Patrol: *Station Break*, Delta 2nd Plt, 2nd Team, 28 Jan–1 Feb 1st Recon Bn, Da Nang, RVN, 221000H Jan '70 (SSgt Mushett, 2 USMC WIA; Hill 119 walk-off patrol).

Operations Order # 0105-70, Patrol: *Spoonbill*, Delta 4th Plt, 2nd Team, 29–31 Jan 1st Recon Bn, Da Nang, RVN, 260900H Jan '70 (1Lt Spolter, emergency ladder extract).

Operations Order # 0191-70, Patrol: *Chili Pepper*, Delta 4th Plt, 2nd Team, 13 Feb '70, 1st Recon Bn, Da Nang, RVN, 231130H Feb '70 (1Lt L'Orange).

Operations Order # 0184-70, Patrol: *Delicatessen*, Delta 3rd Plt, 2nd Team, 15–19 Feb '70, 1st Recon Bn, Da Nang, RVN, 131115H Feb '70 (2Lt M. O. Fallon/Sgt Franklin; contact-7 EKIA).

Operations Order # 0186-70, Patrol: *Pal Joey*, Delta 3rd Plt, 1st Team, 21–22 Feb '70, 1st Recon Bn, Da Nang, RVN, 150740H Feb '70 (2Lt W. X. Lee).

Operations Order # 0201-70, Patrol: *West Orange*, Delta 3rd Plt, 20 Feb–5 Mar '70, Hill 119, 1st Recon Bn, Da Nang, RVN, 181425H Feb '70 (2Lt M. O. Fallon/Sgt Franklin).

Operations Order # 0219-70, Patrol: *Fore Father*, Delta 1st Plt, 3rd Team, 26 Feb–2 Mar '70, 1st Recon Bn, Da Nang, RVN, 231130H Feb '70 (2Lt M. O. Fallon, Hill 119 walk-off, 2 EKIA).

Operations Order # 0221-70, Patrol: *Pal Joey*, Delta 3rd Plt, 3rd Team, 23–26 Feb '70, 1st Recon Bn, Da Nang, RVN, 231100H Feb '70 (2Lt W. X. Lee, captured 2 POWs).

Operations Order # 0246-70, Patrol: *Fig Newton*, Delta 2nd Plt, 2nd Team, 7–12 Mar '70, 1st Recon Bn, Da Nang, RVN, 031320H Mar '70 (1Lt J. Spolter on Charlie Ridge).

Operations Order # 0259-70, Patrol: *Delicatessen*, Delta 1st Plt, 12–14 Mar '70, 1st Recon Bn, Da Nang, RVN, 071110 Mar '70 (1Lt M. O. Fallon; RAID, with 2Lt Rathmell & GySgt Moore).

Operations Order # 0265-70, Patrol: *Terrapin*, Delta 3rd Plt, 2nd Team, 9–15 Mar '70, 1st Recon Bn, Da Nang, RVN, 080700H Mar '70 (2Lt W. X. Lee).

Operations Order # 0280-70, Patrol: *Dublin City*, Delta 2nd Plt, 1st Team, 13–17 Mar '70, 1st Recon Bn, Da Nang, RVN, 110649H Mar '70 (2Lt Garry Parks).

Operations Order # 0313-70, Patrol: *Delicatessen*, Delta 1st Plt, 2nd Team, 17–18 Mar '70, 1st Recon Bn, Da Nang, RVN, 171121H, Mar '70 (1Lt M. O. Fallon; Pathfinder for 1/7).

Operations Order # 0318-70, Patrol: *Dublin City*, Delta 2nd Plt, 1st Team, 23–27 Mar '70, 1st Recon Bn, Da Nang, RVN, 191113H, Mar '70 (1Lt Garry Parks).

Operations Order # 0325-70, Patrol: *Delicatessen,* Delta 3rd Plt, 1st Team, 23–27 Mar '70, 1st Recon Bn, Da Nang, RVN, 220718H, Mar '70 (2Lt Eglevsky).

Operations Order # 0332-70, Patrol: *Fig Newton*, Delta 1st Plt, 2nd Team, 26–31 Mar '70, 1st Recon Bn, Da Nang, RVN, 222115H Mar '70 (1Lt M. O. Fallon, HN Schwartz).

Operations Order # 03xx-70, Patrol: *Chili Pepper*, Delta 4th Plt, 2nd Team, 27–31 Mar '70, 1st Recon Bn, Da Nang, RVN, 23xxxH Mar '70 (1Lt L'Orange).

Operations Order # 0347-70, Patrol: *Summer Breeze*, Delta 1st Plt, 2nd Team, 01–07 Apr '70, 1st Recon Bn, Da Nang, RVN, 281399H Mar '70 (2Lt Paul Eglevsky).

Operations Order # 0349-70, Patrol: *Delicatessen*, Delta 1st Plt, 3rd Team, 01 Apr '70, 1st Recon Bn, Da Nang, RVN, 301030H Mar '70 (SSgt Mushett; 3 Marine WIA booby-trap).

Operations Order # 0355-70, Patrol: *Pal Joey*, Delta, 3rd Plt, 2nd Team, 03–05 Apr '70, 1st Recon Bn, Da Nang, RVN, 281399H Mar '70 (2Lt W. X. Lee; 1 POW, ladder extract).

Operations Order # 0360-70, Patrol: *Policy Game*, Bravo, 04–09 Apr '70, 1st Recon Bn, Da Nang, RVN, 010800H Mar '70 (2Lt Taylor).

Operations Order # 0374-70, *Flakey Snow*, S3 Trng with RIP Training Class, 3–4 April '70, 1st Recon Bn, Da Nang, RVN, 041110H April 1970 (1Lt Rathmell/GySgt Moore, River crossing with 3/5).

Operations Order # 0383-70, Patrol: *Prime Cut*, Delta 4th Plt, 2nd Team, 08–11 Apr '70, 1st Recon Bn, Da Nang, RVN, 060900H Apr '70 (2Lt H. C. L'Orange, emer ladder extract).

Operations Order # 0391-70, Patrol: *Terrapin*, Delta Co 3rd Plt, 2nd Team, 11–16 Apr '70, 1st Recon Bn, Da Nang, RVN, 081525H Apr '70 (2Lt W. X. Lee).

Operations Order # 0400-70, Patrol: *Dublin City*, Delta Co, 12–15 Apr '70, 1st Recon Bn, Da Nang, RVN, 121030H Apr '70 (1Lt M. O. Fallon).

Operations Order # 0401-70, Patrol: *Fig Newton*, Delta Co, 12–15, Apr '70, 1st Recon Bn, Da Nang, RVN, 121010H Apr '70 (1Lt J. Spolter).

Operations Order # 0406-70, Patrol: *Pickwick Papers*, Alpha Co, 14–19, Apr '70, 1st Recon Bn, Da Nang, RVN, 111407H Apr '70 (Lt J. K. Murphy, 2Lt Gump May).

Operations Order # 0424-70, Patrol: *Fig Newton*, Delta Co, 17–19 Apr '70, 1st Recon Bn, Da Nang, RVN, 151345H Apr '70 (1Lt M. O. Fallon, 2 downed helos on extract).

Operations Order # 0464-70, Patrol: *Fig Newton*, Delta Co, 28Apr–2 May '70, 1st Recon Bn, Da Nang, RVN, 240800H Apr '70 (2Lt Garry Parks).

Operations Order # 0466-70, Patrol: *Pal Joey*, Delta Co 1st Plt, 28 Apr–3 May '70, 1st Recon Bn, Da Nang, RVN, 270810H Apr '70 (2Lt P. Eglevsky, PPB).

Operations Order # 0468-70, Patrol: *Terrapin*; Delta Co.,28 Apr–02 May '70, 1st Recon Bn, Da Nang, RVN; 270828H Apr '70 (1Lt J. Spolter).

Operations Order # 0481-70, Patrol: *Vesper Bells-Romeo*, S-3, 28 Apr '70, 1st Recon Bn, Da Nang, RVN, 281815H Apr '70 (1Lt Pete Gray/GySgt Terry Moore, helo recovery).

Operations Order # 0487-70, Patrol: *Dublin City*, Delta Co, 03 May '70, 1st Recon Bn, Da Nang, RVN, 021110H May '70 (2Lt Parks).

Operations Order # 0493-70, Patrol: *Vesper Bells-Divers*, H&S Co, 03–06 May '70, 1st Recon Bn, Da Nang, RVN, 301235H Apr '70 (1Lt C. KERSHAW).
Operations Order # 0504-70, Patrol: *Delicatessen*, Delta Co, 9–12 May '70, 1st Recon Bn, Da Nang, RVN, 091300H May '70 (2Lt H. C. L'Orange, Que Sons Caucasian sighting).
Operations Order # 0514-70, Patrol: *Dublin City*, Delta Co, 10–14 May '70, 1st Recon Bn, Da Nang, RVN, 091070 May '70 (2Lt Garry Parks).
Operations Order # 0522-70, Patrol: *Prime Cut*, Delta Co, 11–12 May '70, 1st Recon Bn, Da Nang, RVN, 091070 May '70 (1Lt Smith).
Operations Order # 0536-70, Patrol: *Summer Breeze*, Delta Co, 15–19 May '70, 1st Recon Bn, Da Nang, RVN, 140415H May '70 (2Lt P. Eglevsky, malaria medevac).
Operations Order # 0541-70, Patrol: *Dublin City*, Delta Co, 16–20 May '70, 1st Recon Bn, Da Nang, RVN, 130827H May '70 (2Lt Garry Parks).
Operations Order # 0566-70, Patrol: *Chili Pepper*, Delta Co, 22 May '70, 1st Recon Bn, Da Nang, RVN, 171020H May '70 (2Lt L'Orange, 1.8 hours shot out LZ).
Operations Order # 0585-70, Patrol: *West Orange*, Delta 4th Plt, 23 May–6 Jun '70, OP Hill 119, 1st Recon Bn, Da Nang, RVN, 230825H May '70 (1Lt Garry Parks, Cpl Grossman, multiple probes).
Operations Order # 0623-70, Patrol: *Terrapin*, Delta Co, 2–6 June '70, 1st Recon Bn, Da Nang, RVN, 311110H May '70 (1Lt Fallon).
Operations Order # 0658-70, Patrol: *Dublin City*, Delta Co, 9–13 June '70, 1st Recon Bn, Da Nang, RVN, 080835H Jun '70 (1Lt Fallon).
Operations Order # 0682-70, Patrol: *Pal Joey*, Delta Co, 17–21 June '70, 1st Recon Bn, Da Nang, RVN, 152025H Jun '70 (1Lt Fallon).
Operations Order # 0724-70, Patrol: *Bag Shaw*, Delta Co, 24–28 June '70, 1st Recon Bn, Da Nang, RVN, 211755H Jun '70 (1Lt Fallon).
Operations Order # 0793-70, Patrol: *Bad Actor*, Echo Co, 7–9 July '70, 1st Recon Bn, Da Nang, RVN, 060745H July '70 (1Lt E. Hailston).
Operations Order # 0821-70, Patrol: *Segment*, Delta Co, 11 July '70, 1st Recon Bn, Da Nang, RVN, 100857H July '70 (SSgt Mushett).
Operations Order # 0860-70, Patrol: *Allen Town*, Delta Co, 23–29 Jul '70, 1st Recon Bn, Da Nang, RVN, 230915H July '70 (1Lt M. O. Fallon).
Operations Order # 0990-70, Patrol: *Big Flower*, Delta Co, 23–27 Aug '70, 1st Recon Bn, Da Nang, RVN, 240805H Aug '70 (1Lt John Hoff).
Operations Order # 1109-70, Patrol: *Pony Boy*, Bravo Co, 29 Sep–3 Oct '70, 1st Recon Bn, Da Nang, RVN, 251415H Sep 70 (1Lt M. O. Fallon).

Meritorious Unit Citation

"For MAG-16, for Typhoon Kate Rescue Operations saving Vietnamese, Oct 1970."
MAG-11, VMO-2 Daily Flight schedules, July 1970.

Messages, 1st Recon Bn Daily Situation Report

Msg: Op Immediate 1stMarDiv (Rein): 1st Recon Bn (Rein) SitRep # 176-68 250001H to 252400H.
Msg: Op Immediate 1stMarDiv (Rein): 1st Recon Bn (Rein) SitRep # 177-68 260001H to 262400H.
Msg: Op Immediate 1stMarDiv (Rein): 1st Recon Bn (Rein) SitRep. # 178-68 270001H to 272400H.
Msg: Op Immediate 1stMarDiv (Rein): 1st Recon Bn (Rein) SitRep # 180-68 290001H to 292400H.
Msg: Op Immediate 1stMarDiv (Rein): 1st Recon Bn (Rein) SitRep # 10-69 100001H to 102400H.

Standard Operating Procedures (SOP)

"Standard Operating Procedures for Sting Ray/Clandestine Long Range Patrolling Operations," 1st Reconnaissance Battalion (REIN), Camp Reasoner, Da Nang, Republic of Vietnam. BNO P3000.4, date 1 Oct 1967, with changes 1970. Declassified: IAW DODI 5200.1-R, by CG 1st Mar Div, H-G. Peterson Jr., By Dir. (author's copy).

Trips to Hill 119

The author has made five trips back to Vietnam. On each trip, he returned to Hill 119 and the ground around the hill. The last four trips were facilitated by the non-profit group at Vietnam Battlefield Tours. https://www.vietnambattlefieldtours.com/.

Garry Parks and Zach Johnson went on a 2016 trip to Vietnam and Hill 119 with the author.

Unpublished Papers

Coffelt, Richard D. "The Coffelt Database of Vietnam casualties," at www.coffeltdatabase.org.

Fallon, Michael O. Personal Notebooks of Da Nang/Camp Reasoner, 1969/1970.

Finlayson, Andrew, R. *The Strategic Importance of An Hoa Combat Base.*

West, Francis James. *The Strike Teams: Tactical Performance and Strategic Potential.* Rand Corporation: research paper published in 1969.

Secondary Sources

Official Marine Corps Histories

Cosmas, Graham A., and LtCol Terrance Murray, USMC. *U.S. Marines in Vietnam: Vietnamization and Redeployment 1970–1971.* Washington, D.C.: History & Museums Division Headquarters, U.S. Marine Corps, 1986.

Melson, Charles D., Maj, LtCol C. G. I. Arnold, USMC. *U.S. Marines in Vietnam, The War That Would Not End 1971–1973.* Washington, D.C.: History & Museums Division Headquarters, U.S. Marine Corps, 1991.

Pearson, William. *The War in the Northern Provinces: 1966–1968 (Vietnam Studies).* Department of the Army, 1975.

Shulimson, Jack, LtCol L. A. Blasiol, USMC, Charles R. Smith, Capt. David A. Dawson, USMC, *U.S. Marines in Vietnam, The Defining Year, 1968.* Washington, D.C.: History & Museums Division Headquarters, U.S. Marine Corps, 1997.

Simmons, E. H., BGen, USMC (Ret.), editor, et al. *The Marines in Vietnam, 1954–1973: An Anthology and Annotated Bibliography, Second Edition.* Washington, D.C.: History & Museums Division, Headquarters, U.S. Marine Corps, 1985.

Smith, Charles R. *U.S. Marines in Vietnam, High Mobility and Standdown, 1969,* Washington, D.C.: History and Museums Division, Headquarters, U.S. Marine Corps, 1988.

Solis, Gary D., LtCol, USMC, *Marines and Military Law in Vietnam: Trial By Fire.* Washington, D.C.: History & Museums Division Headquarters, U.S. Marine Corps, 1989.

West, Bing, Capt. *Small Unit Action in Vietnam, 1966.* History & Museums Division Headquarters, U.S. Marine Corps, 1966.

Books

Adams, Sam. *War of Numbers, An Intelligence Memoir of the Vietnams War's Uncounted Enemy.* Lebanon, New Hampshire: Steerforth Press, 1994.

Allison, William Thomas. *Military Justice in Vietnam: The Rule of Law in an American War.* Lawrence: University Press of Kansas, 2007.

Anderson, David L. *The Colombia Guide to the Vietnam War.* New York: Columbia University Press, 2002.

Bostdorff, Denise M. *The Presidency and the Rhetoric of Foreign Crisis.* Columbia, South Carolina: University of South Carolina, 1994.

Campbell, Tom. *The Old Man's Trail.* Annapolis, Maryland: Naval Institute Press, 1995.

Conboy, Kenneth and James Morrison. *Shadow War: The CIA's Secret War in Laos.* Boulder, Colorado: Paladin Press, 1995.

Cooper, Charles G., LtGen USMC (Ret.). *Cheers and Tears: A Marine's Story of Combat in Peace and War.* Wesley Press, 2002.

Daugherty, Leo J. III. *United States Marine Reconnaissance in the Vietnam War, Ghost Soldiers and Sea Commandos, 1963–1971.* Jefferson, North Carolina: McFarland & Co. Inc, 2024.

Finlayson, Andrew R. *A Marine Long-Range Recon Team Leader in Vietnam, 1967–1968*. Jefferson, North Carolina: McFarland, 2013.

Finlayson, Andrew R. *Rice Paddy Recon: A Marine Officer's Second Tour in Vietnam, 1968–1970*. Jefferson, North Carolina: McFarland, 2014.

Greenberg, Rick. *Silent Heroes, Recon Marine's Vietnam War*. Self-published, ISBN: 1522742808, 2016.

Griffis, Don W. *Eagle Days: A Marine Legal/Infantry Officer in Vietnam*. Tuscaloosa: University of Alabama Press, 2007.

Hastings, Max, *Vietnam, An Epic Tragedy, 1945–1975*. London: Harper Collins, 2018.

Hodgins, Michael C. *Reluctant Warrior: A Marine's True Story of Duty and Heroism in Vietnam*. New York: Ballantine Books, 1996.

Jacques, Maurice J., SgtMaj and Bruce H. "Doc" Norton, USMC (Ret.). *Sergeant Major, U.S. Marines*. New York: Ivy, 1995.

Karnow, Stanley. *Vietnam, A History*. New York: Viking, 1983.

Katrina, Martin. *The Asbury Park July Riots*. The Duke University Libraries, 1970.

Kelley, Michael P. *Where We Were in Vietnam: A Comprehensive Guide to the Firebases, Military Installations, and Naval Vessels of the Vietnam War*. Central Point, Oregon: Hellgate Press, 2002.

Kellum, Michael Dan. *American Heroes: Grunts, Pilots, and "Docs," Book I*. Longview, Texas: Navarro-Hill Publishing Group, 2011.

Kellum, Michael Dan. *American Heroes: Grunts, Pilots, and "Docs," Book II*. Longview, Texas: Navarro-Hill Publishing Group, 2011.

Kiernan, Ben. *Viet Nam: A History from Earliest Times to The Present*. New York City: Oxford University Press, 2017.

Langguth, A. J. *Our Vietnam: The War 1954–1975*. New York: Simon & Schuster, 2000.

Lanning, Michael Lee, and Dan Cragg. *Inside the VC and the NVA*. New York: Fawcett Columbine, 1992.

Lee, Alex, LtCol. *Force Recon Command: A Special Marine Unit in Vietnam, 1969–1970*. Annapolis, Maryland: Naval Institute Press, 1995.

Lembcke, Jerry. *CNN's Tailwind Tale: Inside Vietnam's Last Great Myth*. Lanham, Maryland: Rowman & Littlefield, 2003.

Melson, Charles D., Paul Hannon, and Lee Johnson. *Marine Recon 1940–90*. Osprey Publishing, 1994.

Morris, Michael F. *Corps Competency, III Marine Amphibious Force, Headquarters in Vietnam*. Lawrence: University Press of Kansas, 2024.

Nash, N. S. *Logistics in the Vietnam Wars, 1945–1975*. Philadelphia: Pen & Sword Military, 2022.

Norton, Bruce H. *Stingray*. San Diego: Quadrant Books, 2000.

Peters, Dr. Bill. *First Force Recon Company: Sunrise at Midnight*. New York: Ivy, 1999.

Pribbenow, Merle L., translated by. *Victory in Vietnam, The Official History of the People's Army of Vietnam 1954–1975*. Lawrence: University Press of Kansas, 2002.

Schulzinger, Robert D. *A Time for War, The United States and Vietnam, 1941–1975*. New York: Oxford University Press, 1997.

Simonsen, Robert A. *Every Marine, 1968 Vietnam, A Battle for Go Noi Island*. Westminster, Maryland: Heritage Books, 2008.

Sorley, Lewis. *A Better War, The Unexamined Victories and Final Tragedy of America's Last Years in Vietnam*. New York: Harcourt Brace & Company, 1999.

Spector, Ronald H. *After TET: The Bloodiest Year in Vietnam*. New York: The Free Press, 1993.

Tang, Truong Nhu, David Chanoff, Doan Van Toai. *A Viet Cong Memoir*. New York: Vintage Books, 1985.

Walt, Lewis W. *Strange War, Strange Strategy, A General's Report on Vietnam*. New York: Funk & Wagnalls, 1970.

Walton, Darren, with Michael J. Coffino. *Di Di May, Tigers, Rock Aps, The Jungle,… and War*. San Rafel: BATT Publishing, 2023.

Wawro, Geoffery. *The Vietnam War, a Military History*, New York, Basic Books, 2024.

West, F. J. Jr. *The Village*. University of Wisconsin Press, 1972.

West, Francis James. *The Strike Teams: Tactical Performance and Strategic Potential*. Rand Corporation: research paper published in 1969.

Young, Paul R. *First Recon—Second to None: A Marine Reconnaissance Battalion, 1967–68*. New York: Ivy, 1992.

Magazine Articles

Burzynski, Don. "The Lore of the Corps: Gone to fight the Indians." Special to the *Times*, February 13, 2006.

Correll, John T. "The Shadow War in Cambodia." *Air Force Magazine*, Jan 2018.

Keene, R. R. Keene. "Hill 119 in the 'Nam: The Night Recon Called In 'Guns-A-Go-Go'." *Leatherneck*, LXXXVI: 1, January 2003, 30–34.

Van Den Bout, Vicki. "Ripley at the Bridge." *Leatherneck*, April 2022.

West, Francis J. Jr. "Stingray '70." *Proceedings of the U.S. Naval Institute*, November 1969, 27–37.

Newspaper Articles

"Pullout-of-Troops Proposal Defeated By Senate, 55–39." *Pittsburgh Post-Gazette*, September 4, 1970, 1.

"Nixon orders 1000 FBI agents for college campus." *New York Times*, September 25, 1970, 42.

"Stop Trials of GIs for Viet Killings Senator Henry Bellmon (R-Okla)." *UPI wire*, 29/30 Nov 1969, wire report.

"Hanoi Charges Disputed: Marines Cleared in Slaying." *San Francisco Chronicle*, 24 May 1970.

"L.G. Marine Charged with Murder in Viet." *San Jose Mercury*, 25 May 1970.

"Los Gatos Charged in Viet Death." *San Jose News*, 25 May 1970.

"Defense from S.J." *San Jose News*, 5 June 1970.

"Marine Defense Delay Claimed." *San Jose News*, 11 June 1970.

"Viet Murder Defense Hits Roadblock." *San Jose Mercury*, 12 June 1970.

"400,000 in Capital Join in Honor America Day." *Chicago Tribune*, July 5, 1970, 1.

"Marines Reduce Charges." *San Jose Mercury*, 7 August 1970.

"Wanted To Scare, Not Slay Viet" *San Jose News*, 1 September 1970. AP Da Nang, Vietnam.

Maps

ref: https://maps.lib.utexas.edu/maps/topo/vietnam/

Sheet # 6641 III-series L7014 Da Nang, Prepared by AMS (LU), U.S. Army, 1965, Army Map Service, Washington, D.C.

Sheet # 6640 IV-Series L7014 Dai Loc, Prepared by AMS (LU) U.S. Army, 1965, Army Map Service, Washington, D.C

Sheet # 6540 I-series L7014 Thong Duc, Prepared by AMS (LU) U.S. Army, 1965, Army Map Service, Washington, D.C.

Sheet # 6640 III-series L7014, Hiep Doc, Prepared by AMS (LU) U.S. Army, 1965, Army Map Service, Washington, D.C.

Index